Middleton Public Library
7425 Hubbard Ave
Middleton, WI 53562

Roadside New Mexico

Roadside
New Mexico

A GUIDE TO HISTORIC MARKERS

Revised and Expanded Edition

David Pike

Foreword by Beverly Duran

UNIVERSITY OF NEW MEXICO PRESS • ALBUQUERQUE

© 2015 by the University of New Mexico Press
All rights reserved. Published 2015
Printed in the United States of America
20 19 18 17 16 15   1 2 3 4 5 6

Library of Congress Cataloging-in-Publication Data

Pike, David, 1964–
   Roadside New Mexico : a guide to historic markers /
David Pike ; foreword by Beverly Duran. — Revised and expanded edition.
      pages cm
   Includes bibliographical references and index.
   ISBN 978-0-8263-5569-0 (pbk. : alk. paper) — ISBN 978-0-8263-5570-6 (electronic)
   1. Historical markers—New Mexico—Guidebooks. 2. New Mexico—History, Local.
3. New Mexico—Guidebooks. 4. Automobile travel—New Mexico—Guidebooks.
   I. Title.
   F797.P545 2015
   917.8904'54—dc23
                              2014024698

Cover photo: Lisa C. Tremaine
Designed by Lisa C. Tremaine
Composed in Plantin and Block Berthold

Contents

List of Markers	vii
Foreword by Beverly Duran	xiii
Introduction	xv
Maps of New Mexico Historic Markers	1
Alphabetical Listing of New Mexico Historic Markers	7
Bibliography	469

List of Markers

1. Abiquiú (map 2)
2. Abó Pass Trail (map 4)
3. Abó Ruins (map 4)
4. Acomilla (map 5)
5. Ada McPherson Morley (map 5)
6. Agnes Morley Cleaveland (map 5)
7. Agua Fria (map 2)
8. San Isidro Catholic Church (map 2)
9. Agueda Martinez (map 2)
10. Alameda (map 4)
11. Albuquerque (map 4)
12. Founding Women of Albuquerque (map 4)
13. Ghost Marker: Old Town Plaza—On the Camino Real (map 4)
14. Ghost Marker: Albuquerque Petroglyphs (map 4)
15. Ghost Marker: Sandia Mountains (map 4)
16. Amelia Elizabeth White (map 2)
17. Mary Cabot Wheelwright (map 2)
18. Ana de Sandoval y Manzanares (map 4)
19. Apache Battleground (map 6)
20. Artesia (map 6)
21. Ghost Marker: Chisum's South Spring Ranch (map 6)
22. Ghost Marker: Flynn-Welch-Yates Oil Well (map 6)
23. Aztec (map 1)
24. Aztec Ruins National Monument (map 1)
25. Bartlett Garcia Continental Survey Point (map 5)
26. Basin and Range Country (map 5)
27. Bayard (map 5)
28. Beclabito Dome (map 1)
29. Belen (map 4)
30. Bernalillo (map 4)
31. Bernalillo on the Camino Real (map 4)
32. Ghost Marker: Coronado State Monument (map 4)
33. Bicentennial Celebration (map 2)
34. Bisti Wilderness (map 1)
35. Black Jack Ketchum (map 3)
36. Black Jack's Hideout (map 3)
37. Black Jack Ketchum (map 3)
38. Blackdom Townsite (map 6)
39. Blackwater Draw (map 6)
40. Blazer's Mill (map 6)
41. Bluewater Village (map 1)
42. The Bond House (map 2)
43. Bottomless Lakes State Park (map 6)
44. Ghost Marker: Civilian Conservation Corps Camp #831 (map 6)
45. Brazos Cliffs (map 2)
46. Buffalo Soldier Hill (map 6)
47. Butterfield Trail (map 5)
48. Caballo Mountains (map 5)
49. Camino del Llano (map 4)
50. Camp Lordsburg (map 5)
51. Canadian Escarpment (map 3)
52. Canadian River Canyon (map 3)
53. Cañoncito at Apache Canyon (map 2)
54. Capitan (map 6)
55. Captive Women and Children of Taos County (map 2)
56. María Rosa Villapando (map 2)
57. Capulin Volcano National Monument (map 3)
58. Carlsbad (map 6)
59. Carlsbad Irrigation Flume (map 6)
60. Carlsbad Caverns National Park (map 6)
61. Carlsbad Caverns National Park (map 6)
62. Ghost Marker: Guadalupe Mountains (map 6)
63. Carrizozo (map 6)
64. Carrizozo (map 6)
65. Carthage-Tokay-Farley (map 5)
66. Casa Colorada (map 4)
67. Castaño de Sosa's Route (map 6)
68. Cathay Williams (map 5)
69. The Catwalk (map 5)
70. Cedarvale (map 4)

71. Cerrillos (map 2)
72. Ghost Marker: Madrid National Historic District (map 2)
73. Ghost Marker: Golden (map 2)
74. Chama (map 2)
75. Ghost Marker: Cumbres and Toltec Scenic Railroad (map 2)
76. Chimayó (map 2)
77. El Santuario de Chimayó (map 2)
78. Cimarron (map 3)
79. Cimarron Canyon (map 3)
80. Cimarron Canyon State Park (map 3)
81. Palisades Sill (map 3)
82. City of Bloomfield (map 1)
83. City of Rocks State Park (map 5)
84. Civilian Conservation Corps—Carlsbad Campsite (map 6)
85. Civilian Conservation Corps—Lake Arthur Campsite (map 6)
86. Clayton (map 3)
87. Clayton Lake State Park (map 3)
88. Clayton Dinosaur Trackway (map 3)
89. Clifton House Site (map 3)
90. Cloud-Climbing Railroad (map 6)
91. Clovis (map 6)
92. Ghost Marker: Norman Petty Recording Studio (map 6)
93. Colfax County War (map 3)
94. Colorado Plateau (map 4)
95. Columbus (map 5)
96. Pancho Villa's Raid (map 5)
97. Pancho Villa State Park (map 5)
98. Comanche Country (map 3)
99. Continental Divide (maps 1, 2, and 4)
100. Cooke's Wagon Road (map 5)
101. Ghost Marker: Mormon Battalion (map 5)
102. Córdova (map 2)
103. Corrales (map 4)
104. Iglesia de San Ysidro (map 4)
105. Couse-Sharp Historic Site (map 2)
106. Cuba (map 4)
107. Cumbres Pass (map 2)
108. Curanderas—Women Who Heal (map 3)
109. Dawson (map 3)
110. Dawson Cemetery (map 3)
111. Deming (map 5)
112. Disappearance of Albert J. Fountain and His Son Henry (map 5)
113. Dog Canyon (map 6)
114. Domínguez-Escalante Trail (map 2)
115. Doña Ana (map 5)
116. Doña Ana (map 5)
117. Doña Dolores "Lola" Chávez de Armijo (map 4)
118. The Dorsey Mansion (map 3)
119. Dr. Annie Dodge Wauneka (map 1)
120. Dr. Meta L. Christy (map 3)
121. Dulcelina Salce Curtis (map 4)
122. Eagle Nest Lake State Park (map 3)
123. Early Spanish Route (map 6)
124. Eastern New Mexico University (map 6)
125. Edge of the Plains (map 4)
126. El Camino Real—The King's Highway (map 5)
127. Oñate's Route (map 5)
128. Women of the Camino Real (map 5)
129. El Morro National Monument Inscription Rock (map 1)
130. El Paso del Rio del Norte (map 5)
131. El Rancho de las Golondrinas/Old Cienega Village Museum (map 2)
132. El Rito (map 2)
133. El Rito (map 2)
134. Elephant Butte Dam (map 5)
135. Elephant Butte Lake State Park (map 5)
136. Elizabethtown (map 3)
137. Emory Pass—Black Range Mountains (map 5)
138. Española Valley (map 2)
139. Espejo's Expedition (map 5)
140. Espejo's Expedition (map 5)
141. Espejo's Trail (map 6)
142. Esther Martinez, P'oe Tsáwä (map 2)
143. Eve Ball (map 6)
144. Fabiola Cabeza de Baca Gilbert (map 3)
145. Fabric Artists (map 6)
146. Estella García (map 6)
147. Farmington (map 1)
148. Feliciana Tapia Viarrial (map 2)
149. Fenton Lake State Park (map 4)
150. Fort Bascom (map 3)
151. Fort Bayard (map 5)
152. Fort Bayard National Cemetery (map 5)
153. Fort Craig (map 5)
154. Ghost Marker: Valverde Battlefield (map 5)
155. Fort Craig Rest Area (map 5)
156. Fort Cummings (map 5)
157. Fort Defiance (map 1)

158. Fort Lowell (map 2)
159. Fort Selden State Monument (map 5)
160. Fort Selden Cemetery (map 5)
161. Fort Stanton (map 6)
162. Bosque Redondo Indian Reservation (map 6)
163. Bosque Redondo Indian Reservation (map 6)
164. Old Fort Sumner and "Billy the Kid's" Grave (map 6)
165. Fort Sumner (map 6)
166. Helene Haack Allen (map 6)
167. Fort Union National Monument (map 3)
168. Fort Union Arsenal (map 3)
169. Fort Wingate (map 1)
170. Galisteo Basin (map 2)
171. Galisteo Pueblo (map 2)
172. Gallup (map 1)
173. Garcia Opera House (map 5)
174. Georgia O'Keeffe (map 2)
175. Gila Cliff Dwellings National Monument (map 5)
176. Glorieta Pass Battlefield (map 2)
177. Gold and Turquoise (map 2)
178. Goodnight-Loving Trail (map 6)
179. Goodnight-Loving Trail (map 3)
180. Goodnight-Loving Trail (map 6)
181. Loving's Bend (map 6)
182. Goodnight-Loving Trail (map 3)
183. New Goodnight Trail (map 3)
184. Graciela Olivárez (map 4)
185. Gran Quivira Ruins (map 4)
186. Grants (map 1)
187. Ghost Marker: Mount Taylor (map 1)
188. Greathouse Station and Tavern (map 6)
189. Hachita (map 5)
190. Harriet Belle Amsden Sammons (map 1)
191. Harvey Girls (map 4)
192. Mary Elizabeth Jane Colter (map 4)
193. Hatch (map 5)
194. Hermits Peak (map 3)
195. Hillsboro Historic District (map 5)
196. Historic Los Luceros (map 2)
197. Hobbs (map 6)
198. Hobbs Discovery Well (map 6)
199. Hogback (map 1)
200. Ghost Marker: San Juan Basin (map 1)
201. Hogbacks (map 3)
202. Hyde Memorial State Park (map 2)
203. Inez Bushner Gill (map 2)
204. Maralyn Budke (map 2)
205. Jal (map 6)
206. Jemez Mountains (map 2)
207. Jemez Mountains (map 2)
208. Jemez State Monument (map 4)
209. Jicarilla Apache (Tribe) (map 2)
210. Jicarilla Apache (Tribe) (map 2)
211. Jicarilla Apache (Tribe) (map 2)
212. Jicarilla Apache Reservation Centennial Highway (map 2)
213. John H. Tunstall Murder Site (map 6)
214. Jornada del Muerto (map 5)
215. Jornada del Muerto (map 5)
216. Jornada del Muerto (map 5)
217. Josephine Cox "Grandma" Anderson (map 6)
218. Kelly (map 5)
219. Ken Towle Park (map 6)
220. Khe Sanh Veterans (map 1)
221. Kneeling Nun (map 5)
222. La Angostura (map 4)
223. La Bajada (map 2)
224. La Bajada (map 2)
225. La Cienega School (map 2)
226. La Cueva National Historic District (map 3)
227. La Joya de Sevilleta (map 5)
228. La Luz (map 6)
229. Ghost Marker: Alamogordo (map 6)
230. La Mesilla (map 5)
231. La Mesilla (map 5)
232. La Salineta (map 5)
233. Ladies Auxiliary of Local 890 Mine, Mill, and Smelter (map 5)
234. Laguna del Perro (map 4)
235. Ghost Marker: Salt Lakes (map 4)
236. Las Cruces (map 5)
237. Las Nutrias (map 5)
238. Las Placitas (map 4)
239. Las Trampas (map 2)
240. Las Vegas (map 3)
241. Laura Gilpin (map 2)
242. Lea County Cowgirls—Dessie Sawyer (map 6)
243. Fern Sawyer (map 6)
244. Leasburg Dam State Park (map 5)
245. Lincoln (map 6)
246. Lincoln-Jackson School (map 6)
247. Llano Estacado (map 3)

248. Llano Estacado (map 3)
249. Llano Estacado (map 3)
250. Llano Estacado (map 6)
251. Llano Estacado and Oil (map 6)
252. Lordsburg (map 5)
253. Lordsburg-Hidalgo Library (map 5)
254. Los Padillas (map 4)
255. Louise Massey Mabie (map 6)
256. Lovington (map 6)
257. Lozen, Little Sister (map 6)
258. Magdalena (map 5)
259. Magdalena Fault (map 5)
260. Magnolia Ellis (map 5)
261. Malpais (map 6)
262. Manuelito Area (map 1)
263. María "Concha" Concepción Ortiz y Pino de Kleven (map 4)
264. María Dolores Gonzáles, La Doctora (map 4)
265. Maria Gertrudis Barceló (Doña Tules) (map 2)
266. Marjorie Bell Chambers (map 2)
267. Peggy Pond Church (map 2)
268. Mary White (map 6)
269. Matilda Coxe Stevenson (map 1)
270. McComas Incident (map 5)
271. McNees Crossing (map 3)
272. Mela Leger (map 3)
273. Mesa and Pecos Valley (map 6)
274. Mesa del Contadero (map 5)
275. Mills Canyon (map 3)
276. Mogollon (map 5)
277. Monica Fuentes Gallegos and Carlota Fuentes Gallegos (map 3)
278. Mother Magdalen and the Sisters of Loretto (map 2)
279. Mountainair (map 4)
280. Nara Visa (map 3)
281. Navajo Indian Reservation (map 1)
282. New Mexico School for the Blind and Visually Impaired (map 6)
283. New Mexico Tech (map 5)
284. New Mexico Bureau of Mines and Mineral Resources Museum (map 5)
285. Nina Otero-Warren (map 4)
286. Oil and Gas (map 6)
287. Oil Country (map 6)
288. Old Armijo School (map 4)
289. Old Spanish Trail (map 2)
290. Pajarito (map 4)
291. Palo Flechado Pass (map 2)
292. Paraje de Fra Cristobal (map 5)
293. Paraje de los Brazitos (map 5)
294. Brazito Battlefield (map 5)
295. Paraje de Robledo (map 5)
296. Paraje San Diego (map 5)
297. Parteras of New Mexico (map 1)
298. Emma Estrada (map 1)
299. Pat Garrett Murder Site (map 5)
300. Pecos (map 3)
301. Ghost Marker: Pecos National Historical Park (map 3)
302. Evelyn M. Vigil and Juanita T. Toledo (map 4)
303. Pecos Valley (map 6)
304. Peralta (map 4)
305. Percha Creek (map 5)
306. Philmont Scout Ranch (map 3)
307. Pilar (map 2)
308. Ghost Marker: Cantonment Burgwin (map 2)
309. Ghost Marker: Embudo Stream Gaging Station (map 2)
310. Pinos Altos (map 5)
311. Plains of San Agustín (map 5)
312. Playas Siding (map 5)
313. Point of Rocks (map 3)
314. Portales (map 6)
315. Los Portales (map 6)
316. Pueblo of Ácoma (map 1)
317. Old Ácoma "Sky City" (map 1)
318. Pueblo of Isleta (map 4)
319. Pueblo of Isleta Tuei (map 4)
320. Pueblo of Jemez (map 4)
321. Pueblo of Laguna (map 1)
322. San José de la Laguna Mission (map 1)
323. Susie Rayos Marmon (map 1)
324. Pueblo of Nambé (map 2)
325. The St. Francis Women's Club (map 2)
326. Pueblo of Picurís (map 2)
327. Maria Ramita Simbola Martinez "Summer Harvest," Cora Durand, Virginia Duran (map 2)
328. Pueblo of San Felipe (map 4)
329. Pueblo of San Ildefonso (map 2)
330. María Montoya Martínez (map 2)
331. Pueblo of Santa Ana (map 4)
332. Pueblo of Santa Clara (map 2)

333. Pablita Velarde (map 2)
334. Pueblo of Santo Domingo (map 4)
335. Kewa Women's Co-Op (map 4)
336. Pueblo of Tesuque (map 2)
337. Tesuque Rain Gods (map 2)
338. Pueblo of Tuf Shurn Tui (map 4)
339. Pueblo of Zía (map 4)
340. Trinidad Gachupin Medina (map 4)
341. Pueblo of Zuni (map 1)
342. Zuni Olla Maidens (map 1)
343. Puerto de Luna (map 3)
344. Puyé Ruins (map 2)
345. Quarai Ruins (map 4)
346. Quemado (map 5)
347. Rabbit Ear Mountain (map 3)
348. Raton (map 3)
349. Ghost Marker: Raton Pass (map 3)
350. Ghost Marker: Willow Springs (map 3)
351. First Automobile in New Mexico (map 3)
352. Red River Valley (map 2)
353. Red Rocks (map 2)
354. Reserve (map 5)
355. Ghost Marker: Fort Tularosa (map 5)
356. Riley (map 5)
357. Rincón (map 5)
358. Rio Felix Bridge (map 6)
359. Rio Grande (map 5)
360. Rio Grande Bridge at Radium Springs (map 5)
361. Rio Grande Rift (map 2)
362. Rio Grande Gorge State Park (map 2)
363. Rio Grande Gorge Bridge (map 2)
364. Jack M. Campbell Highway (map 2)
365. Rio Salado Sand Dunes (map 5)
366. Rio Salado Sand Dunes (map 5)
367. Rockhound State Park (map 5)
368. Rocky Mountains (map 3)
369. Rodeo Station (map 5)
370. Rodeo Intermediate Field (map 5)
371. Rodey (map 5)
372. Rose Powers White (map 6)
373. Roswell (map 6)
374. Roswell Pioneer Plaza (map 6)
375. Ruidoso (map 6)
376. Old Dowlin Mill (map 6)
377. Ghost Marker: Chisum Trail (map 6)
378. Sabino y Lemitar (map 5)
379. Sally Rooke, Heroine of the Dry Cimarron Flood (map 3)
380. Salmon Ruin (map 1)
381. San Augustin Pass (map 5)
382. Ghost Marker: Organ Mountains (map 5)
383. San Antonio (map 5)
384. San Antonio de Padua Catholic Church (map 3)
385. San Francisco de Asís Church (map 2)
386. San Gabriel on the Camino Real (map 2)
387. San Miguel del Vado National Historic District (map 3)
388. Settlements of the San Miguel del Vado Land Grant (map 3)
389. San Patricio (map 6)
390. San Pedro (map 5)
391. San Rafael (map 1)
392. Sangre de Cristo (map 2)
393. Santa Cruz (map 2)
394. Ghost Marker: Ojo Caliente (map 2)
395. Santa Cruz de la Cañada (map 2)
396. Santa Cruz Plaza (map 2)
397. Santa Fe (map 2)
398. Ghost Marker: Kearny's Route (map 2)
399. Santa Fe Opera (map 2)
400. Santa Fe Trail (map 3)
401. Santa Fe Trail (map 3)
402. Puertocito de la Piedra Lumbre (map 3)
403. Santa Fe Trail (map 3)
404. Santa Fe Trail (map 3)
405. Santa Fe Trail (map 3)
406. Santa Fe Trail (map 3)
407. Santa Fe Trail Cimarron Cutoff (map 3)
408. Women of the Santa Fe Trail (map 3)
409. Santa Rita Copper Mines (map 5)
410. Santa Rosa (map 3)
411. Santa Rosa Lake State Park (map 3)
412. Louis S. Page and Joe O. Page Highway (map 3)
413. Seton Village (map 2)
414. Seven Rivers Cemetery (map 6)
415. Shakespeare (map 5)
416. Women of Shakespeare (map 5)
417. Shalam Colony (map 5)
418. Ship Rock (map 1)
419. Ghost Marker: Shiprock (map 1)
420. Sierra Blanca (map 6)
421. Sierra Grande (map 3)
422. Silver City (map 5)
423. Ghost Marker: Mangas Coloradas (map 5)

424. Ghost Marker: Old Silver City "Memory Lane" (map 5)
425. Sisters of Charity (map 2)
426. Site of San Augustin Springs (map 5)
427. Smokey Bear Historical Park (map 6)
428. Smuggler's Trail (map 5)
429. The Clanton Hideout (map 5)
430. Socorro (map 5)
431. Ghost Marker: Socorro Plaza (Kittrell Park) (map 5)
432. Soda Dam (map 4)
433. Southern Rockies (map 2)
434. Spanish Entrada Site (map 4)
435. Springer (map 3)
436. Old Colfax County Courthouse (map 3)
437. St. Anthony's Catholic Church (map 2)
438. State History of Education Museum (map 6)
439. Storrie Lake State Park (map 3)
440. Strike Valleys (map 3)
441. Sugarite Canyon State Park (map 3)
442. Sumner Lake State Park (map 6)
443. Sunnyside Springs (map 6)
444. Tajique (map 4)
445. Taos (map 2)
446. Kit Carson Park (map 2)
447. Kit Carson Park Memorial Cemetery (map 2)
448. Taos Canyon (map 2)
449. The Three Fates (map 2)
450. D. H. Lawrence Ranch (map 2)
451. Three Rivers (map 6)
452. Three Rivers Petroglyphs (map 6)
453. Three Wise Women (map 2)
454. Tierra Amarilla (map 2)
455. Tiguex Province (map 4)
456. Tijeras Canyon (map 4)
457. Tomé (map 4)
458. Trail of the Forty-Niners (map 3)
459. Trinity Site (map 5)
460. Jumbo (map 5)
461. Truchas (map 2)
462. Truchas Peaks (map 2)
463. Truth or Consequences (map 5)
464. Truth or Consequences (map 5)
465. Tucumcari (map 3)
466. Tucumcari Mountain (map 3)
467. Tularosa (map 6)
468. Ghost Marker: Round Mountain (map 6)
469. Ute Dam and Reservoir (map 3)
470. Ute Lake State Park (map 3)
471. Valencia (map 4)
472. Valle Grande (map 4)
473. Vásquez de Coronado's Route (map 4)
474. Vásquez de Coronado's Route (map 5)
475. Vásquez de Coronado's Route (map 3)
476. Vásquez de Coronado's Route (map 4)
477. Vaughn (map 3)
478. Velarde on the Camino Real (map 2)
479. Vietnam Veterans National Memorial (map 3)
480. View of the Rockies (map 3)
481. Villanueva State Park (map 3)
482. Virginia T. Romero (map 2)
483. Wagon Mound (map 3)
484. Waldrop Park (map 6)
485. Watrous (map 3)
486. Wheeler Peak (map 3)
487. White Oaks (map 6)
488. Women of Cochiti (map 4)
489. The Honorable Mary Coon Walters (map 4)
490. Chief Justice Pamela B. Minzner (map 4)
491. Women Veterans of New Mexico (map 4)
492. Yetta Kohn (map 3)
493. Yucca—New Mexico's State Flower (map 5)
494. Yucca Plains (map 5)

Foreword

New Mexico is a land of cultural richness and unique historical significance unparalleled in these United States. It is a state with a long and storied history of women of courage, vision, and fortitude working equally with men, determined to achieve in this Land of Enchantment. Women have influenced the course of New Mexico history in every part of our state, within every culture, and across every generation. So when we conceived of the idea of erecting Historic Roadside Markers to honor women who exemplify the great spirit of New Mexico, we sought not only to recognize esteemed historical figures like Pablita Velarde and Georgia O'Keeffe but also to acknowledge the contributions of individuals who were not as well known, such as Dr. Annie Dodge Wauneka, Esther Martinez, Dolores Chávez de Armijo, Dr. Meta L. Christy, Josephine Cox Anderson, and Cathay Williams, among other unsung heroes.

The Committee of the New Mexico Historic Women Marker Initiative is honored to have our work not only highlighted in *Roadside New Mexico* by David Pike, but also expanded. David met with families and colleagues where possible, went to every marker site, and visited the historical places where many of these women lived and worked—and in doing so, he placed them in historical context. We are so grateful for his genuine interest in the telling of their stories: factual and informed, but compassionate and sincere in both his research and his writing, thus enabling readers to learn more of the lives of these fascinating figures than would be possible solely on the Historic Markers texts themselves. We are happy to have partnered with David in bringing their stories to these pages.

And finally, we particularly hope that young girls and women will be inspired by the stories of these women of achievement and distinction and the work of the New Mexico Historic Women Marker Initiative and find in their accomplishments the motivation and the will to succeed themselves. Women still do not live in a world free from the barriers that faced these women on their journeys, but by recognizing those individuals who opened the doors we walk through today, we open new doors for others. In the words of Apama Basu, "History is no longer just a chronicle of kings and statesmen, but of ordinary women and men engaged in manifold tasks. Women's history is an assertion that women have a history."

Beverly Duran
Co-Founder and Chair
New Mexico Historic Women Marker Initiative
International Women's Forum–New Mexico

Introduction

If you've driven anywhere in New Mexico, you've seen one: a big, brown wooden sign along the roadside. Through these Official Scenic and Historic Markers we learn about the people, the geological features, and the historical events that have come together to make New Mexico a state unlike any other. They tell us about our triumphs, our heroes, our discoveries, our villains. They tell us about our cultures and our origins. They tell us about our mysteries, our tragedies, our very way of life. They are an index to our history.

Although the past that is documented on the Historic Markers does not itself change, our understanding of that past certainly does. Changes in our values over time can affect how we interpret what has happened before and how we choose to memorialize it. That is one of the reasons the Cultural Properties Review Committee in Santa Fe has the authority to revisit the texts of each of the Historic Markers every ten years for the life of the Marker. Sometimes no changes to the text are needed; other times, an entire rewrite is done—either for clarity, to add or remove a statement, or to emphasize new ideas. While all this is going on, of course, even more Historic Markers are being erected to recognize other aspects of history in the state. Our historical index is always being revised and updated.

And despite the incredibly diverse range of subjects covered by the Historic Markers already in place, sometimes new Markers are needed to highlight aspects of history that—to present-day eyes—have been overlooked. That accounts for the many new Historic Markers erected since 2005 documenting the contribution of women to the history of the state. For this effort, the Selection Committee of the New Mexico Historic Women Marker Initiative worked with county commissioners, tribal leaders, and historians to identify some of the outstanding women in the history of the state and recognize them with their own Historic Markers. The addition of these new Historic Women Markers represents the most significant change to the Historic Marker program since its inception in the 1930s. It also marks the entry of the program into recognizing events of more modern times: some of the women mentioned in the Markers were making history into the twenty-first century.

With all these exciting additions, changes, and updates, a book on Historic Markers originally published in 2004, as the first edition of this book was, would be showing its age within a decade. I was pleased, then, to be given the opportunity to put together this new version of the book, to include all the updates and additions since the first edition was published.

For those familiar with the first edition of the book, you'll notice a few changes in this book. First, the Markers are now organized by title, not by geographic region, making them much easier to find. Markers are alphabetized by the first letter of their title, even if they mention a person's name—so, "Black Jack Ketchum" appears in the Bs for "Black Jack" rather than the Ks for "Ketchum." Consider the Marker title as the title of a book for alphabetization purposes. In addition, each essay now includes suggestions of similar Historic Markers to help you explore each topic further.

In the first edition of the book, I included only those Historic Markers that I could personally verify were in place. Any that were not "on the ground" did not get included. Unfortunately, a number of those missing Markers remain missing today. But they are simply too intriguing to be left out yet again. So, the book now includes texts and short essays for what I'm calling "Ghost Markers." You won't find these Ghost Markers on the road (at least not as of this writing), but you'll still get to learn the lessons they impart. The Ghost Markers are included as short addendums to other Marker essays that share a similar location or subject. For example, the Ghost Marker for the "Flynn-Welch-Yates Oil Well" is part of the essay for "Artesia," because it was near Artesia that the Flynn-Welch-Yates well was sunk.

I'm pleased that this edition now includes maps that show the general location of each Marker. In cases where a Marker appears in more than one location, usually the maps show only one primary location so as not to be too cluttered. The locations are intended to give the reader an idea of where a Marker can be found and what other Markers are around it. For specific locations and directions to a Marker, consult the essay itself. The initial location information for these maps was compiled by Tonya G. Fallis between March and May of 2014, and I am grateful to her for allowing the use of her data. The maps themselves were drawn by David Carter and by staff at the University of New Mexico Press.

As with the first edition, I am indebted to many people for helping me get all of this done. I will long remember my visit to Camp Mary White on a rainy summer afternoon, being shown around the camp by Liz Lonngren and other former campers as they held their annual reunion. I am grateful to Ralph McClish of the New Mexico Osteopathic Medical Association, who sat with me in the hot sun outside his storage locker as we looked through files for mention of Dr. Meta L. Christy. If I'm healthier now than I was when I started the book, it's because of the curanderism seminar that Eliseo "Cheo" Torres of the University of New Mexico invited me to attend. (Although it might also be from undergoing my first chiropractic alignment under the care of Dr. Connie Moore in the former clinic of Magnolia Ellis, as I learned more about "Magnificent Magnolia"

in the very place she lived and worked. Thanks also to Wendy Waters and Gayle Martin, Ellis's family members, who helped me understand what made Ellis so "magnificent.") I am grateful to Holm Bursum III for giving me a tour of the Garcia Opera House in Socorro and sharing his family's stories of that property. I remember fondly my visit with Dora and Leroy Ortiz, who spoke with me about La Doctora, María Dolores Gonzáles, and I'll long remember the tour Sandra Alvarado gave me through the school named in Gonzáles's honor. I likewise remember my visit to the Couse-Sharp Historic Site in Taos and my guides Virginia Couse Leavitt and Ernie Leavitt. I am grateful to these good people for letting me experience their worlds.

Tom Drake with the Historic Preservation Division at the Cultural Properties Review Committee deserves thanks for his efforts to keep the Historic Marker program active and reflective of the needs of the state and those who travel our highways. Doug Sylvester and his wife, Vicki, generously shared information about Doug's grandfather, who drove the first car into New Mexico. Jeffery Joeckel, an archivist with the National Register of Historic Places, responded graciously to my many requests. Many others helped in countless ways: Kathy Flynn, executive director of the New Mexico Chapter of the National New Deal Preservation Association; Troy Ainsworth of El Centro Real de Tierra Adentro Trail Association (CARTA); Laurie Rufe and Candace Jordan Russell of the Roswell Museum and Art Center; Toni Laumbach of the New Mexico Farm and Ranch Heritage Museum; Kat Thompson of the Folsom Museum; Bruce Thompson, who spearheaded the Rodeo Intermediate Field Marker; Pat Brady, who helped tremendously with the geography and geological texts; Robert Julyan, who provided place-names assistance; David Carter, who provided the maps and illustrations; Tomas Jaehn of the Fray Angelico History Library; Gigi Galassini and the fine crew at the Telephone Museum of New Mexico; Richard M. Chamberlin and Bob Eveleth of the New Mexico Bureau of Geology and Mineral

Resources; Greg Mack of New Mexico State University; State Historian Rick Hendricks; and all the staff at the Center for Southwest Research, including Chris Geherin, Ann Massmann, and Nancy Brown-Martinez, as well as my friends and family. I am particularly grateful to Bev Duran and the members of the Selection Committee for the New Mexico Historic Women Marker Initiative, who trusted me to get this right and who helped me do so. Not to mention countless park rangers, professors, reference librarians, archivists, and historians who helped along the way.

A final note. For accuracy, I have included the text of each Historic Marker exactly as it appears on the faceplate, leaving intact any spelling, grammatical, or factual errors (which I note in the essay). This book reflects the texts and locations as they appeared in the spring of 2014. Changes and additions since that time won't appear here.

I hope you find this book a useful companion on your explorations through the Land of Enchantment. Travel happily.

David Pike

Maps of New Mexico Historic Markers

Map No. 1: Northwest Region

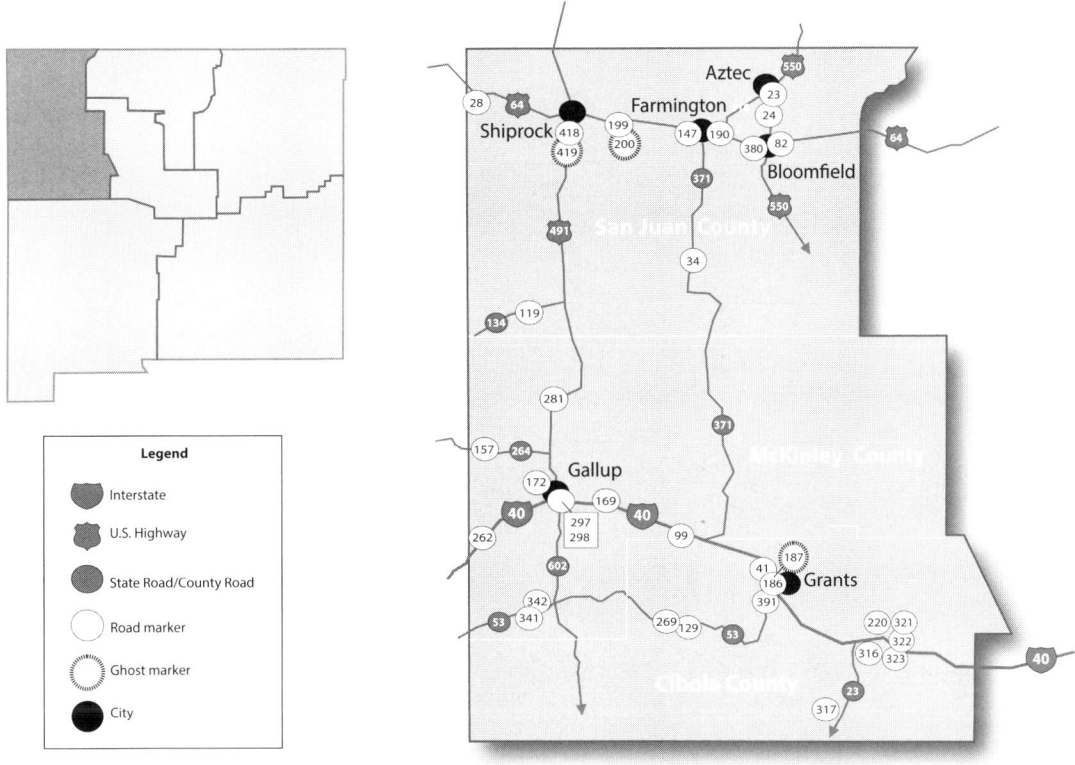

Map No. 2: North-Central Region

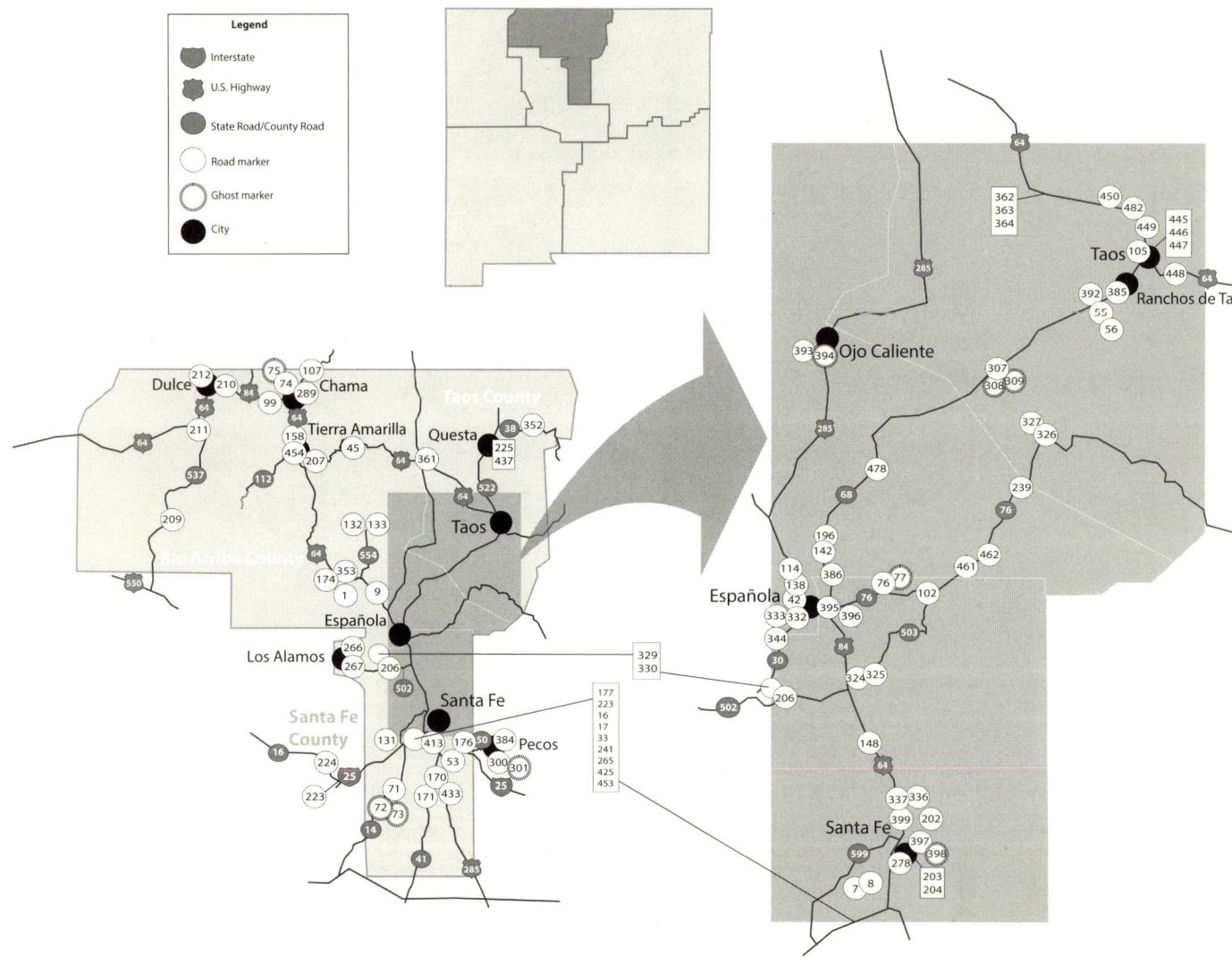

Map No. 3: Northeast Region

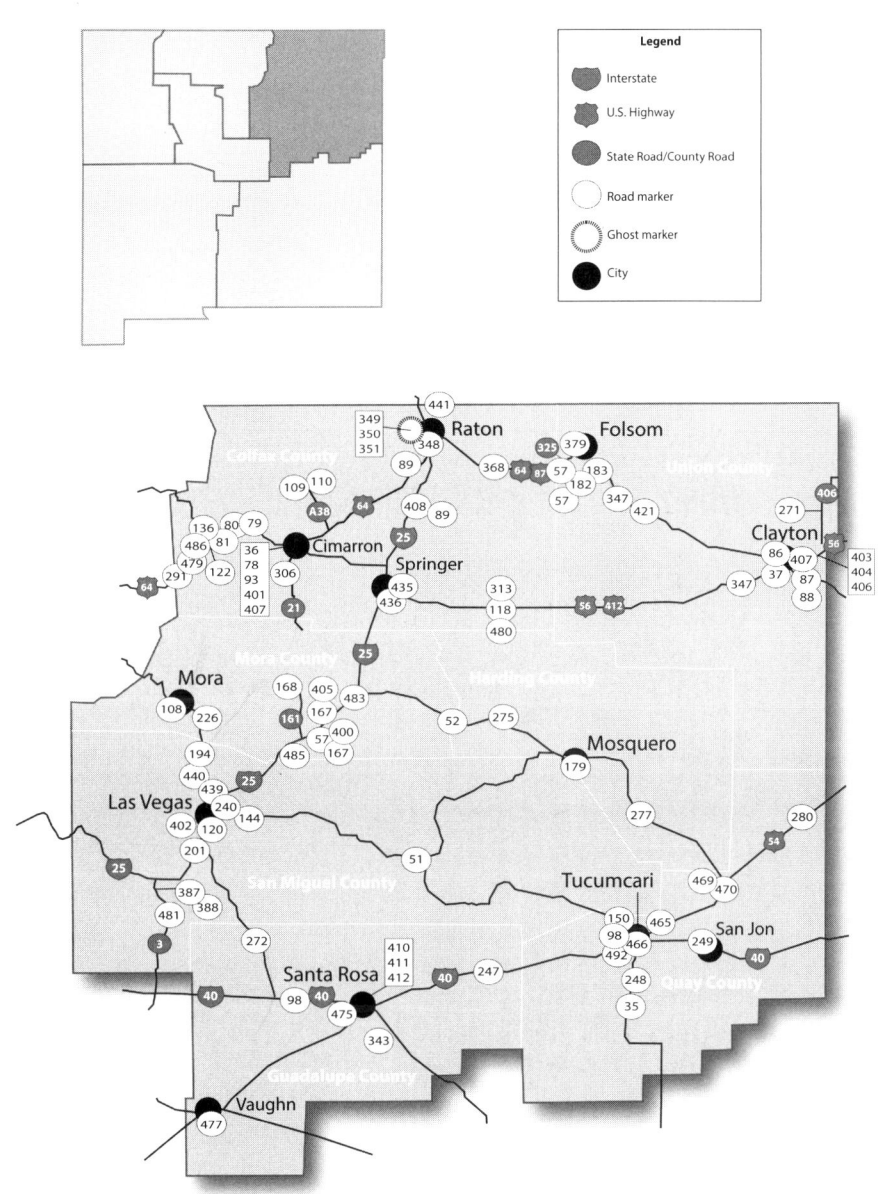

Map No. 4: Central Region

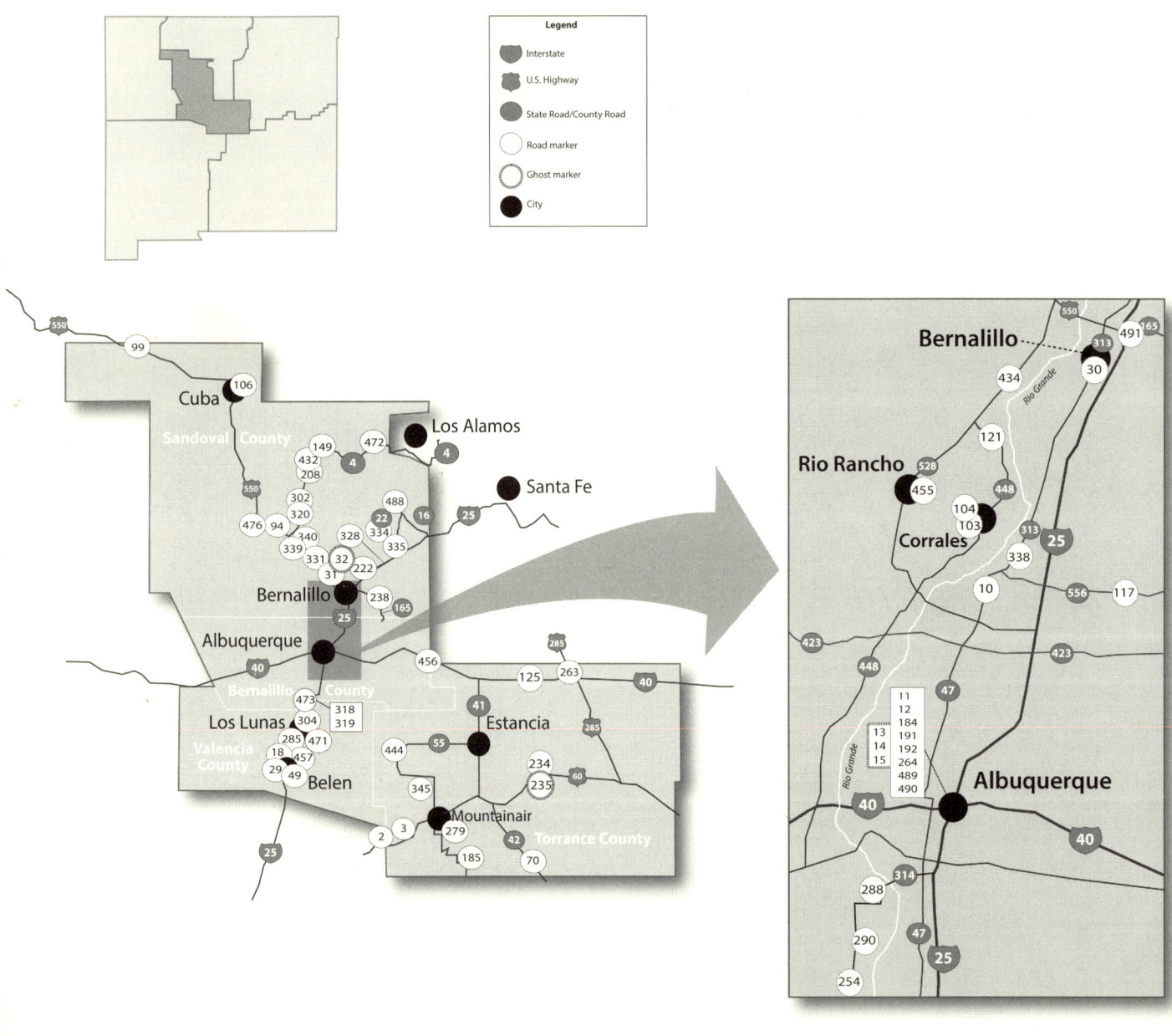

Map No. 5: Southwest Region

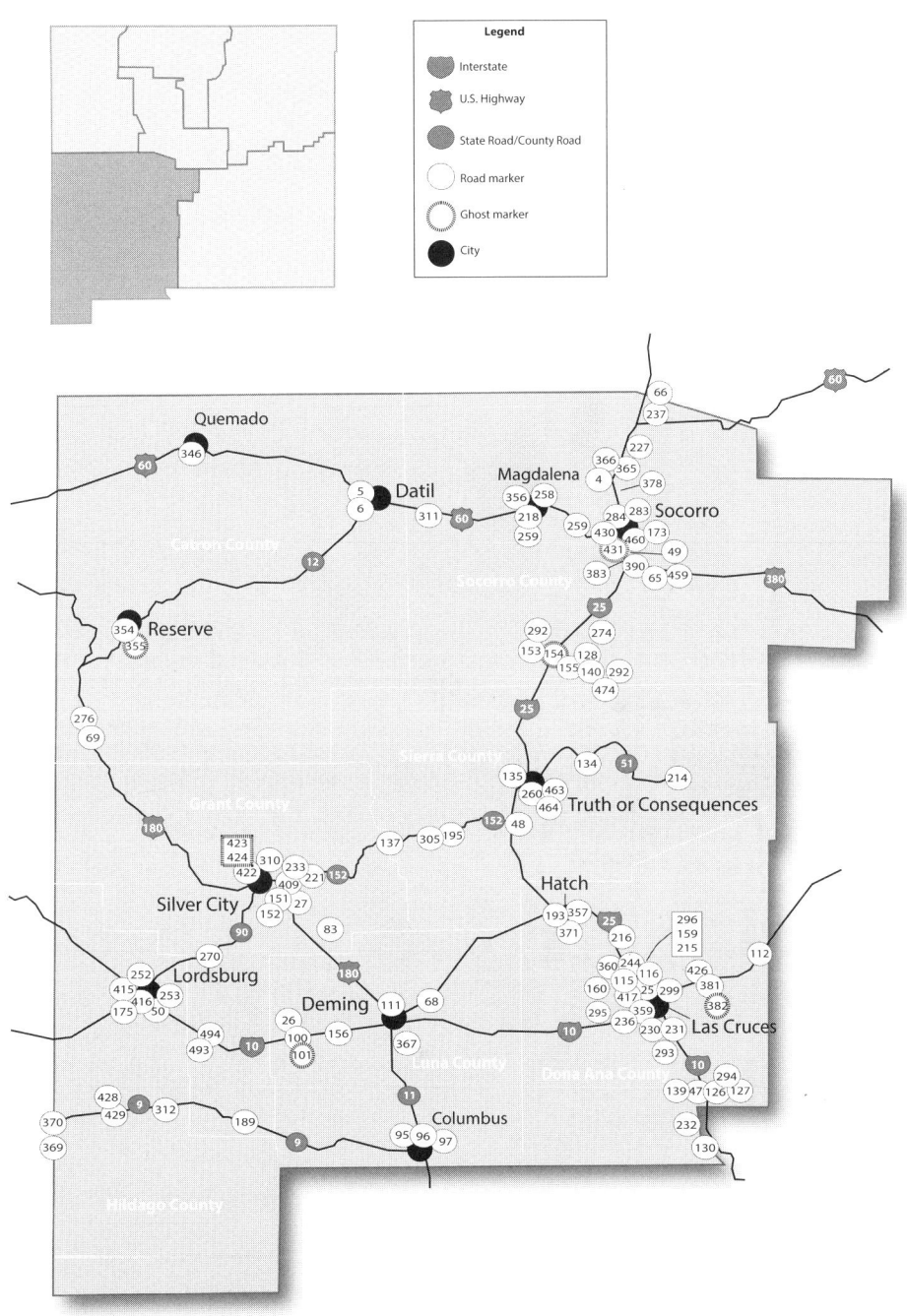

Map No. 6: Southeast Region

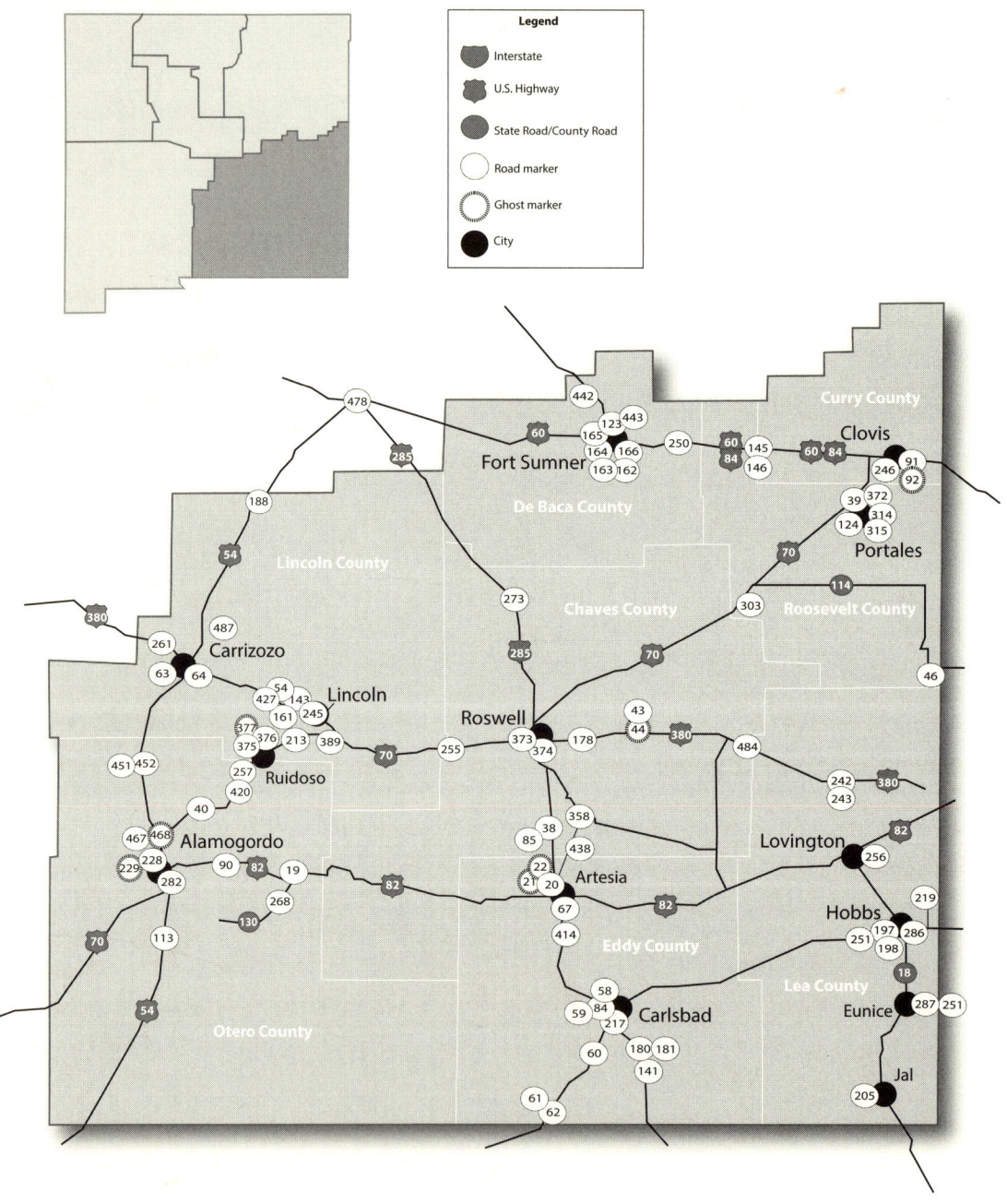

Alphabetical Listing of New Mexico Historic Markers

1. Abiquiú

Location: Rio Arriba County. At the eastern end of Abiquiú, on the north side of US 84, between mile markers 211 and 212. See map 2.

Marker text: Established on the site of an abandoned Indian pueblo, Abiquiú in the mid-18th century became a settlement of Spaniards and *genízaros* (Hispanicized Indians). In 1776, explorers Fray Francisco Atanacio Domínguez and Fray Silvestre Vélez de Escalante visited here. In 1830, the settlement became one of the stops on the Spanish Trail which linked Santa Fe with Los Angeles, California.

Famous as the one-time home of artist Georgia O'Keeffe, Abiquiú remains a rural village, cuddled against the Rio Chama as it flows between the San Juan Mountains to the north and the Jemez Mountains to the south. The rugged mesas and canyon lands, vermilion rock cliffs, and awe-inspiring vistas surrounding Abiquiú, including beautiful 9,857-foot Cerro Pedernal nearby, have become scenic emblems of the Southwest.

It was in this vivid landscape that Tewa-speaking Indians first constructed a series of pueblos, probably, archaeologists suspect, in the late fifteenth century. They also planted fields atop a nearby mesa. The Indians abandoned their pueblos sometime in the 1500s.

In the eighteenth century, the pasturelands along the Rio Chama attracted the attention of Spanish-speaking settlers. By 1734, colonists had established Santa Rosa de Lima de Abiquiú. The word *abiquiú* is believed to be derived from the original Tewa pueblo name, and one linguistic interpretation translates its meaning as "hooting of an owl." Harassment by Apache, Navajo, and Ute Indians in the village, then one of the farthest Spanish settlements northwest of Santa Fe, eventually compelled the Abiquiú settlers to abandon their homes.

In 1750, Governor Tomás Vélez Cachupín ordered resettlement of the grant. A handful of fugitive families returned and formed a new settlement that borrowed in part the name of the old, Santo Tomas de Abiquiú. The Spanish were joined in this effort by thirteen genízaros, or Hispanicized Indians, who established a small community of their own a few miles from the Spanish village near where the earlier Tewa pueblo had stood—the present site of Abiquiú.

In 1776, Abiquiú was one of the first villages visited by the wayfaring priestly duo of Fray Francisco Atanasio Domínguez and Fray Silvestre Vélez de Escalante. The Catholic Church had tasked Domínguez and Escalante to open a route between Santa Fe and Monterey, California, and to proselytize native people they encountered along the way. Departing Santa Fe on July 29, the priests traveled north along the Chama River and arrived in Abiquiú the following day. Here they remained for two days before journeying into Colorado along with two genízaro guides from the Abiquiú area. A piercing-cold snowstorm cut short their expedition in present-day Utah in October, and the priests returned to Santa Fe.

Through the Chama River Valley into Colorado and into lands farther west, the priests were tracing portions of a route that would become what is known today as the Spanish Trail. The first to travel its full length from New Mexico to California was the Mexican trader Antonio Armijo, who led a sixty-man caravan from Abiquiú in November 1829. The men reached the San Gabriel Mission near Los Angeles, California, the last stop on their journey, at the end of January 1830. Thereafter, extensive New Mexico trade processions embarked on this three-month round-trip journey every fall. Use of the Spanish Trail waned after the mid-eighteenth century as travelers began using other routes to the Pacific coast, and the railroad spelled its end altogether.

More to explore: *Deming, Domínguez-Escalante Trail, Georgia O'Keeffe*

2. Abó Pass Trail

Location: Torrance County. West of Mountainair, in a roadside pullout on the north side of US 60, between mile markers 189 and 190. See map 4.

Marker text: This route through the southern edge of the Manzano Mountains links the Rio Grande Valley to the salt lakes and Salinas Pueblo missions east of the mountains. The road began as a Pueblo trade route to the eastern plains and later connected the Spanish-period Camino Real to the region. Evolution of the route continued when the Santa Fe Railway completed its Belen Cutoff route through the pass in 1908 and with subsequent construction of a modern highway.

Highway 60 parallels a much older trail that squeezed through a pass between the Los Pinos Mountains to the south and the Manzano Mountains to the north. The pass and trail took their names, Abó Pass and Abó Pass Trail, from the Tompiro-speaking pueblo of Abó in the valley southeast of the Manzano Mountains. Centuries before the arrival of the Spanish in 1598, Indians at Abó, Gran Quivira, Quarai, and other pueblos of the Estancia Valley were active participants in a trade network between the Pueblo Indians living along the Rio Grande and the Plains Indian tribes like the Comanches to the east. In addition to beans, cotton, shells, and buffalo meat, one of the major commodities of exchange over the Abó Pass Trail was salt mined from the small basin playas nearby, lakes that are remembered in the Spanish name of the Estancia Valley pueblos—Salinas.

In the seventeenth and eighteenth centuries, travel through Abó Pass gave missionaries and traders access to the Camino Real along the Rio Grande, the major road between Mexico and Santa Fe for two hundred years. After the Southwest came under American control in 1846, the pass allowed an expedition headed by Army Major James H. Carleton to visit the Salinas Pueblos, then in ruins. Traveling in December 1853, Carleton left an evocative description of his journey through Abó Pass:

The scene presented by the column winding its circuitous route to the summit, with parts of it lost to view behind some jutting crag, or just emerging into sight from some deep gorge—the foreground filled with the dragoons moving upon different turns of the road, the sun glancing brightly on their appointments—the towering snow-clad peaks on either hand—the background the valley of the Rio Grande, with the distant mountains in the northwest marking with a serrated line the far off horizon—was a picture whose beauty will not easily be forgotten.

Carleton's assertion that this route would be ideal for a railroad came to fruition in early 1903, when crews with the Santa Fe Railway ran track from Belen southeastward through Abó Canyon, which lies north of the pass, and then eastward to Texas. The route, known as the Belen Cutoff because it branched off the main line at Belen, allowed trains to avoid the punishing 3.5 percent grade over Raton Pass in northern New Mexico. The first commercial service on the cutoff began operation on December 18, 1907, with trains following very closely the route Carleton had envisioned many decades before.

More to explore: *Abó Ruins, Belen, El Camino Real—The King's Highway, Laguna del Perro*

3. Abó Ruins
Salinas National Monument
3/4 Mile North

Location: Torrance County. Just west of Mountainair, in a pullout on the north side of the intersection of NM 513 and US 60, the turnoff to Abó National Monument. See map 4.

Marker text: Located adjacent to the major east-west trade route through Abó Pass, the Tompiro Pueblo of Abó (ca. 1300s–1670s) was one of the Southwest's largest Pueblo Indian villages. Extensive Indian house complexes are dominated by the unique buttressed walls, 40 feet high, of the Spanish Franciscan mission church of San Gregorio de Abó, built around 1630.

Abó was once one of the largest Pueblo Indian villages in the Southwest. The Tompiro-speaking Indians who lived in the pueblo and in other nearby villages emerged in the Estancia Basin around 1300 as an amalgam of Puebloan and Mogollon cultures. Indians at Abó hunted rabbits and deer in the Manzano Mountains and preserved the meat with salt gathered from the basin playas in this part of New Mexico. That salt was also a valuable article of trade along the major trade route that ran through Abó Pass between the Manzanos and the Los Pinos Mountains to the east. The Abó Pass Trail fostered a network of exchange, allowing Indians at Abó to broker commodities like cotton, made possible by the longer growing seasons of the pueblos of the Rio Grande Valley, with delicacies like dried beef from the Plains Indians to the east.

As the Spanish began to settle New Mexico in the seventeenth century, Franciscan priests arrived to administer the faith among the Indians of the valley. Fray Francisco Fonte came to Abó around 1622 and directed the Indians in the erection of the mission church, the Mission San Gregorio de Abó. He was joined a few years later by Fray Francisco de Acevado, who oversaw renovations and expansions to the mission. Big was in. The towering forty-foot buttressed chapel walls, made from locally quarried red sandstone, dominated the smaller pueblo complex adjacent to them. A *convento* attached to the chapel contained the priests' living quarters and a classroom for religious instruction.

Secular and holy did not mix well in central New Mexico in the mid-1600s. Nicolás de Aguilar served as *alcalde mayor*, the ranking citizen in the Salinas district, which included Abó. Under the encomendero system of civil authority in effect at the time, Aguilar was entitled to the use of Indian labor and taxes in the form of cloth and corn, provided he protected and educated the Indians in his district. Aguilar quarreled with Fray Antonio Aguado, resident priest at San Gregorio from 1659 to 1662, about the proper use of Indian labor. One testimony from the time relates a breakdown this bitter disparity caused:

Father Fray Antonio Aguado availed himself of an Indian named Bartolomé, who knew Castilian, with whose aid he administered the sacraments to the Indians, and supplied what he lacked of that language in administering to the Indians, and in preaching. Learning this, Nicolás de Aguilar ordered this interpreter on no account to enter the convent, imposing upon him the penalty of two hundred lashes; thereby did Nicolás de Aguilar on his own initiative place an obstacle in the way of the administration of the holy sacraments and the spiritual welfare of those souls.

Beset by a decade of political discord, frequent Apache raids, droughts, disease, and famine, Abó broke. Between the years 1672 and 1675, the Indians left their homes to join other pueblos along the Rio Grande. Apache Indians later burned the abandoned pueblo.

More to explore: *Abó Pass Trail, Gran Quivira Ruins, Quarai Ruins*

4. Acomilla

Location: Socorro County. North of Socorro, in the Walking Sands Rest Area, on the west side of Interstate 25, at mile marker 167. See map 5.

Marker text: Named Acomilla by the Spanish, these buttes form the walls of a narrow passage for the Rio Grande, along which Spanish encountered the Apache. Travelers organized armed caravans to assure their safety along this section of the Camino Real. An earlier pueblo named Alamillo sat below the black basaltic buttes of San Acacia to the southeast.

Until well into the nineteenth century, settlers and merchants traveling between New Mexico and Mexico trod a well-worn path known as El Camino Real, or the Royal Road. Geographic features along the Camino Real became milestones for travelers. As it crossed through this part of the state, the Camino Real weaved along the base of the dark buttes visible about three miles to the southeast from this rest area (they are the smaller buttes to the east of the interstate and not the prominent mountain directly south). The Spanish originally named this region Acomilla, or Little Acoma, for reasons unknown. The most prominent butte later began to carry the name it has today, San Acacia Butte. The name San Acacia comes from Saint Acacius, a soldier in the Roman army who was tortured and beheaded by the emperor Diocletian for refusing to renounce his strong faith.

For many years, a small Piro-speaking Pueblo Indian village known to the Spanish as Alamillo existed somewhere near the butte. That name translates as "little cottonwood" and was likely a reference to cottonwood trees in the area. The pueblo may at one time have had up to three hundred residents and was ministered to by Spanish priests during the seventeenth century. Abandoned in the Pueblo Revolt of 1680, it was never resettled, although its ruins became a stopping point along the Camino Real. Today, those ruins have vanished, and the exact location of the pueblo is unknown, but it was believed to have been on the east bank of the Rio Grande. However, a more recent settlement on the west bank of the river borrowed the name and survives today as the village of Alamillo.

For most of the 1700s and into the 1800s, only a few scattered ranches and campsites lay within the 135-mile stretch of the Camino Real between La Joya, just north of here, and El Paso, to the south. The Spanish knew this desert landscape as *el despoblado*, the unpopulated land. In particular, at Acomilla, the Rio Grande flowed close to the base of the small hills and cramped the passage for caravans, creating an ideal junction for attacks by hostile Apache Indians on unwary travelers. Wagon masters leading the annual caravans over the Camino Real left Santa Fe organized into armed squads to minimize the threat of such attacks and to protect themselves should one occur.

In the early 1880s, after the Atchison, Topeka, and Santa Fe Railway ran rails past the base of San Acacia butte, settlers established the small village of San Acacia near the tracks. Census records for the village show a population that rarely exceeded four hundred through 1950. The small settlement survives to this day.

Because nouns in the Spanish language have gender, the grammatically correct name of the village and butte would actually be San Acacio, the *o* representing the masculine noun *san*, or male saint. (*Santa* is the feminine form of "saint" in Spanish.) Indeed, that was the original name of the village. The naming error likely arose when the village was given a post office in 1881 and has never been corrected, in part because of the cost associated in doing so. Locals often use the correct form, San Acacio, when referring to their village and butte.

More to explore: *El Camino Real—The King's Highway, La Joya de Sevilleta, Mesa del Contadero*

5. Ada McPherson Morley

Location: Catron County. North of Datil, in a pullout on the east side of US 60, between mile markers 69 and 70. See map 5.

Marker text: Ada McPherson Morley ran a ranch outside of Datil, New Mexico where she raised three children, including Agnes Morley Cleaveland. A crusader for women's rights, she opposed the infamous Santa Fe Ring, worked for women's suffrage for over thirty years, and formed societies for the Prevention of Cruelty to Animals as well as the Prevention of Cruelty to Children.

6. Agnes Morley Cleaveland (1874–1958)

Marker text: New Mexican, Agnes Morley Cleaveland grew up on her family's ranch near Datil, New Mexico. Her prize-winning book, No Life for A Lady (1941), is an autobiographical story of a woman's life on a turn-of-the-century ranch. She was educated and lived in other parts of the country, but always returned home to Datil where she spent the last years of her life.

Note: Marker faceplates are on opposite sides of the same sign.

The autobiographical novel *No Life for a Lady* is a classic of New Mexico literature. In strong and heartfelt prose, author Agnes Morley Cleaveland writes of her life growing up with her family on their ranch in this part of southwestern New Mexico as the nineteenth century ended and the twentieth century began. But the background for the story begins much earlier, with Cleaveland's own mother, Ada McPherson Morley.

The railroad brought Iowa-born Ada McPherson Morley to New Mexico. Newly married to railroad surveyor and Civil War veteran William Raymond Morley, Ada in 1871 accompanied her husband to the village of Cimarron in northeastern New Mexico. There, William Morley served as the executive officer of the Maxwell Land Grant and Railway Company. The Morleys arrived at a pivotal time in the history of Colfax County, and their position and professional interests put them squarely in the center of a brewing land rights dispute that would erupt into what became known as the Colfax County War.

The Maxwell Land Grant and Railway Company managed the affairs of the Maxwell Land Grant, the largest tract of privately owned land in New Mexico. Named for its former owner, Lucien Bonaparte Maxwell, the grant encompassed almost two million acres of land in northeastern New Mexico, including that around Cimarron and the gold-rich mountains nearby. Maxwell had earlier sold his grant to a group of English investors, who had mismanaged the legal affairs. With the formation of the Maxwell Land Grant and Railway Company, Morley and others had been brought in to help the company become stable again and wrestle with difficult land rights issues surrounding the grant.

That proved exceedingly difficult. Disagreements about the management of the company arose between Morley and the company president, Stephen B. Elkins, who was also a delegate in the territorial legislature. Morley found himself distrustful of Elkins's alignment with the Santa Fe Ring—the name given to an unofficial cabal of powerful politicians, attorneys, and land speculators operating chiefly out of Santa Fe. Working in collusion with other powerful officials, these men used their political influence to dominate New Mexico politics. They built wealth in part by acquiring land through unscrupulous means; the Ring was, in fact, disputing the size of the Maxwell land grant. Their numbers included district attorney Thomas B. Catron, who would later serve as one of New Mexico's first two senators after statehood, and even the New Mexico governor, Samuel Axtell.

Morley openly editorialized against the Ring on

Smart, civic-minded, and compassionate, Ada McPherson Morley was, as the *Las Vegas Optic* newspaper would later state, "one of the intellectual aristocrats of the Southwest." Ada McPherson Morley. New Mexico State University Library, Archives and Special Collections.

Ada's daughter, Agnes Morley Cleaveland, captured ranch life in Datil, New Mexico, in the nineteenth century in her book, *No Life for a Lady*. Agnes Morley Cleaveland. New Mexico State University Library, Archives and Special Collections.

the pages of the company-owned newspaper, the *Cimarron News and Press*. But it was a letter that proved the inciting factor between the Morleys and the Santa Fe Ring—a letter that was, oddly, never sent. When Ada McPherson Morley's visiting mother wrote a missive critical of the Santa Fe Ring, Ada herself went to the post office to retrieve it before it entered the mail system. Soon enough, none other than Thomas B. Catron himself, no friend of the Morleys, had filed an indictment against her for mail theft. The Morleys believed that the case, if it went to trial, would enrage public sentiment against Catron and undermine the political influence of Stephen Elkins—and indeed,

the case was eventually dropped. Nonetheless, the damage had been done. Morley left the company soon thereafter.

On June 26, 1874, in Cimarron, Ada gave birth to a baby girl, Agnes. Sadly, when Agnes was only eight years old, her father died of an accidental gunshot while surveying a railroad line in Mexico. Ada was left alone with their three children. She remarried and began a new life, convinced by her new husband to move to south-central New Mexico and the small community known as Datil. There, they established the Swinging W Ranch.

A social activist, Ada Morley had long advocated for the women's suffrage movement, writing letters and editorials to newspapers in support of that cause. According to her grandson, who wrote a book about his recollection of the Morley family, she was firm in her belief that "once women obtained the right to vote, all the reforms society so urgently needed would soon be made." Ada also served as the president of the New Mexico Chapter of the Woman's Christian Temperance Union, part of the national temperance movement that hoped to discourage drinking. She formed a state chapter of the Society for the Prevention of Cruelty to Animals, or SPCA, a group established nationally in 1866 by civil activist Henry Bergh to advocate for the proper care and treatment of animals. She also formed a chapter of the related organization, the Society for the Prevention of Cruelty to Children.

Despite having convinced Ada and the family to move to Datil and begin a ranching life there, Ada's new husband soon left the family. Ada found herself alone again to raise her three children, Ray, Agnes, and Lora, and to manage the ranch on her own.

An advocate for a strong education, Ada sent all her children to schools in the East. Agnes attended school in Philadelphia and later graduated from Stanford University, where she met and, in 1899, married Newton Cleaveland. She lived in California for much of her life, but she returned often to the Datil ranch, finding there a true sense of the land and way of life she most admired. She captured that essence in her 1941 book, *No Life for a Lady*.

Upon the death of her husband in 1945, Agnes returned to live on the Datil ranch. In a bit of a historical turnabout, in 1948 she published a book about the Cimarron country, with stories of the people and historical incidents there, including a recollection of her father's involvement in the incidents of the Colfax County War. She titled the book *Satan's Paradise*.

Ada McPherson Morley, the matriarch of this longtime ranching family, passed away on December 9, 1917. Her daughter Agnes survived her by forty-one years, passing away on March 8, 1958, after which her ashes were scattered over her beloved ranch.

A monument to the Morley family can be viewed on the west side of US 60 between mile markers 72 and 73, a few miles down from this pullout.

More to explore: *Cimarron, Colfax County War, Peggy Pond Church (see under Marjorie Bell Chambers)*

7. Agua Fria

Location: Santa Fe County. In Agua Fria, in front of the Agua Fria Elementary School, on the south side of Agua Fria Road. See map 2.

Marker text: Caravans entering and leaving Santa Fe on the Camino Real wound their way through scattered agricultural settlements south of the capital. Although this section of the Santa Fe River Valley was initially utilized as pasture for livestock, in the 17th century farmers were attracted to its arable lands and to the fresh water springs from which the community derives its name.

8. San Isidro Catholic Church

Location: Santa Fe County. In Agua Fria, in front of the San Isidro Catholic Church, on the south side of road, near the intersection of Agua Fria Road and Paseo Mel Senaida. See map 2.

Marker text: This 19th century adobe church is dedicated to San Isidro the ploughman, patron saint of farmers and protector of crops. Christian tradition maintains that in order to allow San Isidro time for his daily prayers, an angel plowed his fields. Agua Fria annually observes this fifteenth day of May as "His Day of Goodwill" to honor his role in this agricultural community along El Camino Real.

Esta iglesia fue construida en el siglo XIX y dedicada a San Isidro, patron de los labradores y protector de la cosecha. Tradición Christiana dice que un angel barbecho la tierra minetras San Isidro rezaba. La communidad de Agua Frida cada año celebra el quince de Mayo como "Dia de Benevolencia," en respeto de su ayuda a este pueblo Labrador a lo largo del Camino Real.

Spanish colonists living in Santa Fe in the seventeenth century found the freshwater springs and irrigable grasslands along this stretch of the Santa Fe River Valley valuable pastureland for livestock. Although historians do not know when permanent Spanish settlement here began, land grant petitions suggest that several families had already moved in before 1700. Eventually a small farming village developed, going by the name Quemado, or "burned," a Spanish word by which the ruins of an earlier Indian pueblo here had sometimes been known. The name of the community later changed to Agua Fria, or "cold water," for the refreshing local springs.

Agua Fria was one of several smaller agricultural villages clustered astride the Camino Real south of Santa Fe. While the land was still under the direction of Spain, the Camino Real, or Royal Road, linked Santa Fe, Taos, and other settlements in New Mexico with the controlling authorities in Mexico. Until the demise of the route coincident with the coming of the railroad in the 1880s, Agua Fria was one of the last stops northbound travelers on the Camino Real made before reaching Santa Fe.

One historical account of the village comes from the journal of Lieutenant James W. Abert, a military officer at the head of an expedition to the Southwest in 1846, who thought to question the farming practices of the residents:

We marched 6 miles and formed our camp at Agua Fria. Here we were obliged to buy corn and wood, for the country around is settled and the grazing ground appropriated. . . . [I]n some of the yards fine apricot trees were growing, but I wonder much if they bear anything, they were planted so close together.

As defined by a survey conducted in 1983 by archaeologist Jane Whitmore, the district boundaries today extend roughly from the intersection of Agua Fria and Siler Roads south along the Santa Fe River to the Santa Fe airport. Although development in western Santa Fe has encroached on historic Agua Fria, Whitmore relates that the community retains today much of its character as a semirural village.

The beautiful Catholic church in Agua Fria bears the dedication of Saint Isidore, the patron saint of farmers and of Madrid, Spain. Born in that city into an impoverished household, Isidore toiled as a farm laborer. He married, but when his first son died at a young age, he devoted his life to serving God. He prayed even as he plowed, and tradition holds that a guardian angel helped guide his farm instruments as he meditated. He died on May 15, 1130. Residents of Agua Fria observe his death and subsequent canonization every year on that day with a service at the San Isidro Catholic Church.

More to explore: *El Camino Real—The King's Highway, Iglesia de San Ysidro (see under Corrales), Santa Fe*

9. Agueda Martinez (1898–2000)
"You Will Find Me Dancing on the Loom"

Location: Rio Arriba County. North of Hernandez, in a pullout at the intersection of US 84/285 and NM 74, between mile markers 203 and 204 on US 84. See map 2.

Marker text: Agueda is the matriarch of Hispanic weaving in New Mexico. From a very young age, she was known for her complex designs and natural dyes. She was the subject of the Academy Award–nominated documentary film, "Agueda Martinez: Our People, Our Country." Her weaving is carried on by fifty-two direct descendants and can be seen today in many museums, including the Smithsonian.

Produced in 1977, the film *Agueda Martinez: Our People, Our Country* documents the life and work of New Mexico weaver Agueda Salazar Martinez. Nominated for an Academy Award in the category of Best Documentary Short Subject, the film shows doña Agueda (Lady Agueda), as she was often called, working in the fields of the farm she ran with her husband, and also in her home weaving. It was the latter craft for which she became best known. Her talent at the loom matched her passion for the art of weaving, a fortunate partnership that resulted in a colorful array of finely woven textiles produced over a lifetime—one that spanned more than a century. For her prolific output, for the number of her descendants who sustain the tradition, and for setting a high creative standard in the fine art of weaving, doña Agueda has come to be regarded as the matriarch of Hispanic weaving in New Mexico.

Doña Agueda was born on March 13, 1898, in the small village of Chamita, New Mexico, across the Rio Chama about two miles east of this Historic Marker. This part of north-central New Mexico has acquired a reputation for its centuries-old traditions of textile weaving. Doña Agueda joined that tradition early in her life: by age twelve, she was producing her first "rag rug" weavings (a rag rug is a weaving made from unused scrap fabrics). She later studied the craft with another weaver in the nearby village of Chimayó and soon was developing a style that would later bring her international acclaim. Initially, she used money from selling her weavings to supplement the earnings she and her husband, Eusebio, made from their farm in Medanales, New Mexico. (Her husband was also a weaver.) Those sales brought outside attention to her work. Soon she was exhibiting her talent in shows, and her weavings became admired by collectors and museums.

A piece acquired by the Smithsonian American Art Museum in 1995, when Martinez was ninety-seven years old, is typical of her style, which incorporates elements of Hispanic and Native American design and features geometric shapes, bold colors, and stripes. In the piece, jagged chevrons of reds, oranges, greens, purples, and browns alternate outward in rows from a center diamond, creating symmetrical patterns repeated across the length of the weaving, each one separated by brown and white stripes. The gentle, symmetrical patterns of the design present a sophisticated beauty.

Doña Agueda worked on a handmade wooden loom in her house, using wools she dyed from plants harvested at her Medanales farm. She might spend six hours a day or more at the loom, but hers was a labor of true love, fueled by a talented passion. She wove almost every day.

"I love to weave, and I never get tired doing this work," she once said. "I will weave until the day I can no longer move. Until then, you will find me dancing on the loom."

Doña Agueda raised a family of ten children. Those children had children of their own, many of whom carried on her interest in and talent for weaving. A large number of her direct descendants (fifty-two by one count) are practicing weavers today.

Doña Agueda passed away in 2000 at the age of 102.

More to explore: *Chimayó, Estella García (see under Fabric Artists)*

10. Alameda

Location: Bernalillo County. Near the community of Alameda, at the north end of Albuquerque, in a pullout on the north side of the intersection of Second and Fourth Streets. See map 4.

Marker text: This 18th century Spanish settlement was established on the site of an ancient Tiwa Indian Pueblo that was destroyed following the Pueblo Revolt of 1680. The pueblo was reestablished in 1702, but in 1708 the Spanish moved its Tiwa inhabitants to help resettle the Pueblo of Isleta. Here the Camino Real passed by cottonwood groves from which the community derived its name.

When don Juan de Oñate made his colonizing expedition to New Mexico in 1598, he passed a pueblo here, on the west bank of the Rio Grande, whose inhabitants spoke the Tiwa language. The pueblo was one of several Tiwa-speaking pueblos in the area, including the ones known today as Tuf Shurn Tui (formerly Sandia Pueblo) and Isleta. An inventory of the pueblos in New Mexico in 1680 mentioned that the pueblo here at the time had three hundred residents and that it was known by the name the Spanish had given it, Alameda. That name is derived from the Spanish word for cottonwood, *alamo*, and likely came from groves of cottonwood trees that, the inventory noted, "shaded the road for four leagues."

That road was the historic Camino Real, or Royal Road, the main trade and colonization route that developed between New Mexico and Mexico after Oñate's expedition and that continued for two hundred years thereafter.

In the same year of that inventory, 1680, an uprising occurred among the Pueblo Indians of New Mexico. In protest against Spanish colonists who were usurping their land and preventing them from worshiping freely, Pueblo Indians throughout New Mexico rebelled and violently expelled the Spanish from the state. The following year, Governor Antonio de Otermín attempted to reenter New Mexico. He found that many of the pueblos along the Rio Grande, along with Spanish haciendas (large ranch homes), had been abandoned or destroyed in the revolt. At Alameda, Otermín's officers found an empty pueblo, the Indians having fled in fear of him and his troops a few days prior. Otermín ordered the pueblo (and others near it) burned. A full return of the Spanish into New Mexico did not take place until 1692.

In 1702, Fray Juan de Sabalita assisted Tiwa Indians in repopulating the Alameda pueblo and establishing a small mission there. But only six years later, the Indians moved to Isleta, another Tiwa pueblo about ten miles south, to join with other Isletans who were returning after the revolt to resettle their pueblo. The pueblo of Alameda was abandoned.

The story of Alameda continues with a Spanish land grant made in 1710 to Captain Francisco Montes Vigil. Originally the grant included land on the west side of the river, but the river later changed course, and the Hispanic farming village of Alameda that had arisen soon found itself on the east side of the river. It remains there today, a small village in the north valley of Albuquerque.

More to explore: *Albuquerque, El Camino Real—The King's Highway, La Salineta, Pueblo of Isleta*

11. Albuquerque

Location: Bernalillo County. In Albuquerque, on the plaza in Old Town Albuquerque. See map 4.

Marker text: In 1706, New Mexico governor Francisco Cuervo y Valdes founded the new Villa de Albuquerque (now Albuquerque), which became the principal settlement of the Rio Abajo, or lower river district. Here, the Camino Real wound its way through a series of farming and ranching communities and led to a nearby ford which linked the Camino Real to settlements on the west bank of the Rio Grande.

Note: The original name of the villa had an *r* before the first *q*—Alburquerque—which has been left out of the text of this Historic Marker.

12. Founding Women of Albuquerque

Location: Bernalillo County. In Albuquerque, at the Albuquerque Museum, 2000 Mountain Road NW. See map 4.

Marker text: In February 1706 several families participated in the founding of Albuquerque but the names of only 22 are preserved in the historical record. Within those families were many women honored as being founders of La Villa San Felipe de Alburquerque. Their success in the face of incredible challenges is testament to their courage and bravery. Their names are recorded on the back of this marker.

Isabel Cedillo Rico de Rojas, María de la Encarnación, Francisca de Góngora, Gregoria de Góngora, María Gutiérrez, Juana Hurtado, Juana López del Castillo, Antonia Gregoria Lucero de Godoy, Leonor Luján Domínguez, Francisca Montoya, Juana Montoya, María Montoya, Clementa de Ortega, María de Ortega, María de Ribera, Jacinta Romero, Gregoria Ruiz, Bernardina de Salas Orozco y Trujillo, Josefa Tamaris, Catalina Varela Jaramillo, María Varela, Petrona Varela

13. Ghost Marker: Old Town Plaza—On the Camino Real

Marker text: The center of Albuquerque's Old Town, the plaza dates from the early 18th century. San Felipe de Neri Church was established in 1706, but construction of the present structure was begun in 1793. In March 1862, General Henry H. Sibley and his Texas volunteers occupied Albuquerque and raised the Confederate flag here.

Note: This marker appears in an inventory of Historic Markers compiled by the Historic Preservation Division but is not in the field. See map 4.

14. Ghost Marker: Albuquerque Petroglyphs

Marker text: Over 15,000 petroglyphs have been carved into the lava rock which covers the mesa west of the Rio Grande. The earliest of these rock drawings were made by prehistoric inhabitants almost 3000 years ago. Many others were added by Pueblo peoples and later by Spanish explorers and settlers. This gallery of ancient art is interpreted at Petroglyph State Park 6 miles south of here.

Note: This marker appears in an inventory of Historic Markers compiled by the Historic Preservation Division but is not in the field. See map 4.

15. Ghost Marker: Sandia Mountains

Marker text: A giant block of the earth's crust tipped up sideways, the Sandia Mountains are a range of the Basin and Range province in New Mexico. The adjoining Rio Grande rift contains deep aquifers that provide water for the large population center of Albuquerque. Sandia Crest elevation is 10,678 feet.

Note: This marker appears in an inventory of Historic Markers compiled by the Historic Preservation Division but is not in the field. See map 4.

Pueblo Indians had been living and farming in the middle Rio Grande Valley for generations before the Spanish arrived in the seventeenth century. Spanish settlement in the region began as colonists built a scattering of estancias, or ranch homes, along the river south of present-day Albuquerque. This early Spanish occupation did not last; settlers were driven away during the Pueblo Revolt of 1680, an insurrection among the Pueblo Indians against Spanish authority in the state.

After twelve years in exile, the Spanish returned to New Mexico and began resettlement of the land. In the colonial demarcations of the era, the region south of Santa Fe was known as the Rio Abajo, or Lower River. (The Rio Arriba, or Upper River, designated the land north of Santa Fe.) To serve as the seat of government for this district, Spanish governor don Francisco Cuervo y Valdés founded here in 1706 the town of San Francisco de Alburquerque. The name, complete with the extra *r* in *Alburquerque*, honored don Francisco Fernández de la Cueva, the duke of Alburquerque, viceroy of Spain. Governor Cuervo designated the settlement as a villa, the most esteemed classification for a Spanish town. Only two other villas had been established to that point in New Mexico—Santa Fe, which served as the capital, and Santa Cruz de la Cañada, an important village east of Española. The governor hoped that a new town here, in addition to encouraging settlement of the area, would likewise shield other towns of the lower river from attacks by unfriendly Indians.

The family members who originally settled the villa included, of course, several women. Historians have so far uncovered twenty-two names of women, recorded on the "Founding Women of Albuquerque" Historic Marker, but they suspect there were more not recorded. The stories of these women and their families, along with their genealogical histories, have been compiled in the book *Aquí Se Comienza* by the New Mexico Genealogical Society. These women were indeed the "founding mothers" of Albuquerque. Their stories offer glimpses into the lives, histories, and lineages that came together when this new Spanish settlement was founded. They include doña Bernadina de Salas Orozco y Trujillo, deemed the "Beloved Matriarch" by the Genealogical Society, whose son was the first alcalde mayor of Albuquerque and whose grown children and their extended families were many of the first residents of this new village. Another is Gregoria Ruiz, wife of one of the soldiers appointed to protect the new settlement, whose grandchild, Manuel Armijo, would be the last governor of New Mexico before it came under American rule. Many of the names of these women are still reflected in the history of the region and the state.

The early villagers here tended their fields and pastured their livestock; the town in its infancy, as described by visiting priest Fray Francisco Atanasio Domínguez in 1776, was little more than "a settlement of farms on the meadows of the river for the distance of a league." In the nineteenth century, as English speakers began arriving, Albuquerque lost its second *r*, but it gained in stature and population as the villa slowly embraced the pastoral farming villages adjoining it. The incipient Albuquerque included a central plaza surrounded by smaller buildings and a church, San Felipe de Neri. The plaza and church remain today in an area known as Old Town.

For a short time in the spring of 1862, the Confederate Army advanced through New Mexico on its way to Colorado. Brigadier General Henry Hopkins Sibley and the Texas Volunteers claimed the village for the Confederacy and raised the Confederate flag in the plaza. It was lowered shortly thereafter when the Confederate supply wagons were burned at Glorieta Pass near Santa Fe and the Confederate Army retreated from the state. The next invasion came with the advent of the railroad toward the end of the nineteenth century, bringing new development to Albuquerque. A new, predominantly Anglo community grew around the Santa Fe Railway about a mile and a half east of Old Town. Among the sites in downtown Albuquerque that retain the distinctive character of this period are the Sunshine Building, erected in 1924, and the KiMo Theatre, built in 1927. It was in Albuquerque, too, that famous hotelier Conrad Hilton, born in the New Mexico community of San Antonio near Socorro, chose to erect his first hotel in the state in 1939. It survives today as the Hotel Andaluz.

In 1854, Albuquerque became the county seat of Bernalillo County. It incorporated as a city in 1891 and has since become the most populous city in the state.

Albuquerque is sheltered to the east by the towering Sandia Mountains. The mountains formed as land along a fault line here dropped downward to form the Rio Grande Rift, tipping up sections of earth as a result, one of which formed these mountains. The Sandias are part of the Basin and Range Province of the southwestern United States, characterized by broad valleys interspersed with north-south mountain ranges. The highest peak is Sandia Crest at 10,678 feet. The landscape to the west of Albuquerque includes the West Mesa, a prominent basalt escarpment upon which the ancient people who lived in the valley centuries ago scratched figures, geometric designs, and animal shapes known as petroglyphs. Pueblo Indians in the Rio Grande Valley later added additional carvings, and Hispanic sheepherders soon scratched their own figures on the basalt rocks. Some designs, like that of a face, take advantage of the edge of a rock to present a three-dimensional appearance. About twenty thousand of these carvings in Rinconada Canyon, Boca Negra Canyon, and other locations are preserved today and open to the public as Petroglyph National Monument.

More to explore: *San Antonio, Santa Cruz de la Cañada, Three Rivers Petroglyphs*

16. Amelia Elizabeth White (1878–1972)

Location: Santa Fe County. Fifteen miles south of Santa Fe, in the Bicentennial Rest Area and Visitors Center, on the east side of Interstate 25. (The rest area is also known as the La Bajada Rest Area.) See map 2.

Marker text: Amelia Elizabeth White worked tirelessly to promote Indian art and to preserve Santa Fe's heritage. A philanthropist and community activist, she donated land for the Laboratory of Anthropology and Wheelwright Museum, gave the city its first animal shelter, and established the Garcia Street Club for neighborhood children. Her estate, once a gathering place for local artists, is now home to the School for Advanced Research.

17. Mary Cabot Wheelwright (1878–1958)

Location: Santa Fe County. Fifteen miles south of Santa Fe, in the Bicentennial Rest Area and Visitors Center, on the east side of Interstate 25. (The rest area is also known as the La Bajada Rest Area.) See map 2.

Marker text: Born in Boston, art heiress Mary Cabot Wheelwright came to New Mexico for an extended visit in the 1920s. She restored and lived in Los Luceros, a centuries old Rio Grande estate. Her understanding and advocacy of Navajo spirituality resulted from her association with ceremonial singer Hastiin Klah. Wheelwright created the Museum of Navajo Ceremonial Art, now the Wheelwright Museum of the American Indian.

Note: Marker faceplates are on opposite sides of the same sign.

The two women memorialized on these Historic Markers connected in several ways, from their overlapping lives in Santa Fe to their cultivation of intellectual thought to their advocacy for the preservation of southwestern cultures. One of their most significant links is their connection to the Wheelwright Museum of the American Indian. Opened in 1937, the museum was founded by art heiress and cultural preservationist Mary Cabot Wheelwright, on land donated to her for the purpose by her friend, philanthropist and community activist Amelia Elizabeth White.

Amelia Elizabeth White was born in New York City in 1878. After graduating from Bryn Mawr College in Pennsylvania, she came to New Mexico with her sister, Martha. Arriving in Santa Fe in 1923, the White sisters quickly immersed themselves in the community, becoming known as activists, philanthropists, and promoters of southwestern culture. They built an estate in the city, modeled on the historic chapel at the pueblo of Laguna west of Albuquerque. Amelia White used part of the estate, which they had named El Delirio (the Madness), as a kennel for Irish wolfhounds. In 1939, in honor of her sister, who had passed a few years earlier, White donated land to the city for use as an animal shelter—the first in Santa Fe.

White, who became known as "Miss E," made it somewhat of a habit to donate property to support causes she felt just—and in so doing, changed both the architectural and the cultural landscape of Santa Fe itself. She deeded some fifty acres for the Laboratory of Anthropology in 1927, a research institution funded in large part by John D. Rockefeller to study and help preserve Indian culture. Wanting to provide a safe place for the education of young children in her neighborhood, White also donated a house to what would become the Garcia Street Club. That beneficial organization continues to this day.

In 1937, White donated another plot of land that she owned next to the Laboratory of Anthropology for the establishment of a new museum. Opened originally as the Museum of Navajo Ceremonial Art, the institution is today known as the Wheelwright Museum of the American Indian. The name honors the woman who founded the museum, a friend of White's, art heiress Mary Cabot Wheelwright.

Wheelwright was born in Boston in 1878 to a wealthy family. She spent most of her youth traveling overseas, but she also visited New Mexico for an extended time in 1920. She found that she enjoyed the Southwest and wanted to help preserve what made it so appealing. To that end, she purchased the historic Spanish colonial hacienda known as Los Luceros, north of Española, which she renovated and used as her New Mexico base of operations.

While traveling across the Navajo reservation on one of her visits to the state, Wheelwright met trading post owner Arthur Newcomb, who in turn introduced her to Navajo healer and ceremonial singer Hastiin Klah. Wheelwright and Klah developed a deep and mutually respectful friendship. For many years, Wheelwright traveled with Klah to various locations on the Navajo Nation and observed his ceremonies. Wheelwright recorded Klah's narratives and documented the rituals he performed, even transferring his sand paintings to patterns on tapestry to make them permanent and to protect them from being lost or forgotten.

Wheelwright wanted a place to store and display her collection, and the donated land from her friend Amelia White helped her achieve that goal. The deed for the land stipulated that it be used for a building that would "constitute a laboratory or museum for the assembling together of articles of every character produced now, in the past or in the future, by the Navajo tribe of Indians." The new museum building reflected that purpose in its very design, an octagonal structure built to resemble a *hooghan*, a traditional Navajo building. The Wheelwright Museum opened to the public on November 29, 1938, and remains open today.

Wheelwright passed away on July 29, 1958, at her home in Maine. Her friend, Amelia White, survived her by more than a decade, passing away on August 28, 1972. Posthumously, White made one last charitable donation of land. Upon her death, her Santa Fe house, El Delirio, became the permanent home of the School of American Research. The school, dedicated to the research of archaeology and ethnology of the people and places of the Southwest, remains in operation today as the School for Advanced Research.

More to explore: *Historic Los Luceros, Navajo Indian Reservation, Santa Fe, Three Wise Women*

18. Ana de Sandoval y Manzanares (ca. 1650–1734)

Location: Valencia County. In Los Lunas, at the Thirteenth Judicial District Court Building, at the intersection of Morris Road and NM 314. See map 4.

Marker text: After surviving the 1680 Pueblo Revolt, the widowed and destitute Ana de Sandoval y Manzanares led her family back to New Mexico. In 1716 this descendant of mulatto and Indian parents asserted her rights to successfully petition New Mexico's governor to restore her father's land, the San Clemente Grant that today includes the site of the Village of Los Lunas.

The Pueblo Revolt of 1680 was a turning point in New Mexico history. In the insurrection, the Pueblo Indians of New Mexico, upset at their treatment at the hands of Spanish colonists, united to drive the Spanish from the state. Fearing for their safety, Spanish families abandoned their ranches and farmlands throughout the state and fled south to what is now Mexico. One family caught in the conflict was that of Ana de Sandoval y Manzanares.

Sandoval y Manzanares, who was probably born in New Mexico around 1650, was a daughter of mulatto and Indian parents. ("Mulatto" is a term used to indicate a person of mixed ancestry.) Her father, Mateo de Sandoval y Manzanares, had earlier been awarded a tract of land by the Spanish government, the San Clemente land grant, in the area of present-day Los Lunas. She married into the Candelaria family, a family name now remembered in Candelaria Road in Albuquerque. With her husband, Blas de la Candelaria, she started a family, with three of their own children and three others whom they adopted (it's not known whether the children were adopted before or after the revolt). Sandoval y Manzanares's husband passed away sometime before 1680, leaving her a widow.

After the revolt drove the Spanish from the state, Sandoval y Manzanares remained in Mexico with other refugees and other members of her family for twelve years. In 1692, Governor Diego de Vargas prepared to lead a contingent of colonists back to the state to begin the resettlement effort. A census of displaced settlers living in El Paso compiled in December of that year lists Sandoval y Manzanares and her family as among those willing to return to New Mexico with the governor. She is listed in the census as being part of a household of thirteen individuals, including her three children: Feliciano (Félix), age sixteen; Francisco, age twenty; and María de la Rosa, age fourteen. "They state that they are his majesty's loyal vassals," the census noted, "and that, being given the means to be able to go, they will go to settle this kingdom."

The desire to return to New Mexico bespoke both a practical as well as a principled decision for Sandoval y Manzanares. She was widowed and destitute, and a return to her home in New Mexico promised the start of a better life. In this desire, she had the benefit of an important judicial tenet: Spanish law at the time recognized the rights of women as heads of households and landowners. Because of this, Sandoval y Manzanares had the legal right to petition the government for the return of her father's prerevolt land holdings to her, the rightful heir.

Which she did. In 1716, after colonists had progressed their settlements into the valley south of Albuquerque (indeed, two of Sandoval y Manzanares's sons were among the founders of that city), Sandoval y Manzanares petitioned Governor Félix Martínez for the restoration of her father's land near Los Lunas. She was living in Albuquerque herself at the time. The governor approved the request on July 13, 1716. Ten days later, her son, Félix Candelaria, officially took possession of the San Clemente land grant, bringing it back into the family—although the new dimensions of the grant were considerably less than the original.

Very likely, Sandoval y Manzanares acted mostly out of interest for her family and descendants. It is not known for certain if she ever returned to the grant land and lived there herself. When the Luna family purchased parcels of the grant land around the mid-eighteenth century, the settlement that formed here took the family name, Los Lunas.

Ana Sandoval y Manzanares passed away in 1734.

More to explore: *Albuquerque, Doña Ana, La Salineta*

19. Apache Battleground

Location: Otero County. In Mayhill, on the south side of US 82 between mile markers 34 and 35. See map 6.

Marker text: In this immediate vicinity, Captain Henry W. Stanton of the U.S. Army, for whom Fort Stanton was named, lost his life in 1855 in a skirmish with the Mescalero Apaches. For several weeks, soldiers commanded by Stanton and Capt. Richard S. Ewell, were in pursuit of Indians who had stolen livestock from the Pecos River area south of Anton Chico. In the final confrontation lives were lost on both sides.

On orders to pursue Mescalero Apache Indians, who were reported to have stolen livestock from the area around Anton Chico, a small settlement along the Pecos River south of present-day Las Vegas (New Mexico), Captain Richard Stoddert Ewell set out east from Fort Thorn, near present-day Hatch, on December 28, 1854. His command included a force of eighty-one soldiers of Companies G and K, along with Lieutenants Moore and Davidson of the First Dragoons (cavalry). Captain Ewell, nicknamed "Old Bald Head" for self-explanatory reasons, would only a few years later serve as a lieutenant general in the Confederate Army after the outbreak of the Civil War. But on this mission at the end of 1854, he was commanding a harsh winter march in a series of battles between the US Army and the Apaches of the Southwest, known collectively as the Apache Wars.

Ewell led his troops initially to Anton Chico, but once there he received word that the Indians had left that area and returned to their homelands in the Sacramento Mountains to the southwest. Ewell then followed new orders to return to the Rio Bonito, where, on January 13, he joined forces with fifty infantrymen and twenty-nine dragoons from Fort Fillmore, near Mesilla. Those troops were under the command of an officer named Captain Henry Whiting Stanton.

Born in New York in 1823, West Point graduate Henry Stanton had come to the Southwest as a second lieutenant, serving at Fort Leavenworth, Kansas, and other posts in Oklahoma. After service in the Mexican-American War and at posts in California, Oregon, and elsewhere, Stanton was promoted from first lieutenant to captain in July 1854 and sent to duty at Fort Fillmore. "Whether in the field or in barracks," wrote Brevet Brigadier General John Garland of Stanton, "the Captain was looked upon by his comrades as the very pattern of an officer, and a gentleman."

Together, Captains Ewell and Stanton led their combined forces along the Rio Peñasco into the Sacramento Mountains, the homeland of the Mescalero Apaches.

Although the men had to this point in their mission seen no Indians, that changed on the night of January 17, 1855. Mescalero Apache Indians that evening attacked the soldiers' campsite with arrows and bullets, attempting even to set the camp on fire. The scuffles continued through the next day, as the march continued. "The Indians appeared in force," Ewell wrote, "with every mark of defiance, and during the whole day opposed our march, disputing every ravine, at times coming under cover within arrow-shot."

Ewell believed, probably correctly, that the

Indians were purposely confronting the men in an attempt to keep the soldiers from reaching the Indians' main camp, where their families were. The Indians were determined in this goal, and some fifteen of them gave their lives in pursuit of it.

Nonetheless, around 3:00 p.m. that afternoon, January 18, the soldiers reached the Indian encampment. The lodges had been abandoned, the Indians fearing for their safety and departing before the soldiers arrived. Hoping to determine the direction in which the Indians had fled, Captain Stanton led his men through a valley to the right of the main camp, where they found an additional Indian lodge. Upon seeing a few Indians quickly leaving the site, Captain Stanton charged his horse forward in pursuit. The few Indians he chased dispersed, and after briefly venturing up the valley, Stanton then turned and started back on foot, the soldiers walking their horses toward the camp, less than a mile away, through a valley known today as James Canyon. In doing so, they passed through a lightly forested area that lay between them and the campsite—and straight into an ambush.

In his report, Captain Ewell described the last moments of Captain Stanton's life:

[Stanton] ordered his party to take to trees; but the Indians being in too great force, he mounted and directed his party to retreat, remaining in the rear himself, firing his Sharp's carbine, when he received a shot in the head, and was instantly killed.

Soldiers rushed to the scene and engaged in a short exchange before the Indians fled. Captain Stanton's lifeless body was retrieved, along with the bodies of Privates Thomas Dwyer and John Hennings, also killed in the skirmish. The three were wrapped in blankets and given a temporary burial.

For a few days thereafter, Captain Ewell and the remaining soldiers continued to pursue the Apaches through the snow and ice to the headwaters of the Rio Peñasco; unable to track the Indians from that point, and losing their own animals to cold and fatigue, Ewell returned to the camp to retrieve the bodies of the fallen men. He found, to his horror, that wolves had been merciless in plundering the graves in the meantime, leaving what one of the soldiers, Private James Bennett, called a "revolting site." Ewell's men burned the flesh from the bodies and then carried the bones for burial back to Fort Fillmore—where Colonel Stanton's wife, who had been without her husband for a month and had not yet received word of his death, was longing to see him again.

A few months later, General Garland selected a spot for a new military fort in the northern Sacramento Mountains. He suggested that the fort be named Fort Stanton, "in memory of a gallant officer who lost his life near the spot." Secretary of War Jefferson Davis agreed, and Fort Stanton was established on May 4, 1855. It is open to the public today as Fort Stanton Historic Site.

More to explore: *Fort Stanton, Hatch, La Mesilla*

20. Artesia

Location: 1. Eddy County. Just north of the town of Artesia, on the west side of US 285.

2. Eddy County. South of Artesia, in the Earl Boulden Park Rest Area, on the west side of US 285, at mile marker 61. See map 6.

Marker text: Artesia, named for the area's many artesian wells, lies on the route of the Pecos Valley cattle trails used by Charles Goodnight, Oliver Loving, and John S. Chisum. The town, established in 1903, is located in what was once part of Chisum's vast cattle empire.

21. Ghost Marker: Chisum's South Spring Ranch

Marker text: In 1875, John S. Chisum, the "Cattle King of the Pecos," made this the headquarters of a cattle ranching empire which extended for 150 miles along the Pecos River. In that year, 80,000 cattle bore his famous Jinglebob-earmark. After Chisum's death, the ranch was acquired by J. J. Hagerman.

Note: This missing marker gives a bit of background on the South Spring Ranch, once owned by cattleman John S. Chisum—land on which the community of Artesia was built. See map 6.

22. Ghost Marker: Flynn-Welch-Yates Oil Well

Marker text: On April 9, 1924, a well drilled at this site by the partnership of Thomas Flynn, Van Welch, and Martin Yates, Jr. struck oil. It became the first commercial oil well in New Mexico and led to subsequent discoveries of vast amounts of oil and gas. The oil and gas industry has developed into the single greatest source of revenue for the State of New Mexico.

Note: This missing marker may have once been placed near the site of the Flynn-Welch-Yates oil well, which was located east of Artesia. See map 6.

En route to Fort Sumner and other points north, nineteenth-century cattle ranchers Charles Goodnight and Oliver Loving drove their herds past a small, cottonwood-lined natural spring nearby known as Eagle Draw. After Loving's death in 1867, Charles Goodnight collaborated with rancher John S. Chisum to continue the profitable drives. Chisum liked southeastern New Mexico. Along the Pecos River in 1875, he established what he dubbed the South Spring Ranch, a rambling cattle empire that stretched from Fort Sumner to Carlsbad and encompassed Eagle Draw. With some eighty thousand head of cattle, Chisum was soon anointed the "Cattle King of the Pecos."

Upon Chisum's death in 1884, his niece, Sally, acquired much of the South Spring Ranch property. She built a house near Eagle Draw and established both a hotel and a post office. She also acquired her own title, "Queen of the Jingle-bob," for the distinctive cut her uncle had made in the ears of his cattle. In the fall of 1890, Sally Chisum sank the first successful well in the region, tapping a large artesian water belt at 124 feet. Locals formed a townsite development company, and in 1903, Artesia percolated forth.

The prospect of free-flowing water, coupled with the luxuriant grasslands of the Pecos Valley, made Artesia a popular location for homesteaders.

John Chisum's Jingle Bob Ranch included the cottonwood-lined Eagle Draw wash, around which the town of Artesia grew. The name of the town comes from the former province of Artois in France, home to many artesian wells. John Chisum. William A. Keleher Pictorial Collection, Box 1, Folder 17, Item 000-742-0040, Center for Southwest Research, University Libraries, University of New Mexico.

The town incorporated in 1905 with a population of more than one thousand residents. Just ten years later, that number had more than doubled. Skipping the awkward growing pains suffered by other, less financially secure towns, Artesia soon had electricity, telephones, an ice plant, a bank, and a newspaper, the *Artesia Advocate*. The town also had, of course, a successful waterworks company.

Not only water lay underneath the Artesian soil. Although several companies had drilled unsuccessfully in the area, the Flynn, Welch, and Yates State no. 3 oil well, drilled near Artesia in 1924, proved that large underground reservoirs of oil and gas existed here. The discovery established Artesia as a commercial center for oil and gas production in southeastern New Mexico, lying atop what geologists call the Artesia-Dayton oil field. The opening of the large Navajo Refining Company in town ensured the continued development of oil resources in this region.

More to explore: *Goodnight-Loving Trail (series), Hobbs, Oil and Gas*

23. Aztec

Location: San Juan County. East of Aztec, on the north side of NM 550, between mile markers 158 and 159. See map 1.

Marker Text: Aztec, named for the nearby National Monument, was founded in 1876 when portions of the Jicarilla Apache Reservation were opened for non-Indian settlement. It is the seat of San Juan County, which was created in 1887 partially as a response to the desire of the residents to be free from the political forces of Rio Arriba County.

Ancestral Puebloan people settled in the fertile lands of the Animas Valley centuries ago. They built a large, multistoried structure, which served as their living quarters, supporting several hundred residents. They cultivated beans and squash along the river for sustenance. The ruins of their sandstone structures are preserved today as Aztec Ruins National Monument.

Much later in time, a presidential executive order in March 1874 created the boundaries of a reservation here for Jicarilla Apaches, who at the time were living in and around the areas of Cimarron and Abiquiú in north-central New Mexico, more than two hundred miles to the east. Only a few Apache families moved to the reservation, however, as it was distant from what they felt was their true homeland. At the same time, Anglo settlers and farmers were attracted to the river valley and to the promise of successful harvests it offered—as well as the potential mineral wealth to be found here. Those settlers began petitioning the government to move the reservation and open the land instead to homesteading. In 1876, just two years after the creation of the reservation, President Ulysses S. Grant abrogated the order that had created it and moved the boundaries of the Jicarilla Apache Reservation.

The land in this region was suddenly opened to settlement. A small community soon formed, taking the name Aztec, the name that had been given to the ruins of the houses built by the Ancestral Puebloans who had settled here centuries before.

Initially, Aztec was part of Rio Arriba County, which at the time encompassed a much larger area than it does today. The very size of the county created jurisdictional problems. The distance from the growing communities of Aztec and Bloomfield and other nearby settlements to the county seat in Tierra Amarilla was some one hundred miles. Political and economic strife led to instances of vigilante justice and greater calls for self-governance among the people living in northwestern New Mexico, all of which eventually compelled the territorial government to create San Juan County in 1887. Aztec vied with another nearby village for county seat. Aztec won, and the losing community, Junction City, became a ghost town.

More to explore: *Aztec Ruins National Monument, City of Bloomfield, Jicarilla Apache (series), Navajo Indian Reservation, Tierra Amarilla*

24. Aztec Ruins National Monument

Location: 1. San Juan County. In Aztec, on the south side of the intersection of NM 516 (West Aztec Boulevard) and NM 574 (North Light Plant Road). See map 1.

2. San Juan County. In Aztec, in a pullout on the north side of the intersection of Ash Street and NM 516 (North Aztec Boulevard). See map 1.

Marker Text: Despite its name, this magnificent site reflects 11th century influence from nearby Chaco Canyon rather than from the later Aztecs of Mexico. The striking masonry pueblos illustrate the classic Chaco architectural style with later Mesa Verde additions. Aztec was finally abandoned by 1300.

Sometime around AD 1111, Ancestral Puebloan Indians began to assemble a multistoried pueblo near the Animas River in northwestern New Mexico. Competent masons, the Indians carved sandstone blocks, laid them one atop the other, and mortared the walls with mud for support. When finished, their pueblo reached grand scales, with hundreds of rooms and dozens of kivas, underground chambers where the Indians worshiped in ceremonial rituals. Centuries later, Anglo settlers would unknowingly give credit where credit was not due and christen the ruins of this pueblo *Aztec*, believing them to be the work of the Aztecs of Mexico.

Aztec supported a community of up to three hundred people. The Indians ate corn and other vegetables grown along the rich banks of the Animas River and supplemented their meals with meat from deer, rabbit, and antelope. Artisans as well as architects, the Ancestral Puebloans wove baskets and crafted beautiful pottery.

Archaeologists are piecing together the relationship between Aztec and the Ancestral Puebloan villages of Chaco sixty miles to the south. Chaco, one of the most advanced prehistoric communities in North America, may have been the original home of the people of Aztec. The pueblos at Aztec and Chaco show architectural similarities. Further, Aztec was part of an array of trails that had its nucleus in Chaco. Although one theory suggests that this "Chaco Road System" was a supply network that used "outlier" pueblos like Aztec to provide raw materials to the residents at Chaco, the exact purpose of these roads is unknown.

Soon after the pueblo was built, the Ancestral Puebloans left Aztec and other pueblos in northwestern New Mexico, possibly in exodus from prolonged drought or in response to a collapse in their social structure. By 1150, the magnificent masonry pueblo was empty.

Then, as now, it was often easier to modify an existing structure than build a new one. Around 1225, a different group of people occupied the site, very likely arriving from or having been influenced by Mesa Verde, another Ancestral Puebloan village in what is now southwestern Colorado. Not content with the pueblo as designed, the new residents sealed doors, modified rectangular rooms to include round kivas, and added extra rooms. They also enlarged the village complex by erecting new structures near the main pueblo. These additional sites await full excavation.

Despite having made these changes to the pueblo, the new people also left Aztec after only a short time. They were not alone. By 1300, the Ancestral Puebloan people had abandoned their villages at Chaco Canyon, Aztec, and other sites throughout the Four Corners region. Archaeologists are not certain what caused the departure, although suspicions fall on drought, changes in the environment, upsets in the Chacoan religious or social structure, or possibly an insurmountable combination of such factors.

Aztec is open to the public today as Aztec Ruins National Monument and is maintained by the National Park Service.

More to explore: *Aztec, City of Bloomfield, Gila Cliff Dwellings National Monument, Salmon Ruin*

25. Bartlett Garcia Continental Survey Point

Location: Doña Ana County. In Doña Ana, at the intersection of Doña Ana Road and Thorpe Road. See map 5.

Marker text: On April 24, 1851, John Russell Bartlett for the United States and Pedro Garcia-Conde for the Republic of Mexico, erected near here a monument designating 32° 22′ north latitude on the Rio Grande as the initial point for the official survey of the U.S.-Mexico boundary. After the Gadsden Purchase of 1853, the international boundary was moved south and the former Mexican lands were ceded to the U.S.

In a hillside ceremony near here on April 24, 1851, John Russell Bartlett, head of the US-Mexico Boundary Commission, and his counterpart from Mexico, Pedro García Conde, signed an agreement, sealed it in an empty sarsaparilla bottle along with a splinter of marble chipped from the Washington Monument, and placed the container inside a small pillar made of stones. By doing so, the men had just agreed that 32° 22′ north latitude, a spot just north of Doña Ana, would be the initial survey point for the boundary line between the United States and Mexico. Surveyors would work from that spot to chart the new border west.

The Mexican-American War was over, and the Treaty of Guadalupe Hidalgo had established the boundary between the United States and Mexico to be that laid down in the 1847 "Map of the United Mexican States," published in New York by J. Disturnell. Yet Disturnell's map had inaccuracies, and ownership of the southern quarter of New Mexico was in dispute. The Boundary Commission, created as a stipulation of the treaty and comprising surveyors from both countries, was to come to agreement on where the border should fall.

Three successive men chosen to lead the commission for the United States either died or dropped out before the $3,000-a-year job was offered to forty-five-year-old bookworm John Russell Bartlett. Bartlett, a scientist who liked to paint, had written essays with twenty-seven-word titles like *The Progress of Ethnology: An Account of Recent Archaeological, Philological, and Geographical Researches in Various Parts of the Globe Tending to Elucidate the Physical History of Man*. He accepted the position.

The hillside accord caused instant controversy. Under the Bartlett–García Conde survey point, the United States stood to lose large parcels of the flat, dry, southwestern land most desired by railroad capitalists for their planned railroad routes—including the land south of what is now Interstate 10 between Las Cruces, New Mexico, and Tucson, Arizona. In 1852, Bartlett's foes in Congress successfully cast him as the enemy of westward expansion and repudiated the initial point agreement. Bartlett countered by pointing out that his survey had kept in US control the lucrative Santa Rita del Cobre copper mines near present-day Silver City, and that the land given up was, at best, "a desert, with scarcely a tree save in the ravines of the lofty mountains, and little other vegetation than the chaparral or thorny bushes." He lost. The following year, after only three years of service, Bartlett was suspended from the Boundary Commission.

The controversy was settled only when President Franklin Pierce sent railroad man and diplomat James Gadsden to procure the desired land from the Mexican government in 1853. The $10 million acquisition, known as the Gadsden Purchase, moved the boundary to 31° 47′, and in so doing added 45,000 square miles to the southwestern corner of New Mexico.

Bartlett went on to become the secretary of state for Rhode Island and later served as a bibliographer for John Carter Brown, whose library opened to the public at Brown University in 1904. Bartlett may have had trouble with lines, but he did manage to end his life in a circle: he died in Providence, Rhode Island, the town where he was born, on May 28, 1886.

More to explore: *Doña Ana, Santa Rita Copper Mines, Wheeler Peak*

26. Basin and Range Country

Location: Luna County. West of Deming, in the rest area on the north side (westbound) of Interstate 10, after the Gage exit, between mile markers 60 and 61. See map 5.

Marker text: Basin and Range province of southwest New Mexico is of broad alluvial plains from which isolated fault block mountains rise like islands in a sandy sea. Indigenous peoples have used both the basin and range in their seasonal cycle. The Victorio Mountains to the south yield zinc, silver, gold, copper, lead, and tungsten.

Southwestern New Mexico is distinguished geographically by isolated mountain ranges separated by broad plains overlaid by alluvium. (Alluvium is loose sediment carried by water to other locations.) This is the Basin and Range Province, one of five physiographic regions in the state. It began to form fifteen million years ago as tension in the crust of the earth caused land throughout southwestern New Mexico, Nevada, Arizona, southeastern California, and western Utah to stretch, break into faults, and alternately sink downward to form valleys or tilt upward to create mountains.

The Victorio Mountains are visible on the southern horizon. The range takes its name from nineteenth-century Mimbreño Apache chief Victorio, to whom this part of the state served as a camping ground and hunting land. The Apaches, as did other southwestern Indian tribes, used the natural ecology of the mountains and valleys in their seasonal cycle, planting crops in the valleys in the spring and hunting deer and other animals in the mountains throughout their homelands in the winter. For many years, Victorio and his followers resisted government campaigns against them, both military and political, and continued their raids against settlements in Arizona, New Mexico, and into Mexico to protest the encroachment of Spanish and Anglo settlers. Victorio died in 1880 in an engagement with US soldiers in Mexico.

As mining camps arose throughout southwestern New Mexico in the nineteenth century, the Victorio Mountains were not to be left behind. Prospectors uncovered silver ore on Carbonate Hill around 1880 and worked the claims "under conditions which would now be considered very adverse," according to a report by the US Geological Survey in 1910. A small settlement of some eighteen buildings developed. In its formative years, the camp took the name Victorio for the mountains, but later became Chance City.

The name proved a foretaste of the longevity of the camp, as activity in the Victorio mining district was overall short-lived. Most prospectors had left Chance City by 1887, although mining continued at sporadic intervals into the 1940s. Estimates of the total production of silver, copper, lead, and zinc from the district range from $500,000 to $2.5 million.

More to explore: *Edge of the Plains, Lozen—Little Sister, Rio Grande Rift, Yucca Plains*

27. Bayard

Location: 1. Grant County. On the north end of the town of Bayard, in a pullout on the west side of US 180, near mile marker 124. See map 5.

2. Grant County. On the south end of the town of Bayard, on US 180, near the middle school. See map 5.

Marker text: Sites in the surrounding hills indicate that Indians of the Mogollon culture (A.D. 300–1450) lived here long before the Europeans. In the late 19th century, this was a stronghold of Apaches led by Victorio and Geronimo. Today Bayard, which was incorporated in 1925, lies in a great commercial mining region.

Potsherds, pit houses, and other ruins in the surrounding hills are archaeological evidence left by the prehistoric Mogollon Indians, who lived in this region centuries before other settlers arrived. The Mogollon culture emerged in the Southwest by 300 BC and had soon spread from southwestern New Mexico into southeastern Arizona, west Texas, and northern Mexico. One of the most exceptional dwelling sites built by the Mogollon is preserved at Gila Cliff Dwellings National Monument north of Bayard in the Gila Wilderness. There, the Mogollon created a small village inside the natural cliffs along the western face of a sheer canyon wall. In the fifteenth century, for reasons still unclear, the Mogollon left the area. Archaeologists generally believe that they were subsumed into other Indian pueblos.

In the 1800s, Apache Indians roamed this part of what is now southwestern New Mexico and considered it a sacred homeland and hunting ground. Geronimo, leader of the Chiricahua Apaches, and Victorio, leader of the Mimbreño Apaches, conducted raids throughout the region to defy the miners and settlers who were arriving to claim the land as their own. Apache raids often targeted Mexican and Anglo settlers in nearby communities like Pinos Altos. To control the hostilities and guard settlers and fortune seekers, the army established Fort Bayard here in 1866. Soldiers patrolled the area, escorted wagon trains, and protected local residents.

When the frontier quieted after 1880, Fort Bayard became an army-operated sanatorium for veterans suffering from tuberculosis. To transport patients to the hospital, the Silver City and Northern Rail Road Company in 1891 laid track to the fort. A small settlement grew around the depot. When a post office opened there in 1902, the town borrowed the name of the fort. Citizens of Bayard incorporated their community in 1925.

Bayard is located in a mineral-rich area, one of the first in the Southwest to be mined. Today, the proceeds from Grant County mines make up nearly the total production of copper in the state. This substantiates the prophetic statement made about the Bayard area by a correspondent to Rossiter Raymond, commissioner of mining statistics, and presented in an 1874 report:

It has been satisfactorily proved that the whole country for a radius of two hundred miles is literally filled with mineral. Gold, silver, copper, iron, and lead abound in the greatest profusion, all awaiting capital and industry to bring to light the hidden treasure buried in this vast area of country.

More to explore: *Fort Bayard, Kneeling Nun, Lozen—Little Sister, Mogollon, Santa Rita Copper Mines, Silver City*

28. Beclabito Dome

Location: San Juan County. At the Beclabito Trading Center in Beclabito, on the north side of US 64, near mile marker 4. See map 1.

Marker Text: Colorful red rocks of Entrada Sandstone are domed up by deep seated igneous intrusions to be exposed by erosion. The same igneous activity created the Carrizo Mountains to the west. Uranium deposits in the Morrison Formation just above the Entrada created New Mexico's first uranium boom in the East Carrizos south of here in the 1950s. Elevation 5,600 feet.

One translation of the Navajo word *beclabito* is "spring under a rock." High temperatures deep within the earth underneath this part of northwestern New Mexico converted rocks to liquid. That liquid welled upward until hardened again by the cooler temperatures above. This igneous intrusion pushed up layers of rock on its voyage, doming them into the shape of an outward-bulging arch: Beclabito Dome.

That diligent mountain-building activity can also take credit for the Carrizo Mountains on the Navajo Nation in northeastern Arizona, about thirty miles west of the town of Shiprock.

One layer of rock pushed upward by this intrusion was the soft shale known as the Morrison Formation, named for having been first described near Morrison, Colorado. The Morrison Formation is well known today for its numerous dinosaur fossils. Morrison shale contains compact and finely grained bentonite created from volcanic ash, as well as uranium, an ore used to fuel nuclear power plants. In the 1950s, discovery of that uranium by sheepherder Paddy Martinez in the East Carrizos sparked a mining boom near Grants.

Beneath the Morrison Formation lies a second distinct layer of rock, the formation known as the Entrada Sandstone. Weathering and time have collaborated to expose this beautiful layer of sedimentary red rock. The Entrada Sandstone was named for having first been described at Entrada Point in Utah.

Incidentally, it was a dome like Beclabito that forever marred the good name of domes everywhere. In the late 1920s, a US senator from New Mexico, Albert Fall, was at the turbulent center of what became known as the Teapot Dome Scandal. Congress investigated Fall's relationship with Mammoth Oil, a company he had allowed to lease and develop the Teapot Dome oil reserve in Wyoming. Fall was found to have conspired to defraud the government and to have accepted bribes from Sinclair Oil and other oil industry leaders. He went to prison in 1931.

More to explore: *Grants, Hogbacks, Red Rocks, Three Rivers*

29. Belen

Location: 1. Valencia County. On the north side of the city of Belen, on the west side of Main Street, between mile markers 2 and 3. See map 4.

2. Valencia County. On the west end of the city of Belen, on the north side of Camino del Llano just before the Interstate 25 interchange (exit 191). See map 4.

3. Valencia County. On the west end of the city of Belen, on the south side of Camino del Llano just before the Interstate 25 interchange (exit 191). See map 4.

Marker text: By the mid 18th century, Spanish colonization had begun along the Rio Grande south of Albuquerque. The Belen land grant was made to encourage this expansion, and colonists from Albuquerque settled here around 1740. The early community also included a group of genízaros, or Hispanicized Indians. Belen is Spanish for Bethlehem.

After the founding of Albuquerque in the early eighteenth century, Spanish settlement progressed south along the Rio Grande, a colonial division of the state known as the Rio Abajo, or Lower River. Eager to promote this expansion of its domain, the Spanish government in November 1740 approved the land grant petition submitted by Captain Diego de Torres, his brother-in-law Antonio de Salazar, and thirty-one other colonists from Albuquerque, to create a settlement alongside the west bank of the river in this vicinity. The site lay along the Camino Real, the main road connecting New Mexico with Mexico. As was customary in taking possession of a land grant, Diego de Torres walked with officials of the governor over the terrain, tossed rocks, pulled grass, and made a physical show of possessing the land as the grant was conveyed.

The colonists named the village Nuestra Señora de Belen, or "Our Lady of Bethlehem."

Six years later, *genízaros* living nearby protested the Belen land grant, claiming that its boundaries overlapped those of their preexisting settlement. Genízaros were detribalized Indians, most of whom had their origins as the children of captives brought into Spanish families, baptized into the Christian faith, and taught to speak Spanish. In the eighteenth century, the Spanish government in New Mexico at times created settlements for the genízaros, with the intention both to keep them from falling into poverty and to establish villages that would serve as bulwarks between Spanish settlements and marauding Indians. The Belen dispute was never resolved, and eventually the genízaros mixed into the Spanish population.

Belen received its first rail connection in the 1880s when the Santa Fe Railway laid track from Raton Pass south through the state. The town came into its own in 1903 when officials of the railroad selected it as a divisional headquarters and western terminus of the Belen Cutoff, an east-west branch of the Santa Fe Railway that left Kansas and traveled through Clovis and eastern New Mexico to rejoin the main tracks at Belen. The town became both a shipping point for livestock as well as a service center for passengers on the line. In 1910, railroad officials remodeled the Santa Fe Hotel near the tracks into the beautiful mission revival–style Belen Harvey House, one of a string of similarly named hospitable dining rooms run by Fred Harvey along the route of the Santa Fe. Belen incorporated as a city eight years later.

Because of its location along the route of both the Belen Cutoff and the Camino Real, Belen has today adopted the slogan, "Where the Trains and Trail Meet."

More to explore: *Abó Pass Trail, Camino del Llano, El Camino Real—The King's Highway, Harvey Girls*

30. Bernalillo

Location: Sandoval County. On the south end of Bernalillo, in a pullout on the east side of NM 313 (near Calle de Bosque), between mile markers 6 and 7. See map 4.

Marker text: Archaeological research indicates that this fertile valley has been the focus of human occupation for at least 10,000 years. Soon after the Spanish colonized New Mexico in 1598, a series of estancias, or farming and ranching communities, flanked the Camino Real along this section of the Rio Grande. These settlements formed the basis of present-day Bernalillo, which was well established by the close of the 17th century.

31. Bernalillo on the Camino Real

Location: Sandoval County. West of the town of Bernalillo, on the south side of US 550 (formerly NM 44), at mile marker 4. See map 4.

Marker text: The Pueblo Indian province of Tiguex, in the area of Bernalillo, served as winter headquarters for Francisco Vasquez de Coronado in 1540–42 during his explorations of the southwest. Bernalillo was founded after the Spanish reconquest of New Mexico by Diego de Vargas in 1692. Vargas died here in 1704.

32. Ghost Marker: Coronado State Monument

Marker text: Kuaua Pueblo was one of the Rio Grande Valley villages visited by Francisco Vasquez de Coronado in 1540. He called this region the Tiguex Province because its inhabitants spoke a common language, Tiwa. Abandoned before the 1680 Pueblo Revolt against Spanish rule, this large and important site has been excavated and partially restored.

Note: This missing marker was once located near the Coronado Historic Site, formerly known as Coronado State Monument. See map 4.

This part of New Mexico has seen human occupation for at least ten thousand years, with archaeologists having identified the ruins of a number of early pueblo villages and agricultural sites. When Francisco Vásquez de Coronado came to New Mexico in 1540 intent on finding the spurious "Seven Cities of Cibola," his officers visited a cluster of Tiwa-speaking Indian villages in a region stretching south from present-day Bernalillo to Isleta Pueblo. The Spanish called the area the Province of Tiguex, probably from their pronunciation of the corresponding Indian name. Coronado and

"This I ask as a favor," don Diego de Vargas requested as he dictated his last will and testament on his deathbed in Bernalillo in 1704: "In a coffin lined with simple woolen cloth, let [my body] be buried according to military honors and the privileges of a titled nobleman of Castile." He died in the town he had founded. Courtesy Palace of the Governors Photo Archives (NMHM/DCA), neg. no. 11409.

his men spent two winters in Tiguex. During that time, they visited the twelve pueblos in this region, including the northernmost, known as Kuaua. Ruins of the pueblo of Kuaua are now part of the Coronado Historic Site (formerly Coronado State Monument) just west of Bernalillo. Visitors can see modern reconstructions of some of the pueblo foundations and admire beautiful murals found several layers deep on the walls of one of the kivas.

Coronado returned to Mexico empty handed in 1542.

The first incarnation of the Spanish village of Bernalillo came after the 1598 colonizing expedition of Juan de Oñate. Descendants of the Bernal family settled near this area, and a small village known as Bernalillo developed a short jaunt north of the present town. Settlers fled that town in 1680 when the Pueblo Indians revolted against the Spanish, but the valley again saw occupation when Spanish officer and governor Diego de Vargas re-settled the area as part of a plan to consolidate Spanish rule in New Mexico. The new Bernalillo included a central plaza, adobe homes, farmlands, and a small church.

In 1704, while on a campaign in the Sandia and Manzano Mountains to retrieve livestock stolen from local ranches by Apache Indians, Governor de Vargas suddenly took ill. The governor's allies carried him to the home of a wealthy landowner in Bernalillo, where he summoned sufficient strength to dictate and sign his last testament. In it, he made a twenty-page flourish of endowments and amends, ordering that on the day of his funeral, the poor of Santa Fe be given "50 measures of corn and 12 head of cattle"; that his three illegitimate children be acknowledged with two thousand pesos between them; that one of his slaves be freed; that his secretary be given his "black hat with blue and white plumes" along with his "Vandyke with linen-lace ruff"; and that a mass be said for his body in Bernalillo before being taken to Santa Fe for burial. The will was dated April 7, 1704. Vargas died the next day.

Bernalillo prospered in subsequent years as the home of many wealthy landowners. Lieutenant James William Abert passed through on a military reconnaissance mission in 1846 and left a pleasing account of the settlement as it existed then:

In the evening we reached the pretty little town of Bernalillo, and we encamped close by the neat haciendas at the northern extreme of town. Here are the handsomest and best arranged vineyards in the whole department, and the houses show a greater appearance of wealth and comfort.

Despite the name and proximity, Bernalillo is not within Bernalillo County but lies instead within Sandoval County. Even more: when the territorial legislature created Sandoval County in 1903, Bernalillo became the county seat.

More to explore: *Spanish Entrada Site, Tiguex Province, Vásquez de Coronado's Route (series)*

33. Bicentennial Celebration

Location: Santa Fe County. Fifteen miles south of Santa Fe, in the Bicentennial Rest Area and Visitors Center, on the east side of Interstate 25. (The rest area is also known as the La Bajada Rest Area.) See map 2.

Marker text: This facility was built by the New Mexico State Highway Department to commemorate the bicentennial birthday of the United States. Located 15 miles south of the plaza in Santa Fe, the nation's oldest capital city, the site atop La Bajada (The Descent) affords a spectacular view of the Ortiz, Jemez and Sangre de Cristo Mountains.

As the country celebrated its two-hundredth birthday in 1976 in a yearlong celebration known as the American Bicentennial, communities around New Mexico were marking the occasion with localized projects. The Jaycees in Alamogordo planted two hundred "Freedom Trees" around the city, one for each year since the signing of the Declaration of Independence in 1776. Roswell residents painted their fireplugs to resemble famous past Americans. Albuquerque even hosted the American Bicentennial Mime Festival.

Project I-015-5(44)265 of the New Mexico State Highway Commission brought the commemoration to a spot off Interstate 25 just fifteen miles south of Santa Fe. This was the site selected for the facility officially known as the Bicentennial Rest Area. Construction had begun the previous year after final approval of the plan by the state on January 14, 1975. That plan called for a rest area accessible to northbound traffic, complete with picnic tables and benches, restrooms, timber parking barriers, a flagpole, underground garbage cans, a charcoal grill, and, of course, a Historic Marker recognizing the site. (Instructions were given that any wood slivers in the Marker posts were to be removed so that visitors who touched them would not get splinters.) The rest area was also to have a drinking fountain, which, given the elevation here, was to be frost proof. So that the rest area would remain in harmony with its surroundings, the plans stated that "care shall be taken by the contractor to remove only those rocks, trees, shrubs, and other vegetation necessary for construction in order to preserve the natural beauty of the rest area." The landscaping edict went so far as to mention a specific juniper tree that was not to be harmed during excavation for the sewage system.

The Bicentennial Rest Area sits atop La Bajada Hill—visitors stopping here from the south have just conquered it, and travelers going south soon will—a prominent escarpment that challenges motorists even today. This hill was a convenient geopolitical dividing point between northern and southern New Mexico in Spanish colonial times. *La bajada* translates to English as "the descent."

Travelers might rest their legs at the Bicentennial Rest Area, but it's hard to rest one's eyes. Recognizing the beautiful surroundings on display here, the Highway Department included a scenic overlook at the northernmost end of the rest area. The views from that overlook in every direction are as striking as any to be found in the state.

The Sangre de Cristo Mountains command the view to the northeast. This range is a southern extension of the Rocky Mountains and stretches from southern Colorado to just north of here. Sunlight hitting the mountains at sunrise or sunset reflects vivid colors of red, offering one origin of the translated name: "blood of Christ." The peaks immediately to the east are the Santa Fe Mountains, named for the city of Santa Fe. South Truchas Peak, at 13,102 feet, is the highest in this part of the range.

To the northwest are the Jemez Mountains. The range stretches roughly from Abiquiú to the pueblo of Jemez, a distance of some fifty miles. Both the city of Los Alamos and Bandelier National Monument are found in the Jemez, as is the Valles Caldera, a giant, collapsed volcano. The caldera contains several valleys within its expanse, including the Valle Grande, or "big valley," the largest of them all. Chicoma Mountain weighs in as the highest in this range, spiring to 11,561 feet.

The Ortiz Mountains to the southeast was the site of some of the first gold mining in the country, performed by Indian slave labor toiling for Spanish settlers in the seventeenth century. As early as the 1820s, gold placer mining was taking place here—decades earlier than the California Gold Rush of 1849. Not surprisingly, the highest peak, at 8,858 feet, bears the name Placer Peak.

The Bicentennial Rest Area is just south of the city of Santa Fe, the capital of New Mexico. Founded by don Juan de Oñate in 1610, Santa Fe is the oldest state capital in the United States.

More to explore: *Fort Craig Rest Area, Gold and Turquoise, Ken Towle Park, La Bajada, Santa Fe, Waldrop Park*

34. Bisti Wilderness

Location: San Juan County. On the west side of NM 371 at mile marker 77. See map 1.

Marker text: The highly scenic badlands of the Bisti were created by the erosion and weathering of interbedded shale, sandstone and coal formations into unusual forms. The area is also rich in fossil flora and fauna. 3,946 acres of the Badlands were designated a Wilderness Area by Congress in 1984 to preserve their scenic and cultural value. The Wilderness is protected by federal law.

Wind, weathering, and the passing of eras have fashioned the rocks of the Bisti Wilderness into fantastic, wraithlike towers of multicolored, banded siltstone. *Bisti* is a Navajo word that translates as "badlands." Most prevalent of the rocks in these badlands are those of the Fruitland Formation, a layer of interbedded sandstone, shale, mudstone, silt, and bituminous coal. Capping these are shales of the Kirtland Formation. Together, they create an otherworldly landscape like something out of a science fiction movie.

Some seventy million years ago, this region looked much different than it does today, making up part of a heavily forested, dank marsh. Artifacts from that foregone age are preserved in the Fossil Forest, a 2,720-acre petrified woodland of upright Cretaceous tree stumps and fossilized dinosaur skeletons within the Bisti Wilderness.

The Bisti Wilderness is adjacent to the De-Na-Zin Wilderness, a similarly colorful if more remote area. Together, the two make up a 45,000-acre expanse of desert landforms, rock formations, and badlands. Nearby is the Ah-Shi-Sle-Pah Wilderness Study Area, with its own hoodoos and columns to delight. Federal law protects these beautiful areas from commercial development. The Bureau of Land Management of the US Department of the Interior today administers most of the property.

More to explore: *City of Rocks State Park, Clayton Dinosaur Trackway (see under Clayton Lake State Park), Malpais, Rockhound State Park*

BLACK JACK KETCHUM: Series of Three Historic Markers (Various Locations)

General Introduction

Thomas Edward Ketchum, alias "Black Jack," built his nefarious reputation around a series of train robberies in New Mexico and Texas in the late 1890s. Ketchum is said to have acquired the nickname "Black Jack" by accident later in his life, after being mistaken for another criminal by that name. The moniker, and the dark reputation that accompanied it, stuck.

Legend claims that "Black Jack" Ketchum once chased a dog through a church during Sunday services. Only people with a ticket were allowed to watch his hanging in Clayton in 1901. "Please dig my grave very deep," he reportedly asked of them. Black Jack Ketchum. Albert Thompson Photo Collection, Box 1, Folder 2, Item 000-079-0004, Center for Southwest Research, University Libraries, University of New Mexico.

Born on October 31, 1868, in San Saba County in central Texas, Thomas Ketchum got off to a rocky start in life: both his parents died while he was still a boy. He came to New Mexico in 1890; his older brother Sam joined him a few years later. The two worked as cattle hands at a number of ranches in the Southwest. But, starting with their suspected involvement in a train robbery near present-day Nutt, New Mexico (west of Hatch) in 1892, the Ketchums seemed destined for a life lived outside of societal boundaries.

Oral histories in the New Mexico Federal Writers' Project from people who encountered the Ketchum brothers give a firsthand glimpse into their dual personalities. "The Ketchum boys were fine fellows to be around just in a social way," Texas rancher W. J. D. Carr summed up in his 1937 recollection, "but they were of a reckless, devil-may-care sort, who thought only of easy money. The Indian Territory was fertile soil for them in the bootlegging days."

The story of the outlaw's exploits in New Mexico is presented through a series of three Historic Markers, which have been combined here into one series so that his remarkable story can be followed comprehensively. The series includes two Markers entitled "Black Jack Ketchum" and one entitled "Black Jack's Hideout." The Markers are presented roughly in chronological order so that the story can be followed from beginning to end.

More to explore (Black Jack Ketchum Series): *The Clanton Hideout (see under Smuggler's Trail), Clayton, Monica Fuentes Gallegos and Carlota Fuentes Gallegos, Smuggler's Trail*

35. Black Jack Ketchum

Location: Quay County. South of Tucumcari, in a pullout on the east side of NM 209, between mile markers 71 and 72. See map 3.

Marker text: The last of the train robbers, Black Jack Ketchum, who terrorized the railroads in the 1880's, killed two men near this spot and hid out in a cave near Saddleback Mesa to the Southwest. The swarthy bandit was wounded in his last robbery and hanged in 1901.

Note: See the general introduction to this series of Markers, as well as the other Markers making up the series, for further background on Black Jack Ketchum's exploits in the state.

In June 1896, after quitting their positions as cattle hands at the sprawling Bell Ranch in Quay County, north of present-day Tucumcari (and stealing ranch supplies on their way out the door), brothers Sam and Thomas Ketchum were drawn to the nearby small town of Liberty. The community of Liberty earned its name from its location just outside the boundaries of Fort Bascom, a now-shuttered military installation in the same area, as a place where soldiers "on liberty" could let loose. The community of Liberty has today completely vanished—but at the time it was doing well for itself, with a stage stop, a saloon, and a combination store and post office run by brothers Morris and Levi Herzstein.

On June 10, Sam and Thomas visited the Herzstein store. The owners may have invited the Ketchums to spend the night in the store, since a storm was coming. Regardless, when the Herzsteins checked their cash register the next morning, they found they had been robbed—and the Ketchum brothers had fled. Levi Herzstein, along with other men from town, formed a posse and set out south in pursuit.

When the posse reached this location and encountered the Ketchum gang around noon that day, the inevitable gunfight ensued. It did not last long. The Ketchums were good with their pistols, and they quickly felled Herzstein and another member of the posse named Merejildo Gallegos, while all but one of the remaining posse members fled. That man, Placido Gurule, lay wounded but not killed, although the Ketchums probably thought he was. The outlaws shot Herzstein again as he lay on the ground to ensure that he was dead. They did not do so to Gurule, fortunately for him, and after the Ketchums fled, the wounded posse member managed to make his way safely back to town to recount the story.

The shooting of Levi Herzstein was one of the first times (and possibly the first, depending on the historical account) that Black Jack Ketchum had murdered another person.

The Ketchums departed New Mexico for Arizona, committing further crimes, and then returned to New Mexico, where their story continued.

36. Black Jack's Hideout

Location: Colfax County. In Cimarron, in the dirt area on the north side of the intersection of Tenth and Euclid Streets, in front of the Cimarron Inn. See map 3.

Marker text: In Turkey Creek Canyon near here, the outlaw gang of Thomas "Black Jack" Ketchum had one of its hideouts. After a train robbery in July 1899, a posse surprised the gang at the hideout. The outlaws scattered after a bloody battle, and the Ketchum gang was broken up.

Note: See the general introduction to this series of Markers, as well as the other Markers making up the series, for further background on Black Jack Ketchum's exploits in the state.

On July 11, 1899, outlaw Thomas "Black Jack" Ketchum, his brother Sam, and a handful of desperados held up a Denver and Gulf train as it pulled out of Folsom in far northeastern New Mexico. The outlaws blew up the train's safe with dynamite and absconded with the loot they recovered.

After the robbery, the Ketchum gang returned to their hideout, a cave in Turkey Creek Canyon north of Cimarron. Here they holed up for several days—the last they would spend together. Black Jack was not present on July 16 and so was spared the gunfire that bombarded the camp when a local posse charged the den in a surprise attack. Bullets killed most of the posse members and wounded several of the Ketchum gang. Sam Ketchum escaped, but not before catching a shot just below his left shoulder. Lawmen snagged him a few days later. A doctor recommended that Sam's arm be amputated before fatal infection spread, but the obdurate outlaw refused. He died in prison sometime during the night of July 23.

37. Black Jack Ketchum

Location: Union County. In Clayton, in the courtyard of the Clayton Tourist Information Center, 1103 South First Street. See map 3.

Marker text: Thomas "Black Jack" Ketchum, leader of a notorious band of train robbers, was wounded in August 1899 while trying to rob a train near Folsom. He surrendered the next day. He was tried and convicted under a law making train robbery a capital offense, and hanged at Clayton on April 26, 1901.

Note: See the general introduction to this series of Markers, as well as the other Markers making up the series, for further background on Black Jack Ketchum's exploits in the state.

Black Jack was still grieving the loss of his brother Sam in July 1899, who had died in a battle with a local posse at Turkey Creek Canyon near Cimarron, when he decided, in mid-August of that year, to return to the scene of the same train robbery he and his former gang had committed the previous month near Folsom, and once again rob the evening passenger train. After stopping the locomotive, Ketchum ordered the engineer, fireman, and express messenger to uncouple the train behind the express car. Conductor Frank Harrington, the same conductor aboard the train that Black Jack had earlier waylaid, seized his opportunity. As the men worked, Harrington snuck with his shotgun to the back of the train and took aim just as Ketchum returned fire. Ketchum's bullet grazed Harrington's arm, causing little damage. Harrington's bullet, in contrast, gruesomely shattered the flesh and bone of Ketchum's upper right arm.

The next morning, crews from a northbound freight train found the wounded outlaw sitting by the tracks, his shirt stained with blood and his hair matted with sweat. They transported him to a hospital in Trinidad, Colorado, where, in a grisly repeat of the diagnosis his brother Sam had received, doctors told Black Jack that his arm would have to be amputated if he was to survive. In late August, after prison officials had taken Ketchum to the Santa Fe penitentiary, the outlaw complied with the doctors' orders.

Ketchum languished in jail for more than a year, visited only by those curious to lay eyes on the infamous bandit. His trial finally began on September 6, 1900. It ended just two days later. The jury found the culpable outlaw guilty of "assault on a railroad train," a felony in New Mexico, punishable by death.

As Black Jack approached the scaffold in Clayton, New Mexico, on the morning of April 26, 1901, legend says that he scoffed at the hangman, requesting that the task be done quickly so he could be in Hell in time for dinner. His was the first hanging in Clayton history. Although officials in Santa Fe had corresponded with the sheriff in Clayton about the proper method of gallows construction, the deputies lacked experience in the task. As Black Jack dropped through the trap door, the violent pull of the noose nearly severed his head.

After being buried in an unmarked grave outside of town, Black Jack's body was reinterred twice, the third and final burial in Clayton Memorial Cemetery, where it remains today. When it came to creating an epitaph, Black Jack's descendents gave Shakespeare the last word: "And how his audit stands, who knows save Heaven."

38. Blackdom Townsite

Location: Chaves County. Sixteen miles north of Artesia, in a pullout on the west side of US 285, between mile markers 86 and 87. See map 6.

Marker text: West of this location stood the now abandoned community of Blackdom. The community was founded circa 1908 by Francis Marion Boyer and his wife Ella. Several dozen African American families homesteaded nearly 15,000 acres of land and built a self-sustaining community that boasted a general store and a Baptist Church. Officially platted in 1920, the community was eventually abandoned due to continued problems with irrigation from the distant Pecos River.

Among the many small settlements that have been born, struggled, then disappeared across the history of New Mexico and its varied cultural landscape, the community of Blackdom is set apart by one distinguishing attribute: it was founded and settled entirely by African Americans.

Hoping to establish a self-sustaining community where African Americans could raise families free from the racial, economic, and political hardships of the post–Civil War South, Georgia-born Francis Marion Boyer set out on foot from Georgia to New Mexico in 1896. Boyer had learned about the open, fertile land of the Southwest from his father—the elder Boyer had traveled through New Mexico in 1846 as a free black wagoneer with the Army of the West under the command of General Stephen Watts Kearny, after the United States had claimed the land from Mexico. Francis Boyer, a college graduate, followed in his father's footsteps, almost literally, walking (and occasionally hopping rides with passing wagon trains) from his home in Pelham, Georgia, to the Pecos Valley of southeastern New Mexico, a distance of more than a thousand miles, from January to October 1900. Upon his arrival, Boyer and his traveling companions hired out as farmhands, earning enough money to send for their wives and children the following year.

Around 1908, Boyer and his wife, Ella, homesteaded a patch of land about sixteen miles south of Roswell. A settlement needs settlers, so Boyer advertised his community, which he called Blackdom, in newspapers in the southern states. He hoped to draw other African Americans to join him in fulfilling the mandate set out in the articles of incorporation for the townsite:

to maintain a colony . . . by means of the cultivation of crops, the growing of town and settlements and the general improvements of the colony; to build, erect and equip schoolhouses, colleges, churches and various education and religious institutions for the improvement and upbringing of the moral and mental condition of the colony.

Settlers arrived, and together they did build a community, homesteading an area that covered about fifteen thousand acres. Boyer helped many of them personally in their resettlement efforts, offering newcomers a place to stay until they could build their own homes, and sometimes loaning them money. Most of the residents of Blackdom subsisted as farmers, either raising their own crops of alfalfa and corn or working on farmlands in nearby Roswell or Dexter. Enterprises important to the nascent years of a new settlement arose: a store, a small hotel, and a one-room school. On Sundays, the school building doubled as the Blackdom Baptist Church. Local revelry included a festive annual "Juneteenth"—likely the first in the state—a celebration to commemorate the abolition of slavery. Just a few short years after its founding, Blackdom had some three hundred residents.

From the beginning, though, the community struggled. The location offered insufficient access to water, and bankers in Roswell refused to loan the money necessary for wells. An infestation of cutworms in 1916, along with a prolonged drought, didn't help. Lacking the financial resources to drill wells on their own, most residents were unable to keep their fields productive and were forced to resettle elsewhere.

Francis Boyer and his wife filed a plat of the Blackdom townsite in 1920, showing a town of 155 lots surrounding a central "public square and park"—but that dream existed only on paper. When the bank foreclosed on his farm, Boyer and his family, no doubt reluctantly, moved away the next year. They resettled in Vado, New Mexico, where many of their descendants remain today.

With the Boyers went the heart of the community. By the end of the decade, after a brief but remarkable life, Blackdom was abandoned.

More to explore: *Buffalo Soldier Hill, Dr. Meta L. Christy, Las Vegas, Roswell, Shalam Colony*

39. Blackwater Draw

Location: Roosevelt County. Northeast of Portales, at the entrance to the Blackwater Draw Rest Area and Blackwater Draw Museum, on the south side of US 70, between mile markers 429 and 430. See map 6.

Marker text: Blackwater Draw consists of several important archaeological sites that have yielded much information about the big-game hunting way of life. Some of the animals that were hunted, like the mammoth, are long extinct. Eastern New Mexico University's Blackwater Draw Museum contains artifacts of the Paleo-Indian cultures that existed here as early as 10,000 B.C.

It was partly the wind that changed what science knows about the earliest history of humankind in North America. For years, gusting winds, along with gravel excavations by the State Highway Department, had been uncovering curious objects on the eastern plains near Clovis. Requests from local amateur paleontologist A. W. Anderson finally induced Dr. Edgar B. Howard of the University of Pennsylvania to visit in 1932. Here, at Blackwater Draw, Howard and his team of archaeologists unearthed not only mammoth skeletons but also tools and weapons made from the bones, as well as flaked spear points and evidence of ancient human campsites. These prehistoric relics confirmed that early humans had coexisted with and hunted creatures now extinct, such as the Columbian mammoth and ancient bison—animals that had lived eleven thousand years ago during the late Pleistocene epoch. The wind had uncovered proof that humans had arrived in North America much earlier than archaeologists had previously believed.

Blackwater Draw Locality Number 1 and its counterpart, Locality Number 2 near Anderson Basin, have since become the "type sites," or scholarly reference points, for the Clovis Paleo-Indian archaeological culture. The name *Clovis* comes from the nearby city of Clovis.

Prehistoric Blackwater Draw was a large, spring-fed pond, the remnant of an ancient river. Giant mammoths and bison came to the waters to drink. Higher up on the food chain, humans came here, in part to hunt them. Using characteristically chipped flint points known as Clovis points, which archaeologically identify their culture, Clovis hunters and gatherers stalked and felled the colossal beasts. They did so as early as 10,000 BC.

Blackwater Draw also contains a small earthen hole that archaeologists believe is one of the earliest wells in the United States. More than five thousand years ago, Indians here dug the well by hand through sand and caliche, apparently, as anthropologists believe, to tap the water table after changes in the climate caused the pond to run dry.

Humans may have visited Blackwater Draw over a span of some six thousand years' time. The Draw is a multicomponent site, which simply means that other human occupation besides the Clovis culture occurred here. As temperatures rose and mammoths became extinct, the Clovis culture gradually gave way, and a new people emerged: the Folsom culture.

Recognizing the historical significance of Blackwater Draw and the Anderson Basin, the National Park Service has designated the site a National Historic Landmark.

More to explore: *Clayton Dinosaur Trackway (see under Clayton Lake State Park), Clovis, Eastern New Mexico University*

40. Blazer's Mill

Location: Otero County. In Mescalero, on the south side of US 70, at mile marker 241. See map 6.

Marker text: An early fight in the Lincoln County War occurred near this sawmill on April 5, 1878, when several men of the McSween faction, including Dick Brewer and Billy the Kid, attempted to arrest Buckshot Roberts. Roberts and Brewer were killed, and two others wounded, in the battle that followed.

Note: The gunfight took place on April 4, not April 5, as the Marker states.

Lincoln County was a relatively quiet place when Dr. Joseph H. Blazer, a retired dentist from Iowa, established a sawmill and post office near here in the early 1870s. Things changed dramatically on February 18, 1878, when Lincoln County sheriff William Brady sent a posse to inventory the ranch of Englishman John Tunstall. Tunstall's rise to economic power locally and his alliance with Lincoln lawyer Alexander McSween had put him at odds with merchants L. G. Murphy and J. J. Dolan, associates of Sheriff Brady, who had previously held a monopoly in retail business in the county. The deputized posse met Tunstall on his way to Lincoln and murdered him. Infuriated, Tunstall's ranch hands, including young Billy the Kid, formed an outlaw posse they named "the Regulators" and made a covenant to avenge the killing. The resulting conflict became known as the Lincoln County War.

Riding in Sheriff Brady's posse that day was Andrew Roberts, once a clerk in J. J. Dolan's Lincoln store. Earlier in his life, Roberts had taken a round of buckshot that, while it prevented him from raising his right arm above the shoulder, had given him a new nickname: Buckshot. Although some historians believe that Roberts had probably not been directly involved in the murder of John Tunstall, a warrant had nonetheless been issued for his arrest.

Many of the events in the saga that is the life of Billy the Kid are fodder for historical debate. We may never know the true story of Blazer's Mill, but the principals remain the same. According to most accounts, Roberts traveled to Blazer's Mill on April 4, 1878. Regardless of his motivations for being at the mill (histories differ), a coincidence of timing put him there just as the Regulators, including Frank and George Coe, Billy the Kid, John Middleton, Charlie Bowdre, and Richard M. "Dick" Brewer, arrived to eat dinner.

Frank Coe attempted to negotiate Roberts's peaceful surrender outside the mill. Roberts was reluctant to comply, as he disliked the Kid and his gang and worried that they meant to kill him. After about a half hour of talk, Charlie Bowdre, George Coe, and the others finally drew the line. Bowdre ordered Roberts to drop his two six-shooters and rifle, but Roberts declined. Each then drew his pistol and moved from words to bullets: Roberts fired on Bowdre the very moment Bowdre returned the shot. The result was later recounted by the hapless George Coe, who had been standing nearby:

Bowdre's bullet struck Roberts right through the middle, while Roberts' ball glanced off Bowdre's cartridge belt, and with my usual luck, I arrived just in time to stop the bullet with my right hand. It knocked the gun out of my hand, took off my trigger finger, and shattered my hand which still bears record of the fight.

Severely injured, Buckshot Roberts crawled into Dr. Blazer's office and propped himself on a mattress he had dragged near a window. When Brewer's head rose from behind a barricade of sawmill logs outside, Roberts fired, killing him instantly.

Dr. Blazer negotiated his way into the room where Roberts lay, but found the man more dead than alive. Despite ministrations from a local doctor, Roberts passed away the following day.

Only ruins of Blazer's Mill can be seen today. They lie behind a fence in Mescalero, on the south side of US 70 between mile markers 243 and 244, three miles west of this Historic Marker.

More to explore: *John H. Tunstall Murder Site, Lincoln, Old Dowlin Mill (see under Ruidoso)*

41. Bluewater Village

Location: Cibola County. In the village of Bluewater, in a pullout on the west side of Main Street, just before the Interstate 25 interchange. See map 1.

Marker text: This community was founded in 1894 on the site of an earlier homestead and stage coach stop. Irrigation from Bluewater Lake and its proximity to the railroad and Route 66 allowed development of extensive agricultural fields, which earned Bluewater the title, "Carrot Capital of the World." The region became known as the "Uranium Capital of the World" after uranium was discovered nearby in 1950.

Ernest Tietjen and Frihoff G. Nelson, residents of nearby Ramah, built a dam on Bluewater Creek around 1894. The reservoir behind the dam became the impetus for the development of a small village. Because many of the new settlers were members of the Church of Jesus Christ of Latter-Day Saints, like Tietjen and Nelson, the new community came to be known as Mormontown. It was only a short distance from the small settlement of Bluewater, a stop along the Atlantic and Pacific Railroad, which had laid rails through the area a decade earlier. Eventually, the two communities merged, with the name Bluewater winning out.

The original dam built by Nelson washed away, and a second one, too, gave out in 1905. Hoping for a more permanent structure, locals in 1927 erected a new dam from concrete. The reservoir of that dam provided the infrastructure necessary for sustainable irrigation of the fields around Bluewater. Among the vegetables grown in those fields were carrots—a vegetable that would change the course of the history of the village.

According to pioneer histories, samples of Bluewater carrots were taken to a growers' convention in California sometime in the 1930s. The orange vegetables were so regarded by the experts that carrots quickly became the cash crop in Bluewater gardens. That continued to be the case for two subsequent decades. The Atlantic and Pacific Railroad had reached Gallup in the 1880s, and historic Route 66 (now Interstate 40 and NM 122) came through in the 1920s, allowing for easy shipping of the carrot harvest out to the world. An article in the *Albuquerque Journal* in 1941 reported that farmers that year were cultivating 1,100 acres of carrots in the Bluewater Valley, each acre yielding some 165 crate loads of carrots. The carrots, an early tourist brochure boasted, "attracted much attention for color, size and quality." The many fields under cultivation during the boom years soon earned Bluewater Village the nickname "the Carrot Capital of the World."

In September 1942, Bluewater farmers used their harvest to help the war effort by sending a freight car of carrots to New York to be auctioned. The proceeds, about $13,000, were donated to the Bataan Relief Organization, serving the families of captured American soldiers held in the Philippines during World War II. Many of those soldiers were members of the 200th Coast Artillery, mostly made up of young men from New Mexico.

In 1950, something else from the ground brought new prosperity to the region. That year, sheepherder Paddy Martinez found uranium in Haystack Mountain. The mining boom that resulted gave nearby Grants its own eminent designation, becoming known as "the Uranium Capital of the World."

More to explore: *Cooke's Wagon Road, Grants, Hatch*

42. The Bond House

Location: Rio Arriba County. In the courtyard of the Bond House in Española, 710 Bond Street, behind the Española Post Office and Plaza. See map 2.

Marker text: Frank Bond (1863–1945), prominent Española merchant, came from Canada in 1882. In 1887 Bond married May Anna Caffal of Pueblo, Colorado and built the home. The house grew from a two-room adobe to this large structure. Acquired by the city in 1957, the building is used as a museum today.

The historic Bond House, a landmark along the street now similarly named, is the architectural handiwork of leading nineteenth-century Española merchant Frank Bond. Bond was born on his parents' farm in Quebec, Canada, on February 13, 1863. He followed his brother George to New Mexico in 1883. The brothers worked briefly with a merchant near San Juan Pueblo before moving to Española, where they purchased the Scott and Whitehead Store and changed the name to G. W. Bond and Brother Mercantile Company. As their profits rose, the Bond brothers opened franchises in Wagon Mound, Roy, and Albuquerque, and later entered the sheep husbandry business. Although George Bond left New Mexico to run the venture from Trinidad, Colorado, Frank remained. Hardworking and intelligent, Frank Bond developed a business sense and social standing that brought economic growth and prominence to the community of Española through the turn of the century.

After marrying Colorado native May Anna Caffal on August 15, 1887, Bond began work on a permanent home in Española for his new bride and their impending family. From its humble beginnings as a two-room territorial-style adobe, the structure swelled as major renovations and additions eventually culminated in a one-and-a-half-story neoclassical revival mansion with more than eleven decorous rooms, elegant fireplaces, a sun porch, a veranda held aloft by Corinthian columns, a pitched roof, and even a small outdoor park.

Frank and May Anna had three children, Maude, Amy, and Richard. In 1918, to improve the health of eldest daughter Maude, Bond moved with his family to Albuquerque.

Frank Bond passed away from a chronic heart ailment in Los Angeles on June 21, 1945, at the age of eighty-two. Mrs. Bond had preceded her husband in death by ten years.

In 1957, a Bond heir deeded the Bond House to the city of Española, after which the structure served as City Hall until 1977. A renovation in 2000 returned the historic Bond House to its early twentieth-century urbane grandeur. The building is listed on the National Register of Historic Places, which notes its important role as "one of the major architectural landmarks of Española."

More to explore: *Dorsey Mansion, Española Valley, Historic Los Luceros*

Bosque Redondo Indian Reservation: *see Fort Sumner and Fort Sumner State Monument (series)*

43. Bottomless Lakes State Park

Location: Chaves County. Twelve miles east of Roswell, in a pullout on the north side of US 380, at the intersection of US 380 and NM 409, the park entrance. See map 6.

Marker text: When 19th Century cowboys attempted to measure these lakes by tying lariats together, they found no bottom and declared the lakes "bottomless." Today we know these sinkholes, formed by collapsed salt and gypsum deposits, are 17 to 90 feet in depth. The park was established in 1933 as New Mexico's first state park.

44. Ghost Marker: Civilian Conservation Corps Camp #831

Marker text: The Civilian Conservation Corps (CCC) was a federal program established during the Great Depression to provide jobs for the nation's young men. #831 was one of the first CCC camps in New Mexico. The men stationed here provided most of the labor to develop Bottomless Lakes State Park. Dedicated in 1933, this park was built on land purchased by the citizens of Chaves County and donated to the State.

Note: This Historic Marker appears in an inventory of Markers maintained by the Historic Preservation Division but may not have been built. Because it provides information about the CCC camp that helped build this state park, it is included here as a Ghost Marker. See map 6.

As the story goes, cowboys herding cattle on the Goodnight-Loving Trail over the grassy plains of southeastern New Mexico in the late nineteenth century camped at water holes and small lakes in this area. The cowboys made a crude attempt to measure the depth of the lakes by tying their lariats together end to end (lariats are long ropes that cowboys use to lasso cattle), possibly attaching a rock to one end as a sinker, and lowering the device into the water. Unable to feel the rope hitting the floor below, the cowboys had no choice but to proclaim the lakes "bottomless."

Geologists later disproved this notion, finding that the lakes did have bottoms after all, which ranged in depth from the eighteen-foot-deep Pasture Lake to the ninety-foot-deep Lea Lake. The lakes are technically sinkholes, formed when the roofs of large underground caverns (themselves formed from the gradual erosion of salt and gypsum deposits) collapsed, then filled with rain and groundwater from the Sacramento Mountains to the west. Geologists use the term "cenotes" to describe lakes that form within sinkholes, like the ones here.

There are nine lakes total, although two are closed to the public. The names of the lakes evoke their individual character or that of their surroundings, including Lazy Lagoon, Figure Eight, Cottonwood, Mirror, Devil's Inkwell, and Pasture. Those last four are stocked with rainbow trout for fishing. Lazy Lagoon and Lea Lake are the largest and sit at opposite ends of the park. Lea Lake, named for Captain Joseph Calloway Lea, scion of Roswell and founder of the New Mexico Military Institute there, is a popular swimming area complete with shoreline. Small boat rentals are also available at Lea Lake, and the lake is open to scuba diving.

The New Mexico State Park Commission, organized in 1933, selected Bottomless Lakes as the site of the first state park created in New Mexico. As the commissioner of public lands noted, the park was

of scientific interest by reason of the fact that upon said lands are situated a series of lakes of unusual depth in proportion to their diameter, formed by collapsed caverns in a gypsum formation in an artesian area, and should be preserved for the use and pleasure of the people of the State of New Mexico.

In December of that same year, the Civilian Conservation Corps (CCC) established Camp no. 831 here. The CCC was a Depression-era program to put young men to work building parks, roads, and other structures around the country. Some two hundred men stationed at the Bottomless Lakes camp erected structures to enhance the accessibility of the new park and allow for its interpretation and enjoyment. These structures, some of which stand today, include the Lea Lake Recreational Building and Lea Lake Tower.

More to explore: *Carlsbad Caverns, Civilian Conservation Corps—Carlsbad Campsite, Elephant Butte Lake State Park, Goodnight-Loving Trail (series), Roswell*

Brazito Battlefield: *see Paraje de los Brazitos*

45. Brazos Cliffs

Location: Rio Arriba County. In Carson National Forest, in a pullout on the west side of US 64 at mile marker 194. See map 2.

Marker text: These precipitous cliffs form the western edge of the Tusas Mountains, a Rocky Mountain highland that enters New Mexico from Colorado. They are composed of some of the oldest rock known in New Mexico, the Precambrian quartzite about 1.7 billion years old. Vertical distance from summit to base is more than 2,000 feet. Elevation here 10,000 feet.

Composed of some of the oldest rock in New Mexico, quartzite created during the Precambrian period about 1.7 billion years ago, the towering Brazos Cliffs are as stunning as they are ancient. These cliffs lie within the transition between the Rio Chama Valley and the rugged highlands of the Rocky Mountains, which enter New Mexico from Colorado in the form of the Sangre de Cristo Range. The cliffs likewise form the western periphery of the Tusas Mountains. The sheer vertical face of these cliffs strains the tape measure at more than two thousand feet from base to summit—about a third of a mile high.

The cliffs are only a small part of the much larger Brazos country, which includes the Tusas Mountains, a spectacular waterfall, and the gushing Rio Brazos, the main tributary of the Rio Chama to the south. The Brazos Box is a spectacular canyon through which the Rio Brazos flows. Rock climbers are especially fond of the Brazos Cliffs.

More to explore: *Palisades Sill (see under Cimarron Canyon State Park), Rocky Mountains*

46. Buffalo Soldier Hill

Location: Roosevelt County. One mile west of the New Mexico–Texas border, approximately seventeen miles west of Morton, Texas, in a pullout on the south side of NM 114, between mile markers 46 and 47. See map 6.

Marker text: Near here in the summer of 1877, Troop A of the US Tenth Cavalry endured substantial hardship and death when they became lost during an attempt to force a band of Kwahada Comanche warriors back to their reservation in Oklahoma. Also known as the Forlorn Hope or Lost Troop Expedition, Troop A was composed of some 40 Buffalo Soldiers (African American cavalry) under the command of Captain Nicholas M. Nolan and 22 bison hunters.

Note: Although Buffalo Soldier Hill itself is on privately owned land, the small hill is clearly visible to the north from this Historic Marker. By following South Roosevelt Road B (a dirt road) from here north for about a mile, you can get a bit closer to it and see the rise from the east.

On orders to pursue a band of Kwahada Comanche Indians who had left their Oklahoma reservation and were raiding buffalo hunter camps on the plains, Troop A of the US Army Tenth Cavalry left Fort Concho, Texas (located today within the present-day city of San Angelo, between Odessa and Austin), on July 10, 1877, on what would become a historic but ill-fated expedition. Under the command of Captain Nicholas M. Nolan, Troop A was composed of some sixty black soldiers. African American soldiers at the time were colloquially known as Buffalo Soldiers, a name given to them by Indians of the Southwest.

About a week into their expedition, Captain Nolan (who was white) and his soldiers met a group of buffalo hunters while making a base camp. These men made a living hunting bison on the plains. Nolan, who knew some of the hunters, jokingly called the ragged men the "Forlorn Hope," a military reference to soldiers who lead an assault in which the risk of casualty is high. Nolan believed that the hunters' knowledge of the land and of Indian trails would be beneficial to his expedition, so the two groups joined forces. Some men stayed at the base camp, while forty soldiers of Troop A and some twenty buffalo hunters proceeded toward the northwest, where Nolan believed the Comanche Indians would be found.

As it happened, the land that Nolan and his men crossed in their pursuit proved a far more formidable opponent than the Indians they were chasing. A drought had left the land of western Texas and southeastern New Mexico, a stretch known as the Llano Estacado, barren of water, and the treeless plains offered no hospitable refuge from the sun. Initially, the men drank from the sparse desert playas, but as their journey progressed they found they were chasing ghosts: of Comanche Indians, who may have suspected they were being pursued and left misleading trails to follow, and also water itself, a precious resource in scarce supply. Disagreements arose between the bison hunters and Captain Nolan about where the Comanches might be. Some of the hunters turned back, fearful of facing the journey with little water and diminished prospects.

While the command camped at Double Lakes, south of present-day Lubbock, Texas, on July 25, they dug wells by hand to reach small pockets of water. It was the last they would have for several days. When word came the next day that the Comanches had been spotted near Rich Lake, some fifteen miles distant, the men left their camp in pursuit—some of them with canteens only half full. Unfortunately, as the expedition reached Rich Lake, they found no Comanches—and no water in the now-dry lake.

The next day, July 27, still hoping to find a Comanche camp and a water source, Nolan pressed his men forward, following an Indian trail. Searing heat from the summer sun bore down on the company and their horses and mules and slowly robbed them of their fortitude. "The command now commenced to suffer exceedingly for water," Nolan wrote in his report of the expedition. "One of the men at this time fell from his horse from the effects of sunstroke."

As they traveled from Texas into New Mexico later that day, Nolan sent the buffalo hunters' guide, José Tafoya, ahead to Silver Lake, hoping to find water there. The expedition reached this location, the rise now known as Buffalo Soldier Hill in southeastern New Mexico, just as night was falling. Here, Nolan sent another detachment of men ahead with instructions to find Tafoya at Silver Lake and return with water.

The hill represented a turning point for the expedition, both literally and figuratively. As the parched and bedraggled men camped for the night, Nolan may well have assessed their bleak outlook and realized he had to make a desperate choice. The next morning, July 28, Captain Nolan at first pressed forward toward Silver Lake, but, not locating the lake, and with no sign of Tafoya or the soldiers he had sent out the night before and fearing them lost, Nolan abandoned hope of finding the Comanches and turned his attention to the urgent task of finding water for their own survival. He ordered his men to turn around and return to Double Lakes, their last dependable source of water—some fifty miles back.

No longer part of an expedition with mutual goals, and thinking their best chance of finding water still lay in finding Silver Lake, the buffalo hunters left the Buffalo Soldiers and started out on their own.

With the unremitting sun bearing down on them, the soldiers of Troop A staggered back toward Double Lakes in temperatures that reached over a hundred degrees. Confused and half-crazed from the sun, some men wandered off; others went missing. Sergeant William L. Umbles, who had earlier in the expedition argued with Captain Nolan and been demoted as a result, left the expedition with a handful of soldiers the night before and set off to find water himself. (Umbles and his men were later court-martialed for desertion.) Desperate, the soldiers were forced to adapt, as Nolan described:

One of Lieutenant Cooper's private horses had become so exhausted he was killed and his blood distributed among the men. Previous to this, the command were suffering so much for water we were compelled to drink our own and our horses' urine, as also did the horses and mules. Having sugar along, I issued a liberal supply to the men, which tended to make the urine palatable.

Ironically, the soldiers Captain Nolan had earlier sent to find water at Silver Lake had actually done so; returning, they encountered Sergeant Umbles and his men and shared the precious fluid. But they were unaware that the main expedition had turned back to Double Lakes, and so they searched desperately for their command—lifesaving water in hand. They were only reunited with their troop several days later at the base camp.

At last, on July 30, after five days without water, the men of Troop A, along with Captain Nolan, arrived at Double Lakes and found there the water they so desperately needed. Stragglers from the command continued to arrive for days later. In total, four men perished from thirst and exhaustion on the expedition.

The soldiers could not have known, as they faced their own desperate circumstances, that their story had meanwhile become a national concern. Word had reached Fort Concho that the men were missing and presumed dead. While that turned out to be mostly untrue, the press nonetheless reacted, calling the incident the "Staked Plains Horror," the Staked Plains being another name for the Llano Estacado. Today, the incident is most commonly referred to as the "Buffalo Soldier Tragedy of 1877" or the "Lost Troop Expedition."

Until 2004, the name of the small hill here included a word today considered pejorative and racist. Oscar Robinson, an employee of Eastern New Mexico University and a member of the Llano Estacado Buffalo Soldier Association, led a successful effort to have the US Board of Geographic Names officially change the name. A ceremony in June of that year marked the new name, Buffalo Soldier Hill, and the approval by the state of this Historic Marker to inform travelers of the fateful incident that played out here.

More explore: *Blackdom Townsite, Cathay Williams, Fort Selden*

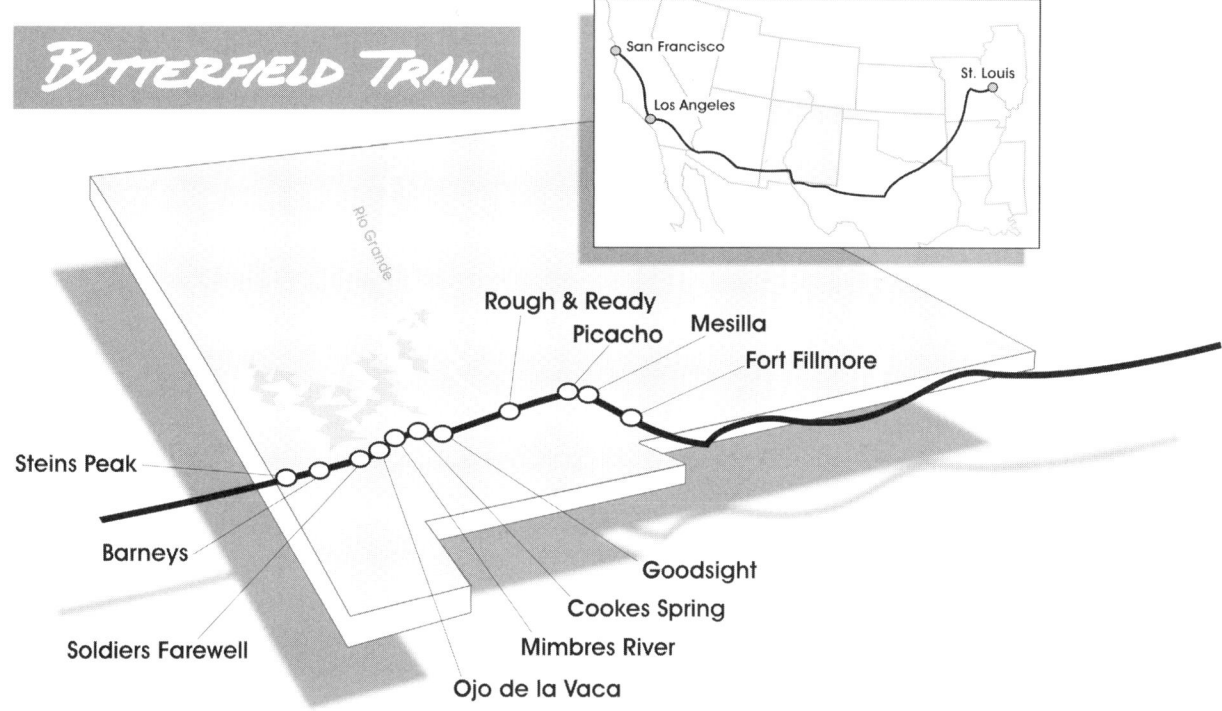

Although New Mexico had other stage lines, none was more famous than the Butterfield Trail. Rolling through the southwestern corner of the state, Butterfield stages made stops roughly every twenty miles to change horses until crossing into Arizona. Illustration by David Carter.

47. Butterfield Trail

Location: Doña Ana County. At the New Mexico Visitors Center on Interstate 10, just north of the New Mexico–Texas border. See map 5.

Marker text: Stagecoaches of the Butterfield Overland Mail Co. began carrying passengers and mail from St. Louis to San Francisco, across southern New Mexico, in 1858. The 2,795-mile journey took 21–22 days. In 1861 the service was rerouted through Salt Lake City. Here the trail followed the Rio Grande northward to La Mesilla.

A founding member of the American Express Company and former mayor of Utica, New York, John Butterfield attached his name firmly to the saga of westward expansion with his catchphrase, "Remember boys, nothing in God's earth must stop the United States mail!" In 1858, Butterfield secured a $600,000 government contract to institute the first transcontinental passenger and mail delivery route between the Midwest and the Pacific coast. Butterfield sent the first of his resplendent Concord wagons forth from Saint Louis on September 16, 1858. It passed through Mesilla on September 30 on its way to the western terminus in San Francisco, opening the mines and frontier settlements of the Southwest to anyone who could afford the $200 ticket.

The 2,800-mile course of the Butterfield Trail, which curved in a semicircle through the southern half of the country in what detractors labeled the Oxbow Route for its resemblance to the collar placed around the neck of an ox, included several stops in New Mexico. Some of these were simply mail stops with small corrals for horses and water troughs; others, if they were stationed in a populated area, offered restaurants and hotel accommodations for passengers. The trail entered the state near El Paso and followed the Rio Grande north to its first New Mexico stop, Fort Fillmore, a now-vanished military installation six miles south of present-day Las Cruces. From there, the stage ran to Mesilla Station, one of the largest in the state, located in what was then one of the most commercially important villages in southwestern New Mexico. The stage then turned west and followed an itinerary that included stops at Picacho, Rough and Ready Station, and Goodsight Station. Goodsight, as described by Roscoe P. and Margaret B. Conkling in their book *The Butterfield Overland Mail*, provides a glimpse of a typical design that Butterfield had used in creating the more than 140 stations along the route:

The station, judging from the ruins, comprised a rock and adobe corral, forty-five feet long by about thirty feet wide. There were two rooms, one at each end of the corral and each provided with a fireplace. An earth-made tank, about thirty by forty feet, stood seventy-five feet north of the station building, the road passing between them.

The line continued to the watering hole at Cookes Spring and Fort Cummings, north of present-day Deming. From there, the powerful team of horses pulled the coach, which could typically seat up to nine passengers, along with the mail—safely stashed under the driver's seat—another eighteen miles to the eastern bank of the Mimbres River and Mimbres River Station. Travelers endured further overland turbulence as they bumped their way to the station at Ojo de las Vacas, later renamed Dinsmore for Butterfield vice president William B. Dinsmore. Fourteen miles later, stages reached Soldiers Farewell Mountain, so named because the military escort from Fort Cummings turned back at this point. The ride then continued past the present-day town of Lordsburg and moved to the station at Steins Peak. This was the last stop in New Mexico before passengers entered what is now Arizona.

A competing mail service emerged in 1860—the Pony Express. Although it had the advantage of a northern route, which avoided the dangers of traveling through the sometimes volatile Southwest, and it allowed for faster delivery of mail, the Pony Express was disbanded after only eighteen months in operation.

In 1861, cutbacks in funding and the advance of Confederates in New Mexico during the Civil War forced John Butterfield to reroute his line north through Salt Lake City. Six years later, in 1867, the man whose name would become synonymous with stagecoach lines in the Southwest suffered an encumbering stroke. He died in November 1869.

More to explore: *Fort Cummings, La Mesilla*

48. Caballo Mountains

Location: Sierra County. North of Caballo, on NM 187, between mile markers 24 and 25. See map 5.

Marker text: To east beyond Caballo Reservoir are rugged Caballo Mountains, uplifted about 3 miles above down-dropped Rio Grande trough, along fault scarp at edge of mountains. Lowest slopes are ancient granites. Black ironstone beds are at base of high cliffs which are formed by Paleozoic dolomites and limestones. Elevation 4,390 feet.

Commanding the landscape to the east beyond the Caballo Reservoir are the majestic Caballo Mountains, rising to heights of 7,500 feet and above. *Caballo* is a Spanish word meaning "horse." The name derived either from the likeness of a horse's head supposedly visible in the contours of the northern side of the range, or from wild horses that legend says once galloped these slopes.

Great upheavals in the land brought about by faulting millions of years ago produced the towering mountains. As earth through the center of New Mexico dropped downward to form an elongated trough known as the Rio Grande Rift, great chunks of land here were uplifted along a fault to create this rugged, north-south tending range. Because of this disjointed alignment of land, the same rocks seen on the slopes of the mountains lie buried in the trough under sediment eroded from the range, separated from their counterparts by about three miles. The mountains stretch between the towns of Engle, east of Truth or Consequences, and Hatch, south of here, a distance of some thirty miles.

Exposed along the lower slopes on the western face of the mountains are ancient Precambrian granites. Creosote bush, saltbush, sand sage, yucca, and cholla grow at these lower elevations. A dark-brown band of ironstone geologists call the Bliss Sandstone overlies the granite slopes. Higher still are cliffs of Paleozoic dolomite and limestone. Chokeberry, yucca, and juniper vegetate these upper elevations. The highest peak of the range is the 7,565-foot-high Timber Mountain, but the most recognized is probably Turtle Mountain east of Truth or Consequences. Commonly called Turtleback Mountain, this peak has eroded into a shape reminiscent of a turtle crawling north.

A small mining district known as Shandon arose in the Caballos in 1901 when Encarnación "Bernardo" Silva discovered gold in Trujillo Gulch near the present site of Caballo Dam. Silva reportedly worked the placer deposits in secret for more than a year until other eager miners in Hillsboro somehow enticed him into revealing the location. As related by a US Geological Survey report from 1910, "a stampede to the new diggings immediately followed." In 1905, that stampede had raised the population in Shandon to 150 people. But production petered quickly as the gold was exhausted, and the camp was gone by 1915.

About twenty-five years later, engineers and state workers began construction of Caballo Dam, an adjunct storage facility to the larger Elephant Butte Dam near Truth or Consequences. Completed in 1938, Caballo Dam created a reservoir with a maximum storage capacity of around 300,000 acre-feet. The state created Caballo Lake State Park around the reservoir in 1964. The state park remains a popular recreational site today.

More to explore: *Elephant Butte Lake State Park, Rio Grande, Rio Grande Rift, Truth or Consequences*

49. Camino del Llano

Location: Valencia County. In west Belen, in a pullout on the south side of Camino del Llano near the intersection of Camino del Llano and the Interstate 25 interchange (exit 191 from the interstate). See map 4.

Marker text: Camino del Llano (Road to the Plains) played a significant role in the history of Belen and the surrounding communities. While the history of its use extends into colonial New Mexico, it continued to be defined by trade and commerce into the 20th century. Locally, it remains a symbol for the development and growth that occurred as a result of the commerce connecting area ranches to both the Belen stockyards and the railroad.

This Historic Marker, placed along the road named Camino del Llano, recognizes the importance of this road in the history of Belen and the surrounding region. *Camino del llano* is a Spanish phrase that translates as "road to the plains." The plains, in this case, were not the Great Plains to the east but instead the llanos, or grasslands, of the West Mesa area west of Belen. As Belen developed in the nineteenth century, cattle ranchers near the West Mesa used the road to drive their herds east to the stockyards near Belen, where the cattle were corralled and held until they were later herded to the railroad and shipped to market.

The road also traveled south from Belen to other settlements along the Rio Grande. It reached the Rio Puerco about twenty-five miles south of here. The road was an access point to the Ladrones Mountains, where trees provided firewood for Belen residents in the winter. In more recent years, the road connected Belen with the regional Alexander Municipal Airport built just west of the interstate.

This Historic Marker is here in part because of strong local interest in preserving the name of the road—an interest that became evident as the result of a name change in 1985. In that year, the city renamed the road, which had long been known as Camino del Llano, to Sosimo Padilla Boulevard. The name honored Belen native Sosimo Padilla, an accomplished and respected businessman and political leader who had assisted with many projects in Valencia County. Further, Padilla had a direct connection with the road that now bore his name: as a member of the State Highway Commission, Padilla had notably helped secure funding for a new interchange that would allow interstate traffic to enter Belen near the south of the city by exiting at Camino del Llano. Wanting to honor Padilla's contributions and recognize his importance to the region, the city council changed the name of the road.

Although the new name had been in place for fifteen years, a petition drive arose in early 2000 to restore the old name. The effort was led by longtime Belen residents, who recalled using the road in their own childhoods. By restoring the old name, they felt, they would also be restoring an important part of the history of their community. The city council agreed, voting to restore the name Camino del Llano—the name by which it remains known today. A portion of the road running east of South Main Street retains the name Sosimo Padilla Boulevard.

This Historic Marker was also erected afterward to bring attention to the history of Camino del Llano in Belen.

More to explore: *Belen, Rio Salado Sand Dunes*

50. Camp Lordsburg

Location: Hidalgo County. At the eastern edge of Lordsburg, south of the Interstate 10 interchange, at the intersection of Frontage Road (East Motel Boulevard) and POW Road. See map 5.

Marker text: Near this site the U.S. Army operated a camp during World War II. It opened as an internment camp for the Japanese and Japanese-American civilians from 1942–43. It later reopened as the Lordsburg Prisoner of War Camp for Germans and Italians from 1943–45. This camp is one of the few sites in the U.S. to house Japanese, Germans and Italians during its operations.

Just a few miles east down this road, today known as POW Road, the US Army in June 1942 established Camp Lordsburg. Originally, Camp Lordsburg served as an internment camp for Japanese and Japanese American civilians in the United States—one of several such war relocation camps across the United States erected in response to the events that precipitated the US entry into World War II, notably the attack on Pearl Harbor the previous winter. The Japanese civilians who were sent to the camp, most of whom were deemed suspicious by the FBI simply by virtue of their heritage but also including some actual Japanese POWs, numbered almost two thousand.

The use of Camp Lordsburg to hold Japanese internees was short-lived: by July 1943, the internees had been relocated to other camps, and the camp then began receiving prisoners of war. At first, the prisoners were Italians, arriving after the defeat of the Axis powers in the North African campaign. The following summer, however, most of the Italian prisoners were themselves relocated (or had joined the Allies after Italy's surrender in September), and the camp was host to German prisoners of war.

This change of populace over the course of its existence has given Camp Lordsburg the distinction of being one of only a few camps in the country to have held Japanese, German, and Italian internees and prisoners.

As a base camp and center of a number of smaller branch POW camps in southwestern New Mexico (at Fort Bayard, Deming, Hatch, Las Cruces, and Anthony), Camp Lordsburg was a large operation. The site included barracks, a hospital, a mess hall, a gymnasium, and various administrative and service buildings, along with a vegetable garden. (Although relations between locals and the POWs were generally genial, some locals considered the accommodations excessively grand.) At its peak around the fall of 1944, the camp held more than four thousand prisoners and was staffed by some seven hundred military service personnel. Inmates received medical care, regular hot meals, and the opportunity to attend religious services. To pass time inside the camp, the Italian prisoners ran their own camp newspaper and formed a small orchestra; the Germans after them held classes, taught by the more educated prisoners, in such subjects as math and biology. A guard tower allowed officers to spot any inmates attempting to scale either of the two fences surrounding the compound. There were, in fact, several escape attempts, and a few were successful, although the prisoners were later captured.

Oral histories of former employees at the camp archived at the New Mexico Farm and Ranch Heritage Museum paint a picture of the relationship between the camp and the town of Lordsburg itself. During the time Camp Lordsburg served as a POW camp, able-bodied prisoners were allowed and encouraged to work. Given the importance of agriculture in Hidalgo County, many POWs were escorted out of the camp each day in trucks to provide labor—while under guard—to area farms and ranches, or on other construction projects in the town, to supplement the labor force diminished by the number of men and women serving in the war effort. Prisoners were paid for their efforts, and the camp had a canteen where the prisoners could spend their earnings.

In June 1945, as World War II was ending, the

army deactivated Camp Lordsburg and released all remaining prisoners. Local Lordsburg residents removed building materials from the site and repurposed them into their own homes. Only a few scant cement foundations remain today to mark the former site of the camp.

More to explore: *Khe Sanh Veterans, Lordsburg*

51. Canadian Escarpment

Location: San Miguel County. Just south of Trementina on the east side of NM 104, between mile markers 46 and 47. See map 3.

Marker text: Prominent landform of north-eastern New Mexico that extends for almost 100 miles between Las Vegas and Clayton. From this point, the grasslands of the High Plains reach northwestward to the foot of the Southern Rocky Mountains which rise to elevations of more than 13,000 feet. Elevation here 6,300 feet.

The scene-stealing precipice in the foreground to the immediate north is part of an elongated cliff known as the Canadian Escarpment. This prominent landform runs diagonally for almost one hundred miles from Las Vegas (New Mexico), west of here, toward the town of Clayton. Along its length lie deep, entrenched valleys and dramatic, flat-topped mesas. The cliff takes its name from the Canadian River, which flows roughly north-south through the plains of north-eastern New Mexico until reaching Conchas Dam, where it turns eastward.

From this point, the lush blue gramma and buffalo grasses of the High Plains section of the Great Plains stretch northwestward to the Sangre de Cristo Mountains, a southern extension of the Rocky Mountains. The Taos Range within the Sangre de Cristo Mountains contains the highest peak in New Mexico, 13,161-foot-high Wheeler Peak. That elevation brings Wheeler Peak into the arctic-alpine life zone, the highest and coldest possible. No trees grow atop the peak, and its highest elevations remain snowy through late summer.

The elevation here is 6,300 feet, making this location part of the upper Sonoran life zone, a region characterized by small, scattered trees, mostly piñon, juniper, Apache plume, and mountain mahogany.

More to explore: *Canadian River Canyon, Mills Canyon, Rio Grande Rift, Wheeler Peak*

52. Canadian River Canyon

Location: Mora County. On NM 280, between mile markers 62 and 63. See map 3.

Marker text: Flowing out of the Rockies, the Canadian River has cut a gorge 600 feet deep through sedimentary strata of the High Plains. Rim elevation is 5,400 feet.

The spectacular Canadian River Canyon has earned its nickname: the mini–Grand Canyon.

The canyon is the slow, artistic creation of the Canadian River. The headwaters of the Canadian River originate on the northeastern slopes of the Sangre de Cristo Mountains in north-central New Mexico. The river navigates many contrasts as it wends through the northeastern corner of the state, transitioning from mountain slopes to deep gorges to rolling plains, and dropping in the process from an elevation of 9,000 feet to 3,660 feet.

Just south of Springer, the upper reaches of the river have cut a series of steep canyons, notably the spectacular Canadian River Canyon, a dramatic six-hundred-foot gorge carved into the sandstone rock layers of the High Plains.

The view today is no less inspiring than it was on August 28, 1845, when seen by a lieutenant traveling with Lieutenant James William Abert's expedition to the Southwest after the United States had claimed the land from Mexico:

It was . . . sufficiently deep to excite our admiration, and impress us with an idea of the wonderful effect of running water. The rock had been furrowed to the depth of 250 feet, nearly perpendicular, and the craggy sides were every where covered with cedars [junipers] and pines that had caught root in the crevices. At the foot, and between the two precipices, lay a smiling valley, covered with a luxuriant growth of fresh grass, through which, in silent beauty, the stream wound its way from bluff to bluff. A detached rock started a deer, and, as he bounded from his covert, broke in upon the dream in which I was indulging on the unbroken solitude of the scene before me.

More to explore: Canadian Escarpment, Mills Canyon

53. Cañoncito at Apache Canyon

Location: Santa Fe County. In Cañoncito, on the south side of the Old Las Vegas Highway. See map 2.

Marker text: Strategically located where the Santa Fe Trail emerges from Glorieta Pass, Cañoncito is where the New Mexican governor Manuel Armijo weakly defended New Mexico against the American army in 1846. In 1862, Union forces destroyed a Confederate supply train contributing to the Confederate loss at the Battle of Glorieta, six miles to the east.

As settlers and traders on the Santa Fe Trail emerged from Glorieta Pass to the east and continued with their wagons west to Santa Fe, they moved through a forested gap in the Sangre de Cristo Mountains known as Apache Canyon. Already a geographically strategic vantage point, this defile would witness two major turning points in New Mexico history.

The first occurred in the summer of 1846, as American forces advanced into New Mexico, a land then under the purview of Mexico, to claim the Southwest for the United States. Traveling with the expedition, Lieutenant William H. Emory wrote: "Reports now reached us at every step that . . . Armijo was collecting a formidable force to oppose our march at the celebrated pass of the Canon, 15 miles from Santa Fe."

Mexican Governor Manuel Armijo was indeed preparing to defend New Mexico against the American invasion. Armijo was a complex and controversial man. As historian Daniel Tyler points out in his article "Gringo Views of Governor Manuel Armijo," the American government often cast the governor in an unflattering light to help bolster support for their occupation. Still, Armijo gave them plenty to work with. If accounts of his exploits can be believed, he once poisoned a nephew's horse rather than face the chance that his might lose in a race. "God rules the Heavens," Armijo once reportedly said, "and Armijo rules the earth."

Despite his pretensions, Armijo was unprepared to fight the large American army. Although his troops did gather in the canyon, Armijo soon disbanded the brigade and fled south to Mexico. It is possible that the American government bribed him, as some historians have conjectured, and that the gathering of troops in Apache Canyon was only for show. A Mexican court later tried Armijo on charges of treason for having abandoned New Mexico. In his defense, Armijo displayed yet another side to his personality—a practical one. Armijo claimed that resisting the occupation

Manuel Armijo, the last Mexican governor of New Mexico before the American occupation, gathered a force to oppose the U.S. troops in Cañoncito. That battle never happened, but another one in this pass a decade and a half later would decide the fate of the Confederate Army in New Mexico. Governor Manuel Armijo. William A. Keleher Pictorial Collection, Box 1, Folder 1, Item 000-742-0001, Center for Southwest Research, University Libraries, University of New Mexico.

would have resulted in a pointless waste of lives. He was acquitted.

During the Civil War just sixteen years later, Apache Canyon was again the site of military chaos. In late March 1862, Confederate and Union troops were engaged in the Battle of Glorieta Pass, about six miles to the east. On March 28, Union Major John M. Chivington and a regiment of Colorado Volunteers flanked the south side of Apache Canyon. Spying the lightly guarded Confederate supply train below, Chivington and his men made their way down the cliffs of the mesa in a surprise attack, quickly trouncing the few Confederate wagon guards. The Union soldiers burned the supply carts and with them the ammunition, food, and medicine the Confederates needed to continue their advance to capture Fort Union.

Two weeks later, the Rebel army retreated from New Mexico, and Confederate hopes for victory in the Southwest ended.

More to explore: *Emory Pass, Fort Craig, Fort Union National Monument, Glorieta Pass Battlefield, Site of San Augustin Springs*

54. Capitan

Location: 1. Lincoln County. On the east side of Capitan, past the cemetery, on US 380. See map 6.

2. Lincoln County. On the west side of Capitan on US 380. See map 6.

Marker text: Many incidents in the Lincoln County War, 1876–79, occurred in the area around Capitan. The promoters Charles B. and John A. Eddy platted the townsite in 1900, after building a spur of the El Paso & Northeastern Railroad from Carrizozo in order to open the Salado coal fields. The mines were abandoned in 1901.

In 1950, a little bear cub, his feet badly burned, was rescued from a forest fire near here. The cub was nursed back to health and flown to Washington, D.C. to become the living symbol of "Smokey Bear" in the U.S. Forest Service's fire prevention program.

Homesteader Seaborn T. Gray and his family were among the first to settle in the area now known as Capitan. Gray opened a store and post office along Salado Creek in 1894, a few miles northwest of where the US Army had earlier established Fort Stanton. A community formed, which became known as Gray.

Soldiers from Fort Stanton had mined coal in this vicinity from at least 1885; others had likely done so much earlier. The Salado coalfields soon attracted the interest of railroad promoters Charles B. Eddy and his brother John A. Eddy. The Eddy brothers needed fuel for the trains of their El Paso and Northeastern Railroad (later renamed the El Paso and Southwestern) as it ran from El Paso, Texas, to Santa Rosa, New Mexico, where it connected with the Rock Island Railroad. In 1899, the Eddy brothers platted Gray into a larger townsite and completed a twenty-one-mile spur from Carrizozo to the Salado coalfields. They renamed the town at the railhead Capitan, for the pine- and piñon-covered Capitan Mountains north of the village.

In the late 1870s, those mountains had provided a safe refuge for William Bonney, better known as Billy the Kid. The Kid was a participant in the feud known today as the Lincoln County War. This land and cattle dispute between competing groups in the town of Lincoln sometimes festered into the surrounding countryside. Incidents related to the war included a shootout on the plaza at San Patricio to the south, and the killing, possibly by the Kid or members of his gang, of blacksmith James Carlyle north of White Oaks. The town of White Oaks, northwest of the Capitan Mountains, was at the time one of the largest settlements in New Mexico.

The Salado coal reserves were largely exhausted after the turn of the century. Most of the mines had closed by 1910. The Eddy brothers turned instead to the coalfields near Dawson in northern New Mexico and left Capitan behind. The rebuke did not impede the growth of the village. Citizens of Capitan incorporated their community on February 1, 1937.

A devastating inferno in the Capitan Mountains in May 1950 introduced the world to a new icon of safety—one with four paws and a growl. On May 9, firefighters battling the blaze found a black bear cub, only a few months old and weighing just four pounds, clinging to a tree. After officials nursed the cub to health, they flew him to Washington, D.C., to become the living counterpart of the cartoon character Smokey Bear. Smokey lived in the National Zoo in Washington until his death on November 9, 1976. At the request of local residents, his body was returned to Capitan for burial. Each year, more than 25,000 people visit Smokey Bear Historical Park and the grave of the most famous native son of Capitan.

More to explore: *Fort Stanton, Lincoln, San Patricio, Smokey Bear Historical Park, White Oaks*

55. Captive Women and Children of Taos County

Location: Taos County. South of Ranchos de Taos, in a rest area on the south side of NM 68 between mile markers 33 and 34. See map 2.

Marker text: In August 1760, around sixty women and children were taken captive in a Comanche raid on Ranchos de Taos. That raid is an example of the danger of living on New Mexico's frontier during the 17th and 18th centuries, for Hispanic and Indigenous communities alike raided each other and suffered enormous consequences. Thousands of women and children were taken captive. Most were never returned.

56. María Rosa Villapando (ca. 1725–1830)

Location: Taos County. South of Ranchos de Taos, in a rest area on the south side of NM 68 between mile markers 33 and 34. See map 2.

Marker text: One known captive of this raid, María Rosa Villapando was traded to the Pawnees and, after ten years, was ransomed by her future husband, a French trader from St. Louis. She was reunited with her New Mexican son, Joseph Julian Jacques in 1802. Her grandson, Antoine Leroux, returned to Taos and married into the Vigil family, making her the ancestral matriarch of several prominent Taos families.

Note: Marker faceplates are on opposite sides of the same sign.

In the mid-eighteenth century, relations between Indian tribes and Hispanic settlers in New Mexico could best be described as "complex." The Pueblo and Plains Indians like the Comanches often fought one another, as did the Indians and Hispanic settlers, but these cultural groups also often traded together. Each year, a summer trade fair in Taos served as a place where Plains Indians, Spanish settlers, and Pueblo Indians met and bartered goods, including buffalo meat, muskets, horses, and, unfortunately, often captive slaves.

Pedro Tamarón y Romeral, the bishop of Durango, traveling through New Mexico in 1760 on a visit to missions in his southwestern diocese, left the Taos area just a few weeks before one terrible Comanche raid. That raid centered on the home of a Spanish merchant, Pablo Francisco Villapando, in Ranchos de Taos, just south of Taos Pueblo. Tamarón, upon later learning of that raid, left this account of the attack:

And on the fourth day of August, according to what they say, nearly three thousand Comanche men waged war with the intention of finishing the pueblo of Taos. They diverted, or provoked, them from a very large house, the greatest in all that valley, belonging to a settler called Villapando, who luckily for him, had left that day on business. But when they saw so many Comanches coming, many women and men of that settlement took refuge in this house as the strongest. And, trusting in the fact that it had four towers and in the large supply of muskets, powder, and balls, they say that they fired on the Comanches. The latter were infuriated by this to such a horrible degree that they broke into different parts of the house, killed all the men and some women, who also fought. And the wife of the owner of the house, seeing that they were breaking down the outside door, went to defend it with a lance, and they killed her fighting. Fifty-six women and children were carried off, and a large number of horses which the owner of the house was keeping there. Forty-nine bodies of dead Comanches were counted, and other trickles of blood were seen.

Among the women captured in the raid that fateful August day was one of the two daughters of the owner of the home, María Rosa Villapando. María Rosa was probably in her early twenties at the time; the assault would change her life forever. It's not clear, in fact, why the attack even occurred. One story, which is probably untrue, suggested that María Rosa had been promised to a Comanche chief, and the raid was in retaliation for her refusing to marry him. Another suggested that it was done to avenge a taking of Comanche scalps by Taos Indians.

Regardless, in being taken captive, María Rosa left behind a husband and mother, both slain that day, as well as her son, Joseph Julian Jacques, who survived. It would be more than forty years before she would see her child again.

Initially, María Rosa lived with the Comanches as their captive, but sometime later she was traded to the Pawnee Indians. Then, around 1767, a French trader from Saint Louis, Missouri, Jean Sale dit Lajoi, who traded among the Pawnee, met the captive María Rosa. By that time, she had had a second son, whom she had named Antoine Xavier. The French trader Sale and María Rosa lived together for some time as a couple within the Pawnee camp, and the two had their own son together, Lambert. Wanting to make permanent their relationship, Sale ransomed María Rosa and returned with her to his home in Saint Louis. They married in July 1770.

For reasons unknown, Jean Sale returned to France in the year 1792, leaving Marie Rose (her name after the marriage) alone with the children in Saint Louis. If Sale had intended to return, he never did. But one other protagonist in this drama did resurface: Marie Rose's first son, Joseph Julian Jacques, whom she had been torn from in the raid in Taos four decades earlier. Somehow, Jacques learned his mother's whereabouts and traveled from Taos to Saint Louis in 1802 to reunite with her. He settled his inheritance with her the following year.

Another layer was added to this remarkable story in 1824 when one of Marie Rose's grandsons, Antoine Leroux, left Saint Louis and moved, of all places, to Taos. There, he married into the Vigil family. His descendants still live in the area, making Marie Rose Sale—the woman taken captive from the area as a young girl—the matriarch of many Taos family lines.

Marie Rose Sale passed away on July 27, 1830, in Saint Louis.

More to explore: *McComas Incident, Point of Rocks, Taos*

57. Capulin Volcano National Monument

Location: Union and Mora Counties. Four locations:

1. Mora County. North of Fort Union on Interstate 25, in the rest area between mile markers 359 and 360, on the east side of the interstate. See map 3.
2. Union County. Just south of Capulin Volcano National Monument, on US 64, between mile markers 376 and 377. See map 3.
3. Union County. Near the intersection of NM 325 (toward Folsom) and US 64/87. See map 3.
4. Union County. East of Capulin on US 64, between mile markers 377 and 378. See map 3.

Marker text: An outstanding example of an extinct volcanic cinder cone, Capulin Mountain was formed as early as 10,000 years ago. In cinder cones, lava pours from cracks in the base rather than over the top. Capulin itself was the escape hatch for gases that blew lava fragments into the air where they solidified and landed red hot on the cone.

Note: Capulin last erupted between 58,000 and 62,000 years ago.

Capulin Mountain formed between 58,000 and 62,000 years ago, as gases within the earth spewed red-hot ash, cinders, pellets, and molten rocks with astonishing force high into the air. The debris solidified as it hit the cooler atmosphere, then fell back onto the central vent to form a tapering mound known as a cinder cone. Because less-gaseous magma flowed outward through fissures in this mound and not through the main crater, the symmetry of the one-thousand-foot-high cinder dome, Capulin, remained intact. In fact, given its remarkably balanced shape, geologists consider Capulin Mountain one of the best examples of an extinct volcanic cinder cone in the United States.

Capulin eventually formed a mountain that rose in altitude more than 1,200 feet and stretched at its base about a mile and a half wide. Slowly, vegetation took hold and helped reduce the effects of erosion, thereby stabilizing the shape of the mountain. Some of that vegetation also gave the mountain its name: *capulin* is Spanish for "chokeberry," a plant found on the slopes of the volcano.

Capulin is one of many volcanoes in a large volcanic field that stretches to present-day Clayton.

More to explore: *Malpais, Sierra Grande*

58. Carlsbad
Elevation: 3,120 feet

Location: Eddy County. Just east of Carlsbad, in a pullout on the north side of US 62/180, between mile markers 36 and 37. See map 6.

Marker text: Native people have lived in this area for thousands of years. In 1590, the expedition of Gasper Castaño de Sosa followed the Pecos River near what would later become Carlsbad. Carlsbad was originally named Eddy after the Eddy brothers, pioneer cattlemen and railroad promoters. In 1899 it was renamed Carlsbad for the famous European resort of Karlsbad because the mineral content in its water was found to be similar.

59. Carlsbad Irrigation Flume

Location: Eddy County. At the north end of Carlsbad, at the intersection of US 285 (Pierce Street) and University Drive. See map 6.

Marker text: The massive concrete flume in the distance carries water from the Pecos River to irrigate much of the farmland in this area. It is a vital link in an extensive irrigation system which made possible development of the region's agricultural resources. A wooden flume constructed in 1890 washed away in 1902 and was replaced by the more substantial concrete structure in 1903.

Note: The flume is visible to the east from this Historic Marker.

The Pecos River deserves credit for man's exploration and development of southeastern New Mexico. The waters wind southward from the Sangre de Cristo Mountains in northern New Mexico, past present-day Carlsbad, and then into Texas. In 1590, Gaspar Castaño de Sosa, lieutenant governor of what later became the Mexican state of Nuevo León, led families from that region north along the Pecos with the intent of establishing the first Spanish colony in what is now New Mexico. Castaño had done so of his own accord, lacking the express permission of the Spanish Crown for his effort. Spanish officials arrested him the next year on charges of leading an unauthorized expedition and escorted him, with his followers, back to Mexico.

Long before Castaño made his way through this region, Paleo-Indians had hunted bison and mammoths and gathered edible plant materials on the plains of eastern New Mexico. Much later, in the nineteenth century, the plains became a grassy homeland for cattle ranchers. Texans Charles Goodnight and Oliver Loving drove herds along the Pecos over their famous Goodnight-Loving Trail. In 1867, John Chisum established his own ranching empire in the area, the South Spring Ranch, which stretched some 150 miles along the river.

Land and railroad promoter Charles B. Eddy also saw value in the water-rich Pecos Valley. New York–born Eddy had moved to New Mexico with his brother John Arthur in 1880. In 1887, he partnered with an investment team that included Pat Garrett, most famous for dispatching outlaw Billy the Kid six years earlier, to form the Pecos Valley Land and Ditch Company. Hoping to lure settlers to the Pecos Valley with the promise of reliable water, the men engineered an Olympian network of irrigation canals in the land surrounding present-day Carlsbad. Company workers first dammed the Pecos River to form reservoirs such as Lake Avalon and Lake McMillan, and then erected the Main Canal and attendant tributaries to convey water from the lakes into irrigation ditches along a twenty-mile stretch of inland waterways. Waters reached the west bank of the Pecos River by coursing over a wooden flume, something like a highway overpass, two miles north of what is now Carlsbad. One of the largest arms of the project, this massive wooden aqueduct was the centerpiece of the irrigation system.

At the same time, the Eddy brothers founded a new townsite along the river and gave it the proprietary name Eddy. When the territorial legislature created Eddy County a year later, the original county seat soon transferred from Seven Rivers to Eddy. Given the prominent backing of the Eddy Brothers and James J. Hagerman, a wealthy railroad and land developer who had sunk a good portion of his own money into the canal system, the prosperous town soon had hotels, a telegraph office, a bank, and the county courthouse. For his part, Hagerman also organized the Pecos Valley and Northeastern Railway, running from Texas into southeastern New Mexico, to link the region by rail to outside commerce and travel.

In a luckless turn in 1893, a flood of the Pecos wiped out the infrastructure of the irrigation project. Even as crews reconstructed the canals, Hagerman and Eddy disagreed on how operations should be run. Partners became enemies. "If you will quit lying about me," Hagerman reportedly wrote Eddy, "I will quit telling the truth about you."

In April 1894, Charles Eddy resigned from his position with the Pecos Valley company and left his namesake town. He never returned. In 1900, Hagerman sold his railroad and went to live on land he had purchased south of Roswell—John Chisum's South Spring Ranch. The two major defining influences in the town left it an orphan.

Also orphaned was the name. In 1899, residents of Eddy voted to rename their city Carlsbad, after the curative waters and mud at the spas of Karlsbad, Bohemia (now Karlovy Vary in the Czech Republic)—waters visited by such historical dignitaries as Beethoven and Napoleon. One story says that the mineral content in the waters of the two cities was found to be similar, which is possible, given that limestone deposits exist in both locations. Eddy residents hoped that the association with the more famous waters (and famous bathers) in central Europe would attract tourists. But it was also supposed that Hagerman preferred the new name to the former, the name of his estranged business partner.

In 1902, Chicago engineer Thomas T. Johnson

Nature had given settlers in southeastern New Mexico the Pecos River for their fields. The water was there, it just had to be controlled. Building the flume across the Pecos River, near Carlsbad, New Mexico, 1903. Photo by J. R. Riddle, courtesy Palace of the Governors Photo Archives (NMHM/DCA), neg. no. 76081.

oversaw construction of a steadfast concrete flume to replace the damaged wooden original. The behemoth, when completed the following year, stretched four hundred feet on its span across the Pecos River, fluming water to fields of sorghum and alfalfa on the west bank of the river. It featured four giant arches holding aloft the flume itself and metal rails embedded in the concrete to keep the structure from collapsing. Completed at a cost of $50,000, the flume, as aptly described by a visiting reporter with the *American Shepherd's Bulletin*, was "the largest and only thing of its kind in the world." The remarkable structure remains in operation to the present day.

Today, this wet web continues to bring Pecos River water to the farmlands of the Pecos Valley. The system is run under the auspices of the Carlsbad Irrigation District.

More to explore: *Castaño de Sosa's Route, Chisum's South Spring Ranch (see under Artesia), Early Spanish Route, Goodnight-Loving Trail (series), Mesa and Pecos Valley*

CARLSBAD CAVERNS NATIONAL PARK: Series of Four Historic Markers (Locations East and West of Carlsbad Caverns)

General Introduction

Jim White, a cowboy building fences near Carlsbad in the late 1890s, first thought the dark, spiraling eddy he saw on the horizon one evening was ash from an erupting volcano. When he investigated, he discovered not smoke but bats, thousands of them, winging en masse from a yawning hole in the side of a mountain. White lit a piece of cactus and tossed it into the abyss to determine the depth of the chasm. The cactus extinguished before reaching the bottom.

White had come across one of the deepest limestone caves in the nation, a cavern penetrating 1,567 dark and damp feet into the earth. His discovery is preserved today as Carlsbad Caverns National Park. In addition to the publicly accessible caverns, the park includes famous Lechuguilla Cave, one of the longest and deepest caves in the United States, along with numerous other limestone caves in the area. Many of these caves are open only to exploration teams approved by the Park Service.

The background of the park and the history of a nearby subsidiary camping area, Rattlesnake Springs, along with that of the Guadalupe Mountains in which the caverns are found, is documented in a series of four Historic Markers, although two have the same text. They are grouped here in a series for easy reference.

More to explore (Carlsbad Caverns National Park Series): *Carlsbad, Castaño de Sosa's Route, Civilian Conservation Corps—Carlsbad Campsite, Early Spanish Route, Goodnight-Loving Trail (series), Josephine Cox "Grandma" Anderson, Mesa and Pecos Valley*

60. Carlsbad Caverns National Park

Location: 1. Eddy County. Just east of the turnoff to Whites City, in a pullout on the north side of US 62/180, between mile markers 15 and 16. See map 6.

2. Eddy County. Just west of Whites City, in a pullout on the south side of US 62/180. See map 6.

Marker text: These vast magnificent caverns contain over 21 miles of explored corridors. The chambers have countless stalactites and stalagmites unrivaled in size and beauty. The caverns are within a reef that formed in an ancient sea 240 million years ago. Millions of years later, the reef was fractured, allowing ground water to begin work fashioning the caverns.

Note: See the general introduction to this series of Markers, as well as the other Markers making up this series, for further background on the caverns.

The long history of the caverns that today make up Carlsbad Caverns National Park begins in the depths of an ancient sea that covered this area some 240 million years ago. As sea life died, shells, skeletons, and other debris amassed to form what is today known as the Capitan Reef. Over time, the sea evaporated, the earth buckled, and the reef rose to form the Guadalupe Mountains. Weathering and groundwater fractured the rock within the landform to create these mammoth underground caverns and chambers.

Mescalero Apache Indians in the 1400s roasted mescal within circles of rocks known as ring middens near the entrance to the cave. Whether the Apaches ever entered the cave is not known. However, Jim White certainly did. His partnership with a fertilizer company to mine bat guano for California fruit growers gave the cowboy many opportunities to explore further this subterranean frontier. According to his autobiography, White descended into the cave on a rickety rope-and-stick ladder and dispelled the darkness, which he compared to "a million tons of black wool," with a small kerosene lantern. Water and time had festooned those dark interiors with elegant calcite deposits whose figurative names leave little doubt of their appearance: soda straws, drapery, popcorn, and totem poles. One of the more impressive features White encountered was the 2,013-foot-wide, 254-foot-high Big Room, today considered the largest subterranean chamber in the United States.

For years, White conducted personal tours of the site and worked to bring recognition to the scenic wonders he found there. In the spring of 1923, he led employees of the General Land Office through an official on-site survey. The scientists were impressed enough to recommend that the site be designated as a national monument. Later that fall, on October 25, President Calvin Coolidge officially declared the site the Carlsbad Cave National Monument. In 1930, Congress changed the designation to Carlsbad Caverns National Park.

After the redesignation, the National Park Service extended trails, erected staircases, installed electric lighting, and built an elevator to hoist visitors to and from the surface. Tourists converged on the new monument, fascinated by the wonders they found in the Main Corridor, King's Palace, Queen's Chamber, Big Room, and elsewhere. Several couples even chose to be married near the spectacular formation known as the Rock of Ages, until that practice was ended in 1944.

Jim White, the earliest known spelunker of the caves, died in April 1946 at age sixty-four.

61. Carlsbad Caverns National Park

Location: Eddy County. West of Whites City, in a pullout on the north side of US 62/180, between mile markers 10 and 11. This is also the entrance road to Rattlesnake Springs campsite, which is open to the public and makes a good place for a picnic. See map 6.

Marker text: The Civilian Conservation Corps provided employment for more than 50,000 young men in New Mexico during the Great Depression of the 1930s. At the National Park Service CCC camp, they developed nearby Rattle Snake Springs into a permanent water source for Carlsbad Caverns, built roads, parking areas, and trails. Which made the park more accessible to the public.

Note: This marker was previously titled "CCC—Rattlesnake Springs Campsite," and indeed it has more to do with the CCC and the campsite than the caverns themselves. The name of the park is incorrect on the Marker—it should be "Rattlesnake Springs."

Note: See the general introduction to this series of Markers, as well as the other Markers making up this series, for further background on the caverns.

62. Ghost Marker: Guadalupe Mountains

Marker text: Guadalupe Mountains to southwest rise from Pecos Valley, with higher southern peaks at 8,750 feet. Bold escarpment is famous Capitan limestone, an ancient reef similar to Great Barrier Reef of Australia, and host to Carlsbad Caverns as well as deep petroleum and underground water. Elevation 3,270 feet.

Note: See the general introduction to this series of Markers, as well as the other Markers making up this series, for further background on the caverns. See map 6.

Indiana-born settler Henry Harrison arrived in the southeastern foothills of the Guadalupe Mountains in the 1880s and homesteaded a patch of ground near a refreshing marsh with a venomous name: Rattlesnake Springs. In short order, Harrison had erected a house for himself, his wife, and a family that grew to include six children. He dammed the springs and fed water through an irrigation system to his fruit tree orchard and vegetable gardens. He also raised cattle—one of the first settlers in southeastern New Mexico to do so, according to the National Park Service. Although the region was sparsely populated, Harrison had neighbors in the Apache Indians who frequented the Guadalupe Mountains.

The property fell to the National Park Service a few years after Harrison's death in 1931. Seven years later, the site acquired a new history when Ensign Albert Schlott arrived with sixty-two young men aged seventeen to twenty-three to establish Civilian Conservation Corp camp NP-1-N. The CCC was a Depression-era relief project through which young men gathered in rural camps to build trails, plant trees, and develop the land. Schlott supervised as workers graded a dirt plaza at the springs and erected their camp, comprising barracks, a kitchen, a school, a garage, and other outbuildings.

Using the camp as a base, the men of the CCC set to work improving what Harrison had created. They tilled and landscaped the earth, planted cottonwoods, graded the service road to the camp, repaired the irrigation canals, and laid trails through the foothills of the Guadalupe Mountains. After five years of hard work, Rattlesnake Springs became a bucolic recreational park open for public access.

The end of the Depression and the outbreak of World War II forced the disbanding of CCC camps throughout New Mexico. Workers left the Rattlesnake Springs CCC camp in early May 1942; many of them enrolled in the military. The Park Service closed the camp on May 22.

Today, Rattlesnake Springs serves as a division of Carlsbad Caverns National Park. A pipeline carries water from the site to the Visitors Center at the park six miles away, as it has since 1934. The Nature Conservancy manages a portion of the property as a nesting area for songbirds, including the southwestern willow flycatcher. Most of the CCC structures have been removed, but the cottonwoods landscaping the picnic ground and providing a pleasant environment for songbirds are those planted by CCC workers many years ago.

63. Carrizozo

Location: 1. Lincoln County. Just west of Carrizozo, in a pullout on the north side of US 380, between mile markers 65 and 66. See map 6.

2. Lincoln County. Just west of Carrizozo, in a pullout on the south side of US 380, between mile markers 64 and 65. See map 6.

3. Lincoln County. Southwest of Carrizozo, in a pullout on the east side of US 54, near the train tracks, between mile markers 122 and 123. See map 6.

Marker text: Carrizozo, county seat of Lincoln County, was established in 1899, a new town on the El Paso and Northeastern Railroad. The ghost town of White Oaks, once a booming mining camp, is nearby. Billy the Kid, Pat Garrett, Governor Lew Wallace and Albert Bacon Fall all figured prominently in the history of the area.

64. Carrizozo

Location: Lincoln County. In Carrizozo, at the corner of Central (US 54) and E Avenues. See map 6.

Marker text: The crossroads of History. Northeast is the Ghost Town of White Oaks, a once booming mining camp, where Emerson Hough lived and laid the scene of his book, Heart's Desire. Famous names like Billy the Kid, Pat Garrett and Lew Wallace are closely associated with the area.

In the late nineteenth century, land and railroad promoters Charles B. Eddy and his brother John A. Eddy financed construction of the El Paso and Northeastern Railroad across this part of southeastern New Mexico. The line ran north from El Paso through the flat, dry Tularosa Basin and farther still to the town of Santa Rosa. A small railroad town developed along the line in this vicinity in 1899. Located just south of Carrizo Springs, that town took the appealing name Carrizozo. According to place-names historian Robert Julyan, the additional -*zo* may have joined the root when residents platted their town in 1907, probably to emphasize the great number of reed grasses—*carrizo* in Spanish—growing in the area.

Just as Carrizozo owes its life to the railroad, the town of White Oaks, eleven miles northeast, partially owes its decline to the same. White Oaks thrived after prospectors discovered gold in the Jicarilla Mountains in 1879. The camp quickly became one of the more high-flying towns in Lincoln County. Yet Eddy's railroad bypassed the settlement some twenty years later, leaving White Oaks residents dependent on the stagecoach for transportation. The town further sagged as the mines played out. Today, White Oaks is a quiet community with many picturesque buildings, including a four-room brick structure once used as a schoolhouse.

Albert Bacon Fall, a prominent cattleman and lawyer and one of the first two senators for New Mexico after the territory became a state in 1912, owned the Tres Ritos cattle ranch in Three Rivers south of Carrizozo. Fall was forced to sell his ranch to pay debts he acquired after being convicted of wrongdoing in the Teapot Dome Scandal while he was secretary of the interior under President Warren Harding in 1921.

In the late 1870s, Lincoln County was the site of a pitched feud known today as the Lincoln County War. Chief among the participants was young Billy the Kid, who helped form a gang he called "the Regulators" to seek revenge for the killing of his rancher boss, John Tunstall. Tunstall had been murdered by members of a posse connected with Lincoln merchants L. G. Murphy and J. J. Dolan. The hostilities climaxed into full-scale violence on the streets of Lincoln between July 15 and 19, 1879, as members of the Murphy-Dolan faction laid siege to the home of Tunstall's business partner, Alexander McSween. McSween was killed. After the battle, President Rutherford Hayes replaced New Mexico governor Samuel Axtell, who had played a part himself in the incident, with Lewis "Lew" Wallace. The new governor offered amnesty to all the major players in the feud except Billy the Kid, who had murdered the Lincoln County sheriff during the conflict. Lawman Pat Garrett tracked Billy the Kid after the young outlaw escaped from the Lincoln jail and, on the night of July 14, 1881, in Fort Sumner, New Mexico, shot the Kid dead.

Lincoln County quieted considerably when the last shovel of dirt fell on the Kid's coffin. In 1909, residents voted to move the county seat from Lincoln to Carrizozo, due to its proximity to the railroad. Carrizozo retains the county seat today.

More to explore: *Fort Sumner and Fort Sumner State Monument (series), Lincoln, Three Rivers, White Oaks*

Arrow-straight houses show the order that was late nineteenth-century Carthage. Like its Tunisian namesake, this Carthage, too, would become a memory. Upper camp from west, Carthage, New Mexico, ca. 1886. Photo by J. R. Riddle, courtesy Palace of the Governors Photo Archives (NMHM/DCA), neg. no. 76081.

65. Carthage-Tokay-Farley

Location: Socorro County. West of San Antonio, in a pullout on the south side of US 380, between mile markers 9 and 10. See map 5.

Marker text: Important coal-mining towns from the 1880s to 1925 when the mines closed. Originally developed by the Santa Fe Railroad and later operated by the Carthage Fuel Company mainly to fire the Kinney brick kilns in Albuquerque. Farley was a limestone quarry. The Hilton Mine belonged to the father of Conrad Hilton.

Note: The limestone quarry of Fraley is incorrectly spelled "Farley" on this Historic Marker.

Left to represent the memory of the ghost town of Carthage today is a small cemetery, visited mostly by the wind. Locals had worked coal deposits in these small mountains east of San Antonio for years, as had soldiers from nearby Fort Craig, who opened the Government Mine in the 1860s to fuel their smithing shop. The mining town of Carthage arose here in 1882, when the Santa Fe Railway in May of that year completed a ten-mile branch line east from San Antonio across the Rio Grande to the deposits. The town likely took its name from the ancient Phoenician seaport and birthplace of the warrior Hannibal.

By 1885, Carthage was home to three hundred people, most of whom made a living in the mines. Workers sent the majority of coal by rail to fire the

Billing Smelter in nearby Socorro. The sound of large Murphy fans ventilating the mines bounced across the arroyos as a hoisting engine lifted two hundred tons of coal to the surface each day. John James IV, who had pulled scattered members of his family and friends together from Colorado, Illinois, and Pennsylvania to work the mine and build the settlement, supervised operations for the Santa Fe Railway. James was, as the August 1885 Socorro *Bullion* described him, "a courteous gentleman who excels in his profession."

Around 1893, the railroad ran a spur to a quarry northeast of the coalfields, where J. B. Fraley had built kilns to fire limestone deposits. A small post office opened there and took the name Fraley—but it was not in service long. The devaluation of silver that year as the country turned to the gold standard lessened production at the Billing Smelter in Socorro, which, in turn, caused a decrease in the demand for coal. The Santa Fe Railway also entered a new agreement to use coal from mines near Cerrillos, New Mexico, and transferred many of the Carthage buildings and equipment to that area. Fraley was abandoned, and Carthage nearly so. The August 22, 1893, *Santa Fe Daily New Mexican* posted a burial notice:

Within another week, the town of Carthage, once the busiest coal mining camp in New Mexico, will have ceased to exist. All the dwelling houses, coal chutes and machinery have already been removed. This place has practically been razed to the earth, and the depot, adobe hotel, and Gross, Blackwell & Co.'s Store are about all that remain.

But that notice proved premature. Mining continued in the Carthage coalfields on a limited scale, with the proceeds hauled by wagon to San Antonio. In fact, a report by the state mine inspector in 1895 showed twenty-one active mines at Carthage employing a total of 1,659 men. The area soon got a second wind when investors with the Carthage Coal Company rejuvenated the town. New, one-story adobe homes appeared along a street known as 'Dobe Row, and the superintendent's house and a hard-earth tennis court were built on a small rise at the end of town. A company subsidiary, the New Mexico Midland Railroad, returned rail service to the region in 1906. A spur turned east to serve the Hilton Mine, owned by San Antonio merchant Augustus H. Hilton, father of soon-to-be-famous hotelier Conrad Hilton.

Around 1916, Bartley Hoyt Kinney, superintendent of the Carthage mines, uncovered a new deposit of coal two miles west of town. According to a descendent, Kinney put a baking soda can on the ground near the discovery while he went to Socorro to make valid the claim. Another small town grew around that can, complete with a store, homes, and a two-story building that housed a barbershop and pool hall on the lower floor and a school, serving the first through the fifth grades, on the upper. Legend says that Kinney named the settlement Tokay for a box of Tokay grapes he saw while conversing with the postal inspector. Kinney's descendents later operated the Kinney Brick Company in Albuquerque.

Mining at Carthage and Tokay waned in the twentieth century as railroads switched from coal to diesel to fuel their lines. The New Mexico Midland pulled up the rails to the town in 1931, but scattered activity continued at both Carthage and Tokay for the next few decades. The Carthage post office closed in 1950, and the community, like the ancient seaport from which it drew its name, was gone.

More to explore: *Dawson, Elizabethtown, Fort Craig, Riley, San Antonio, Shakespeare*

66. Casa Colorada

Location: Valencia County. In Casa Colorada, on the east side of NM 304, between Benavidez Road and Daisy Lane, in front of the school building. See map 4.

Marker text: A Spanish settlement, with houses built of red adobe or earthen bricks, was established in this vicinity in the 1740s. This community was soon abandoned, probably as a result of Apache raids, but was reoccupied in 1823 and developed into a bustling trade center along the Camino Real.

Traveling though this part of central New Mexico on a tour of his diocese in May 1760, Bishop Pedro Tamarón y Romeral passed this location. In his journal, Tamarón left an early description of what he saw:

On the nineteenth we passed the house they call Colorado, also in ruins, and from that point on we began to see pens of ewes, corrals, and small houses, for there is good pasturage.

By "house," likely the Bishop was referring to an estancia, or large ranch, and perhaps even a small settlement that had existed around it sometime in the 1740s. How that place came to be abandoned by the time of his visit is lost to history, but possibly it was as a result of raids by Apache warriors. And how it came to acquire the name Colorada—a word that translates in English as "red"—is also lost to time, although one source for the origin of the name credits it to the red stones used to build the ranch building. Casa Colorada translates as "Red House." Another, later story says that the red house was actually a station on an early stagecoach line.

Regardless, the name survived through the centuries. When José María Perea and forty-two other former residents of nearby Manzano applied for a community land grant in this area in July 1823, they used the name Casa Colorada for their new settlement. In 1841, a member of the Texas Santa Fe Expedition left an account of that new village and surrounding region as it appeared at the time, having rebounded since Tamarón's visit: "Late in the afternoon . . . we reached the Casa Colorada, or Red House, a large hacienda and trading establishment. . . . Passing the little collection of houses, we entered a grove of cotton-woods near the Rio Grande, and there encamped for the night."

The small settlement lay along the Camino Real, the historic trail primarily following the course of the Rio Grande through the middle of New Mexico, from Mexico City to Santa Fe. The trail brought trade, commerce, and settlers to and from the two end points and to villages along the way. Casa Colorada was one of the stops on the trail as it wound its way through the largely agricultural settlements that lay along the river south of Albuquerque. The course of the trail between Casa Colorada and La Joya to the south largely followed the path that NM 304 traverses today.

When a post office opened in 1927, the small community was officially given the name Turn. The name was chosen both because the post office and store in which it was located were situated on a bend in the course of Highway 304, and also because postal authorities at the time discouraged two-word names (particularly if they were non-English). But, as related by place-names historian Robert Julyan, residents never fully adopted the name and petitioned to have it changed to Casa Colorada, the name by which they had always known their community. They were successful. Despite the vague origins of the original name of this historic village, it has staying power.

More to explore: *El Camino Real—The King's Highway, La Joya de Sevilleta*

67. Castaño de Sosa's Route

Location: Eddy County. Just south of Artesia on the east side of US 285. See map 6.

Marker text: In 1590–91, Gaspar Castaño de Sosa led an expedition in an unsuccessful attempt to establish a colony in New Mexico. During the winter of 1590, as he pushed north along the Pecos River, the group passed along this route in the vicinity of present-day Artesia and Roswell.

While late sixteenth-century Spain was busy organizing the first official expedition to colonize the region that is now New Mexico, Gaspar Castaño de Sosa jumped the gun. Castaño, Portuguese by birth, served as lieutenant governor for the region that later became the Mexican state of Nuevo León. Promising that the land to the north held great abundance, wealth to be easily won, he convinced the citizens of Nuevo León to accompany him on a mission to colonize what is now New Mexico.

Castaño and his followers left Nuevo León on July 27, 1590. They reached the Pecos River in present-day south Texas on October 23, no doubt grateful for its refreshing waters. Finding those waters salty, Castaño named the river Rio Salado, or "Salty River." The party followed the Pecos northward. In late November and early December, they passed through the vicinity of what is now Artesia and Roswell. On December 3, near present-day Lake McMillan, the party had a small scare. The evening darkness had fallen, and Castaño, who had ridden ahead earlier that day, had not yet returned to the fold. The chronicler of the expedition described the incident:

[Castaño de Sosa] went so far ahead that it was more than two hours after nightfall and he had not returned, at which we were all deeply grieved and to some extent vexed at having let him go alone. . . . Many luminaries [lights] were lit in order that he might come to them, and having noticed his continued absence, the grief of all was doubled. So Juan de Carbajal, Pedro Ynigo [and] Pedro Flores decided to go to search . . . they found him about a quarter of a league off on his way back to camp. . . . He replied that he had not thought to go so far ahead, and when he went, it was in order to find a road, because there was bad sandy ground in that place that could not be traveled and moreover the river made a bend.

Historians believe that the episode marks the first time traditional luminaries were used in New Mexico! Luminarias are small lights, often used as decorations for the seasons. They are customarily made by setting a candle into sand inside a paper bag. In parts of New Mexico, they are often known as *farolitos*.

Upon reaching northern New Mexico, Castaño and some of his colleagues explored the pueblos along the upper Rio Grande, including San Felipe Pueblo, San Juan, Picurís, pueblos in what is now the Galisteo Basin, and others now abandoned.

One day in mid-March, Spanish captain Juan de Morlete arrived in the camp and arrested Castaño on charges of leading an unauthorized expedition. Castaño surrendered willingly, even kissing the documents read to him outlining his imprisonment. Their leader being escorted back to Mexico in chains, Castaño's weary followers returned as well, and New Mexico was left for the colonizing expedition of don Juan de Oñate in 1598.

More to explore: *Artesia, Carlsbad, Early Spanish Route, Oñate's Route (see under El Camino Real—The King's Highway), Pueblo of Nambé, Pueblo of Picurís, Pueblo of Tesuque, Roswell*

68. Cathay Williams
(ca. 1850–Death Date Unknown)

Location: Luna County. East of Deming, in a pullout on the east side of NM 26, between mile markers 10 and 11. The location is also used as an inspection station by the US Border Patrol. See map 5.

Marker text: Born into slavery, Cathay was liberated in 1861 and worked as a cook for the Union army during the Civil War. In 1866 she enlisted in the U.S. Army as Private William Cathey serving with the Buffalo Soldiers at Fort Cummings and Fort Bayard until 1868. She is the only documented woman to serve as an enlisted soldier in the Regular U.S. Army during the 19th century.

Note: Cathay Williams's enlisted name was William Cathay, not Cathey, as the Marker incorrectly states.

Private William Cathay served honorably with the Thirty-Eighth US Infantry, a regiment of "Buffalo Soldiers"—African American soldiers who served in the army after the Civil War. Stationed first at Fort Cummings and later at Fort Bayard in southern New Mexico in the mid-nineteenth century, Private Cathay bore the rigors of a soldier's duties with fortitude. But Private Cathay had a secret: he was not actually William Cathay. That was a pseudonym. The private's real name, in fact, was Cathay Williams. The soldier calling himself Private William Cathay and living life as a man was, in reality, a woman.

The story of Cathay Williams is little known but is among the most fascinating in southwestern military history.

Williams was born a slave sometime around 1850 near Independence, Missouri. Although her father was a free man, her mother was a slave, the property of landowner William Johnson. When Johnson moved to Jefferson City, Missouri, sometime later, Williams was taken as well, forced to work as a domestic servant for the Johnson family. But a change came in 1861 with the outbreak of the Civil War. Williams and other blacks were taken by soldiers of the Eighth Indiana Infantry and made to serve the troops. Williams worked as a cook and laundress. She traveled with the regiment on their marches through Arkansas, Louisiana, and Georgia. Later, the Eighth Indiana became part of the army led by General Phil Sheridan, the celebrated Civil War officer, and Cathay was firsthand witness to some of the prominent battles of the Civil War.

After the war, Cathay Williams was a free woman. She moved to Saint Louis, but work was hard to come by for a former slave. Her desire, strongly felt, was to be self-sufficient, not a burden to family or friends. With few other choices, Cathay turned to the one occupation she thought could sustain her. On November 15, 1866, in Saint Louis, Cathay Williams enlisted in the US Army as Private William Cathay.

The name she had chosen was derived by simply reversing her first and last names. As to the question of cover, she had the benefit of wearing the Zouave uniform. Designed for the French Army earlier in the century, the open jacket and baggy trousers of the uniform were loose enough to hide her figure. "And only two persons, a cousin and a particular friend, members of the regiment, knew that I was a woman," she later recounted to a reporter with the *St. Louis Daily Times* in 1876. "They never 'blowed' on me."

Cathay was assigned to Company A of the Thirty-Eighth Infantry, a regiment of African Americans known as Buffalo Soldiers. The name had been given to these soldiers by Indians of the Southwest because their short, curly hair was reminiscent of that of buffalo. Although Cathay was hospitalized for smallpox shortly after her enlistment, she later rejoined her regiment in Kansas. From there, Cathay and her regiment marched over the Santa Fe Trail to Fort Union in northeastern New Mexico, arriving in July 1867, then to Fort Cummings in southwestern New Mexico. The fort was north of the location of this Historic Marker.

The US Army in the mid-nineteenth century was engaged in battles against Apaches that were collectively known as the Apache Wars, and soldiers at Fort Cummings—including Cathay Williams—participated in guard duty and as scouts. Later, her company marched to garrison Fort Bayard, about sixty miles to the northwest. Despite the challenges that must have come from living daily as a man in conditions that were less than ideal, and expected to perform all the duties of a soldier, Cathay was never discovered to be a woman.

"I was a good soldier," she summarily told the reporter.

In October 1868, tired of army life and somewhat sickly, Cathay decided to end the deception. Pretending to be sick, she reported to the post surgeon at Fort Bayard—knowing that a medical examination would reveal the truth.

The news was not well received among her fellow soldiers. Having lived with her, scouted with her, eaten and laughed with her, her companions were incensed to find that the soldier they knew as Private William Cathay had been deceiving them. Probably there was a degree of misogyny in the hostile response as well. "The men all wanted to get rid of me after they found out I was a woman," Cathay recalled. "Some of them acted real bad to me."

After leaving the army, Cathay moved to Pueblo, Colorado, where she made a living as a washerwoman and seamstress. She married, but when her husband stole from her, she had him put in jail, and then she returned to Saint Louis. Although the date and location of her passing is not known, it is safe to assume that she was never, as she had feared, a burden to her family or friends.

Cathay Williams is the only documented woman to serve as an enlisted soldier in the regular US Army in the nineteenth century. Unfortunately, that distinction did not help her while she was alive. In 1892, Cathay applied for a military pension from the army. Her request was denied.

More to explore: *Fort Bayard, Fort Cummings*

69. The Catwalk

Location: Catron County. In Glenwood, at the intersection of US 180 and NM 174. See map 5.

Marker text: This steel causeway follows two pipelines which supplied water and water power to the old town of Graham where gold and silver ores were milled from nearby mines in the 1890s. The causeway clings to the sides of a sheer box canyon in Whitewater Creek and is accessible by a foot trail from the Whitewater picnic ground.

The Helen Mining Company knew that the sheer, rugged walls of Whitewater Canyon made up in vigor what they lacked in accessibility. After the company purchased the Confident and Bluebird Mines above the canyon in 1893, company officials made plans to harness that vigor by converting the waters gushing through the upper reaches of the canyon into a power source for the hydroelectric generators in the company-owned mill downstream. The waters in the canyon represented one of the few dependable water sources in the Mogollon mining district, so the canyon was about the only place such a mill could be built.

In what the National Park Service would later call "one of the most ingenious but difficult engineering feats in the history of New Mexico mining," workers met the challenge of the canyon head on. First, they drilled iron bars into the sheer western face of the canyon wall, then they suspended on these a timber platform running some three miles into the upper reaches of the ravine. Wet from mist, that slippery and narrow platform required every nimble movement that workers could muster and thus brought honor to its nickname, "the catwalk." Atop the wooden planks, crews constructed the core of their funnel system: a four-inch-wide metal pipeline, cushioned in insulating sawdust and placed within an elongated wooden box. The effort was a success. Buoyed by their momentum through this conduit, the crystal canyon waters provided sufficient power to process seventy-five tons of ore a day at the Graham Mill downstream.

The mill took its name from its first supervisor, John T. Graham, who was also the superintendent of the Confidence Mine. The small mining camp that developed at the foot of the canyon became known originally as Whitewater, for the canyon, but soon changed to Graham. Never a big settlement, Graham was home to a couple hundred people at its peak. Most were mill workers.

In 1897, the Graham Mill got a new mouth to feed with the installation of a second generator. Workers laid an additional eighteen-inch iron pipeline through the canyon, parallel to the original, to provide accessorial waterpower to process the ores arriving from the mines.

The twin pipelines served the mill and provided water to the community of Graham through the turn of the century. Eventually, production and transportation costs involved in hauling the ores from the canyon made the company ledger sheet even more precarious than the catwalk. The mill closed in 1913, and settlers left the town of Graham. Company workers tore most of the original catwalk and pipeline system down from the canyon and sold it for scrap.

During the Depression, young men stationed at the local Civilian Conservation Corps camp known as FS-25-N built a more accessible catwalk along the course followed by the original pipeline. The Forest Service replaced that structure with the current steel causeway in 1961. Today, Whitewater Canyon, the catwalk, and the picnic area at the base of the canyon are recreational attractions in the Mogollon Mountains. The remains of one wall of the Graham Mill are still visible on the cliff face near the parking area at the foot of the canyon.

More to explore: *Cloud-Climbing Railroad, Dulcelina Salce Curtis, Mogollon*

70. Cedarvale

Location: Torrance County. In Cedarvale, on the east side of the intersection of NM 42 and CR C0006, in front of the old schoolhouse. See map 4.

Marker text: Edward Smith, William Taylor, and Oliver P. DeWolfe of Cedarvale, Kansas laid out this farming community in 1908. Hundreds of homesteaders arrived on immigrant trains. Most farmed pinto beans, shipping their crop to distant markets. In 1917, the community successfully petitioned to build a large schoolhouse. The WPA added classrooms and a gym in 1935–36. In the 1930s, drought and the Depression substantially reduced the population.

Here in the southeastern corner of Torrance County, there's a little bit of Kansas in New Mexico. In June 1908, three Kansas men, Edward Smith, William Taylor, and Oliver P. DeWolfe, founded a new settlement along the route of the New Mexico Central Railroad. When the post office opened the next year, with Mrs. DeWolfe as the first postmistress, the community took the name Cedarvale, for their Kansas hometown, Cedar Vale, some 670 miles away.

The men and their families had been drawn to this region of central New Mexico by the promise of a small farm on homesteaded land. They were not alone. What was happening at Cedarvale was part of a larger population trend in central New Mexico after the turn of the century. Hundreds of other homesteaders were being actively lured to these lands by the territorial government of New Mexico, a body eager for residents as New Mexico drew nearer to statehood. The arrival of the Santa Fe Central Railway (later renamed the New Mexico Central Railroad) in August 1903 between Santa Rosa and Santa Fe (following approximately the route of NM 42 today) had connected the region to outside rail traffic and continued to bring "immigrants" from neighboring states; eventually, the population in Cedarvale contained as many as five hundred residents. The railroad changed one other thing as well: one of the founders of the railway was Francis J. Torrance, a man remembered today in the name of the county surrounding Cedarvale—Torrance County.

As in other towns in central New Mexico, including nearby Mountainair and Estancia, the cash crop in Cedarvale in its formative years was pinto beans. Favorably suited to the altitude and the short growing season in this part of New Mexico, pinto beans could be dry farmed and had a ready market both in New Mexico and nationwide. At the fall harvest, the beans were threshed, stored in one of Cedarvale's three bean elevators, and then shipped by truck and rail across the country, with a good part of the crop being used to feed soldiers during World War I.

Originally, a small, one-room building served as the Cedarvale school, but as the community grew, a larger structure was needed to hold the children of the many farms in this part of the county. Oliver P. DeWolfe, one of the original Cedarvale founders, donated twenty acres of land at the north end of town for use as the site of a new school building. On August 25, 1917, the Torrance County Board of Education heard testimony from Mr. L. O. Foster, clerk of the Cedarvale school board, "asking for the approval of this Board of their action in issuing bonds in the amount of $5000.00 for the purpose of issuing money to erect a school building in that district." The board approved the request.

That school was completed in 1921, with additions added by the Depression-era Works Progress Administration in 1935. Oral histories given by former residents to the New Mexico Farm and Ranch Heritage Museum in Las Cruces in recent years paint a picture of the school when it was operational. It had four rooms and a gymnasium, with about fifty students in three grades per room, kindergarten through eighth grade (high school students traveled to Corona). Former Cedarvale resident Austin Vick recalls the school "bus" being a truck, and students riding in the back sitting on half-gallon Karo syrup cans. In addition to educating students, the school also served as a social gathering place for the community.

A drought, combined with the economic downfall brought about by the Depression, forced many farmers in Cedarvale to leave their homesteads and resettle elsewhere. The school closed in 1953. The school building still stands, but it has fallen into disrepair, serving today as a reminder of more prosperous years.

More to explore: *La Cienega School, Mountainair, Nara Visa, State History of Education Museum*

71. Cerrillos

Location: Santa Fe County. Twenty miles south of Santa Fe on NM 14, at the south end of Cerrillos. See map 2.

Marker text: Before the arrival of the Spanish, the mineral rich area around Cerrillos produced turquoise, which was broadly traded across the American Southwest and into Mexico. An early settlement of Los Cerrillos harbored Spanish refugees from the 1680 Revolt, but the present community was not founded until the lead strike of 1879.

72. Ghost Marker: Madrid National Historic District

Marker text: Madrid is located in the Ortiz Mountains, one of the United State's oldest mining regions. Its unique coal deposits are both bituminous and anthracite. Established about 1892 at the site of Coal Gulch, Madrid grew as a company-owned mining town. Its Christmas lighting displays drew national attention during the 1930s. When the mines closed in 1954, Madrid nearly became a ghost town.

Note: Although this Marker was approved by the state in 1992, it was either never erected or has since gone missing. See map 2.

73. Ghost Marker: Golden

Marker text: Golden derives its name from the gold mining operations that have taken place here since the 1820s. Permanently settled in the 1840s under its original name of Real de San Francisco, the settlement was also known as New Placers in the mid-19th century. The historic village church of St. Francis may date from the early 1840s.

Note: Although this Marker was approved by the state in 1990, it was either never erected or has since gone missing. See map 2.

As early as AD 900, Native Americans living in pueblo villages in the Galisteo Basin, south of what is now Santa Fe, were using stone axes and hammers to pry turquoise from the bowels of Mount Chalchihuitl, a hill two and a half miles north of present-day Cerrillos. The Indians valued the beautiful blue gemstone for its religious symbolism as well as for its decorative use in their beads and pendants, and they traded it through extensive trade networks. According to historian Marc Simmons, the activity at Mount Chalchihuitl constitutes "the most extensive prehistoric mining operation on the continent."

Spanish settlement first occurred here sometime before 1680 in the form of a small village taking the name Los Cerrillos, or "Little Hills." The Spanish colonists continued mining for turquoise, lead, and silver in mines like the Castilian.

The history of New Mexico changed inalterably in 1680, when Indian pueblos in the state rose in revolt against the Spanish. Colonists fleeing the revolt from points north holed up temporarily at Los Cerrillos, one of the few settlements between Santa Fe and Albuquerque, before continuing to El Paso. The village itself was likewise abandoned.

Modern Cerrillos emerged in the spring of 1879 when Frank Dimick (sometimes seen as Dimmitt) and Robert Hart, two prospectors leaving labor strikes in the mining camp of Leadville, Colorado, discovered silver and lead in the Cerrillos foothills. They called their claim the Galena Chief. The two laid out the Cerrillos mining district, into which a flood of other prospectors arrived to stake claims like the Cash Entry and the Grand Central. Even the illustrious Tiffany of New York had operations in the district, among them the old Castilian Mine, from which the company is said to have reaped some $2 million in extracted turquoise for use in jewelry.

Cerrillos burned brightly in its vigorous years, with population estimates ranging from 800 to 2,500 people. A hardware store, several saloons (twenty-one by one count!), a grocery store, four hotels, and a barbershop bordered Main Street.

Someone planted cottonwood trees along the streets to bring shade to early residents. Anthracite coal mining became the dominant activity with the arrival of the Atchison, Topeka, and Santa Fe Railway in Cerrillos in 1880. A post office opened that same year.

The nearby communities of Madrid and Golden also grew from mining operations in the Ortiz Mountains and could be said to be sister cities to Cerrillos. Like Cerrillos, Madrid developed as a coal-mining town, while Golden, as its name implies, grew from local gold strikes (dating even earlier than the California Gold Rush in 1849). It was said that in Golden, residents could find free gold in the gulches after a rainstorm, the raindrops being nature's panning. Madrid was a company town, built in Coal Gulch by the Cerrillos Coal Railroad. The settlement became known for its festive display of holiday lights around Christmas, with colored bulbs on a nearby hilltop depicting a glowing nativity scene. The tradition continues to this day.

As silver and lead ores played out during the Depression and the mines around Madrid closed in the 1950s, the villages of Cerrillos, Madrid, and Golden settled into their new roles as quiet and historic communities. The company town of Madrid was later put up for sale, and today has become a tourist attraction with numerous shops and a distinctive character. The historic church of Saint Francis in Golden still holds Mass today. The three lie along an official Scenic Byway appropriately named "the Turquoise Trail."

More to explore: *Dawson, Gold and Turquoise, Trail of the Forty-Niners*

74. Chama

Location: 1. Rio Arriba County. On the south end of Chama, in a pullout on the west side of US 64 between mile markers 162 and 163. See map 2.

2. Rio Arriba County. In Chama, in the park next to the train terminal, at the intersection of Fifth and Terrace Avenues. See map 2.

Marker text: From a small crossroads town, Chama became an important site on the Denver & Rio Grande Western Railroad after 1880. The Cumbres & Toltec Scenic Railroad is the remnant of the San Juan Extension, a narrow-gauge line which once served the mining areas of southwestern Colorado.

75. Ghost Marker: Cumbres and Toltec Scenic Railroad

Marker text: In 1880–82, the Denver & Rio Grande Railroad built the San Juan Extension to serve the mines of southwestern Colorado. The Cumbres & Toltec Scenic Railroad still operates 64 miles of the narrow-gauge system between Chama, N.M., and Antonito, Colorado. Jointly owned by the two states, it is a "living museum" of railway history.

Note: This Historic Marker once stood in the small park near the train terminal but has since been removed. See map 2.

The history of Chama is echoed in the hefty chug of rolling stock: specifically, that of the San Juan Extension of the Denver and Rio Grande Western Railroad. Laid between Denver and Santa Fe in the early 1880s, the San Juan Extension was erected with the express purpose of serving local mining districts, including those centered at well-known Colorado camps such as Leadville and Silverton. The San Juan Extension was the first railway to open this heavily forested and sparsely populated part of New Mexico to outside commerce and travel.

As such, the railroad transformed the character and development of the preexisting hamlet of Chama, founded originally as a Hispanic settlement known as San Pedro de Chama, or Saint Peter of Chama (for the nearby Chama River). Given its location near the line, the village became a tent city to house railroad workers. A post office opened in 1880 under the name Chama.

As the population in Chama grew, buildings of a more commercial nature arose. Two hotels opened to cater to the needs of railroad crews and travelers. One was later destroyed by fire, but the second survived as the historic Foster Hotel, today one of the few intact commercial structures from the developmental years of Chama history.

The town would outlast the railroad. As mining booms ended and the country moved from railroads to trucks for shipping goods, the San Juan Extension fell victim to decades of economic downturns and track closures. During the 1960s, mounting public nostalgia for the lore of railroad trains, coupled with a sincere interest in preserving the "iron horse" legacy of north-central New Mexico, led to efforts to resurrect passenger service on the line. In a move that created what has since become one of the most beloved tourist attractions in New Mexico, the state legislatures of Colorado and New Mexico in 1970 jointly appropriated funds to purchase a portion of the railroad and bring it into public ownership.

Today, the sixty-four-mile stretch of track between Chama and the eastern terminus of the line at Antonito, Colorado, operates as the Cumbres and Toltec Scenic Railroad. It is open to the public during the summer months. Both New Mexico and Colorado have a hand in operating this "living museum" of railway history.

More to explore: *Belen, Cloud-Climbing Railroad, Playas Siding, Vaughn*

76. Chimayó

Location: Rio Arriba County. In Chimayó, at the intersection of County Road 94E and County Road 98. See map 2.

Marker text: Indians occupied the Chimayó valley centuries before the arrival of the Spaniards. The village of Chimayó, founded in the early 18th century, shortly after the reconquest of New Mexico, has been a center of the Spanish weaving tradition for over 250 years. The village retains the historical pattern of settlement around a defensible plaza.

77. El Santuario de Chimayó

Location: Rio Arriba County. In the parking lot of the santuario in Chimayó. See map 2.

Marker text: In 1816, Bernardo Abeyta and the other residents of El Potrero, then a separate community, finished this massive adobe chapel honoring Nuestro Señor de Esquípulas. It is noted for its 6-foot crucifix and its tradition of healing the sick. The Santuario remained in the Abeyta family until the 1920s.

The name Chimayó has become synonymous worldwide with fine, handwoven textiles. Families in Chimayó now regarded for their artisanship, like the Ortegas and the Trujillos, have carried the tradition through many generations.

The Chimayó Valley was originally home to Tewa-speaking Indians, who built a pueblo among the foothills of the Sangre de Cristo Mountains in what is now the Santa Cruz Valley. Living here centuries before the Spanish arrived, these Indians named the region *Tsimayo*. One translation of the word equates it to "flaking stone"; another, to "place where the big stones stand." To the native people, this land was the backdrop of a battle between their twin war gods and a truculent giant. A volcanic hot spring bubbled muddily forth at the spot where the giant, slain in the brawl, fell to the ground. Indians believed that the mud from that spring had healing powers, and another Chimayó tradition had its inception—that of eating or rubbing the dirt on afflicted areas of the body to stimulate healing regeneration.

Around 1692, the Spanish government awarded tracts of land in the Santa Cruz Valley to settlers so they might establish defensive villages on the northern frontier—that is, the region north of Santa Fe. Several closely knit agricultural communities developed under the umbrella name Chimayó, including La Puebla, El Potrero, Plaza Abajo, Los Ranchos, El Llano, and Plaza de San Buenaventura, now known as Plaza del Cerro. Settlers in Chimayó, like those in many of these villages, laid out their settlement as a fortified outpost, with flat-roofed adobe houses adjoining a plaza. This arrangement is found frequently in colonial villages, especially those where attacks by hostile Indians made such defensibility necessary.

The chapel of El Santuario de Chimayó in nearby Potrero has today become a sacred place for those seeking the healing holy dirt from the dried-up volcanic spring. The story of El Santuario begins with Bernardo Abeyta, one of the original Chimayó settlers and a wealthy trader in the village. One of several popular legends relates that Abeyta one day beheld a refulgent crucifix floating near his home. He put the glowing cross into a small shelter attached to his house, but the crucifix had returned to its original location by the following morning. He tried once more with similar results. When these events repeated a third time, Abeyta erected a chapel, dedicated to Nuestro Señor de Esquípulas, to hold the miraculous crucifix. His church opened in 1816. Pilgrims then and now came to seek the dirt, taken from a hole in a room to the left of the altar that is said to lie under the spot where the miracle crucifix appeared. Discarded crutches, braces, eyeglasses, and other ex-votos lining the wall of the sacristy testify to the faith of those who believe that they have been healed from their visit.

A few years after Abeyta's death in 1856, legend says, Chimayó resident Severiano Medina prayed to El Santo Niño de Atocha (the Holy Child of Atocha) and was subsequently cured of rheumatism. Devout then in his admiration for Santo Niño, Medina purchased a statue of the saint and secured it in a private chapel, known as Capilla del Santo Niño de Atocha, next to El Santuario. Worshippers at El Santuario followed by purchasing a statue of El Niño for their church. Side by side, the Capilla del Santo Niño de Atocha and El Santuario both claimed miraculous cures. Over time, El Niño replaced the crucifix as the venerated healer.

El Santuario remained in the Abeyta family until 1929, when a committee of artists from Santa Fe purchased the sanctuary and donated it to the Catholic Church.

More to explore: *Agueda Martinez, Iglesia de San Ysidro (see under Corrales), San Isidro Catholic Church (see under Agua Fria)*

78. Cimarron

Location: Colfax County. In Cimarron, in the park next to the Cimarron Visitors Center at the intersection of Ninth and Lincoln Streets. See map 3.

Marker text: This village on the Mountain Branch of the Santa Fe Trail was settled around 1844. In 1857 it became the home of Lucien B. Maxwell, and headquarters for the famous Maxwell Land Grant of almost 2,000,000 acres. An agency for Utes and Jicarilla Apaches was located here from 1862 to 1876.

Land baron Lucien Maxwell entertained lavishly in his Cimarron mansion for soldiers at Fort Union and travelers over the Santa Fe Trail. He could afford to: his extensive holdings in northeastern New Mexico had made Maxwell the owner of one of the largest tracts of land ever possessed by one private individual. Lucien Bonaparte Maxwell. William A. Keleher Pictorial Collection, Box 1, Folder 52, Item 000-742-0089, Center for Southwest Research, University Libraries, University of New Mexico.

Cimarron began as a small village, settled in the mid-1800s along the banks of the Cimarron River. The village witnessed caravan traffic both from the Mountain Branch of the Santa Fe Trail and from a wagon road serving Fort Union, some forty miles to the south. Given its location near the western foothills of the Sangre de Cristo Mountains, Cimarron served as a gathering place for beaver trappers, who stocked their inventories from the flowing mountain streams.

The name Lucien B. Maxwell ascends to prominence early in the history of Cimarron. Maxwell, a fur trapper from Illinois, settled in the Rayado area south of the village in March 1848. Through his marriage to the daughter of French Canadian trapper and landowner Carlos Beaubien, Maxwell inherited the majority of the sizeable Beaubien-Miranda land grant after his father-in-law's death. Maxwell bought out what he did not inherit, eventually acquiring 1,714,765 acres of northeastern New Mexico. In 1857, Maxwell moved his family into a large, twenty-two-room adobe mansion and flour mill in Cimarron and made the village his headquarters for his far-reaching ranching and land operations.

Several period buildings from the developmental years of Cimarron remain intact today and reflect the fervent history of the town. The Frenchman Henri Lambert, who claimed to be the former cook for General Grant and President Lincoln, built the Saint James Hotel in 1872 at a cost of $17,000. Reportedly, no fewer than twenty-six murders occurred in the hotel during its raucous early years. The stone jail just south of the hotel held the village ne'er-do-wells, one of whom dynamited through a wall during a jailbreak in the early 1900s. The word *cimarron*, perhaps not coincidentally, translates from Spanish as "wild."

In 1861, the US government established a reservation for Utes and Jicarilla Apaches in Ponil Canyon north of Cimarron on land owned, not incidentally, by Lucien Maxwell, and stationed the agency for the reservation in the village itself. Maxwell became the chief supplier of flour and meat to both the army and the Indians and profited greatly from the arrangement. Yet problems beset the reservation from the outset. Rancid food and inadequate blankets and supplies hastened the devastating spread of smallpox among the Indians. Meanwhile, the influx of prospectors seeking their destiny on the slopes of nearby Baldy Mountain conflicted with the set-aside of reservation land. One of these mining promoters was Maxwell himself, upon whose land the activity was taking place and who even established his own short-lived mining camp, Virginia City, on the mountain. In 1876, the US Indian Office moved the reservation to northwestern New Mexico and closed the agency at Cimarron.

By that time, however, Lucien Maxwell had passed away. He died in the southeastern New Mexico community of Fort Sumner in July 1875, where he had moved after having sold his land grant to an English conglomerate five years earlier. The sale was the impetus for the Colfax County War, as miners, settlers, and the new landowners disputed rights to the land. The battle, centered in Cimarron, was settled only when the Supreme Court upheld the original grant, thereby forcing settlers to buy their properties or move.

More to explore: *Ada McPherson Morley, Agnes Morley Cleaveland, Black Jack Ketchum (series), Colfax County War, Fort Sumner and Fort Sumner State Monument (series), Jicarilla Apache (series)*

79. Cimarron Canyon

Location: Colfax County. West of Cimarron, in a pullout on the south side of US 64 at mile marker 305. See map 3.

Marker text: You are now at the Great Plains–Rocky Mountain boundary. The Cimarron Range is one of the easternmost ranges of the Sangre de Cristo Mountains in this part of New Mexico. Elevation 6,800 feet.

80. Cimarron Canyon State Park

Location: Colfax County. West of Cimarron and east of Ponderosa Campground, in a pullout on the north side of US 64, between mile markers 295 and 296. See map 3.

Marker text: This high mountain park is part of a state wildlife area and is managed by the New Mexico State Park Division in cooperation with the New Mexico Department of Game and Fish. Trout fishing is excellent in the Cimarron River, and the park offers fine opportunities for backcountry hiking and wildlife viewing. The crenellated rock formations known as the Palisades are popular.

81. Palisades Sill

Location: Colfax County. West of Cimarron, in a pullout on the east side of US 64, between mile markers 293 and 294. See map 3.

Marker text: These spectacular cliffs are cut by the Cimarron River through igneous rock known as a sill and composed of the rock type monzonite which was emplaced some 40 million years ago as these Southern Rocky Mountains were being uplifted. Elevation 8,000 feet.

The landscape at Cimarron Canyon and the state park that surrounds it changes from vertical to horizontal as the rugged Rocky Mountains to the west give way to the rolling Great Plains to the east. Cimarron Canyon cuts through the Cimarron Range, one of the easternmost in the Sangre de Cristo Mountains, to separate the communities of Eagle Nest and Cimarron. The Sangre de Cristos make up the southernmost limits of the Rocky Mountains.

The Cimarron country harbors many treasures, among them the Palisades Sill. In geological terms, palisades are lines of steep cliffs, usually found along a river—in this case, the Cimarron River. True to their descriptive name, these incredible four-hundred-foot-high crenellated granite cliffs resemble in their towering reach the defensive parapets that secure a castle. A sill, meanwhile, is a layer of igneous rock formed when magma rising from the mantle intrudes into horizontal sedimentary rock layers, then cools and hardens into a thin sheet. The sill from which the Cimarron Palisades was formed stretches from Baldy Mountain to the eastern edge of the Cimarron Range. It was created as part of the upheavals some forty million years ago that uplifted the Rocky Mountains into existence. The sill is made up in part of finely grained monzonite. The towering vertical columns are actually weathered cooling vents within the sill.

The Cimarron River, with its tributaries Clear Creek and Tolby Creek, offers anglers the chance to hook rainbow and brown trout. Elk, deer, bear, turkey, and grouse all wander this pristine wilderness. A portion of the river, as well as the Palisades Sill, are within the boundaries of Cimarron Canyon State Park, established in 1979. The park has a total of ninety-four campsites and offers fishing and camping. Trails, including the Tolby Creek Trail and the Clear Creek Trail, allow visitors to explore this beautiful country.

More to explore: *Jemez Mountains, Rocky Mountains*

Cimarron Canyon State Park: *see Cimarron Canyon*

82. City of Bloomfield

Location: San Juan County. At the west end of Bloomfield, on the south side of US 64. See map 1.

Marker Text: Prehistoric farmers established major communities along the rivers of this region in the eleventh century. Eight hundred years later, historic settlement was also made possible by abundant water. Bloomfield was established in 1879 near a site which afforded a safe crossing of the San Juan River. The hard lives of the early settlers gradually gave way to increasing prosperity made possible by irrigation farming and horticulture.

The first villages in the San Juan Basin were those built by the Ancestral Puebloan people in the eleventh century. These early Indians built several large, multistoried pueblos of stone and adobe along the San Juan River, the Kutz Canyon Arroyo, and other water sources in the Four Corners region. Partially excavated ruins of two can be seen at nearby Salmon Ruin and Aztec Ruins National Monument. Considered "outlier" communities by archaeologists, both Salmon and Aztec appear to have been connected with the Ancestral Puebloan network that had its nucleus in the villages at Chaco Canyon, about ninety miles south of present-day Bloomfield. The Ancestral Puebloan people migrated from the area after 1250.

With the creation of the Jicarilla Apache Indian Reservation in March 1874, the government held in reserve a parcel of land in this part of northwestern New Mexico to serve as the exclusive home of the Jicarilla Apache tribe. Pressure from the public to open the land to homesteading was mounting, however, and two years later President Ulysses S. Grant abrogated the executive order that had created the reservation and redefined the reservation boundaries elsewhere. Homesteaders and ranchers arrived swiftly, eager to reap their prospects in small farmsteads along the San Juan River. An agricultural settlement formed around 1879 near a crossing on the river and took the name Bloomfield. The name, like that of nearby Farmington, spoke of the rewards made possible by the generosity of the waters.

Despite the pastoral setting of Bloomfield, violence marred the earliest years of the town. Local bad guy Port Stockton, alias Stogden, along with his dark-hearted Stockton Gang, ran through the litany of frontier criminal acts: holding up stage lines, rustling cattle, spitting. The end came in January 1881 when Stockton formed a collusion with another outlaw named Truitt, a wretched cuss on the lam for murder. A sheriff hunting for Truitt came upon Stockton and shot him to death.

More to explore: *Aztec Ruins National Monument, Jicarilla Apache (series)*

83. City of Rocks State Park

Location: Grant County. At the entrance to the City of Rocks State Park. See map 5.

Marker text: Wind and water gradually sculpted the volcanic tuff at City of Rocks, creating the rows of monolithic blocks that gave this park its name. Camping/picnicking sites are tucked away among these Stonehenge-like formations and the park also features a cactus garden, hiking trails and a playground.

Nature seems to be in a mischievous mood at City of Rocks State Park, south of Bayard. Here, towering boulders rise Stonehenge-like from the surrounding valley, giving the appearance of a gathering of shrouded mystics in the middle of a vast open desert. Clustered over a one-mile-square area, the boulders—some as high as forty feet—create a labyrinth of passageways and secret hiding spots that is mysterious, playful, spooky, and awe inspiring all at once.

What keeps the City of Rocks from being too otherworldly is that geologists know how it was created.

About thirty-four million years ago, a volcano located near Kingston and Hillsboro—some fifty miles northeast of here and on the opposite side of the Black Range Mountains—erupted, spewing ash high into the air. Some of that ash collected here, coalescing into a giant mass. Over millions of years, weathering sculpted the ash into these giant blocks, softening them into the fantastic shapes they have today.

City of Rocks became a state park on March 20, 1953, with the passage of Senate Bill 89 in the state legislature, which established the site and conferred the name "City of Rocks." Its wonders continue to captivate visitors, who come to explore the formations, pitch a tent at one of the camping areas, or picnic in the shade of their own personal boulder. The setting is also ideal for stargazing—City of Rocks State Park is home to the Gene and Elisabeth Simon Observatory, the first observatory built at a New Mexico state park. It was named for a local ranching couple who donated money for the observatory to be built.

More to explore: *Bisti Wilderness, Clayton Lake State Park, Rockhound State Park*

84. Civilian Conservation Corps
Carlsbad Campsite

Location: Eddy County. In Carlsbad, in the courtyard of a local hotel, 2429 W. Pierce Street. See map 6.

Marker text: The Civilian Conservation Corps (CCC) provided employment for more than 50,000 young men in New Mexico during the Great Depression as part of President Roosevelt's New Deal Program. Three CCC companies were located where the Carlsbad Hospital now stands. They worked on flood control and reclamation projects along the Pecos River and in the Guadalupe Mountains and helped build Carlsbad's "President Park."

The Civilian Conservation Corps, a pet project of President Franklin Roosevelt during the Great Depression, employed young men throughout the country in building city parks, laying trails, erecting dams, and otherwise improving the public lands of the nation.

Carlsbad was one of only a handful of New Mexico cities to secure more than one CCC camp. The first Carlsbad camp, Company 2868 of Camp F-37-N, arose in Dark Canyon of the Guadalupe Mountains southwest of town. According to the *1935 CCC Official Annual*, young men at the camp—most of whom had come from Texas—had as their mission "developing and improving transportation facilities, improving general range conditions, and opening to the public one of the most beautiful and primitive recreational areas in the southwest."

Two other camps operated within the city itself. The first was at the spot where Carlsbad Hospital now stands; the second, a smaller campsite, was adjacent to the first. This second camp, Company 1830 of Camp BR-3-N, held a unique designation in New Mexico CCC history: it was made up of soldiers who had served in World War I. The veterans' camp ran under the command of Captain Jerome H. Parker, with Second Lieutenant A. L. Lewis as exchange officer, First Lieutenant R. J. Laurentz as camp surgeon, and J. D. Brimhall as the education adviser. As reported in the *Official Annual*:

The CCC organization constructed a dam parallel with the hills, preventing the escape of water, insuring the valley a steady water supply. The men have been engaged in dam construction, flood control, ditch cleaning, and rodent control.

Camp workers also laid rocks along the river in an area on the opposite bank of what would later become President's Park. The park, erected in the 1960s after the camps had gone, was a small-scale amusement complex, with rides, an ice cream parlor, and a Ferris wheel.

The CCC dismantled most of its camps throughout the state during World War II as men of the corps enlisted and the military appropriated camp materials for its operations. During the war, the army reused the buildings and materials of the Carlsbad Hospital CCC camp for construction of an air base southwest of town. The veterans' camp served briefly as a prison camp for German POWs before it, too, was disassembled.

Although these and other camps are little more than memories now, the CCC left a significant and long-lasting mark on New Mexico history. According to one estimate, more than thirty thousand young men were enrolled in the CCC throughout the state between the years 1933 and 1942.

More to explore: *Camp Lordsburg, Carlsbad Caverns National Park (series), Civilian Conservation Corps—Lake Arthur Campsite*

85. Civilian Conservation Corps
Lake Arthur Campsite

Location: Chaves County. Sixteen miles north of Artesia, in a pullout on the west side of US 285, between mile markers 86 and 87. See map 6.

Marker text: The Civilian Conservation Corps was established to provide employment for the nation's young men during the Great Depression of the 1930s. More than 50,000 were enrolled in the program in New Mexico between 1933 and 1942. CCC enrollees at the Lake Arthur camp improved grazing lands and developed water resources for livestock and wildlife.

In 1932, President Franklin Roosevelt proposed to Congress an ambitious new economic relief program for the country. Roosevelt wanted to help young men endure the Depression by putting them to work planting forests, grading new roads, building dams, and generally rejuvenating the parks and public domain areas of the nation. Congress approved the plan and passed the Emergency Conservation Work Act to help combat, as the language read, the "acute condition of widespread distress and unemployment . . . existing in the United States." The act was a precursor to the Civilian Conservation Corps Act, passed in June 1937, which officially formed the Civilian Conservation Corps, or CCC.

It was a camp under the direction of the Grazing Service of the Department of the Interior that opened at a spot known as Hackberry Wells, fourteen miles west of Lake Arthur. When work at the camp commenced on September 1, 1935, the roster included some eighty young men from Roswell and Albuquerque. Officially known as DG-41-N, the camp itself included a schoolroom with a library, a recreation hall, and a carpentry shop. When not improving the land in this part of southeastern New Mexico, the young men at the camp learned typewriting and other vocational skills and published their own newspaper. Lieutenant Sherman B. Wetmore served as commander, First Lieutenant Jack I. Davis as exchange officer, and Dr. F. L. Hinkley as camp surgeon.

The Lake Arthur CCC camp was in operation for only a short time before the Department of the Interior disbanded it on July 31, 1936. But a lot had been accomplished in that brief period. As reported in the CCC Annual Report for that year, work projects at the camp had included "the completion of 21 miles of telephone lines, 29 miles of truck trails, erosion work on thousands of acres, loco weed eradication, rodent control, and the construction of 1,120 rods of fence." To top it off, the men of camp DG-41-N also won the 1935 sub-district championship in basketball and softball.

More to explore: *Carlsbad Caverns National Park (series), Civilian Conservation Corps—Carlsbad Campsite*

Clanton Hideout: *see Smuggler's Trail*

86. Clayton

Location: 1. Union County. At the northeastern end of Clayton, in a pullout on the north side of US 56/64/412 (Main Street), between mile markers 83 and 84. See map 3.

2. Union County. Southeast of Clayton, in a pullout on the north side of US 87 (South First Street), between mile markers 4 and 5. See map 3.

3. Union County. Northwest of Clayton, in a pullout on the south side of US 64/87, between mile markers 427 and 428. See map 3.

4. Union County. West of Clayton, in a pullout on the south side of US 56/412, at mile marker 81. See map 3.

Marker text: Trade caravans and homesteaders traveling the Cimarron Cutoff of the Santa Fe Trail passed near here. Clayton was founded in 1887 and named for the son of cattleman and ex-Senator Stephen W. Dorsey, one of its developers. It became a major livestock shipping center for herds from the Pecos Valley and the Texas Panhandle.

The grasslands surrounding present-day Clayton first saw caravan travel over the Santa Fe Trail after 1821 after Mexico opened its borders to trade from the East. A southern-tending branch of the trail left Dodge City, Kansas, and traversed the northwestern reaches of Oklahoma into New Mexico north of here. Traders and homesteaders crossing this, the Cimarron Cutoff, had sacrificed the comfort of regular water stops and safety from Indian attacks offered by the Mountain Branch of the trail in exchange for the swiftness made possible by the level prairies of the cutoff. Rabbit Ear Mountain and McNees Crossing north of Clayton were key landmarks along the route.

The advent of the railroad in New Mexico in the 1880s meant the end of the Santa Fe Trail but the beginning of small railroad communities like Clayton. The settlement was named for Clayton Chauncey Dorsey, the son of one of the developers of the town and former US senator from Arkansas Stephen W. Dorsey. The elder Dorsey had come to New Mexico in 1877 and constructed an elaborate ranch manor, the Dorsey Mansion, about twenty-five miles east of Springer. With his range manager, John Hill, and others, Dorsey convinced officials of the Colorado and Southern Railroad in the late 1880s to establish a division point in this location as the company set down track between Fort Worth and Denver. The townsite lay midway between two other railroad division points at Trinidad, Colorado, and Amarillo, Texas.

The budding railroad town of Clayton developed as a shipping center for livestock. According to a 1902 bulletin issued by the Bureau of Immigration of the territory of New Mexico, Clayton ranchers shipped two million pounds of wool, 160 carloads of cattle, and 400 carloads of sheep and lambs annually. The same bulletin described the settlement thus:

It has electric light and water works, a telephone system, a splendid public school system and a fine public school building, a Methodist and Christian church, a number of secret societies, many business establishments and contains many nice homes.

Despite the nice homes, Clayton today holds one notorious historical distinction. Here, in 1901, law enforcement officials hanged desperado Thomas Edward "Black Jack" Ketchum. Tried and sentenced to death for robbing a train out of Folsom near the New Mexico border with Colorado,

Ketchum was the first person to be hanged in Colfax County. He is buried between two sections of the Clayton Memorial Cemetery, an unusual location said to have been chosen so the outlaw's body would not lie close to hallowed graves.

More to explore: *Black Jack Ketchum (series), Clayton Lake State Park, Dorsey Mansion, McNees Crossing, Rabbit Ear Mountain, Santa Fe Trail (series)*

87. Clayton Lake State Park

Location: Union County. Southeast of Clayton, in a pullout on the north side of US 87 (South First Street), between mile markers 4 and 5. See map 3.

Marker text: The rolling grasslands around Clayton Lake were once a domain of the huge buffalo herds that ranged the Great Plains. Many years prior to this, dinosaurs ruled the area as indicated by a series of tracks embedded in the rock near the lake. Clayton Lake is stocked with rainbow trout and channel catfish and also provides good bass and walleye fishing. The lake serves as a wintering area for waterfowl.

88. Clayton Dinosaur Trackway

Location: 1. Union County. In Clayton, in the courtyard of the Clayton Tourist Information Center, 1103 South First Street. See map 3.

2. Union County. At the entrance to the trackway at Clayton Lake State Park.

Marker text: One of the best dinosaur track sites in the world can be viewed at Clayton Lake State Park. More than 500 fossilized footprints, made by at least eight kinds of dinosaurs, are visible on the lake's spillway. These tracks were embedded in the mud over 100 million years ago, when most of New Mexico was a vast sea.

One day a hundred million years ago, a plant-eating dinosaur slipped in the mud north of present-day Clayton. The big creature steadied itself with its tail, leaving a "tell-tail" impression of its prehistoric lapse in physical grace. Other moments of ancient significance recorded in the layers of silt and clay at the Clayton Dinosaur Trackway are the takeoff of a winged pterodactyl and the hesitation, dubbed the "dinosaur shuffle," of another plant eater as it rocked in place several times before turning right. With more than five hundred such impressions, the Clayton Dinosaur Trackway at Clayton Lake State Park is one of the most extensive and best-preserved trackways in the world.

This was the dinosaurs' world before it was ours. The landscape of brown hills and rolling plains that are the New Mexico of today was, in the time of dinosaurs, a shallow inland sea of warm, salty water. Walking along the muddy western edge of that sea, the heavyset dinosaurs left depressions of their strolls in the mud. Their mucky footprints slowly filled with sand, which eventually coalesced into sandstone. In 1954, the construction of Clayton Lake Dam on Seneca Creek exposed these sandstone layers to the air. Wind and weather did their work, eventually breaking away the sandstone within the depressions and freeing the footprints for our admiration.

At first glance, the trackway may appear little more than a scrap of earth with shallow depressions along the spillway of Clayton Lake. Closer observation, though, especially as evening shadows bring dimension to the dimpled earth, reveals those depressions as the imprints of dinosaur feet—called "traces" by paleontologists. Surveys of the site show that at least eight different kinds of dinosaurs left a record of their visit to the Cretaceous mudflat. They include the herbivorous, bipedal iguanodont, a name that translates to "iguana tooth." Carnivores are represented in part by the sharp-toothed, hollow-boned coelurosaur. Preserved as well are the rare tracks of a baby dinosaur, probably an iguanodont.

Paleontologists suspect that the beasts may have been migrating along a stretch of land between Clayton and Fort Collins, Colorado—a sweep suitably nicknamed the Dinosaur Freeway. Much later in time, this area was a freeway to creatures of a different sort, as buffalo roamed the rolling grasslands of northeastern New Mexico in great herds.

Clayton Lake was set aside as parkland and managed locally by the New Mexico State Game Commission in 1955, and it was designated a state park ten years later, in August 1965. The lake offers boating from March to the end of October, and the waters are stocked with rainbow trout and channel catfish for fishing. In the colder months, the lake serves as a wintering area for geese and other migratory waterfowl, making it popular with birdwatchers. In 2006, the park installed the Star Point Observatory, complete with a Meade telescope, from which stargazers can observe the night skies for constellations and wayward pterodactyls.

More to explore: *Bisti Wilderness, Blackwater Draw, Clayton*

Clayton Dinosaur Trackway: *see Clayton Lake State Park*

89. Clifton House Site

Location: 1. Colfax County. At mile marker 344 on US 64, just off exit 446 from Interstate 25. See map 3.
2. Colfax County. South of Raton, in a highway rest area on the west side of Interstate 25, between mile markers 434 and 435. See map 3.

Marker text: Three-quarters of a mile west of here at the Canadian River crossing was the popular overnight stage stop on the Old Santa Fe Trail. Clifton House was built in 1867 by rancher Tom Stockton, with materials bought overland from Dodge City. For years it served as headquarters for cattle roundups. After abandonment of Santa Fe Trail in 1879, it fell into disuse and burned.

Note: Because this Historic Marker uses a distance reference and appears in two locations, the referenced location in the Marker in the rest area is off. From the rest area, the site was about twelve miles north.

Steeped in the hospitality of his native Tennessee, rancher Tom Stockton dreamed of building a sumptuous mansion on his northeastern New Mexico ranch south of Raton, a community gathering place where cowboys driving cattle through the area could stop for a good meal and local families could hold weddings and dances. Stockton rolled up his sleeves on the project in 1866, using shingles, glass, and furniture freighted in prairie schooners over the Santa Fe Trail from as far east as Dodge City, Kansas. Built mostly of adobe, the building when completed in 1870 stood two stories high over a raised, half-story basement. A veranda held aloft by Doric columns ran across the front and sides of the building on both levels to create a beautiful promenade balcony. Inside, the mansion held washbasins in the front hall, a saloon, a resplendent parlor, sleeping rooms with fireplaces, and a grand dining room with a high ceiling. Tom Stockton's Clifton House stood as a bit of southern opulence on the banks of the Canadian River.

Built along the Mountain Branch of the Santa Fe Trail near the southern base of Raton Pass between New Mexico and Colorado, Clifton House became a "home-station stop" on the Barlow and Sanderson stage line, which ran over the pass and south along Raton Creek. Travelers no doubt welcomed a warm meal and comfortable night's sleep at Clifton House as a reprieve from the physical demands the trail had made on them. As its popularity and use grew, the house soon employed cooks and waitstaff to maintain operations and added a trading post, a blacksmith shop, and even a post office. A small settlement grew near the mansion and took the name Clifton. Abandoned now, that settlement never grew larger than a few small adobe homes and a cemetery.

Only small stone corner remains of what was once one of the finest hostelries in north-central New Mexico. Tom Stockton's Clifton House served traveler and rancher alike, and even a couple of outlaws. Clifton House. Albert Thompson Photo Collection, Box 1, Folder 4, Item 000-079-0031, Center for Southwest Research, University Libraries, University of New Mexico.

Guests at the house one evening in the early 1870s likely heard the gunshot that killed an unfortunate young member of the waitstaff. As related by a Stockton descendent in 1937, the bullet had been intended for notorious outlaw Chunk Colbert:

Chunk was in trouble in Trinidad [Colorado]; the sheriff wanted him, he had heard that Chunk was at the Clifton House, and he came over after him. The sheriff arrived after bed time, inquired of the proprietor if his man was there, disregarding the negative answer, took a candle in one hand and his cocked-gun in the other and started through the house to see for himself. He was nervous; it was a nervous job to go looking for Chunk Colbert at night or anytime. He opened a bed room door, saw a man in bed, and in his nervousness, fired.

Although the sheriff had shot the wrong man, Chunk Colbert did finally get his, killed by fellow gunman Clay Allison in the dining hall on January 6, 1874. Despite being enemies, the two had spent the day in riotous behavior together before sitting down to a meal. Allison waited to shoot Colbert until after he finished his dinner because, as the outlaw later recounted, "I didn't want to send him to Hell on an empty stomach."

The first train over Raton Pass arrived in 1879, and the Barlow and Sanderson stage soon faded to obsolescence. Tom Stockton's Clifton House fell into disuse. The empty structure apparently proved too great a temptation, for an arsonist torched the remains in 1885.

More to explore: *Dorsey Mansion, Raton, Santa Fe Trail (series)*

Roller coasters had nothing on the winding ascent of Charles B. Eddy's "Cloud-Climbing Railroad," the highest standard-gauge railroad in the country in the late nineteenth century. Here, officials celebrate the opening of the line. Dedication Day, Alamogordo and Sacramento Railway, Toboggan, New Mexico, November 16, 1898. Photo by Bushong and Feldman, courtesy Palace of the Governors Photo Archives (NMHM/DCA), neg. no. 14914.

90. Cloud-Climbing Railroad

Location: Otero County. Just west of the village of Cloudcroft, on the north side of US 82, between mile markers 5 and 6. See map 6.

Marker text: In order to provide timber for the construction of his El Paso & Northeastern Railroad north of Alamogordo, Charles B. Eddy in 1898 built a spur into the Sacramento Mountains. The line operated as far as Cloudcroft until 1947. The Cloudcroft Trestle is all that remains.

Few other railroad lines in the early 1900s could match the ear-popping exhilaration of the thirty-two-mile standard-gauge spur that ran through the Sacramento Mountains. Rolling in from the Tularosa Valley to the west, trains ascended from 4,322 feet to 9,069 feet in their two-and-a-half-hour journey over the line, up and up and up, through the sweet and invigorating mountain air, conquering no fewer than 330 dizzying curves in their twisting ascent. Although known officially as the Alamogordo and Sacramento Railway, the line was more descriptively known as the Cloud-Climbing Railroad.

This majestic branch line was a physical example of the importance of railroads in the development of southeastern New Mexico—and of the entrepreneurial dreams of railroad promoter Charles B. Eddy. Eddy had arrived in New Mexico with his brother John A. Eddy from New York in the late nineteenth century. Among the entrepreneurial projects he undertook on his rise to tycoon status was the construction of the El Paso and Northeastern Railroad from El Paso through the Tularosa Valley to Santa Rosa in the late 1890s. The hungry railroad required timber for ties, and although the flat Tularosa Valley was favorable land for railroads, it lacked trees. The solution lay in the heavily forested Sacramento Mountains east of the valley. So, in 1898, Eddy hired engineer Horace A. Sumner to build one of the most breathtaking railroad spurs in New Mexico.

The weathered wooden railroad trestle spanning Mexican Canyon here, fifty-two feet high, was just one of fifty-eight in the line Sumner engineered. A report from the National Park Service describes the structure:

In order to form the curve, the top part was built in 21 sections with 8 x 16" timbers. There are 10 main timbers 15 feet in length in each of the 21 sections resting on footing blocks set 4 to 8 feet underground. Lateral, longitudinal, and diagonal wooden braces prevented sway and shifting of the trestle. A wooden guard rail ran along the track to keep the ties from bunching. Metal guard rails running outside the standard gauge rails prevented derailed trains from falling off the trestle.

The Cloud-Climbing Railroad soon began operating as a passenger line with a stop at a small townsite the railroad crew had established at the summit of the mountain. That town, nestled in a small clearing, took the name Cloudcroft. Many of the tourists riding the line were honeymooners, who no doubt found the dizzying dangers of the ride a suitable metaphor for their recent nuptial excursions.

After 1930, when the state had constructed a new road between Alamogordo and Cloudcroft, hauling lumber became a task more for trucks than for trains. The last car of the Cloud-Climbing Railroad rolled down the mountain on September 12, 1947, and the great ride was ended.

More to explore: *Alamogordo (see under La Luz), Belen, Capitan, Chama, Cumbres and Toltec Scenic Railroad (see under Chama), Playas Siding, Vaughn*

91. Clovis

Location: Curry County. In the parking lot of the New Mexico Visitors Center east of Clovis on the north side of US 60 between mile markers 395 and 396. See map 6.

Marker text: During the 1700s and early 1800s, Comanche Indian buffalo hunters used trails that passed near here. In 1907 the Santa Fe Railroad established Clovis to serve as the eastern terminal of the Belen Cutoff, which would connect with the transcontinental line at Belen. Formerly the domain of ranchers, the railroad opened the area to farmers.

92. Ghost Marker: Norman Petty Recording Studio

Marker text: At thirteen, Norman began cutting records in his father's filling station. With money earned from the Norman Petty Trio's "Mood Indigo," Petty converted a family grocery store next door into a modern recording studio, where he experimented with echo and microphone settings. In 1957, Petty made rock 'n roll history recording Buddy Holly and the Crickets' "That'll Be the Day." The sound influenced a generation.

Note: This Historic Marker has been approved by the state of New Mexico but was not yet placed as of the publication of this book. See map 6.

Comanche Indians had acquired the horse by 1700, and, with the mobility the animal begat, their dominion in the Southwest soon stretched over the plains of eastern New Mexico and much of present-day Texas, Oklahoma, and southern Colorado. They, like other Plains Indians, hunted the buffalo that once thrived on these grasslands. One of the most frequently used Comanche buffalo hunting trails passed near the present site of Clovis. Slowly, as soldiers from Fort Bascom near Tucumcari and other military installations in the Southwest increased their campaigning and Anglo and Mexican hunters slaughtered most of the buffalo needed for their survival, Comanches were forced to accept a less itinerant lifestyle. Most had moved to reservations by the end of the nineteenth century.

Modern Clovis arose in the early twentieth century as officials of the Atchison, Topeka, and Santa Fe Railway began work on the Belen Cutoff, a branch line that would leave the main track at Belen and run east through New Mexico to the Texas border at the settlement of Texico. The chief engineer of the AT&SF Railway asked crews to "locate and buy the first level section of land west of Texico for a townsite and facilities for the eastern terminal" of the line in New Mexico. The townsite thus selected, originally known as Riley Switch, had taken the name Clovis by the time workers finished trackage through the region on March 20, 1907.

Legend credits the name Clovis as a nod to the Frankish king Clovis I, who ruled between AD 461 and 511 and counted among his victories the defeat of both the Visigoths and the Burgundians. Clovis was very much a New Mexico city, however: it featured north-south streets named for New Mexico territorial governors. They included Wallace Street, named for Governor Lew Wallace, who served from 1878 to 1881 and still found time to work on his biblical epic novel *Ben-Hur*; and Ross Street, named for Edmund Gibson Ross, who served from 1885 to 1889 and signed the bill that established the University of New Mexico, the Agricultural College (which later became New Mexico State University), and the School of Mines (now New Mexico Tech). With the creation of Curry County in 1909, Clovis became the county seat. A year later, Clovis census rolls listed 3,255 residents.

Many of those residents engaged in cattle ranching on the plains surrounding the town. Farming also developed, as the railroad allowed farmers to access outside markets for their crops of alfalfa, wheat, and potatoes. In the late 1920s, Portair Field outside Clovis brought more traffic when it opened to passenger flights. Today, it is Cannon Air Force Base, home of the Twenty-Seventh Fighter Wing.

Rock 'n' roll lovers know the Clovis address of 1313 West Seventh Street well, for it was at this location that local musician Norman Petty converted a family grocery store into a recording studio in the 1950s. He financed the project with money he had earned performing with his very own Norman Petty Trio, which included his wife Violet ("Vi") and one other musician. Their most famous song was a cover of Duke Ellington's "Mood Indigo." At the Norman Petty Recording Studio, Buddy Holly shook his way into the musical consciousness of the nation by recording his rock 'n' roll hits "Peggy Sue" and "That'll Be the Day." Petty also produced and recorded songs for Roy Orbison, Waylon Jennings, and other famous rock and country singers and songwriters of the era.

More to explore: *Belen, Blackwater Draw, Fort Bascom, Lincoln-Jackson School, Louise Massie Mabey*

93. Colfax County War

Location: Colfax County. In Cimarron, in the dirt area on the north side of the intersection of Tenth and Euclid Streets, in front of the Cimarron Inn. See map 3.

Marker text: For twenty years after the 1869 sale of the Maxwell Land Grant, homesteaders, ranchers, and miners fought the new owners for control of this enormous region. The resulting murders and general breakdown of law and order led to the removal from office, in 1878, of Territorial Governor Samuel B. Axtell.

In the Cimarron cemetery on the hill south of town stands a monument marking the burial site of Reverend F. J. Tolby. Engraved across the front is the word "Assassinated." It is a memorial not just to Tolby but also to the larger fray that brought about his death, a dispute known as the Colfax County War.

Until 1870, much of the land surrounding Cimarron and into large tracts of north-central New Mexico was under the authority of one man, former fur trapper turned landowner Lucien B. Maxwell. Through marriage to the daughter of an original land grant recipient, Maxwell inherited or bought out all other scions of the Beaubien-Miranda land grant and eventually acquired control of almost two million acres of land. In the meantime, homesteaders and miners had taken up residence throughout the grant land. That became a problem when Maxwell sold his grant in 1870 to a group of British investors who operated the Maxwell Land Grant Company. The new owners gave the homesteaders an ultimatum: buy their land or face eviction.

The first true martyr to the cause was Cimarron's Methodist minister, Reverend F. J. Tolby. An outspoken critic of the Maxwell Land Grant Company and its efforts to oust settlers, Tolby was shot from behind while riding his horse through Cimarron Canyon in September 1875. His horse and personal belongings had not been taken—damning evidence of foul play. Suspicions fell on officials of the Maxwell Company, who, some felt, had acted to silence Tolby's objections permanently.

Next to fall was mailman Cruz Vega, who indignant citizens believed had information that would bring to light a suspect in the death of Tolby. A renegade posse lynched Vega, but not before torturing a confession from him: Vega proclaimed his own innocence in the affair but implicated Manuel Cardenas, another local man. Cardenas confessed to the murder in a legal hearing while also accusing others from the Maxwell Company, but he too was killed by a violent mob before he could be brought to justice. Hostilities continued, fueled in part by instigating sermons from the pulpit of Parson Oscar P. McMains, another Cimarron minister and friend of Reverend Tolby, who preached that the land should be opened to settlement at once. Riots broke out in and around Cimarron when grant officials tried to prevent miners from working their claims.

At last, the murders and lawlessness in Colfax County induced President Rutherford B. Hayes to remove New Mexico territorial governor Samuel B. Axtell from office. Hayes replaced Axtell with General Lew Wallace, a name most famous for appearing on the title page of the biblical novel *Ben-Hur*.

In March 1887, to bring about a judicial end to the violence, the US Supreme Court heard the case of *United States v. the Maxwell Land Grant Company*. In their decision, the justices confirmed the validity of the Maxwell grant. The land company, then, had sole rights and ownership of the land. Over time, homesteaders were forced to purchase their land outright or leave it. After a violent two decades, the Colfax County War ended.

More to explore: *Ada McPherson Morley, Agnes Morley Cleaveland, Cimarron, Fort Sumner and Fort Sumner State Monument (series), Springer*

94. Colorado Plateau

Location: Sandoval County. Northwest of San Ysidro on US 550, just before reaching the Zia Indian Reservation, on the west side of the road near mile marker 25. See map 4.

Marker text: From this point, the Colorado Plateau extends across northwestern New Mexico into northeastern Arizona, southeastern Utah, and southwestern Colorado. A colorful landscape of mesas and canyons, it is underlain by natural mineral, oil, and gas resources locked within sedimentary strata deposited millions of years ago. Elevation 6,400 feet.

With its 130,000 square miles of colorful desert canyons and mesas, the Colorado Plateau is among the more visually exciting physiographic regions in the country. Four different states contribute land to the plateau: northern Arizona (including the Grand Canyon), southern Utah, southwestern Colorado, and northwestern New Mexico. The Rocky Mountains form the eastern border of the plateau; and the Basin and Range Province, a region of low-lying valleys between mountain ranges, the southern border. Over thousands of years, weathering and erosion have carved the marvelous land formations that make up the variegated landscape of the plateau. Oil and gas reserves trapped within the sedimentary rocks underlying the plateau have given those living on its surface even more reason to appreciate this land.

Extensive ruins of communal stone villages at Chaco Canyon and other sites throughout the Four Corners region are traces of the Ancestral Puebloan people. By AD 1050, the Ancestral Puebloan civilization was at its peak. Yet, about a hundred years later, the culture was in decline, and the Indians had begun to migrate from the region. Historians consider the Pueblo Indians of today their descendants.

More to explore: *Mount Taylor (see under Grants), Red Rocks*

COLUMBUS AND PANCHO VILLA'S RAID: Series of Five Historic Markers (in Columbus and Pancho Villa State Park)

General Introduction

In the dark reaches of the morning of March 9, 1916, Francisco "Pancho" Villa and some five hundred mercenaries crossed the Mexican border and crept toward the village of Columbus, New Mexico. Quietly, the *Villistas* surrounded the town and the American military outpost of Camp Furlong, established at Columbus to keep the peace along the border. Residents and most soldiers were asleep, unaware of what was about to strike.

Details of the attack that forever changed the village of Columbus are presented through a series of five Historic Markers in Columbus and Pancho Villa State Park (also in Columbus), although two of the Markers have identical text. You can follow the story of the attack and the resulting "punitive expedition" through the Markers, which have been combined here into one series. This series includes the Markers entitled "Columbus," "Pancho Villa's Raid," and "Pancho Villa State Park." You might do so while relaxing in Pancho Villa State Park, which preserves the ruins of Camp Furlong and is the location where most of the Historic Markers are found.

More to explore (Columbus and Pancho Villa's Raid Series): *Hachita*

95. Columbus

Location: Luna County. At the north end of Columbus, in a pullout on the west side of NM 11, between mile markers 5 and 6. See map 5.

Marker text: Columbus was founded in 1891 as a U.S./Mexico border station but eventually coalesced around the railroad station three miles to the north in 1903. The area's history is tied to a March 9, 1916, raid on Columbus by Mexican revolutionary leader Francisco "Pancho" Villa. President Woodrow Wilson dispatched General John J. Pershing and 10,000 troops into Mexico to pursue Villa. This punitive expedition ultimately failed.

96. Pancho Villa's Raid

Location: Luna County. Two markers with identical text, both in Pancho Villa State Park. One is on the opposite side of the marker for Pancho Villa's Raid. See map 5.

Marker text: On March 9, 1916, Francisco "Pancho" Villa, a major figure in the Mexican Revolution, crossed the international border with a large force, attacking and looting Columbus, New Mexico. Eighteen U.S. soldiers and civilians, and approximately 100 Villistas were killed. Gen. John J. "Black Jack" Pershing led an expeditionary force into Mexico in pursuit of Villa.

When residents of Columbus went to sleep the night of March 8, 1916, theirs was still a village with no particular historical distinction. A devastating hour of chaos the next morning changed that. New Mexico State University Library, Archives and Special Collections.

Born Doroteo Arango in Chihuahua, Mexico, in 1878, Pancho Villa was a prominent figure in the Mexican Revolution. As a contender for the presidency of Mexico, Villa had grown resentful of the support the United States had given his opponent, Venustiano Carranza. The target of his revenge, the village of Columbus, was still a developing community in 1916. It had begun in the 1890s when Colonel Andrew O. Bailey homesteaded near the border and began to develop a small community there. The small village moved three miles north in 1903 when the rails of the El

Paso and Southwestern Railroad arrived at this location and a station was built. At the time of Villa's raid, the settlement claimed seven hundred residents, four hotels, a bank, three restaurants, two barbershops, and an ice-cream parlor.

Private Fred Griffin of the Thirteenth Cavalry was posted as guard at Camp Furlong on the morning of March 9, 1916. Griffin, seeing the Villistas approaching, shouted a warning to his fellow soldiers. Villa's men shot him in the stomach.

The siege began. Mexican mercenaries burned the Commercial Hotel, killing several inside. A gunshot killed the Columbus druggist, Charles C. Miller, as he ran from the Hoover Hotel to his drugstore to get rifles for defense. The rebels marauded down Broadway Avenue, burning much of the town. Soldiers at Camp Furlong grabbed their Springfield rifles and began to return fire. Although frightened and trapped inside her building, Susan Parks, the Columbus telephone operator, rang residents to warn them of the danger.

The battle continued until just after dawn, when Villa and his men retreated to Mexico.

Although it lasted little more than an hour, the raid had left Columbus a scarred village. The Columbus State Bank served as a temporary morgue for those killed: eight American soldiers, ten Columbus residents, and ninety Mexican soldiers. One Columbus woman was among the dead—Bessie James, along with her unborn child.

General John J. ("Black Jack") Pershing, who would later lead soldiers to fame in World War I, entered Mexico in search of Villa on what was called the Punitive Expedition. With him were ten thousand soldiers and an entourage that included motorcycles, trucks, and Curtis JN-3 biplanes. It was the first time the military had used mechanized transport on an official expedition. For almost a year, Pershing and his force sought their prey, but Villa eluded them. Pershing returned to the United States on February 5, 1917, with only a few Mexican prisoners.

97. Pancho Villa State Park

Location: Luna County. There are two markers for Pancho Villa State Park, both inside the park grounds. One is on the opposite side of the marker for Pancho Villa's Raid at the entrance to the park; the other is in the center of the park. See map 5.

Marker text: Pancho Villa State Park commemorates the historic Columbus Raid of 1916. Ruins of Camp Furlong, headquarters for General John Pershing's expeditionary force, still exist at the park. The old Columbus Customs Service building has been restored to house exhibits about the raid and Pershing's Punitive Expedition into Mexico in pursuit of Pancho Villa and his raiders. Camping/picnicking sites are scattered throughout a beautiful desert botanical garden.

Pancho Villa State Park is a peaceful site, in contrast to the riotous evening of March 9, 1916, when Pancho Villa raided the small village of Columbus in which the park that now bears his name sits. Despite being named for Villa, the park surrounds and protects the ruins of Camp Furlong, the US Army base where soldiers valiantly attempted to protect the village from Villa's onslaught. Among the fort buildings preserved at the park are the headquarters building and the recreation hall.

Pancho Villa State Park was founded in 1959 and dedicated in November 1961. The park is popular with RVers for its spacious lots. Camping and picnicking sites are available, as is a walking trail through the ruins of the camp on Coote's Hill. The park has been landscaped with creosote bush, yucca, and other vegetation common to the Chihuahuan Desert.

The old Customs Service Building within the park, built in 1902, now serves duty as a museum, with displays about Villa, the raid, the camp, and the history of Columbus.

98. Comanche Country

Location: 1. Quay County. In Tucumcari, in Wailes Park at the corner of South Date Street and East Tucumcari Boulevard (the Interstate 40 business loop). See map 3.

2. Guadalupe County. In the Interstate 40 rest area east of Santa Rosa, on the north side of the highway between mile markers 301 and 302. See map 3.

Marker text: By 1700 the Comanches had acquired the horse and began moving into this area. They drove out the Jicarilla Apaches, and their raids on New Mexico's eastern frontier posed a threat to Indian, Spanish, and Anglo settlements for over a century. The Comanches were finally defeated by the U.S. Army in 1874.

After acquiring horses from Spanish settlers in the early eighteenth century, Comanche Indians divided into smaller bands and spread through the eastern plains of New Mexico, Texas, Oklahoma, and southern Colorado. Comanches became skilled and agile equestrians and parlayed their facility into a lifestyle, dominating the plains through sheer force for more than a hundred years. They were universally feared for their fierce raids. In 1723, bands of Comanches began a series of attacks against the Jicarilla Apaches, who were then living in eastern and northeastern New Mexico. These raids weakened the Jicarillas, forcing them from the eastern plains farther into New Mexico by the middle of the eighteenth century.

The word *Comanche* likely comes from the name given to the tribe by Ute Indians. That name, *Komantcia*, has been interpreted to mean "enemy." An early account of the Comanches can be found in the journal of Spanish officer Pedro de Rivera, as translated by Thomas W. Kavanagh:

Each year at a certain time, there comes to this province a nation of Indians. . . . Their name is Comanche. They never number less than 1,500. . . . They halt at whichever stopping place and set up their campaign tents, which are of buffalo hide and carried by large dogs, which they raise for this purpose. The clothing of the men does not pass the navel, and that of the women passes the knee.

Comanche raids continued after Spanish and later Anglo settlers reached what is now eastern New Mexico. Resentful of this intrusion into their territory, Comanche bands descended on villages and raided livestock from ranches on the Great Plains and in the Texas Panhandle. So devastating were these attacks that the US Army constructed Fort Bascom north of present-day Tucumcari in 1863 to protect settlers and travelers along the eastern frontier of New Mexico. Soldiers at the fort also did their futile best to curtail the dealings of the *comancheros*, desperado traders who rode into Comanche camps and bartered illegally in goods, horses, and even at times captive slaves.

The year 1874 brought a pivotal change to the last of the free-roaming Comanche bands. According to Comanche historians Joseph H. Cash and Gerald W. Wolff, a prophet appeared to the Comanche people that year with an inducement to further aggressions against Anglos. The US Army responded to the increase in hostilities with a stepped-up series of military campaigns, at least two of which involved soldiers from Fort Bascom. But it was a decisive battle between the army and Comanches and other Plains Indians in Palo Duro Canyon in Texas in 1874, where troops attacked and destroyed an Indian encampment in the canyon, that drove the last of the nomadic Comanches from the Great Plains and onto reservations.

Today the Comanche Nation maintains its headquarters in Lawton, Oklahoma.

More to explore: *Captive Women and Children of Taos County, Fort Bascom, Llano Estacado, Tucumcari*

99. Continental Divide

Locations: 1. Sandoval County. West of Cuba, in a pullout on the south side of US 550 at mile marker 76. See map 4.

2. McKinley County. At the Continental Divide exit (exit 47) from Interstate 40. See map 1.

3. Rio Arriba County. West of Chama, in a pullout on the south side of US 64 between mile markers 152 and 153. See map 2.

Marker text: Rainfall divides at this point. To the west it drains into the Pacific Ocean, to the east, into the Atlantic.

The Continental Divide, also called the Great Divide, is a geographic stripe separating the continent into two major basins. Waters on the eastern side of the divide discharge into the Atlantic Ocean via the Rio Grande and the Gulf of Mexico. Their counterparts on the western side drain into the Pacific through the Colorado River and the Gulf of California. Standing on the divide during a rainstorm, a saturated observer will witness the phenomenon of rainwater parting to flow either east or west.

The divide is a requirement, not an option, of an earth that is constantly rising. The drainage of the continent "divides" in a path that follows a series of mountain ridges (mostly the Rocky Mountains), beginning in Alaska, crossing Canada and the western United States, and continuing through Mexico. Land along the divide is rising faster than erosion, weather, and streams can wear it back down, forcing rivers and rainwater into separate drainage basins.

On its journey through New Mexico, the divide snakes a crooked eight-hundred-mile path through a miscellany of landscapes. Moving from the top of the state to the bottom, the divide begins west of Chama and weaves through the Jicarilla Apache and Navajo Indian Reservations. Then it crosses Interstate 40 through a town that straddles the divide: the aptly named settlement of Continental Divide. From Interstate 40, the divide wends its way through Cibola National Forest around Mount Taylor and runs through the southeastern section of the Ramah Navajo Indian Reservation. At Alegres Mountain near Pie Town, it reaches its highest elevation in the state—10,244 feet. After it crosses Interstate 10 about eighteen miles west of Deming, the divide enters the expanse of the Playas Valley and reaches its nadir in the state—4,460 feet. Near Antelope Wells, the divide enters Mexico.

In 1978, Congress officially designated 3,100 miles of the Continental Divide Trail as a National Scenic Trail.

More to explore: *Basin and Range Country, Jicarilla Apache Reservation, Navajo Indian Reservation, Yucca Plains*

100. Cooke's Wagon Road

Location: Luna County. West of Deming, in the rest area on the north side (westbound) of Interstate 10, after the Gage exit, between mile markers 60 and 61. See map 5.

Marker text: In 1846, while leading the Mormon Battalion to California during the Mexican War, Lt. Col. Philip St. George Cooke blazed a wagon road from New Mexico to the West Coast. The potential use of the route for the railroad construction was one of the reasons for the Gadsden Purchase in 1853. Cooke entered Arizona through Guadalupe Pass.

101. Ghost Marker: Mormon Battalion

Marker text: The Mormon Battalion, composed of 500 volunteers, left Council Bluffs, Iowa, June 5, 1846, as part of the expeditionary force of Brigadier General Kearny. They followed the Santa Fe Trail to Santa Fe and won the Rio Grande here, where it turned west ending in San Diego, California, January 30, 1847.

Note: This marker appears in an inventory of Historic Markers compiled by the Historic Preservation Division but is not in the field. See map 5.

During the Mexican-American War, the US Army placed Lieutenant Colonel Philip St. George Cooke at the head of one of the most atypical battalions in military history. Cooke, a tall, slim man with a full beard, was to lead a regiment of some 340 Mormon soldiers in blazing a wagon trail to the Pacific coast. The army had earlier convinced Mormon leader Brigham Young to lend these soldiers to the American cause in helping open the Southwest. In return, the army would march the soldiers to the coast, where they could establish new Mormon settlements.

Cooke first met his new regiment in Santa Fe on October 13, 1846. The battalion, having trooped to Santa Fe with the expeditionary force of Brigadier General Stephen Watts Kearny all the way from Council Bluffs, Iowa, presented a ragged sight. Cooke's initial impressions of the unit showed his apprehension of the task before him:

Some were too old,—some feeble, and some too young. . . . [The Battalion] was undisciplined; it was much worn by traveling on foot. . . . [T]heir clothing was very scant . . . their mules were utterly broken down.

Cooke dispatched the more sickly members and set out on October 19 with the rest, including five officer's wives and a handful of scouts. Their march largely followed the Rio Grande south through New Mexico. The regiment turned west near Hatch and passed the base of a prominent peak at the southern end of the Mimbres Mountains on November 16. That peak now bears a record of their passing in its name: Cookes Peak. Portions of the route followed by the battalion through the state had earlier been traversed by Governor Juan Bautista de Anza in 1780 as he opened his own road between Santa Fe and Sonora, Mexico. In history yet to come, the US Army in 1863 would later erect Fort Cummings in the southern shadow of Cookes Peak to protect settlers in this part of southwestern New Mexico from Indian attacks.

According to accounts of the trip, the men of the Mormon Battalion often marched double file before the wagons to press the grass and dirt flat for the wagon wheels. They fed and watered their mules and horses where they could, battled terrain that ranged from sand to mud, and burned sticks for fuel in the cool autumn evenings.

In late November, the battalion reached the Guadalupe Mountains in the far southwestern corner of New Mexico. Cooke described the location as "a very precipitous and rocky descent of perhaps a thousand feet into the heart of a wild confusion of mountains." Soldiers carefully let down their wagons through the canyon on pulley ropes. Even then, one wagon broke in the rocky crag and had to be abandoned.

The battalion crossed Arizona and reached the San Diego Mission in San Diego, California, on January 29, 1847. Cooke, proud of the accomplishment, stated: "History may be searched in vain for an equal march of infantry."

More to explore: *Deming, Fort Cummings, Trail of the Forty-Niners*

102. Córdova

Location: Rio Arriba County. About a mile and a half west of Córdova, in a pullout on the north side of US 76. See map 2.

Marker text: Originally named Pueblo Quemado, after an ancient burned-out Indian pueblo located nearby, Cordova was settled prior to 1748, but was abandoned due to Indian attacks. Permanently re-settled by 1750, the village was renamed Cordova after a prominent local family. The village chapel, San Antonio de Padua, is an outstanding example of Northern Mexico art and architecture. Cordova is home to a unique style of woodcarving begun by Jose Dolores Lopez (1868–1937).

Note: Córdova can be reached from County Road 80 off NM 76, about a mile and a half east of this Historic Marker.

Tucked away in the Quemado Valley, the small village of Córdova straddles the Rio Quemado as it flows westward from the Truchas Peaks. The word *quemado* is Spanish for "burned." The reference may be either to burned vegetation in the area or, as is sometimes suggested, the ruins of an ancient Indian pueblo once in this vicinity that may have been set afire.

The word is also found in the original name of the small Spanish village that first formed here around 1748. That village took the name Pueblo Quemado. Beset by Indian raids, primarily from Utes, the villagers abandoned their settlement soon after establishing it. Resettlement occurred only a few years later, and by 1750 the village had taken hold. One estimate showed a population of just over two hundred by 1776. The settlement retained its original name until 1900, but when a post office opened here that year, it did so under the name Córdova. (The name Quemado was already in use by another town in southwestern New Mexico.) The new name, Córdova, recognized the surname of one of the prominent families in the village.

The village church in Córdova is today a prominent historical feature on the plaza. Work on the structure began in 1832. The large church took shape in brown earth adobe at the head of the plaza. Although the building today sports a pitched tin roof, the original was flat, supported by six-foot-wide walls and large vigas that ran across the inside. At the uppermost part of the chapel, above a center window located over the front door, is a pitched-roof bell tower supporting a small cross. A small *campo santo*, or cemetery, makes up the enclosed courtyard. The original dirt floor of the nave has since been upgraded to wood. The choir loft, held in place by large timbers, rests to the left of the front entrance. Among the outstanding art that adorns the interior are hand-painted altar screens and handcrafted santos, or religious figures. Feeling that the chapel served as "a significant example of a passing era in the mountain villages of northern New Mexico," the National Park Service added the San Antonio de Padua del Quemado Chapel to the National Register of Historic Places in 1978.

One of the santos in the church was sculpted by local artist and woodcraftsman José Dolores López. Born in the village in 1868, López developed his skill in wood crafting initially as a furniture maker, but he grew to prominence as a *santero*, an artist who specializes in religious paintings and figurines. López left his figurines unpainted and otherwise unadorned, allowing the natural beauty of the wood he used, often aspen, to highlight his craftsmanship and lend an elegant simplicity to the figures. His work appealed to the stylistic preferences of a growing Anglo interest in southwestern art around the turn of the century. One of his most famous carvings, *Expulsion from the Garden of Eden*, done around 1920, depicts the exile of Adam and Eve by an angel from the Garden of Eden through the use of three standing figurines. The angel is shown with a large wing projecting from his back, his outstretched and pointing hand commanding the first couple into the world out of the garden. Eve rests her face in one hand in agony while the other hand reaches out plaintively, and

Adam is shown looking out at the barren world, his hand shielding his eyes from the sight. The art is all the more beautiful for the powerful emotions it conveys using minimal adornment.

Descendants of López continue the distinctive wood-crafting tradition to this day.

More to explore: *Chimayó, Truchas Peaks*

103. Corrales

Location: Sandoval County. At the south end of Corrales, on the west side of US 448, at mile marker 8. See map 4.

Marker text: Spanish colonization of this region, once the location of many Tiwa Indian pueblos, began in the 17th century. Corrales is named for the extensive corrals built here by Juan González, founder of Alameda. In the 18th century this rich farming area was subject to Comanche attacks and was raided by Navajos as late as 1851.

San Isidro, patron saint of farmers, is the traditional guardian of the valley. The present church is the third to bear his name. Spanish and later United States garrisons used the valley as a base of defense to protect the river settlements of Albuquerque and Bernalillo and nearby pueblos and towns from Navajo raids.

104. Iglesia de San Ysidro

Location: Sandoval County. In Corrales, in the courtyard of the Iglesia de San Ysidro on Old Church Road. See map 4.

Marker text: This church was constructed in 1868 following a flood which demolished an earlier building. Dedicated to San Ysidro, patron of farmers, the church incorporates materials salvaged from the original structure. The building is one of the finest surviving examples of mid-19th century New Mexico religious architecture. It is maintained by the Corrales Historical Society and used for community functions and other cultural events.

The upset resulting from the Pueblo Revolt of 1680 dispersed the Indians living between Bernalillo and Isleta Pueblo, an area the Spanish had called the Province of Tiguex. The region lay relatively empty until the founding of Albuquerque in 1706, after which Spanish settlement progressed into the neighboring river valleys north and south of that town. In 1710, military officer Captain Francisco Montes Vigil received the 106,274-acre San Carlos de Alameda land grant encompassing this area. Two years later, Bernalillo resident Captain Juan Gonzáles purchased the grant from its recipient, who had not yet settled it, and built a large ranch home near the southern end of the land. The village of Alameda arose around the Gonzáles homestead. The community survives today.

To pen the horses, cattle, and sheep of their stock, settlers in Alameda erected corrals just north of their village. A small assembly of ranches grew around the stockyards as the grant was parceled and sold. Those homes took the descriptive name under which the region had earlier fallen: Los Corrales, Spanish for "the Corrals."

Raids by hostile Comanche and Navajo Indians punctuated the otherwise pastoral agricultural lives of early Corrales residents. Spanish soldiers patrolled the area in an attempt to prevent these attacks, using Corrales as a base for their operations. Later, when New Mexico came under the control of the United States, American soldiers continued this protection. The valley was subject to Navajo raids as late as 1851, some five years after the American occupation.

Corrales residents and those of other settlements in the middle Rio Grande Valley regard San Isidro, sometimes seen as San Ysidro or, in English, Saint Isidore, as their patron saint. San Isidro was a farmer in eleventh-century Madrid whose devotion led him to pray even as he plowed his fields. Sometime in the 1700s, the people of

Corrales built their first church and dedicated it to his patronage, but an unrepentant flood in early July 1868 destroyed the small building beyond repair. Residents erected a new, cruciform-shape church, the Iglesia de San Ysidro, on higher ground and laid its adobe walls three feet thick as a buttress against future inundations. Workers adorned the interior with statues of saints that had survived the flood. They also incorporated salvaged timbers into the new structure, including a lintel over the doorway. The distinctive twin bell towers and pitched tin roof, which replaced the original flat roof to give the structure protection against rain, appeared with later renovations. For its historic value to the community, the church was added to the National Register of Historic Places in 1980.

The Iglesia de San Ysidro ministered to Corrales until a new church building took over the role in 1966. Today, the old church, now desanctified, functions as a community center.

More to explore: *Albuquerque, Bernalillo, Dulcelina Salce Curtis, San Isidro Catholic Church (see under Agua Fria)*

105. Couse-Sharp Historic Site
146 Kit Carson Road

Location: Taos County. In Taos, at the Taos County Administrative and Judicial Complex, 105 Albright Street. See map 2.

Marker text: The Site's many structures include three studios of Taos Society of Artists founders Eanger Irving Couse, its first president, and Joseph Henry Sharp. Both artists trained in Europe and became nationally recognized for their paintings of native cultures and the Taos landscape. Couse lived on the property in a residence dating from the 1830's. His home was a gathering place for the Society's artists. Their art and reputation led to Taos becoming a famous art colony.

The artist economy that flourishes in Taos today got a major boost in September 1898 when the wagon carrying artists Bert Greer Phillips and Ernest L. Blumenschein, on their way from New York to Mexico, broke down in the area. Even though the broken wagon wheel was quickly repaired, it didn't get much use. Phillips and Blumenschein were smitten by the landscape of the Taos area and decided to stay. They invited their artist friends and colleagues, most from studios in the East, to join them, and in July 1915 they collectively formed the Taos Society of Artists. The society, through which the artists marketed their works, brought prominence and worldwide recognition to the art industry in Taos.

Serving as the society's first president was Michigan native Eanger Irving Couse, who had studied painting in Chicago and Paris before accepting Blumenschein's invitation to come to Taos in 1902. While some members of the society, including founder Blumenschein, did not remain in New Mexico, others—like Couse—split their time between Taos and other parts of the country. Couse moved into an older adobe home on Kit Carson Street dating from 1839, a block from the plaza. He added a studio to the property in 1909, and there he began the work for which he would become most famous. Using local Indians from Taos Pueblo as models, Couse painted scenes depicting Native Americans painting, playing flutes, tracking animals, or simply out in the natural landscape of the Southwest. He often posed his models in his studio, took their photograph, and then painted from the photograph. His studio, in fact, included a darkroom where Couse developed his own negatives. When the Santa Fe Railway began to purchase some of Couse's art for their promotional material, his work became internationally recognized.

Along with the Couse studio, the Couse-Sharp

Historic Site also preserves the house and gardens in which Couse and his family lived while in Taos. The house contains a number of small surprises, including a playroom hidden behind a bookcase and a bed that folds into a table.

The Couse property adjoined that of Couse's friend and fellow society member Joseph Henry Sharp. Ohio-born Sharp visited New Mexico periodically starting in the 1890s and bought a house next to the Couse property in 1908. Between his house and the Couse home was a small adobe church, which had been built by the original owner of the Couse home. The following year, Sharp purchased the church from the Catholic diocese and converted it into his studio. He called it the "Studio of the Copper Bell" for the bell he purchased at Taos Pueblo and hung in the church belfry. The studio offered a quiet, reflective place to paint, with walls almost three feet thick and light entering through enlarged windows that Sharp had added near what had been the altar. Sharp also built and used a second studio with a loft south of the church. In his studios, Sharp, like Couse, painted portraits of Taos Indians, often showing them against the landscape of the Southwest.

The Couse-Sharp property was added to the National Register of Historic Places in 2005.

More to explore: *Georgia O'Keeffe, Pablita Velarde (see under Pueblo of Santa Clara), San Patricio, Taos, The Three Fates*

106. Cuba

Location: 1. Sandoval County. On the north end of Cuba, in a pullout on the south side of US 550, between mile markers 65 and 66. See map 4.

2. Sandoval County. On the south end of Cuba, in a pullout on the east side of US 550, between mile markers 63 and 64. See map 4.

Marker text: In 1769, Spanish Governor Pedro Fermin de Mendinueta made the San Joaquin del Nacimiento land grant to 35 pioneering families who had settled the headwaters of the Rio Puerco in 1766. The community was later abandoned, owing to raids by frontier Indian tribes, but was resettled in the late 1870s. Originally known as Nacimiento or La Laguna, it was renamed Cuba when the post office was established in 1887.

Spanish settlement in the Cuba region began around 1766, when thirty-five families came to build homes near the headwaters of the Rio Puerco, or "Muddy River," where those turgid waters flowed from the Sierra Nacimiento. These settlers established a small farming and ranching village along the river and, in 1769, appealed to Governor Pedro Fermín de Mendinueta for official possession of the land they had occupied. The governor obliged, awarding the Pueblo de Señor San Joaquín del Nacimiento del Rio Puerco grant.

Although these early settlers of Nacimiento, as the village was commonly known, made valiant attempts to maintain their property, constant raids by Navajo Indians made life in the frontier village a battle hard fought. In desperation, settlers abandoned their homes and fields only a few years later and migrated to other communities.

The region remained unoccupied until 1879, when two families from nearby Jemez settled east of the original village. Early histories describe the region then as replete with lakes and cattail-lined swamps, which may explain why these settlers named their community Laguna. Laguna formed the nucleus of several smaller closely knit villages, including Lagunitas, Gonzalitas, Agua Pa, and Los Pinos, communities that have now condensed. Residents made a living by harvesting wheat and corn, raising sheep, and logging timber in the surrounding mountains. Mining boosted the credentials of the town, with the earth here bearing coal, gold, silver, and copper.

When the settlement opened its first post office in 1887, residents chose Cuba as the official name. No association with the country of Cuba was intended. Rather, the name in Spanish can mean a watery draw and likely referred to one of the basins so generous in the area.

The same mountains and streams that attracted early settlers to the region today attract tourists and outdoor enthusiasts. The Forest Service has established a ranger station in Cuba, and the town serves as a gateway to the Santa Fe National Forest.

More to explore: *Curanderas—Women Who Heal, Jemez Mountains, Valle Grande*

Cumbres and Toltec Scenic Railroad: *see Chama*

107. Cumbres Pass

Location: Rio Arriba County. At Cumbres Pass, just along the New Mexico–Colorado border, on the south side of NM 17 between mile markers 8 and 9. See map 2.

Marker text: A major encounter between the U.S. Army and a large group of Utes and Jicarilla Apaches occurred here in July 1848. Old Bill Williams, the famous scout and guide, was badly wounded while fighting the Utes, who had once adopted him as a tribesman.

As rugged as the mountains he called home, William Sherley Williams, better known as "Old Bill" Williams, was the archetypal mountain man, a slim, bearded, solitary figure hunting beaver pelts in the rocky frontiers of the Southwest. Williams was born in North Carolina on January 3, 1787. He spent his early years spreading the Baptist gospel with missionary ardor along the Missouri circuit. Later, after learning to speak the languages of many Indian tribes, Williams lived with both the Osage Indians and later the Ute Indians of the southern Colorado mountains while trapping along sparkling mountain streams.

Author Albert Pike, who met the mountain man on his travels in the Southwest in the mid-nineteenth century, vividly captured Williams's character in a first-hand sketch:

He is a man about six feet one inch in height, gaunt, and red-headed, with a hard, weather-beaten face, marked deeply with the small pox. He is all muscle and sinew, and the most indefatigable hunter and trapper in the world. He has no glory except in the woods, and his whole ambition is to kill more deer and catch more beaver than any other man about him. Nothing tires him, not even running all day with six traps on his back.

In early 1848, Williams betrayed the Ute tribe by exchanging pelts they had entrusted to him for liquor. He did not return to the Indians after his act, but instead enlisted as a guide with an American army expedition under the command of Major W. W. Reynolds. On July 8, Major Reynolds, Williams, and some 150 soldiers marched out of Taos into the Sangre de Cristo Mountains to strike against the Utes, his former adopted tribe.

The decisive battle occurred July 23 here, in Cumbres Pass, a scenic corridor cutting through the San Juan Mountains. As recounted in the *Santa Fe Republican* on August 1, 1848:

The engagement lasted but 2 or 3 hours, the Indians fighting like a set of desperadoes, and the Americans with equal spirit. The loss of the Indians were some twenty or twenty-five killed, and a large number wounded. The Americans had two killed and six wounded. . . . Also, Old Bill Williams was shot in the arm, shattering it most horrible, at the first fire, but he managed to use it so as to keep his rifle hot during the engagement.

The following year, Williams and an ally entered the Raton Mountains to retrieve supplies stored by an earlier expedition. Several Ute Indians came upon Williams and opened fire. Williams took a fatal bullet to the skull. The trapper died on March 14, 1849.

More to explore: *Jicarilla Apache (series)*

108. Curanderas—Women Who Heal

Location: Mora County. In Mora, in a pullout on the north side of NM 518, between mile markers 29 and 30. See map 3.

Marker text: In New Mexico, women blessed with special knowledge of herbs, household remedies, human health and strong faith are trusted to cure real or imagined maladies. Known as Curanderas, these women have been an integral part of the Hispanic fabric in Mora County and in the more remote communities around the state. They oversee the well-being of their respective villages where medical doctors and clinics are scarce.

Curanderas have been part of the cultural fabric of traditional Hispanic villages in New Mexico since the state's colonial days. Curanderas combine their knowledge of holistic and spiritual remedies, mixed with an ounce of empathy and a pinch of common sense, to maintain the health and well-being of people in their community. One particular subset of curanderas includes *parteras*, or midwives. Indeed, the partera for a village might also be the curandera, but not always. Curanderas are women; their male counterparts are known as *curanderos*. The root of the word comes from the Spanish *curar*, meaning "to heal."

In the healing process, a curandera attempts to balance the energies of her patient, often by removing negative energy, which is believed to be the cause of many maladies. This is done in a number of ways. The curandera might rub an egg (still in the shell) over her patient in order to draw negative energy out of the body. Or she might stroke herbs and flowers and sprinkle fragrant water over her patient as part of a spiritual *limpia*, or cleansing. She might also ask a patient to drink a special tea she has prepared from herbs to banish anger or to ease pain.

The origins of *curanderismo*, the name of the practice itself, are difficult to pinpoint, but experts believe that they have deep roots. When the Spanish arrived in Mexico in the sixteenth century, they may have brought with them medicinal knowledge of plants and ritualistic healing. Many of those practices, in turn, show an earlier Moorish influence. When Spanish settlement began in New Mexico after 1598, the healing practices followed and then developed organically as local practitioners incorporated elements from the practices of the native people of the Southwest. Even today, new practices merge with the old as the art continues to evolve.

In the early years of New Mexico, doctors and priests were few. Curanderas filled a need in smaller, more remote villages in New Mexico by providing healing services where access to modern medicine was difficult to come by. New Mexico is a large state with many rural areas; poverty, language barriers, poor infrastructure, and other impediments have challenged medical professionals in their attempts to provide quality health care to people living away from the state's metropolitan centers. A curandera, then, might fill the role of doctor, priest, midwife, pharmacist, and even counselor.

Curanderas were (and are) often well known and respected in their villages, practicing a craft that may have been handed down and taught to them from previous generations of their family. Often they were not paid for their services, but they might barter for another service.

A story gathered by the Works Progress Administration (WPA) from northern New Mexico in 1940 gives insight into the work of curanderas at that time:

Before [the curandera] left home, she gathered all the remedios [natural remedies] she thought might be needed, and took them with her. She stayed at the patient's bedside treating them with the remedios, until the sick one either got better, or died. She would use one remedio after another, and sometimes two or three at the same time. If the sick got well, she was praised for it. If she or he died, it was because God willed it so, and she was not to blame. The curandera never charged for her work. When asked how much was owed her—they knew she would not charge them—she would reply that it was nothing "just what you want to give me."

Recently, a desire to reclaim the tradition of curanderismo is leading to a revival of interest in the practice in New Mexico.

More to explore: *Chimayó, Magnolia Ellis, Parteras of New Mexico*

109. Dawson

Location: Colfax County. At Dawson Cemetery, about fourteen miles northeast of Cimarron, at the end of County Road A38, five miles west of US 64. See map 3.

Marker text: Dawson was established by the Phelps Dodge Corporation in 1901 to develop the region's vast coal deposits. In its heyday, it was the largest company mining town in New Mexico, with many modern amenities and a population of more than 6000. Named after John Dawson, who owned part of the historic Beaubien-Miranda land grant on which it is located, the town was abandoned when the mines closed in 1950.

110. Dawson Cemetery

Marker text: This was the cemetery for the coal mining town of Dawson. Its grave markers reflect the diverse immigrant populations which came to this country seeking a better life, and which fueled American industrial development. Hundreds of identical crosses, which mark the graves of miners killed in mine accidents in 1913 and 1923, demonstrate the great sacrifices of these pioneers.

Note: Marker faceplates are on opposite sides of the same sign. See map 3.

Often, it is the cemetery that bears the responsibility of relating the story of a town, especially when that town exists no longer. The story of Dawson Cemetery, and of the town of Dawson itself, begins officially in 1906, the year the Stag Canyon branch of the Phelps Dodge Corporation purchased the settlement, then only a five-year-old mining camp, from developer Charles B. Eddy for $16 million. Eddy had bought the mineral rights to the land in 1901 from John Barkley Dawson, for whom he had named the camp. Dawson had been the first to discover coal on this land, which he, in turn, had purchased in 1869 from an heir to the larger Beaubien-Miranda land grant for a comparatively cheap $3,700.

Dawson was the only coal-producing town owned by Phelps Dodge, which may explain why the company transformed it into one of the most beautiful company towns in the country. Dawsonites, as residents called themselves, enjoyed luxuries not typically found in mining camps, including a movie theater, a bowling alley, a twenty-six-bed hospital, an excellent school system (the high school football team was named the Miners)—even a golf course.

Phelps Dodge wrapped its protective arms around the coal-mining camp of Dawson, making the settlement one of the largest and most prominent company towns in the United States. Dawson, New Mexico, 1917. Adella Collier Photograph Collection, 1978-030, Album 1, Image 32046. Courtesy New Mexico State Records Center and Archives.

"There are no shacks," one 1917 account of the town summed up.

As was true with the populations of many New Mexico mining camps, miners who worked the ten separate mines in Dawson had immigrated from Italy, Greece, and Mexico, among other countries. This diversity is evidenced by the surnames on grave markers in the cemetery. The most heartbreaking of those markers may be the rows and rows of identical white trefoil crosses. Making up half the cemetery burials, they are reminders of the two greatest tragedies of the town, mining disasters that rank among the worst in US history.

Crosses closest to the mountain recall the victims of the first tragedy, an explosion in Mine no. 2 on October 22, 1913. Two hundred and sixty three miners lost their lives when coal dust throughout the mine burst into flames from an overcharged shot, an explosion that was said to have sent flames roaring more than two hundred feet out from the tunnel opening. Phelps Dodge paid all burial expenses and offered bereaved widows money to return to Europe if they desired. Almost a decade later, on February 8, 1923, tragedy again befell the town when a derailed train inside Mine no. 1 knocked over feed wires to ignite coal dust. The resulting explosion ripped through a tunnel, being worked by 124 men. Only two survived.

The most recent graves in the cemetery date to 1949, a year before Dawson became a casualty of a changing world. With the demand for coal diminishing as railroads shifted to diesel fuel, Phelps

Dodge was forced in late February of the following year to alert Dawsonites that the mines were closing and the town was to be abandoned. Bit by bit, the town came apart, literally, as workers dismantled homes, stores, and schools and moved elsewhere—all within the span of a month's time. Phelps Dodge officials sold what property remained for scrap. By the end of April 1950, Dawson was gone.

More to explore: *Carthage-Tokay-Farley, Elizabethtown, Riley, Seven Rivers Cemetery, Shakespeare*

111. Deming

Location: Luna County. On the north side of Deming, on the west side of US 180. See map 5.

Marker text: In 1780, Governor Juan Bautista de Anza passed near here while searching for a trade route between Santa Fe and the mines of Sonora, Mexico. Deming was founded in 1881 when the Santa Fe and Southern Pacific Railroads were connected, giving New Mexico its first railway access to both the Atlantic and the Pacific.

A true wayfarer, Governor Juan Bautista de Anza laid a path near Deming that would later be followed in part by the Mormon Battalion and subsequent generations of travelers. Juan Bautista de Anza, from a painting by Fray Orci, Mexico City, 1774. Courtesy Palace of the Governors Photo Archives (NMHM/DCA), neg. no. 50828.

Juan Bautista de Anza, one of the governors of New Mexico while the land was under the authority of the Spanish Crown, had been in office only two years when he set out from Santa Fe on November 9, 1780, to open a wagon road that would run the seven hundred miles between the capital and Arizpe, in Sonora, Mexico. Anza, a Sonora native with prior military and path-finding experience, hoped that his new road would allow greater movement of trade goods into Santa Fe and link the New Mexico economy with that of the lucrative Sonora silver mines.

Commanding a battalion of some sixty soldiers, fifty-five militiamen, and about half as many Indian guides, Governor Anza followed the course of the Rio Grande southward from Santa Fe along the Camino Real, or Royal Road, a trade route running to Mexico. Near Hatch, the expedition veered westward to pass the southern rim of the Mimbres Mountains. After pausing overnight to drink the bracing waters at what would later be known as Cookes Spring, Anza led his men south through the area of present-day Deming. Anza and his tired crew made their successful arrival in Arizpe on December 6, 1780.

A hundred and one years after Anza passed through, officials with the Atchison, Topeka, and Santa Fe Railway, along with their counterparts at the Southern Pacific Railroad, congregated in what was soon to become the town of Deming to mark another historic crossing. The date was March 8, 1881, and the crews with great ceremony drove into the ground a silver spike—connecting their two lines into the second transcontinental railroad in the country.

In anticipation of that spike, settlers had already formed a small camp at the site, which they named New Chicago. When the Southern Pacific Railroad selected a spot several miles west of Little Chicago for its depot, the village withered as settlers put together a new town around the roundhouse and repair shops of the railroad. The settlement grew quickly, with a townsite platted within two weeks of the spike-driving ceremony. Charles Crocker, an official with Southern Pacific, named the new town for his wife, Mary Anne Deming.

A year later, Deming had a school system, several hotels, a newspaper, and soon thereafter a customhouse to process goods that travelers were bringing into the country from Mexico. By 1901, the town had the wherewithal to become the county seat of the newly formed Luna County.

More to explore: *Cooke's Wagon Road, El Camino Real—The King's Highway*

D. H. Lawrence Ranch: *see The Three Fates*

112. Disappearance of Albert J. Fountain and His Son Henry

Location: Doña Ana County. East of Las Cruces, on the south side of US 70 at mile marker 178. See map 5.

Marker text: Albert Jennings Fountain was a Civil War veteran, New Mexico legislator and prominent lawyer. On February 1, 1896, Fountain and his eight-year-old son, Henry, were traveling home to Mesilla from Lincoln. They carried grand jury indictments against cattle rustlers. Both disappeared at Chalk Hill, and their bodies were never found. In 1899 Oliver Lee and James Gililland were tried for their murder. Both were acquitted.

Having secured indictments for "larceny of cattle" against wealthy southeastern New Mexico rancher Oliver M. Lee at the Lincoln County courthouse in Lincoln, Albert J. Fountain was driving his wagon home to Mesilla on Sunday, February 1, 1896. Beside him sat his eight-year-old son, Henry. Fountain was anxious to get home, as the cold winter air had given young Henry a chill.

Neither one arrived.

Few other incidents in the history of southwestern New Mexico have inspired the anger, grief, or controversy that surrounds the disappearance and presumed murder of Albert Jennings Fountain. More than a hundred years after Fountain and his son left Lincoln, the location of their bodies, as well as the truth about what happened to them along that lonely road that lonely winter evening, remain unknown.

Fountain had come to New Mexico in 1862 as a member of the Union Army's California Column. After the Civil War, Fountain settled in Mesilla to practice law. He rose quickly in community standing, marrying into a wealthy Hispanic family and founding a newspaper in Mesilla, *The Republican*. Around 1896, the Southeastern New Mexico Stock Growers Association, comprising mostly small ranchers from the Tularosa Valley, enlisted his services to investigate charges of cattle rustling within the ranching operations of Oliver Milton Lee. Lee, a magnate of southeastern New Mexico, had moved to the Tularosa Valley from Texas in 1892 and established a vast cattle domain—so vast that many believed his holdings included cattle that properly belonged to other ranches. Fountain traveled to Lincoln County in late January with his son to obtain grand jury indictments against

Albert Jennings Fountain was a soldier, legislator, newspaper editor, and lawyer. His willingness to challenge men as prominent as he was may have led to his death. Albert J. Fountain. Courtesy Palace of the Governors Photo Archives (NMHM/DCA), neg. no. 9873.

Lee and several other men for cattle rustling. He had started the return trip to Mesilla with those papers in hand.

Suspicions in Fountain's disappearance fell immediately on Lee. Still, Doña Ana County sheriff Pat Garrett, most famous for having killed Billy the Kid fifteen years earlier while sheriff of Lincoln County, uncovered little evidence against the rancher despite two years of searching and a $10,000 reward for recovery of the Fountain bodies. When Garrett did finally file charges against Lee and his ranch hand, James Gilliland, the men enlisted the services of prominent southern New Mexico lawyer Albert Fall in their defense. The prosecuting attorney would be Santa Fe lawyer Thomas Benton Catron, who hoped to aid his case by charging the men not with the murder of Albert Fountain but with that of his son, Henry.

The trial venue moved to Sierra County, away from the sympathies traditionally falling to Fountain in Doña Ana County and those falling to Lee in the newly created Otero County. During the proceedings in 1898 in Hillsboro, then the Sierra County seat, spectators filled the brick courthouse to capacity. On the final day of the three-week trial, Fall offered an impassioned speech implicating Catron and others in a "conspiracy to send an innocent man to the gallows."

The jury deliberated eight minutes before reaching a verdict. With no bodies to produce as evidence of foul play, they acquitted Oliver Lee and James Gilliland of murder and dropped all other charges.

More to explore: Hillsboro Historic District, La Mesilla, Pat Garrett Murder Site, Three Rivers, Tularosa

113. Dog Canyon

Location: Otero County. South of Alamogordo, in a pullout on the west side of US 82, between mile markers 55 and 56, across from the entrance to Oliver Lee State Park. See map 6.

Marker text: For the Mescalero Apaches, Dog Canyon was a favorite camping area and trail through the Sacramento Mountains. It was the scene of several battles in the 19th century. In 1861, a group of Mescaleros was attacked by soldiers, and the survivors were sent to the Bosque Redondo Reservation.

Dog Canyon cuts through the western foothills of the Sacramento Mountains, forming a natural pass from the Tularosa Basin eastward into the heavily forested mountains. Mescalero Apache Indians, who lived and hunted in this part of southern New Mexico for many years before the arrival of Spanish and Anglo settlers, used the canyon and its natural springs as a camping area, the sheer canyon walls providing defensive cover for their campsites.

As Hispanic and Anglo settlers began moving into the Southwest in the mid-nineteenth century, including the Tularosa Basin, they encroached on the traditional homelands of Apaches and other Indians of the region. Indian raids attempting to forestall this encroachment were met with retaliation, and the US government stepped in to attempt to quell a hostile frontier. One ill-advised plan included moving the Navajos of northwestern New Mexico and the Mescalero Apaches to the Bosque Redondo Reservation at Fort Sumner, about 150 miles northeast of here. To help enact that plan, General James H. Carleton, commander of the Military District of New Mexico, ordered army officer and former scout Colonel Kit Carson to conduct a series of harsh scorched-earth campaigns against the Navajo and Apache tribes to force them from their homes and onto the new reservation.

Carson was ordered to occupy Fort Stanton in 1862, a military post about fifty miles north of Dog Canyon near the town of Lincoln. That fort had been abandoned when Confederate troops moved through New Mexico during the Civil War. Fort Stanton became a base of operations for Carson and other soldiers garrisoning the fort in their attempts to gather Mescalero Apache Indians and move them to Bosque Redondo. The orders Carson had received, in fact, were quite specific. "All Indian men of that tribe are to be killed whenever and wherever you can find them," Carleton had written in a memo in October 1862. "The women and children will not be harmed, but you will take them prisoners, and feed them at Fort Stanton until you receive other instructions about them."

Several skirmishes had occurred in this canyon prior to that memo; in one, soldiers found a small dog in an Indian campsite, a discovery now remembered in the name of the canyon itself: Dog Canyon. A major battle took place in November 1862, when three separate commands from Fort Stanton approached the site from the north, south, and east—the latter moving toward the camp through Dog Canyon. That company, under the command of Captain William McCleave, came upon an Indian encampment at the mouth of the canyon populated by an estimated five hundred Mescalero Apache Indians. The soldiers attacked the camp. After the battle, the Indians who had survived made their way through the Sacramento Mountains to Fort Stanton and Colonel Kit Carson himself, to whom they appealed for peace. They were taken to the Bosque Redondo Reservation.

The reservation at Bosque Redondo was short-lived—ill-conceived from the start, it quickly buckled under the weight of its own flaws. Disease and crop failures decimated the Navajo and Apache Indians forced to live there. Finally, in 1868, the government closed the reservation. The Navajos returned to their homelands in northwestern New Mexico, and the Mescalero Apaches who had not already escaped the confines of the reservation returned to the Sacramento Mountains.

Today, Dog Canyon is part of Oliver Lee State Park. Named for prominent area rancher and politician Oliver Lee, the park preserves Lee's ranch house, which he built at the mouth of the canyon in 1893. Visitors can hike the Dog Canyon National Recreational Trail through the canyon.

More to explore: *Fort Stanton, Fort Sumner and Fort Sumner State Monument (series), Tularosa*

114. Domínguez-Escalante Trail

Location: Rio Arriba County. Just north of Española, in a pullout on the east side of US 84/285, at mile marker 192. See map 2.

Marker text: On July 29, 1776, two Franciscans, Fray Francisco Atanasio Domínguez and Fray Silvestre Velez de Escalante set out on horseback on an expedition from Santa Fe, New Mexico to Monterey, California. The purpose of the expedition was two-fold: to open communications between the two missions (Santa Fe and Monterey) and to covert the Indians (Utes and Havasupais) between pueblo land and the Pacific Coast. The party did not reach Monterey, however, but only got as far as the Utah Basin. Due to the onset of winter weather, lack of provisions and frequent desertion of Indian guides, their goal was reconsidered, causing much dissension. Lots were cast to continue or return to Santa Fe. Thus it was decided to turn back to Santa Fe.

On July 29, 1776, a journey that would eventually reach more than two thousand miles began when two Franciscan priests left the plaza in Santa Fe on horseback, headed northwest. The Spanish government had asked Fray Francisco Atanasio Domínguez, head of the Franciscan Order in New Mexico, to investigate the possibility of an overland route between Santa Fe and the recently founded mission in the seaport of Monterey, California. Domínguez selected twenty-five-year-old Fray Silvestre Vélez de Escalante, a former priest at the missions of Laguna and Zuni Pueblos in New Mexico, as his partner in the effort. A handful of associates traveled with the duo, including a cartographer, Bernardo Miera y Pacheco, whose maps of the journey would later give the European world its first glimpse of these uncharted reaches.

With horses, pack mules, and supplies, the priests passed Tesuque Pueblo, Pojoaque Pueblo, and Nambé Pueblo on their first day out, and spent the night at Santa Clara Pueblo. From there, they continued along the course of the Rio Chama along the base of the Jemez Mountains to Abiquiú, the last Spanish settlement before the northern frontier. On August 1, the expedition left the Rio Chama, then crossed into present-day Colorado four days later. There, the party of intrepid explorers received guides in the form of two *genízaros*, Hispanicized Indians, who led the men across the Colorado River and into western Utah.

On October 6, while still in the Utah Basin, the priests awoke to an unexpected snowfall. Heavy flakes scattered over their camp without pause for three straight days as driving winds assailed the shivering men. The guides fled, fearing the onslaught of an early winter. Dissension arose within the group over whether to abandon or continue the journey. Some men, not wanting to call it quits after having come so far, urged the others to continue, even though they were unsure of their exact location and did not know what lay ahead. Others, including Domínguez and Escalante, thought it prudent to turn back. As Escalante explained in his diary:

We feared that long before we arrived, the passes would be closed and we would be delayed for two or three months in some sierra . . . and so we would expose ourselves to death from hunger if not from cold.

In 1776, two Franciscan friars embarked on a remarkable journey, narrowly avoided disaster, and returned with maps that would give the European world its first glimpse of the uncharted territory between Santa Fe and California. The Domínguez-Escalante voyage covered some two thousand miles. Illustration by David Carter.

At last, the men agreed to cast lots between two choices: continue to Monterey or return to Santa Fe. No records survive to specify how the decision was made, but the outcome is known. Fate chose the latter, and the defeated expedition began the trek home.

In November, the forlorn party reached Zuni Pueblo, Escalante's former missionary post. Exhausted, the men rested for three weeks before resuming their travels. They celebrated Christmas at Isleta Pueblo, south of Albuquerque, and arrived back in Santa Fe on January 2, 1777.

More to explore: *Abiquiú, Old Spanish Trail, Pueblo of Isleta Tuei, Pueblo of Zuni*

115. Doña Ana
On the Camino Real

Location: Doña Ana County. In Doña Ana, at the intersection of Doña Ana Road and Thorpe Road. See map 5.

Marker text: This site, named after the legendary woman Doña Ana, is first mentioned as a paraje along the Camino Real. Spanish rested near here as they retreated from New Mexico following the Pueblo Revolt of 1680. The community was founded in 1843 as the Doña Ana Bend Colony Grant. Today, both the village and the historic Catholic church, Nuestra Senora De Purificatión, are on the National Register of Historic Places.

116. Doña Ana (1604–1680)

Location: Doña Ana County. In Doña Ana, in a pullout on the north side of NM 320 (Thorpe Road), between mile markers 1 and 2. See map 5.

Marker text: The name of the county of Doña Ana originates from Doña Ana Robledo, who died near here while fleeing south with other settlers during the 1680 Pueblo Revolt. She was buried below the peak that now bears her surname in the Robledo Mountains, so named in memory of her grandfather who was buried there in 1598.

When the lower Rio Grande again overflowed its banks and rushed through the fields of El Paso–area farmer Jose Maria Costales, he and 116 of his frustrated neighbors petitioned the governor of Chihuahua in 1839 for a grant of unsettled land to the north where they could plant new fields. The land conferred to them was near a *paraje*, or camping spot, along the route between Mexico and Santa Fe known as El Camino Real, the Royal Road. That paraje had become known as Doña Ana sometime in the seventeenth century.

The title *doña* in Spanish is similar to "Lady" in English. There are two possible women who may have been the lady known as doña Ana. One is doña Ana Córdova, a widowed woman believed to have been the owner of a large hacienda and orchard in the area. The second is doña Ana Robledo, the woman recognized in the Historic Marker.

If doña Ana Robledo existed, her story is a sad one. It begins with the documented death of a man named Pedro Robledo, a colonist with the 1598 expedition of Juan de Oñate. Robledo passed away near this location in that year while traveling with Oñate and other settlers north from Mexico to establish the first Spanish settlement in what is now New Mexico. Robledo was buried near here, and the mountains to the west, the Robledo Mountains, were later named in his honor. That much is true. In a tragedy worthy of folklore, it has also been said that his granddaughter, Ana Robledo, then a widow more than seventy years old, perished near this same location in 1680 while fleeing south from Santa Fe from the Indian uprising known as the Pueblo Revolt. The thought of a woman dying near the very site where her grandfather had died many years earlier, one traveling north, the other south, is certainly hard to bear, if it happened—and certainly worthy of being remembered as a toponym. Whether true or not, and regardless of which doña Ana is being recognized here, it's worth noting that the name survives as well in the larger county that surrounds this village: Doña Ana County.

In the spring of 1843, thirty-three of the original petitioning families arrived to settle the Doña Ana Bend Colony Grant. They built small, flat-roofed adobe houses, and later a church. To irrigate their fields, they constructed an acequia, or irrigation ditch, to channel water from the Rio Grande, and then they planted staples of corn and beans. Within a year, the struggling colony at Doña Ana had a population of 261 residents. Although Apache attacks hampered development of the village, the colonists adapted. Each day, thirty men went together to farm while the rest stayed home to protect the village.

Doña Ana was for many years the principal settlement between Socorro and El Paso along the Camino Real. Between it and Socorro to the north lay a lonely and treacherous ninety-mile stretch of the Chihuahuan Desert today known as the Jornada del Muerto, or Journey of the Dead Man. This *despoblado*, or unpopulated region, was the frequent site of attacks by hostile Indians. Doña Ana was one of the last places for travelers headed north to find water or shelter before entering the arid desert; and, for those heading south, the first place to count their blessings for having survived the journey.

An account by John Russell Bartlett, who helped survey the boundary between the United States and Mexico in 1851, offers a description of the village as it then appeared:

Doña Ana is a small town of five or six hundred inhabitants and stands upon a spur of the plateau, fifty or sixty feet above the bottom lands, thereby commanding a wide prospect of the adjacent country. It has been settled but a few years, and was selected on account of the broad and rich valley near, and the facilities that existed for irrigating it. Its houses are mostly of a class called jacales, *i.e., built of upright sticks, their interstices filled with mud, though a better class of adobe buildings have just been erected along the main street for the occupation of the military, and for places of business.*

In the 1860s, settlers constructed the Nuestra Señora de Purificatión Church, or "Our Lady of Purification." The prominent building, constructed of adobe in a cruciform design and featuring a small bell tower (since replaced), still stands. It is considered the oldest church building in southern New Mexico.

The arrival of the railroad in the late nineteenth century shifted the population and economies of southern New Mexico from Doña Ana to Las Cruces. In 1985, the National Park Service included the Nuestra Señora de Purificatión Church in the National Register of Historic Places, noting that it "has become a landmark to the people of the Mesilla Valley." The historic village of Doña Ana itself was added to the national register in 1996.

More to explore: *Bartlett Garcia Continental Survey Point, El Camino Real—The King's Highway, Jornada del Muerto, Paraje de Robledo*

117. Doña Dolores "Lola" Chávez de Armijo (1858–1929)

Location: Bernalillo County. In northeastern Albuquerque, in a pullout on the south side of NM 556 (Tramway Road), between mile markers 5 and 6. See map 4.

Marker text: In 1912, State Librarian Lola Chávez de Armijo filed a gender discrimination law suit after the governor sought to replace her by court order, claiming that as a woman, she was unqualified to hold office under the constitution and laws of New Mexico. The New Mexico Supreme Court ruled in her favor and legislation followed, thereafter allowing women to hold appointed office.

Libraries are usually quiet places, where people research and study and where conversations are held in hushed tones. But a library in New Mexico in 1912 became a noisy battleground, metaphorically, and a librarian spoke out loudly for her rights—and for the rights of all women in New Mexico.

Upset that his nominee to replace the incumbent state librarian had been rejected by the state legislature, newly elected governor William C. McDonald tried a different approach. He took the matter to court. The librarian at the time, Dolores "Lola" Chávez de Armijo, had been in the position already for three years, having succeeded another woman. But McDonald nonetheless made the claim that the new state constitution did not allow women to hold that office (or any appointed office in the state). Oddly, the person he had sought to replace Mrs. Armijo with had been, in fact, a woman—suggesting that political motivations were a major factor in the move.

Indeed, 1912 was a year of great transition. New Mexico had achieved statehood that year, and McDonald, the first governor of the new state, was testing his authority. He was a Democrat, and the state legislature was largely Republican. Although the State Library would seem an unlikely place for the conflict to unfold, it was a well-known office among the parties involved. Then housed in the State Capitol Building, the library contained law books, maps, and government documents and stayed open during the day for use by legislators. The librarian, who was paid an annual salary of $900, was required to speak both English and Spanish. (The library is not to be confused with the current State Library in Santa Fe, which was established in 1929.)

Mrs. Armijo fought the attempt to replace her—and won, when Judge Edmund C. Abot of the Santa Fe District Court ruled in her favor and dismissed the case.

Governor McDonald did not back down, and neither did Mrs. Armijo. Unwilling to admit defeat, McDonald took the matter to the State Supreme Court. It would prove to be a move that would change New Mexico history—just not in the way McDonald likely intended.

Lacking a statute in the new state constitution expressly allowing women to hold office in New Mexico, the State Supreme Court instead reviewed common law for a precedent of women being allowed to hold office, as well as the laws that had created the librarian position while New Mexico was still a territory. In *State v. Armijo*, 18 N.M. 646, the court ruled that because the position was "ministerial"—that is, it did not require the librarian "to exercise his or her judgment in any respect"—the duties of the office, then, were "not incompatible with the ability of a woman to perform." Further, the court pointed to the previous appointment of Anita Chapman in the position as precedent for a woman holding the office, as well as other examples of women in public positions in the state. The court also specifically referenced Section 9, Article 22 of the new state constitution, which allowed all existing territorial office holders to retain their positions after statehood.

In the opinion of the court, the justices wrote:

The people of the Territory, the chief executive of the Territory, and the courts, have long recognized the right of women to hold various offices and the office in question having been acceptably filled many years by women, it is clear that this Court should not oust a woman from the office, because of her sex solely, unless it is clearly and unmistakably demonstrated that she holds the office without right of lawful authority.

Although the decision was a victory for Mrs. Armijo, it bespoke a prevailing prejudice against women in the state (not to mention a poor understanding of what librarians do). In 1913, the legislature passed H.B. 150, expressly allowing women to hold appointed office in New Mexico. Later, the State Library was moved under the jurisdiction of the State Supreme Court, where it remains today.

The victor in a battle unwittingly thrust upon her, Lola Chávez de Armijo continued her duties as state librarian until her retirement in 1917. She passed away on September 8, 1929, in Albuquerque.

More to explore: *Ladies Auxiliary of Local 890, Lordsburg-Hidalgo Library, Women of the Judiciary*

118. The Dorsey Mansion

Location: Colfax County. East of Springer, in a pullout on the north side of US 56/412, between mile markers 23 and 24, at the turnoff to Dorsey Road, which leads to the mansion. See map 3.

Marker text: Built by controversial Arkansas Senator Stephen W. Dorsey in the late 1870s and early 1880s, the part log and part stone mansion was once a center of social life in the Southwest. Since its completion, it has been a unique architectural feature in New Mexico.

The man behind the mansion, Stephen Wallace Dorsey, was born in Benson, Vermont, on February 28, 1842. Dorsey distinguished himself in the Union Army during the Civil War before being mustered out with the rank of captain in 1865. That same year, he married Helen Mary Wack, with whom he had three children and adopted a fourth. In 1871, Dorsey moved to Arkansas and, buoyed by the politics of the Reconstruction era, won election to a Republican seat in the United States Senate. Only thirty-one years of age, Senator Dorsey purchased land near Chico Springs in New Mexico, where he constructed over many years an opulent thirty-six-room Gothic Victorian palace, part Lincolnesque log cabin and part Arthurian stone fortress—an architectural confection known today as the Dorsey Mansion.

Dorsey lavished his home with grandeurs of all manner. A marble fireplace from Italy warmed guests in the dining room, which was, according to the National Park Service, the largest such room in west Texas, New Mexico, and Arizona in its day. The art gallery, complete with cathedral ceiling, showcased paintings imported from overseas. On the outside facade of the tower, gargoyle faces of Dorsey, his wife, and his brother John glared in stone relief over the artificial pond and fountain that bubbled in the front yard. A billiard room provided contemplative entertainment for guests. Sumptuous parties bestowed the mansion with a deserved reputation as the center of social life in the Southwest.

Yet Dorsey's mansion, no matter how majestic, could not shelter him from the controversies that sullied his public life. The senator became involved in a controversial scandal involving mail contracts, agreements between the Postal Service and private citizens to ensure economical mail delivery between post offices not accessible by stage or railroad. The Post Office called these "certainty, celerity, and security routes," and often indicated them on timetables with three asterisks, leading to their nickname "Star Routes." Dorsey, his brother, and other associates apparently won lucrative bids through fraudulent contracts. In 1881, President Chester A. Arthur ordered the prosecution of Dorsey and eight others in the matter, and the senator found himself ostracized, albeit alliteratively, as "Star Route Stephen."

Although he had since left the Senate and was living in his New Mexico cabin (the stone portion of his edifice was not completed until 1886), Dorsey and his wife returned to Washington in June 1881 to stand trial. Dorsey's lawyer, the famed Robert Ingersoll, secured a hung jury. The jury in a second trial acquitted the senator of wrongdoing. "There isn't much doubt there was some crookedness," Ingersoll told reporters, "but they can't prove a conspiracy."

Dorsey hoped to return to politics by vying for leadership of the Republican Party in New Mexico, but debts and lawsuits arising from his trial and other land transactions stymied his climb. From the security of his mansion, Dorsey operated his sprawling Mountain Spring cattle ranch under the Triangle Dot brand, once stating that he was happy to be on the ranch because "my cattle do not vote." In the late 1880s, he established the nearby town of Clayton, named for his son. Dorsey eventually moved to Los Angeles, and his mansion temporarily became a health retreat for tuberculosis patients before again falling to private ownership.

Senator Dorsey died in California on March 20, 1916, age seventy-three. His obituary in the *Little Rock Gazette* described him, simply but fittingly, as "a lawyer and a businessman who interested himself in the promotion of large enterprises."

More to explore: *Bond House, Chisum's South Spring Ranch (see under Artesia), Clayton*

119. Dr. Annie Dodge Wauneka (1910–1997)
"Legendary Mother of the Navajo Nation"

Location: San Juan County. About thirty miles north of Tohatchi, on the Navajo Indian Reservation, in a pullout on the north side of NM 134, between mile markers 9 and 10. See map 1.

Marker text: Dr. Annie Dodge Wauneka was elected to the Navajo Tribal Council in 1951 and served for three terms. She worked tirelessly to improve the health and education of the Navajo people and led the fight against tuberculosis on the reservation. Among her many distinctions, she received the U.S. Presidential Medal of Freedom in 1963 and was inducted into the National Women's Hall of Fame in 2000.

In March 1951, Annie Dodge Wauneka ran for and won election as a delegate to the Navajo Tribal Council, the legislative governing body of the Navajo Nation. She was one of the first women ever elected to the council. In securing the position, she was also beginning the work that would make her one of the most respected Navajo leaders of her time and help her become a crucial link between cultures at a critical time in the history of the Navajo Nation.

Wauneka's family had a history of service. Born near Sawmill, Arizona, on April 10, 1910, she grew up admiring the work of her father, Henry Che Dodge, a tribal leader himself, who exerted a great influence on her. In 1929, Annie married George Wauneka, and the couple began a ranch together. They also started a family, raising a total of six children. Although their home was in Klagenoh, Arizona, Wauneka traveled throughout the Navajo Reservation, about a third of which extends into New Mexico.

Around the time of Wauneka's election to the council, tuberculosis had begun to spread across the Navajo Reservation. The Tribal Council appointed Wauneka as chair of the Tribal Health and Welfare Committee in an effort to address the problem. Rather than simply attending to the issue from a distance, Wauneka determinedly and personally invested herself in the well-being of the Navajo people, educating herself about the disease of tuberculosis, spending time with doctors, and visiting patients individually to hear their concerns. A critical part of her success lay in her ability to work within two cultures, Navajo and Anglo, and push from both sides to mutual benefit. She encouraged white medical practitioners who were treating Navajo patients in hospitals and on the reservation to better understand and appreciate Navajo culture, which often emphasized more traditional cures under the guidance of a medicine man. At the same time, she encouraged those Navajos sick with the disease to seek both their own traditional care as well as the care they would find in hospitals and through trained and expert practitioners.

"We have to accept modern medicine," Wauneka told the *Albuquerque Journal*, "so our Indian people can have a better health standard."

Through speeches, lectures, a weekly radio program, and personal interventions, she spoke out (often in the Navajo language) against poor sanitary conditions on the reservation, including

For her work on behalf of the Navajo Nation, particularly in helping create access to life-saving tuberculosis medicines, Annie Dodge Wauneka became known as the "Legendary Mother of the Navajo Nation." In December 1963, she received the Medal of Freedom from President Lyndon B. Johnson. Photograph, Medal of Freedom Presentation, December 6, 1963. White House Photo Office, LBJ Presidential Library, CA41–26-WH63.

impure water and poor dietary habits. She pushed her people to accept the tuberculosis treatment offered through modern medicine. She even worked with doctors to write a dictionary translating medical terms into Navajo.

Her conscientious and diligent work earned her recognition at the highest levels. In 1963, President Lyndon B. Johnson awarded Wauneka the Presidential Medal of Freedom, the highest peacetime honor given to a civilian. She was the first Native American woman to receive the medal. In 1984, Wauneka received another high award when the Navajo Tribal Council, the very council on which she herself had served for three terms, bestowed on her the honorary title Legendary Mother of the Navajo Nation.

Wauneka was active as an advocate for better health care until her death on November 10, 1997. Three years after her passing, Wauneka was posthumously entered into the National Women's Hall of Fame. In their induction, the Hall of Fame noted: "All recognize that through her efforts in education and health, the lives of every Navajo, as well as the nation at large, have been improved."

More to explore: *Dr. Meta L. Christy, Josephine Cox "Grandma" Anderson, Navajo Indian Reservation, Sisters of Charity*

120. Dr. Meta L. Christy (1895–1968)

Location: San Miguel County. In Las Vegas, at the City of Las Vegas Museum, 727 Grand Avenue. See map 3.

Marker text: Meta L. Christy, DO, is recognized by the American Osteopathic Association as the first black osteopath. Dr. Christy graduated in 1921 from the Philadelphia College of Osteopathic Medicine as its first black graduate. The College gives an annual award in her name. She established her lifelong private practice with quiet dignity when there were no women physicians or osteopaths in local hospitals and few blacks in Las Vegas.

Note: The Philadelphia College of Osteopathic Medicine was originally known as the Philadelphia College of Osteopathy.

The first black osteopath in New Mexico and possibly the country, Dr. Meta L. Christy brought her form of hands-on healing to Las Vegas, where she established her own clinic. This photo shows her as a graduate of the Philadelphia College of Osteopathy in 1921. Dr. Meta L. Christy. Courtesy Philadelphia College of Osteopathic Medicine.

On June 2, 1921, the twenty-one graduates of the Philadelphia College of Osteopathy assembled in Witherspoon Hall, eager to receive their degrees as doctor of osteopathic medicine (DO) and bring their form of hands-on healing to the world. Among them, one stood out: a young black woman, twenty-six years old, the only black student in the class, and, indeed, the first black graduate of the college. Her name was Meta Loretta Christy. Some historians believe that Dr. Christy was achieving another first that day as well, very likely becoming the first black osteopath in the country.

Osteopathy is a form of manual healing that treats patients holistically, based in part on a belief that the mind, body, and spirit are a whole and capable of self-healing. Osteopaths use what they call "manipulative treatment" (stretching, muscle contraction, and other physical interactions with the musculoskeletal system), often in combination with more traditional forms of treatment, to return a body suffering from back pain, migraines, and other ailments to wellness. When first developed in the late nineteenth century, osteopathy shifted the treatment focus from viewing patients as a set of symptoms, to emphasizing their complete well-being as a person.

Having a brother who lived in Las Vegas, New Mexico, Dr. Christy moved to the state sometime after her graduation. (The brother, Oran, had possibly come to Las Vegas to work on the railroad.) She settled into a house on Shulzbacher Avenue, near New Mexico Normal University (today known as New Mexico Highlands University), in the small black settlement that had formed in that part of the city. Her house doubled as her clinic.

Osteopathy was fairly new in New Mexico when Dr. Christy arrived. Until 1903, there was only one osteopath practicing in the entire state. Dr. Christy might have come to New Mexico, as osteopath Dr. Charles A. Wheel later wrote of other osteopaths venturing to the state, "equipped only with ten good fingers and about as many dollars, and an abiding faith in their profession." She would have benefited from a law passed in the state in 1933 governing the practice of osteopathy in New Mexico and creating a board to oversee its professional development. Her life in Las Vegas was certainly different from what she had known growing up in the town of Kokomo in north-central Indiana, where she had been born in October 1895. Still, her practice did well, and it is believed that she was able to buy her own home by 1947. Her clinic was open for more than thirty years.

Dr. Christy became a member of the American Osteopathic Association as well as the New Mexico Association of Osteopathic Physicians and Surgeons, later known as the New Mexico Osteopathic Medical Association. From her peers in the latter organization she earned a degree of recognition, being awarded their Distinguished Service Award in 1956.

Dr. Christy passed away in 1968, but her legacy has not been forgotten. Each year, students in the Student National Medical Association at the Pennsylvania College of Medicine select a practitioner they want to recognize for "exemplary practice of osteopathic medicine, service to the community and inspiration to future DOs," and award that person the Meta L. Christy Award.

More to explore: *Blackdom Townsite, Curanderas—Women Who Heal, Dr. Annie Dodge Wauneka, Las Vegas, Sisters of Charity*

121. Dulcelina Salce Curtis (1904–1995)

Location: Sandoval County. At the north end of Corrales, just past the municipal limit, at the intersection of Paseo Cesar Chavez and NM 448, in a pullout on the west side of NM 448, between mile markers 12 and 13. See map 4.

Marker text: Teacher, agriculturalist, farmer and conservationist, Dulcelina Curtis led efforts to control flooding of arroyos in Corrales where a flood-control channel is named in her honor. The first woman appointed to a board of the U.S. Agricultural Stabilization and Conservation District, she received the National Endowment for Soil Conservation Award for New Mexico in 1988. She served on the Village Council and helped launch many of the town's civic organizations.

In the northwest corner of Corrales can be found one of the hardest-working structures in the village. Here, rainwater and runoff from the Lomitas Negras watershed flow into a large V-shaped conduit, about the width of a city block, visually similar to a funnel cut in half and laid flat. From that conduit, the waters enter a long, narrow, brick-walled channel built into the earth, through which they are carried southwestward, their journey contained within the nine-foot-high, fourteen-foot-wide confines of the channel. The channel snakes for more than a mile, crossing from Rio Rancho into Corrales, until it empties its watery cargo into the Montoya Arroyo channel, and from there to the Rio Grande. By diverting water away from populated areas and directing it safely along a defined pathway, this diversionary channel helps prevent flooding in Corrales during heavy rains and protects homes and property from destruction by watery deluge. The channel, begun in 1989 and constructed over three years, was a joint effort between the Corrales Watershed District Board, the Ciudad Soil and Water Conservation District, and the Soil Conservation Service of the US Department of Agriculture. It is named the Dulcelina Curtis Channel, a name that honors former Corrales farmer, civic leader, and conservationist Dulcelina Salce Curtis.

When she passed away on April 16, 1995, Curtis left behind a lifetime of accomplishments. In addition to helping start the Corrales Library and the Corrales 4-H Club, she was an original member of the Corrales Village Council, having been elected to that organization in 1971. But she is remembered in particular for her work on flood control in and around Corrales.

Flooding is a problem that has long plagued this area. Rainwater and mountain runoff, often propelled through small earthen ditches known as arroyos, can inundate areas of lower elevation, like Corrales, causing significant damage. Curtis herself had firsthand knowledge of that damage. In the fall of 1904, when she was only an infant, a torrent of floodwater demolished her family's house in Corrales.

The family had not been in the area long when they suffered this loss. The Salces had arrived in New Mexico around 1896. Curtis's Italian father, Angelo Salce, along with his brother, soon began acquiring land around Corrales. Angelo and his mail-order bride, Maria, started a family, with Dulcelina—"Dulce" as she was commonly known—the eldest of six children. Dulce left school at age fourteen to care for her brothers and sisters after the death of her mother, but she nonetheless went on to earn a teaching certificate at New Mexico Normal University (now New Mexico Highlands University) in Las Vegas, New Mexico. She returned to Corrales and put the degree to use teaching in area schools. She met and married her husband, Vincent Curtis, in the village in 1928, and the couple had two daughters of their own. They also started a farm and apple orchard, known as Curtis Farm, and for a time sold cider and apples from a store on their property.

Another massive flood swept through the area in 1962. In response, Corrales residents organized the Corrales Watershed District Board, with Dulcelina its first chair. Her experience with irrigation and flood control on her own farm had given her expertise in this area. In 1973, she was appointed to the board of directors of the Agricultural Stabilization and Conservation Service, an agency of the US Department of Agriculture—the first woman to hold that position. (In 1994, the service was subsumed into the Farm Service Agency.) In 1988, her civic work earned her the National Endowment for Soil Conservation Award for New Mexico. The following year, digging began on the flood control channel that would bear her name.

Dulce Curtis lived to see that channel completed. She passed away four years later, in 1995. She is buried beside her husband in San Ysidro Cemetery in Corrales. A ceremonial urn above the couple's graves reads, "Here lie the souls of Corrales."

The best place to see the Dulcelina Curtis Channel is near a small park and walkway at the corner of Rio Ruidoso and Rio Vista Drive NE in Rio Rancho, a short distance southwest of this Historic Marker. The park, set alongside the channel, includes a monument to Curtis, and a short walkway leads north to the mouth of the channel itself.

More to explore: *Corrales, Iglesia de San Ysidro (see under Corrales), Sally Rooke—Heroine of the Dry Cimarron Flood*

122. Eagle Nest Lake State Park

Location: Colfax County. East of Eagle Nest, on the east side of US 64 just above Eagle Nest Lake. See map 3.

Marker text: Eagle Nest was a place where members of several Indian tribes were said to have come to collect ceremonial feathers. Before 1919, Charles Springer acquired the land and built a dam for irrigation. It now has a capacity of 78,000 acre feet and provides irrigation for many farmers in eastern New Mexico. Today Eagle Nest State Park is known for its premier trout fishing.

Credit for the creation of Eagle Nest Lake goes to prominent twentieth-century New Mexico rancher and landowner Charles Springer, who first put in motion a plan to dam the Cimarron River and harness its waters into a dependable water source for irrigating his C. S. Cattle Ranch as well as the fields of other local landowners. In 1906, Springer formed the Cimarron Valley Land Company. Under company auspices, Springer purchased six hundred acres of land in the Moreno Valley and bankrolled the construction of the huge concrete colossus at the southern end of the property. Begun in 1918 under the supervision of engineer Neal Hanson, the dam—with a reservoir capacity of 78,000 acre feet—was completed in 1920.

Waters backed up by the dam collected into a small, placid lake, which took the name Eagle Nest, and a community of the same name soon developed nearby. That pleasant sobriquet, according to legend, was inspired by the belief that Native Americans had once collected eagle feathers in the valley. The 2,500-acre, five-mile-long, two-mile-wide Eagle Nest Lake is today owned by the state of New Mexico and is stocked with rainbow trout and three-inch fingerlings.

More to explore: *Clayton Lake State Park, Springer*

123. Early Spanish Route

Location: De Baca County. Just north of the city of Fort Sumner, in a pullout on the west side of US 84, between mile markers 1 and 2. See map 6.

Marker text: In 1582, Antonio de Espejo and his exploring party left New Mexico to return to Mexico by way of the Pecos River. Eight years later, Gaspar de Sosa led another group into New Mexico alongside the same river, a route little used again until the Territorial period.

In 1582, Antonio de Espejo led the third authorized Spanish expedition into New Mexico. He came in search of two priests, Fray Agustín Rodríguez and Fray Francisco López, who had remained behind on an expedition the previous year. The priests had made their home at a Tiwa-speaking Indian pueblo the Spaniards called Puaray. The exact location of Puaray is not known, but historians believe that it was near present-day Bernalillo. After entering New Mexico from the south, Espejo retraced the steps of the previous expedition north along the course of the Rio Grande. He received bad news before even reaching Puaray in 1583: word arrived that the Indians had martyred the two priests in the intervening year. Espejo briefly explored northern New Mexico and parts of Arizona for gold and other riches, and then he returned south, following the course of the Pecos River through the plains of eastern New Mexico.

The Pecos River originates near and was named for the pueblo of Pecos southeast of Santa Fe, the ruins of which are preserved today at Pecos National Historical Park. The river flows from the Sangre de Cristo Mountains southward into Texas, making the valley it follows a natural concourse for early explorers traveling the flat grasslands of this part of the state. Espejo's chronicler left this impression of the Pecos: "It is a medium sized river with exquisite water, surrounded by numerous trees and many vines, roses, rosebush fruit, and much pennyroyal."

In 1590, eight years after Espejo's journey commenced, Gaspar Castaño de Sosa launched his own remarkable expedition. Castaño, lieutenant governor of Nuevo León in Mexico, was apparently a cogent leader: he had convinced the citizens of that village to follow him into New Mexico to establish what they hoped would be the first Spanish colony in this interior province. The colonists left Nuevo León on July 27 and followed the Pecos north into New Mexico. Intent though Castaño and his wards might have been on their mission, they had undertaken the venture without the approval of the Spanish Crown. In mid-March of the following year, Captain Juan de Morlete arrived to arrest Castaño on charges of leading an unauthorized expedition. Soldiers returned Castaño to Mexico in chains.

After the Southwest came under the control of the United States, cattle barons drove their herds along the Pecos to supply meat to army forts and Indian reservations in the New Mexico Territory and in other western states. In 1866, Charles Goodnight and Oliver Loving led their first herd of cattle northward from Texas through the Pecos Valley more than 130 miles to the Bosque Redondo Navajo Indian Reservation at Fort Sumner. Having made a profit on the deal, Goodnight and Loving returned twice more.

More to explore: *Castaño de Sosa's Route, Espejo's Expedition, Espejo's Trail, Fort Sumner and Fort Sumner State Monument (series), Goodnight-Loving Trail (series)*

124. Eastern New Mexico University

Location: Roosevelt County. In Portales, on the campus of Eastern New Mexico University, visible from US 70. See map 6.

Marker text: This University was established at Portales in 1927 by the State Legislature as the Eastern New Mexico Normal School. It opened for the 1934–35 school year with 274 students. Originally established to train teachers for rural schools, Eastern now has a wide range of undergraduate and graduate programs to serve the instructional, public service and research needs of the state and the nation.

When legislators drafted the New Mexico constitution just before statehood in 1912, they included a provision calling for the founding of an institution of higher education somewhere in eastern New Mexico. On March 1, 1927, members of the state legislature in Santa Fe followed through, approving a bill that would, among other things, "locate and establish the Eastern New Mexico Normal School at Portales, Roosevelt County, New Mexico." As a "normal school," the institution would have as its primary mission the preparation of educators to teach in underserved areas of the state.

Seven years later, the school, renamed Eastern New Mexico Junior College, opened the doors of its sole academic building in Portales to a fall class of 274 eager young students.

The institution progressed as a two-year college until 1939, when the academic regiment expanded to include a third year of studies. A fourth year followed in 1940. The development of the school thereafter is recounted in a history of the university by Donald W. Whisenhunt:

The curriculum was expanded, special community services were inaugurated, and summer schools were offered at other locations in the state such as Ruidoso and Taos. The first four-year graduating class in

1942 consisted of 41 persons, a very respectable number for a new college.

By the time Floyd Golden took over as president that same year, Eastern was on a par with other degree-granting institutions in the state. Dr. Golden, long affiliated with the school, good naturedly referred to his tenure there as the "Golden Years." Accreditation came in 1947, and the first master's degree programs were added two years later.

Today, Eastern New Mexico University is the third-largest educational institution in the state after the University of New Mexico in Albuquerque and New Mexico State University in Las Cruces. Floyd Golden is remembered in the name of the university library, Golden Library. The school is also home to the Blackwater Draw Museum, which features exhibits interpreting the important Paleo-Indian archaeological site of Blackwater Draw near Clovis.

ENMU offers both undergraduate and graduate programs, with degrees in business, technology, education, and arts and sciences. The Center for Teaching Excellence brings the best of the modern century to the original normal school mandate of the university.

More to explore: *Blackwater Draw, Clovis, New Mexico Tech, Rose Powers White*

125. Edge of the Plains

Location: Torrance County. Just east of Wagon Wheel, in the highway rest area on the north side of Interstate 40, at mile marker 220. See map 4.

Marker text: Grassy plains meet pine dotted uplands in this transition from Great Plains to Basin and Range provinces. Plains to the east are capped by caliche, sand, and gravel which are deeply eroded into the underlying bedrock in places. To the west, faulting has produced alternating highlands and intermountain basins of the Basin and Range province. Elevation 6,500 feet.

Geologists divide the United States into eight broad regions, which themselves break down into provinces, or physiographic divisions. There are twenty-five provinces altogether, each one characterizing the topography of a particular part of the country. The Coastal Plain Province, for example, includes parts of many of the states along Atlantic coast, while the Pacific Border Province, the Lower California Province, and others make up areas of the west coast. (Provinces are further subdivided into smaller sections, which allow even more specific description.) This breakdown is a helpful way of categorizing the many different geophysical characteristics found in the varied topography of the country.

New Mexico includes a total of four provinces. This Historic Marker is within a transition zone between two of them: the Great Plains Province to the east, and the Basin and Range Province to the west.

The name "Great Plains" does a good job summarizing the region to the east: it is part of a vast area of varying, mostly low-lying grassland plains, some 450,000 square miles' worth. The plains are capped by a thin layer of soil on top of caliche (a sedimentary rock formed when calcium carbonate binds gravel, sand, and other minerals together), which overlies sand and gravel eroded from the Rocky Mountains to the west. Provinces do not respect state boundaries. The Great Plains Province, for example, stretches through much of the central part of the country, from the Mississippi River all the way to the Rocky Mountains. It covers most of the eastern third of New Mexico, top to bottom.

The Basin and Range Province to the west,

as this Historic Marker notes, is characterized by alternating "highlands" (mountains) and "intermountain basins" (the valleys between them). (The word "intermountain" means "located between mountains.") Most of the work in fashioning this discontinuous landscape was done by faulting, which occurred as portions of the earth's crust stretched. This caused large chunks of land to drop downward, forming basins, while the earth edging the basins uplifted, sometimes tilting in the process, forming mountains.

The other two provinces in New Mexico are the Rocky Mountains Province and the Colorado Plateau Province.

More to explore: *Basin and Range Country, Continental Divide, Llano Estacado, Mesa and Pecos Valley*

126. El Camino Real—The King's Highway

Location: Doña Ana County. At the New Mexico Visitors Center on Interstate 10, just north of the New Mexico–Texas border. See map 5.

Marker text: The oldest historical road in the United States, running over 2000 miles from Mexico City to Taos. Parts of the Camino Real were used by Spanish explorers in the 1580s, but it was formally established in 1598 by Juan de Oñate, New Mexico's first colonizer and governor. It was later referred to as the Chihuahua Trail.

127. Oñate's Route

Location: Doña Ana County. At the New Mexico Visitors Center on Interstate 10, just north of the New Mexico–Texas border. See map 5.

Marker text: Juan de Oñate, first governor of New Mexico, passed near here with his colonizing expedition in May 1598. Traveling north, he designated official campsites (called *parajes*) on the Camino Real, used by expeditions that followed. In Oñate's caravan were 129 men, many with their families and servants.

128. Women of the Camino Real

Location: Socorro County. South of San Antonio, in the Fort Craig Rest Area on the east side of Interstate 25, between mile markers 113 and 114. See map 5.

Marker text: In 1598, the first Spanish settlers in New Mexico traveled up the Camino Real from north-central Mexico. Of the 560 people so far identified on that expedition, at least 20 percent were women. They came on foot, on wagons or horseback, and were the first of thousands of women who suffered the arduous journey traveling back and forth, sometimes more than once, on the trail.

The legacy of these women is evident from place names, communities like Socorro, which bear their names. Some women came as heads-of-households while others followed their husbands and families. Some even came as slaves. They all played an important role in expanding and colonizing New Mexico. Women defined the culture, history and traditions of New Mexico throughout the 17th and 18th centuries.

In January 1598, don Juan de Oñate departed Santa Barbara, Mexico, at the head of a two-mile convoy of armor-clad soldiers, proselytizing priests, 129 men with their families and servants, and cattle and oxen pulling eighty wagons packed to the brim with personal possessions and supplies. Among them as well were a number of women, traveling as wives or daughters with their families. In some cases, the women were servants to a family. These settlers were likely compelled in part to take on such an effort by the pride they felt fulfilling the desire of the Spanish government to plant a colony

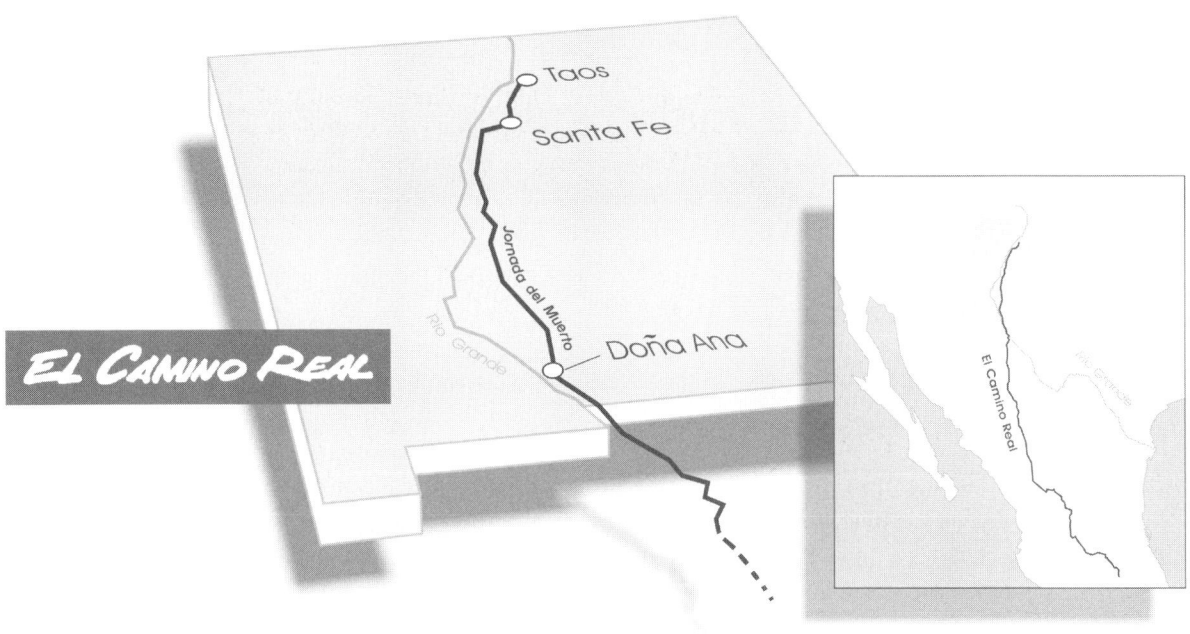

Without the Camino Real, authorities in Mexico would have had no easy way to administer or supply the Province of New Mexico to the north. Caravans on the route traveled through the center of the state to Santa Fe, and later to Taos. Illustration by David Carter.

deep in the heart of this northern land. The route Oñate followed took a name that bespoke this goal. It was El Camino Real de Tierra Adentro, or "the Royal Road to the Interior."

Much of the four-hundred-mile earthen stretch of the Camino Real that ran through New Mexico adhered to the course of the Rio Grande. Native Americans had laid foot trails along this corridor long before Oñate arrived and had used the passage in their trade networks. Earlier Spanish explorers, like Captain Francisco Sánchez Chamuscado in 1581 and Antonio de Espejo in 1582, had also followed sections of these trails as they visited Indian pueblos and searched for mineral wealth in this interior land. When later extended to its full length, the Camino Real ran some two thousand miles from Mexico City to Taos, although several shortcuts and detours evolved along its path over time—a phenomenon known as trail braiding. It was the first road developed by Europeans in what is now the United States and is therefore often considered to be the oldest historical road in the country.

As his caravan headed north into New Mexico, Oñate established encampments along the route, known as *parajes*, where travelers could catch their breath before moving forward. As use of the trail continued into subsequent generations, these parajes became vital landmarks for later travelers. A few eventually acquired names, like the Paraje San Diego near Hatch and the Paraje de Fra Cristobal north of the Fra Cristobal Mountains. One, the Paraje de Robledo, recognized Pedro Robledo, an older gentleman who died on the initial journey northward. That paraje lay near the village that became known as Doña Ana—a name often ascribed to Robledo's own granddaughter, Ana Robledo, who, legend says, perished near the same spot almost a hundred years later fleeing the state during the Pueblo Revolt.

For almost three hundred years, the Camino Real was the uniting means of support between Mexico City and Santa Fe. For the earliest part of those three centuries, trade with the East was forbidden, and the flow of commerce over the Camino Real represented the only legal means by which people in New Mexico could secure goods. Every fall, caravans from Taos and other points north traveled the route to obtain supplies for the colony at trade fairs in Chihuahua, Mexico—and for a time, the route became known by those headed south as the Chihuahua Trail. Settlements along the route of the Camino Real, sometimes established as presidios to guard the Spanish frontier, were the foundations of cities like Belen and La Joya. Twelve years after the Pueblo Revolt of 1680, exiled colonists returned to New Mexico over the Camino Real—some of them women who had lost their husbands in the insurrection and now found themselves the new heads of household. When the Southwest came under US control in 1846, the Camino Real saw companies of soldiers and scientists here to explore, map, and build wagon roads to the Pacific coast. Later, would-be prospectors partially followed its course through the state before turning west to the gold fields of California.

One firsthand account of the Camino Real comes from Susan Shelby Magoffin, wife of trader Samuel Magoffin, who was traveling with her trader husband from Missouri to Mexico in 1847. Magoffin wrote of the portion of the Camino Real just north of Doña Ana:

We are almost at the mouth of the Jornada (the long journey without water) [and] have been traveling slowly, the roads being exceedingly heavy, with two or three severe hills; one we passed this morning about a half mile in length, and the sand so heavy all the teams doubled and were then just able to get over with resting half a dozen times. 'Tis an ugly road very, but they say 'twill be better after this.

As railroads arrived in New Mexico in the late 1800s, travel on the Camino Real receded and finally ended.

More to explore: *El Paso del Rio del Norte, Jornada del Muerto, Paraje de Fra Cristobal, Paraje de Los Brazitos, Paraje de Robledo, Paraje San Diego, Trail of the Forty-Niners, Women of the Santa Fe Trail (see under Santa Fe Trail)*

129. El Morro National Monument Inscription Rock

Location: Cibola County. Pullout at the entrance to the monument, off NM 53, on the north side of the road. See map 1.

Marker text: Until it was by-passed by the railroad in the 1880s, its waterhole made El Morro an important stop for travelers in the Ácoma-Zuni region. Numerous inscriptions carved in the sandstone date from the prehistoric, Spanish, Mexican, and Territorial periods in New Mexico's history. An important example is Oñate's inscription, carved in 1605.

Ancestral Puebloan Indians were the first to carve in the dramatic two-hundred-foot sandstone bluff known as El Morro, starting a tradition that would continue until the early part of the twentieth century. Their petroglyphs featured animals and geometric designs. The Indians built two pueblos atop the spacious mesa, each containing about 250 rooms and providing a home for between 1,000 and 1,500 people. The pueblos were probably in use for only fifty or sixty years before the builders left the area. The Zuni Indians, descendants of the Ancestral Puebloans, later named the larger of the two pueblos A'ts'ina.

El Morro is a cuesta, a bluff with a gentle slope on one side and a steep cliff on the other. A small depression at the base of the towering precipice collects rainwater and other runoff from the bluff. That catchment made El Morro a dependable source of fresh water for travelers through this part of northwestern New Mexico. Many of these travelers passed nearby on the Zuni-Acoma Trail, an ancient and well-traveled path between the Zuni Pueblo villages, Acoma Pueblo, and farther east to Santa Fe.

The earliest Spanish inscription scratched into El Morro is that of don Juan de Oñate, the first official Spanish colonizer and governor of New Mexico, who camped here in 1605 while returning from an expedition to the Gulf of California. Oñate, or one of his soldiers, wrote:

Paso por aquí el adelantado Don Juan de Oñate del descubrimiento de la mar del sur a 16 de Abril de 1605.

Passed by here the governor don Juan de Oñate, from the discovery of the Sea of the South on the 16th of April, 1605.

In September 1849, the US Army's Lieutenant James H. Simpson and R. H. Kern veered off the course of their military reconnaissance to Navajo country, bivouacked at the base of the rock, and spent two days exploring the ruins and copying the inscriptions for their report. Simpson described the spring at the rock as "an accessory not more grateful to the lover of the beautiful than refreshing to the way-worn traveler." Before leaving, the two added their own signatures in what were the first English-language inscriptions to join the loquacious rock.

In 1857, Lieutenant Edward Fitzgerald Beale left his autograph during an unusual army expedition. Beale and his caravan were trying to prove that camels would be more efficient than horses in moving soldiers and supplies throughout the Southwest. Although Lieutenant Beale felt that the tests had been successful, the army never advanced the proposal.

In all, historians have cataloged some two thousand inscriptions on what the National Park Service called "a commanding register of three hundred years of European and American exploration and expansion in the southwestern United States."

More to explore: Albuquerque Petroglyphs (see under Albuquerque), Oñate's Route (see under El Camino Real—The King's Highway), Pueblo of Zuni, Three Rivers Petroglyphs

130. El Paso del Rio del Norte

Location: Doña Ana County. In Sunland Park, on Old McNutt Road, along the banks of the Rio Grande. See map 5.

Specific directions: From Racetrack Road in Sunland Park, follow NM 273 (McNutt Road) east for about a mile. Just before the highway crosses the river (whereupon it becomes Anapra Road), turn right (south) onto a dirt road. This is still McNutt Road, although this portion is sometimes called Old McNutt Road. Follow the dirt road for half a mile until it forks, then take the right fork another mile, traveling along the base of the mountain. Pass under one railroad bridge; another is visible in the distance. The marker is just past the second bridge, on the left, near the bank of the river.

Marker text: The canyon cut here by the Rio Grande marks the crossing of the historic Camino Real, or Royal Road, to La Tierra Adentra. Trackers and traders crossed the river here to begin the arduous journey north to Santa Fe. Permanent settlement of this area began with establishment of the Mission of Nuestra Señora de Guadalupe in 1659 in present-day Ciudad Juarez.

Note: This Marker takes a little work to reach, and the road can be rutted and uneven in spots, but the effort is worthwhile. The Marker is less than a mile from the Mexican border in an area frequented by the US Border Patrol, who will probably make their presence known to you.

The border cities of El Paso, in Texas, and Ciudad Juárez (also just called Juárez), in Mexico, share more than a common boundary: they also share a common history, and at one time, a common name. That duality has its origins in their location at a place where the Rio Grande cut a gorge through what are today the Franklin Mountains (in the United States) and the Sierra de Juárez (in Mexico); in effect, a "pass." When don Juan de Oñate came through here on his colonizing expedition for Spain in 1598, he named the river Rio del Norte, or "River of the North" (because it flowed from the north); the pass itself later became known as El Paso del Rio del Norte, or "the Pass of the River of the North." Today, the name El Paso is remembered in the city on the east bank of the river, and we know the Rio del Norte as the Rio Grande.

Oñate, after reaching the river at a site near present-day San Elizario, Texas, about twenty miles downstream from here, in late April 1598, sent scouts across to the east bank of the river to travel upriver and find a suitable place where his caravan of some five hundred new settlers, with their wagons and livestock, could safely ford. The land was too narrow between the river and the uplift on the west side of the river ahead for the caravan to pass; they would need to continue north on the east bank. The ideal spot to ford would be a place with a small amount of sand, a hard surface to the riverbed, and a low current. Local Mansos Indians, who had encountered Oñate's caravan earlier, helped the scouts determine a spot—very near the location of this Historic Marker.

Oñate began the crossing on May 4, 1598. It took four days to move the caravan, including sheep and wagons, across the river, so treacherous were the waters, probably running full with spring thaws. In subsequent years, the location of the historic crossing came to be known as Oñate's Crossing.

The full route of the colonists became a well-traveled trail known as the Camino Real de Tierra Adentro, or the Royal Road to the Interior Land—that "interior land" being what Spanish, and later Mexican, officials called the region that is now New Mexico. Through the nineteenth century, as settlers, priests, and traders traveled its course, the Camino Real served as the thoroughfare connecting the colonies Spain had established in the interior land with the controlling authorities in what is now Mexico.

As it continued north from this point, the Camino Real largely followed the east bank of the river to Santa Fe, although variations on the route arose that included travel on the opposite bank.

The journey north was an arduous one, particularly across the stretch of the Chihuahuan Desert known today as the Jornada del Muerto, between present-day Rincon and San Antonio. Along that ninety-mile stretch, the Camino Real strayed from the banks of the river, opting for a straighter path north rather than a route that followed the difficult bend of the river for that distance. The trail rejoined the Rio Grande south of present-day San Antonio and continued to the capital in Santa Fe.

Permanent settlement of this region began when Franciscan missionary Fray García de San Francisco built the Nuestra Señora de Guadalupe ("Our Lady of Guadalupe") Mission in 1659. The settlement that grew around the mission came to be known as El Paso del Norte. Much later, at the end of the Mexican-American War in 1848, the Treaty of Guadalupe Hidalgo designated the Rio Grande as the boundary between the United States and Mexico, which put El Paso del Norte in Mexico. In an example of a naming phenomenon that can occur with towns that share a border, the settlement that had been forming on the east side of the river, still part of the United States, was later platted under a similar name: El Paso. For years, the two communities, El Paso del Norte and El Paso, coexisted on opposite sides of the river, probably causing frequent misdelivery of mail. Finally, in 1888, El Paso del Norte changed its name to Ciudad Juárez, the name it retains today.

More to explore: *Bartlett Garcia Continental Survey Point, El Camino Real—The King's Highway, Jornada del Muerto, La Salineta*

131. El Rancho de las Golondrinas/Old Cienega Village Museum

Location: Santa Fe County. South of Santa Fe, at the entrance to El Rancho de las Golondrinas. See map 2.

Marker text: Established in the 1700s, Rancho de Las Golondrinas was a *paraje*, or stopping place, which provided a welcome respite to weary travelers along the Camino Real well into the 19th century. The site is now a living historical museum which features a reconstructed Spanish fortified hacienda and other structures. The museum is open to the public from April 1st to October 31st.

A walk through El Rancho de las Golondrinas and the Old Cienega Village Museum today is a walk through the Spanish colonial history of New Mexico. Here, visitors can talk to workers in a *carreteria*, or wheelwright shop, admire the desks of an old schoolhouse, smell the fragrant fortunes of a fruit orchard and vineyard, and observe a Morada de la Conquistadora, or Penitente Meeting House.

The village of La Cienega emerged as one of several scattered farming communities in the water-rich valley south of Santa Fe in the seventeenth and eighteenth centuries. The village grew around the hacienda, or ranch home, erected along the banks of the Santa Fe River by the Vega y Coca family in the early 1700s. The patriarch of the family, Miguel Vega y Coca, had come to New Mexico in 1693 as part of the Spanish reconquest of the state after the Pueblo Revolt more than a decade earlier. Vega y Coca's large ranch included living quarters, guest rooms, and probably a *torreón*, or defensive tower, from which the family could guard against Indian violence. The family named their enterprise El Rancho de las Golondrinas, "the Ranch of the Swallows."

Travelers along El Camino Royal, the Royal Road, the foremost trade and settlement route between Mexico City and Taos, stopped at the village and enjoyed the coffers of hospitality at the Vega y Coca ranch. Such stops along the route were known as *parajes*, or resting places. The paraje at El Rancho de las Golondrinas offered those traveling south their last bit of Santa Fe hospitality, and those going north, their first.

Fray Francisco Atanasio Domínguez visited La

Cienega in 1776 on an inspection tour of missions in New Mexico. He left behind one of the earliest accounts of the village and its farms:

The settlement lies in a kind of nook between two cañadas [valleys]. None of the rivers mentioned reach it, nor does it have any water except some springs which suffice for the irrigation of the little farms. . . . Here it is called Cienega Grande *and that is just what it is, for there is a good swamp. . . . These lands . . . usually yield fairly good crops.*

In 1932, New Mexico folklorist Leonora Curtin and her family purchased the ranch and began a restoration of the historic hacienda and outbuildings, remaining true to the style and materials of the original. With the guidance of the residents of La Cienega and descendants of the original Vega y Coca lineage, they self-financed the rebuilding of many of the older structures to period authenticity. They even salvaged entire buildings and equipment from outlying mountain villages and reconstructed them on the ranch. Through their efforts, El Rancho de las Golondrinas opened to the public in 1972 as a living history museum.

The acequia, or irrigation system, built by La Cienega residents to pull water from local marshes for their fields of corn, beans, and wheat, is today listed on the National Register of Historic Places. The nomination notes that the ditches "still water the same small fields planted with traditional crops which have sustained the community for over 200 years."

More to explore: *El Camino Real—The King's Highway, Historic Los Luceros, Three Wise Women*

132. El Rito

Location: Rio Arriba County. At the south end of El Rito, in a pullout on the east side of NM 554, at mile marker 11. See map 2.

Marker text: Tewa people lived in this area before the village of El Rito Colorado was settled in the 1830s by residents from the Abiquiú area. The Territorial Legislature of 1909 established the Spanish-American Normal School here to train teachers for northern New Mexico schools. El Rito has evolved into a vibrant art community while retaining its traditional agricultural roots.

133. El Rito

Location: Rio Arriba County. In El Rito, in a pullout on the west side of NM 554, in front of Northern New Mexico Community College. See map 2.

Marker text: This village was settled in the 1830s by residents from the Abiquiú area. The Territorial Legislature of 1909 established the Spanish-American Normal School here to train teachers for northern New Mexico schools. After several changes in name and purpose the institution is now the Northern New Mexico Community College.

The small northern New Mexico community of El Rito lies within the 1.5-million-acre Carson National Forest. The village takes its name from the rambling stream running northeast of town, El Rito, a Spanish name that translates to "Little River." The population in El Rito today includes some 1,300 residents. The community has endured as a ranching center, a gateway to Carson National Forest, and, more recently, a haven for artists. A Depression-era writer summed up the genial setting by noting: "This little town and settlement is situated in a beautiful valley, bountifully supplied with fertile land, timber and water."

The ruins of rock dams and terraced gardens

in the hills surrounding El Rito provide evidence of centuries-old Tewa Indian agriculture here. The native people who tilled these grounds some six hundred years ago lived in a grand two-thousand-room, three-story pueblo known today as Sapawe. After Gregorio Quintana purchased land here in 1808, settlers, many of them migrating from nearby Abiquiú, began to tend fields along the river. The village of El Rito Colorado (Spanish for "the Red Creek," a name later shortened to its present form) developed as an agricultural community, with a population of about four hundred by 1820. Within twenty years, that number had more than tripled.

In 1903, the New Mexico territorial legislature appropriated funds for the construction of a school for youthful offenders, to be located in northern New Mexico. El Rito was chosen as the site of the school, and a new building, Delgado Hall, erected. Yet, shortly after completion of the building in 1907, the territorial legislature rescinded the designation and transferred the school to the community of Springer. Delgado Hall opened instead in 1909 as the Spanish American Normal School, which would have as its mission, as stated by the legislature, "preparing Spanish-speaking young people of New Mexico for the vocation of teaching in the Spanish-speaking counties of the State."

The institution grew over time. An essay in the *New Mexico Highway Journal* of October 1930 noted that the school in that year had five buildings and two dormitories for teachers, and that students paid boarding costs of fourteen dollars a month.

The Normal School closed in 1969. The buildings served briefly as the New Mexico Technical-Vocational Institute before becoming part of Española-based Northern New Mexico Community College. Highly regarded for its programs in traditional folk arts, NNMCC is the only school in the country today to offer degrees in Spanish colonial furniture making.

More to explore: *Córdova, Eastern New Mexico University, New Mexico Tech*

El Santuario de Chimayó: *see Chimayó*

134. Elephant Butte Dam

Location: Sierra County. In Elephant Butte, in a parking area overlooking the dam from the east, just north of the intersection of NM 177 and NM 51. See map 5.

Marker text: Pueblo Indians irrigated and farmed the Rio Grande Valley for several hundred years before the Spaniards arrived and continued the tradition. Built between 1910–1916, Elephant Butte Dam when completed was the world's largest irrigation reservoir. It was the first large-scale effort to harness and control the Rio Grande, and its construction was critical to the historic debate over interstate and international aspects of water use.

135. Elephant Butte Lake State Park

Location: Sierra County. In Truth or Consequences, in the lawn of the Sierra County Courthouse, at the intersection of Date and Third Streets. See map 5.

Marker text: Situated beside the huge, 36,000-acre Elephant Butte Reservoir, this is one of the largest and most popular parks in New Mexico. It combines boating, waterskiing, fishing and other water-based sports with land activities such as camping, picknicking, and hiking. Fish caught year-round at Elephant Butte Lake include various species of bass, channel catfish and crappie.

Sixteenth-century Spanish explorers in New Mexico found Pueblo Indians living in the Rio Grande Valley and subsisting on the agriculture made possible by the arable soil. Later, Spanish and Anglo settlers sought the life-giving Rio Grande for their own farmlands. But the river could be meanspirited: dry years meant dead fields; wet years meant floods, sometimes vengeful enough to destroy crops, roads—even entire villages. Harnessing the river into a dependable water source was a requirement for stable, sustainable development of the lower Rio Grande Valley.

After years of legal wrangling, which included discussions about the complex issues of interstate and international water use rights, Congress gave final approval in 1905 for the construction of a dam at an appropriate site somewhere along the lower Rio Grande. Engineers with the US Bureau of Reclamation first considered, and then rejected, a spot near the Mexican border. They settled instead on a location just east of present-day Truth or Consequences, near the core of an ancient volcano eroded into the shape of the head and back of an elephant: Elephant Butte.

Under the supervision of R. J. Schmalhausen, workers began construction of the dam in 1912. Crews first built a diversion dam and flumed the water from the Rio Grande away from the drilling area. After casting footings, workers poured enough cement to create a megalith 306 feet high and 1,674 feet long. Materials came to the site over the short-lived Elephant Butte Railroad, which ran from nearby Engle to the construction camp at the base of Elephant Butte that served as home for the crews while they labored. In addition to houses, the camp had a hospital, a telephone system, and a jail. The workers' "dam kids," as they were good-naturedly known, even studied at their own school.

Crew members building Elephant Butte Dam lived at a small townsite near the base of the butte. When completed in 1916, the dam created the largest lake in the state. Workers' camp during the construction of Elephant Butte Dam, Elephant Butte, New Mexico, ca. 1911–1915. New Mexico State University Library, Archives and Special Collections.

Designed to restrain a capacity of more than two million acre-feet of water, the dam at completion stretched 16 feet wide at the top and 205 feet at its base. Functionally, it worked in conjunction with other dams to the south, like Leasburg Diversion Dam near Las Cruces, to release water in a controlled flow for irrigation throughout the lower Rio Grande Valley. When dedicated on October 16, 1916, Elephant Butte Dam was the largest concrete structure in the United States.

No longer needed, some of the barracks used in the workers' city were floated down the river to nearby Truth or Consequences, where they were resuscitated as apartment and office buildings. Not as lucky were the abandoned towns of Alamocita, San José, San Albino, and Zapata, entombed by the waters of the forty-mile-long Elephant Butte Reservoir. Also down in the murky darkness are the remains of Fort McRae, a military post in operation from 1863 to 1884.

In April 1965, a recreational area around the dam and lake was dedicated as Elephant Butte Lake State Park and opened to visitors. Today, the 31,000-acre reservoir created by the dam, along with two hundred miles of shoreline, are popular with campers, hikers, swimmers, boaters, and fishers. Elephant Butte Lake is the largest lake in New Mexico, and the state park is one of the busiest in the state.

More to explore: *Caballo Mountains, Leasburg Dam State Park, Rio Grande, Truth or Consequences*

136. Elizabethtown

Location: Colfax County. Just west of Eagle Nest, at the intersection of NM 64 and NM 38. See map 3.

Marker text: The discovery of gold on Baldy Mountain in 1866 brought such a rush of fortune-seekers to the Moreno Valley that "E-town" became a roaring mining camp almost overnight. Because of water and transportation problems, and a decline in ore quality, it had become virtually a ghost town by 1875.

Near the summit of the 12,441-foot Baldy Mountain, in the fall of 1866, Captain John William Moore, sutler at nearby Fort Union, and a partner, William Kroenig, opened the Mystic Copper Mine. By the following May, other fortune seekers, lured by the additional discovery of gold flakes in Willow Creek, had staked claims in hundreds of promising locations across the mountain. Moore and Kroenig quickly decided that the greater prospects lay above ground; Moore opened a store and Kroenig a sawmill to serve the needs of the town that had bounded to life almost overnight. That settlement took the name Elizabethtown, for John Moore's four-year-old daughter, Elizabeth Catherine.

By 1868, the buildings in Elizabethtown, or E-Town as it was colloquially known, ran the litany required by an upstart settlement: stores, hotels, a school, and several saloons. Placer mining was augmented with lode mines like the War Eagle, Red Bandanna, Only Chance, and Puzzler; and E-Town's first newspaper, the *Lantern*, was soon dishing the dirt to several thousand residents. In 1869, E-Town became the first incorporated city in New Mexico.

By 1910, it was a ghost town.

E-Town suffered from location. The town rested in the Moreno Valley high in the Sangre de Cristo Mountains, making the cost of transporting ores from the site prohibitive. Additionally, water sources were few, and miners were left without adequate means of separating gold from gravel. Industrious settlers, led by William Moore and others, attempted to flume water over an elaborate funnel system from the Red River eastward through some forty miles of splintery wooden track to the mines at Baldy Mountain. But this, the "Big Ditch," was a big bust, its watery cargo victim to evaporation and leakage along the run. As fortunes in Colfax County shifted to the village of Cimarron, E-Town became a faded settlement by 1875.

The town enjoyed a small renaissance in 1901 when a new woman came to visit, promising a rebirth of mining on Baldy Mountain. She was the brainchild of H. J. Reiling, who orchestrated an elaborate plan to dredge the Moreno River for gold. Reiling dammed the river to create a small lake and placed there a sixty-five-bucket dredge he named Eleanor. "May thy wheels never turn without profit to thy owners," said Mrs. W. A. Maughey in her christening prayer, after breaking a bottle of champagne on Eleanor's wooden legs. "May there be no loss of gold in thy boxes; no leakage of water in thy seams. May harmony and success prevail."

It did, for a time. Eleanor spun her buckets without pause, yielding what one estimate claimed was one-third of the total production of gold in New Mexico at the time. By 1904, however, she was dredging more stone than gold. A greedy fire a year earlier had engulfed the wooden structures in town. Reiling's lake was drained, and the gold-producing Ferris wheel shut down and sold.

Elizabeth Catherine Moore, for whom the town was named, lived in the settlement until her death in 1934. She is buried in the E-Town cemetery atop a hill east of town.

More to explore: *Carthage-Tokay-Farley, Cimarron, Dawson, Riley, Shakespeare*

Emma Estrada: *see Parteras of New Mexico*

137. Emory Pass—Black Range Mountains
Elevation: 8,228 feet

Location: Sierra County. West of Kingston, at the turnoff to Emory Pass Lookout in the Mimbres Mountains, between mile markers 31 and 32 on NM 152. See map 5.

Marker text: At the top of the pass are Tertiary volcanic and Paleozoic sedimentary rocks that also form the high cliffs of the Caballo Mountains seen 35 miles to the east. The two ranges were joined until the Rio Grande Rift formed a graben that settled about four miles lower than the pass. McKnight Peak is the Black Range's highest point at 10,165 feet. The pass is named for Army officer William Hemsley Emory, who crossed it in 1846.

The Black Range Mountains began to form more than thirty-five million years ago as the result of volcanic activity in the southwestern part of the state. The uplifted range borders the Rio Grande Rift, an area of sunken land known by the geological term *graben*, over which flows the Rio Grande. The Paleozoic rocks exposed at the pass here are the same as those that form the high cliffs of the Caballo Mountains on the opposite side of the rift, thirty-five miles to the east. The rock that once joined the two has settled roughly four miles vertically and is now covered by graben sediments. The highest point of the range is the peak of McKnight Mountain, about ten miles northwest of here, reaching 10,165 feet.

The name of this cut through the Black Range Mountains honors nineteenth-century army officer William Hemsley Emory. Nicknamed "Bold Emory" by his West Point classmates, Adjutant General Emory crossed this mountain pass in 1846. He was traveling as part of the Army of the West, a force sent to bring the Mexican

Southwest under the control of the United States. As a member of the Army Corps of Topographical Engineers, Emory compiled for Congress an extensive scientific record and map of his journey, entitled *Notes of a Military Reconnaissance from Fort Leavenworth in Missouri to San Diego in California*. His chronicle included details about the people, landscape, and natural resources of the region—Emory called cacti his "new and disagreeable friend."

From Emory Pass, visitors can enjoy a panorama very much like the one Emory himself probably admired: the Rio Grande Valley, including the Caballo Reservoir and the San Andres Mountains, behind which glisten the gypsum sands of White Sands National Monument.

More to explore: *Basin and Range Country, Caballo Mountains, Jornada del Muerto, Rio Grande*

West Point graduate William Hemsley Emory traveled to New Mexico with the Army Corps of Topographical Engineers as part of the American occupation in 1846. His name on this cut through the Black Range Mountains recalls his contributions to opening the West. Photograph, General William H. Emory, ca. 1860–1865, ARC Identifier 528334, Local Identifier 111-B-4189. Matthew Brady Photographs of Civil War–Era Personalities and Scenes, 1921–1940, War Department, Records of the Office of the Chief Signal Officer, 1860–1985, Record Group 111, National Archives at College Park, Maryland.

138. Española Valley

Location: Rio Arriba County. North of Española, on the west side of US 285, between mile markers 191 and 192. See map 2.

Marker text: When it was described by Gaspar Castano de Sosa in 1591, the Española Valley contained about ten Tewa-speaking pueblos, several of which are still occupied today. Juan de Oñate established New Mexico's first colony here in 1598. Long on the northern frontier of Spanish settlement, the Valley has continuously reflected its Indian and Spanish heritage.

North of Santa Fe, the Rio Grande traverses a valley flanked on the west by the volcanic Jemez Mountains and on the east by the beautiful Sangre de Cristo range. This is the Española Valley. Long the backdrop for seminal interactions between Native American and Spanish-speaking people in the state, the Española Valley reflects in its people, its architecture, and its heritage the shared history of Indian, Spanish, and Anglo cultures in New Mexico.

One of the first meetings between Europeans and the Tewa-speaking Pueblo Indians of the Española Valley came with the visit of Gaspar Castaño de Sosa in 1591. Castaño, lieutenant governor and captain general of Nuevo León in Mexico, was leading an unlicensed colonization expedition into New Mexico. In all, he made stops at eleven Tewa pueblos, including Tesuque, San Ildefonso, and Santa Clara, before authorities tracked him down and carted him back to Mexico.

A more favorable venture took place seven years later, when don Juan de Oñate arrived leading the expedition that would bring permanent European settlement to New Mexico. Oñate reached the Tewa-speaking pueblo of Ohke in July 1598. He renamed the pueblo San Juan and established his headquarters there, along with some four hundred soldiers, priests, settlers, and servants. By 1601, the colonists had moved the Spanish capital, the first in New Mexico, across the Rio Grande to the Tewa pueblo of Yunque-Ouinge. Oñate renamed Yunque-Ouinge as San Gabriel de los Españoles, or "Saint Gabriel of the Spaniards," which some historians credit as a possible source of the name Española.

Relations between Spanish, Indian, and later Anglo cultures in the Española Valley in the centuries since have been marked by both conflict and alliance. In 1998, with the release of a new postage stamp commemorating four hundred years of Spanish settlement in New Mexico, state representative Nick Salazar of San Juan Pueblo summed up the experience in a speech he presented that day, saying that the mesh of Spanish and Indian nations

caused great conflict and suffering among all our people, both Spanish and Indian. But it was also the beginning of the merging of two cultures with mutual benefits in art, agriculture, trading, framing of government, and the introduction of Catholicism.

Today, the logo of the city of Española displays a pueblo wedding vase beside the helmet of a Spanish conquistador.

More to explore: *Castaño de Sosa's Route, Oñate's Route (see under El Camino Real—The King's Highway), San Gabriel on the Camino Real*

139. Espejo's Expedition

Location: Doña Ana County. At the New Mexico Visitors Center on Interstate 10, just north of the New Mexico–Texas border. See map 5.

Marker text: Trying to locate two Franciscan friars, Antonio de Espejo in 1582 led an expedition up the Rio Grande near here. The two friars had remained among the Tiwa Indians near Bernalillo after the Rodriguez-Sanchez Chamuscado expedition returned to Mexico in 1581. When he reached the Tiwas in 1583, Espejo learned that the missionaries were dead.

140. Espejo's Expedition
On the Camino Real

Location: Socorro County. South of San Antonio, in the Fort Craig Rest Area on the west side of Interstate 25, between mile markers 113 and 114. See map 5.

Marker text: In 1582 and 1583, Antonio de Espejo and his party followed the Rio Grande north to the Bernalillo area. Espejo was trying to learn the fate of two Franciscan friars who had stayed with the Pueblo Indians after the Rodriguez-Sanchez/Chamuscado expedition returned to Mexico in 1581.

When don Antonio de Espejo led his expedition into New Mexico in 1582, he was intent on finding two Franciscan friars who had remained behind from another expedition the previous year. Those priests, Fray Agustín Rodríguez and Fray Francisco López, had come to New Mexico with Captain Francisco Sánchez Chamuscado and a small battalion of soldiers to investigate the region and substantiate claims of golden cities. Chamuscado and his soldiers had returned to Mexico after their explorations, but the two priests had remained, hoping to spread Christianity among the Indians. They made their home among the Tiwa-speaking Indians near present-day Bernalillo at an Indian pueblo the Spaniards called Puaray. The exact location of Puaray is not known.

Like the Chamuscado expedition, Espejo and his crew, which included Franciscan priest Bernardino Beltán and a handful of soldiers, followed the Rio Grande north through New Mexico. Before even reaching Puaray, however, Espejo received word that the two priests they were seeking had been killed in the intervening year—martyred by the Indians they had hoped to convert.

After visiting the now-abandoned pueblos of the eastern Piro and eastern Tigua near present-day Mountainair, Espejo and his men returned to the Rio Grande and continued north. They reached Puaray on February 17, 1583. It was empty, the Indians having left to seek haven from the soldiers in the Sandia Mountains. Espejo dubbed the pueblo Puaray of the Martyrs.

Espejo began to travel, probing the region for a fabled golden lake and other evidence of mineral wealth. His tour took the explorer to Cochiti, Zia, and Acoma Pueblos, and then into what is now Arizona. When Espejo returned to Puaray in June, he was countered by a defiant group of some thirty Indians, who stood on the roofs of their pueblo mocking the Spanish soldiers and refusing to give food. Espejo, concerned that such sedition might set a precedent among other pueblos, garroted sixteen Indians and set fire to the village. The explorer's regretful act had the desired effect: pueblos he visited from that point forward were, as the expedition's chronicler put it, "so afraid that all served and regaled us."

From Pecos Pueblo in the summer of 1583, Espejo turned southward and traveled home along the course of the Pecos River. In doing so, he became the first Spanish explorer to visit the Pecos Valley. The ensemble arrived back at their home base of San Bartolomé that September.

More to explore: *Bernalillo, Early Spanish Route, Espejo's Trail, Mesa and Pecos Valley, Pueblo of Acoma, Pueblo of Zia*

141. Espejo's Trail

Location: Eddy County. South of Loving and just north of Malaga, at the Black River, on US 285. See map 6.

Marker text: Don Antonio de Espejo, leader of the third expedition to explore New Mexico, passed near here on his return to Mexico City in 1583. After learning of the martyrdom of two Franciscan friars from an earlier expedition, he explored the Pueblo country and then followed the Pecos River Valley south.

Don Antonio de Espejo and his small company of men were returning from the third expedition by Spain into New Mexico in 1583 when they became the first Spanish explorers to visit the Pecos Valley. Their excursion was an attempt to tie up loose ends from the journey of Francisco Sánchez Chamuscado the previous year. Two Franciscan priests traveling with Chamuscado, Fray Agustín Rodríguez and Fray Francisco López, had remained in New Mexico after Chamuscado left, hoping to erect a mission in an Indian pueblo the Spaniards called Puaray. Although historians know that Puaray was somewhere near present-day Bernalillo, they do not know the exact location. Espejo, with a group of fourteen soldiers and another Franciscan, had come to New Mexico in November 1582 to learn the priests' fate.

They discovered it before even reaching Puaray. Word arrived that the priests were dead, martyred by the Indians they had hoped to convert. Despite the bad news, Espejo, intent on searching the region for mineral riches, led his associates onward. They visited several pueblos in central and northern New Mexico, including Cochiti, Zia, and Zuni, and then continued into Arizona. The explorer uncovered small traces of copper near present-day Prescott, Arizona. While not the glorious riches he had dreamed of, the discovery gave him reason to boast of the untapped wealth of this magnificent land.

By the summer of 1583, Espejo had returned east and reached the pueblo of Pecos, southeast of Santa Fe. From there, he began his return trip to Mexico southward along the Pecos River. The men named the river Rio de las Vacas, or "River of the Cows," although the "cows" were likely buffalo.

Espejo reached his return destination of San Bartolomé in September 1853 with zealous tales of silver and other riches in the land to the north. He even had a new name for that land, a term he coined in his own account of the journey: *Nuevo Mejico*—New Mexico.

More to explore: *Bernalillo, Early Spanish Route, Espejo's Expedition, Mesa and Pecos Valley, Pueblo of Zuni*

Estella García: *see Fabric Artists*

142. Esther Martinez, P'oe Tsáwä (1912–2006)

Location: Rio Arriba County. Near the entrance to Ohkay Owingeh Pueblo, on the east side of US 68 between mile markers 4 and 5, near the intersection of US 68 and NM 74. See map 2.

Marker text: Esther Martinez served her community as an educator, linguist and storyteller. Her foremost contributions to our state are documenting and preserving the Tewa language and the art of storytelling. Esther was named a National Heritage Fellow in 2006 by the National Endowment of the Arts, the nation's highest honor for artists.

Hearts were gladdened around New Mexico as Esther Martinez, the ninety-four-year-old storyteller from the Pueblo of Ohkay Owingeh, was honored in Washington, D.C., in September 2006 with a National Heritage Fellowship. Martinez received a standing ovation at the ceremony held at the Library of Congress as she accepted the fellowship, which she did on behalf of all of Ohkay Owingeh. It was a happy occasion for the state and particularly for the pueblo. The award, offered by the National Endowment for the Arts, is one of the most prestigious honors in the nation for artists—and Martinez had certainly earned it.

Martinez was born in 1912 in Utah. She moved with her family as a girl to Ignacio, Colorado, but she spent much of her time growing up with her grandparents in Ohkay Owingeh. With her family, she spoke Tewa, the traditional language spoken at the pueblo. (Her Tewa name, P'oe Tsáwä, means "Blue Water.") Tewa is the traditional language of six of the nineteen pueblos in New Mexico, including Ohkay Owingeh. It was in the very preservation of that language that Martinez later found her calling.

In the 1960s, while she was working at the John F. Kennedy School in Pueblo, Colorado, Martinez got an interesting offer. A linguist working at the school, Randall Spiers, upon learning that Martinez spoke Tewa, encouraged her to learn to read and write it as well. So Martinez traveled to North Dakota in 1974 to attend the Summer Institute of Linguistics and later enrolled in a similar program at the University of New Mexico. Returning to Ohkay Owingeh, she accepted a position in 1978 as a bilingual teacher at the Ohkay Owingeh Day School, teaching the Tewa language to young students. She would hold this position for more than two decades—and through it, help preserve a language that might otherwise have fallen to disuse.

Martinez engaged herself in a number of linguistics projects. Through the San Juan Pueblo Bilingual Program (San Juan was the former name of Ohkay Owingeh Pueblo), she developed curriculum guides for the teaching of Tewa to young children as well as children's books in Tewa, helping young students in the pueblo schools learn their native language. She compiled a dictionary, with Spiers (the man who had inspired her earlier), of the dialect of Tewa spoken at the pueblo. And she translated a version of the New Testament into Tewa. All this while raising three girls and seven boys.

Martinez also became regarded for her storytelling abilities. Storytelling is part of the tradition of Ohkay Owingeh, as it is in many native communities; it offers a way to preserve cultural heritage, pass along values and lessons, entertain, inform, and build community. Martinez's own grandfather was a storyteller, and she credited many of the stories she told to him. Martinez worked as a storyteller for the public school system as well as for the National Park Service. She traveled throughout the United States to participate in storytelling conferences, bringing her stories to a wider audience. Today, the community library at Ohkay Owingeh is named in her honor.

Her dedication and passion led to many awards, including the New Mexico Governor's Award for Excellence in the Arts in 1998. And later, she received recognition as a National Heritage Fellow with the National Endowment for the Arts, the honor for which she, at age ninety-four, traveled to Washington, D.C.

As happy as New Mexicans were in September 2006 when Martinez was honored with that fellowship, they were abruptly saddened only days later. As Martinez was being driven home from the airport on September 16, 2006, after returning to New Mexico from her trip, a drunk driver struck the car in which she was riding. Martinez did not survive the crash.

"Traveling my [life's journey] was not easy," Martinez wrote in her 2004 book, *My Life in San Juan Pueblo*. "Seeking new adventures was."

More to explore: *María Dolores Gonzáles, Pablita Velarde (see under Pueblo of Santa Clara)*

143. Eve Ball (1890–1984)
Author and Preservationist

Location: Lincoln County. East of Fort Stanton, in a pullout on the north side of US 380, between mile markers 91 and 92, just across from the turnoff to Fort Stanton–Snowy River Cave National Conservation Area. See map 6.

Marker text: A pioneer in the preservation of the history of people in Southeastern New Mexico, Eve wrote over 150 articles and numerous books chronicling Mescalero and Chiricahua Apaches, Anglo and Hispanic settlers. Her honesty, patience and determination to learn from them won the confidence of Apache elders, saving oral histories certain to be lost without her.

Oral historians work in a tradition that values the role of the first-person narrator. Stories captured through oral histories can offer nuanced versions of historical events by presenting a glimpse of those events from an informed and sometimes very personal point of view. Such was the case with much of the work of historian and author Eve Ball. Although not exclusively an oral historian, Ball did conduct numerous oral history interviews, finding in them the source material for many of her books about the people of the Southwest. Without her enterprising work in this area, many important historical voices would have gone unheard.

In the preface to one of her most respected books, *In the Days of Victorio: Recollections of a Warm Springs Apache*, Ball mentions that the Apaches who lived on the Mescalero Apache Reservation near Ruidoso were not well known to the people of that town. As Ball visited with elders and others on the reservation, getting to know them and earning their confidence, she found that the stories they told her of events in the Apache Wars (a mid-nineteenth-century series of engagements between Apaches and the US Army in the Southwest) sometimes differed from the written accounts of those episodes—proving true the adage that history is written by the victors. Bell sought to bring the untold stories she was hearing to a wider world. "I have hoped to make the reader live their story with them," she wrote, "to see the Apache's experiences through their eyes."

Ball was born in Clarksville, Tennessee, on March 14, 1890. After graduating from Kansas State Teachers College in 1918, she became a schoolteacher in Kansas and Oklahoma, and then completed a master's in education at Kansas State University. In 1949, at age fifty-nine, she retired from education and moved to Ruidoso, New Mexico—a place she chose specifically because of the opportunities she believed existed here to reach out to the Mescalero Apaches, along with other notable denizens of southern New Mexico, and help tell their story. She spent time with her subjects, encouraging them to speak honestly about their experiences. In so doing, she bridged gaps between races, genders, generations, and cultures, and then shared with the world what she learned.

Ball researched, wrote, and published the histories of the people and the places around her, eventually seeing more than 150 of her articles and books in print. Her first book, *Ruidoso: The Last Frontier*, published in 1963, told the history of the town she had moved to, and the place where she made her home until her death. She followed that with her 1966 biography of Roswell rodeo cowboy "Wild Horse Bob" Crosby. Another biography, *Ma'am Jones of the Pecos*, followed, detailing the life of southeastern New Mexico pioneer woman Barbara Jones. In addition to the book *In the Days of Victorio*, she cowrote *Indeh: An Apache Odyssey*, a series of oral histories from the Mescalero and Chiricahua Apaches, with Nora Henn and Lynda Sánchez.

Ball's writing was recognized for its valuable contribution to our understanding of the American Southwest. Among the awards she received was the prestigious Saddleman Award, given in 1982, from the Western Writers of America. Acknowledging "outstanding contributions to the American West," the award had previously been bestowed on such literary luminaries as Dorothy M. Johnson (author of "The Man Who Shot Liberty Valance") and Louis L'Amour. That same year, Ball was inducted into the Cowgirl Hall of Fame.

In the fall of 1983, the US Senate passed S.R. 243 commending Eve Ball, noting that "the people of the United States owe Eve Ball a tremendous debt of gratitude for writings which enrich our knowledge of the Indian, the West, and those courageous persons who settled that vast land, and for the invaluable legacy such writings will be for future generations."

Ball passed away the following year, on Christmas Eve, 1984, in Ruidoso.

More to explore: *Lozen—Little Sister, Rose Powers White, Ruidoso*

Evelyn M. Vigil and Juanita T. Toledo: *see Pecos*

144. Fabiola Cabeza de Baca Gilbert (1895–1991)

Location: San Miguel County. About eight miles east of Las Vegas, at the intersection of NM 104 and NM 67, in a pullout on the south side of NM 104. See map 3.

Marker text: Raised on a ranch at La Liendre, Fabiola received a degree from New Mexico Normal School. She worked as a rural teacher and an agricultural Home Extension agent. In the 1930s, she became a charter member of La Sociedad Folklorica. An author and teacher, she dedicated her life to preserving Hispanic traditions. In 1954, she wrote "We Fed Them Cactus," a book about growing up at La Liendre.

It often falls to writers to capture the vanishing traditions of the cultures that make up a multicultural state like New Mexico before they are lost to history. In this, New Mexicans are indebted to Fabiola Cabeza de Baca Gilbert, teacher, folklorist, and writer, for her work in recording the lives, customs, rituals, and traditions of New Mexico in the twentieth century.

Fabiola Cabeza de Baca was born on May 16, 1894, on a ranch in La Liendre, New Mexico, a small ranching settlement about twelve miles south of this Historic Marker. Fabiola received her bachelor's degree in pedagogy from the New Mexico Normal University (now New Mexico Highlands University) in Las Vegas, a school to train teachers. After working as a teacher in parts of rural New Mexico, she enrolled in the Agriculture College at New Mexico State University in Las Cruces, earning a second bachelor's degree in home economics in 1929. With her degrees in hand, she began work as a home extension agent with the New Mexico Extension Service.

Her work with the extension service allowed her to travel through rural communities in northern New Mexico, teaching food preparation, canning, nutrition, and cooking techniques. In addition to speaking both Spanish and English, she also learned the Tiwa and Tewa dialects, which allowed her to include some of the northern Indian pueblos among her outreach efforts. In 1942, she published the book *Historic Cookery*, which included recipes she had created for the extension service. The recipes reflect the diverse cultural makeup of the state, including Native American, Spanish, Mexican, and Anglo cuisine.

Immersed in the culture of New Mexico and eager to preserve the *cuentos*, or stories, of the Hispanic people of the state, she and others founded La Sociedad Folklorica (the Folklore Society) in Santa Fe in 1936. Still in operation today, La

Fabiola Cabeza de Baca Gilbert's combination of training in education and home economics, along with her command of several languages, enabled her to make a true difference in the state. Her remembrances growing up near La Liendre formed the basic of her classic book, *We Fed Them Cactus*. Fabiola Cabeza de Baca Gilbert. New Mexico State University Library, Archives and Special Collections.

Sociedad Folklorica helps to preserve the traditions and cultures of Hispanic New Mexico.

Fabiola's work for the New Mexico Extension Service continued for thirty years, during which time she became well known and highly regarded across the county. An article in the *California Farmer* in 1954 referred to her as "New Mexico's Famous Home Economist." In May 1957, her efforts were recognized by the US secretary of agriculture, who awarded her the USDA Award for Superior Service.

Despite her prodigious work with the extension service, Fabiola Cabeza de Baca Gilbert is probably best known today as the author of the literary classic *We Fed Them Cactus*, first published in 1954. The book is a memoir about her own experiences growing up on the plains surrounding La Liendre, a part of New Mexico encompassed by a vast, treeless expanse known as the Llano Estacado. The book, she later wrote, was "inspired by the love I had for ranch life and to retrieve the history of Hispanic pioneering on the Llano." That life could be hard: the title refers to cactus that her family was forced to use as cattle feed during a sustained drought. In the book, she writes of her family, and even of her experience teaching school. That she loved the llano is clear. "The whole world seems to be there," she writes, "full of promise and gladness."

Fabiola Cabeza de Baca Gilbert passed away in Santa Fe in 1991.

More to explore: *Agnes Morley Cleaveland, Eve Ball, Peggy Pond Church (see under Marjorie Bell Chambers)*

145. Fabric Artists
Women of the Works Progress Administration

Location: Curry County. At the east end of Melrose, in a pullout on the north side of US 60/84 at mile marker 366. See map 6.

Marker text: Under the umbrella of the WPA, the National Youth Administration, and the Federal Art Program, instructors and students were recruited to work in community-based art centers that produced fabric arts, including weaving, colcha embroidery, and lace-making. While the artistic creativity of these mostly unrecognized women was considered "women's work for home use" by WPA administrators, this now popular New Mexican art form has been revitalized.

146. Estella García
Dates Unknown
Fabric Artists: Women of the WPA

Location: Curry County. At the east end of Melrose, in a pullout on the north side of US 60/84 at mile marker 366. See map 6.

Marker text: Estella García taught colcha embroidery at Melrose, New Mexico, for the Federal Art Program in the 1930s. Anglo and Hispana women in García's class collaborated to design and produce embroidered theater curtains, wall hangings, and seat coverings for institutions across the state including the Albuquerque Little Theatre. García is one of the few Hispanic women artists recorded in FAP documents. Unfortunately, few examples of her work remain.

Note: Marker faceplates are on opposite sides of the same sign.

Facing a country mired in the economic downturn of the 1930s, President Franklin D. Roosevelt created the Works Progress Administration (WPA) in 1935 in an effort to put Americans back to work. Two of the programs operating under the WPA were the National Youth Administration (NYA) and the Federal Art Project (FAP). (In 1939, the program was renamed the Federal Art Program.) The National Youth Administration helped young people aged sixteen to twenty-five find employment. In some cases in New Mexico, like at the NYA camp known as Camp Capitan in Capitan, that included instructing youth in fiber arts and helping them sell their creations.

Similar in concept to the Federal Writers' Project, which paid local writers to write about their communities or about local history, and the Federal Theater Project, which supported actors and directors, the Federal Arts Project allowed artists to produce public art or teach art instruction in exchange for a livable income. As part of that mission, the FAP sponsored a number of community art centers across the country—about a hundred altogether. With the goal of bringing art instruction to local communities, these centers were meeting places where art instructors and community members could gather for instruction. New Mexico had community arts centers in Roswell, Las Vegas, Taos, Gallup, and a few other smaller communities.

One was founded here, in Melrose—the Melrose Art Center. Housed in a two-story wooden building, the center advertised itself by a hand-painted wooden sign out front reading, "Melrose Art Center—Federal Art Project WPA."

While much of the art produced under the auspices of the FAP nationwide was visual art and included such products as murals, posters, and sculptures, instruction in the fabric arts took place as well. At the Melrose Art Center, local instructor Estella García taught community members a traditional Spanish colonial style of embroidery

Estella García and her colcha embroidery class, Federal Art Project of the Works Progress Administration, Melrose, New Mexico. García is standing; the fourth artist from the left is identified as Rita Rodríguez Chávez. Ca. 1936. Courtesy Palace of the Governors Photo Archives (NMHM/DCA), neg. no. 090204.

known as colcha. Most often done with dyed wool, colcha embroidery usually features a long stitch with a second stitch in the middle. It has a long history, being traditionally associated with Spanish nobility.

Despite a prevailing belief within the WPA that fabric work was mostly for domestic use, García and her students at the Melrose Art Center produced a number of beautiful handiworks that were used in public institutions. These included curtains, wall hangings, and seat coverings for theaters throughout the state. One of the curtains adorned the recently built Albuquerque Community Playhouse (now the Little Theater). Opening in 1936, the playhouse was a local performing arts center and, not coincidentally, the first structure built by the WPA in Albuquerque.

Most of the community arts centers around the country closed with the outbreak of World War II. (One in New Mexico remains in operation today—the Roswell Museum and Art Center.) Unfortunately, much of the fabric work done by García and her students has been lost to history. A few examples of her work have been preserved and can be admired in the collection of the Museum of International Folk Art in Santa Fe. These pieces are among the few examples of work produced by a Hispanic woman artist working for the FAP.

More to explore: *Agueda Martinez, Roswell*

147. Farmington

Location: San Juan County. At the west end of Farmington, on the south side of US 64, between mile markers 46 and 47. See map 1.

Marker text: Until 1876, this area comprised part of the Jicarilla Apache Reservation. Anglo settlement quickly began at the confluence of the San Juan, Animas, and La Plata Rivers. Farmington became a ranching and farming area and, later, an important producer of oil, gas, coal, and uranium.

Navajo Indians know the Farmington area by the word *to-tah*, which references the three rivers that converge here: the San Juan, Animas, and La Plata. For generations before the arrival of other settlers, this region of northwestern New Mexico was home to the Ancestral Puebloan people. These early Native Americans built extensive pueblo village complexes throughout the sun-drenched plateaus and mesas of the Colorado Plateau until migrating from the area around AD 1300.

A presidential executive order in March 1874 established a reservation for the Jicarilla Apache Indians in this region, with boundaries that began at the headwaters of the San Juan River and ran south along the river to the eastern edge of the Navajo Indian Reservation. Despite the restrictions on this area, miners and settlers alike restlessly wanted to set foot on the land, believing that the Four Corners area held great stores of mineral wealth. Bowing to the determined spirit of the times, President Ulysses S. Grant in July 1876 redefined the boundaries of the Jicarilla Apache Reservation and opened the land to homesteading.

One of the first settlers to arrive was Colorado farmer William Locke, who planted an eighty-four-acre orchard of fruit trees in the San Juan Valley in 1878 and named his fragrant enterprise Sunnyside Orchards. According to early pioneer histories, Locke's fruit trees were among the first in the region. Other farmers soon followed, planting peach, apple, and walnut trees. In 1879, fellow resident Milt Vernon suggested that the community that had similarly taken root here be named Farmington, a contraction of "farming town."

Farmington made good on that contraction. Horticulture and ranching carried the settlement safely across the turn of the century, with coal and uranium mining later adding their boost to the town's economy. In the 1940s, natural gas companies began to tap the petroleum reserves underlying the San Juan Basin and added a new asset to the ledger sheets.

Today, given its location in the Four Corners region, Farmington shares its history and traditions with the Navajo Nation. The Totah Festival held in Farmington in late summer celebrates this endemic cultural mix.

More to explore: *Aztec Ruins National Monument, Colorado Plateau, Harriet Belle Amsden Sammons, Jicarilla Apache (series)*

148. Feliciana Tapia Viarrial (1904–1988)
Pojoaque Pueblo

Location: Santa Fe County. In Pojoaque Pueblo, on the north side of Cities of Gold Road, just east of the intersection of Cities of Gold Road and W. Gutierrez Street. See map 2.

Marker text: Feliciana Viarrial helped establish today's Pueblo of Pojoaque. Pojoaque, or Posuwageh, water drinking place, is a Tewa village founded circa A.D. 1000. By 1913, the Pojoaque homelands were severely diminished. Most members left for neighboring Pueblos and Colorado. The families, including Feliciana's, returned after 1932 when the federal government restored their homelands. Mother of eleven, Feliciana was a matriarch of the community as it revitalized its culture.

Pojoaque Pueblo is a vibrant and thriving community, and visitors today would hardly guess that it had ever been otherwise. But the pueblo went through a rough turn in the early 1900s. That it survived is credit to the dedication of several families, including that of matriarch Feliciana Tapia Viarrial.

The pueblo of Pojoaque was originally established sometime before AD 1000 in this part of north-central New Mexico. The pueblo is known to residents as Posuwageh, or water-drinking place. It is one of the six New Mexico pueblos where the Tewa language is spoken.

Situated near water, the pueblo began to feel encroachment after 1900, as Anglo and Hispanic settlers used the pueblo lands to graze their livestock. Diseases like smallpox, along with a loss of population, conspired against the pueblo as well. By 1913, with the boundaries of the pueblo fractured, the situation was untenable. Although many of the remaining residents at Pojoaque kept their homes at the pueblo, several moved with their families to other pueblos, including Nambé, another Tewa-speaking pueblo a few miles to the east. Among those forced to leave was Pojoaque leader Antonio José Tapia, who moved with his family and a few other Pojoaque families to Colorado. The pueblo, so long an integral part of the history of this area, was in danger of disappearing.

It would be another two decades until the fortunes of Pojoaque reversed. In the early 1930s, when a nearby pueblo began to show interest in acquiring the Pojoaque lands, determination grew among former residents to resettle their pueblo before it was lost forever. That interest coincided with efforts by the federal government at that time related to Indian sovereignty. In 1933, Commissioner John Collier of the Bureau of Indian Affairs began to implement federal policies based on the premise that Indian tribes should be self-governing entities. His efforts culminated in the Indian Reorganization Act, passed in 1934. Under Collier, the BIA made a concerted effort to locate former Pojoaque residents or their descendants and entice them to return to their tribal lands.

Antonio José Tapia, who was still in Colorado, led the effort to bring former Pojoaque residents back home. With a small number of other families, all of whom made the decision to leave the lives they had created in the meantime and return to their home at Pojoaque, Tapia left Colorado in 1932 and returned to the pueblo. Soon thereafter, the federal government formally recognized the Pojoaque reservation, officially protecting its boundaries. Pueblo lands, which had been given over to grazing by local sheepherders, were granted back to Pojoaque residents. The recognition, coming after the resettlement, helped solidify the foundations of the restored pueblo.

But it took people to resurrect the pueblo itself. One of them was Tapia's daughter, Feliciana Tapia Viarrial, who returned to Pojoaque with her father, along with her husband, Fermin, and their four children. Viarrial became instrumental in the resettlement of the pueblo. After being elected to the Tribal Council, she was able to help direct the legislative and political affairs of the village and influence its future. As a community leader, respected and admired, Viarrial helped the pueblo return to its traditions and reestablish its cultural identity.

Feliciana and Fermin's own family grew to eleven children—making Feliciana Viarrial the matriarch of the pueblo.

From the hard work of the small number of former residents, Pojoaque Pueblo grew, and a community that had been on the brink of disappearing reemerged strong and proud.

That tradition of service continued in the next generation. Viarrial's son, Jacob Viarrial, was elected governor of the pueblo in 1978. He served in that position for twenty-two years. Upon his death in 2004, a stretch of US 84/285 through the reservation was named the Jacob Viarrial Memorial Highway in his honor.

Feliciana Tapia Viarrial, the woman considered instrumental in the development of today's Pojoaque Pueblo, passed away in 1988.

More to explore: *Founding Women of Albuquerque (see under Albuquerque)*

149. Fenton Lake State Park

Location: Sandoval County. At the entrance to Fenton Lake State Park, in a pullout on the east side of NM 126, between mile markers 28 and 29. See map 4.

Marker text: Surrounded by imposing mountains and beautiful ponderosa pine woodlands, Fenton Lake has long been a popular fishing and camping retreat. This area offers both lake and stream fishing for rainbow trout, and many deer, turkey and elk inhabit the immediate vicinity. The park area is also used for winter sports such as cross-country skiing and dogsled racing.

Note: Although the park once hosted winter dogsled races, it no longer does so.

Picturesque Fenton Lake lies along the Rio Cibola, surrounded by ponderosa pine woodlands, deep within the beautiful Jemez Mountains. The mountains formed some eleven million years ago as a result of volcanic eruptions. They are home to many natural wonders, like nearby Soda Dam, as well as the lake that is the centerpiece of this state park.

Fenton Lake takes its name named for missionary Elijah McClean Fenton Sr. Fenton built a home here in 1907 and lived near the lake with his family for many years. In 1940, he sold the land to the New Mexico State Game Commission, although the family still lived here for some time thereafter. The lake served as a protected migrating area for waterfowl for many years before becoming a state park in 1984.

Fenton Lake State Park offers outdoor enthusiasts plenty of opportunities to connect with nature. Fishing is available in the streams and also at the lake, which is stocked with rainbow trout. Wildlife lovers can expect to see mule deer and elk, among other woodland creatures. Birders might catch a glimpse of a bald eagle, the endangered Mexican spotted owl, or a black-headed grosbeak.

More to explore: *Jemez Mountains, Soda Dam*

150. Fort Bascom

Location: Quay and San Miguel Counties. North of Tucumcari, in a pullout on the east side of NM 104, between mile markers 100 and 101. See map 3.

Marker text: Fort Bascom was built to protect this area from Comanches. In 1864, Kit Carson led a campaign against the Comanches, as did General Philip Sheridan in 1868. The fort was also established to control the Comancheros, New Mexicans involved in illegal trade with the Comanches. Fort Bascom was abandoned in 1870.

In August 1863, Company F of the Seventh US Infantry and Company I of the First New Mexico Volunteers arrived along a bend on the east bank of the Canadian River to garrison the newly commissioned Fort Bascom. The name of the fort recognized Captain George N. Bascom, a West Point graduate and member of the Sixteenth US Infantry, who had died the previous year at the Battle of Valverde in New Mexico. Made up of officers' quarters ("badly constructed," according to an 1872 inventory), a guardhouse, commissary, hospital, quartermaster's building, and adobe barracks around a central parade ground, Fort Bascom originally was under the command of Captain Peter W. L. Plympton.

Soldiers at the fort spent much of their time forestalling aggression by bands of Comanche Indians. The Comanches stole livestock and raided settlements and ranches along the eastern plains of New Mexico as well as in Texas and Oklahoma, in part to resist the intrusion of Texas cattle ranchers into territory they had previously roamed. Very likely, the Comanches were unfairly blamed for other acts with which they had no connection. Still, Brigadier General James H. Carleton, head of the military in New Mexico, warned in an 1865 letter to the commander of Fort Bascom: "If they attack our [supply] trains we will make war upon them which they will always remember."

A year earlier, mountain man and military officer Kit Carson commanded a company of some 350 Fort Bascom soldiers in what became known as the Battle of Adobe Walls. The clash took place on November 12, 1864, when Carson and crew raided a Kiowa village along the Canadian River in Texas. Comanche Indians, allies of the Kiowas, banded with the Kiowas to stage an aggressive return attack. Severely outnumbered, Carson and his troops survived the onslaught by hiding behind the adobe walls of an abandoned trading post and firing on the Indians with howitzers. Two soldiers were killed and twenty-one lay wounded when the battle ended. An estimated sixty Indians were killed or wounded.

Meanwhile, soldiers at Fort Bascom faced a second adversary: the *comancheros*, Mexican and American roustabouts who traded illegally with Comanches and other Plains Indians. As described by Lieutenant James William Abert in 1845, these men were "dressed in conical-crowned sombreros, jackets with the stripes running transversely; large bag breeches extending to the knee; long stockings and moccasins." Soldiers stopped trade wagons on the road from Arkansas and Texas typically used by the comancheros. Traders without a valid government-issued trading license had their goods confiscated.

In the 1860s, a small settlement near the fort arose to serve the off-duty needs of the soldiers. It took the name Liberty, presumably because it represented as much to soldiers who sought it out as a place to have fun away from the confines of the military reservation.

On Christmas Day, 1868, in a canyon near the Wichita Mountains, two companies of Fort Bascom soldiers dispatched by General Philip Sheridan engaged a band of Comanches and set fire to their village. This battle, in addition to a decisive battle at Palo Duro Canyon in Texas in 1874 between the US Army and the Comanches and other Plains Indians, forced a somber peace onto the plains.

Although comanchero trade dwindled in the mid-1870s as the Plains Indians moved to reservations, soldiers at Fort Bascom never saw the decline. In December 1870, citing both heavy operating expenses and bad location, the army decommissioned the fort. The town of Liberty likewise depopulated soon after, and Tucumcari became the area's prominent settlement.

More to explore: *Comanche Country, Fort Bayard, Kit Carson Park (see under Taos), Tucumcari*

151. Fort Bayard

Location: Grant County. Ten miles east of Silver City on NM 180, between mile markers 120 and 121, at the entrance to Fort Bayard. See map 5.

Marker text: One of several posts created on the Apache frontier, Fort Bayard protected the Pinos Altos mining district. Company B of the black 125th Infantry served here, as did Lt. John J. Pershing. In 1900 the fort became a military hospital, and today serves as Fort Bayard Medical Center.

152. Fort Bayard National Cemetery

Location: Grant County. Ten miles east of Silver City on NM 180, between mile markers 120 and 121, at the entrance to Fort Bayard. See map 5.

Marker text: Originally established in 1866 as the military cemetery for Fort Bayard, many troopers, veterans, and civilians are buried here. It became a national cemetery, one of two in New Mexico, in 1973.

Note: Marker faceplates are on opposite sides of the same sign.

As part of an extensive plan to protect settlers and miners on the Apache frontier in the mid-nineteenth century, the army established a constellation of military outposts in southwestern New Mexico, among them Fort Cummings near Deming and Fort Selden near Las Cruces. On August 21, 1866, Fort Bayard, east of present-day Silver City, joined the muster roll. Established by soldiers of Company B of the 125th Colored Infantry, the fort was named to honor Brigadier General George D. Bayard, a soldier in the First Cavalry killed during the Civil War Battle of Fredericksburg.

Fort Bayard was, as its first post return asserted, "beautifully situated on the southern slope of the Pinos Altos mountains, with wood, water and feed in abundance." The fort grew to include a library and hospital, officers' quarters, enlisted men's barracks, storerooms, and cavalry stables. By 1879, the Fort Bayard roster showed 325 enlisted men in one infantry and three cavalry companies, 17 officers, and 25 Navajo scouts. Soldiers protected settlers and miners in the Pinos Altos mining district, which included the gold mines of Pinos Altos and the Santa Rita del Cobre copper mines to the east. Among those to serve at Fort Bayard in the summer of 1886 was Lieutenant John J. "Black Jack" Pershing, who helped establish the heliograph relay signaling stations between Fort Bayard and Fort Stanton, near Lincoln.

Indian hostilities were settled with the killing of Apache leader Victorio in 1880 and the surrender of Geronimo in 1886. In response, the army discontinued Fort Bayard as a military post in 1900 and transferred the facility to the surgeon general for use as the first army pulmonary tuberculosis sanitarium. Heading the outfit was respected army surgeon Major Daniel M. Appel. With 1,800 beds by 1919, Fort Bayard treated soldiers, sailors, and marines with "climatological therapy," a regimen that required patients to remain outdoors in the fresh air throughout the day.

In 1922, the Veterans Administration (VA) acquired the site, replaced most of the original fort buildings with more modern structures, and operated Fort Bayard as a Veterans Hospital. In its later history, the fort served as a treatment center for veterans under the management of the New Mexico Department of Public Welfare. Although it was designated a National Historic Landmark in 2004, the hospital closed in 2010, and the fate of the abandoned fort is still to be determined.

Fort Bayard Cemetery, established with the original fort in 1866, was designated a national cemetery in 1973. Now under the care of the VA, it is one of two national cemeteries in the state. The other is in Santa Fe.

More to explore: *Fort Cummings, Fort Selden State Monument, Pinos Altos, Santa Rita Copper Mines, Silver City, Site of San Augustin Springs*

Fort Bayard National Cemetery: *see Fort Bayard*

153. Fort Craig

Location: Socorro County. South of San Antonio, in the Fort Craig Rest Area on the west side of Interstate 25, between mile markers 113 and 114. See map 5.

Marker text: Fort Craig was established in 1853 and garrisoned in 1854 with troops from Fort Conrad located about nine miles north. Named after Capt. Louis S. Craig, it was used to control Indian raids along the Jornada del Muerto. Troops from Fort Craig were defeated in 1865 by Confederates at the Battle of Valverde, 7 miles distant. Between 1863 and 1865, it was headquarters for campaigns against the Gila and Mimbres Apache.

154. Ghost Marker: Valverde Battlefield

Marker text: The first major battle of the Civil War on New Mexico soil occurred at Valverde on February 21, 1862, when a Confederate force of Texas Volunteers under General H. H. Sibley defeated Union forces commanded by Col. E. R. S. Canby stationed at Fort Craig. From here, Sibley marched north and was defeated in Glorieta Pass near Santa Fe.

Note: This marker, which once stood at the Fort Craig Rest Area (near the Fort Craig Historic Marker), has since been removed. See map 5.

Fort Craig owes its existence to the demise of another military installation, Fort Conrad, built in 1850 nine miles to the north. Constructed of flimsy cottonwood timbers in a marshy area, Fort Conrad was literally falling apart by 1853. The army selected a tableland west of the Rio Grande as the site of a replacement fort and named it for Captain Louis S. Craig of the Third US Infantry, First US Dragoons, an officer killed by deserters he was chasing in California. Occupied in March 1854, Fort Craig consisted of twenty-two buildings, including a bakery, hospital, library, officers' quarters, and enlisted men's barracks.

At the outbreak of the Civil War, Fort Craig's mission changed from averting Indian raids and protecting travelers through this part of central

New Mexico to halting the advance of the Confederate Army in the Southwest. By January 1862, Brigadier General Henry Hopkins Sibley had amassed an army of Rebel soldiers some 2,500 strong and was moving north from El Paso with the intent of capturing Fort Union, near present-day Las Vegas, New Mexico. He hoped also to take the capital at Santa Fe along the way and eventually secure the gold fields in Colorado. His biggest obstacle to these plans lay in Fort Craig.

Meanwhile, Colonel Edward R. S. Canby, commander of the military in New Mexico, had come to Fort Craig to stop him. Soldiers quickly built earthen bastions around the fort and placed on them false wooden cannons, known as "Quaker Guns," to give the appearance of a heavily armed fortification. The ruse worked. When General Sibley reached the area on February 16, his men halted for three days to assess the garrison. Sibley, who had wrestled most of his life with illness and alcoholism, lay sick in a tent, but he knew that his soldiers did not have the ammunition or manpower to effect a direct attack. Instead, he sent Colonel Thomas Green and a battalion of men to move around the fort, cross the river, and cut off the Union supply route from the north. Sibley stayed in the tent. Realizing the Confederate plan, Colonel Canby ordered Captain Alexander McRae on February 21 to lead more than three thousand men in companies of cavalry and infantry, along with six brass cannons, upriver along the west bank of the Rio Grande to engage the Rebel troops. Canby himself remained at the fort. The two forces met that morning, at a small river crossing and settlement known as Valverde.

Federal troops held an early advantage in the battle that followed. Sibley rode to the battlefield later in the morning, but his illness persisted, and he soon withdrew to his tent. Canby joined his men that afternoon. Confederates launched a series of frontal attacks against Captain McRae's men. In one, the Confederates captured the Union's six brass cannons and turned them on the federal troops. The Union line broke, and soldiers fled for safety to Fort Craig. Among those killed that day was Canby's trusted ally, Captain McRae.

Exhausted, Confederate troops did not attempt to occupy the fort. Leaving Valverde, they marched north, taking Albuquerque and the capital in Santa Fe. They would reach Glorieta Pass, east of Santa Fe, in March, where a surprise attack by Union troops on their supply wagons would force them to retreat from the state.

The battle at Valverde took a sizeable physical toll. Confederate losses totaled 79 killed, 107 wounded. Union losses totaled 85 killed, 143 wounded.

After the war, soldiers at Fort Craig returned to protecting settlers and travelers along the Jornada. Apache hostilities eventually subsided, and the army deactivated the fort in 1884. The ruins are now open to the public under the direction of the Bureau of Land Management.

More to explore: *Cañoncito at Apache Canyon, Glorieta Pass Battlefield, Jornada del Muerto*

155. Fort Craig Rest Area

Location: Socorro County. South of San Antonio, in the Fort Craig Rest Area on the west side of Interstate 25, between mile markers 113 and 114. See map 5.

Marker text: Fort Craig is on alluvial gravelly sands, derived from mountains to west, sloping toward Rio Grande to east. Magdalena Mountains to northwest and San Mateo Mountains to west are mainly thick piles of volcanic rocks. San Andres Mountains on southeast horizon are of older limestones and shales. Elevation 4,810 feet.

Rainwater and snowmelt from the Magdalena Mountains to the northwest and the San Mateo Mountains to the west have carried debris and sediment down the eastern slopes of those ranges to create a veneer of sand and gravel on both sides of the interstate in this part of the Rio Grande Valley. This debris is known as alluvium, a word geologists use to define deposits specifically derived as sediments from streams and other running water. This rest stop, as well as the one across from it on the east side of the interstate, sits atop these alluvial gravels. These two rest areas are commonly called the Fort Craig Rest Areas. Their name comes from the nearby ruins of the mid-nineteenth-century military installation of Fort Craig about nine miles north.

The Magdalena and San Mateo Mountains are mainly thick piles of eroded volcanic rock from the Datil-Mogollon volcanic field. The highest point of the Magdalena Mountains is South Baldy at 10,783 feet. Weighing in for the San Mateo Range is Blue Mountain at 10,309 feet.

The San Andres Mountains on the southeast horizon are composed in part of older, Paleozoic limestones and shales. The highest peak is Salinas Peak, at 8,958 feet.

More to explore: *Fort Craig, Magdalena Fault, Rio Salado Sand Dunes*

156. Fort Cummings

Location: Luna County. In a pullout on the north side of Interstate 10, between mile markers 110 and 111. See map 5.

Marker text: This small and isolated post was built on the Mesilla-Tucson road to protect the Butterfield Trail against Apaches. Notorious Cookes Canyon, located nearby, was a particularly dangerous point on the trail. Only ruins now remain of the ten-foot adobe walls which once surrounded it.

Travelers ventured cautiously through Cookes Canyon in the mid-nineteenth century. Mining booms in the Black Range and Mimbres Mountains had placed settlers and Apache Indians in this part of southwestern New Mexico in precarious contact. Apaches made frequent attacks on travelers who stopped at nearby Cookes Spring, the only dependable water source for almost fifty miles. Stage drivers of the Butterfield Overland Stage Company running a road between Mesilla and Tucson, Arizona, also stopped at the spring as they ventured through the treacherous canyon. Although the Butterfield stage was re-routed farther north at the outbreak of the Civil War, Cookes Spring continued to serve as a stopping point for immigrants on the way west.

The army accordingly chose a spot near the base of Cookes Peak in 1863 as the site of a new fort to protect travelers and help secure the area from Apache attacks. In early October of that year, Captain Valentine Dresher and troops of Company B, First Infantry, California Volunteers, quartered here and began construction of Fort Cummings. In its designation, the fort honored Major Joseph

Although the ten-foot-high adobe wall that surrounded Fort Cummings offered a degree of protection in this isolated and precarious part of New Mexico, an account from one soldier relates that the men often woke to find tracks of Indian moccasins crisscrossing the parade ground. Fort Cummings. Bainbridge Bunting Photo Collection, Box 6, Folder 90, Item 000-385-1505, Center for Southwest Research, University Libraries, University of New Mexico.

Cummings, former commander of the First New Mexico Cavalry, who had been killed by Navajo Indians near Pueblo, Colorado, only months before work on the fort began. When finished two years later, the camp featured a rarity made necessary by location: an encircling, whitewashed adobe wall, standing 10 feet high and running 320 feet by 366 feet. Crouched inside the confines of the walls were quartermaster's storerooms, workshops, officers' and enlisted men's quarters, a hospital, and corrals, most constructed of adobe and wood. Such were the comforts of military living: soldiers fastened blankets into the dirt-packed floors of their rooms with pegs, and a story persists that bites from red ants and spiders during the night forced the men to put the legs of their bed in tins of water to ward off the varmints.

Regular and volunteer troops garrisoned the fort over its history, riding out on campaigns and escorting stagecoaches through treacherous Cookes Canyon. So treacherous was the area that soldiers traveled in small, well-armed packs, even when gathering scrub oak and cedar for their fires.

Stagecoach passengers even complained of the human skeletons they could see on the ground as they passed through the canyon.

Indian hostilities ebbed in the late 1880s as the majority of Apaches settled on reservations. In May 1885, the post was abandoned, and its adobe walls were used by local ranchers as a cattle corral. The construction of an army heliograph relay station atop Cookes Peak in 1886 brought some one hundred men temporarily back to the post, but by July 1887 the buildings were again drained of activity. On October 7, 1891, President Benjamin Harrison ordered Fort Cummings permanently closed.

Today, some of the ruins of Fort Cummings are on land owned by the Bureau of Land Management. Travel to the site is over a difficult roadway, but once there, visitors can wander among remnants of the fort, a spring house, and the sites of the cemetery and the Butterfield stagecoach station—all slowly fading back into the earth.

More to explore: *Butterfield Trail, Cathay Williams, Cooke's Wagon Road*

157. Fort Defiance

Location: McKinley County. Just across the New Mexico border from Arizona, on the east side of NM 264, between mile markers 0 and 1. See map 1.

Marker text: Now in the State of Arizona but then in the Territory of New Mexico, Fort Defiance was once described as "the most beautiful and interesting post as a whole in New Mexico." It was established in 1851 to control the Navajos, and abandoned as a military post in 1864.

When Colonel Joseph King Fenno Mansfield of the US Army visited Fort Defiance on an inspection tour of military posts in 1853, he wrote:

The buildings are good and mostly of logs and mud, but some good stone store houses have recently been completed. . . . The post has the disadvantage of being commanded within musketry range by a rocky ridge on the east; but this evil can readily be remedied by the erection on the ridge of two small block houses. This is the most beautiful and interesting post as a whole in New Mexico.

Established by the US Army on September 18, 1851, Fort Defiance was built in Cañon Bonito, or "Beautiful Canyon," a place Navajos knew by a name that meant "Meadow Between the Rocks." Members of the First and Second Dragoons, the Second Artillery, and the Third, Fifth, and Eighth Infantry garrisoned the post and rode on campaigns to deter raids by free-roaming bands of Navajos. One battle, however, came to them. It happened on April 30, 1860, when more than a thousand Navajo Indians, led by Indian warrior Manuelito, assailed the fort. In the aftermath, about twenty Navajos and one American soldier lay dead, and several more on both sides were wounded. Manuelito survived.

The army officially deactivated Fort Defiance on April 25, 1861, to turn its attentions instead to the Civil War. Just two years later the post reopened, this time to play a role in the comprehensive army crusade to quiet Indian conflicts in the area. Colonel Christopher "Kit" Carson used the post temporarily in what was known as the Navajo Campaign. Carson and his soldiers forced several thousand Navajo Indians from their homelands in the Four Corners region to the Bosque Redondo Reservation in southeastern New Mexico, where the army hoped to resettle the Navajos and Mescalero Apaches as farmers. Pestilence, tainted water, and raids by other tribes decimated the captive Indians. In 1868, the army negotiated with Navajo leaders, including Manuelito, to close the reservation and create instead a permanent Navajo reservation in the Four Corners region.

With the return of the Navajos to the region, the mission of Fort Defiance changed yet again. Ironically, the post that had once played a part in efforts to subdue hostilities by the Navajos became the agency responsible for their peaceful resettlement. Soldiers at the fort distributed supplies and food to the Indians in their care. As often happened at military installations in New Mexico, a small community developed near the fort. Although most of the buildings of the original fort have since been razed, the settlement that arose adjacent to it endures today as Fort Defiance.

In 1875, Major Chandler Robbins, the commissioner charged with surveying the border between New Mexico and Arizona, determined "that Fort Defiance is found to stand in Arizona."

More to explore: *Fort Sumner and Fort Sumner State Monument (series), Manuelito Area, Navajo Indian Reservation*

158. Fort Lowell

Location: Rio Arriba County. Just north of Tierra Amarilla, at the intersection of US 84 and NM 112, on the west side of US 84 between mile markers 172 and 173. See map 2.

Marker text: Fort Lowell was established in 1866 to protect the Tierra Amarilla area settlements from the Southern Utes. Originally named Camp Plummer, this post was garrisoned by a detachment of New Mexico Volunteers, some of whose descendants live in the area. The fort was abandoned in 1869 and its log, or "fuerte" buildings sold to local residents.

On November 6, 1866, Colonel Edward H. Bergman and company established a small military installation on leased land along the Chama River about three miles north of Tierra Amarilla. Known then as Camp Plummer, the fort had been named to recognize Augustus H. Plummer of the Thirty-Seventh US Infantry, who died only a few days after the camp was founded. Soldiers at Camp Plummer were tasked with maintaining peace between settlers and Indians, principally the Southern Utes of Colorado and the Jicarilla Apaches of northern New Mexico.

First to garrison the camp in 1866 was a detachment of New Mexico Volunteers, mostly Hispanic, who erected the log buildings that defined the construction of the fort. Company C of the Thirty-Seventh US Infantry arrived the following year to replace the New Mexico Volunteers. Another kind of replacement quickly followed: on July 13, 1868, the army rededicated Camp Plummer as Fort Lowell to honor Brigadier General Charles R. Lowell, a Massachusetts native, killed in the Civil War Battle of Cedar Creek (Virginia) on October 20, 1864.

The new name did little for the longevity of the fort, however. The commander of the military in New Mexico in the late 1860s, Brevet Major General George W. Getty, stated his belief that "the only Ute tribe of Indians in the vicinity are now, and have been peaceable for a number of years and are not likely to give trouble in the future." As the army began abandoning the post, local residents made clear their objections in letters to the military in 1869, reprinted in the *Santa Fe New Mexican*:

Since the establishment of said post, the people have been secure in their persons and property . . . but with the abandonment of said post, they fear they will have to abandon their homes and seek protection elsewhere.

The protests went unheeded. On July 27, 1869, the army decommissioned Fort Lowell, and Company C marched away to garrison Fort Lyon in Colorado.

For a short time thereafter, the log buildings of the fort housed an Indian agency for the Ute and Apache tribes. After the agency moved in 1878, the army dismantled those buildings, called *fuertes* in Spanish, and sold them to locals. Although the term *fuerte* is used for "fort," it can also mean a structure used to store farm equipment, which is likely what the buildings became.

More to explore: *Jicarilla Apache (series), Tierra Amarilla*

Fort Selden Cemetery: *see Fort Selden State Monument*

159. Fort Selden State Monument

Location: Doña Ana County. Ten miles north of Las Cruces, in the rest area on the west side (southbound) of Interstate 25, at mile marker 23. See map 5.

Marker text: Fort Selden was established to protect settlers and railroad construction crews in the Mesilla Valley and the Jornada del Muerto from Apaches. The first regular army troops to garrison it were four companies of the black 125th Infantry. General Douglas MacArthur spent two years of his childhood here. The fort was finally abandoned in 1891.

Note: The four companies of black soldiers served throughout the history of Fort Selden, not all at once when the fort opened, as the Marker implies. Fort Selden State Monument is today known as Fort Selden Historic Site.

160. Fort Selden Cemetery

Location: Doña Ana County. North of Las Cruces, at the entrance to Leasburg Dam State Park on NM 157. See map 5.

Marker text: Fort Selden was established nearby in 1865 to help protect the settlements of the Mesilla Valley and travelers along the Jornada del Muerto from Apache raids. The post cemetery was located in this field until the fort was abandoned in 1891. Military personnel were reinterred at the National Cemetery at Santa Fe. A number of unmarked graves in an adjacent potters field apparently still remain.

Vermont native Colonel Henry Raymond Selden, for whom the army named Fort Selden, graduated near the bottom of his 1843 West Point class. Such an inauspicious beginning did not prevent Selden from distinguishing himself in the Fifth Infantry during the Mexican-American War, commanding battalions in the Civil War battles of Valverde and Glorieta Pass in New Mexico, or commanding Fort Union, near Las Vegas. It was at Fort Union that Colonel Selden, after a life dedicated to military service, passed away in early 1865.

Only a few months after Selden's death, soldiers, military prisoners, and civilian employees arrived at an elevated patch of ground along the Rio Grande north of present-day Las Cruces to erect the fort named in his honor, Fort Selden. Soldiers at the post were to guard settlers in the Mesilla Valley and escort travelers through the Jornada del Muerto, or "Journey of the Dead Man," an unsettled stretch of desert between Doña Ana and Socorro. When completed, the buildings at Fort Selden formed a rectangle that enclosed a large parade ground. Three contiguous one-story flat-roofed adobe units at the north end served as the officers' quarters. Corrals, a two-ward hospital, enlisted men's barracks, a two-story stone guardhouse, prison cells, a bakery, and a sutler's shop completed the layout.

First among those to garrison the fort were members of the 125th Infantry, a unit of African Americans whom the Indians called "Buffalo Soldiers" because the soldiers' curly hair seemed similar to that of buffalo. Most of these men had fought in the Civil War and remained in the army after its conclusion. Through the history of Fort Selden, three other companies of Buffalo Soldiers saw duty there: the Thirty-Eighth Infantry, the Ninth Cavalry, and the Twenty-Fourth Infantry.

The post cemetery, established northeast of the fort, measured an even 150 square feet. Although the cemetery lay on some of the highest ground within the reservation, an officer at the fort in

1868 requested permission from the adjutant general for an adobe wall to be built around the field as added protection against floods and desert animals. Concerned that the material used be the best available, the officer requested that the work be contracted out, because any soldiers who could be found to make the adobe bricks "would require a long time to complete them; and when done, from the inexperience of the makers, [the adobes] would probably be very inferior." Burials at the cemetery reflected the cross section of life found at a frontier military installation. Soldiers killed in the line of duty lay near nonmilitary personnel, including local citizens who had worked at the fort. The majority of burials were "unknowns," many of them probably nameless bodies found along the Jornada. Soon, a patch of land within the cemetery became a "potter's field," a burial place for those who could not afford a traditional interment or whose identities remained obscure.

Although a decrease in Indian hostilities led to an abandonment of the post in the late 1870s, a resurgence of Apache raids and a decision by the army to install a heliograph system among frontier posts in New Mexico and Arizona brought Captain Arthur MacArthur and Company K of the Thirteenth Infantry to regarrison the post in 1884. MacArthur's son, Douglas, who was only four years old at the time, later wrote in his *Reminiscences* that his march to the post with his father was one of his first memories. He relates an incident that occurred at Fort Selden:

One day, while on herd the horses and mules panicked at the sight and smell of a strange new animal moving along the sandy wastes like some shaggy ghost out of the pages of wonderland. It was a camel, lonesome survivor of a herd that in 1855 Jefferson Davis, then Secretary of War, had brought from Egypt to serve as pack animals to supply the chain of isolated forts in this vast desert country.

Douglas MacArthur earned prominence in the years that followed as the supreme commander of Allied troops in the Pacific during World War II.

With the surrender of Apache leader Geronimo in 1886, the role of Fort Selden ebbed, and on January 20, 1891, the army ordered the fort abandoned. Two days later, Lieutenant James E. Brett filed the last post return for Fort Selden, writing: "All public property at this post having been disposed of, it was abandoned on this date."

An inventory shows 103 people buried in the cemetery and adjacent potter's field at the time of abandonment. Thirty-three of those were soldiers, fifty-nine were unknown, and ten were citizens. One, William Touqua, was an Indian scout. The army offered a citizen contractor the remaining roofs and woodwork from the fort as payment for removing the bodies of soldiers for reinterment in the National Cemetery in Santa Fe. Bodies in the potter's field were left behind.

Fort Selden is today a state historic site, administered by the Museum of New Mexico.

More to explore: *Buffalo Soldier Hill, Fort Cummings, Jornada del Muerto*

161. Fort Stanton (1855–1896)

Location: Lincoln County. On NM 220, at the entrance to Fort Stanton. See map 6.

Marker text: Fort Stanton, named for Captain Henry Stanton, was established to control the Mescalero Apaches. It was burned and evacuated by Union troops in 1861, held briefly by the Confederates, and then reoccupied by Colonel Kit Carson for the Union in 1862. Since its abandonment as a military post, it has been used as a hospital.

When Brevet Brigadier General John Garland selected this spot for a fort in April 1855, he chose to name the new installation in honor of Captain Henry Whiting Stanton of the First US Dragoons. Four months earlier, Captain Stanton had been killed in a battle with Mescalero Apache Indians in the Sacramento Mountains near present-day Mayhill, New Mexico, about fifty miles to the south. "The post is easy of access," Garland wrote of the location he had selected; "its vicinity affords abundance of grass, wood, and timber; the water is pure, and the roads good." The new fort, intended to help calm the region from Apache attacks and offer protection to settlers, was located in the very homeland of the Mescalero Apaches.

When construction was completed, Fort Stanton consisted of a large, central parade ground with official buildings aligned around it. The commanding officer's quarters were at the head of the grounds, with the officers' quarters to the right. Barracks for the enlisted men took up a portion of the opposite side. A hospital, jail, and library also lay along the rectangular grounds. A laundresses' building and a kitchen were set back from the other buildings on either side. The post also had stables for horses and mules. Most of the buildings were constructed of stone. Garrisoning the post were soldiers of the First Dragoon, and the Third and Eighth Infantry Regiments.

Lydia Spencer Lane, wife of Lieutenant William Bartlett Lane, stayed at Fort Stanton for a short time in 1858 and offers an insider's view of life at this isolated post in her diary:

Fort Stanton was a beautiful post, with the best quarters in the army at that time, but it was like being buried alive to stay there. Nothing ever passed that way, and it was seldom a stranger came among us. There was but one mail a month, and on the day it was expected we dropped all work and fixed our eyes on a certain hill, round which the man with the mail, carried on a mule, was bound to appear, if the Indians had not caught him. Whoever first spied him spread the news that the mail was coming. Then all was excitement until the post-office was opened and each had his own letters and papers in his hand.

As it happened, one of the largest threats to the fort came not in the form of Indian raids but instead from the Confederate Army during the Civil War. In July 1861, Confederates had forced the surrender of Fort Fillmore, near Mesilla. Union solders at Fort Fillmore attempted to retreat to Fort Stanton, a distance of more than 140 miles, but were overtaken by and surrendered to Confederate forces just a few miles outside of Mesilla. The Confederates then continued their advance north through the state, intending to take military installations along the way to Santa Fe, capture Fort Union near Las Vegas, claim the land for the Confederacy, and then move into Colorado to secure the gold fields there.

Learning of the approach of the Confederates toward Fort Stanton, the army withdrew from the post on August 2, 1861, but not before setting fire to the supplies and buildings. This effort at sabotage was unsuccessful, however, and Confederate forces, under the command of Captain James Walker, raised the Confederate flag here within a week. The fort remained under Confederate control until the spring of 1862, when Union troops burned the Confederate supply wagons at Glorieta Pass and the Confederates retreated from the state.

Soon after, Colonel Kit Carson, famous for his mountain man exploits (and somewhat infamous today for his treatment of the native populations of the state), was ordered to return Fort Stanton to Union control. Carson and the First New Mexico Cavalry arrived in October 1862 to regarrison and rebuild the fort, which now had a new mission. General James H. Carleton, commander of the military in New Mexico, had ordered the forced resettlement of Mescalero Apaches from their homelands to the newly constructed Bosque Redondo Reservation near present-day Fort Sumner, about one hundred miles north. Using the fort as a base of operations, Carson charged through the Sacramento Mountains, rounding up Mescalero Apaches and forcing them to the reservation. The Bosque Redondo Reservation was a dismal failure, and the government shut it down in 1869, at which time Mescalero Apaches returned to the region.

Soldiers at Fort Stanton found themselves peacekeepers of a different sort with the outbreak of what became known as the Lincoln County War in 1878. The "war," centered in the small village of Lincoln six miles to the east, pitted merchants L. G. Murphy and J. J. Dolan against Englishman John Tunstall and his ranch hands, later known as "the Regulators"—one of whom was Billy the Kid. At issue, among other things, was the question of who would secure the lucrative government contracts for the sale of cattle to feed the soldiers at Fort Stanton. At the height of hostilities in July 1878, the commanding officer of Fort Stanton, Colonel Nathan Augustus Monroe Dudley, went to Lincoln with troops to help quell the hostilities in town. Dudley's loyalties probably lay with the Murphy-Dolan faction (both had earlier worked at Fort Stanton), and his actions in Lincoln helped break apart the Regulators.

The army decommissioned Fort Stanton in August 1896, but the post has had several rebirths since then. In 1898, it reopened as a US Merchant Marine hospital for the care of sailors with tuberculosis—the first federal tuberculosis hospital in the country. A common treatment for the disease at the time included allowing patients to convalesce in a pristine, outdoor environment, often at a higher altitude—requirements easily met by the spot Brevet Brigadier General Garland had selected more than forty years earlier. The post also served brief duty during World War II as an internment camp for captured German soldiers. The hospital remained in operation until 1953, after which time patients were transferred to the hospital at Fort Bayard, near Silver City.

Today, the buildings of Fort Stanton are some of the best preserved of any former military installation in the state, offering visitors a firsthand look at the layout of a frontier military post of the nineteenth century. The site is open to the public today as the Fort Stanton Historic Site.

More to explore: *Apache Battleground, Dog Canyon, Fort Selden State Monument, Fort Sumner and Fort Sumner State Monument (series), La Mesilla, Lincoln, Site of San Augustin Springs*

FORT SUMNER AND FORT SUMNER STATE MONUMENT:
Series of Six Historic Markers (in the city of Fort Sumner and at the Bosque Redondo Memorial at Fort Sumner Historic Site, formerly known as Fort Sumner State Monument)

General Introduction

A stretch of the Pecos River known as the Bosque Redondo, or "Round Woods," has today become a place that many people speak of with the strongest emotions—among them anger, confusion, and grief. It was here, on November 30, 1862, that men of Company A, Fifth US Infantry, under the command of Captain Joseph Updegraff, arrived to begin work on a fort that would oversee what would be the first Indian reservation in New Mexico. These were Fort Sumner and the Bosque Redondo Reservation.

Six separate Historic Markers document the story of the Bosque Redondo Reservation, the growth of the community of Fort Sumner nearby, and the later arrival of Billy the Kid to the area. These Markers have been combined here into one series, so this remarkable story can be followed comprehensively. The Markers are presented here roughly in chronological order.

In 2013, the state of New Mexico changed the name of Fort Sumner State Monument to the Bosque Redondo Memorial at Fort Sumner Historic Site.

More to explore (Fort Sumner and Fort Sumner State Monument Series): *Cimarron, Fort Stanton, Kit Carson Park (see under Taos), Lincoln, Navajo Indian Reservation, Sumner Lake State Park*

162. Bosque Redondo Indian Reservation
Old Fort Sumner, 1862–1869

Location: De Baca County. At the eastern end of the city of Fort Sumner, in a pullout on the south side of US 84/60, between mile markers 330 and 331. See map 6.

Marker text: The U.S. Army established Fort Sumner in 1862 as a supply and control point for the Bosque Redondo Indian Reservation. About 10,000 Navajo were forcibly relocated from the Four Corners Region during the tragic march known as the Long Walk. About 500 Apaches from southern New Mexico were also brought here. Approximately 3000 Navajos and Apaches died here. The ill-conceived reservation was closed in 1868, and the Navajos and Apaches returned to their homes. The fort was abandoned in 1869.

Note: See the general introduction to this series of Markers, as well as the other Markers making up the series, for further background on the Bosque Redondo Indian Reservation and the town of Fort Sumner.

163. Bosque Redondo Indian Reservation
Fort Sumner, 1862–1868

Location: De Baca County. In the parking lot at the entrance to the Bosque Redondo Memorial at Fort Sumner Historic Site (formerly Fort Sumner State Monument). See map 6.

Marker text: You are entering the grounds of historic Fort Sumner, headquarters of the Bosque Redondo Indian Reservation. Over 400 Mescalero Apache and 7,000 Navajo were held here as prisoners of war. The museum tells their stories.

Note: See the general introduction to this series of Markers, as well as the other Markers making up the series, for further background on the Bosque Redondo Indian Reservation and the town of Fort Sumner.

At first, only a few tired and ragged Navajo Indians trickled in to the 1,600-square-mile Bosque Redondo Reservation. By February 1864, there were thousands, some of whom were put to work constructing the fort itself. Fort Sumner. Bainbridge Bunting Photo Collection, Box 6, Folder 92, Item 000-385-1529, Center for Southwest Research, University Libraries, University of New Mexico.

As commander of the Military District of New Mexico in 1862, Brigadier General James H. Carleton faced the challenge of managing a new western frontier. Among his problems were the conflicts, often brutal, between settlers, miners, and the native people of the West. Indians had been forced from their lands by the migration of new settlers and were frequently the victims of racial aggression. Some hostile Indian bands had responded by attacking villages and raiding livestock, actions that netted their own fatal rejoinders from New Mexico settlers. Carleton believed that the solution lay in resettling nomadic Indian tribes, such as the Navajos in northwestern New Mexico, in permanent reservations while teaching them to make a living farming—and, in the process, opening former tribal land to the public for settlement and mining.

A month before construction began at the fort in November 1862, Carleton tapped former mountain man turned soldier Colonel Christopher "Kit" Carson and the First New Mexico Cavalry to lead attacks against the Mescalero Apache Indians in the Sacramento Mountains of southern New Mexico. With his soldiers, Carson swept through the mountains, burned fields, and shot those who resisted. Yielding finally to Carson's command in mid-November, Mescalero Apache men on foot and women in wagons, some 450 in all, arrived at Fort Sumner in December. Their first responsibility, after building their own shelters, was to help soldiers construct the buildings of the fort. Eventually the installation grew to include officers' quarters, barracks for the enlisted men, a guardhouse, a bakery, and stables.

Colonel Carson then turned to the Navajos in their homelands in the Four Corners region. In a scorched-earth campaign undertaken in the fall of 1863, Carson and his men raided and torched Navajo villages. With the threat of approaching winter, many Navajos surrendered and left for the Bosque. Even more left in mid-January 1864, after Carson and his troops trapped a large number of Navajos in Canyon de Chelly in northeastern Arizona.

Navajos call the journey to the reservation the Long Walk. More than 8,500 made the forced march from northern New Mexico and Arizona over three hundred miles of terrain to the reservation in southeastern New Mexico. Navajo oral histories recall the intense suffering of the Long Walk; they tell of a people expelled from their homeland, weak and hungry, struggling to walk for up to twenty miles at a time into captivity. They tell of brutal atrocities committed against them along the way, of men and women shot by soldiers for having complained of sickness, of the frailest dying from hunger, thirst, or exposure. The Long Walk remains one of the most tragic episodes in New Mexico history.

Conditions at Bosque Redondo quickly deteriorated. Cramped quarters fostered the spread of malaria and other diseases. The Indians had few blankets to protect themselves from the cold winter air. Cutworms and hail demolished crops three years in a row, and Comanche raids on the livestock lessened the meager food supplies kept in inventory. The failures took a lamentable physical toll: some two thousand Indians lost their lives while in captivity at the Bosque Redondo Reservation.

In the fall of 1865, spurred by an outbreak of measles, most of the 450 Mescalero Apaches slipped out of the reservation and returned to their sacred Sacramento Mountains.

Recognizing the failure of Carleton's resettlement plan at the Bosque, the federal government created a peace commission in May 1868 to help bring resolution to the situation. At its head was General William T. Sherman, best remembered for his march of devastation through the South during the Civil War and for uttering one of the most famous expletives in military history: "War is hell." Sherman felt similarly about the reservation. "I found the Bosque a mere spot of green grass in the midst of a wild desert," he wrote, "and that the Navajos had sunk into a condition of absolute poverty and despair."

Sherman met with Navajo leaders, including Barboncito and Manuelito, to negotiate a treaty that would end their confinement and create a permanent reservation in northwestern New Mexico. The Navajos agreed to end further raids and to send their children to government-sponsored schools. On June 18, 1868, the Navajos left Bosque Redondo in a long-awaited return to their home.

164. Old Fort Sumner and "Billy the Kid's" Grave

Location: De Baca County. South of the city of Fort Sumner, near Old Fort Sumner Cemetery, on the west side of NM 272 between mile markers 5 and 6. See map 6.

Marker text: Fort Sumner was established in 1862 to guard the Navajo and Apaches on the Bosque Redondo Reservation. It was discontinued as a military post in 1868 and the buildings and site sold to Lucien B. Maxwell. William "Billy the Kid" Bonney was killed here by Sheriff Pat Garrett the night of July 14, 1881. Bonney is buried in the nearby cemetery.

Note: See the general introduction to this series of Markers, as well as the other Markers making up the series, for further background on Fort Sumner and the Bosque Redondo Memorial at Fort Sumner Historic Site.

165. Fort Sumner

Location: 1. De Baca County. At the eastern end of the city of Fort Sumner, in a pullout on the north side of US 84/60, between mile markers 329 and 330. See map 6.

2. De Baca County. At the western end of the city of Fort Sumner, in a pullout on the south side of US 60, between mile markers 326 and 327, near the intersection of US 60 and NM 20. See map 6.

Marker text: Named for the fort built in 1862 to guard the Bosque Redondo Indian Reservation, the town of Fort Sumner grew out of settlements clustering around the Maxwell family properties. It moved to its present site with the construction of the Belen Cutoff of the Santa Fe Railroad around 1907.

Note: See the general introduction to this series of Markers, as well as the other Markers making up the series, for further background on Fort Sumner and the Bosque Redondo Memorial at Fort Sumner Historic Site.

166. Helene Haack Allen (1891–1978)
Philanthropist, Civic Leader, Businesswoman

Location: De Baca County. In Fort Sumner, on the grounds of the Bosque Redondo Memorial at Fort Sumner Historic Site (formerly Fort Sumner State Monument), near stop 16 (the former office building). See map 6.

Marker text: Helene was a pioneer businesswoman, moving to Fort Sumner at 21. She married a homesteader and they ran diverse businesses, including theaters and a mortuary. She established the first Billy the Kid museum on the site of the Old Fort and won legal battles to keep him interred there. Late in life, she donated land, which became Fort Sumner State Monument and Bosque Redondo Memorial Museum.

Note: See the general introduction to this series of Markers, as well as the other Markers making up the series, for further background on Fort Sumner and the Bosque Redondo Memorial at Fort Sumner Historic Site.

When the army deactivated Fort Sumner in 1869 and returned the reservation land to the public domain, a small settlement grew around the old post buildings. It, too, took the name Fort Sumner. The buildings of the post soon became the family home and ranch headquarters of Lucien Bonaparte Maxwell, who purchased the property in October 1870 for $5,000. Before retiring to Fort Sumner, Maxwell had amassed and then sold an extensive stretch of land in northern New Mexico, giving him a place in the record books as one of the preeminent landholders in New Mexico history. In 1907, the community of Fort Sumner moved a few miles to the north of the Maxwell ranch with the arrival of the Belen Cutoff, an alternate route of the Santa Fe Railway from Belen to Texas. Maxwell did not live to see the railroad arrive. He passed away in 1875.

After Maxwell's death, his son Peter continued the Maxwell ranching operations. Peter Maxwell was a friend of New Mexico's notorious Billy the Kid, and it was in Peter's bedroom at Fort Sumner that Lincoln County sheriff Pat Garrett shot and killed the outlaw on the evening of July 14, 1881. Locals buried the Kid in Fort Sumner Cemetery, not far from Lucien Maxwell's grave. This has created a curious juxtaposition: one of the most notorious outlaws in the history of New Mexico is spending eternity scarcely feet from one of the richest men in the state.

More recent history of the site of Fort Sumner includes the name Helene Haack Allen, a businesswoman in the village of Fort Sumner. Born in Wisconsin in 1891, Allen came to Fort Sumner at age twenty-one to live with her brother, Ted Haack, who owned a farm in the area. According to a family history, after being thrown from her buggy while out riding one day, Haack found herself the recipient of attentive care from a local homesteader, John Allen, who had seen the accident and quickly took her to a doctor. Haack and Allen married in 1913. Together, the two owned and operated a number of enterprises in Fort Sumner over the succeeding years, including a drugstore, a farm, the Zia Theater, and a mortuary. John Allen also served as sheriff of De Baca County for a time during their marriage. The ruins of the old Fort Sumner and the Bosque Redondo Reservation lay on farm property they owned.

John Allen passed away in 1945, leaving Helene to run the family enterprises, which she did successfully for many years. She also successfully defended herself in court against at least one lawsuit attempting to move the remains of Billy the Kid to the cemetery in Lincoln County, site of the Lincoln County Wars. Before her own passing in 1978, by which time she was living in Carlsbad, Allen transferred ownership of the land containing the fort, the cemetery, and the reservation ruins to the village of Fort Sumner.

Today, the old fort and portions of what was the Bosque Redondo Reservation make up the Bosque Redondo Memorial at Fort Sumner Historic Site (formerly Fort Sumner State Monument). The site is open to the public under the administration of the Museum of New Mexico.

Fort Union Arsenal: *see Fort Union National Monument*

167. Fort Union National Monument (1851–1891)

Location: 1. Mora County. North of Watrous, in a pullout on the east side of Interstate 25 (no facilities), between mile markers 360 and 361. (The Marker at this location also indicates that Fort Union is eighteen miles to the northeast.) See map 3.

2. Mora County. North of Watrous, in a rest area on the west side of Interstate 25, between mile markers 375 and 376. See map 3.

Marker text: Once the largest post in the Southwest, Fort Union was established to control the Jicarilla Apaches and Utes, to protect the Santa Fe Trail, and to serve as a supply depot for other New Mexico forts. The arrival of the railroad and the pacification of the region led to its abandonment in 1891.

168. Fort Union Arsenal

Location: Mora County. Across from the arsenal, two miles south of the fort itself, on NM 161. See map 3.

Marker text: West of Fort Union near the base of the mesa are the ruins of Fort Union Arsenal. The first Fort Union was built at this location in 1851. In 1867 this wooden fort was razed and the adobe Arsenal erected. This Arsenal played a vital role in supplying armaments to military posts throughout New Mexico until 1882.

In August 1851, soldiers raised pine-log buildings with dirt-covered roofs along the base of a nearby mesa and established the first of three installations to bear the name Fort Union. Mounted troops from the fort escorted travelers along the Santa Fe Trail and protected the region against the hostile warriors of the Jicarilla Apache tribe, the Utes of southern Colorado, and the Comanches of the eastern plains.

With the outbreak of the Civil War, Major Henry Hopkins Sibley, who had previously commanded the fort, defected to the Confederate Army and began to gather troops to capture military installations throughout New Mexico—including his former post, Fort Union. Although many men stationed at Fort Union had been pulled to supplement the ranks of Fort Craig farther south, citizen soldiers quickly erected a second Fort Union to withstand an attack should the Confederates break through. Built in the valley east of the first, this second fort followed a French blueprint: a massive earthen eight-pointed star with barracks built underground. Cannons placed in the parapets offered soldiers a 360-degree firing range. Although constructed hastily, the elaborate design was nonetheless considered impenetrable.

The boast was never proven. Union troops burned the supply wagons of the Confederates at Glorieta Pass, east of Santa Fe, in March 1862. Sibley, without his reserves of ammunition and food, retreated from the state.

General James H. Carleton, commander of the New Mexico military in 1862, then ordered a new fort built to replace the "Star Fort." Constructed over a six-year period, this third and final incarnation of Fort Union, built largely in territorial style, featured storehouses, corrals, an icehouse, laundresses' quarters, a bakery, a prison, a thirty-six-bed hospital, officers' quarters, and a parade ground—enough to make it the largest post in the Southwest.

On May 8, 1866, the War Department ordered that a section of the Fort Union reservation one mile long and half a mile wide be put into service as an arsenal. Congress appropriated $10,000 for its construction at the site of the original pine-log fort. Supplies, weapons, and ammunition were freighted from larger arsenals in the East and stored here before being distributed to other forts in the Southwest. The arsenal also served as a workshop where damaged weapons could be repaired. Heading operations at the arsenal was Captain William R. Shoemaker, a man most famous for having designed the popular military-style Shoemaker bit for horses.

As the Indian threat in the area subsided in the 1880s and railroad lines replaced the Santa Fe Trail, the usefulness of the fort to a quieted frontier diminished. Army General Order 71, issued on July 3, 1882, abolished the arsenal. Fort Union itself was abandoned in 1891.

Now run under the direction of the National Park Service, the ruins of the fort and portions of the reservation became a national monument in 1954.

More to explore: *Jicarilla Apache (series), Santa Fe Trail (series), Wagon Mound, Watrous*

169. Fort Wingate

Location: 1. McKinley County. In Fort Wingate, at the intersection of NM 400 and Main Street, at the entrance to Fort Wingate Veterans Park. See map 1.

2. McKinley County. On old Route 66, just west of Exit 33 from Interstate 40, on a pullout on the north side of the road. See map 1.

Marker text: The first Fort Wingate was established near San Rafael in 1862 to serve as the base of Col. Kit Carson's campaigns against the Navajos. In 1868 the garrison was transferred to the second Fort Wingate near Gallup. In that same year, the Navajos returned here after their imprisonment at Fort Sumner.

On October 22, 1862, soldiers formally established a military post at Ojo del Gallo, or "Spring of the Rooster," near present-day San Rafael, about forty miles southeast of here. The post took the name Fort Wingate to honor Brevet Major Benjamin Wingate, mortally wounded by Confederate soldiers at the Battle of Valverde that February. The army needed the fort as a base from which to launch campaigns against hostile bands of Navajo Indians from northwestern New Mexico.

Brigadier General James H. Carleton, commander of the Military District of New Mexico, believed that Indian hostilities in the Southwest would cease only if the Navajos were moved to a reservation and taught to farm for a living. In addition, Carleton was feeling public pressure to open the land to prospecting, as many settlers believed that the region harbored gold and silver.

With that untenable goal in mind, Carleton appointed Colonel Kit Carson to drive Navajos from their homeland to the Bosque Redondo Reservation in southeastern New Mexico. Leading a force of one thousand men from Fort Wingate in the early summer of 1863, Carson waged an unrelenting campaign, forcing Navajo men, women, and children to walk a distance greater than three hundred miles to Bosque Redondo. Conditions at the reservation quickly turned dire as lack of food, impure water, and the spread of disease decimated the captive Indians. In 1868, the Navajos negotiated with the US government to establish a permanent reservation in northwestern New Mexico.

To oversee operations at the new Navajo reservation, the army reopened a previously abandoned post at Ojo del Oso, or "Spring of the Bear," at the present site of the community of Fort Wingate. That post, established in 1860 as Fort Fauntleroy and later renamed Fort Lyon, was renamed yet again to Fort Wingate, and the garrison from the original Fort Wingate transferred to the new fort.

By June 1868, Fort Wingate consisted of accommodations for four full companies, officers' quarters, storehouses, a hospital, a guardhouse, and a bakery.

In 1909, the fort experienced a bit of unwanted excitement, as noted in the post returns for July:

On July 8, 09, the Quartermaster Storehouse and Office at this post was completely destroyed by fire. Cause of fire unknown. Office records saved. About $29,200.00 worth of property lost.

Two years later, the army abandoned the post, but Fort Wingate was not to slip unremembered into the past. For five months in 1914, the army used the fort as an internment site for some eight hundred Mexican soldiers, along with their families, who were fleeing the Mexican Revolution. These soldiers had been part of Mexican president Victoriano Huerta's Federal Army of the North.

In 1921, the army transferred a section of the fort to the Department of the Interior to serve the Navajo Nation as a boarding school. Although most of the original post buildings have since been torn down to make way for more permanent, modern structures, the community of Fort Wingate survives today.

More to explore: *Fort Sumner and Fort Sumner State Monument (series), Kit Carson Park (see under Taos), Navajo Indian Reservation*

170. Galisteo Basin

Location: Santa Fe County. South of Santa Fe, on US 285, near the turnoff to Lamy. See map 2.

Marker text: The extensive lowland south of here is called the Galisteo basin, a sag in the earth's crust where rock layers are depressed and thickened. It is one of the northernmost basins of the Basin and Range province in New Mexico and is bordered by the Rocky Mountains immediately to the north. Elevation 6,400 feet.

171. Galisteo Pueblo

Location: Santa Fe County. In the village of Galisteo, on the west side of NM 41 between mile markers 56 and 57. See map 2.

Marker text: Spanish explorers found several Tano-speaking pueblos in the Galisteo Basin in 1540. They were among the leaders of the Pueblo Revolt of 1680. 150 Tano families were eventually resettled in Galisteo Pueblo in 1706. Droughts, famine, Comanche raids, and disease led to its abandonment by 1788, with most of the survivors moving to Santo Domingo.

The stretch of sunken land south of Santa Fe, northeast of the Sandia and Manzano Ranges and southwest of the Sangre de Cristo Mountains, is known as the Galisteo Basin. This extensive lowland formed from the collective weight of sediments carried from the slopes of the mountains. The basin is a far northern valley in the Basin and Range Province of New Mexico, a region characterized by isolated mountain chains separated by broad, flat valleys, such as this one.

Archaeologists have today cataloged more than ten major multistoried pueblos and many other associated structures built by Indians in the Galisteo Basin many hundreds of years ago. In place by AD 1300, these quarried stone and adobe buildings rose to enormous size and constitute some of the largest pueblo ruins in the country. Although not completely excavated, San Marcos Pueblo, for example, contained an estimated two thousand rooms and perhaps as many as ten plazas. The pueblo known today as Galisteo, the central-most in the complex, held more than 1,600 rooms. The Indians who lived in these villages farmed squash and corn along the banks of Galisteo Creek and its tributaries, carved impressive rock art into nearby boulders, and crossed the piñon- and juniper-covered lowlands to mine turquoise from Mount Chalchihuitl near present-day Cerrillos.

Into this intricate structure in the sixteenth century came waves of Spanish explorers, including Gaspar Castaño de Sosa in 1591, who gave many of the pueblos their Spanish names. Around 1600, after the Spanish had colonized the state, Franciscan priests established mission churches in four of the Galisteo Basin pueblos to spread Christianity among the Indians. These efforts continued for some eighty years, until tensions between the Spanish and the native people exploded in the Pueblo Revolt of 1680. In August of that year, most of the pueblos along the Rio Grande rose in unison, laid siege to Santa Fe, and drove the Spanish from the state. Indians of the Galisteo Basin were among the instigators of the insurrection, given their proximity to the capital. During the melee, many of them abandoned the basin pueblos and joined other pueblos or Indian tribes, perhaps in fear of reprisal by the Spanish.

In 1706, with the Spanish again in command of the region, Governor Francisco Cuervo y Valdés resettled some 150 Tano-speaking Indians from Tesuque Pueblo and elsewhere into the basin pueblo he named Nuestra Señora de los Remedios de Galisteo, or "Our Lady of the Remedies of Galisteo." The resettlement was short-lived. Fray Francisco Atanasio Domínguez, who inspected the missions of New Mexico in 1776, wrote of the mission church that "to live in it is to enter expecting death and to remain buried there as soon as one sits down, because it is so near to falling," and that the pueblo was, as a whole, "caught on a reef of misfortunes." Steady raids by nomadic Comanche tribes, poor proceeds from farming, and the spread of disease brought an end to pueblo life in the Galisteo Basin. By 1788, the region lay empty, most of its residents having joined Santo Domingo Pueblo.

Today, the small village of Galisteo, first settled as a Spanish garrison post around 1795, recalls by name the Indian villages of centuries ago.

More to explore: *Castaño de Sosa's Route, Santa Fe*

Galisteo Pueblo: *see Galisteo Basin*

172. Gallup

Location: 1. McKinley County. On the east side of the city of Gallup, on the north side of US 66, near the Interstate 40 interchange. See map 1.

2. McKinley County. In Gallup, at the Tourist Information Center, exit 22 from Interstate 40. See map 1.

Marker text: Long a major trading center for the Navajo and Zuni Indians living in communities north and south of the town, Gallup emerged in 1881 from a railroad construction camp. It is named for David Gallup, who in 1880 was paymaster for the Atlantic & Pacific (now the Santa Fe) Railroad.

Gallup took root in the 1880s when crews with the Atlantic and Pacific Railroad (an affiliate of the Atchison, Topeka, and Santa Fe) laid tracks in the region as the railroad bustled through to California. Payday for these workers meant well-earned money in well-worn pockets, and they got it from railroad auditor and paymaster David L. Gallup. When a post office opened at the small railroad camp in 1882, it took the name Gallup—making this the only community in New Mexico named in recognition of payday.

Gallup grew as its early settlers developed a residential section and built a school and hotels. Branches of the railroad served the prodigious area coal mines and allowed for such quantities of production that Gallup earned the backhanded nickname "Carbon City." Citizens of Gallup incorporated their settlement on July 9, 1891. When McKinley County was carved from Bernalillo County eight years later, Gallup was by then a settlement substantial enough to be named county seat.

Owing to its location near the Navajo Nation, Zuni Pueblo, Acoma Pueblo, and Laguna Pueblo, Gallup developed early as a brokerage center for Native American arts and crafts. Gallup business owners H. E. Phenecie and Mike Kirk felt that a public festival of Indian arts and dances might draw tourist attention and give the residents of Indian country in northwestern New Mexico a chance to share and celebrate their heritage. After much planning and preparation, Gallup hosted its first Inter-Tribal Indian Ceremonial on September 28, 1922. The annual event continues today.

Although the interstate later bypassed Gallup, the snub did not mar the success of the town as a hub for Indian trade. Today, Gallup is known as a commercial center for the sale of authentic Native American jewelry, art, pottery, and weavings.

More to explore: *Navajo Indian Reservation, Pueblo of Acoma, Pueblo of Laguna, Pueblo of Zuni*

173. Garcia Opera House

Location: Socorro County. In Socorro, in the parking lot of the Garcia Opera House, 110 Abeyta Avenue. See map 5.

Marker text: Using the gold he had left her, the widow of Juan Nepomuceno Garcia began construction of the Garcia Opera House in 1884. It was completed three years later in 1887. It served as the main center for cultural and community events including theatrical productions, balls, marriages, etc. The curved shape of the massive 34-inch walls strengthened the building and improved acoustics. The "rake" stage is one of very few still in existence in the U.S. Restoration began in 1983 and was completed in 1985 by Holm Bursum, Jr. The Garcia Opera House is a National Historic Site.

It was the dream of wealthy businessman Juan Nepomuceno Garcia and his wife, Francisca, scions of two of the original founding families of Socorro, to provide a venue for cultural performances in their community in the early 1880s. Socorro at the time was one of the largest and most influential towns in this part of the state, flush with money from local mining enterprises. The town was in the midst of a coming-of-age, transitioning from rough-edged western town to modern (by nineteenth-century standards) heavy-weight community with significant political clout. Resplendent Victorian homes were being built, new businesses were erected, and, in a few years, the New Mexico School of Mines (now the New Mexico Institute of Mining and Technology) would open. The town had also recently installed sidewalks.

When Juan Garcia passed away in 1886, his widow, after remarrying, used money from his estate to complete work on the edifice that would be the structural fulfillment of their dream: the Garcia Opera House. Built only a couple blocks away from a resplendent house the Garcias had erected and lived in near the downtown plaza, the opera house was grand, with an interior stretching 140 feet long by 40 feet wide and walls 34 inches thick. The topmost portions of those walls curved as they reached the ceiling to improve interior acoustics. The stage, which faced west, was raked, simply meaning that it was raised so that the back was higher than the front, in this case by about a foot, giving patrons an unobscured view of performers across the entire stage. A beautiful fresco across the top and sides of the stages displayed figures of the muses of Drama and Music.

Opening-night ceremonies for the Garcia Opera House were held on December 1, 1886. The program for that evening opened with the orchestral "Travels Through New Mexico," which included popular airs, and continued with performances from local and state singers and musicians, including the Socorro Cornet Band. "The seats were then removed and dancing commenced," the *Socorro Bullion* noted in its review of the evening, "which was kept up until 1 a.m. when everybody retired expressing themselves highly delighted with the evening's amusement."

In 1917, the opera house was sold to Holm Olaf Bursum, a prominent name in New Mexico politics. Born in Iowa in 1867, Bursum was orphaned at a young age and sent to live with his uncle in nearby San Antonio. That uncle, Augustus H. Hilton—father of soon-to-be-successful hotelier Conrad Hilton—owned a store and mining properties. After working in the mercantile business, Bursum was elected sheriff of Socorro County in 1894 and began a lifelong career in public service. He was elected to the New Mexico Territorial Senate in 1899, then served as mayor of Socorro in 1906, and later followed his political star to Washington, D.C., representing New Mexico in the US Senate from 1921 to 1925.

Under Bursum's ownership, the Garcia Opera House continued to provide residents of Socorro with a setting for a litany of social events over the years, from weddings to political rallies to concerts—and even, believe it or not, to indoor basketball games! For many years after World War II, the hardwood floors of the opera house even served as a roller-skating rink. After that, the building was used as the B and M (Bursom and Murray) Feed Store, providing ranchers with supplies and feed. In later years, it was used as a storage facility.

In 1983, Holm Bursom Jr. began a series of restorations on the building, which was showing signs of wear after a century of community service, intending to restore the structure to its original grandeur and purpose. Bursom replaced the roof, keeping the style similar to that of the original, and added concrete abutments to the outside walls for support. Inside, workers laid new pine flooring in the hall itself as well as on the stage, placing the boards directly over and on top of the original flooring. While renovating the stage, workers uncovered old programs that had slipped beneath the floorboards. These were framed and put on display in the hall. Since the completion of renovations in 1985, the opera house has continued in its original role as a playhouse and community gathering site.

Although the Garcia Opera House is not a "National Historic Site," as incorrectly noted on the Historic Marker, its significance has nonetheless earned it a distinguished spot in both the Historic American Buildings Survey and the National Register of Historic Places. But perhaps the greatest endorsement of the value of the Garcia Opera House to the Socorro community is the fact that many couples today choose it as the site for their wedding—wanting to be married in the same building where their own grandparents tied the knot many years before.

More to explore: *Carthage-Tokay-Farley, Kelly, New Mexico Tech, Santa Fe Opera, Socorro*

174. Georgia O'Keeffe (1887–1986)

Location: Rio Arriba County. North of Abiquiú, on the east side of US 84, between mile markers 215 and 216. See map 2.

Marker text: One of America's great and most celebrated painters of the twentieth century, Georgia O'Keeffe is known for her unique depictions of natural and architectural forms. She began spending summers painting in Northern New Mexico in 1929 and moved from New York to make it her permanent home in 1949. The Georgia O'Keeffe Museum was founded in 1997 in Santa Fe to honor her legacy and extraordinary achievement.

Few discussions of art in the Southwest can overlook the contributions of Georgia O'Keeffe, so fundamental and transformative was her creative output to the genre. O'Keeffe's art has come in many ways to represent the Southwest itself, her brushstrokes capturing the brilliant colors and forms of both the architecture as well as the landscape and flora of the region—particularly that of the Abiquiú area, where she lived for many years. She managed through her extraordinary talent and innovative vision to move the beauty of the Southwest out of the natural world and onto canvas so that others could experience it through her eyes.

Georgia O'Keeffe was born near Sun Prairie, Wisconsin, on November 15, 1887. In 1905, she graduated from high school at Chatham Protestant Episcopal Institute. Several years of art training followed as she experimented with different styles, attending the Art Institute of Chicago as well as the Art Students League in New York and working then mostly with abstracts. But it was a class at Columbia University in 1914 studying under Arthur Wesley Dow where she was introduced to and strongly influenced by Dow's ideas on the use of lines and colors to create a "building up of harmony." Her work came to the attention of photographer Alfred Stieglitz, who arranged a one-woman show of her charcoal drawings in his gallery in New York in 1916. The two later married, and Stieglitz's portraiture of O'Keeffe has itself become iconic.

In the summer of 1929, O'Keeffe accepted an invitation from Taos art patron Mabel Dodge Luhan to visit New Mexico. O'Keeffe immediately felt inspired by the landscape she found in the state and continued visiting for many years thereafter, alternating her time between New York and New Mexico. She bought a house at an old dude ranch named Ghost Ranch and rambled around this part of northern New Mexico in her Ford Model A, looking—and finding—subjects for her canvas in the red rocks and canyons of the land she called "the faraway." By then she was working in her own distinctive style, her work part of a larger movement known as American Modernism. Mesas, flowers, trees, bleached cow skulls, and adobes all made their appearance in oil on her canvas. Among her most famous works created while she was in New Mexico are *The Lawrence Tree*, painted on the New Mexico ranch of novelist D. H. Lawrence, and *Pedernal*, a representation of Cerro Pedernal peak near Abiquiú, which was part of the view she enjoyed at her Ghost Ranch house.

After her husband's death in July 1946, O'Keeffe moved to New Mexico permanently, continuing to paint despite her diminishing eyesight.

O'Keeffe passed away on March 6, 1986, age ninety-eight, in Santa Fe. Her obituary in the *New York Times* praised both her talent and her legacy, reading in part: "As an interpreter and manipulator of natural forms, as a strong and individual colorist and as the lyric poet of her beloved New Mexico landscape, she left her mark on the history of American art and made it possible for other women to explore a new gamut of symbolic and ambiguous imagery."

The Georgia O'Keeffe Museum in Santa Fe holds a number of items in its collection, including *Black Mesa Landscape* and other pieces representative of the different phases of her artistic development. The museum is a fairly recent entry in the Santa Fe landscape of museums, founded in 1997. It is located at 217 Johnson Street, not faraway from the plaza.

More to explore: *Abiquiú, Red Rocks, The Three Fates*

175. Gila Cliff Dwellings National Monument

Location: Hidalgo County. At the New Mexico Welcome Center just west of Lordsburg, on the south side of Interstate 10, exit 20. See map 5.

Marker text: Gila Cliff Dwellings National Monument was established in 1907 by Theodore Roosevelt to protect the prehistoric material culture of the Mogollon people and others who inhabited this area. The first scientific description of a pueblo ruin on the upper Gila River was written in 1874 by Henry Wetherbee Henshaw of the Wheeler Geographical Surveys of the Territories of the United States West of the 100th Meridian.

For some eighty years, a small population of families of the prehistoric Mogollon culture found shelter in five natural caves along the southern wall of what is now known as Cliff Dweller Canyon. Their name, *Mogollon*, comes from the prominent presence of these early people in the Mogollon Mountains of southwestern New Mexico, although they lived also in parts of what are now Arizona, Texas, and northern Mexico. The spectacular dwellings they constructed in this canyon, along with other nearby archaeological sites within what is now the Gila Wilderness, are preserved today as the Gila Cliff Dwellings National Monument.

The Mogollon showed inventive technique in designing their house on the hill. After they arrived here around 1270, they quarried rocks from the canyon or simply appropriated stones that had already fallen from the roofs of the caves. They mortared the walls with clay dug by hand from the nearby Gila River and hewed beams for the cave ceilings from timber, which they gathered in abundance from the surrounding forest. Through their labors, these architects constructed an incredible forty-two rooms high above the canyon floor.

The Gila sustained them. The river nourished crops of corn, beans, and squash, while the mountain supplied jackrabbits, turkeys, and mule deer. Their canyon homes offered cover from extremes of weather. Theirs was a small community, and their cliffside penthouses domiciled a population that archaeologists believe rarely exceeded sixty people at any one time.

For reasons still uncertain, the Mogollon left the general area sometime around 1350. Possibly the drought that withered the land between 1276 and 1299 had made life here too difficult, or perhaps other factors compelled them into migration. Archaeologists cannot trace the Mogollon much further in time beyond 1350. Many suspect that they may have joined other Indian groups, like the Ancestral Puebloans, and lost their distinct cultural identity.

In 1874, ornithologist Henry Wetherbee Henshaw of the Wheeler Geographical Survey, along with a companion, visited the ruins the Mogollon left behind as part of the "Great Surveys" to map the West. Henshaw's account of the dwellings, published in 1879, is the first scientific description of a pueblo ruin on the upper Gila River. Reaching the canyon, Henshaw wrote of having noticed

a wall of cemented rocks, which evidently had been raised to inclose a natural cavity in the rocks. . . . The wall, which was perhaps 30 feet above the valley, was 15 or 18 feet long, and composed of volcanic debris plastered together with mud, and further strengthened and supported by stout timbers, which had been cemented into the interior face. Two principal openings had been left, one to serve as a doorway, through which we entered by stooping slightly, the other, perhaps a foot in diameter, which apparently answered the double purpose of admitting the light and serving as a loop-hole for the discharge of arrows. . . . On entering we found ourselves in a small room, about 14 feet long by 10 wide, out of which a second smaller apartment opened, the two being separated by a wall similar in construction to the first.

Henshaw went on to explore the upper part of the cave, noting also the steps carved into the rock and finding a number of bows and arrows.

Regrettably, some nineteenth-century locals who scouted the canyon dwellings pillaged the ruins, taking away artifacts and even a mummified baby that the Mogollon had left behind. To protect the integrity of the site, President Theodore Roosevelt on November 16, 1907, officially set aside land to preserve what was then known as the Gila Hot Springs Cliff-Houses.

Today, the National Park Service administers the renamed Gila Cliff Dwellings National Monument. The Visitors Center offers explanatory exhibits, and an interpretive trail allows viewers to walk through the ruins of the dwellings.

More to explore: *Mogollon*

176. Glorieta Pass Battlefield
National Historic Landmark, 1961

Location: Santa Fe County. West of Pecos, in a pullout on the west side of NM 50, near mile marker 1. See map 2.

Marker text: The Civil War battle fought in this pass is often referred to as the "Gettysburg of the West." Union forces dashed Confederate strategy to seize the Southwest's major supply base at Fort Union; Colorado and California were to be next. The Texas vanguard captured Santa Fe, March 10, 1862, but after two days of battle here U.S. troops and Colorado Volunteers burned a poorly guarded Confederate supply camp and slaughtered hundreds of their horses and mules on March 28. Rebel Troops retreated from New Mexico within two weeks.

Note: Glorieta Pass Battlefield was named a National Historic Landmark in 1961.

Union prospects looked bleak in New Mexico in the spring of 1862. Confederates were fresh from their engagements with Union troops at Valverde, near present-day Socorro, and had steamrolled through Belen, Albuquerque, and the capital of Santa Fe. Next on the agenda: Fort Union, near Las Vegas.

When the morning sun of March 26, 1862, rose over Glorieta Pass east of Santa Fe, Union and Confederate soldiers awoke in camps situated scarcely ten miles apart. The advance guard of some two hundred Confederate soldiers, under the command of Major Charles Pyron, had bivouacked near Johnson's Ranch at a spot known as Cañoncito in Apache Canyon. They were oblivious to the vanguard of Union Colorado Volunteers, led by Major John M. Chivington, who were stationed a short distance to the east, near the stage stop along the Santa Fe Trail known as Kozlowski's Ranch.

The opposing sides met later that morning, when Chivington's men captured one of Pyron's scouting parties in Glorieta Pass, a defile through the southern foothills of the Sangre de Cristo Mountains, and then advanced on the main Confederate force. Union troops, initially harassed by the fire from two Rebel howitzers, regrouped and repeatedly flanked the Confederate line, forcing the Rebels to withdraw to the west. After charging with their cavalry, federal troops managed to corral some seventy Rebel soldiers in Apache Canyon before darkness fell. This fragment of the larger three-day engagement is sometimes known as the Battle of Apache Canyon.

That evening, both sides withdrew to their respective camps to care for their casualties, most of whom were no older than twenty-five. Excavations of skeletons at the site by the Museum of New Mexico in 1994 offer a glimpse of those who died in the fighting at Glorieta. Private Enos R. Slaughter, for example, was twenty-six. He was killed when a bullet tore into his head. Private J. S. L. Cotton, twenty, died when a cannonball hit his lower back.

During the evening, Colonel John P. Slough marched in from the north with the main body of Union troops, including 950 men of the First Regiment of Colorado Volunteers and the New Mexico Volunteers. Pyron's Confederate troops also received reinforcements when Colonel William Scurry arrived from the south with additional soldiers, a team of horses and mules, and a welcomed sight: some eighty wagons filled with ammunition, food, clothing, and medicine.

The day of March 27 was quiet in both camps. No doubt it was a day filled with portent, as the two sides waited in vain for enemy movements.

The next day, Slough's Union troops engaged the Confederates in a lengthy battle near Pigeon's Ranch. Meanwhile, Major Chivington, along with Lieutenant Colonel Manuel Chavez of the New Mexico Volunteers and some 450 troops, arced to the south and crept over the rim of Glorieta Mesa, initially following orders to attack the Confederate flank. But when they reached the top of the mesa, they found that the main body of troops had moved en masse to meet the Union forces near Pigeon's

Ranch—leaving behind the lightly guarded Confederate supply wagons, still stationed near the Confederate camp at Cañoncito.

Chivington decided at that point to attack the supply wagons. Caught unaware, the few Confederate wagon guards and teamsters who did not flee were taken prisoner. Then, in a move that would effectively halt the Confederate advance in the Southwest, Union soldiers set fire to the wagons and their stores of supplies and slaughtered a number of horses and mules.

By nightfall, word of the loss had reached the Confederate camp. Knowing well that he could not advance without supplies, Colonel Scurry called for a truce. Two weeks later, the Confederate Army began a retreat from New Mexico.

The Battle of Glorieta Pass is sometimes called the "Gettysburg of the West," a reference to the decisive Civil War battle fought at Gettysburg, Pennsylvania, in July 1863.

More to explore: *Cañoncito at Apache Canyon, Fort Craig, Fort Union National Monument, Peralta, Site of San Augustin Springs*

177. Gold and Turquoise

Location: Santa Fe County. Fifteen miles south of Santa Fe, in the Bicentennial Rest Area and Visitors Center, on the east side of Interstate 25. (The rest area is also known as the La Bajada Rest Area.) See map 2.

Marker text: First gold placer mining west of the Mississippi began with the discovery of the precious metal in the rugged Ortiz Mountains south of here in 1828, 21 years before the California gold rush. Since then, the district has produced more than 99,000 ounces of placer gold and gold is currently produced from lode deposits.

The prominent hills to the east and to the left are the Cerrillos Hills, site of ancient turquoise mines worked by the Indians centuries before the arrival of the Spanish. The Cerrillos ("little hills") are regarded as the oldest mining district in the United States, and New Mexico is a major turquoise producer. Elevation 6,200 feet.

Note: New Mexico is no longer a major turquoise producer.

Although small and inconspicuous amid the Los Cerrillos Hills visible to the east, the hill grandly known as Mount Chalchihuitl nonetheless has played a prominent role in the history of this part of New Mexico. The name *chalchihuitl* is derived from the Aztec word for turquoise. From at least AD 900, Native American cultures mined Mount Chalchihuitl for that precious gem, a rare and valuable commodity in prehistoric trade networks. Historians consider these efforts some of the earliest mining activity in North America. At one time, turquoise mined near present-day Cerrillos made New Mexico one of the foremost turquoise producers in the country. The state no longer holds that distinction, but the value of turquoise to our history is evident: the state legislature adopted turquoise as the official state gem in 1967.

Not to be outdone, gold has likewise contributed its share to the mining history of the area. Sheepherder José Francisco Ortiz is generally credited as the person to have first discovered the precious metal in the Ortiz Mountains to the south when he came across gold flakes in streams on the eastern slopes of the mountains in 1828—a full twenty-one years before golden specks in the riverbed near John Augustus Sutter's sawmill set off the California Gold Rush of 1849! Miners descended on what became known as the Old Placers mining district, extracting what chips they could from Cunningham Canyon, Dolores Gulch, Arroyo Viejo, and other locations. The Old Placers district had its nucleus in the settlement of Dolores. This small camp showed early promise of becoming a stable, stalwart settlement, offering a saloon, a general store, and a population that ranged between two thousand and four thousand people. Lieutenant James W. Abert, leading a military reconnaissance through the Southwest in 1846, left this backhanded compliment: "The houses were the most miserable we had yet seen, and the inhabitants the most abject picture of squalid poverty, and yet the streets of the village are indeed paved with gold."

According to an account published by the US Geological Survey in 1972, the total yield from all this effort reached almost $2 million dollars in gold.

Dusty mining camps rose and fell in the mountains almost overnight, their names chosen, no doubt, in hopes they would prove prophetic: Bonanza City, Chance City, Eureka. Most of the surface gold at Old Placers was depleted by the mid-1840s, but a second mining district developed around that time when prospectors uncovered lode gold deposits on the slopes of the San Pedro Mountains. This district, dubbed New Placers, gave rise to the community of Real de San Francisco. The settlement, which survives today, has been renamed Golden.

More to explore: *Cerrillos, Santa Rita Copper Mines*

GOODNIGHT-LOVING TRAIL: Series of Six Historic Markers (Various Locations)

General Introduction

Famous among its contemporaries, the Goodnight-Loving Trail was the creation of two men and a couple thousand cattle. The men were Charles Goodnight and Oliver Loving, and their partnership resulted in some of the most famous cattle drives in western history.

Goodnight, born in 1836 in Illinois, had moved to Texas in his youth to work on a small ranch. He served as a Texas Ranger during the Civil War before returning to ranching at the end of the conflict. Kentucky-born Loving was the elder of the duo, seasoned by twenty years of seniority and experience. Loving brought previous cattle driving know-how to the partnership, having pioneered the Shawnee Trail from Texas to Chicago in 1855.

Six separate Historic Markers document the duo's travels (and travails) in New Mexico. Those Markers have been combined here into one series, so the story of Goodnight and Loving and their famous cattle trail can be followed comprehensively. The series includes the Markers entitled "Goodnight-Loving Trail," "Loving's Bend," and "New Goodnight Trail." The Markers are listed here roughly in chronological order.

More to explore (Goodnight-Loving Trail Series): *Artesia, Bottomless Lakes State Park, Playas Siding, Vaughn*

178. Goodnight-Loving Trail

Location: Chaves County. On US 380 east of Roswell, on the north side of the highway, between mile markers 167 and 168. See map 6.

Marker text: The famous old cattle trail, running 2000 miles from Texas to Wyoming, was blazed in 1866 by Charles Goodnight and Oliver Loving. In New Mexico, the trail followed the Pecos River north to Fort Sumner, where the government needed beef to feed the Navajos at the Bosque Redondo Reservation.

Note: See the general introduction to this series of Markers, as well as the other Markers making up the series, for further background on the Goodnight-Loving Trail.

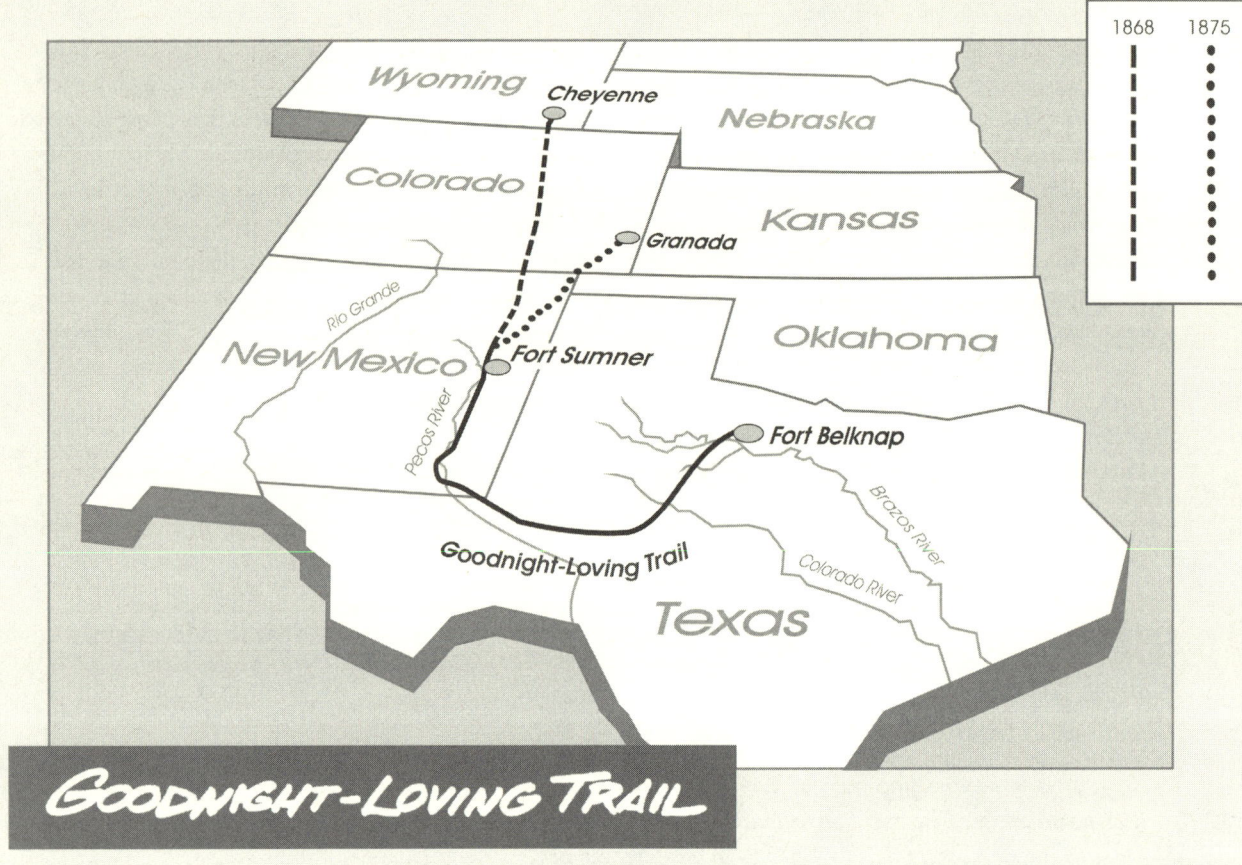

Goodnight-Loving Trail

Charles Goodnight and Oliver Loving's cattle trail crossed the southeastern plains of New Mexico at a time when such drives were still the most efficient way of moving large herds. Cattle depended on the waters of the Pecos River and various springs to quench their thirst along the way. Illustration by David Carter.

On their first trip together, Goodnight and Loving set out from Fort Belknap, Texas, on June 6, 1866, with a two-thousand-head mixed herd and eighteen fellow cowboys, intending to travel more than two hundred miles to supply beef for government contracts in New Mexico and other western states. Rather than traverse the west Texas plains, the men planned to veer to the southwest, cross the Colorado River, and eventually meet the Pecos River, which they would follow north from Texas into southeastern New Mexico. Such a route meant more time in transit, but it also meant avoiding the threat of Comanche raids on the Texas plains.

Goodnight and Loving left Fort Belknap in June. Heat and lack of water initially conspired against the two-thousand-head convoy—with the searing summer sun killing three hundred cattle before the men even reached the Pecos River. Upon smelling the waters of the Pecos, the parched herd stampeded to the river in an onslaught that killed another hundred cattle.

Undaunted, the drovers continued their trek north along the course of the Pecos through west Texas and southeastern New Mexico. They followed the Pecos north over the plains of southeastern New Mexico to Fort Sumner and the Bosque Redondo Indian Reservation. At the

Bosque Redondo Reservation, Navajo and Mescalero Apache Indians forcibly removed from their homelands were starving from a paucity of crops and edible meat. Pestilence and malnourishment had decimated the Indians, and soldiers at the fort readily purchased half the herd to feed the starving families in their care. Goodnight and Loving turned a substantial profit.

179. Goodnight-Loving Trail

Location: Harding County. In Mosquero, in Village Hall Park, next to the City Hall/Volunteer Fire Department Building, on the west side of NM 39. See map 3.

Marker text: After leaving Fort Sumner, the Goodnight-Loving Trail forked in two directions. This branch, developed by Oliver Loving in 1866, followed the Pecos River to Las Vegas, and the Santa Fe Trail to Raton Pass. The great Texas cattle drives followed this and other routes to Colorado and Wyoming until 1880.

Note: See the general introduction to this series of Markers, as well as the other Markers making up the series, for further background on the Goodnight-Loving Trail.

180. Goodnight-Loving Trail

Location: Eddy County. North of Loving, in a pullout on the west side of US 285, between mile markers 23 and 24 on US 285, at the intersection of US 285 and NM 31. See map 6.

Marker text: After leaving Fort Sumner, the Goodnight-Loving Trail forked in two directions. This branch, developed by Oliver Loving in 1866, followed the Pecos River to Las Vegas, and the Santa Fe Trail to Raton Pass. The great Texas cattle drives followed this and other routes to Colorado and Wyoming until 1880.

Note: This Marker references a branch of the trail that was actually located much farther north of this location, the divide near Fort Sumner, about 175 miles away. Don't let that deter you from enjoying this Marker, as the Goodnight-Loving Trail did pass through this area, following the Pecos River north to Fort Sumner, where the two branches divided.

Note: See the general introduction to this series of Markers, as well as the other Markers making up the series, for further background on the Goodnight-Loving Trail.

181. Loving's Bend

Location: Eddy County. At the north end of Loving, on the west side of US 285. See map 6.

Marker text: In July 1867 Oliver Loving, a partner in the Goodnight-Loving cattle concern, was attacked by Comanches while driving cattle to Fort Sumner. Wounded, Loving held off the attack for two days and nights. With the help of Mexican traders, he made it to Fort Sumner, where he died of gangrene. Fulfilling his promise, Charles Goodnight exhumed Loving's body, reburying him a year later in Weatherford, Texas.

Note: See the general introduction to this series of Markers, as well as the other Markers making up the series, for further background on the Goodnight-Loving Trail.

After their successful first sale of cattle to the army at Fort Sumner in 1866, Charles Goodnight and Oliver Loving decided to multitask. While Goodnight returned to Texas to start a second drive, Loving pushed the remainder of the herd north from Fort Sumner through New Mexico. His route paralleled the Pecos River to Las Vegas and then traced the Mountain Branch of the Santa Fe Trail over Raton Pass to Denver, Colorado, where he sold the remainder of the herd.

The two men reunited on the trail and returned together with the new cattle Goodnight had herded here to the Bosque Redondo Reservation. When this second herd sold as successfully as the first, Goodnight and Loving planned a third drive for the next year.

This time, however, Loving was in a hurry. Government beef contracts would be let in August, and Loving wanted to beat the competition to Fort Sumner and Santa Fe. So, when the cattlemen and their herd reached the Pecos in July of 1867, Loving forged ahead with another cowboy, Bill "One-Armed" Wilson. Goodnight warned his associates not to travel during the day, when the potential for a Comanche attack was greater than under cover of night. Loving complied—for a time. Soon enough, though, both men had foregone night riding and were traveling in the open light of day.

Their luck held until they crossed the Texas border into New Mexico. A band of Comanches, sighting the lone figures on the grasslands of the eastern plains, rained down upon them in a surprise attack. Wilson and Loving sought refuge from the onslaught among scrub oak growing along a bend in the Pecos River. There they holed up as the Indians, perhaps as many as a hundred, surrounded them. Wilson attempted diplomacy, emerging that evening to address his adversaries directly. His efforts at conciliation met with a round of gunfire. One of the bullets shattered Loving's wrist and entered his side. It would be a mortal wound.

At Loving's insistence, Wilson escaped later that evening by swimming the river past the unsuspecting Indians. Now alone, Loving continued to bleed out as the Indians pelted rocks and arrows at him and snuck ever closer. He survived two days barricaded at the riverbank. Finally, on the third night, Loving too evaded his attackers by braving the waters of the Pecos himself, somehow managing to swim for six miles upstream even in his grim condition. He stumbled to a nearby trail, waylaid a passing wagon master, and paid him $250 for passage to Fort Sumner.

When Goodnight received word of the incident, he traveled quickly to the fort to be with his injured friend. Doctors had been forced to amputate Loving's arm in the meantime, but the operation had not successfully stayed the onset of gangrene. Knowing he was near death, Loving confessed to his partner his last regret: that by dying in New Mexico, he would be buried "in a foreign country" and not in his home state of Texas.

On September 25, 1867, several months after Loving's death, Charles Goodnight returned to the Fort Sumner Cemetery, where his partner had been temporarily interred, and placed his friend's wooden casket into a large metal encasement that Goodnight had fashioned from flattened oil cans. Goodnight carried the casket by wagon to Loving's home in Weatherford, Texas, where his body was laid to final rest—safely distant from the strange foreign country of New Mexico.

182. Goodnight-Loving Trail

Location: Union County. East of Capulin, in pullout on the north side of US 64, between mile markers 377 and 378. See map 3.

Marker text: In order to avoid the high toll charged for each animal on the Raton Pass branch of the Goodnight-Loving Trail, Charles Goodnight blazed this route through Trinchera Pass in 1868. Because it was shorter, had easier grades, and was toll-free, later cattle drives followed Goodnight's example.

Note: See the general introduction to this series of Markers, as well as the other Markers making up the series, for further background on the Goodnight-Loving Trail.

183. New Goodnight Trail

Location: Union County. Just west of Des Moines, in a pullout on the north side of US 64/87, between mile markers 384 and 385. See map 3.

Marker text: Charles Goodnight, the great Texas cattleman, used the Trinchera Pass branch of the Goodnight-Loving Trail until 1875. In that year, he blazed this trail northward from Fort Sumner, passing near Tucumcari and Clayton. This was the last trail created by Goodnight, marking the end of his operations in New Mexico.

Note: See the general introduction to this series of Markers, as well as the other Markers making up the series, for further background on the Goodnight-Loving Trail.

After the death of his partner, Oliver Loving, cattleman Charles Goodnight continued driving cattle through New Mexico. In the meantime, though, Richens Lacy "Uncle Dick" Wootton had obtained permission from the Colorado territorial legislature to establish a toll road over mountainous Raton Pass in northern New Mexico, the route through which the earlier Goodnight-Loving cattle drives had passed. Although Wootton blasted through the worst of the barriers in the craggy pass and eased the treacherous grades over the Raton Mountains, his toll of ten cents a head for cattle proved too steep for Goodnight's financial tastes. On Goodnight's next cattle drive in 1868, he thus chose to forgo Raton Pass and instead laid a new trail into Colorado over Trinchera Pass, a cut at the eastern end of Johnson Mesa in the far northeastern part of what is now Colfax County in New Mexico.

Goodnight later teamed with cattleman John Chisum and continued driving cattle for another decade, as did other stockmen who used his trail. With the arrival of the railroad in New Mexico in the 1880s, large-scale cattle drives became a romantic part of western history.

184. Graciela Olivárez (1928–1987)

Location: Bernalillo County. In Albuquerque, near the Gateway Overpass, in a park at the northwest corner of Broadway and Avenida Cesar Chavez. See map 4.

Marker text: Attorney, public servant, and activist, Graciela Olivárez was a high school dropout who became the first woman graduate of Notre Dame Law School where an award is presented each year in her name. She led national anti-poverty efforts and ensured equal representation of men and women on the National Council of La Raza's Board of Directors. In 1980, she started the nation's first Spanish-language television network.

Each year, the Hispanic Law Students Association at Notre Dame Law School selects one Hispanic judge or lawyer in the country who has "made a significant contribution to the Hispanic legal community" and honors them with the Graciela Olivárez Award. It is a distinguished award, named for a distinguished alumna of the school: Graciela Olivárez, public servant and community activist. Olivárez was, in 1970, the first female and Latina graduate of Notre Dame's law school—a feat rendered all the more remarkable by the fact that Olivárez was a high school dropout.

Born Graciela Gil on March 9, 1928, in Sonora, Arizona, Olivárez at first seemed destined for a career in radio. Dropping out of Ray High School at age fifteen, she soon thereafter secured employment at a Phoenix radio station. Filling in for her boss one day, she found a permanent place on the air, hosting the show *Hora de Los Teenagers* (Hour of the Teenagers) and later a talk program known as *Action Line* at the Spanish-language station KIFN. The radio show and her work as the women's program director gave her the opportunity to reach out to the Spanish-speaking community, discussing issues like poverty and civil rights. In 1965, after passage of the Economic Opportunity Act the previous year, Olivárez left radio to serve as the Arizona state director of the federal Office of Economic Opportunity, where she worked on a state level to address social welfare issues among low-income people, helping the poor attain self-sufficiency. It was a cause she cared about deeply and one she would return to throughout her life.

At an airport in Chicago, Olivárez met Father Theodore Hesburgh, the president of the University of Notre Dame. He knew her work and encouraged her to apply to Notre Dame's law school, despite having only a general equivalency diploma. With Father Hesburgh's backing, Olivárez was admitted. She was a single mother, raising a son from a previous marriage, and attending law school full time. Her graduation in 1970 made history.

But she didn't stop there.

In 1972, Olivárez moved to New Mexico and became the director of the Institute for Social Research and Development at the University of New Mexico. That same year, she led a successful effort to ensure that the board of directors of the National Council of La Raza, an organization that advocates on behalf of Mexican Americans, which had just that year become a national organization, consisted of an equitable number of men and women. In 1975, she accepted a position as the state planning officer in Santa Fe, overseeing the strategic planning efforts of many state agencies. She was, at the time, the highest-ranking woman in state government. She moved even higher, becoming in 1977 the highest-ranking Hispanic woman in the administration of President Jimmy Carter, when in April of that year he appointed her the director of the Community Services Administration (the successor agency to the Office of Economic Opportunity), allowing her to address poverty issues nationwide. In 1978, the University of Notre Dame, her law school alma mater, awarded her an honorary doctor of law degree.

She didn't stop there either.

Olivárez saw a hole in the offerings of Spanish-language television in the United States. So, in 1980, she left Washington to fill it—by creating her own television network, the Olivárez Television Company. The station broadcast as KLUZ out of Albuquerque. It was the first all-Spanish-language television network in the nation.

Graciela often went by the name Grace. But to her friends and family, she was "Amazing Gracie"—a nickname truly deserved. Her work and her accomplishments inspired many.

Graciela Olivárez passed away on September 19, 1987.

More to explore: *María Dolores Gonzáles, Marjorie Bell Chambers*

185. Gran Quivira Ruins
Salinas National Monument
1 Mile South

Location: Torrance County. At entrance to Gran Quivira on NM 55. See map 4.

Marker text: The Tompiro Indian "Pueblo de las Humanas" (ca. 1300–1670s) had 1,500 to 2,000 inhabitants and was a trading center with Plains Indians. The village evolved for centuries on the fringe of the Mogollon and Anasazi cultures. There are two large Spanish Franciscan mission churches, San Isidro built in 1629, and San Buenaventura constructed in 1659.

Built around 1300 atop a small hill now known as Chupadero Mesa, Gran Quivira was the southernmost pueblo village erected in the Estancia Valley as the Ancestral Puebloan and Mogollon cultures merged in this part of central New Mexico. Known to its Tompiro-speaking residents as Cueloze, the original circular blockhouse pueblo saw subsequent modifications as generations of Indians remodeled and enlarged the structure. Cueloze was the largest of a handful of pueblos scattered through the Estancia Valley, its population reaching at times up to two thousand people. Plains Indians like the Comanches and Apaches brought bison meat and hides to the pueblos in the valley, which served as major trading centers, and exchanged them for pottery, cotton, and piñon nuts carried from pueblos along the Rio Grande.

In 1598, don Juan de Oñate arrived in New Mexico to colonize the land for Spain. Oñate visited Cueloze that October. Seeing the stripe the Indians painted across their noses, he dubbed the village Pueblo de Las Humanas, or "Town of the Striped Ones."

Fray Francisco Letrado arrived in Las Humanas in 1629 to serve as the first resident priest. Letrado began work on the earliest mission church in the village, but Fray Francisco de Acevado, who replaced Letrado a few years later, saw it to completion. The mission bore a dedication to San Isidro. Finished in 1634, the outside walls of the structure rose almost thirty feet high, tall enough to allow for a choir loft, supported by wooden posts, above the inside of the front door. Decorative red-and-black-painted ornamentations covered the inside white plaster walls. Coincident with the construction of the mission, the priest destroyed the pueblo kivas, underground structures where the Indians worshiped and gathered for social occasions. Archaeological evidence, however, indicates that the crackdown was not successful: Indians constructed hidden kivas within the pueblo itself.

In 1659, twenty-two-year-old Fray Diego de Santander became resident priest at Las Humanas. Availing himself of Indian workers, Santander pulled up the shrubbery from a hillside west of the pueblo and began the construction of a second mission at that spot, one that was intended to bear the dedication San Buenaventura. Although Santander's grandiose plans for the mission included thirty-foot-high limestone walls, a baptistery to the right of the door, an altar at the far end, and side altars on both ends of the transept, he never saw the church completed. Injured in an accident in 1662, the priest left Las Humanas that year. Work on the church and convento continued sporadically after his departure, but only the foundations and the convento were completed. Left unfinished, the mission was never officially dedicated.

By the 1670s, residents of the Estancia Valley looked upon a landscape made impotent by drought. The priest at Las Humanas even blocked the windows of the food storeroom to prevent desperate Indians from stealing from the dwindling food supplies. Enfeebled by famine and widespread disease, the last five hundred residents of the pueblo left in 1672. The proud mission church and house blocks they left behind eventually collapsed.

The ruins of the pueblo later acquired the name Gran Quivira and became part of Salinas National Monument, which includes the Estancia Valley pueblos of Abó and Quarai. The National Park Service today administers the site.

More to explore: *Abó Ruins, Mogollon, Quarai Ruins*

186. Grants

Location: Cibola County. In Grants, on the east side of city, on the Interstate 40 business loop, in the parking lot of the Holiday Inn Express. See map 1.

Marker text: Located just north of the great lava bed known as the malpais, Grants began as a coaling station for the Santa Fe Railroad. Around 1880 it was known as Grant's Camp, after the Canadian bridge contractor Angus A. Grant. In 1950, the area's vast uranium deposits were discovered.

187. Ghost Marker: Mount Taylor

Marker text: One of the great volcanic cones of the Colorado Plateau, Mount Taylor rises to an elevation of 11,301 feet and last erupted some 2 million years ago. Numerous fissure eruptions since that time and as recently as about 1,200 years ago have created lava flows that form malpais or badlands along portions of this route.

Note: This Marker appears in an inventory of Historic Markers compiled by the State Historic Preservation Office but is not in the field. See map 1.

As crews for the Atlantic and Pacific Railroad laid track through northwestern New Mexico on their way from Isleta Pueblo to Needles, California, in the 1880s, they established a base camp and coaling station at a small, preexisting village along the south bank of the Rio San José. Locals knew that settlement as Los Alamitos, or "Little Cottonwoods." Among the workers at the camp were Canadian-born engineers Angus A. Grant and his brothers and business partners, John R. and Louis A. Grant. Angus had worked for the rail line since 1870, fresh from the payrolls of the Kansas Pacific Railway as well as the Denver and Rio Grande. In short order, Los Alamitos came to be known as Grants Camp. Although a post office opened in 1882 as Grant, in the singular, it changed by popular request to Grants, the plural, in 1935. The Grant brothers, by that time, had moved to Albuquerque, where they helped institute the first waterworks and electric plants in the city.

Grants lay just north of where volcanic activity many centuries ago had left a forty-mile stretch of furrowed lava beds and cinder cones known collectively as the malpais—a Spanish word that translates to "badlands." The lava flows came from volcanoes of the Mount Taylor volcanic region; the 11,300-foot Mount Taylor itself rises like a dormant giant northeast of Grants. The malpais includes several underground caves, where cooler temperatures and insulating lava rock have kept water frozen into blocks of ice. This scarred lot eventually received federal recognition when, in 1987, Congress designated 114,277 acres of the landscape as the El Malpais National Monument and Conservation Area.

Mining and drilling in the land surrounding Grants have yielded pumice, fluorite, and natural gas. In 1950, Navajo sheepherder Paddy Martinez discovered unusual rocks at the base of nearby Haystack Mountain and added uranium to that list. Uranium is an ore used to fuel nuclear power plants. With the discovery, Grants took to calling itself "the Uranium Capital of the World."

Today, given its location near the lava flows, El Morro National Monument, and Acoma and Laguna Pueblos, Grants has become a gateway to area attractions. It is also home to the New Mexico Mining Museum.

More to explore: *Bluewater Village, Colorado Plateau, El Morro National Monument Inscription Rock, Pueblo of Acoma, Pueblo of Laguna*

188. Greathouse Station and Tavern

Location: Lincoln County. Just south of Corona, on the west side of US 54, between mile markers 168 and 169. See map 6.

Marker text: In late November, 1880, William "Billy the Kid" Bonney, David Rudabaugh and William Wilson were hiding out here at a store and tavern operated by James Greathouse and a partner named Kuch. The night of November 27, they were surrounded by a posse. Deputy James Carlyle was accidentally killed when he attempted to negotiate the outlaws' surrender. Bonney and his companions escaped unharmed.

By the winter of 1880, William H. Bonney, better known as Billy the Kid, was an outlaw on the lam. Wanted for the murder of Lincoln County sheriff William Brady two years earlier, the Kid had eluded capture by wandering southeastern New Mexico and trading rustled cattle and stolen horses, all the while trying to convince New Mexico governor Lew Wallace to drop the indictment against him.

In late November, the Kid and his friends Dave Rudabaugh and Billy Wilson stopped at a stage station and ranch owned by James Greathouse and his business partner, Fred Kuch, about a mile southwest of present-day Corona. As befitted his nickname, "Whiskey Jim" Greathouse savored no stellar reputation and had reportedly conspired with the Kid in various crimes. The outlaw trio remained at the tavern with Greathouse for a couple of days before setting out for White Oaks to sell horses. They returned to the tavern on November 27—followed by an agitated eight-man White Oaks posse that hoped to arrest the Kid.

After arriving at the tavern, Deputy William Hudgens sent a note inside demanding that the Kid give himself up. The outlaw and his friends returned their own note asking that a member of the posse come inside, at which time they would consider negotiating surrender. They wanted young James Carlyle, a White Oaks blacksmith.

To his dismay, Carlyle entered an errant den of drunk and fractious outlaws who had no intention of surrendering and were content instead simply to bully him. Several hours of unsuccessful negotiations passed between the Kid and the posse members outside. Finally, around two in the afternoon, men outside the tavern threatened to kill James Greathouse, whom they had taken hostage to ensure Carlyle's safe return. In a fatal response from the Kid and his gang, Carlyle's body crashed through a window of the station house, the target of three gunshots on its journey. The White Oaks blacksmith had become a casualty of the standoff, being either thrown through the window or jumping through it in a pitiful attempt to escape. History is in doubt whether the bullets that killed him came from the Kid, from his gang, or from the White Oaks posse outside—who may have mistaken him for a hostile member of the Kid's gang.

In the gunfight that ensued, James Greathouse and Fred Kuch escaped unharmed. After a few hours, the posse gathered their horses and lit out for home, leaving James Carlyle's body behind. Sometime after midnight, the Kid and his friends Rudabaugh and Wilson also fled.

In retribution for the death of their neighbor, a vengeful mob from White Oaks descended on the Greathouse Tavern the next morning and burned it to the ground.

More to explore: *John H. Tunstall Murder Site, Lincoln, White Oaks*

189. Hachita

Location: Grant County. In Hachita, at the intersection of NM 9 and NM 146. See map 5.

Marker text: Located in the Little Hatchet Mountains, Hachita was founded around 1875 as a mining camp. The mountains supplied the camp not only with silver and copper, but also its name, "little hatchet." By 1884 Hachita grew to 300 residents. Soon after 1900, when railroad tracks were laid nine miles east of Hachita, another settlement sprang up, drawing away residents and dividing the community into Old Hachita and New Hachita. Hachita also served as the base for forces when the "punitive expedition" was organized in retaliation for Pancho Villa's raid upon Columbus in 1916.

Discovery of silver, lead, copper, and turquoise ores in the Little Hatchet Mountains west of here around 1875 provided the impetus for the development of a small community in the foothills of those mountains. Residents built homes out of local stone and adobe, and also constructed a saloon and store. Originally the community took the name Eureka, an exclamation common to mining lore, as well as the name of the larger Eureka mining district that encompassed the mines. When a post office opened in 1882, though, the name of the small town was formalized as Hachita. The name is the Spanish translation of the name of the mountains, "Little Hatchet."

Hachita went through a typical boom-and-bust mining cycle. By 1884, some three hundred people lived in the town, most of them working in one of the three most productive mines: the Hornet, the King, and the American. But in the 1890s, the prosperity faded as the mines ran dry, and by the turn of the century the population had dwindled significantly to about twenty-five people.

In 1900, construction crews with the El Paso and Southwestern Railroad arrived in this part of southwestern New Mexico, running a rail line between El Paso, Texas, and Douglas, Arizona. The line ran nine miles east of Hachita, bypassing the mountains for the level plains more suitable for railroad construction. Desiring to be closer to the economic benefits the railroad would bring, most of the remaining residents of Hachita moved from the mountains down to the valley south of the tracks (today known as the Hachita Valley).

They took the name of their settlement with them, forming New Hachita. Eventually, Old Hachita, as the mining camp in the mountains came to be called, was abandoned, and New Hachita became simply Hachita.

An event in the early morning hours of March 9, 1916, in a town forty miles away had repercussions on Hachita as well. That morning, Francisco "Pancho" Villa led a band of revolutionaries (called *Villistas*) on a raid of the border town of Columbus, New Mexico, and the military post of Camp Furlong there, burning the town and killing eighteen people. For weeks thereafter, fear spread among the residents of other border towns, including Hachita, of further possible attacks.

President Woodrow Wilson responded by organizing what was called the Punitive Expedition, an assemblage of troops that would march into Mexico from New Mexico to find Villa and bring him to justice. At the head of the expedition was Brigadier General John J. "Black Jack" Pershing, who would later lead American troops in World War I. In Columbus, the forces were organized into two columns: the eastern column would march into Mexico from Columbus, while some two thousand troops of the Seventh Cavalry, Tenth Cavalry, and Battery B of the Sixth Field Artillery were sent to Hachita to make up the western column and enter Mexico through Culberson's Ranch south of town. The expeditions were to rejoin and reach the settlement of Colonia Dublan, a Mormon colony near Nuevas Casas Grandes in Mexico, where they would establish a field camp.

As instructed, the western column, under the command of Colonel George A. Dodd, arrived at Culberson's Ranch on the evening of March 14. In Columbus, Pershing gave the order to march the next day, then left to command the troops at Culberson's Ranch himself. He was delayed slightly getting there, as he later explained in his expedition report:

Telegraphic orders were sent Colonel Dodd at Culberson's Ranch to hold his command in readiness to start upon my arrival early that evening, but owing to an automobile accident my arrival was delayed until nearly 12 o'clock P.M., so that the column did not start until about midnight.

The accident was likely not even in Pershing's own car. As the *El Paso Herald* of March 22 reported, Pershing lacked cars to move officers and himself to Hachita after dispatching the troops from Columbus, so he asked at least two of the sightseers who had driven to Columbus to watch the troops depart to drive him and some of his men to Hachita.

Pershing spent less than a year pursuing Villa before being recalled to the United States. Villa was never caught.

The El Paso and Southwestern Railroad pulled up its tracks through Hachita in the 1960s. With the loss of the railroad, Hachita settled into the quieter existence it maintains today.

More to explore: *Columbus and Pancho Villa's Raid (series), Rodeo Station, Yucca Plains (see under Yucca—New Mexico's State Flower)*

190. Harriet Belle Amsden Sammons

Location: San Juan County. In Farmington, near the entrance to the City of Farmington Municipal Operations Center, 101 Browning Parkway, at the northwest corner of the intersection of Browning Parkway and Browning Road. See map 1.

Marker text: Harriet Belle Amsden Sammons was the first female bank president in New Mexico, operating the First National Bank in Farmington from 1922 until 1951. She began working at the bank in 1912 and proved to be a humane and astute financial manager. During the Depression she bought out the San Juan National Bank, keeping it solvent and approving loans. She supported the newly formed United Indian Traders Association and kept many Farmington citizens out of bankruptcy.

In 1908, Harriet Belle Amsden Sammons and her husband, George, arrived in Farmington, New Mexico, from Seneca, Kansas, and changed the small town forever.

The couple settled in a house that Harriet herself designed on North Orchard Street. George went to work as the first doctor in Farmington and helped open the first hospital in the city two years after their arrival. In 1912, Harriet herself entered the Farmington professional world. Her brother, Avery Amsden, who already lived in Farmington, had founded the First National Bank on Main Street (along with a hotel and lumber company)—and Harriet accepted a position at that institution. Her astute financial management skills helped her rise within the bank hierarchy, and in 1922, after ten years on the job, she became the bank president. In so doing, she distinguished herself as the first female bank president in the state of New Mexico.

The Depression brought new challenges to the banking industry. A loss of revenue and an uncertain financial future took their toll on another bank in town, the San Juan National Bank. Before it closed, Sammons bought it—keeping it solvent and protecting the life savings of many Farmington residents. Her actions saved many in Farmington from certain bankruptcy. Over time, because of her humane nature, generosity, and respected stature within the community, Sammons came to be known as "Ma" Sammons.

According to her great-niece, Dr. Diana Avery Amsden, Sammons was a generous person. She enjoyed giving anonymous gifts—often checks—to friends and relatives. The checks often included a directive to the recipient that the money "be spent foolishly." A recollection printed by the *Farmington Daily Times Magazine* in October 1985 told of her once leaving a $100 bookmark in a book she had borrowed from a local minister. She also had a good sense of humor. She was not, however, particularly fond of a certain prank her employees at the bank played. In nominating the bank to the National Register of Historic Places in 2001, the National Park Service noted: "The Halloween prank of sneaking an outhouse into the bank vestibule became an annual tradition as did Ma Sammon's outrage."

During her tenure as president, Sammons became involved in supporting the newly formed United Indian Traders Association. Incorporated in 1931 with headquarters in Gallup, New Mexico, the association grouped together business leaders involved in the sale and promotion of Indian goods. The association retained lawyers who helped represent and protect the interests of marketers involved in the trade, and it held annual meetings at which traders could exchange ideas and information. Sammons supported the mission of the association by generously loaning money to traders to help them establish their trading posts and sustain their profitability. Association lawyer Charles "Bud" Tansey recalled his work with the United Indian Traders Association in an oral history recorded for Cline Library at Northern Arizona University in 1998. Tansey said that by generously offering loans to traders, Ma Sammons "carried a heck of a lot of traders, and carried them on good faith without really having security, except the traders. And she was that kind of a person."

Sammons also helped promote Indian art around the country. In one documented instance, she shipped a Navajo blanket, along with jewelry, to the Tea Chest "tea room" Restaurant in Coconut Grove, Florida.

Sammons remained president of the bank until her retirement in 1951. She passed away three years later.

More to explore: *Farmington, Inez Bushner Gill, Maralyn Budke (see under Inez Bushner Gill)*

191. Harvey Girls

Location: Bernalillo County. In downtown Albuquerque, at the Alvarado Transportation Center, on the southeast corner of the intersection of First Street and Gold Avenue. See map 4.

Marker text: In 1883, the Fred Harvey Company hired women to serve in its diners and hotels along the Atchison, Topeka and Santa Fe Railway. Thousands of respectable, intelligent women were recruited from the Midwest and East Coast to come west. Known as Harvey Girls, many of these women stayed and became founding members of their adopted communities, forever changing the cultural landscape of the Wild West.

192. Mary Elizabeth Jane Colter (1869–1958)

Marker text: In 1902, the Fred Harvey Company hired Mary Colter as interior designer of the Alvarado Hotel in Albuquerque. She was an architect for the company when few women worked in the field. She designed many famous resorts and inns, including the hotel interiors of La Fonda in Santa Fe. In 1987, four of her buildings in Grand Canyon National Park were designated a National Historic Landmark.

Note: Marker faceplates are on opposite sides of the same sign. See map 4.

What is today the site of the Alvarado Transportation Center in Albuquerque was once the location of a sprawling, two-block extravagant showcase of a hotel known as the Alvarado. The hotel, named for Captain Hernando de Alvarado of the Coronado expedition in 1540, exists only in memory today—the city demolished it in 1970. But in its day, the Alvarado was regarded as one of the most beautiful hostelries in the Southwest. Resplendently decorated by renowned architect Mary Elizabeth Jane Colter, the Alvarado was also a Harvey House. Built to cater to railroad travelers, Harvey Eating Houses (often commonly called Harvey Houses) sprang up at whistle-stops along the course of the Atchison, Topeka, and Santa Fe Railway between Kansas and California.

Harvey Houses were the eponymous creation of restaurateur Fred Harvey. After his first hotel in Kansas proved successful, Harvey in 1881 signed a contract with the AT&SF Railway to provide meals and lodging along the route of the railroad. To hire waitstaff for his diners, Harvey in 1883 ran this ad in papers across the East Coast:

WANTED—young women, 18 to 30 years of age, of good moral character, attractive and intelligent, as waitresses in Harvey Eating Houses on the Santa Fe Railroad in the West. Wages $17.50 per month with room and board. Liberal tips customary. Experience not necessary.

Thousands of women applied, were hired, and

Although the Harvey Girls wore several different uniforms, the black-and-white uniform shown here became their trademark. These Harvey Girls worked at the Harvey House in Belen. Harvey Girls at the Belen Harvey House. Courtesy Belen Harvey House and Museum and the City of Belen.

went west. Collectively, these women became the famous Harvey Girls.

Something about the Harvey Girls struck a chord with America. Fondly recalled today as genteel, polite, and respectable young women, many married after their first year in their new locations (their contract with the Fred Harvey Company forbade them from marrying in their first year). Many made their moves permanent, settling down as founding members of communities throughout the Southwest. As late as 1946, Hollywood was musicalizing their story in the MGM movie *The Harvey Girls*, starring Judy Garland—the movie that featured the song "On the Atchison, Topeka, and the Santa Fe."

A number of Harvey Houses were in operation in New Mexico towns along the railroad: Clovis, Deming, Gallup, Las Vegas, Raton, Rincon, and Vaughn, among others. They advertised "the luxury of clean comfort and modern convenience in the atmosphere of the Old Southwest." The former Harvey House in Belen, about thirty-six miles south of Albuquerque, has been preserved and today serves as the Harvey House Museum.

The Alvarado Hotel here in Albuquerque, near the corner of Gold and First Streets and alongside the railroad tracks, opened in 1902, replacing an earlier, much smaller, and much less resplendent wooden depot and Harvey Eating House that had stood in this location. The new depot and hotel complex overall followed the design standards of the Santa Fe Railroad, built in mission revival style. The Alvarado had more than eighty guest rooms (with those on the first floor reserved for traveling salesmen), and in these, according to a Fred Harvey booklet about the hotel, "the most artistic taste has been maintained in the finishing and furnishing." The grand four-poster beds in the rooms even included a Spanish coat-of-arms embossed into the headboard. Other rooms included living quarters for the Harvey Girls and other staff, parlors, a ballroom, a large kitchen, a barbershop, and a dining hall.

"No modern luxury is absent," the booklet truthfully boasted.

To capitalize on the tourist trade, the hotel had an "Indian and Mexican Building and Museum," which functioned as an emporium of Native American pottery, baskets, blankets, and other artifacts, and featured Native American artisans making pottery and bracelets as tourists watched. To decorate the interior of the Indian Building, the Fred Harvey Company hired Pennsylvania-born designer Mary Colter, a graduate of the California Institute of Design and then a teacher at the Mechanic Arts High School in Minnesota. Colter arranged the room to appeal to travelers. "In the half dozen rooms in the Indian and Mexican Building," the Harvey booklet explained, "special collections of inestimable value have been grouped. No one can afford to pass by the superbly woven, gossamer shawls, the exquisite drawn-work, the old paintings, engravings, jewelry, weapons, and woodwork of the Spanish and Mexican Room. The Navajo Room, with its blanketed walls and decorations of pottery and basketry, furnishes an admirable idea for a luxurious home 'den.'"

After designing the Indian Building, Colter returned to teaching. But in 1910, the Fred Harvey Company reconnected with her, hiring her full time. She returned to the Alvarado in 1924 when the hotel underwent modernization. She added bathrooms, redecorated the lobby, and installed fountains in the courtyard.

Colter's other works for the company included the interiors of the historic La Fonda Hotel on the plaza in Santa Fe—a preexisting hotel, which, in 1925, became a Harvey House when the railroad purchased the property—and the El Navajo Hotel in Gallup. She also built four company buildings at the Grand Canyon in Arizona: the Desert View Watchtower, the Hopi House, the Lookout Studio, and the Hermit's Rest structure. On May 28, 1987, in recognition of their historical significance to the country, the National Park Service official designated all four buildings as National Historic Landmarks.

For years, the Alvarado Hotel competed with the Hilton Hotel, Conrad Hilton's first eponymous hotel in New Mexico, only a couple blocks away. (The Hilton was not a Harvey House.) Sadly, only one of those downtown hotels remains—the Hilton, now the Hotel Andaluz. When rail traffic declined, the Santa Fe Railway closed the Alvarado, and the structure was slated for demolition. Despite protests and a last-ditch nomination of the hotel to the National Register of Historic Places, a wrecking crew in February 1970 returned the splendid hotel to the elements.

Mary Colter, who lived in Santa Fe after her retirement, didn't live to see the demolition. She passed away on January 8, 1958.

The current Alvarado Transportation Center, site of these two Historic Markers, has been built to be reminiscent of the Alvarado Hotel in style.

More to explore: *Albuquerque, Belen, Rincón*

193. Hatch

Location: Doña Ana County. In Hatch, in a small park near the intersection of NM 187 and NM 26. See map 5.

Marker text: Originally established as Santa Barbara in 1851, Apache raids drove the settlers away until 1853 when nearby Fort Thorn was established. Abandoned again in 1860 after the fort closed, it was reoccupied in 1875 and re-named for General Edward Hatch, then Commander of the New Mexico Military District.

In 1851, the fertile river valley along the Rio Grande in southern New Mexico supported the development of a small settlement known as Santa Barbara. Raids by Apache warriors on the settlers, mostly Hispanic families making their livings as farmers, kept the population levels in the village low. Some help arrived in December 1853, when Colonel Edmond V. Sumner of the US Army established Fort Thorn a short distance northwest of Santa Barbara. The fort was walled for defense, one of few military installations in the Southwest to have such a design.

Fort Thorn was not in operation for long. The post suffered from its poor location atop a small mesa near the marshy—and apparently unfavorably fragrant—western bank of the riverbed. When Lydia Spencer Lane visited with her soldier husband in the early years of the fort, she wrote simply: "We were delighted it was not to be our station, and were glad to leave." Overflow from the river sometimes left stagnant pools of water, which encouraged the spread of a number of sicknesses among the soldiers stationed there, including malaria. In one month alone, seventy-eight of the ninety men at the post were sick. Writing about the health conditions there in 1856, the assistant surgeon, T. Charlton Henry, did not mince words:

Were there no surgeon at this, the sickliest post in the Territory at this time, and the prevailing malady not properly treated, every man here, very nearly, would, after a series of attacks of ague or fever be seized . . . with a congestive type of fever, and die off like so many sheep with the rot.

The army responded by closing Fort Thorn in March 1859 and moving the troops to Fort Fillmore, near Mesilla. Although its hospital continued in operation for a short time thereafter, Fort Thorn was never regarrisoned. After the post was fully abandoned, sun and rain went to work on the adobe walls, and over time floodwaters from the Rio Grande washed the fort away. Nothing today remains of the former post.

Despite these inauspicious beginnings, settlement did at last take root in the valley some fifteen years later, with a new village forming around 1875. A few years thereafter, in 1880, the rails of the Santa Fe Railway reached this location on their way south to Las Cruces and El Paso. The railroad built a depot here and called the stop Hatch's Station. Later, it became known simply as Hatch.

The name honored Colonel Edward Hatch, the commander of the Military District of New Mexico. Colonel Hatch, born in Maine in 1832 as the oldest of four children, was educated at what is today the Norwich Military Academy in Northfield, Vermont. After volunteering in the Union Army during the Civil War, Hatch earned a series of promotions and, in 1865, was placed in charge as colonel of the Ninth Cavalry, a regiment of African American "Buffalo Soldiers." In 1876, Colonel Hatch was made commander of the Military District of New Mexico, a post he held until 1881.

(Of side interest: a station farther south down the line was originally named Thorne, likely a misspelling of the name of the former fort here. That town is today known as Rincon.)

Today, the town that bears Colonel Hatch's name is known worldwide for the quality of chile peppers grown here. Each Labor Day Weekend, hundreds of people attend the Hatch Chile Festival, where the green and red vegetables are celebrated and pain receptors are tested. Hatch today bills itself as the "Chile Capital of the World," and few would dispute that title.

More to explore: *La Mesilla, Rincón, Rio Grande*

Helene Haack Allen: *see Fort Sumner and Fort Sumner State Monument (series)*

194. Hermits Peak
Elevation: 10,212 feet

Location: San Miguel County. North of Las Vegas, in a pullout on the east side of NM 518, near the intersection of NM 518 and County Road A2. See map 3.

Marker text: From 1863 to 1867 this mountain was the home of Juan Maria Agostini, an Italian Penitent who lived there as a hermit, carving crucifixes and religious emblems which he traded for food. Leaving this area, he moved to the Organ Mountains in southern New Mexico, where he was found murdered in 1869.

Note: The US Board of Geographic Names officially recognizes the peak by the name Hermit Peak. It is the prominent mountain seen to the northwest of this Marker. The elevation listed on the Marker is incorrect; the correct elevation of Hermit Peak is 10,260 feet.

He was a pious man. His eyes were blue; his beard, white. He was a man who cradled both sainthood and superstition. His given name was Giovanni Maria Agostini, but most people called him El Ermitaño, the Hermit.

Born into a noble family in Novara, Italy, in 1800 or 1801, the Hermit around the age of thirty embarked on a religious pilgrimage to monasteries throughout Italy, France, Spain, Mexico, and Cuba. In each country, he became friends with the wealthiest patrons of society while ministering to the physical and spiritual needs of the penniless. After a brief time in Canada, the Hermit came to America. When a wagon train left Kansas for New Mexico in 1862, he walked alongside it more than five hundred miles into the northern part of the state. By then, he was in his sixties.

The Hermit originally settled into a cave in the east wall of a canyon south of present-day Las Vegas. Word of his miraculous healing touch spread, and when locals began to pitch tents beside his cave, the Hermit moved into a less-accessible crevice along the eastern slope of Tecolote Mountain—today known as Hermit Peak in his honor. There, in the cool darkness, he spent hours in prayer, suspending his meditations only long enough to carve crucifixes and rosaries from tree branches. These he used to barter with villagers for cornmeal. Locals helping the Hermit build his home in the mountain cave claimed that the Hermit touched a rock with his staff and drew water from it, and that he fed them from a pot of stew that never emptied.

In 1867, the Hermit moved again, walking alongside another wagon train to southern New Mexico. He again sought shelter in a cave, this time at the rocky base of the Organ Mountains east of Mesilla. The site is today open to the public as part of the BLM Organ Mountains Recreation Area. Using natural herbs he found in the area, the Hermit obliged the requests of the poor and suffering who came to him for absolution from their pain.

To reassure concerned residents of Mesilla that he was alive and safe, the Hermit agreed to light

The legendary Giovanni Maria Agostini, one of the most revered, most beloved loners in New Mexico history, may have predicted his own death. Juan Maria de Agostini, the Hermit of Hermit Peak, New Mexico. Courtesy Palace of the Governors Photo Archives (NMHM/DCA), neg. no. 110764.

a fire at the entrance to his cave every Friday evening. "If the fire fails to appear," the Hermit reportedly warned them, "it will be because I have been killed."

On the evening of April 17, 1868, no flames broke the purple evening sky.

Among the secrets closely guarded by the shadows and canyons of the Organ Mountains is the identity of the assailant who took the life of the beloved Hermit. A posse riding to the cave the next morning found his body in an arroyo, face down, a dagger in his back, and a small cross clutched in his weathered hands.

More to explore: *La Mesilla, Las Vegas, Magnolia Ellis, Organ Mountains (see under San Augustin Pass)*

195. Hillsboro Historic District

Location: Sierra County. On the east end of Hillsboro, near the intersection of NM 152 and NM 27. See map 5.

Marker text: Hillsboro was founded in the 1870s after gold and silver were discovered in the surrounding Black Range. The town developed into an important mining and ranching center and served as the Sierra County seat from 1884 to 1939. It was the site of several renowned trials, and is said to have had the last operating stage line in the United States. It became a historic district in 1986.

Note: A few typographical errors have crept into the title and text of this Historic Marker. The version produced here includes corrections. (While the *trails* in the area are worthy of attention, it's the historic *trials* here that are renowned.)

Prospecting near Percha Creek in 1877, Dan Dugan and Dave Stitzel uncovered glittering gold flakes on the eastern slopes of the Black Range—and in so doing, became the names most often associated with the founding of a mining camp here. That camp was Hillsborough, a name early settlers chose, according to legend, from slips of paper mixed together in a hat. Silver, copper, and lead mining in the foothills of the Black Range and outlying areas also gave rise to the community of Kingston a few miles to the west, as well as Lake Valley, a town centered on a large silver strike, to the south. Together, the three camps made the Black Range one of the most productive and commercially successful mining districts in the state. As Hillsborough expanded, its name contracted, becoming Hillsboro.

In 1884, the territorial legislature carved Sierra County from portions of Socorro, Grant, and Doña Ana Counties and made Hillsboro, by then a spirited mining and ranching town, the new county seat. Within the walls of the brick county courthouse erected on the hill overlooking town, juries heard several renowned trials, including the sensational and still unsolved Albert J. Fountain murder case. Colonel Fountain and his young son Henry disappeared en route from Lincoln to Mesilla in January 1896. Suspicion fell on prominent rancher Oliver Lee, against whom Fountain had secured indictments for cattle rustling. Lee and a ranch hand were brought to trial in the Hillsboro courthouse, but since neither of the victims' bodies had been found, the prosecution lacked sufficient evidence of foul play. The jury acquitted both men.

In the late 1880s, Mr. and Mrs. S. J. Orchard, who operated a mail stage in nearby Silver City, opened a second line to carry passengers between Hillsboro, Kingston, Lake Valley, and sometimes farther south to the railhead at the small settlement of Nutt. Sadie Orchard, who had come to New Mexico from London in 1886, was often the one wielding the reins of the six-horse Concord coaches. "My trips were surely trying," Sadie related of the daily runs to a Works Progress Administration writer in 1936, "especially through picturesque Box Canyon between Kingston and Hillsboro."

According to an account of the line written by William Wallace, the Orchards used the money garnered from the $5.50 round-trip fares they collected between Lake Valley and Kingston to pay crews to clear rocks from the stage route and to purchase soles from men's used shoes for use as brake linings. The stage stayed in operation until the early years of World War I, although under different ownership, and is thus said to be one of the last operating stagecoach lines in the country. After retiring from stage operations, the Orchards later opened the Orchard Hotel in Hillsboro.

Over time, the town of Hot Springs (now Truth or Consequences) eclipsed Hillsboro as the economic and political hub of Sierra County. Hillsboro lost the county seat to Hot Springs in 1936. Its usefulness spent, the brick courthouse eventually collapsed.

Hillsboro continues today as a quiet, secluded community and a retreat for artists and tourists. Because of the number of historic properties in the town, the National Park Service designated Hillsboro as a historic district in 1986.

More to explore: *Disappearance of Albert J. Fountain and His Son Henry, Emory Pass—Black Range Mountains, Percha Creek*

196. Historic Los Luceros

Location: Rio Arriba County. North of Española, on the south side of US 68, between mile markers 8 and 9. See map 2.

Marker text: Historic Los Luceros includes a Pueblo Indian ruin and an 18th century rancho/hacienda on Sebastián Martín Serrano's 1703 land grant. Evolving out of family inheritance, local artistry and preservation efforts, the complex contains five adobe structures, including Casa Grande, a fine example of 19th century territorial architecture, which has served as Rio Arriba's County Courthouse (1846–1854).

At Los Luceros, architecture has become history. Listed on the National Register of Historic Places as "one of the most complete nineteenth century haciendas in northern New Mexico," this Spanish ranch complex of five buildings includes an adobe ranch house, a cottage, a chapel, a guest house, and a building that may have once imprisoned the lawbreakers of Rio Arriba County.

Construction of Los Luceros began in 1703 when Captain Sebastián Martín Serrano received a large parcel of grant land in this vicinity, near where Tewa-speaking Indians of the now-abandoned pueblo that historians know as Pfioge had erected outlying field houses. Serrano, his wife, María Luján, and their ten children established a small community on their property and named it Puesto de Nuestra Señora de la Soledad del Rio del Norte Arriba—"the Outpost of Our Lady of Solitude of the Upper River of the North." Such a ranch was indeed an outpost, fortified by hefty construction to provide defense against assaults by Apaches and Comanches as they swept through the upper Rio Grande Valley. The original house, a hand-built adobe with thick walls and twenty-four rooms, also featured two protective towers at either end, from which Serrano and his family could strike before being struck.

When Serrano died in 1763, the hacienda was divided among heirs. One granddaughter married Santiago Lucero, and the small community of farms and homes that had formed on the original land grant became known as Plaza de los Luceros. Later descendants through blood or marriage added their histories to the property. From 1855 to 1860, with New Mexico now under the auspices of the United States, Judge Elias T. Clark presided from the ranch house, which served double duty as the Rio Arriba County Courthouse. A Clark daughter married Luis M. Ortiz, who was later elected Rio Arriba county sheriff. Historians believe that Sheriff Ortiz, in fulfillment of his peace-keeping mission, may have erected the slender building west of the ranch house and put it into service as a jail.

A flood in 1886 demolished village homes in the upper Rio Grande Valley but left intact the Ortiz hacienda. Legend says that the family showed their gratitude for having been spared by erecting a small adobe church, now known as the Capilla de Nuestra Señora de Guadalupe, southeast of the house beside what is now an apple orchard. Around 1900, an additional building, the L-shaped adobe guesthouse, joined the property, although its original intended use is not known. Historians believe that it may have provided a home for the ranch supervisor.

In 1923, the property was purchased and renovated by art heiress Mary Cabot Wheelwright, who later opened the Wheelwright Museum of the American Indian in Santa Fe.

To recognize the history today preserved at Los Luceros, the National Park Service entered the property on the National Register of Historic Places in 1983.

More to explore: *Bond House, El Rancho de las Golondrinas, Española Valley, Mary Cabot Wheelwright (see under Amelia Elizabeth White)*

197. Hobbs

Location: Lea County. West of Hobbs, on the north side of US 62/180, between mile markers 106 and 107. See map 6.

Marker text: Named for the family of James Hobbs which homesteaded here in 1907, Hobbs became first a trading village for ranchers and then a major oil town after the discovery of oil by the Midwest Oil Company in 1928.

198. Hobbs Discovery Well

Location: Lea County. In Hobbs, in front of the Hobbs Chamber of Commerce, at the intersection of East Snyder and North Marland. See map 6.

Marker text: Following earlier oil discoveries in the Lea County area, Ronald K. DeFord, of Midwest refining co., now Amoco, came to Hobbs to survey for a new drilling site. Drilling began October 12, 1927, oil was discovered at 4,063 feet, and the new well produced over 500,000 barrels of oil in its lifetime. Hobbs was transformed from an unknown community into a bustling boomtown boasting many restaurants and bars, several hotels and movie theaters.

The frontier grasslands of southeastern New Mexico attracted many early twentieth-century homesteaders eager to break the sod and start a new life. One of them, James Hobbs, his wife, Fannie, and their family, which included twin daughters Minnie and Winnie, had originally intended to settle in Alpine, Texas, in hopes that the chaste prairie air would improve Mrs. Hobbs's health. Upon meeting a wagon master coming from that town and hearing his hard-luck story of life there, the Hobbs family decided instead to try the frontier grasslands of southeastern New Mexico. This was ranching land, and when James Berry Hobbs, son of James and Fannie, opened a store and post office around 1909, many of his early customers were area cowboys. The agricultural and ranching settlement that grew near the store took the name of the Hobbs family.

Hobbs might have remained a small but contented trading village had it not been for the discovery of substantial oil reserves beneath the southeastern plains in the early twentieth century. The first commercially successful oil well in New Mexico, the Flynn-Welch-Yates, was drilled between Hobbs and Artesia in 1924. That well tapped the Permian Basin, an almost oval patch of oil reserves underlying a vast region of west Texas and southeastern New Mexico. With proof that the region contained a large body of oil reserves, the "black gold rush" was on.

Hobbs became an oil town on June 13, 1928, when the Midwest State no. 1, sunk by Ronald K. DeFord with the Midwest Oil Company (later Amoco, which later merged with British Petroleum), struck oil at 4,065 feet. The well, which had begun drilling on October 12, 1927, was the "discovery well" for the underlying reserves of oil that soon became known as the Hobbs Pool.

A sister well, the Bowers no. 1-A, proved equally productive. The result was effectively summarized in the March 15, 1929, edition of the *Lovington Leader* in nearby Lovington:

Reports coming from the town of Hobbs indicate a rapid and healthy growth of that enterprising little city. A census which was recently taken showed it to have a population of more than 300 and that number has increased since that date. When it is taken into consideration that the town is less than a year old and that most of this growth has taken place within the last two months, it will be readily seen that the record is something to be proud of.

Residents and oil workers erected buildings of more permanence, and a larger Hobbs emerged as population and production proliferated. By April 1930, the month that the Texas–New Mexico Railway arrived in town, Hobbs had, by one estimate, more than ten thousand residents. The city today retains its mix of ranching and oil economies.

The air of the plains, by the way, did improve the health of Fannie Hobbs. She lived in the community she helped form until her death in 1942. Residents lovingly referred to her as "Grandma Hobbs."

More to explore: *Flynn-Welch-Yates Oil Well (see under Artesia), Llano Estacado and Oil (see under Llano Estacado [series]), Oil and Gas, Oil Country*

199. Hogback

Location: San Juan County. East of Shiprock, on the north side of the junction of US 64 and County Road 6950, at mile marker 32. See map 1.

Marker text: Steeply dipping strata define the western edge of the San Juan basin. To the west older geologic formations are exposed toward the Defiance uplift whereas basinward they are downwarped thousands of feet beneath younger rock units. Vast coal, uranium, oil and gas resources occur in the strata buried within the basin. Elevation 5,050 feet.

200. Ghost Marker: San Juan Basin

Marker text: Thousands of feet of sedimentary strata have been downwarped into the San Juan basin of northwestern New Mexico, a total area of some 20,000 square miles. The San Pedro and Nacimiento Ranges of the Southern Rockies rise in fault contact above the basin to elevations of more than 10,000 feet.

Note: This Marker appears in an inventory of Historic Markers compiled by the State Historic Preservation Office but is not in the field. See map 1.

One of the defining geological features of northwestern New Mexico and southwestern Colorado is the San Juan Basin, an immense depression in the land stretching approximately one hundred miles across and encompassing a total area of some 7,500 square miles. The western edge of the basin is defined by a north-south tending ridge in Arizona known as the Defiance Uplift. The name derives in part from the nineteenth-century army post Fort Defiance, which once stood in northwestern New Mexico but later became part of Arizona when officials surveyed the boundary line between the two states. Closer at hand is the prominent north-south tending ridge known as the Hogback.

The relationship between these geologic formations is explained by a geologist from the New Mexico Bureau of Geology and Mineral Resources:

Older rock layers that underlie low ground to the west and younger rock layers to the east are mostly formed by easily eroded shale beds that are nearly horizontal. The western basement block—the Defiance uplift—was squeezed eastward and upward over the western margin of the San Juan Basin along a narrow north-tending fault zone that breaks across basement rocks [about two miles below the surface of the earth]. The nearly horizontal top of the 1.6–1.4 billion year old basement rocks is about 3000 feet higher on the west side of this hidden fault. The relatively flexible sedimentary layers, which lie above the nearly vertical face of the hard rock created by the fault, were simply draped over the concealed escarpment something like layers of carpet over a step.

As the land of western North America rose, weathering and erosion removed the shale layers to expose the "draped" sandstone layers. Some of those layers, inclined in one direction (to the east) and thus considered "monoclines," form the Hogback monocline. The name is metaphorical, as these steeply tilted rocks are said to resemble the hairs on the back of a hog.

It is no coincidence that the San Juan Basin is one of the largest gas-producing fields in the country. There is a geological advantage to being a basin. Some of the same sediments that collected to depress the land later transformed into underlying reserves of coal, oil, and natural gas. As plant and animal remains, small rocks, and volcanic ash decomposed, the heat inside the earth transformed the viscous organic "goo" into pockets of liquid petroleum trapped in the sedimentary rock strata.

More to explore: *Beclabito Dome, Hogbacks*

201. Hogbacks

Location: San Miguel County. About six miles south of Las Vegas, at the intersection of Interstate 25 and US 84. See map 3.

Marker text: Interstate 25 cuts through dipping strata that form hogback ridges between the Great Plains and the south end of the Rocky Mountains. The Santa Fe Trail from here to Santa Fe followed a natural valley eroded in less resistant strata between the mountains to the north and Glorieta Mesa to the south. Elevation 6,200 feet.

Along Interstate 25 just west of this Historic Marker, road cuts carved through a handful of small ridges offer an unobstructed peek at a cross section of steeply tilted layers of rock known as hogbacks. The dipping strata resemble the prickly hairs on the back of a hog, which accounts for the unusual name, although they might just as accurately be compared to porcupine quills standing on edge. Hogbacks form when layers of rock resist weathering while weaker sections wear away to form steep slopes like the ones seen between interstate mile markers 340 and 341.

These hogback ridges lie along the eastern border of the Sangre de Cristo Mountains, a southern extension of the Rocky Mountains. This is also the westernmost edge of the Great Plains. Characterized by flat and rolling prairies, tablelands, and low bluffs, the Great Plains covers the eastern third of New Mexico and forms the geographical interior of the country. Across those plains in 1821, William Becknell, a bankrupt merchant, led a group of traders from Franklin, Missouri, to Santa Fe in hopes of establishing a regular trade network between East and West. Becknell's route, later called the Santa Fe Trail for its western terminus, became a principal trade and migration course into New Mexico. From this point northwestward, the trail cut through a valley cradled between the Sangre de Cristo Mountains on the north and Glorieta Mesa on the south. Interstate 25 largely covers the same route today.

More to explore: *Hogback, Santa Fe Trail (series)*

202. Hyde Memorial State Park

Location: Santa Fe County. Just north of Santa Fe, at the entrance to Hyde Memorial State Park, in the parking area next to the Visitors Center and Lodge. See map 2.

Marker text: This park is named after Benjamin Talbot Hyde, devoted educator of America's youth. His family donated the 350 acres which constitute the park to the State of New Mexico in 1934. Situated at an elevation of 8500 feet in the scenic Sangre de Cristo Mountains, it is one of the oldest state parks in New Mexico. Facilities include a picnic area, campground, skating pond and sledding area.

Benjamin Talbot Babbitt Hyde was the heir to a fortune, his millionaire grandfather having been financially successful in the manufacture of Babbitt's Best Soap and other household products in New York in the early nineteenth century. Although the younger Hyde served as president for a time at his grandfather's firm, his financial standing allowed him to pursue his own calling—and the Harvard-educated Hyde found it in the world of the naturalist. Of particular interest to Hyde was introducing children to the natural world around them, and cultivating in them respect and appreciation for the creatures within it.

After serving as the educational director for the Boy Scouts of Greater New York for many years, Hyde in 1927 moved with his wife from New York to Santa Fe. There he founded the Children's Nature Foundation and became scoutmaster for the local troop. Hyde and his wife purchased 350 acres in the scenic Sangre de Cristo Mountains and used the land as a type of nature preserve where they could help children explore the natural world.

On July 27, 1933, Hyde—known as "Uncle Bennie" to the scouts—was killed in a car accident. In keeping with his expressed wishes, Hyde's family the following year donated the land he had purchased to the state of New Mexico for use as a park. That park, the Hyde Memorial State Park, was dedicated and opened to the public in 1936, making it one of the oldest parks in the state. An article in the October 1936 edition of *Boys' Life* magazine described the dedication ceremony:

Hundreds of Scouts were present to handle the traffic of visitors, and most of the program was carried on by active Scouts and Scouters. The Master of Ceremonies was Daniel T. Kelly, president of the Northern New Mexico Council, Boy Scouts of America. The presentation of the Park was made by A. J. Connell, the council Camping chairman, for the Hyde family. The Park was accepted by Honorable Clyde Tingley, governor of New Mexico, on behalf of the state. The Park will always be a fitting tribute to a wonderful man and a true scout, our Uncle Bennie.

Since then, thousands of people have come to this part of the Santa Fe National Forest to enjoy the park dedicated to Dr. Hyde and appreciate the beauty he too appreciated. Visitors can picnic, hike, camp, bird watch, and enjoy nature, and if it's winter, go sledding or cross-country skiing.

More to explore: *Philmont Scout Ranch, Seton Village*

Iglesia de San Ysidro: *see Corrales*

203. Inez Bushner Gill (1918–1982)

Location: Santa Fe County. On the grounds of the State Capitol Building, on the west side of the Roundhouse, facing Don Gaspar Avenue. See map 2.

Marker text: Inez Bushner Gill impressed governors, legislators and journalists with her fiscal expertise. Among the original staff of the Legislative Council Service when it was founded in 1951, she served as fiscal analyst and principal staff for its finance committee. In 1957, she helped establish separate staff for what today is the Legislative Finance Committee. Inez developed many of the financial procedures that modernized state government and helped create the Department of Finance and Administration, bringing order to the chaos of state finances.

204. Maralyn Budke (1936–2010)

Location: Santa Fe County. On the grounds of the State Capitol Building, on the west side of the Roundhouse, facing Don Gaspar Avenue. See map 2.

Marker text: Maralyn Budke, Inez Gill's first intern, joined the Legislative Finance Committee in 1959 and was its first woman director from 1968–1982. A brilliant strategist and trusted advisor, Maralyn was a confidant to legislative leaders and chief of staff for Governors Cargo and Carruthers. Highly valued for her knowledge and insight, she mentored legislative and executive staff during 40 years of exemplary public service. Maralyn and Inez were two of the most important and influential women in New Mexico state government.

Note: Marker faceplates are on opposite sides of the same sign.

For more than forty years, New Mexicans were well served by the financial acumen and dedicated service of two notable employees of the state government: Inez Bushner Gill and Maralyn Budke.

That legacy of service began in 1951, when the state legislature formed an office known as the Legislative Council Service. The division was tasked with drafting legislation and performing legal research for state legislators. One of the first four staff members when the office opened that year was Inez Bushner Gill. An astute fiscal analyst who grew up in Gallup and graduated from the University of New Mexico with a bachelor's degree in political science, Gill later became the assistant director of the office. Throughout her nearly thirty-year tenure as the chief fiscal analyst for the state, Gill implemented a series of modern policies and procedures to help provide adequate fiscal oversight of the state government's budget operations.

"It was just a mess," Gill told the *Albuquerque Journal* in 1978 when describing the state's fiscal operations when she began work there. In 1957, Gill helped create the Legislative Finance Committee to provide fiscal analysis of legislative initiatives and to help oversee the creation and execution of the state budget. Originally, the committee was under the auspices of the Legislative Council Service, and Gill served as its primary fiscal analyst. But later, Gill worked to separate the two entities and ensure that the committee was fully and independently staffed. To help state agencies in the executive branch with their budgets, she assisted with the formation of the Department of Finance and Administration (DFA), a state-level department tasked with the fiscal oversight of all the state government, including the governor's office. She later served as assistant to the director of the DFA.

In addition to these efforts at modernizing state government and helping legislators implement sound fiscal policy, Gill also created an internship program to allow undergraduate college students to experience the work of that government firsthand. In 1958, she welcomed the first of those students into the Legislative Finance Committee offices—a young woman studying political science at the University of New Mexico in Albuquerque. Her name was Maralyn Budke.

Gill liked what she saw in the Texas-born Budke, so the following year, after Budke had graduated, Gill hired her as an assistant fiscal analyst for the Legislative Finance Committee. Together, the two women would become, as a memorial in their honor passed by the state legislature in 2013 noted, "two of the most important and influential women ever to serve in New Mexico state government."

For her part, Maralyn Budke—who, after the separation of the Legislative Finance Committee from the Legislative Council Service, served as the executive secretary of the committee—implemented a number of oversight processes and procedures herself. Described as fierce but compassionate by those who knew her, she was a brilliant strategist and a sharp and competent policy analyst to whom legislators often turned for sound advice on any range of issues.

For a short period in 1967, Budke shifted positions and moved from the Legislative Finance Committee to serve as the chief of staff for newly elected governor David Cargo. But she returned to the committee the following year—this time as the director. She was the first woman in the history of the state to hold that position.

Budke remained at the helm of the Legislative Finance Committee for fourteen years, until her retirement from state government in 1982. She didn't stay retired long. With the election of Garrey Carruthers as New Mexico governor in 1987, Budke accepted an offer to serve as the new governor's chief of staff. She did so for an annual salary of one dollar the first year, two dollars the second, three the third, and four the fourth. She never cashed the checks. In 2006, Budke was honored as a "Santa Fe Living Treasure."

Inez Gill retired from the state government in 1973 and passed away in 1982. Maralyn Budke survived her by twenty-eight years, passing away on January 9, 2010.

More to explore: *Harriet Belle Amsden Sammons, Women of the Judiciary*

Jack M. Campbell Highway: *see Rio Grande Gorge State Park*

205. Jal
Jal Lake Park

Location: Lea County. At the south end of Jal, in a pullout on the east side of NM 18, between mile markers 7 and 8, near the entrance to Jal Lake Park. See map 6.

Marker text: In the 1880s, the Cowden brothers, with their distinctive JAL brand, operated one of southeast New Mexico's largest cattle ranches in this region. A post office and store established nearby in 1910 was named Jal, after the JAL brand, and the town which developed around the site acquired the name. Jal Lake State Park was also designed in the shape of the JAL brand.

Cattleman brothers George, John, and William Henry Cowden left their mark on this part of New Mexico, both figuratively and literally.

Their mark, specifically, was the brand they used to identify their free-range-roaming cattle: JAL. Various stories account for the origin of the brand, with perhaps the most likely being that the letters were the initials of a rancher from whom the Cowdens bought their cattle, along with the attendant brand (in part so that they would not be accused of owning cattle belonging to another ranch). The JAL brand incorporates three letters into a distinct shape. The *J* and *L* are tilted toward one another and connect at their topmost points, while the intersection formed by this collusion shapes the letter *A*.

The Cowden brothers, operating as the Cowden Cattle Company, first came to southeastern New Mexico from Texas in the 1880s and established a ranch. The JAL Ranch, also known as the Cowden Ranch, soon grew to become one of the largest in the state, claiming at one time around forty thousand head of cattle. A small settlement developed around the ranch itself, giving rise to a store and school. When a post office opened there in 1910, the community took the name of the ranch, to become Jal.

The Cowden brothers also left their mark on the landscape itself. On a patch of land at the south end of the city of Jal lies a man-made lake created by the city for recreational use. In an appealing form of landscape art, the lake has been designed in the outline of the JAL brand. Seen from the air, the flat desert terrain of this part of southeastern New Mexico appears to have its own watery brand—JAL—in the form of the figurative shape of Jal Lake.

More to explore: *Chisum's South Spring Ranch (see under Artesia), Ute Lake State Park*

206. Jemez Mountains

Location: Santa Fe County. On the north side of NM 502 between Nambé and Los Alamos, between mile markers 13 and 14. See map 2.

Marker text: On the skyline to the west are the Jemez Mountains where tremendous volcanic eruptions a million years ago created a huge caldera some 15 miles in diameter that now forms beautiful Valle Grande, set amid a ring of volcanic peaks. Geothermal energy has been tapped from hot rock beneath the mountains.

Flow and ash-fall deposits surrounding the volcanic range form the Pajarito Plateau, site of numerous, ancient cliff dwellings and the atomic city of Los Alamos. The Jemez Mountains are part of the Southern Rockies and form one of the western ranges of the Rockies in New Mexico. Elevations exceed 11,000 feet.

207. Jemez Mountains

Location: Rio Arriba County. South of Tierra Amarilla, on the east side of US 64 between mile markers 33 and 34. See map 2.

Marker text: Formed from cataclysmic volcanic eruptions some one million years ago, the Jemez Mountains are part of the westernmost New Mexico Rockies that enter the state from Colorado near Chama. Chicoma Peak (11,561 feet), prominent on the western horizon, is the highest in the Jemez Mountains. Elevation here 5,800 feet.

The beautiful Jemez Mountains were born from volcanic fury, shaped through a chain of eruptions that began some eleven million years in the past and continued until about 400,000 years ago. These violent outbreaks left a docile legacy: a range of mountains comprising rugged volcanic peaks, shadow-drenched canyons, and luxurious sweeping valleys—the Jemez.

The Jemez Mountains extend southward from the flat-topped Cerro Pedernal, near the settlement of Abiquiú, to the pueblo of Jemez, from which the mountains take their name. The highest summit, Chicoma Mountain (sometimes seen as Tschicoma or Santa Clara Peak), rises to 11,561 feet. The second highest, Polvadera Peak, follows closely behind at 11,232 feet. Deer, beaver, bears, hawks, eagles, and cutthroat trout all make a home in this verdant wilderness.

Also found here is the Jemez Caldera and the beautiful Valle Grande within it. The caldera took shape about a million years ago with the eruption and subsequent massive collapse of a large composite volcano. The caldera encompasses five meadowlands within its grand circumscription: Valle San Antonio, Valle Toledo, Valle Jaramillo, Valle de los Posos, and the most famous, Valle Grande. In width an incredible sixteen miles long, the breathtaking Valle Grande makes good on its translated name—"Big Valley."

Over time, lava flows and ash deposits from the Jemez eruptions coalesced to form the lofty Pajarito Plateau on the eastern flank of the mountain. The Puyé Ruins and Bandelier National Monument on the plateau today preserve cliff houses and pueblo-style dwellings built here in the late 1300s by ancestors of the Pueblo Indians.

On the opposite end of the historical continuum, the Pajarito Plateau is also home to the "atomic city" of Los Alamos. It was here in 1942 that the US government created a top-secret laboratory where scientists clandestinely engineered the world's first atomic bomb. Today, Los Alamos National Laboratory (LANL) is one of the principal scientific institutions in the nation. Owned by the US Department of Energy and managed by the University of California, LANL has worked to convert the large geothermal resources in the Jemez into an alternative energy resource. Scientists have many opportunities for study: the Jemez Mountains contain one of the highest concentrations of geothermal hot springs in the state.

More to explore: *Jemez State Monument, Peggy Pond Church (see under Marjorie Bell Chambers), Soda Dam, Valle Grande*

208. Jemez State Monument

Location: Sandoval County. On NM 4, near the Jemez Historic Site (formerly Jemez State Monument). See map 4.

Marker text: The village of Giusewa was occupied by ancestors of the Jemez Indians before the arrival of the Spanish in 1541. Its ruins lie close to those of the great stone mission church of San Jose de Los Jemez, which was built by the Franciscans around 1622.

Note: Jemez State Monument is now known as Jemez Historic Site.

For at least two hundred years before Spanish conquistadores arrived in New Mexico in the sixteenth century, the Indian pueblo of Giusewa supported a thriving community of Towa-speaking Indians. In translation, the Towa word *giusewa* alludes to the many geothermal hot springs that percolate nearby.

Built sometime in the fourteenth century, Giusewa was one of several closely related Indian villages in the mountainous region of north-central New Mexico. Spanish captain Francisco de Barrionuevo, traveling with the expedition of Francisco Vásquez de Coronado into New Mexico in 1541, noted several of these pueblos in a region he called the Provincia de los Hemes. Around 1600, after the Spanish had begun their colonization of the land, Franciscan priest Fray Alonso de Lugo was assigned to the conversion of the Jemez Indians. Arriving shortly afterward was Fray Geronimo de Zárate Salmerón, the priest generally credited with having directed Indian women and children around 1621 in the construction of a large mission church east of the pueblo: San José de los Jémez.

Reflected in the design of the mission is the priests' architectural response to the all-too-frequent attacks by Navajo Indians on the population at Giusewa. Built for both devotion and defense, the fortress-like sandstone and adobe walls ran four to eight feet thick and rose in places thirty feet high, a towering hulk broken only by thin, impenetrable windows. A unique feature of the mission was the fifty-foot-high octagonal tower, complete with observation room from which sentinels could survey the surrounding region for the approach of unfriendly Indians. The entrance to the chapel was 11 feet wide; the nave 33 feet wide and 110 feet long. A convento with living space for the priests adjoined the church. Inside this bulwark, creativity still found its spark. On plastered walls inside the mission, Indians painted delicate alfresco murals of floral patterns and designs.

In 1622, the Spanish government ordered the Jemez pueblos consolidated to ameliorate the administrative burden the colony had undertaken in its missionary effort and to gain additional protection against attacks by Navajo Indians. The Spanish resettled members of the Jemez pueblos into two main Jemez villages, Astialakwa and Giusewa. Further Navajo depredations eventually forced the villages to unite into a single congregation. The Spanish called that pueblo San Diego de los Jémez—the present Jemez Pueblo.

Abandoned, Giusewa and the San José de los Jémez mission fell to ruin. They are open to the public today as the Jemez Historic Site.

More to explore: *Evelyn M. Vigil and Juanita T. Toledo (see under Pecos), Pueblo of Jemez, Vásquez de Coronado's Route (series)*

JICARILLA APACHE: Series of Four Historic Markers (Various Locations on the Jicarilla Apache Reservation)

General Introduction

The beautiful Jicarilla Apache Reservation protects the homelands of the Jicarilla Apaches. Four Historic Markers across the reservation document the history, ancient and modern, of the Jicarilla Apache tribe and their reservation. These Markers have been combined here into one series, so the story of the Jicarilla Apaches can be followed more easily. The Markers are presented here roughly in chronological order.

Public ceremonies at the Jicarilla Reservation include the Little Beaver Rodeo and Powwow in late July and the Gojiiya Feast Day on September 14 and 15.

More to explore (Jicarilla Apache Series): *Aztec, Cimarron, City of Bloomfield, Cumbres Pass, Farmington, Fort Lowell, Pilar*

209. Jicarilla Apache (Tribe)

Location: Rio Arriba County. On the Jicarilla Apache Reservation, on NM 537 between mile markers 27 and 28. See map 2.

Marker text: The Jicarilla Apache, a Southern Athabascan people, migrated to the Southwest from northwest Canada. The Jicarilla Apache's pre-reservation homeland ranged from southeastern Colorado through northeastern New Mexico, to the Texas/Oklahoma panhandle. The Jicarilla Apache, named by the Spanish for the reed baskets they wove, are composed of two clans—the Llanero (plains) and the Ollero (mountain).

Note: See the general introduction to this series of Markers, as well as the other Markers making up the series, for further background on the Jicarilla Apache and their reservation.

Jicarilla Apaches trace their ancestry to cultural groups that migrated from Canada around AD 1300 to 1400. As these groups, classified as Athabascan, reached the Rocky Mountain region and other places in North America, they developed linguistic differences and separated into distinct tribes. Among these were Navajos, who settled in the northwestern portion of the state, and Apaches, who roamed vast portions of New Mexico, Arizona, Colorado, Oklahoma, and Texas Panhandle. Separate branches of the Apache tribe arose, including the Chiricahua in southwestern New Mexico, the Mescalero in south-central New Mexico, and another group in northeastern and eastern New Mexico. After the Spanish encountered the latter group in the seventeenth century, they named the Indians Jicarilla. The Spanish word *jicarilla* means "little cup" and likely refers to baskets woven by the Apaches from reeds.

210. Jicarilla Apache (Tribe)

Location: Rio Arriba County. Just east of Dulce on the north side of US 64 between mile markers 136 and 137. See map 2.

Marker text: The Jicarilla Apaches, primarily a hunting and gathering group, once occupied vast portions of northeastern New Mexico and southern Colorado. Pressure from Comanche Indians and European settlers eventually pushed them from their homeland. In 1887, the Jicarillas were given a permanent reservation in north-central New Mexico, near Dulce.

Present day (1989) size of the reservation is 842,315 acres. The northern one-half of the reservation was established by Presidential Executive Order in 1887 and the southern one-half in 1907. New additions to the reservation are the El Poso Ranch in 1982 and the Thesis Ranch in 1986.

Note: See the general introduction to this series of Markers, as well as the other Markers making up the series, for further background on the Jicarilla Apache and their reservation.

Jicarilla Apaches were primarily hunters and gatherers and frequently crossed the plains on buffalo hunts. Archaeological evidence shows that Apaches also built small farming villages south of present-day Cimarron. In 1723, Comanche warriors began a series of attacks against the tribe. By the middle of the eighteenth century, these attacks, together with encroachments by the French and Spanish onto the plains, had driven the Apaches over the Sangre de Cristo Mountains and into the Rio Grande Valley.

After the Southwest became part of the United States in the mid-nineteenth century, the government created land set-asides to provide permanent homes for Native Americans. The Jicarillas were the last tribe in the state to receive their own reservation.

211. Jicarilla Apache (Tribe)

Location: Rio Arriba County. On the east side of US 64 at the intersection of US 64 and NM 537. See map 2.

Marker text: During the 19th century, the United States government attempted to establish reservations to separate Indian tribes from settlers along the frontier. The Jicarilla Apache initially agreed to settle on a reservation in 1851, but unratified treaties and local political squabbles hampered the process of obtaining a reservation for 36 years. President Grover Cleveland finally issued the Executive Order which established a permanent home for the Jicarilla on February 11, 1887.

Note: See the general introduction to this series of Markers, as well as the other Markers making up the series, for further background on the Jicarilla Apache and their reservation.

An executive order issued by President Grover Cleveland on February 11, 1887, established the current Jicarilla Apache Reservation in north-central New Mexico. The town of Dulce became the headquarters for the Jicarilla Agency. A second executive order issued on November 11, 1907, augmented the size of the reservation to almost twice its original allotment. The newly gained land ran south from roughly around Tapicito Ridge to just below present-day US 550. More recently, the Jicarilla have acquired El Poso Ranch and Thesis Ranch, bringing the size of their reservation to more than 840,000 acres.

212. Jicarilla Apache Reservation Centennial Highway

Location: Rio Arriba County. In Dulce, in a small rest area on the side of US 64. See map 2.

Marker text: The Jicarilla Apache Tribe commemorated the Centennial Anniversary of their present reservation on February 11, 1987. The Centennial was also observed at the annual Little Beaver Pow-wow and Round-up in July and the Go-Jii-Ya Fiesta September 13–15. The Jicarilla Apache Centennial Wagon Trek, a 200 mile horse and wagon journey from Cimarron to Dulce, was undertaken May 26–June 14, 1987, to acknowledge earlier homelands around Cimarron, Taos, and Abiquiú.

Note: See the general introduction to this series of Markers, as well as the other Markers making up the series, for further background on the Jicarilla Apache and their reservation.

As part of the 1987 centennial celebrating the executive order that had created their reservation, a caravan of some 130 Jicarilla Apaches driving wagons and pickup trucks left Cimarron for Dulce on May 26 in a symbolic reenactment of the journey of their ancestors to their present home. Led by Adolphus Caramillo, who rode a horse he named "Amtrak," the caravan wound its way through the mountain resort areas of Eagle Nest, Angel Fire, Taos, Abiquiú, Tierra Amarilla, and Chama, arriving in Dulce on June 14 after covering some two hundred miles. Later, the tribe worked with the New Mexico State Highway Department to designate NM 537 between US 550 (formerly NM 44) and US 64 as the Jicarilla Apache Reservation Centennial Highway.

213. John H. Tunstall Murder Site

Location: Lincoln County. Near San Patricio, on the south side of US 70, between mile markers 272 and 273. See map 6.

Marker text: In one of the Lincoln County War's earliest violent encounters, John H. Tunstall was shot and killed at a nearby site on February 18, 1878. Tunstall's death set off a series of violent reprisals between his friends, among whom was William "Billy the Kid" Bonney, and forces of the Murphy/Dolan faction of this tragic conflict. Tunstall, an English businessman, came to New Mexico in 1876.

When young Englishman John H. Tunstall established his ranch on the Rio Felix south of Lincoln in 1876, he soon found himself at odds with other Lincoln County ranchers over grazing and water rights. Chief among his rivals were Lincoln businessmen Lawrence G. Murphy and James J. Dolan. Murphy and Dolan found important political backing in a larger group of politicians out of Santa Fe that included Governor Samuel B. Axtell and US District Attorney Thomas B. Catron.

For his part, Tunstall aligned with John Chisum, one of the foremost cattle ranchers in southeastern New Mexico at the time—and since. The two partnered in founding the Lincoln County Bank in Lincoln. Tunstall also opened a dry goods store in Lincoln with his friend Alexander McSween, a Scottish-born lawyer whom he had first met in Santa Fe. McSween himself was no friend of Murphy or Dolan, and the new Tunstall store directly competed with an existing store owned by Murphy.

Within two years of Tunstall's arrival in Lincoln, the stage was set for his death.

In February 1878, McSween was defending himself in court over charges that he had embezzled the proceeds of a life insurance policy. Dolan was behind the accusation, having convinced Sheriff William Brady to inventory McSween's store to reach the $10,000 indemnity ordered by the judge. Brady also sent a posse to Tunstall's ranch to inventory his stock, given his partnership with McSween. Tunstall set out with his ranch hands for Lincoln on February 18 to meet with the deputized men. The posse, having reached Tunstall's ranch in the meantime, turned back to catch up with him.

Among those Tunstall had hired to help run his

Englishman John Henry Tunstall moved to America in 1876 in hopes of becoming wealthy, but he soon found himself embroiled in a feud destined to become legendary. His murder in a canyon south of Lincoln was the spark that ignited the violent Lincoln County War. Courtesy Palace of the Governors Photo Archives (NMHM/DCA), neg. no. 110764.

ranch was young William "Billy the Kid" Bonney. Billy the Kid and the other ranch hands were riding with their boss that February day when they ventured into a canyon southwest of San Patricio.

Having caught up, the sheriff's posse approached. The cowboys warned Tunstall of the dangers of the situation, but he proceeded toward the posse to speak with them, his men remaining in a different part of the canyon. How the sequence of events played out from that point is conjecture to all but the canyon itself, but one thing is certain: Tunstall did not emerge alive. Posse members shot him twice, once in the chest and once in the head—his own cowboys not positioned where they could defend him. Tunstall was three weeks short of his twenty-fifth birthday.

Efforts to avenge Tunstall's death by Billy the Kid and his gang, who took the name "the Regulators," set off a spate of paybacks known today as the Lincoln County War.

Tunstall was buried on February 21 in a lot east of his store in Lincoln. The grave is on private property, but a marker for his body and that of his business partner, Alexander McSween, can be visited in the small alley between the Lincoln Post Office and the Tunstall Store. The canyon where Tunstall lost his life now bears his name.

More to explore: *Blazer's Mill, Greathouse Station and Tavern, Lincoln, Old Dowlin Mill (see under Ruidoso), San Patricio*

214. Jornada del Muerto

Location: Sierra County. Just west of Engle, in a pullout on the south side of NM 51, at mile marker 15. See map 5.

Marker text: This section of the Camino Real was named the Journey of the Dead by the Spanish because of the countless travelers who lost their lives along the 100 miles of desert between the Paraje de Fra Cristobal to the north and the Paraje Robledo to the south. This route was also utilized by the American Army, the Confederates in 1862, and the railroad in 1881.

Note: The correct English translation of Jornada del Muerto is "Journey of the Dead Man."

215. Jornada del Muerto

Location: Doña Ana County. North of Las Cruces, in the rest area on the east side of Interstate 25, at mile marker 28. See map 5.

Marker text: This stretch of the Camino Real leaves the Rio Grande and cuts across 90 miles of desert with little water or shelter. Despite its difficulty, the dreaded "Journey of the Deadman" was heavily used by Spanish, Mexican, and Anglo travelers between El Paso and the northern New Mexico settlements.

216. Jornada del Muerto

Location: Doña Ana County. North of Las Cruces, in a pullout on the east side of Interstate 25 just north of the Border Patrol checkpoint. See map 5.

Marker text: High plains of the Jornada del Muerto, elevation 4,340 feet, lie 400 feet above the Rio Grande Valley. It is a transitional area from the Basin and Range region to the west into tilted mountain ranges, such as the San Andres Mountains to the east, flanked by broad alluvial and wind-blown basins.

The stretch of the Chihuahuan Desert between Las Cruces and Socorro goes by the ominous name Jornada del Muerto, "the Journey of the Dead Man." Every one of its ninety miles a challenge, the Jornada was for travelers a treacherous departure from the Rio Grande, and along its parched course one visitor estimated a burial cross lay every five hundred feet. But the man most often identified as the *muerto* is Bernardo Gruber, a German trader who perished toward the southern end of the Jornada while a fugitive from officers of the Spanish Inquisition. Traders crossing the desert on July 16, 1670, found his blue doublet and trousers, a shock of hair, and several desiccated rib bones that had been gnawed by desert animals.

Geographically, the Jornada is a vast basin. It is part of the Rio Grande Rift, an area of sunken land that extends from central Colorado through the center of New Mexico. The Caballo and Fra Cristobal mountains separate the Jornada from the Rio Grande on the west, and the San Andres Mountains flank its eastern boundary. The Jornada is part of the Basin and Range Province, a geographical region of the southwestern United States characterized by low-lying basins, like the Rio Grande Valley, separated by large sections of land tilted up to form mountains. Despite its name and bad reputation, the arid Jornada abounds with life. Scattered cacti, soapweed yucca, Mormon tea, greasewood, and desert shrubs like creosote bush and mesquite all thrive here. Animals living in the Jornada include kangaroo rats, blacktail jackrabbits, pronghorn sheep, bullsnakes, horned larks, and even the roadrunner, the state bird of New Mexico.

Juan de Oñate, leading the first official colonizing expedition by Spain into New Mexico in 1598, was the first European to brave the Jornada. His route from Mexico through the state became recognized as the Camino Real, or Royal Road. As generations of settlers, missionaries, and traders followed him, camping places, known as *parajes*, emerged along the Camino Real. These rest areas offered travelers a respite from the journey and gave them a convenient place to tally and water their animals. The Paraje de Robledo near the present-day ruins of Fort Selden marked the southern end of the Jornada, and the Paraje de Fra Cristobal near Socorro, the northern. Crossing the Jornada took three days, or, more accurately, nights, since most travelers moved during the cooler hours of darkness. Still, it was a better option than following the Rio Grande. The serpentine course of the river in this part of the state could take much longer and would require navigating, in places, troublesome humpbacked land.

The Jornada saw traffic from Spanish, Mexican, and later, Anglo travelers following Oñate's path. During the Mexican-American War in 1846, Colonel Alexander Doniphan led his Missouri Volunteers south through the Jornada on their way to capture Chihuahua, Mexico. Later, soldiers from Fort Craig near Socorro and Fort Selden near Las Cruces escorted travelers through the Jornada to protect them against Apache attacks. As part of the Civil War in the Southwest, Confederate soldiers marched north along the Camino Real through the Jornada in the early months of 1862, hoping to capture Union forts in New Mexico and claim the territory for the Confederacy.

Today, the Jornada sees far fewer travelers. The Atchison, Topeka, and Santa Fe Railway built a line through the basin between 1881 and 1882, and, later, the interstate bypassed the Jornada altogether. While ranchers occupy parts of the western half of the Jornada, the eastern stretch lies within the restricted confines of White Sands Missile Range.

More to explore: *El Camino Real—The King's Highway, La Joya de Sevilleta, Oñate's Route (see under El Camino Real—The King's Highway), Paraje de Fra Cristobal, Paraje de los Brazitos, Paraje de Robledo, Paraje San Diego*

217. Josephine Cox "Grandma" Anderson

Location: Eddy County. Just east of Carlsbad, in a pullout on the north side of US 62/180, between mile markers 36 and 37. See map 6.

Marker text: During the terrible "la grippe" flu epidemic of 1918, Grandma fearlessly led other women in nursing and feeding the sick in tents and shacks along the banks of the Pecos River. She did not lose a single patient, later opening a sanatorium in Carlsbad. Humanitarian, nurse, teacher; she earned the nickname "The Angel of the Pecos."

When Josephine Cox Anderson and her husband, Lucius, arrived in the southeastern New Mexico community of Carlsbad in the late 1880s, they were on the brink of a wave of changes that would test the fortitude of the new settlement (which at the time was still known as Eddy). Lucius, hired to help plat and build the town, was elected the town's first mayor in 1897. Josephine, a former teacher turned nurse, assisted the only doctor in town in tending to the needs of the sick—a position that put her squarely in the path of one of the earliest challenges the nascent city would face.

Just after the turn of the century, the flu strain that came to be known as the Russian flu swept through Carlsbad. Josephine Cox, one of the few nurses in town at the time, knew that the community offered special challenges. Some settlers, too poor to find housing, lived in tents or ramshackle cabins alongside the Pecos River. The substandard housing meant poor sanitation, which helped the spread of the flu. Worse, Carlsbad had no hospital to care for the ill.

So Anderson, along with a few companions, took their healing cures out where they were needed—to the patients themselves. Riding in her buggy to visit the sickly families in their homes, she fed them soup and ministered to their illnesses with medicines donated by the town pharmacist. For bravely putting herself among the sick and infected and caring tenderly to their needs, Anderson became known as "the Angel of the Pecos."

Within about a year, the Russian flu had subsided in Carlsbad. But that was not the end of Anderson's story. Indeed, something worse was on the way.

It arrived in the year 1918. That year, an especially virulent strain of flu known as the Spanish flu spread in three separate waves, mutating each time, the second and third waves progressively more lethal, until even otherwise healthy individuals were affected. Today it is estimated that the Spanish flu pandemic killed between thirty and fifty million people worldwide. Fortunately, in the intervening years, Anderson and her husband had built a sanatorium at the corner of Shaw and Main, across from their own house. When the building opened in 1904, it was the first hospital in Carlsbad. This time, those who contracted the Spanish flu came to the sanatorium, where they could receive care under more sanitary conditions than Anderson had faced before. Anderson continued her ministrations to the patients who were presented to her, showing the care and attentive diligence for which she became beloved. She was successful in her work. Despite the possible devastation the flu could have inflicted, not a single one of the sixty patients under Anderson's care died.

For all of her nurturing treatments, the Angel of the Pecos was honored with yet another title, that of "Grandma" for the town of Carlsbad.

Over time, age slowly robbed Grandma Anderson of her sight and hearing, preventing her from indulging in her first true passion, painting. The sanatorium was later converted to apartments, and Anderson lived there—the very place where she had cared for so many in need—until her death on November 16, 1941. She was ninety-two.

More to explore: *Carlsbad, Dr. Annie Dodge Wauneka*

Jumbo: *see Trinity Site*

218. Kelly

Location: Socorro County. In Magdalena, in a pullout on the south side of US 60, at the intersection of US 60 and NM 114, the road to Kelly. See map 5.

Marker text: Silver was discovered in Kelly around 1866 and the town site was laid out in circa 1879. Kelly boomed with silver mining and eventually zinc mining, becoming one of central New Mexico's most prosperous mining towns. At one time, it boasted a population of 3,000. When zinc played out in the 1930s, Kelly began to die and is now a ghost town.

Although today a ghost town, Kelly can rest on its laurels: miners here produced almost $30 million worth of silver and lead ore. Main Street, Kelly, New Mexico, ca. 1880s. Courtesy Palace of the Governors Photo Archives (NMHM/DCA), neg. no. 110764.

Abandoned head frames, mine tailings, adobe ruins, and a small church offer piecemeal testament to the wealth of what was once the most prosperous mining town in central New Mexico. Kelly dates to the spring of 1866, when Colonel J. S. "Old Hutch" Hutchason staked two claims, the Juanita and the Graphic, on lead deposits he uncovered on the western slopes of the Magdalena Mountains. Hutchason knew a local sawmill operator named Andy Kelly, who staked his own claim close to the Juanita. By 1870, the Kelly Mine was the largest producer in the fledgling camp that had grown up around it.

In addition to lead ore, Kelly miners were soon pulling silver from the mountains. With the mining boom in full swing, the burgeoning town grew to include some eight hundred residents. Two hotels, a school, two dance halls, and several stores went up along the dirt main street, which curved its way up the hill. A visiting priest from nearby Magdalena, a town that had grown along with Kelly and often rivaled it for population, held services at the Little Mission Church of Saint John the Baptist.

In 1882, German immigrant Gustav Albert Billing acquired the Kelly Mine. Billing had earlier erected a smelter about thirty miles to the east in Socorro, which made possible large-scale treatment of silver and lead ores from his and other mines in the Kelly area. Teams of oxen and mules hauled ore-laden carts from Kelly to Socorro almost daily until 1885, when that task was taken up by the Atchison, Topeka, and Santa Fe Railway. On a promise from Billing himself that the district would yield sufficient wealth to return the investment, railroad officials had run the line from Socorro to Magdalena and included a short spur from the railhead to Kelly.

A silver crash in 1893 hit Billing's smelter and mines in the town of Kelly hard, but Kelly miners found solace in an unlikely place: the discard piles of their own mines. In 1903, Cony T. Brown, who then owned the Graphic Mine, sent green rocks from discard piles to Missouri to be assayed. The rocks were smithsonite, a form of zinc carbonate used as a pigment in the manufacture of paint. The Sherman-Williams Paint Company purchased the Graphic Mine the following year for $150,000.

The population in Kelly swelled to a peak of three thousand people in 1905. Zinc mining operations in Kelly exceeded those of any other camp in the state at the time. An account written by the US Geological Survey in 1910 stated: "The dumps of the Kelly mine alone would supply a sufficient number of fine specimens of copper and zinc carbonates to stock a dozen museums."

The early 1930s brought a dimmer prosperity. As smithsonite deposits became too difficult to reach, the once-bustling town of Kelly faded. Although the Kelly Mine remained open until 1939, most miners by that time had already moved elsewhere—many of them to nearby Magdalena. Kelly is now a ghost town.

More to explore: *Elizabethtown, Magdalena, Riley, Shakespeare, Socorro*

219. Ken Towle Park

Location: Lea County. East of Hobbs, in Ken Towle Park, on the north side of US 62/180, between mile markers 108 and 109. See map 6.

Marker text: Dedicated to Highway Commissioner Kenneth Towle, whose efforts made possible this rest area for visitors to New Mexico.

Ken L. Towle grew to prominence as the owner of an oil company in Hobbs in the 1960s. He later entered public service, representing the interests of Hobbs citizens with his election as a Democrat to the Hobbs City Council. He served also on the Hobbs Chamber of Commerce and later chaired that organization.

When a vacancy opened on the State Highway Commission in 1967 after the resignation of a former commission member, Towle accepted an appointment to that office to represent Highway District 2. A state agency, the Highway Commission (today known as the Transportation Commission) represents the six highway districts in New Mexico. Commissioners act on behalf of residents of their district on matters concerning highways and transportation.

Towle's appointment was intended to be temporary. But New Mexico governor David Cargo formalized the appointment in January of the following year. After being elected vice chairman of the commission two years after his appointment, Towle remained on the Highway Commission another eight years, until his retirement in 1977.

This rest area is dedicated to the work that Towle undertook on the Highway Commission, including securing funding for the rest area itself. A unique feature of the rest area, which doubles as a port of entry for trucks, is a stone map at the walkway leading to the entrance of the office. The map shows the highways connecting the major towns and cities of southeastern New Mexico, including Eunice, Jal, Hobbs, Lovington, and Tatum.

Additionally, this stretch of US 62/180 is known as the K. L. Towle Highway. A small plaque at the rest area, placed in July 1974, notes Towle's "outstanding public service and dedication in the field of highway construction and maintenance."

More to explore: *Bicentennial Celebration, Jack M. Campbell Highway (see under Rio Grande Gorge Bridge), Waldrop Park*

Kewa Women's Co-Op: *see Pueblo of Santo Domingo*

220. Khe Sanh Veterans

Location: Cibola County. East of Curbero and Budville, in a pullout on the south side of NM 124, at mile marker 17. See map 1.

Marker text: The Battle of Khe Sanh, Vietnam 1968. "Home was where you dug it." Eternally Bonded.

The Battle of Khe Sanh claimed the lives of 2,097 United States servicemen. This historic marker is dedicated to honor and preserve the memory of New Mexico servicemen who were wounded in action or later died of their wounds. The Khe Sanh Vietnam Veterans will forever live in each others' hearts.

These servicemen from New Mexico were killed in action at Khe Sanh.

Cpl. Carlos C Aguirre, USMC, February 24, 1968, Silver City
Capt. Edmund D. Bilbrey, USA, March 11, 1971, Albuquerque
Cpl. James L. Foster, USMC, May 19, 1968, Roswell
S. Sgt. Robert L. Graham, USA, June 18, 1969, Roswell
Cpl. David C. Grijalva, USMC, April 27, 1967, Santa Rita
L/Cpl. John A. Le Compte, USMC, July 01, 1968, Albuquerque
Pfc. Stephen Orosco, USMC, June 18, 1969, Tularosa
Cpl. Bobby A. Taylor, USMC, February 03, 1968, Silver City
HM-3 Ronald D. Whitlow, USN, August 6, 1968, Albuquerque

In Quang Tri Province of South Vietnam in the early 1960s, about fourteen miles south of the demilitarized zone between North and South Vietnam, the US military built a base and airstrip from which to conduct operations during the Vietnam War. The base took the name of the nearby village of Khe Sanh. Despite its remote location, the Khe Sanh Combat Base, its airstrip, and the smaller outposts on the hills that surrounded it would soon become the center of a months-long siege that would claim the lives of 2,097 US servicemen, nine of whom were from New Mexico.

In the winter of 1967, the North Vietnamese Army began amassing forces around the Khe Sanh base. In response, American reinforcements arrived to augment the US Marines of the

Twenty-Sixth Marine Regiment already stationed at the outpost. Then, early in the morning of January 21, 1968, fighting broke out when the NVA began their assault, first on Hill 861 south of the base, and later, through an aggressive mortar and rocket attack, on the base itself. The onslaught decimated several of the buildings on the base, including the ammunitions dump and the valuable weaponry inside, and killed several American servicemen. Further Marine reinforcements arrived in the next few days before the North Vietnamese began a ground artillery assault, entrenching themselves around the outpost and effectively isolating the base.

Under orders from General William Westmoreland, commander of the US military in Vietnam, to hold the base, the Americans used artillery, tanks, and mortars to maintain their position. As the siege continued over subsequent weeks, both sides engaged in almost daily battles around the base and in outposts in the hills nearby. Although hampered by winter monsoons and ground fire, American supply planes dropped food, medical supplies, and weaponry to sustain the men at Khe Sanh as weeks turned to months. From their trenches, the North Vietnamese fired on the American camp and encroached ever closer to the base perimeter. In February, the North Vietnamese reinforced their troops with another twenty thousand soldiers as they continued to expand their assault, although an anticipated all-out ground attack never came.

In an air assault known as Operation Niagara, the US Air Force and Navy sent fighter bombers on a sustained series of sorties against North Vietnamese positions around Khe Sanh, eventually dropping some 25,000 tons of bombs into suspected enemy locations. Although the NVA maintained their artillery assault, they were unable to break through the perimeter of the base.

At last, in early April, overland reinforcements of marines and army soldiers, supported by air assaults on the North Vietnamese, advanced on the base in an effort called Operation Pegasus. Pushing successfully through North Vietnamese ground forces, the troops reached the base on April 8. Although shelling of the base and gunfire in the surrounding hills continued sporadically for some time thereafter, the siege was effectively over.

On June 19, the marines evacuated the base at Khe Sanh and destroyed the remaining buildings.

In memory of the servicemen killed in the battle, the state of New Mexico on May 26, 2010, dedicated the Interstate 40 overpass at exit 104 near this Historic Marker as the Khe Sanh Bridge. The names of the servicemen from New Mexico who lost their lives are recorded on this Historic Marker.

More to explore: *Vietnam Veterans National Memorial, Women Veterans of New Mexico*

Kit Carson Park: *see Taos*

Kit Carson Park Memorial Cemetery: *see Taos*

221. Kneeling Nun

Location: Grant County. East of Bayard, in a pullout on the south side of NM 152, between mile markers 2 and 3. See map 5.

Marker text: Most famous of the many historic landmarks in the Black Range country is the Kneeling Nun. So named for its resemblance to a nun kneeling in prayer before a great altar. Many legends have grown up around the giant monolith which rests near the summit of the Santa Rita Range.

She may have gone by the name Sister Teresa or Sister Raquel. She may have worked at a mission or walked the hushed hallways of a convent. Regardless, the legend of her downfall remains the same. Overtaken by passion for a young, handsome suitor, she sought forgiveness from God at the base of Ben Moore Mountain. As punishment for the nun's indiscretion, the Almighty changed her kneeling figure to stone. Forever repentant, forever lacking absolution, the Kneeling Nun is one of the most beloved landmarks in southwestern New Mexico.

It was Lieutenant José Manuel Carrasco who gave the penitent monolith her descriptive name. Carrasco was a Spanish military officer who came to the area around 1800 and learned from local Apache Indians of copper deposits here. Although Carrasco may not have ever mined the extensive copper reserves at Santa Rita, history credits him as the first European to view them. Mining began at Santa Rita around 1804 and continues today.

John Russell Bartlett, on an expedition to map the border between the United States and Mexico in the early 1850s, left one of the first written accounts of the Kneeling Nun. He describes Ben Moore Mountain, part of the Santa Rita Range, then states prosaically: "On one side of this bluff, a portion of the rock is separated from the mountain and stands detached from it like a column."

More to explore: *Bartlett Garcia Continental Survey Point, Santa Rita Copper Mines*

222. La Angostura

Location: Sandoval County. North of Bernalillo, in the small village of Angostura (south of Algodones), in a pullout on the west side of NM 313 between mile markers 13 and 14. See map 4.

Marker text: Near here the Rio Grande Valley closes into a narrow pass (angostura). Control of this pass was critical to the safety of the trade along the Camino Real, so this area has been the focus of fortifications since the early 17th century. The 18th century settlement of Algodones developed as a result of continuing Spanish efforts to control the pass and nearby fords of the Rio Grande.

Angostura is a Spanish word meaning "narrows" or "narrow pass." The small village of Angostura lies within such a narrow stretch of the Rio Grande Valley. The river here offered a solid bed of gravel, making it possible for early settlers and wagons to ford safely. This strategic bit of geography made the area a key location along the Camino Real, the leading trade and settlement route between Mexico and Santa Fe for more than two hundred years.

Although a grant of land had been awarded here in the eighteenth century to Andres Montoya of San Felipe Pueblo, with boundaries stretching from Algodones to the Jemez River, disputes over proper ownership of the land delayed permanent settlement. The site was of interest to Spanish settlers, in part because of the ford it offered at the river. A village finally did take shape sometime around 1824. As late as 1851, the US Army maintained a small quartermaster depot in the area.

As the Camino Real came north from Bernalillo in the nineteenth century, it passed a number of small settlements in the Rio Grande Valley between that city and San Felipe Pueblo. Angostura and the small village of Algodones, its close neighbor to the immediate north, were among them, both lying about halfway between Bernalillo and San Felipe Pueblo. Most of that stretch comprised small farms and orchards. The route of NM 313 largely parallels the course of the Camino Real through here today.

More to explore: *El Camino Real—The King's Highway, Pueblo of San Felipe, Rio Grande*

223. La Bajada

Location: 1. Santa Fe County. South of Santa Fe, just off Interstate 25 at the Cochiti exit (258), in a pullout on the south side of NM 16, at mile marker 8. See map 2.

2. Santa Fe County. Fifteen miles south of Santa Fe, in the Bicentennial Rest Area and Visitors Center, on the east side of Interstate 25. (The rest area is also known as the La Bajada Rest Area.) See map 2.

Marker text: La Bajada, or "the descent," marks the division between the Rio Arriba, or "upper river," and the Rio Abajo, or "lower river," sections of New Mexico. This steep and dangerous grade was long an obstacle to caravan traffic going from the Rio Grande Valley to Santa Fe.

224. La Bajada

Location: Santa Fe County. South of Santa Fe in a pullout on the south side of NM 16, between mile markers 4 and 5, near the entrance to Tetilla Park Recreation Center. See map 2.

Marker text: This black volcanic escarpment is one of New Mexico's most important landmarks. The descent (bajada) of this escarpment marked the traditional division between New Mexico's upper (Rio Arriba) and lower (Rio Abajo) districts. Over the centuries several trails and roads were developed to overcome this most difficult of the obstacles along the Camino Real.

The most dramatic geographical division between upper and lower New Mexico is the infamous La Bajada, a rocky volcanic cliff just south of Santa Fe. *Bajada* is a Spanish word meaning "descent," an appropriately Dantesque term considering the hellish route over this precipitous escarpment that in years past caused both man and machine to overheat. For more than three centuries oxcarts, caravans, and later automobiles navigated the winding circles up and down this black basalt hill, each level a new punishment for travelers following this most direct route between Santa Fe and Albuquerque.

Caravan travel between New Mexico and Mexico over El Camino Real, the Royal Road, traversed the rugged slopes of La Bajada Hill throughout the seventeenth and eighteenth centuries. Southbound wagon masters braked their descent with ropes and braced the wheels of their carts with rocks when they needed to stop. Going up, freighters often required two teams of horses or mules to haul their wagons to the summit. Even then, reaching the top might take an entire day.

The steep slope of La Bajada made a convenient separation point between the two major economic and civil divisions in colonial New Mexico. Affairs in the upper elevations north of the hill were under the control of the governor. This was the Rio Arriba, or "Upper River"—that river being the Rio Grande. Maintaining judicial order in the lower elevations south of the hill, an area known as the Rio Abajo, or "Lower River," was the responsibility of the lieutenant governor.

As automobiles replaced wagons, a journey over La Bajada meant piloting a Tin Lizzie over twenty-three hairpin switchbacks, a stretch improved only slightly by the later addition of a gravel surface. Accidents and breakdowns were common. Motorists sometimes chose to drive their cars backward up the mile-and-a-half road to take advantage of the additional power the reverse gear provided in early automobiles. So significant was this ascent that history even records the name of the first woman believed to have made it: Gladys Epstein, who hustled her father's Velie sports car up the slope in 1910.

In early 1932, the road over La Bajada was replaced by a more gradual grade on a hill five miles to the southeast, and later still by Interstate 25.

More to explore: *Bicentennial Celebration, El Camino Real—The King's Highway, First Automobile in New Mexico (see under Raton)*

La Bajada was an example of early New Mexicans' ability to balance the hardships imposed by the geography of the state with their desire to remain mobile. La Bajada, New Mexico. Courtesy Palace of the Governors Photo Archives (NMHM/DCA), neg. no. 8231.

225. La Cienega School

Location: Taos County. In Questa, at the intersection of Gallegos Road and NM 38. See map 2.

Marker text: Construction began on the La Cienega School in 1934 as a Works Progress Administration (WPA) project. The school was built on donated land with donated building materials and opened its doors in 1936. La Cienega School graduated its first senior class in 1950. The school closed in 1999, having educated several generations of students from many communities throughout northern Taos County.

Note: The old school itself is a short distance down Gallegos Road from this Historic Marker.

By January 1937, the Works Progress Administration (WPA), a project of President Franklin D. Roosevelt's New Deal created to fund and implement workforce projects around the country, had either completed or begun construction on 309 rural schools and 43 city schools in New Mexico, with a waiting list of more than 200 still to come. One of the reasons the WPA was so active in building new schools in New Mexico was the strong backing the program received from New Mexico governor Clyde Tingley, who personally wrote to each school district and asked officials to use the WPA to help fund school construction and repairs. Tingley's efforts at school construction and improvement were supported by Lea Rowland, the WPA state administrator for New Mexico, who wrote that he had seen "literally hundreds of rural schools [in New Mexico] that are a disgrace to any state." The WPA took time to boast of its successes in school construction in

New Mexico. A WPA map showing all the schools being built or repaired in New Mexico proudly declared: "Modern Schools Supplant Old Shacks."

The following year, one more school was added to the "completed" list. Known officially as WPA Project 65-85-351, the school was more commonly known as La Cienega School in Questa. (*Cienega* is a Spanish word meaning "marsh.") Construction on the school had begun in 1934 on land donated by the county and materials donated, in part, by county residents.

From its first graduating class in 1950, the school educated several generations of students in Questa and the surrounding communities. By the 1990s, however, new schools in Questa had been built, and upkeep costs and repairs were proving expensive for the original building. The school closed in 1999, and students moved to other schools. A portion of the building remained open as the La Cienega Community Center for some years thereafter, serving as a meeting place for the town.

Although now closed to the public, the school can still be viewed from behind a fence. The empty halls are reminders of one of the institutions that once provided, as the old WPA school map declared, "Opportunity to Ambitious Boys and Girls."

More to explore: *Cedarvale, Nara Visa, Old Armijo School, State History of Education Museum*

226. La Cueva National Historic District

Location: Mora County. In La Cueva, beside the La Cueva Mill, at the intersection of NM 518 and NM 434, at mile marker 24 on NM 518. See map 3.

Marker text: This ranching community was established by Vicente Romero in the early 1850s. The grist mill was built in the 1870s. Its proximity to Fort Union and the Santa Fe Trail helped the ranch develop into one of the region's most important commercial centers. The mill, mercantile buildings, two-story residence and San Rafael Church were designated a National Historic District in 1973.

Sheepherder Vicente Romero began to purchase tracts of land in the Mora area in the mid-nineteenth century, eventually claiming a domain of more than thirty thousand acres near the eastern foothills of the Sangre de Cristo Mountains. On land he owned along the banks of the Mora River, Romero planted fields of vegetables and fruit trees and built a large two-story adobe hacienda, or Spanish ranch home, in the early 1850s. A wall surrounded the ranch and offered protection from Indian attacks to Romero, his wife, Josefa, and their three sons, Rafael, Antonio, and José Maria. Romero named his ranch La Cueva de los Pescaderos, or "the Cave of the Fishermen." Legend says that the appellation came from Romero's practice of sleeping in caves in the mountains while pasturing his flock.

In 1851, the US Army established Fort Union a short distance east of La Cueva to protect travelers along the Santa Fe Trail. Fort Union was one of the largest military posts in the Southwest, and as such often turned to outside contractors to supply its operations. Romero housed horses and wagons at his ranch and issued them to the fort when requested. He also supplied grain, which he ground in his two-story stone and adobe gristmill added to the property in the 1870s. A small farming community developed around the Romero ranch. The settlement took the name La Cueva.

Vicente Romero passed away in March 1880. His son Rafael incorporated the ranch with two other business partners and continued operations of the mill for almost three decades. When the ranch passed from Romero's hands in 1908, it was the second largest in New Mexico in terms of area under cultivation, according to the National Park Service.

Colonel William Salman acquired the ranch property and mill in 1948. Still the current owners, the Salman family has since cultivated extensive and renowned raspberry fields on the property. Guests to the mill can tour the property, picnic near the river, and purchase souvenirs and sweet raspberry jams.

In April 1973, the National Park Service added La Cueva to the National Register of Historic Places. Properties nominated included the gristmill, the mercantile store, Romero's ranch house and outbuildings, and the San Rafael Church.

More to explore: *Fort Union National Monument, Santa Fe Trail (series)*

227. La Joya de Sevilleta

Location: Socorro County. Just east of the village, on the north side of NM 304. See map 5.

Marker text: Present-day La Joya is located near the site of an ancient Piro Indian Pueblo that the Spanish named Nueva Sevilla, or Sevilleta. During the eighteenth century, this was the southernmost settlement along the Camino Real before travelers entered the *despoblado*, or uninhabited area, between here and El Paso del Norte. Every fall, caravans assembled here in preparation for this portion of the journey.

"New Seville" was what don Juan de Oñate saw in 1598 when he looked out over the Piro-speaking Indian pueblo of Seelocú. Lying along the west bank of the Rio Grande in New Mexico, Seelocú reminded Oñate of the Spanish river port of Seville. Here to colonize New Mexico, Oñate christened the pueblo Nueva Sevilla. It was undoubtedly a compliment. Seville was the wealthiest city in Spain in the sixteenth century.

By contrast, Nueva Sevilla in New Mexico lay abandoned by the end of the seventeenth century. Although Franciscan missionaries had established a small mission in the village in the 1600s, San Luis Obispo, Indian and Spanish residents abandoned the village and chapel during the Pueblo Indian uprising in 1680. Caravans trekking over the trade and colonization route of El Camino Real between Mexico and Santa Fe continued to pass nearby, but these environs were not resettled until 1800. Then, Governor Fernando Chacón established a new village known as La Joya de Sevilleta, or "the Basin of Little Seville."

Zebulon Pike, an American army officer captured by the Spanish in 1807 and escorted through New Mexico, stopped in La Joya de Sevilleta on March 10 of that year. In his diary, he described the settlement as "a regular square, appearing like a large mud wall on the outside, the doors, windows, etc., facing the square. . . . [It] is the neatest and most regular village I have yet seen."

For most of the 1700s and into the 1800s, the Spanish and, later, Mexican governments ran annual supply caravans over the Camino Real. La Joya de Sevilleta became a principal village along the route. Between it and El Paso to the south lay the region sometimes referred to as *el despoblado*, the unpopulated land, where nomadic Apache Indians reigned and only a few haciendas and campsites existed for a stretch of nearly 135 miles. Upon reaching La Joya, usually after leaving Santa Fe in November, the officer leading the military escort of the trade caravan assembled the wagons and made a thorough inspection to ensure that everyone was properly equipped for the forty-day journey. Forewarned and forearmed, the caravan left La Joya and pushed southward into the despoblado.

The name "Sevilleta" survives today in the name of the Sevilleta National Wildlife Refuge, which all but surrounds La Joya on both sides of Interstate 25. Managed by the US Fish and Wildlife Refuge, the area comprises almost 230,000 acres. Hiking trails allow visitors to enjoy wildflowers, wetlands, and the scenery of this part of central New Mexico. Coyote, deer, prairie dogs, and other creatures all call the refuge home.

More to explore: *El Camino Real—The King's Highway, Jornada del Muerto*

228. La Luz

Location: Otero County. North of Alamogordo, in a pullout on the north side of the intersection of US 54/70 and Alamo Street, which is the turnoff to La Luz. See map 6.

Marker text: In 1719, Spanish Franciscan missionaries built a chapel here dedicated to Nuestra Señora de la Luz, Our Lady of Light. The naming of the village is also attributed to the will o'wisp light in the canyon, a perpetually burning lamp in an elderly woman's home and a signal fire left by the male settlers, which when seen by the female settlers exclaimed, "¡La luz! ¡Alla esta la luz!, The light, there is the light!" Settlement of the village did not begin until around 1860, when settlers arrived from other villages devastated by floods on the Rio Grande.

229. Ghost Marker: Alamogordo

Marker text: In 1898 the brothers Charles B. and John A. Eddy, promoters of the El Paso and Northeastern Railroad, laid out and platted a town here. Alamogordo served as a junction with a railroad line to the lumbering operation in the Sacramento Mountains. The first atomic bomb was exploded 60 miles northwest of here on July 16, 1945.

Note: This Marker appears in an inventory of Historic Markers compiled by the State Historic Preservation Office but is not in the field. See map 6.

La Luz, the name of this village situated between Alamogordo and Tularosa, translates in English to "the Light." Several possible explanations account for the origin of the name, each of them indicative of the historical character of this small community in the middle of the Tularosa Basin. One story attributes the name to signal fires lit by the men who originally settled the village in the mid-nineteenth century. Having reached the site where they would found their new settlement late in the evening, the story goes, the men lit fires so the woman and children, still on the trail behind them, could find them. Upon seeing these small fires flickering in the darkness ahead, the women exclaimed in Spanish: "The light! There is the light!" Another account says that the name derives from the presence of mysterious lights, known as will-o'-the-wisps or spook lights, in the canyon (now called La Luz Canyon).

A story persists that two Franciscan missionaries passing through the area in 1719 built a chapel here, which they named Our Lady of Light—offering another possible origin of the name. However, little evidence remains to prove or disprove that assertion. The National Park Service, in nominating the La Luz Townsite Historic District to the National Register of Historic Places, called the story an "unsubstantiated rumor."

What is known, however, is that a small village formed here around 1866 as Hispanic farmers migrated to the area from Belen. Similar to the migration that was responsible for the settlement of nearby Tularosa, these settlers were moving here to escape the frequent flooding of the Rio Grande Valley. This area, safely distant from the capricious Rio Grande, offered a less truculent water source in the nearby creeks, along with a fertile valley for farming. Originally the settlement was known as Presidio, but it later took the name La Luz.

These early settlers built their townsite in an arrangement similar to other smaller Hispanic settlements, with a central plaza surrounded by adobe homes.

La Luz subsisted mostly as a farming village through the late 1800s. But changes came to the Tularosa Valley with the arrival of the railroad in the late 1890s. To the south, a new settlement was being built as the Eddy brothers, Charles B. and John A., laid the El Paso and Northeastern Railroad through the valley and north to Santa Rosa. The Eddy brothers platted the townsite of Alamogordo in 1898, running a spur from the town to the neighboring Sacramento Mountains to haul timber down to the valley to use for railroad ties. The railroad brought an influx of Anglo ranchers, who purchased land in the valley and in La Luz.

Not long after the turn of the century, La Luz was home to the renowned La Luz Pottery Factory, which mined clay from La Luz Canyon and processed it into roof and flooring tiles as well as other ceramics. The man who opened the factory was Rowland Hazard III of Rhode Island, a figure later involved in the founding of Alcoholics Anonymous. Although successful in its operations, the factory closed in 1942.

One other light plays a role in the history of the community, in more modern times. La Luz residents likely witnessed the flash of light that ushered in the atomic age when the first atomic bomb was detonated at the Trinity Site, about seventy miles to the northwest, on the morning of July 16, 1945.

More to explore: *Cloud-Climbing Railroad, Santa Rosa, Trinity Site, Tularosa*

230. La Mesilla

Location: Doña Ana County. In Mesilla, on Mesilla Plaza. See map 5.

Marker text: After the Treaty of Guadalupe Hidalgo, which concluded the Mexican War in 1848, the Mexican government commissioned *Cura* Ramón Ortiz to settle Mesilla. He brought families from New Mexico and from Paso del Norte (modern Ciudad Juárez) to populate the Mesilla Civil Colony Grant, which by 1850 had over 800 inhabitants.

231. La Mesilla

Location: Doña Ana County. In Mesilla, in a small grassy area at the intersection of Calle del Norte (NM 359) and Avenida de Mesilla (NM 28). See map 5.

Marker text: On November 16, 1854, a detachment from nearby Fort Fillmore raised the U.S. flag here confirming the Gadsden Purchase; thus the Gadsden territory was officially recognized as part of the United States. In 1858, the Butterfield stage began its run through Mesilla. During the Civil War, Mesilla was the capital of the Confederate Arizona Territory.

At the conclusion of the Mexican-American War in 1848, Mexico ceded New Mexico and much of the Southwest to the United States. Hoping to resettle Mexican citizens displaced by the new patterns of land ownership, Ramón Ortiz, a *cura*, or priest, gathered families from El Paso del Norte, present-day Juárez, as well as settlers from nearby Doña Ana, to settle the Mesilla Civil Colony Grant near a small bend of the Rio Grande. Their village took shape as a string of flat-roofed adobe buildings surrounding a central plaza. It was named La Mesilla, "the Little Table," for the small plateau on which it arose.

At the time of its founding, Mesilla lay within disputed Mexican territory—but things looked promising for settlers who wished to remain part of Mexico. In April 1851, surveyor John Russell Bartlett agreed with his counterpart from Mexico that the border should lie just north of Doña Ana, which left Mesilla within Mexico. When the news reached the Mesilla settlers, Bartlett recorded:

Their fears were removed, and a day was set apart for public rejoicing. For the whole population had determined to abandon the place if the boundary line had run south of the village. . . . The day came, and the event was celebrated by firing of cannon and a grand ball.

That changed on November 16, 1854, when soldiers from Fort Fillmore, six miles southeast of Mesilla, ceremoniously raised the United States flag on Mesilla's plaza to mark the signing of the Gadsden Purchase. Through that agreement, negotiated by diplomat James Gadsden, the United States purchased an additional 29,640 square miles of the Southwest from Mexico. Surveyors moved the border between Mexico and the United States south to its present location, and Mesilla and Doña Ana residents again found themselves part of the United States. Some moved farther into Mexico to remain Mexican citizens, but most, already settled, remained.

With the land now in control of the United States, stages of the Butterfield Overland Stage Company began to roll across southwestern New Mexico in 1858. Mesilla, then a prominent settlement and the seat of Doña Ana County, became the regional headquarters for the line, with an adobe building and corral at the south end of the plaza serving duty as the station stop. The Civil War forced officials of the Butterfield stage to remove the line and reroute it through Salt Lake City.

The Civil War brought other changes to the village. In July 1861, Lieutenant Colonel John R. Baylor of the Confederate Army marched his Fourth Regiment of Texas Cavalry from San Antonio, Texas, into New Mexico with a plan to conquer the Southwest for the Confederacy. Union troops from Fort Fillmore tangled with the Confederates in Mesilla on July 25 and lost; post commander Major Isaac Lynde ordered Fort Fillmore abandoned early the next morning and pulled out with his men. Baylor proclaimed himself the governor of the territory of Arizona, which included southern New Mexico, and made Mesilla the capital. His pretensions notwithstanding, the Confederates were forced to retreat from the state a year later, after Union soldiers burned Confederate supply wagons at the Battle of Glorieta Pass east of Santa Fe.

With the coming of the Santa Fe Railway in 1881, the economic center of the county shifted from Mesilla to Las Cruces. Mesilla today remains an attractive village steeped in history and a favorite spot for tourists and their cameras.

More to explore: *Bartlett Garcia Continental Survey Point, Butterfield Trail, Las Cruces, Site of San Augustin Springs*

232. La Salineta

Location: El Paso County (Texas). In Vinton, Texas, in a pullout on the west side of NM 20 (Doniphan Drive), just north of Hemley Road. See map 5.

Marker text: In September, 1680, refugees fleeing the Pueblo Revolt assembled at La Salineta, a *paraje*—or stopping place—named for the salt deposits along the Rio Grande. Antonio de Otermín, a governor and captain-general of New Mexico, ordered a muster of those present; he counted 1,946 individuals. Here too, the decision was made to retreat to El Paso del Norte (present-day Juarez) rather than attempt an immediate reconquest of the province.

On August 10, 1680, after more than eighty years under Spanish rule, the Pueblo Indians of New Mexico—unhappy with their treatment and resentful of not being allowed to practice their religion—united in revolt against the Spanish settlers. After holding out for a few days, the governor of New Mexico, Antonio de Otermín, organized colonists, priests, Indian allies, and government officials and fled south along the Camino Real, the major trade and settlement route between Santa Fe and Mexico. Otermín and his officers reasoned that they should first reach a place of safety, and after receiving military assistance from the Spanish king, attempt a reconquest from a stronger position.

After traveling south for several weeks and meeting up with other refugees from the southern part of the state along the way, Otermín rode ahead from southern New Mexico to meet with Fray Francisco de Ayeta—to whom Otermín had earlier sent word of their need for supplies. The Franciscan missionary was coming from farther south with twenty-four wagons of provisions for the refugees. The two met near here on September 18, near an established *paraje*, or campsite, one of many that had developed along the course of the Camino Real. (The exact site of the paraje is not known.) Because of salt deposits in marshes near the river in this area, this campsite had come to be known as La Salineta. Fray Ayeta almost drowned in the process of crossing the river with the wagons to the east bank.

The remainder of the refugees arrived in the next few days, having trekked some three hundred miles in their journey.

As a place to rest and regroup, La Salineta offered several advantages. It was far enough south that Otermín felt he was comfortably safe from the insurrection. It was close to a water source in the Rio Grande. Further, it was near El Paso del Norte, "the Pass to the North," where the Franciscan mission of Nuestra Señora de Guadalupe had earlier been established on the west bank of the river opposite and about ten miles downstream from the campsite.

Safe and reprovisioned, and with the luxury of time to reassess his options, Otermín set about tending to administrative tasks. On September 29, he ordered a muster performed so that he would have an accurate accounting of the number of people in his charge. (Despite Otermín's orders forbidding it, some refugees had continued south on their own.) The accounting took several days, with each of the colonists reporting with their families to Otermín in turn. In total, the governor counted 1,946 individuals and 471 horses.

Otermín and his officers and priests, along with leading citizens among the refugees, now considered the prospect of attempting a reconquest of the land. The men met on October 2 and discussed their options. A few days later, on October 5, Otermín announced his decision: lacking sufficient arms and noting the approach of winter, the governor felt it best to delay the reconquest. Instead, they would remain where they knew they were safe and could secure food, and plan the reconquest from a new provisional base centered across the river at camps near the mission of Nuestra Señora de Guadalupe.

Otermín's attempted reconquest the following year was unsuccessful. The resettlement of New Mexico would not occur for another twelve years.

More to explore: *El Camino Real—The King's Highway, El Paso del Rio del Norte, Rio Grande, Santa Fe*

"Everyone had a gun, except us," striker Mariana Ramirez later recalled. "We had knitting needles. We had safety pins. We had straight pins. We had chile peppers. And we had rotten eggs." Empire Zinc Strike, Hanover, New Mexico, 1951. Los Mineros Photograph Collection, Chicano/a Research Collection, Arizona State University Libraries.

233. Ladies Auxiliary of Local 890 Mine, Mill, and Smelter

Location: Grant County. East of Bayard, in a pullout on the south side of NM 152, between mile markers 2 and 3. See map 5.

Marker text: After eight failed negotiating sessions and the expiration of their labor contract, Mexican-American workers at the nearby Empire Zinc mine struck for wage and benefit equality. When an injunction prohibited union members from picketing, the women—wives, mothers, sisters and daughters—took the union workers' places on the line.

The "striking" women persevered despite life threatening situations, violence, incarceration and tension at home. Their determination made national news and resulted in the popular documentary film, Salt of the Earth. These courageous women not only survived in solidarity until the strike ended, but they commanded recognition as well as respect.

A now-abandoned mine about a mile or so west of here, near the small town of Hanover, was the site of a pivotal episode in the history of US labor relations in the twentieth century—pivotal in part because women played a major role.

The impetus was a strike among the Mexican American mine workers at the Empire Zinc Mine in protest against discriminatory labor practices at the mine. The Mexican American mine workers received lower pay than their Anglo counterparts, worked longer hours, and labored under working conditions that were less safe. After eight separate negotiating sessions between union and company officials failed to achieve a resolution, about a hundred Mexican American workers, members of the International Union of Mine, Mill, and Smelter Workers, Local 890, began their strike on October 17, 1950. The Ladies Auxiliary, formed in support of the Local and comprising the striking miners' wives, mothers, sisters, and daughters, provided meals and other assistance at the picket line.

The strike continued for about nine months before a court order was issued on June 12, 1951, prohibiting union members from blocking the road to the mine with their picket. Prospects for a successful resolution to the matter seemed dim.

But nothing in the injunction prevented non-union members from picketing. So, standing strong against threats of violence, hostility, and the prevailing attitudes of a country that was still decades away from the women's movement, another group took up the picket—the only other people whose interests were as strongly affected by the outcome as those of the striking miners themselves. One by one, the women of the Ladies Auxiliary of Local 890 took their husbands' and brothers' and sons' signs and began to march in their own picket line.

Theirs was a brave—and risky—act of solidarity, undertaken at a dangerous time, and it added a new ingredient to the cauldron of raw emotions brewing at the time. The company and local law enforcement reacted to the new picket aggressively, throwing tear gas into the line, arresting about a hundred women (some with their children), beating them, and attempting to starve them and their families by denying credit at local stores.

Privately, some of the women also found that their act had created tension at home as well. With the women on the picket line, the men were forced to take over the duties of the household and of childrearing—a role reversal that created challenges in homes where a more traditional family structure was valued.

But the brave actions of the women proved to be the turning point of the dispute. Their picket brought national attention to what to that point had been a local issue. And their defiance ultimately proved successful, forcing the company in January 1952 to open negotiations with the striking miners. It may have also adjusted perceptions among the men of the role of the women in their lives. As auxiliary member Angela Sanchez later recalled, "after the strike, men didn't see us as weaklings anymore."

The strike was the basis of the movie *Salt of the Earth*, written by Michael Wilson and directed by Herbert J. Biberman. Even the movie itself created controversy. Released during the Joseph McCarthy "red scare" era and displaying a strong emphasis on the plight of the striking miners, the film was seen as sympathetic to communism. The film was blacklisted—the only film in American history to receive this dubious honor—and the filmmakers labeled as un-American. Today, the film is rightly considered a classic. Filmed very soon after the strike ended, part of the unique character of the movie comes from its mixture of professional actors with real participants in the original strike, including a strike leader, Juan Chácon, some of the striking women, and other members of the Local 890.

More to explore: *Bayard, Santa Rita Copper Mines*

234. Laguna del Perro
Elevation: 6,110 feet

Location: Torrance County. On US 60 between Encino and Willard, in a pullout on the north side of the road, between mile markers 225 and 226. See map 4.

Marker text: Numerous salt ponds and lakes, of which Laguna del Perro is the largest, occur in the lowest part of Estancia Basin, a closed depression between the Manzano Mountains to the west and the low Pedernal Hills to the east. The Basin was filled by a 150-foot-deep lake in the late Pleistocene time and native peoples have always mined salt here. The community was founded in 1879.

Note: The last line of this Historic Marker, which mentions a community that was founded in 1879, appears to be an error and was possibly meant for another Marker. No community existed here.

235. Ghost Marker: Salt Lakes

Marker text: The Pedernal Hills form the eastern edge of Spanish New Mexico's 17th century "Salinas Jurisdiction." Pueblo Indians used salt from these *salinas* in trade with Plains Indians. This salt was also prized by the Spaniards because of its use in silver processing for the rich Chihuahuan mines farther south in Mexico.

Note: This text was once part of the Laguna del Perro Historic Marker, but has been removed. It's included as a Ghost Marker here because it gives good background on the salt lakes themselves. See map 4.

Late Pleistocene epoch rains and snowmelt collected in this basin twenty thousand years ago to form a massive 275,994-acre body of water known today as Lake Estancia. Enclosed by the low Pedernal Hills to the east and the Manzano Mountains to the west, Estancia Lake reached a depth of 150 feet in some places. As the climate warmed, the waters of the lake evaporated or escaped through limestone caverns underground, leaving behind a heritage of small playas replete with concentrated deposits of salt. The largest of these, at twelve miles long, later became known as Laguna del Perro, or "Dog Lake." The origin of the canine reference is unknown. Prehistoric Paleo-Indians of the Clovis and later Folsom cultures were likely the first to reap salt from these playas as they crossed the valley hunting for buffalo some ten thousand years ago.

Between 1100 and 1500, Tiwa- and Tompiro-speaking Indians built large-scale pueblos in the Estancia Valley along major trade routes between the pueblos of the Rio Grande and the Indians of the Great Plains. Ruins of three pueblos, Quarai, Abó, and Gran Quivira, remain today. During the dry months of the year, Indians harvested salt from the playas. Salt was a valuable commodity in early pueblo trade networks and netted buffalo meat, flints, and shells. The Indians also used salt to tan hides and preserve meat.

Salt continued to be important in the Spanish history of New Mexico after the sixteenth century. Don Juan de Oñate, the first governor of New Mexico, named the Estancia Valley Las Salinas, or "Salt Lakes." Using Indians as slave laborers, the Spanish of the Salinas jurisdiction pulled huge blocks of salt from the playas. Spanish miners valued salt for its use in extracting silver from its ores in what was known as the patio or amalgamation process. The procedure involved crushing the silver ores, mixing the mass with salt, treating the concoction, and then setting it out to dry in the sun for a month or more. Workers loaded mules with salt harvested for this purpose and sent them south to the mines in Chihuahua, Mexico.

Although sporadic salt mining has continued at the playas to this day, large-scale production, like the prehistoric lake that created it, has dried up.

The circular highway route around the Estancia Valley between Tijeras, Mountainair, Willard, and Moriarty is known today as the Salt Missions Trail.

More to explore: *Abó Pass Trail, Abó Ruins, Gran Quivira Ruins, Mountainair, Quarai Ruins, Tajique*

236. Las Cruces

Location: Doña Ana County. West of Las Cruces, in the rest area atop the hill overlooking the city on the west, on the south side of Interstate 10, between mile markers 135 and 136. (The rest area is accessible only to eastbound traffic.) See map 5.

Marker text: In 1849, following the Mexican War, fields were first broken in Las Cruces. The town became a flourishing stop on the Camino Real, deriving its name, "The Crosses," from the markings of graves of victims of an Apache attack. Las Cruces since 1881 has been the county seat of Doña Ana County.

Generally it's not a good idea to build anything over a graveyard, but Las Cruces seems to be faring OK. The second-largest city in the state, home to New Mexico State University, and the county seat of Doña Ana County, Las Cruces is today a thriving community. But the name, which translates from Spanish to "the Crosses," speaks to the inauspicious beginnings of the town.

Although there are a number of possible explanations for the name, the one most generally accepted holds that it is a reference to gravesites located in this vicinity in the mid-nineteenth century. That such graves did exist is confirmed by a firsthand account from Susan Shelby Magoffin, the young wife of trader Samuel Magoffin, who traveled through the region in January 1847 and noted:

Yesterday we passed over the spot where a few years since a party of the Apaches attacked Gen. Armijo as he returned from the Pass with a party of troops, and killed some fourteen of his men, the graves of whom, marked by a rude cross, are now seen.

Those gravesites lay south of the settlement of Doña Ana, a village that figures prominently in the history of Las Cruces. At the end of the Mexican-American War in 1849, the Treaty of Guadalupe Hidalgo established the boundary of Mexico west of the Rio Grande, with Doña Ana—on the east side of the river and until then part of Mexico—now being part of the United States. Angered at this change in citizenship, several families in Doña Ana moved across the river to found Mesilla. Those who had stayed behind in Doña Ana might have thought better of it when, in 1854, the boundary was moved again, and they quickly found their village overrun with an influx of new American settlers. The alcalde (mayor) of Doña Ana, don Pablo Melendres, appealed to the government for help addressing the overcrowding in his village. In response, the US Army charged Lieutenant Delos Bennett Sackett to plat a new townsite—the beginnings of the city now known as Las Cruces.

The site selected for the new settlement lay along the route of the Camino Real, the historic road between Mexico and Santa Fe. For two hundred years, the Camino Real saw settlers and traders moving over its more than 1,500-mile course. Lying just south of the unpopulated area known as the Jornada del Muerto, or Journey of the Dead Man, where the trail left the waters of the Rio Grande for some ninety miles, Las Cruces became an important stopping point for travelers—either before they entered the harsh region if going north, or just after they came out of it if going south.

The presence of Fort Fillmore to the south, established in 1851 in an effort to protect the newly American settlements of the border region from Apache raids, helped bring peace to the Mesilla Valley and allowed Las Cruces to grow. The fertile lands along the Rio Grande were promising for agriculture. New enterprises opened in Las Cruces, and the settlement soon saw the appearance of hotels, schools, and businesses. With the arrival of the railroad in the city in 1881, travel over the Camino Real diminished and eventually stopped altogether. By the following year, Las

Cruces had the wherewithal to become the county seat of Doña Ana County, a distinction formerly held by the village of Mesilla. It continues in that role today.

More to explore: *Disappearance of Albert J. Fountain and His Son Henry, Doña Ana, Fort Selden State Monument, Hermits Peak, La Mesilla*

237. Las Nutrias

Location: Socorro County. In Las Nutrias, in the parking lot of the Las Nutrias church, on the east side of NM 304. See map 5.

Marker Text: During the late 17th century, this area had become well known to the Spanish. Called La Vega de Las Nutrias, or meadow of the beavers, it was a welcome *paraje*, or stopping place, for caravans on the Camino Real. Eighteenth century attempts at settlement in this region failed, but by 1860 the current village had been established and a church had been built by the new settlers.

When Spain began colonizing this "new" Mexico to the north in the late sixteenth century, trade and settlement took place over El Camino Real, the Royal Road, a continuous route from Mexico to Santa Fe. Although Native Americans living along the Rio Grande had used sections of the trail earlier, the first official Spanish use was in 1598, when don Juan de Oñate led a colonizing expedition into New Mexico and served as the first governor. Along the four-hundred-mile stretch of the Camino Real that ran through New Mexico, Oñate and later travelers established a string of encampments, or *parajes*. These were resting places where those along the route could unwind during the journey and water and inventory their livestock. As the Camino Real largely followed the course of the Rio Grande through the state, parajes were often established near the river.

One such paraje on the east bank of the river between the Spanish village of Casa Colorada to the north and the farming community of La Joya to the south became known as La Vega de las Nutrias, "the Meadow of the Beavers." The descriptive name likely derived from the presence of beavers or otters making their home along the riverbanks in this part of central New Mexico. Around 1765, a small settlement of Spanish-speaking farmers and their families arose near the paraje and took the name San Gabriel de las Nutrias. Attacks by Comanches and other Indian tribes on the settlers shortened the life of the village, and residents abandoned their town soon after it was established.

Spanish settlers returned to the area a hundred years later. By 1860, they had erected a new village, with farmsteads, irrigated fields, and a church. This settlement borrowed the name of the paraje and became Las Nutrias.

More to explore: *El Camino Real—The King's Highway, Oñate's Route (see under El Camino Real—The King's Highway), Rio Grande*

238. Las Placitas

Location: Sandoval County. On the west end of Placitas, in a pullout on the north side of NM 165, between mile markers 3 and 4. See map 4.

Marker text: The Sandia Mountains have been occupied by human beings for thousands of years. This area was settled by 1767, when Governor Pedro Fermin de Mendinueta made the land grant known as La Merced de San Antonio de las Huertas. The area is called "las placitas" because it contains several villages, also known as "plazas." Descendants of the stockmen and farmers who first settled the grant still live in the vicinity.

Por milenos, seres humanos han ocupado la Sierra Sandia. En 1767 el Gobernador Pedro Fermin De Mendinueta concedio La Merced de San Antonio de las Huertas, en la cual estaban ubicadas varias aldeas o "placitas"—origen del nombre actual. Los primeros pobladores eran rancheros y labradores, cuyos descendientes todavia habitan la vecindad.

Las Placitas, commonly referred to simply as Placitas, lies at the northern end of the Sandia Mountains. This north-south-tending range has provided a home to human beings for thousands of years. In one location, now called Sandia Man Cave, archaeologists have found arrow points and other artifacts used by Paleo-Indians. Later, Indians built small pueblos along the western foothills of the mountains.

In 1767, New Mexico governor Pedro Fermín de Mendinueta awarded the land grant of La Merced de San Antonio de las Huertas to Juan Gutiérrez and twenty-one other families. Many of those families were from nearby Bernalillo and had been living on the land here for two years already. But attacks on the village of Las Huertas by hostile Indians forced the settlers to abandon their homes in 1823. Although Las Huertas itself was never resettled, descendants of the original settlers returned in the succeeding decades to found other communities nearby, including La Madera and Tejon. In the 1840s, the village that would become Las Placitas began to take shape about a mile from the abandoned ruins of Las Huertas, likewise occupied by descendants of the original settlers of the grant. The name *las placitas*, which translates to "the villages" or "the little plazas," was a reference to the small villages in the region.

Early Placitas settlers found the irrigable land good for their crops, and the grazing lands near the mountains was suitable for raising cattle and sheep. By 1881, some five hundred people lived in the village.

In the 1970s, Placitas became known as a site popular with members of the counterculture movement. A number of communes arose to house these mostly Anglo residents, with some preferring to build unique geometric dome as houses. Of these new residents, an article in the *Albuquerque Journal* in July 1973 noted: "Despite the general prevalence of long hair and alternative lifestyle, few could be described as 'hippies' according to the current concept of unwashed, unproductive communards."

Placitas today remains a quiet village. Some of the descendants of the original villages still call this community home.

More to explore: *Sandia Mountains (see under Albuquerque)*

239. Las Trampas

Location: Rio Arriba County. In Las Trampas, just in front of historic Las Trampas church, off NM 76, between mile markers 23 and 24. See map 2.

Marker text: The village of Las Trampas was established in 1751 by 12 families from Santa Fe, led by Juan de Arguello, who received a land grant from Governor Tomás Vélez Cachupín. The Church of San José de Gracia is one of the finest surviving 18th-century churches in New Mexico.

La población de Las Trampas fue establecida en el año de 1751 con doce familias de la Villa de Santa Fe, cónducidas por Juan de Arguello. Los pobladores recivieron un amerced para este lugar del Gobernador Tomás Vélez Cachupín. La iglesia de San José de Gracia, que fue construida en el siglo diez y ocho, es una de las mas finas que se hallan en Nuevo México.

Juan de Arguello was seventy-four years old in 1751, the year he convinced twelve Spanish families to accompany him to a secluded valley amid the foothills of the Sangre de Cristo Mountains in north-central New Mexico and establish a new village there. The settlement emerged alongside the Rio de las Trampas, or "River of the Traps," a mellifluous stream likely named for the beaver snares waiting to spring to action in the river waters. Arguello's community was called Santo Tomás Apostol del Río de las Trampas, or "Saint Thomas the Apostle of the River of Traps." For simplicity, it was called Las Trampas.

New Mexico Governor Tomás Vélez Cachupín had granted land to these settlers in part to place a settlement where it might be of strategic worth in defending the frontier north of Santa Fe. Las Trampas and other settlements in the Santa Cruz Valley lay at the time along the boundary of Spanish New Mexico, and settlers living there were frequently menaced by hostile warriors of the Comanche tribe. Governor Cachupín hoped that the settlement and others like it might serve as living parapets to protect the capital at Santa Fe.

The church nearest to Las Trampas was the mission at Picurís Pueblo, about nine miles to the north. The untenable journey over those nine miles, fraught with the ever-present threat of Comanche attack in the secluded reaches of the mountains, inspired settlers at Las Trampas in 1760 to request permission to erect their own church. Bishop Pedro Tamarón y Romeral of the See of Durango obliged, stating: "We charge the citizens of the place to try to maintain the . . . chapel with all possible seemliness and cleanliness so that the devotion of the faithful may thus be aroused to frequent it."

Completed in 1776, the San José de Gracia Church was a physical representation of the strong spiritual convictions of the Las Trampas settlers. The adobe walls ran, in places, six feet thick. The nave stretched one hundred feet long and fifty-two feet wide, and a transverse clerestory window allowed sunlight to brighten the sanctuary. A ladder led to the choir loft, which hung suspended over the main entryway. Hand-hewn vigas held aloft the roof. A small chapel to the right of the main entrance enclosed the baptistery. Amid the earthen smell of dirt and stone from the original packed-dirt floor, the Las Trampas faithful expressed their religious devotions.

Juan de Arguello, who had led the original settlers to this isolated valley, lived to see the church completed. He lived, by some accounts, a remarkable 112 years, passing away in 1789.

The remoteness of the village helped ensure that the integrity of the church lingered even as the centuries turned. In 1961, the Historic American Buildings Survey called San José de Gracia "probably the best preserved of the eighteenth century Spanish Colonial churches built in New Mexico." So close did the church, and indeed Las Trampas itself, remain to its roots despite the best efforts of the modernizing twentieth century that the National Park Service in 1967 seriously considered an unprecedented request to maintain the entire village as a protected National Historic Landmark. The proposal did not go forward.

More to explore: *Comanche Country, Pueblo of Picurís, Santa Fe*

240. Las Vegas

Location: 1. San Miguel County. At the north end of Las Vegas, in the parking area of the hotel near the Interstate 25 interchange. See map 3.

2. San Miguel County. In front of the Tony Martinez Visitors Center, at the intersection of NM 329 and South Grand Avenue. See map 3.

Marker text: Las Vegas served as an important stop on the Santa Fe Trail and later as a major railroad center. Here General Kearny announced the annexation of New Mexico by the U.S. in 1846. In 1862, during the Confederate occupation of Santa Fe, Las Vegas served as a Territorial capital. New Mexico Highlands University was established here in 1893.

One of the more formative events in New Mexico history took place on a Las Vegas rooftop. On August 15, 1846, Brigadier General Stephen Watts Kearny climbed atop a building lining the plaza and proclaimed:

I have come amongst you by the orders of my government, to take possession of your country and extend over it the laws of the United States. We consider it, and have done so for some time, a part of the territory of the United States. We come amongst you as friends, not as enemies; as protectors, not as conquerors.

With that statement, the United States declared its intention to annex from Mexico the land that is now New Mexico, along with that of other southwestern states.

When Kearny made his announcement, the settlement of Las Vegas was still young, having arisen along the Gallinas River a few decades earlier from two overlapping Mexican land grants. Luis María Cabeza de Baca had received the first allotment in 1825, but Apache raids on the small village he formed came too unremittingly for permanent settlement to take hold. In 1835, residents from the rural community of San Miguel del Bado (sometimes seen as del Vado) about twenty-five miles to the south petitioned for new pasturelands and uncultivated fields using the same boundaries that Baca had earlier. Their community became Nuestra Señora de los Dolores de las Vegas, "Our Lady of the Sorrows of the Meadows." Later, after Congress upheld the veracity of both grants, descendants of Baca relinquished their title in exchange for other tracts in New Mexico.

By 1822, settlers and traders were reaching Las Vegas over the Santa Fe Trail, a major trade route between Missouri and Santa Fe. Las Vegas was one of the first and largest settlements they encountered in New Mexico.

To protect these travelers, the army built Fort Union north of Las Vegas in 1851. During the Civil War ten years later, the fort became a target of the Confederate Army's advance through the state. As the Rebels approached the capital city of Santa Fe in March 1862, Governor Henry Connelly fled for safety to Las Vegas and made the town a provisional state capital. Had Union troops not forced the Rebels from the state by burning Confederate supply wagons at the Battle of Glorieta Pass east of Santa Fe in late March,

Las Vegas, too, might have fallen to Confederate hands.

Today, Las Vegas is one of the largest communities in north-central New Mexico and is the county seat of San Miguel County. Its downtown plaza remains much as it has since the founding of the town, with a historic central plaza surrounded by commercial buildings. New Mexico Highlands University, founded in Las Vegas in 1893, today serves approximately three thousand students. Highlands offers degrees in the liberal arts and sciences, along with programs in business, teacher education, engineering, and social work.

More to explore: *Dr. Meta L. Christy, Fort Union National Monument, Glorieta Pass Battlefield*

241. Laura Gilpin (1891–1979)

Location: Santa Fe County. In the Bicentennial Rest Area fifteen miles south of Santa Fe on the east side of Interstate 25. (The rest area is also known as the La Bajada Rest Area.) See map 2.

Marker text: An outstanding photographer of the twentieth century, Laura Gilpin is best known for capturing southwestern cultures and landscapes on film. When her car ran out of gas on the Navajo reservation in 1930, she began photographing the local people. She published four books culminating with The Enduring Navaho in 1968. A master of the art of platinum printing, her photographs are found in museums around the world.

The world would be a less beautiful place had Laura Gilpin's car not run out of gas one day in 1930 while driving near Chinle, Arizona. But because it did, Gilpin, a photographer, and her companion befriended several Navajo families and were invited to return the following year. It was an invitation that would afford entrance into a way of life that Gilpin longed to capture in her photographs. The proof of her success in that effort can be found today in museums around the world.

Gilpin's love of photography started when she received a Brownie camera for her twelfth birthday in 1903. Two years later, she left her parent's ranch in Colorado to attend private schools in Pennsylvania and Connecticut, and then moved to Massachusetts to study at the New England Conservatory of Music. But it was photography that had captured her heart. She moved to New York in 1916 and studied at the Clarence H. White School of Photography, where she first learned the art of platinum printing. A little-used process at the time, the technique allowed for a wider range of tones across a print than was otherwise possible.

Gilpin began publishing her first photographs in New York, but her efforts were cut short when a bout of influenza sent her back home to Colorado to recover. There, a private nurse, Elizabeth W. Forster, nursed her to health. The two remained friends until Forster's death in 1972.

While traveling with Forster on a portion of the Navajo reservation in Arizona in 1930, Gilpin's gas tank ran empty. The women befriended the Navajo families who came to assist them, and Forster returned the following year to Red Rock, Arizona, to work as a visiting nurse. Gilpin often accompanied her, using the opportunity to capture through her lens the faces, lives, and landscapes of the Navajo Nation and, later, other parts of the state.

Although Gilpin took a range of photographs (she once worked for Boeing taking photos of their aircraft), it was for her landscapes and portraits of Navajo and pueblo people of the Southwest that she became best known. Her first book, *The Pueblos: A Camera Chronicle*, published in 1941, captured images of prehistoric and modern archaeological and Puebloan sites. In 1949, she published a second book, *Rio Grande: River of Destiny*, with photos documenting the course of the Rio Grande from Colorado to the Gulf of Mexico. That book ended with one of Gilpin's best-known photographs, *The Rio Grande Yields Its Surplus to the Sea*, showing the serpentine river winding into the distance.

Through her many photographs taken in New Mexico, Gilpin captured the landscape of the state in stunning black and white—including the ripples of dunes at White Sands, the soft contours of the San Francisco de Asís Church in Ranchos de Taos, and a dramatic rainstorm over La Bajada south of Santa Fe. In 1950, she returned with Forster to the Navajo Nation, where she reconnected with old friends and completed the photos that were published in her groundbreaking 1968 book, *The Enduring Navaho*.

Gilpin passed away on November 30, 1979, at her home in Santa Fe.

More to explore: *Georgia O'Keeffe, Navajo Indian Reservation, Pablita Velarde (see under Pueblo of Santa Clara)*

242. Lea County Cowgirls—Dessie Sawyer (1897–1990)

Location: Lea County. In Tatum, at the intersection of Avenue A and Broadway. See map 6.

Marker text: Dessie Sawyer was a rancher, philanthropist and political activist. Her work with community and charitable organizations advanced her into politics. She became the National Committee Woman of New Mexico's Democratic Party. Her advocacy of the western way of life was recognized by her induction into the National Cowgirl Hall of Fame in 1981.

243. Fern Sawyer (1917–1993)

Location: Lea County. In Tatum, at the intersection of Avenue A and Broadway.

Marker text: Dessie's daughter, Fern Sawyer, became a celebrity cowgirl. She was the first woman to win the National Cutting Horse world title. She also became the first woman appointed to the State Fair Commission and the State Racing Commission. She was inducted into the National Cowgirl Hall of Fame in 1976.

Note: Marker faceplates are on opposite sides of the same sign. See map 6.

Known as the Lea County Cowgirls, Dessie and Fern Sawyer were a mother-daughter team who epitomized the hardworking, community-oriented western character of rural southeastern New Mexico in the twentieth century.

Dessie was born in 1897 in Texas. She met and married a rancher, U. D. Sawyer, in 1928 and became the matriarch of their Crossroads Ranch near Tatum in Lea County. Dessie's work in the community with the March of Dimes and other charitable organizations, along with her prominence in the community, soon made her a respected civic leader. She turned her attention to politics and served for twenty-five years as the chairwoman of the New Mexico Democratic Party, attending the party's national conventions as a state delegate.

Probably only one person could surpass the intensity Dessie Sawyer displayed for the western way of life—her own daughter, Fern, born on May 17, 1917.

Growing up, young Fern Sawyer learned horsemanship and ranch work from her parents. She participated in the rodeo circuit, most often competing against men, riding her personal horse, Bélen. In an oral history related to author Teresa Jordan, Fern recalled volunteering to ride a bull at one rodeo event when no uninjured men remained to do so—she gripped the rope so tightly during the ride that she broke her hand in nine places! Fern was a founding member of the National Cutting Horse Association, overcoming resistance among her colleagues to her membership because of her gender. (Cutting requires a horse and rider to work in tandem to separate an animal, usually a cow, from a herd.) Soon after, in 1945, at the Fat Stock Show and Rodeo in Fort Worth, Texas, Fern won the National Cutting Horse world title—the first woman to do so.

Fond of wearing colorful western attire, Fern mixed panache with hard work to create a spirit and style all her own. Much later, noted cowboy songwriter and poet Red Steagall would call her "the woman who set the standard for the American cowgirl."

Like her mother, Fern, too, participated in politics both at the local and the national level. She was the Democratic chairwoman for Lincoln County (where she owned her own ranch), and likewise served as a delegate to the party's national conventions. She was also the first woman to serve as a commissioner for the New Mexico State Fair—a position she held for fifteen years. A street on the fairgrounds in Albuquerque is named for her. In addition to her induction into the Rodeo Cowboy Hall of Fame and the National Cutting Horse Hall of Fame, Fern Sawyer was also inducted into the National Cowgirl Hall of Fame, in 1976. (She also donated some of her colorful clothing and thirty pairs of boots to the National Cowgirl Museum.) Her mother Dessie followed five years later. Dessie and Fern Sawyer are a rare example of a mother-daughter team to be listed in the Cowgirl Hall of Fame.

A scholarship in the name of U. D. and Dessie Sawyer continues to help students from Hobbs attend the New Mexico Junior College in that city. And the Fern Sawyer Award, offered by the National Cowgirl Museum, is awarded to "an individual or organization that has worked toward and contributed to the advancement of the National Cowgirl Museum and Hall of Fame."

More to explore: *Louise Massey Mabie*

244. Leasburg Dam State Park

Location: Doña Ana County. In Leasburg Dam State Park, on the east side of the road leading to the park, just before the park offices and Visitors Center. See map 5.

Marker text: Built in 1908, the historic Leasburg Diversion Dam channels water from the Rio Grande to irrigate the vast farming area of the Upper Mesilla Valley. The dam also provides a pleasant spot for fishing, and canoes and kayaks may be used on the river. Picnicking and camping facilities are also available.

Leasburg Dam State Park takes it name from the historic Leasburg Dam, which sits at the north end of the park. Construction on the dam began in 1905, but flooding and delays in the delivery of materials deferred its completion until February 1908.

The dam was erected as part of an effort by the US Bureau of Reclamation, begun in the early 1900s and known as the Rio Grande Project, to build a network of dams and canals along the course of the Rio Grande in southern New Mexico. By controlling the flow of water in the Rio Grande, this watery network would both prevent the river from flooding and also provide regular and sustainable irrigation water to farmers. Leasburg Dam serves as a diversion dam in the network. As such, its purpose is not to impound water, like Elephant Butte Dam near Truth or Consequences upriver, but rather to divert the flow of water from the river toward another area. In the case of Leasburg Dam, this diverted water is further funneled through Leasburg Canal to the farmlands of the Mesilla Valley for irrigation.

What Leasburg Dam lacks in height (only nine feet), it makes up for in length (six hundred feet). Because of its historical significance, the dam is listed on the New Mexico State Register of Cultural Properties.

The state park surrounding the dam opened to the public in 1973. Set in a quiet desert locale, the park includes several campsites, a cactus garden, and a number of hiking trails, with one leading to the dam itself.

More to explore: *Elephant Butte Lake State Park, Rio Grande Bridge at Radium Springs, Sumner Lake State Park, Ute Lake State Park*

245. Lincoln

Location: 1. Lincoln County. At the west end of Lincoln, near the Murphy-Dolan Store, in a pullout on the south side of US 380, between mile markers 97 and 98. See map 6.

2. Lincoln County. At the east end of Lincoln, near the museum, in a pullout on the north side of US 380, between mile markers 98 and 99. See map 6.

Marker text: Spanish-speaking settlers established a town here in the 1850s, after the U.S. Army began to control the Mescalero Apaches. First known as Las Placitas del Rio Bonito, the name of the community was changed to Lincoln when Lincoln County was created in 1869.

Center of the turbulent Lincoln County War, 1876–79, a land and cattle feud marked by violence on both sides. Lincoln historic landmarks include the Murphy-Dolan store, which later became the Lincoln County Courthouse, the store of John Henry Tunstall, whose murder set off the hostilities, and the house of Alexander McSween, where the final battle was fought.

Only the torreón, the round brick fortification in the center of town, today gives any indication of the violence that has marred the history of Lincoln. Yet it was in Lincoln that one of the most brutal sagas in the history of New Mexico played out, a struggle for power between rival ranching and political factions that turned so vicious it became known as the Lincoln County War.

Settlement of this part of south-central New Mexico began after the Mexican-American War as Spanish-speaking people established the farming village of La Placita del Rio Bonito, "the Little Village by the Pretty River," along the nearby Rio Bonito. Although the torreón they erected offered a protected spot from which these early settlers could fire on hostile Apaches, raids still drove the villagers from their homes several times until the army established Fort Stanton nearby in 1855. The territorial legislature approved the creation of Lincoln County in 1869 to recognize recently assassinated President Abraham Lincoln. La Placita, renamed Lincoln, became the new county seat.

In 1876, young Englishman John Henry Tunstall moved to Lincoln and built a ranch along the Rio Felix south of town, hoping to take advantage of the beef market at nearby Fort Stanton. Among the hands Tunstall employed was a young man named William Bonney, better known to history as Billy the Kid. Tunstall also built a store in Lincoln, which included offices for his associates: Scottish-born attorney Alexander McSween, whom he had met in Santa Fe upon entering the

United States and who had enticed him to move to Lincoln, and cattleman John Chisum, whose far-reaching southeastern New Mexico ranch was one of the largest in the country.

Two merchants dominated the economy in Lincoln at the time: Lawrence G. Murphy and James J. Dolan. Murphy owned a large, two-story adobe mercantile outlet he called the "Big Store" down the street from that of Tunstall. In league with politicos from Santa Fe, Murphy and Dolan also supplied government contracts to Fort Stanton—at a substantial profit and reportedly using inferior goods. Tunstall's new store and economic intentions stood in direct competition, and tensions between the men grew. For his part, Chisum already disliked Murphy and Dolan, who, he believed, had sent operatives to rustle cattle from his ranch.

A life insurance policy proved the precipitating factor of the violence that was to come. McSween had been hired by Dolan about a year earlier to settle the estate of his former business partner, Emil Fritz. When McSween held up the settlement pending receipt of his fees, an angry Dolan had him charged with embezzlement, then got a writ for the attachment of McSween's property as surety. Lincoln County sheriff William Brady entered McSween's house, took stock of his possessions, and then sent a posse to do likewise at Tunstall's ranch. On February 18, 1878, when the deputized posse met up with Tunstall in a canyon on the road to his ranch, posse members assassinated the young Englishman.

Angered by the turn of events, Billy the Kid and other Tunstall-McSween supporters formed their own gang to avenge Tunstall's death. They called themselves "the Regulators."

An arrest warrant was issued for Alexander McSween for his role in the life insurance fuss, and a trial date was set for April 1. That morning, as Sheriff Brady and his deputies walked down the street, the Kid and his cohorts fired at them. Sheriff Brady fell, mortally wounded, to the ground.

Scuffles in the surrounding countryside marked the next few months of the battle. The final showdown began on July 15, when the new Lincoln County sheriff, George W. Peppin, fired on the McSween house in Lincoln. Billy the Kid and other Regulators returned fire, and the exchange continued sporadically around Lincoln for a full five days. Members of the Regulators eventually holed themselves up inside the McSween house. To rout them out, Sheriff Peppin and his deputies on the evening of July 19 set fire to the building. As the Regulators charged from the home to escape the flames, Peppin and Dolan's men gunned them down. Billy the Kid got out unharmed; Alexander McSween was killed.

In the aftermath, President Rutherford Hayes replaced New Mexico governor Sam Axtell with Lewis "Lew" Wallace, and Sheriff Peppin with Pat Garrett. Governor Wallace pardoned all the participants except Billy the Kid, whose murder of Sheriff Brady, Wallace felt, could not go unpunished. Sheriff Garrett finally trapped the Kid in a mansion in nearby Fort Sumner on July 14, 1881, and shot him to death.

More to explore: *Blazer's Mill, Fort Stanton, Fort Sumner and Fort Sumner State Monument (series), Greathouse Station and Tavern, John H. Tunstall Murder Site, Old Dowlin Mill (see under Ruidoso), Pat Garrett Murder Site, San Patricio, Seven Rivers Cemetery*

246. Lincoln-Jackson School

Location: Curry County. In Clovis, in the courtyard of the Lincoln-Jackson Family Center, at the corner of Alphon and West Grand. See map 6.

Marker text: The African-American Community of Clovis started its first school, Lincoln-Jackson, in 1924 with two students. In 1926, the school was named for Ida Jackson, a favorite teacher, and Abraham Lincoln. By 1954, K-12 enrollment had reached 292 students. After the Supreme Court's Desegregation Decision in 1954, the school board eliminated Lincoln-Jackson High School. In 1966 it became Lincoln-Jackson Elementary, and is now a magnet school for the arts.

In 1924, the African American community in Clovis appropriated rooms in a local Baptist church to create a school for black children. Six years later, the students were treated to their own small, one-room schoolhouse, which joined the Clovis school system as the Lincoln-Jackson School. The name honored both President Abraham Lincoln and the sole teacher at the school at the time, Ida O. Jackson. The Clovis school, which in 1935 had thirty-five students, was one of a handful of segregated schools in New Mexico (others existed in communities where the black population was large enough to support them, including Las Cruces, Hobbs, Carlsbad, Roswell, and Alamogordo).

As the number of enrolled students grew, so did the need to augment the teaching staff, and by 1944 Ida Jackson had been joined by two other faculty members. In 1950, the first class of three students graduated. Growth continued, and a few years later new brick buildings were constructed to serve the school.

But in 1954, the history of the school changed. On May 17 of that year, the Supreme Court decided the case of *Brown v. Board of Education*, declaring that the practice of "separate but equal" education—which allowed black students to be educated in segregated schools, provided the education was equal in quality to that of white students—was in fact a violation of the equal protection clause of the Fourteenth Amendment and therefore unconstitutional.

As a result, Lincoln-Jackson stopped offering high school–level classes, and students were integrated into other Clovis public schools. Lincoln-Jackson now served exclusively as an elementary school, offering classes to students of all races.

In 2001, the school shifted in purpose again to become the Lincoln-Jackson Arts Academy. Still an elementary school, the institution revised its curriculum to incorporate a number of arts-infused courses. Students at the school were introduced to fine arts, including music and literature, regardless of their grade level. In fact, in 2005, second and third graders from the Lincoln-Jackson Shakespeare Troupe performed some of the Bard's soliloquies at the Lensic Youth Arts Festival in Santa Fe. The historic school, which had grown from its humble beginnings in a church, had become a highly regarded magnet school for the arts. (A magnet school is a public school that offers an innovative and unique curriculum with the purpose of attracting—hence the term "magnet"—students of varying backgrounds.)

Today, the Lincoln-Jackson School operates as the Lincoln-Jackson Family Center, offering prekindergarten classes, kindergarten, and child-care services, along with elementary school classes. The center also offers family literacy programs.

More to explore: *Blackdom Townsite, Clovis, Old Armijo School, State History of Education Museum*

LLANO ESTACADO: Series of Five Historic Markers
(Various Locations around Southeastern New Mexico)

General Introduction

"I traveled . . . until I reached some plains," wrote Spanish explorer Francisco Vásquez de Coronado about his journey through eastern New Mexico in 1541, "with no more landmarks than as if we had been swallowed by the sea."

This devouring sea is known today as the Llano Estacado. One translation of the name is "Stockaded Plains," a term derived, perhaps, from the fact that the steep caprock cliffs that define its northern and western edges are said to resemble fortress walls. Another translation is "Staked Plains." The "stakes" may have been posts driven into the ground by Spanish explorers for use as tethers for their horses or, perhaps, as guideposts to track the course of their journey. But a third and perhaps more likely explanation suggests that the correct name should actually be Llano Estacando, or "Ponded Plains"—those ponds being the many playas that lie scattered across the plains. These playas, or small pools of water, can fill with rainwater after a storm.

This broad, level plain covers some 32,000 square miles in southeastern New Mexico and western Texas. In New Mexico, the Llano Estacado runs roughly from Tucumcari to the Mescalero Escarpment, also known as the Caprock, near Hobbs—a region encompassing parts of Quay, Curry, Roosevelt, Lea, and Chaves Counties. About one-third of the Llano Estacado appears in New Mexico; the rest belongs to Texas.

Because of the size of the Llano Estacado and its prominence in defining the landscape of southeastern New Mexico, five separate markers have been placed in various locations in eastern New Mexico to help travelers appreciate it. Three of those share similar text and so have been grouped here under one entry.

More to explore (Llano Estacado Series): *Oil and Gas, View of the Rockies, Waldrop Park*

247. Llano Estacado

Location: Guadalupe County. East of Santa Rosa, in a highway rest area on the south side of Interstate 40, between mile markers 301 and 302. See map 3.

Marker text: Rising above these red-earth lowlands to the south is the Llano Estacado or Staked Plains, a high plateau covering some 32,000 square miles in eastern New Mexico and adjacent areas in Texas. Topographically, it is one of the flattest areas in the United States and rises to 450 feet above the surrounding Great Plains.

Note: See the general introduction to this series of Markers, as well as the other Markers making up the series, for further background on the Llano Estacado.

248. Llano Estacado

Location: Quay County. South of Tucumcari, in a pullout on the east side of NM 209, between mile markers 82 and 83. See map 3.

Marker text: Sediments shed from the rising mountains to the west formed the Llano Estacado, later to be bypassed by streams such as the Pecos and Canadian River and left standing in bold relief with a relatively level, uneroded caprock surface. Croplands on the plains are irrigated by "fossil" water pumped from underground aquifers.

Note: This Marker has a location specific reference to the "rising mountains to the west." Those include the Rocky Mountains.

Note: See the general introduction to this series of Markers, as well as the other Markers making up the series, for further background on the Llano Estacado.

249. Llano Estacado

Location: Quay County. In San Jon, in San Jon Park, at the intersection of NM 469 and Main Street. See map 3.

Marker text: Rising above these red-earth lowlands to the south is the Llano Estacado or Staked Plains, a high plateau covering some 32,000 square miles in eastern New Mexico and adjacent areas in Texas. Topographically, it is one of the flattest areas in the United States and rises to 450 feet above the surrounding Great Plains.

Sediments shed from the rising mountains to the west formed the Llano Estacado, later to be bypassed by streams such as the Pecos and Canadian River and left standing in bold relief with a relatively level, uneroded caprock surface. Croplands on the plains are irrigated by "fossil" water pumped from underground aquifers.

Note: This Marker has a location-specific reference to the "rising mountains to the west." Those include the Rocky Mountains.

Note: See the general introduction to this series of Markers, as well as the other Markers making up the series, for further background on the Llano Estacado.

Forming the southernmost reach of the High Plains region of the Great Plains, the grassy plateau known as the Llano Estacado stretches across thirty-two thousand square miles of eastern New Mexico and western portions of the Texas Panhandle. Its northern limits in the state lie near Tucumcari and the Canadian River, from which point it extends south to encompass portions of Quay, Curry, Roosevelt, Chaves, and Lea Counties.

The Llano Estacado began to form as Pleistocene epoch streams carried huge quantities of sediment and debris from the uplifting Rocky Mountains eastward into the interior of the country, where it accumulated into thick rock layers. For millions of years, rivers like the Pecos and the Canadian downcut these deposits, but bypassed areas of the plains where harder rock prevented their migration. Left in isolation between was the broad, upraised plateau known as the High Plains. The southern extension of the High Plains, south of the Canadian River, is the region known as the Llano Estacado. It is one of the flattest areas of the country.

Farmers and ranchers on the Llano Estacado today pull water from deep within the earth. The water is trapped in porous sandstone layers of the large body of Miocene and Pliocene epoch rock debris known as the Ogallala Formation. This "fossil water" aquifer is known as the Ogallala Aquifer.

250. Llano Estacado

Location: De Baca County. On US 60, approximately twenty-five miles east of Fort Sumner, in a pullout on the north side of the highway. See map 6.

Marker text: Nomadic Indians and countless buffalo herds dominated this vast plain when the Vasquez de Coronado expedition explored it in 1541. Later it was the focus of Comanchero activity, and in the 19th century it became a center for cattle ranching. The name Llano Estacado, or stockaded plains, refers to the fortress-like appearance of its escarpments.

Note: See the general introduction to this series of Markers, as well as the other Markers making up the series, for further background on the Llano Estacado.

Across the vast reaches of the Llano Estacado roam black-tailed prairie dogs, badgers, striped skunks, bobcats, coyotes, foxes, and other grassland denizens. When Spanish conquistador Francisco Vásquez de Coronado traversed the Llano Estacado in his fruitless search for gold more than four hundred years ago, this endless plain was also the territory of numerous herds of wooly-haired buffalo. In May 1541, Coronado's chronicler did his best to describe the mysterious creatures:

They have very long beards, like goats, and when they are running they throw their heads back with the beard dragging on the ground. . . . They have a great hump, larger than a camel's. . . . They have a short tail, with a bunch of hair at the end. When they run, they carry it erect like a scorpion.

Apache Indians once roved these grasslands until displaced by Comanche raids in the early 1700s. In the eighteenth century, Comanches engaged in trade with New Mexicans who roamed the prairies. Because Comanches allowed them peaceably into their camps, these capitalists of the plains became known as *comancheros*. Many traded illegally in gunpowder, stolen livestock, and sometimes even captive women and children.

251. Llano Estacado and Oil

Location: 1. Lea County. East of Eunice, in a small pullout near the intersection of NM 18 and NM 234. See map 6.
2. Lea County. West of Hobbs, on the north side of US 62/180, between mile markers 101 and 102. See map 6.

Marker text: Llano Estacado, Stockaded Plain, is southern part of High Plains section, a high plateau of 32000 square miles in eastern New Mexico and western Texas. Crops are irrigated by "fossil" water pumped from underground sandstones. Deeper are prolific oil and gas pools, the liquid black gold of southeastern New Mexico.

Note: See the general introduction to this series of Markers, as well as the other Markers making up the series, for further background on the Llano Estacado.

One translation of Llano Estacado is "Staked Plains," which is perhaps a reference to stakes early explorers might have driven into the ground as pathfinding tools.

Today, modern stakes mark the course of human history over these grassy plains: windmills and pump jacks. Windmills pull water for livestock and irrigation from aquifers deep beneath the earth's surface. The water lies in the porous sandstone layers of the Ogallala Formation, a large body of sediments eroded from mountains to the west during the Miocene and Pliocene epochs, one million to twenty-five million years ago. Pump jacks, too, crosshatch the land. These "rockers" lift oil from rich reserves trapped in rock below the surface. The larger part of these reserves lies within the Permian Basin, an extensive region of oil underlying much of the western prairies of Texas and southeastern New Mexico. Reserves of the Permian Basin came from the organic remains of plant and animal life that collected on the floor of an ancient sea. Pressure compacted the debris, slowly converting it into oil and petroleum—a product sometimes called the "black gold" of southeastern New Mexico.

252. Lordsburg

Location: 1. Hidalgo County. At the north end of Lordsburg, in a pullout on the west side of US 70, between mile markers 27 and 28. See map 5.

2. Hidalgo County. At the west end of Lordsburg, in a pullout on the south side of Motel Boulevard, about a quarter mile east of the Interstate 10 interchange. See map 5.

3. Hidalgo County. Just west of Lordsburg, in the New Mexico Tourist Information Center, exit 20A off Interstate 10 (reachable from Lordsburg by driving on West Motel Boulevard over the interstate). See map 5.

Marker text: Lordsburg was founded in 1880 on the route of the Southern Pacific Railroad, near that used by the Butterfield Overland Mail Co., 1858–1861. The town was named for Delbert Lord, an engineer with the railroad. In 1927, Charles Lindbergh landed his famed Spirit of St. Louis on Lordsburg. For years, the town catered to motorists traveling the Old Spanish Trail highway and later U.S. 80.

253. Lordsburg-Hidalgo Library

Location: Hidalgo County. At the west end of Lordsburg, in a pullout on the south side of Motel Boulevard, about a quarter mile east of the Interstate 10 interchange. See map 5.

Marker text: The Lordsburg-Hidalgo Library was founded in 1928 under the leadership of Bethel Ernon Fuller (1888–1976). Mrs. Fuller, president of the Library Board of Trustees from 1928–1969, raised funds to build the WPA Pueblo Revival style building, which was completed in 1937. The historic building continues to serve as a center for learning and library services. It is listed on both the State and National Registers.

Note: The Lordsburg-Hidalgo Library is at the corner of Third and Pyramid Streets in Lordsburg.

Natural springs along the Pyramid Valley made this area an important stopping point for travelers heading west in nineteenth century, as it had been for Apaches years before Spanish and Anglo settlers arrived. The Butterfield Overland Stage Company came through southwestern New Mexico in 1858, establishing an alternative stage stop at Shakespeare, then known as Mexican Springs, just south of present-day Lordsburg. Later, as crews with the Southern Pacific Railroad laid track from California to Texas in the fall of 1880, a small tent camp grew here. Settlers opened a post office the following year, and the town acquired a name: Lordsburg. Probably the name recognized Delbert Lord, an engineer for the railroad.

As Lordsburg grew into a supply center for agriculture and mining operations in the region, it siphoned settlers from Shakespeare. Today, the empty dirt streets of Shakespeare testify to the important economic impact railroads had on a developing nineteenth-century New Mexico.

Not only stagecoaches and railroads carried people into Lordsburg. Because it had one of the first airports in the state, opened in the 1920s, Lordsburg became a destination for one of the most famous aviation pioneers in the country. On September 24, 1927, Lordsburg Landing Field hosted Charles Lindbergh and his famed *Spirit of St. Louis*, the Ryan NYP monoplane in which Lindbergh had earlier that year successfully completed the first solo transatlantic flight, between New York and Paris. Both plane and aviator had come to Lordsburg courtesy of the Daniel Guggenheim Foundation for the Promotion of Aviation, which, to further the cause implicit in the name of the organization, sponsored Lindbergh's tour through each of the then forty-eight states.

Lordsburg lay along an early automobile route known as the Old Spanish Trail Highway, a name chosen to highlight some of the Spanish mission pueblos along its length and intended to encourage tourism. In use by 1920, the route carried motorists from Saint Augustine, Florida, to San Diego, California, over three thousand miles of motorway. A portion of the Old Spanish Trail ran through the southern reaches of New Mexico, from south of Anthony to Las Cruces (a stretch now covered by NM 478), then to Deming, then to Lordsburg (a stretch now covered by NM 418), south to Rodeo (a stretch now covered by NM 80), and into Arizona. Later, sections of the route across the country were replaced by US 80 and US 90, and the arrival of the interstates in the 1950s pushed the trail into the history books.

Wanting to ensure that the citizens of Hidalgo County remained well read, members of the Lordsburg Women's Club in the early 1920s began to raise money and solicit book donations for a local library. Leading the charge was Mrs. Bethel Vernon Fuller, president of the Women's Club. Fuller had come to Lordsburg from Alamogordo in 1912, age twenty-four. When she wasn't busy with civic projects, Fuller worked as a silent film pianist at the local movie theater.

For many years, various buildings around town served the function of a library, but in 1935, largely thanks to the efforts of Fuller and the Women's Club, the city of Lordsburg contributed funds toward a Works Progress Administration project to construct a permanent library building. Modeled after the library in nearby Deming, the Lordsburg-Hidalgo Library featured design elements typical of the pueblo revival style, including adobe walls, a flat roof, and vigas (supporting roof beams made of wood). Mrs. Fuller served as the emcee at the library dedication on August 14, 1937, an occasion described as a "most brilliant event" by the *Lordsburg Liberal*, which also noted that the opening of the library was "an important epic in the history of our city and county."

As its name implies, the Lordsburg-Hidalgo Library serves and is supported by both the city of Lordsburg and the surrounding county of Hidalgo, of which Lordsburg is the county seat. Noting that the library "remains the focal point for reading and education of citizens throughout the region," the National Park Service added the library to the National Register of Historic Places in 2004.

After serving on the Lordsburg Library Board of Trustees for an incredible forty-one years, Mrs. Fuller moved to California, where she passed away in 1976.

More to explore: *Butterfield Trail, Camp Lordsburg, Doña Dolores "Lola" Chávez de Armijo, Shakespeare*

254. Los Padillas

Location: Bernalillo County. In Los Padillas, in a parking lot next to the Los Padillas Community Center and Elementary School, on Los Padillas road, near the intersection of Los Padillas Road and NM 14 (Isleta Boulevard). See map 4.

Marker text: Los Padillas is an extended family settlement which was resettled in 1718 by Diego de Padilla. His grandparents had lived on the site prior to the 1680 Pueblo Revolt at which time they were forced to abandon it. In the 1790 census the town, referred to as San Andres de los Padillas, had a population of 168. This is the site of the old Los Padillas School, originally built in 1901 and replaced in 1912.

After Governor Francisco Cuervo y Valdés in 1706 founded the Villa de Alburquerque, complete with second *r*, many extended family farming communities likewise took hold in the middle Rio Grande Valley. Their names recalled the surnames of their predominant founders: Los Armijos, Los Sanchez, Los Lunas, Los Barelas. A few survive today; others have been engulfed by greater Albuquerque.

In an area just north of Isleta Pueblo in 1718, Diego de Padilla established his own such community, Los Padillas. Situated in the fertile green fields west of the Rio Grande, where water was plentiful, Los Padillas by 1790 was home to 168 people.

Diego Padilla was not the first in his family to settle in this valley. During the seventeenth century, his grandparents and other early Spanish colonists had established smaller estancias, or ranch homes, in the same region. Like their descendents years later, these early settlers had been drawn to the Rio Grande Valley for its rich, irrigable farming lands. They were forced to abandon their homes and fields, however, when the Pueblo Revolt of 1680 drove the Spanish from the state for twelve years.

In 1912, the newly elected superintendent of county schools for Bernalillo County, Atanacio Montoya, oversaw the renovation of the public school in Los Padillas—both in form and in function. Montoya was a progressive educator and introduced many improvements to rural schools in New Mexico, including well-lighted and well-ventilated classrooms and a cadre of trained educators to teach in them. Under Montoya's guidance, workers expanded the one-room building, which had served originally as a boarding school for orphans, into a six-room public schoolhouse. Montoya went on to become the state superintendent of public instruction for New Mexico. Los Padillas School is a surviving symbol of Montoya's dedication to the education of the youth of New Mexico after statehood.

More to explore: *Albuquerque, Old Armijo School, State History of Education Museum*

Los Portales: *see Portales*

255. Louise Massey Mabie (1902–1983)
The Original Rhinestone Cowgirl

Location: Chaves County. Twelve miles east of Roswell, in a pullout on the north side of US 380, at the intersection of US 380 and NM 409, the entrance to Bottomless Lakes State Park. See map 6.

Marker text: One of the first female radio stars in the 1930s, Louise's career spanned from 1918–1950. Her recordings in English and Spanish sold millions of copies. Heading the Roswell-based group, Louise Massey and the Westerners, she became known for spectacular costumes and a ladylike demeanor, garnering the title "the Original Rhinestone Cowgirl." She was inducted into the Cowgirl Hall of Fame in 1982.

With her husband, father, and two brothers playing guitars, accordion, violin, banjo, piano, and bass fiddle and sometimes offering backing vocals, country-western singer Louise Massey Mabie offered a crisp but velvety lead vocal. Those who had the pleasure of seeing Louise Massey and the Westerners in person or on TV had a visual delight to match the auditory: the men in full cowboy regalia, including chaps and hats, and Massey's spectacular costumes, calm demeanor, and ladylike presence. Massey's outfits and professional presence later earned her the nickname "the Original Rhinestone Cowgirl."

Victoria Louise Massey was born in Midland, Texas, on August 10, 1902, but moved with her family to a ranch near Roswell as a child. Her rancher father, Henry, played the fiddle and taught Louise and her seven siblings to read and play music. In 1918, Massey and three of the closest men in her life—her father and her brothers Allen and Curt—formed a family band. The next year, she married Milt Mabie in Roswell, and he joined the Roswell-based group as well. Massey wrote a number of the group's songs herself, in a style that might today be called "good old-fashioned country." Originally, the group called themselves by the straightforward name "The Massey Family." But that didn't stick, and worse, it didn't highlight their main attraction—their lead singer. So they changed their name to "Louise Massey and the Westerners."

In 1928, their success at a tent chautauqua—a traveling talent show—launched them to stardom. The group toured and performed on several radio programs and in 1930 signed a contract with CBS Radio. In 1933, they became part of the regular talent at the station WLS in Chicago. By that time, Massey's father had left the band, and musician Larry Wellington had replaced him. A brochure produced by the station in 1935 shows a photograph of the group, with a smiling Louise seated at a piano surrounded by the Westerners and their instruments. The caption promised: "If you knew them personally, you would love them just as much as from hearing them on the air."

Other radio and TV appearances followed, along with recording contracts. Louise even appeared in the 1938 Tex Ritter Western, *Where the Buffalo Roam*, playing a resident of Santa Fe named, coincidentally, Louise Massey. The group performs in a dance scene in the movie.

Louise Massey and the Westerners recorded songs in both English and Spanish, selling millions of records. In 1941, they wrote what was probably their most famous song, "My Adobe Hacienda." The song climbed *Billboard*'s Hillbilly and Pop charts, showing the broad appeal for their music. In beautiful lilting style, the song describes a typical evening at Mabie's house in the Hondo Valley and the comfort she felt there as evening fell:

In my adobe hacienda
nestled in the western hills
Evening breezes softly murmur
harmonize with whippoorwills
When setting sun
says the long day is done

Sweet music starts to fill the air
In my adobe hacienda
harmony is everywhere

The group disbanded by choice in 1947, after thirty years of performing together. Massey and her husband settled on their ranch near Roswell. In recognition of her lifetime achievements, she was inducted into the Cowgirl Hall of Fame in 1982. She passed away the next year.

More to explore: Lea County Cowgirls

Anyone near a working radio in the 1930s was probably treated to the smooth crooning of country-western singer Louise Massey Mabie. Known as "the Original Rhinestone Cowgirl," Mabie delighted audiences for more than thirty years. Louise Massey Mabie. National Cowgirl Museum and Hall of Fame, Fort Worth, Texas.

Louis S. Page and Joe O. Page Highway: *see Santa Rosa Lake State Park*

Loving's Bend: *see Goodnight-Loving Trail*

256. Lovington

Location: 1. Lea County. At the south end of Lovington, in a pullout on the east side of NM 18. See map 6.

2. Lea County. At the north end of Lovington, in front of the Nor-Lea Medical Center, in a pullout on the west side of NM 18. See map 6.

Marker text: Lovington is named after Robert Florence Love, who founded the town on his homestead in 1908. It was a farming and ranching community until the discovery of the Denton pool after World War II turned it into an oil town. It is the county seat of Lea County.

Wanting his share of the plains, Texan Robert Florence Love arrived in southeastern New Mexico in 1900 to grab a patch of homestead. Eight years later, Love's brother, James, joined him and opened the Jim B. Love Grocery Store. The Love brothers established a small settlement and proposed that the post office be named Loving. By coincidence, another community bearing that name already existed in New Mexico, about a hundred miles southwest of the

Loving brothers' homestead. That community had been named for prominent cattle rancher Oliver Loving, who, with his partner Charles Goodnight, had blazed the Goodnight-Loving cattle trail through the Pecos Valley in 1866. Undaunted, the Love brothers simply added *-ton* to their choice, and Lovington—the city of brotherly love, so to speak—was born.

Florence Love later proposed a bill to the New Mexico legislature to form a new county around his community, carved from land currently in Chaves and Eddy Counties. He asked that the county be named Heard, for a local rancher friend, Allen C. Heard. In March 1917, the legislature obliged, but named the county Lea instead, to acknowledge prominent Roswell land promoter Captain Joseph Calloway Lea. Love did not suffer a complete defeat, however: his community, Lovington, won a fight with Hobbs to become the county seat.

In April 1924, the Flynn, Welch, and Yates State no. 3 well, drilled east of Lovington near Maljamar, became the first commercially successful oil well in the state. Other wells soon uncovered additional pockets of oil underlying Lovington and the surrounding plains. An article published in the June 1930 edition of the *Lovington Leader* showed the impact oil was having on community spirit:

The better class of oil men are seeking a place where their families can find a home with all the things that make a home pleasant. They want their families with them in a town where their children may have the very best educational advantages, and to such Lovington has a direct appeal. Here they can find an ideal place for their families to live, away from the usual things that make a shack oil town so repulsive to the average oil man and his family.

September 1949 brought the real boom, which arrived in the form of the Denton Pool, a large underground reservoir of oil discovered about nine miles northeast of Lovington. A 1953 estimate by Lovington city attorney Bob Ward noted an average of 120 wells drilled in Lea County in just two years, making it home to what Ward calculated to be one-twentieth of all the wells drilled in the nation at that time. Lovington had become an oil town.

More to explore: *Flynn-Welch-Yates Oil Well (see under Artesia), Hobbs, Llano Estacado and Oil (see under Llano Estacado [series]), Loving's Bend (see under Goodnight-Loving Trail [series])*

257. Lozen, Little Sister
"A Shield to Her People" (ca. 1840–1889)

Location: Otero County. On the Mescalero Apache Reservation, in a pullout on the west side of US 70, at mile marker 256. See map 6.

Marker text: Lozen, a warrior and sister of the famous Warm Springs Apache chief Victorio, fought alongside her brother until his death in 1880 and later with his successors, Nana and Geronimo. Lozen also was a medicine woman and healer and, it was said, with outstretched hands she could determine the location of an enemy. She died a prisoner at Mt. Vernon barracks in Alabama.

She was a warrior, a healer, a medicine woman—and a little sister.

Her name was Lozen. Born somewhere along the US-Mexico border in the southwestern United States around the year 1840, Lozen grew up in the company of her brother, the famous Warm Springs Apache chief Victorio. Her lifetime coincided with the mid-nineteenth-century series of conflicts known as the Apache Wars. These engagements occurred between troops of the US Army and Victorio and other Apache warriors in the Southwest, who refused to settle on reservations and instead defended their homeland from the intrusions of Anglo and Mexican settlers.

What little is known about Lozen comes mainly through the recollections of Warm Springs Apache James Kaywaykla, as captured by historian Eve Ball in her book *In the Days of Victorio*. According to Kaywaykla, who rode with Victorio and his band, Lozen had many suitors but chose to remain unmarried, preferring to ride by her brother's side, fighting alongside the male warriors of the tribe. At one point, as the Apaches were fleeing the San Carlos Reservation in Arizona with US Army troops in pursuit, Lozen helped lead a group of frightened women and children across the Rio Grande by bravely riding before them through the river currents on a horse, a rifle held high over her head.

"Lozen is as my right hand," Victorio reportedly stated. "Strong as a man, braver than most, and cunning in strategy, Lozen is a shield to her people."

Besides being a skilled and brave warrior, Lozen was also a medicine woman and a healer. Kaywaykla recounts a story Victorio told of her skill in dressing a bullet wound the chief had received in his shoulder, using the thorn from a prickly-pear cactus to bind the wound and nursing the chief back to health in just one night.

Lozen was said to possess one other extraordinary gift as well: the ability to locate the whereabouts of an enemy. As a douser seeks out water, Lozen would, with outstretched arms, recite a prayer as she scanned the surrounding country until she felt she had identified the direction in which the enemy could be found.

Lozen was not part of the conflict with Mexican soldiers that led to her brother's death in Mexico in 1880—possibly she was elsewhere (one story has her escorting a mother and child from Mexico to the Mescalero Apache Reservation in New Mexico). Afterward, Lozen continued to ride with Victorio's successors, Nana and Geronimo, until 1886, when Geronimo surrendered to army troops in Arizona. With other Apaches, Lozen was taken as a ward of the state and sent first to Fort Marion in Saint Augustine, Florida, then later to Mount Vernon Barracks in Mobile, Alabama.

Lozen would not see her homeland in the Southwest again. Infectious disease spread rapidly among the Indians held at Mount Vernon Barracks. Very likely, it was tuberculosis that caused Lozen's death—although history did not pause to capture the exact date. She passed away sometime around 1889.

More to explore: *Eve Ball, Silver City*

258. Magdalena

Location: Socorro County. On the west end of Magdalena, in a pullout on the south side of US 60, near the intersection of NM 169 and US 60. See map 5.

Marker text: Named for Magdalena Peak, Magdalena is located in a mineral-rich area which became a center for silver and zinc mining in the 1860s. In 1884, a railroad spur was built from the smelter in Socorro, and Magdalena became an important railhead for cattle, sheep, and ore. In protohistoric times the Navajo and Apache people moved into the area. The Alamo Navajo Reservation, a noncontiguous section of the much larger Navajo Nation, is nearby.

A providential combination of rocks and bushes on a northern slope of what is now the Magdalena Mountains has shaped a profile many believe to resemble popular depictions of Mary Magdalene. When miners from the nearby lead- and silver-mining camp of Kelly at the foothills of the mountain established an ancillary community a mile or so farther north around 1866, they recognized the woman overlooking their activities in the name of their settlement: Magdalena Mines.

Kelly and Magdalena Mines prospered as the mountains relinquished their stores of silver, lead, and zinc. In the early 1880s, entrepreneur Gustav Billing purchased the Kelly Mine and processed his ores in a smelter he had opened in Socorro. Because of the exertion required to haul the ore by mule train thirty miles to the smelter, Billing convinced the Atchison, Topeka, and Santa Fe Railway to build a branch line from Socorro to Magdalena Mines. By the time those rails arrived in January 1885, the community had already shortened its name to Magdalena.

Permanent buildings rose, including three stores, two livery stables (one billing itself "Hotel de Horse"), blacksmith shops, a church, and a schoolhouse. The town had an estimated peak population of two thousand residents. A Works Progress Administration writer describing early Magdalena showed tongue-in-cheek wit:

Magdalena became a town of prosperity and was run "wide-open" as a western frontier town, with the element of cowman and miner predominating. Money flowed freely; law and order were administered in accordance with whatever local procedure was considered most expedient; saloons flourished and many ladies of easy virtue were attracted to the village. Some justices of the peace attempted to sentence men to the state penitentiary, and it is known that others granted divorce decrees.

The railhead helped Magdalena develop a dual character as both mining camp and livestock shipping point. The US Department of the Interior in 1916 officially restricted some 71,000 acres of land in west central New Mexico from homesteading and opened it for use as a thoroughfare over which ranchers on the Plains of San Agustín and western Arizona could drive cattle and sheep to the Magdalena railhead. This was the founding of the Magdalena Stock Driveway, or, in the vernacular, the "Hoof Highway." The route of the Stock Driveway is largely the same as that followed by US 60 today. Large herds of livestock lumbered over the highway into town "as into a funnel," the WPA writer noted, from which point dusty cowboys stockaded them, loaded them into trains, and shipped them to market. According to the National Park Service, Magdalena was second only to Chicago in the number of livestock shipped by rail.

Today it is mostly motorists who shuffle along US 60. The cattle-town heyday of Magdalena declined as ranchers turned to more efficient shipping methods, and mining petered out after the 1940s. With the line no longer profitable, the Santa Fe Railway closed the spur to Magdalena in 1971.

Apart from its mining and cattle-moving history, the Magdalena region is also characterized by its long presence of Native people. In protohistoric times—the period of time before a recorded history emerges within a culture—the Navajo and Apache people were prominent in this region of New Mexico. Today, about two thousand members of the Alamo Band of the Navajo Nation live on the Alamo Navajo Indian Reservation north of Magdalena in northwest Socorro County. The reservation is a noncontiguous section of the Navajo Nation in the Four Corners region, about a third of which is in northwestern New Mexico. The reservation has an independent school system, with a board that runs a number of community services, including a roads department and a wellness center. The local radio station broadcasts as KABR: K–Alamo Band Radio.

More to explore: *Kelly, Magdalena Fault, New Mexico Tech, Riley, Socorro*

259. Magdalena Fault

Location: 1. Socorro County. East of Magdalena, in a pullout on the west side of US 60, at Water Canyon Turnoff, between mile markers 123 and 124. See map 5.

2. Socorro County. At the east end of Magdalena, in a pullout on the north side of US 60, between mile markers 113 and 114. See map 5.

Marker text: The Magdalena Mountains to the west are topped by South Baldy at 10,783 feet; Magdalena Peak at 8,152 feet. La Jencia plain to the east is bisected by Water Canyon three miles below this marker. The bench along the edge of the mountains is the Magdalena fault, dividing the uplifted mountains from the plains below.

With its counterpart to the east, the Socorro Canyon Fault, the Magdalena Fault has appreciably impacted the geography of this part of central New Mexico. More commonly known as La Jencia Fault, the fault tends roughly north-south, dips to the east, and stretches about twenty-two miles long. Geologists know La Jencia as a range-bounding fault, because the mountain block that forms the Magdalena Mountains has eroded back from the fault itself. The crust of the earth is extending across the fault, pushing up the mountains.

The down-dropped area east of the fault forms the La Jencia Plain. This displacement of earth along the fault accounts for the fact that rocks in Water Canyon west of the fault are found three miles underneath the surface of La Jencia Plain.

The Magdalena Mountains take their name from the profile of a woman's face formed by shrubbery and rocks on the northern slope of Magdalena Peak. Believing the visage to be that of Mary Magdalene, early settlers named the mountain La Sierra de María Magdalena, or "the Mountain of Mary Magdalene." The highest peak in the north-south-tending range is South Baldy, rising to a height of 10,783 feet. Its associate, North Baldy, is 9,858 feet.

More to explore: *Magdalena, Rio Grande Rift, Strike Valleys*

260. Magnolia Ellis
"Magnificent Magnolia" (1893–1974)

Location: Sierra County. In Truth or Consequences, in a small triangular island at the intersection of Main Street and Broadway, between East Riverside Drive and South Riverside Drive, across from the fire station. See map 5.

Marker text: Magnolia Ellis was a healer with a special gift. She opened a clinic in Hot Springs, today's Truth or Consequences. Patients claimed to have a feeling of electricity when she touched them. Recognized by most notable doctors of the day, she put Hot Springs on the map, and was known as "Magnificent Magnolia."

Sometimes patients would arrive as early as five in the morning to receive the healing care offered by "Magnificent" Magnolia Ellis; she would open her clinic early to treat them. Magnolia Ellis. Property of Wendy Waters. Used with permission.

On the south side of the intersection of Broadway and Jones Street in downtown Truth or Consequences stands a two-story building with a sign atop the roof reading "Magnolia Ellis." This was the former clinic and home of one of the most fascinating people in the history of this city—a woman who, some claim, possessed a remarkable ability to heal people. She did so by moving her hands over a patient's body as though pushing out something bad within, a process that some said created a "tingling" sensation on their skin. For the devoted care she offered to those who sought her out, Magnolia Ellis earned her nickname: Magnificent Magnolia.

Born prematurely in Hill County, Texas, and not expected to survive, Magnolia Ellis showed a tough side early. Her parents kept her warm by placing her tiny body inside a wooden box lined with cotton and resting it (no doubt with great care) on the bun warmer of a wood-burning stove. Ellis gained strength through tender nursing and, probably, her own special will. Later, after divorcing her first husband and raising her daughter on her own, Ellis enrolled for a time in college, where she studied home economics. She moved to New Mexico from Texas in 1938 and settled here, in Truth or Consequences—a community that at the time went by the name Hot Springs. That name came from the many geothermal hot springs underneath the town, springs long sought after for their restorative powers. Hot Springs was—and still is—a place of healing comfort for many. It was inevitable, then, that Ellis would find here a community that not only accepted her but was appreciative of what she (and many others) believed she offered: the ability to heal.

That ability was said to be the result of what some have called a "magnetic imbalance" in Ellis's body. (Ellis asked her patients to remove their wristwatches before treatment because watches often stopped working when she was near.) Ellis's daughter Mavis, in a booklet she wrote about her mother, described the daily scene inside her clinic in downtown Hot Springs:

The waiting room will seat about 75 people and there's always a full house. At times there is not even standing room inside, and some wait in their cars and sit on benches which are out in front of her office. There are no appointments made, as she has several hundred people visit her each day. People draw numbers as they come in which number 1–100. Magnolia sees each one when his number is called. People who are on crutches, in wheel chairs, or those who are in great deal of pain are taken in at once and are not asked to draw number. There are six booths with tables in them. When one's number is called he is shown to a booth and lies down on a table. Magnolia moves quietly from one booth to the next and passes her hands over the person's body. The treatment she gives is very short, she uses no mechanical devices of any kind, only her hands.

Magnolia Ellis—described in a 1956 newspaper article as a "tall, impressive woman"—was a study in contrasts. To the people who knew and worked with her, she was outspoken, graceful, sometimes quick to anger, with a taste for chocolate and coffee. Ellis was politically active, charismatic, even somewhat domineering. A friend embroidered some of her common sayings onto a blouse for her, quotations that reveal a woman comfortable speaking her mind: "There is nothing wrong with your big toe." "You eat too much." "I may run for president." At the same time, Ellis was humble about her "gift." She never named her powers and rarely spoke of them, even to her own family, fearing that by speaking of her powers, she might lose them. She was known in town for her generosity of spirit and community service. She only accepted pay from those patients who could afford it. And when tragedy befell a family, it was said that that family might find themselves the beneficiary of a large, anonymous monetary donation—suspected to have come from Ellis herself. She had risen to become a woman of recognition and, indeed, some financial means. Often alone in the clinic at night, she slept with a gun under her pillow.

As to her place in the larger medical community, which generally tends not to support the type of healing she practiced, at least not when performed exclusive of more traditional medical treatment, Ellis seemed nonetheless to find compatibility there. Her daughter wrote: "She is quite honest in her opinion and while she is in the booth, if she feels she can be of no help to them, she says so immediately. If she believes a person requires medical attention or surgery she refers them to a medical doctor at once." Ellis likely benefited from being in a state with a long history of healers and healing practices and a tradition of cultural support for them, and in a town that developed in part around the therapeutic properties of its abundant geothermal springs. She even partnered with some of the mineral springs bathhouses in town and sent patients to them.

Ellis herself seems to offer her own personal thoughts on the subject through one of the quotations embroidered on her blouse: "I cure the doctors, too."

"Magnificent" Magnolia Ellis passed away in Kansas in 1974.

A view inside the upstairs portion of the Magnolia Ellis clinic can be seen in the 1995 film *Mad Love*, directed by Antonia Bird. The room rented by the young couple (played by Drew Barrymore and Chris O'Donnell) toward the end of the movie is the apartment above the clinic where Ellis shared her gift with many grateful patients.

More to explore: *Curanderas—Women Who Heal, Hermits Peak, Truth or Consequences*

261. Malpais
Valley of Fires

Location: Lincoln County. West of Carrizozo, in a pullout on the north side of US 380, at mile marker 64. See map 6.

Marker text: Spanish explorers called this extensive lava flow malpais, or badlands. The river of lava that flowed down this "Valley of Fires" erupted from a volcano some 7 miles north of here about 1000 years ago. Extending through the valley for 44 miles, the malpais averages 3 miles in width. This ropy type of lava is called "pahoehoe."

Note: Recent evidence suggests that the lava flows were produced five thousand years ago, not one thousand years ago as the Marker notes.

Seen from above, the forty-four-mile run of lava that makes up the Valley of Fires Recreation Area looks like ink spilled across the Tularosa Basin. In fact, that ink is a solidified river of lava expelled in two eruptions from a small cinder cone volcano, called Little Black Peak, at the north end of the valley, as well as from other lava vents. These were not the giant, spewing eruptions often associated with volcanoes, but rather a more prolonged discharging of molten rock. The eruptions occurred very recently, geologically speaking—only about five thousand years ago—and may have continued for thirty years.

Geologists know the dark, wrinkled lava found in the flows as pahoehoe (pronounced *pa-hoy-hoy*). If the name sounds Hawaiian, that's because it is. The same type of lava flow is common among volcanoes in Hawaii. The rope-like folds form when hot lava flows beneath cooler lava, bending the cooler lava above into creases and wrinkles.

As with other such lava flows in the state, this rough stretch of land became known as malpais, or badlands. Although the flows are too gnarled to traverse on anything but foot, their "badness" has not deterred wildlife and plants from living among them. Cactus, mesquite, and creosote are here, and mule deer, quail, lizards, and many other animals all make the lava flow their home.

The flows, which stretch an average of three miles in width, are today part of the Valley of Fires Recreation Area and administered by the US Bureau of Land Management. The flows are open for public exploration, and the Valley of Fires offers camping sites, RV hookups, nature trails, and a Visitors Center.

More to explore: *Capulin Volcano National Monument, Carrizozo, City of Rocks State Park, Grants, Three Rivers*

262. Manuelito Area

Location: McKinley County. West of Gallup, in rest stop along Interstate 40 just before crossing the border into Arizona, on the south side of the highway. See map 1.

Marker text: This area contained many Indian pueblos dating from around A.D. 500 to 1325, when it was abandoned. Navajos settled here by 1800. This was the home of Manuelito, one of the last of the chiefs to surrender for confinement at the Bosque Redondo Reservation near Fort Sumner. The Navajos returned here in 1868.

Archaeological sites in the area surrounding Gallup preserve the ruins of pueblo villages constructed by the Ancestral Puebloan people, ancestors of the Pueblo Indians in New Mexico, who predate European occupation by many centuries. The Ancestral Puebloans lived in the Four Corners region from about AD 500 and remained there until migrating from the area after 1300. According to the National Park Service, one of the largest of the pueblos they built in the region contained some 1,500 rooms stacked at least three levels high. Archaeologists know these and other related ruins as the Manuelito Complex. The name comes from one of the most stalwart and highly regarded of Navajo leaders, Manuelito.

Manuelito was born around 1818 near Bears Ears, Utah. In 1855, he became headman of his Navajo clan. But outbreaks of violence in the 1800s between Anglo and Spanish-speaking settlers on the one hand and the Navajos of northwestern New Mexico on the other, especially as settlers and miners moved into territories previously occupied or regarded as sacred by the Indians, would alter his life significantly. Manuelito and his followers were the targets of a raid in 1859 by soldiers from Fort Defiance, near the present border between Arizona and northwestern New Mexico. The following year, Manuelito retaliated with a siege on the fort that left one American soldier dead and many others wounded.

In 1862, the US government established the Bosque Redondo Reservation in southeastern New Mexico in a misguided attempt to resettle the Navajos away from their ancestral homelands. Colonel "Kit" Carson burned Navajo villages and

A respected Navajo leader, Manuelito's war name translated to "Angry Warrior." It was a sentiment that foreshadowed his relations with a nineteenth-century U.S. government that was struggling to control its newest frontier. Chief Manuelito, Washington, D.C., December 1874. Photo by Charles Bell, courtesy Palace of the Governors Photo Archives (NMHM/DCA), neg. no. 15949.

killed livestock, then forced the Navajos to walk great distances from the Four Corners region to the reservation.

Manuelito was not among them. Opposed to the hostile actions of the government and mistrustful of any attempts at negotiation—whether they came in the form of American soldiers or fellow Navajos—the defiant Indian leader and a small band of followers withstood the advances of the military. Manuelito spent years roaming the mesas and canyon lands of the Four Corners area that he knew so well, hiding in caves and living on stores of dried food, repeatedly flouting efforts by the government to defeat him. "I have nothing to lose but my life," he once said, "and they can come and take that whenever they please."

Only in the fall of 1866, facing starvation and suffering physically, did Manuelito capitulate.

At the Bosque Redondo Reservation, Manuelito found his fellow Navajo Indians sick, poorly fed, and subsisting in desperate conditions. In 1868, likewise recognizing the failure of the reservation, the government negotiated with Manuelito and other Navajo leaders to end the Indians' confinement at Bosque Redondo and establish instead a permanent reservation in their homeland of northwestern New Mexico.

Manuelito died in 1893, after a bout of pneumonia.

More to explore: *Fort Sumner and Fort Sumner State Monument (series), Navajo Indian Reservation*

263. María "Concha" Concepción Ortiz y Pino de Kleven (1910–2006)

Location: Torrance County. Four miles north of Clines Corners, in a pullout on the east side of US 285, between mile markers 254 and 255. See map 4.

Marker text: "Concha" was a rancher and the first female Majority Whip of a state legislature in the nation. She helped implement legislation for women's rights, the handicapped, and bilingual education and also championed the arts and Hispanic culture. She served on sixty local and national boards helping to improve the lives of others. Vista Magazine honored her as "Latina of the Century" in 1999.

María Concepción Ortiz y Pino de Kleven passed away on September 30, 2006, leaving behind a legacy of almost nine decades of work on behalf of women's equality, the rights of persons with disabilities, bilingual education, Hispanic culture and art, and a host of other social issues at both the local and national levels.

This remarkable woman, widely known as "Concha," was born on her family's Agua Verde Ranch in Galisteo, south of Santa Fe, on May 20, 1910, to a family with deep roots in the state. Growing up, she showed early interest in community development. In a house donated by her father in Galisteo, she established a small arts school, in which local artisans were trained in art of the Spanish colonial period (including furniture making, sewing, and leather tanning) and encouraged to produce and sell the art they created. "The little school was one of the most satisfying and fulfilling experiences in my life," Concha later wrote. "It was not only a valuable training ground for many other projects which came later on in my life; it was a way in which I contributed in providing help to the poor and the aged, and the means by which I helped people become proud of their Hispanic culture."

Following a family tradition of public service, including that of her father, who had served in the state legislature, Concha ran for the New Mexico House of Representatives in 1936—and won. She was elected majority whip in the legislature in 1940, a position responsible for keeping the members of the majority (in this case, the Democrats) focused on the policy priorities of the party. She was the first woman to hold this position in New Mexico. Later, she took another stride for women's rights, sponsoring a bill to allow women to serve on juries in New Mexico.

While attending George Washington University in Washington, D.C., she met and, in 1943, married Victor Kleven, a faculty member at the school.

Because she believed strongly in bilingual education, one of Concha's legislative initiatives was the passage of a bill enabling New Mexico schools to teach Spanish at the junior high school level. She also championed the rights of persons with disabilities, serving as the only woman on the National Commission on Architectural Barriers. The *Albuquerque Journal* called her a "crusader" in this area, a passion she credited to her grandmother's concern for the sick and less fortunate in Galisteo. Concha later sponsored a bill requiring that public buildings in New Mexico be barrier free and accessible, one of the first such laws enacted in the country.

Concha's list of civic and legislative achievements grew as she helped the state improve the lives of its citizens. She served on the boards of the Albuquerque Symphony and Albuquerque Little Theater, the New Mexico Executive Committee on Crippled Children and Adults, the New Mexico Arts Commission, the State Commission on Streams and Water Pollution Council, and the National Council on the Humanities, just to name a few. She enjoyed a long and productive collaboration with the University of New Mexico, helping establish the School of Inter-American Affairs and later becoming that school's first graduate, serving as the president of the UNM Faculty Women's Club and also serving on the Board of Regents. For her dedicated service to the institution, the university conferred on her an honorary doctorate. She also found time to serve on the Advisory Committee on Women's Participation for the New York World's Fair in 1939. Throughout her life, Concha served on some sixty local and national boards. Little wonder that she became known among New Mexicans as the grande dame of the state.

In recognition of the breadth of Concha's civic and social endeavors, New Mexico governor Gary Johnson in 1996 issued a proclamation declaring October 12 of that year Concha Ortiz y Pino de Kleven Day. Her work gained national recognition as well. In 1999, the New York–based *Vista Magazine*, a magazine for Latina women, honored Concha as their "Latina of the Century."

Admired by many whose lives she had significantly improved, Concha passed away in 2006. She is buried in Santa Fe, not far from her hometown of Galisteo.

More to explore: *Doña Dolores "Lola" Chávez de Armijo, Galisteo Basin, María Dolores Gonzáles—La Doctora, Mela Leger, Nina Otero-Warren*

264. María Dolores Gonzáles, La Doctora (1917–1975)

Location: Bernalillo County. In Albuquerque, at the Dolores González Elementary School (named in her honor), located at 900 Atlantic Avenue SW. The Marker is at the southwest corner of Atlantic Avenue SW and Tenth Street SW. See map 4.

Marker text: Dr. Gonzáles was a pioneer in bilingual and bicultural education. She developed educational materials for students in New Mexico and Latin America and trained teachers in the curriculum. Born in Pecos, "Lola" taught in the area for many years and at the University of New Mexico. She held a master's degree from Columbia University and a doctorate from Pennsylvania State University. Dolores Gonzáles Elementary School in Albuquerque is named in her honor.

This Historic Marker is located outside Dolores Gonzáles Elementary School in Albuquerque, one of the first public schools in the city to offer students bilingual instruction in both English and Spanish. Today, more than four hundred students from kindergarten to fifth grade attend school here, most of them participating in a bilingual, bicultural immersion program that splits the school day in two halves: one with lessons taught only in English, the other with lessons taught only in Spanish. Students in the program leave the school not only fluent in two languages but also appreciative of the diverse cultures that make up New Mexico, including their own. In its mission and its name, the school honors and carries on the legacy of one of the foremost educational pioneers in New Mexico history: Dr. María Dolores Gonzáles.

Gonzáles was born in Pecos, New Mexico, on February 25, 1917, to a large family. Declaring that "our future life will be as pleasant as we shall make it" to her classmates as the valedictorian of Pecos High School in 1934, she set out to create her own pleasant future, beginning her teaching career working with students in small, one-room schoolhouses around San Miguel County. She received a bachelor's degree in elementary education and English from New Mexico Highlands University in Las Vegas in 1949, taught and served as a principal in the Pecos school system, and then went on to earn her master's from the Teachers College at Columbia University in New York in 1953. On assignment with the US Agency for International Development (USAID) in Honduras and Costa Rica, she trained Spanish-speaking teachers in educational methods and helped develop course curricula for Spanish-speaking students. Gonzáles returned to the United States in 1964 to attend Pennsylvania State University, where she received her doctorate two years later—along with a new nickname, "La Doctora." From there, Gonzáles became an associate professor of elementary education at the University of New Mexico in Albuquerque.

Bilingual education had not yet fully taken shape in New Mexico schools. Materials for teaching English to Spanish students, and vice versa, were almost nonexistent; books were imported from other Spanish-speaking countries and lacked information on local dialects and references. Also missing was the idea that a student's own culture could be a valuable resource for use by educators. Instead, students might be punished for speaking Spanish in the classroom, or removed from classrooms and taught apart from their social groups. La Doctora hoped to bring about the paradigm shift necessary to reverse this kind of thinking. "We don't need to change the kids," she once said. "We need to change the schools."

Working within the College of Education at the University of New Mexico, La Doctora produced a series of pedagogical materials for use in New Mexico to train educators in bilingual and bicultural instruction. Additionally, she helped write storybooks for bilingual children in schools around the state, using as their subject the scenic beauty and local customs of the state. They included *Dias de Sol* (*Sunny Days*), *A la Sombra de un Piñon* (*In the Shade of a Pine Tree*), and *Cielo Azul* (*Blue Sky*).

Each contained short *cuentos*, or stories, illustrated with full-page drawings, introducing young people to new Spanish vocabulary words by using New Mexico scenes familiar to them. She also edited a revised edition of a Depression-era Works Progress Administration guide to songs and games for Spanish-speaking children. In her introduction to this book, *Canciones y Juegos de Nuevo México* (*Songs and Games of New Mexico*), Gonzáles summarized the goal of her work: "It has become important to value the children's linguistic diversity and their culture, using them as legitimate content material in the educational process."

Remembered by her students and colleagues as intelligent, quiet, serious, and proper, La Doctora's personality straddled two worlds. She was traditional in her manner and appearance, but progressive in her thinking.

La Doctora died on March 18, 1975, at age fifty-eight. Dolores Gonzáles Elementary School opened the same year of her passing. In her memory, the Dr. Dolores Gonzáles Memorial Scholarship at the University of New Mexico is awarded to a student who is involved with bilingual/bicultural education.

More to explore: *Fabiola Cabeza de Baca Gilbert, María "Concha" Concepción Ortiz y Pino de Kleven, Mela Leger, Women of the Judiciary*

265. Maria Gertrudis Barceló (Doña Tules)
ca. 1800–1852

Location: Santa Fe County. Fifteen miles south of Santa Fe, in the Bicentennial Rest Area and Visitors Center, on the east side of Interstate 25. (The rest area is also known as the La Bajada Rest Area.) See map 2.

Marker text: Maria Gertrudis Barceló or Doña Tules, a notorious gambler and courtesan, operated a gambling house and saloon on Burro Alley in Santa Fe. She traveled up El Camino Real from Sonora, Mexico in 1815. Bishop Jean-Baptiste Lamy allowed this controversial lady to be buried in the south chapel of La Parroquia, the Santa Fe parish church, and used the money from her funeral for badly needed repairs.

She was a literate woman of wealth and social standing who could also deal a mean game of monte. Her name was Maria Gertrudis Barceló, but most people called her doña Tules ("Lady Reeds"). She owned and operated a gambling hall on Burro Street in Santa Fe, only blocks from the historic downtown plaza. An illustration of her in *Harper's Monthly* in 1854 depicts her with a crucifix on her necklace and a cigarillo dangling from her lips. Among the many fascinating and influential women of nineteenth-century New Mexico, Tules was certainly one of the most colorful—and complex.

"The principal monte-banke keeper in Santa Fe," was how the restrained Susan Shelby Magoffin, traveling with her trader husband through New Mexico in 1846, described Barceló in her diary. "A stately dame of a certain age, the possessor of a portion of that shrewd sense and fascinating manner necessary to allure the wayward, inexperienced youth to the hall of final ruin."

The "stately dame" Barceló was born around 1800 in Sonora, Mexico. In 1815, she traveled with her family to New Mexico over the Camino Real, the main road connecting Mexico and New Mexico. The family settled in the small farming village of Valencia, where Barceló later met Manuel Antonio Sisneros. The two were married in June 1823. Although the couple tried to start a family, unfortunately, their first two children—both boys—died in infancy. By 1833, they had moved to Santa Fe, where they lived near Barceló's

Courtesan or misjudged woman of means? History has not taken a definitive side. "La Doña Tules," *Harper's Monthly*, April 1854. Courtesy Palace of the Governors Photo Archives (NMHM/DCA), neg. no. 50815.

mother, who had remarried. The move put Barceló in the center of a powerful city at a seminal time in the history of the Southwest.

The Army of the West, under the command of Brigadier General Stephen Watts Kearny, entered Santa Fe in 1846 and proclaimed New Mexico and the Southwest free from Mexican rule and thereafter part of the United States. Santa Fe was the terminus of the famous Santa Fe Trail, bringing merchants and settlers from the east into the new American territory of New Mexico. Santa Fe became a political, cultural, and economic transition zone and a mixing bowl of new ideas and old traditions, all playing out in the interactions between residents, traders, muleteers, merchants, settlers, Mexican and American army officers, and politicians—many of whom at one time or another found themselves in the gambling hall and saloon that Barceló had opened on Burro Street.

How Barceló came to be adept at gambling isn't known, but she had apparently earlier dealt monte, a popular card game at the time, in the gold mining camp of Dolores, a few miles south of Santa Fe, in the 1820s. Regardless, her gambling hall, which she opened in 1839, became the lavishly appointed backdrop of the emerging political environment in the newly American city of Santa Fe.

Kearny's soldiers were among those who frequented the hall. Barceló's support for the American occupation helped her gain influence with the US Army and increased her own social standing, although she remained excluded from some Santa Fe social circles. It is said that she once loaned money to the US Army to help then continue a march to Mexico.

A few historians have suggested that Barceló was, in fact, a courtesan—an upper-class mistress. But, as historian Fray Angélico Chávez argues, that perception was likely the result of differences in viewpoints about drinking and gambling between the cultures that were merging in Santa Fe at the time. Regardless, Barceló used the money she earned from the gambling hall to acquire three other houses and raise a number of adopted children, her strong business sense eventually making her quite wealthy.

Death came for Barceló in her home on January 17, 1852. Although some controversy had surrounded her in life, Santa Fe archbishop Jean-Baptiste Lamy afforded Barceló an elaborate funeral and a burial in the south chapel of the Santa Fe parish church La Parroquia (now Saint Francis Cathedral). In death, Barceló bequeathed to history one final irony: with the money the church received as payment for her funeral expenses, Lamy financed repairs to the chapel.

More to explore: *El Camino Real—The King's Highway, Las Vegas, Santa Fe, Santa Fe Trail (series)*

Maria Montoya Martinez: *see Pueblo of San Ildefonso*

María Rosa Villapando: *see Captive Women and Children of Taos County*

266. Marjorie Bell Chambers

Location: Los Alamos County. In Los Alamos, in the park surrounding Ashley Pond, near the intersection of NM 502 (Trinity Drive) and Twentieth Street. See map 2.

Marker text: Marjorie Bell Chambers advised Governors and Presidents, participated in the formation of The United Nations, and headed two women's colleges. She was president of the Los Alamos Girl Scouts, a founding member of the Historical Society and a project historian of the US Atomic Energy Commission for Los Alamos. She served on the County Council, campaigned for Congress, and traveled worldwide advocating for women's rights.

267. Peggy Pond Church (1903–1986)

Location: Los Alamos County. In Los Alamos, in the park surrounding Ashley Pond, near the intersection of NM 502 (Trinity Drive) and Twentieth Street. See map 2.

Marker text: Peggy Pond Church, author of the Southwest classic The House at Otowi Bridge and daughter of Los Alamos Ranch School founder Ashley Pond, will forever be "The First Lady of New Mexican Poetry." As she rode the Pajarito Plateau and camped beneath tall pines, she came to understand that "it is the land that wants to be said." She captured it in her sensitive poems.

Note: Marker faceplates are on opposite sides of the same sign.

The two women memorialized on these Historic Markers, Marjorie Bell Chambers and Peggy Pond Church, both in their own way made the world a better place: Chambers through civic and educational leadership, and Church through the power of beautiful words.

Marjorie Bell Chambers, remembered on her death by the Los Alamos Historical Society as a "restless, multifaceted, and indomitable spirit," was born in New York on March 11, 1923. She graduated from Mount Holyoke College in Massachusetts in 1943. The following year, Chambers had a small—but critical—role in the formation of the United Nations. While working at the League of Nations, the post–World War I international peace organization, Chambers took down by shorthand (over the phone, no less!) the official proposals drafted by participating leaders that formed the United Nations. Five years later, in 1948, Chambers was awarded a master's degree in history from Cornell University.

That same year, she married William Chambers, a physicist, and the couple later moved to Los Alamos. There, Chambers's husband began working at Los Alamos National Laboratory. While simultaneously raising four children, Marjorie Chambers set out on her own career. When a branch of the American Association of University Women (AAUW) opened in Los Alamos in 1950, she joined, serving in various roles in that organization, including local branch president. She earned her doctorate from the University of New Mexico in 1974, writing her dissertation on the history of Los Alamos. She ran for the Los Alamos County Council that same year and won—her first public office.

In 1976, Chambers became president of the Colorado Women's College in Denver, helping saving the institution from bankruptcy. That same year, President Gerald Ford appointed her to the National Advisory Council on Women's Educational Programs. After Chambers participated in the influential National Women's Conference in Houston in 1977, Ford's successor, President Jimmy Carter, continued the White House's association with her by appointing her to the National Advisory Committee for Women, formed to help enact the recommendations from the Houston conference—among them support for passage of the Equal Rights Amendment. These positions, along with her continuing role in the American Association of University Women, made her an important advocate for women's rights at a national level.

Chambers tried, albeit unsuccessfully, to win election to federal office. When New Mexico's Third Congressional District was formed in the early 1980s, Chambers ran for the office in 1982 as a Republican against Democrat Bill Richardson, but she lost. Her success at the university level continued, however. In 1985, she served as interim president of Colby-Sawyer College, then an all-girls school, in New London, New Hampshire. The following year, she tried her hand at winning public office again, running for lieutenant governor of New Mexico. Although she lost that race, she did win the distinction of being the first woman in the state to run for lieutenant governor.

Chambers's work at the local level also left an impressive legacy. She was president of the Los Alamos Girl Scouts and a founding member of the Los Alamos Historical Society. The latter organization published two of her books, including (with Linda K. Aldrich) *Los Alamos, New Mexico: A Survey to 1949*, which offered a history of her adopted city. In 1965, she also worked as the project historian for the US Atomic Energy Commission in Los Alamos. Later, she served on both the New Mexico Commission on Higher Education and the New Mexico Endowment for the Humanities. Also, she was a faculty member at the Los Alamos campus of the University of New Mexico.

With all of these accomplishments to her credit, it's no surprise that in 2003 Chambers was awarded the Lifetime Achievement Award from the New Mexico Commission on the Status of Women. Sadly, three years later, that lifetime ended. Chambers passed away in Los Alamos on August 22, 2006.

In her book on the history of Los Alamos, Chambers wrote about the Los Alamos Ranch School, a boarding school for young boys, established on the Pajarito Plateau (the future site of Los Alamos) in 1917. One of the founders of that school was former Teddy Roosevelt Rough Rider, Ashley Pond. Pond's daughter, Peggy, grew to become one of New Mexico's foremost poets—so much so that she is remembered today as "the First Lady of New Mexico Poetry."

Margaret "Peggy" Hallett Pond was born in Valmora, New Mexico, in 1903 and attended school on the East Coast, but she enjoyed childhood summers on the Pajarito Plateau with her family at the Ranch School. She rode horseback, camped, and explored the plateau, later marrying Fermor Spencer Church, a teacher at her father's school, all the while finding a communal connection to the land. In writing later about her connection to the area, she said:

It's not Santa Fe, nor Taos, nor the Capitans, nor any part of New Mexico but that Jemez and Pajarito country that has my heart. It's the smell of the piñon and juniper, the blended cry of the sheep in the Valles, the arrowhead suddenly speaking its message on the lonely trail, eagles turning and soaring on the immense bright air, the Apache plume feathering out in early summer, the lemon cool smell of chamisa, the bright golden vein of the cottonwood along the Rio Grande, the snow that blows down so white and silent upon the branches of fir and spruce.

In her writing, Pond speaks to that beauty. Her poem "Sheep Country" describes the sheep trails made in Capulin Canyon and surrounding mountains as the animals are driven to pastures in early spring. Another, "Abiquiu—Thursday in Holy Week," mentions the mesa near Abiquiú and Pond's vision of a traditional Penitente religious ceremony one evening in that village. "It is the land that wants to be said," Pond once stated.

In 1942, the government purchased the land where the Los Alamos Ranch School was located and established there the top-secret laboratory that would later become Los Alamos National Laboratory. The move forced Pond and her family off her beloved plateau. Pond was unsettled by the idea of the atomic bomb. She wrote about the work of the scientists at LANL in a poem entitled "The Nuclear Physicists," in which she states that the scientists at the labs "invoked for man's sake the most ancient archetype of evil."

Pond wrote eight books of poetry, three memoirs, and a children's book, *The Burro of Angelitos*. A second children's book, *The Pancake Stories: Cuentos del Panqueque*, was published after her death.

In what is probably her best-known book, *The House at Otowi Bridge*, Pond told the story of another woman of importance in the history of the Los Alamos area: her friend, the writer and former teacher Edith Warner. The house in the title is the home where Warner lived alongside a railroad stop after moving to New Mexico in 1928. In that house, Warner hosted numerous members of the community—from scientists building the bomb at Los Alamos (including Robert Oppenheimer and Enrico Fermi) to members of the San Ildefonso tribe. The book is today a classic of New Mexico literature.

More to explore: Eve Ball, Fabiola Cabeza de Baca Gilbert, Mary White, Nina Otero-Warren, Trinity Site

Mary Cabot Wheelwright: *see Amelia Elizabeth White*

268. Mary White (1894–1988)

Location: Otero County. Southwest of Mayhill, at the intersection of NM 130 and NM 24. See map 6.

Marker text: In 1927, "Miss Mary" established one of the earliest Girl Scout camps in America and the first in New Mexico. Situated on 200 acres in Otero County, a stately pine lodge, Ingham Hall, nestles amid cabins and outbuildings of Camp Mary White. Generations of girls, who learned stewardship of nature and community at the camp, continue to be energized as activists by Mary White's pioneer spirit.

Note: Camp Mary White, now closed to the public, was located about five miles west of this Historic Marker.

Among the camps and retreat centers nestled throughout the ponderosa pines of the Sacramento Mountains in south-central New Mexico stands historic Camp Mary White. Established in 1927, Camp Mary White was the first Girl Scout camp in New Mexico, and one of the oldest Girl Scout camps in the United States. It was named for benefactor Mary White, a beloved figure known to girls at the camp as simply "Miss Mary."

White was born in Midland, Texas, on September 24, 1894. At age four, she moved with her family to Roswell, New Mexico, where her father bought and ran a hotel. After graduating from high school, White went to a finishing school in Washington, D.C., and then returned to Roswell, where she became active in community affairs, including being appointed as the Roswell postmaster in 1921. Attending a convention of the Federated Women's Clubs around that time, White learned about a newly formed national organization known as the Girl Scouts, which had been created only a few years earlier in Georgia as a way to offer girls across the country opportunities to engage in acts of citizenship, trek in the outdoors, socialize, do crafts, and play sports. White decided that New Mexico needed such a group, so she formed a troop in Roswell—the first Girl Scout troop in the state. It had sixteen girls.

White's father, known to most as "Daddy" White, owned the Muleshoe Ranch in the Sacramento Mountains. In 1927, he donated two hundred acres of his property, located about a quarter of a mile west of the ranch headquarters, for use as a camp. This, the first Girl Scout camp in the state, took the name of his daughter: Camp Mary White.

Camp Mary White opened for a trial session in the summer of 1927. Sixty-five girls from across the state attended the two-week outing, sleeping in tents donated by the National Guard. With the experiment considered a success, permanent buildings were soon erected. The first was an impressive log-cabin lodge known as Emily Ingham Hall, named for the daughter of Daddy White's fellow rancher, Arthur Ingham, who had paid the $2,500 necessary for its construction. Ingham Hall served as a dining hall and common meeting area as well as the location of the library, the nurse's office, and a trading post where girls could buy stationery with which to write home. Following that, crews built Adirondack cabins, their fronts open to the mountain air, on the hillsides of the two canyons surrounding Ingham Hall. These served as the girls' sleeping quarters, each cabin fitting about four cots, with one cabin reserved for the counselors and counselors in training. The girls were divided into units, based on either age or activity. Each unit consisted of several cabins, a cooking area, and a "lat" (latrine).

A typical day at Camp Mary White began with the girls walking in procession to the flagpole in front of Ingham Hall for a morning flag ceremony, then singing around the Singing Tree while breakfast was prepared and tables set inside the hall. Girls were summoned to three meals a day by clangs on a giant metal wheel, but one meal per unit per day was cooked at that unit's outdoor cooking area. Mornings and afternoons were spent in outdoor activities such as horseback riding, hiking, and archery, or maybe woodburning, pottery, or macrame in the Arts and Crafts Building. After evening skits around the fire ring, nightfall found tired scouts asleep in their mountainside cabins. Sundays included a hike up the switchback trail to a picturesque mountaintop spot known as "Halfway to Heaven."

Mary White ran the camp as its director from 1930 to 1939, while also serving as the regional director for the Girl Scouts' national organization. She lived in a small cabin just down from Ingham Hall. In 1940, Miss Mary resigned from the Girl Scouts and went on to accept positions with New Mexico State University in Las Cruces, and then at Texas Western College (now the University of Texas at El Paso), until retiring to the Muleshoe Ranch. Later generations of campers fondly remember walking the short distance from the camp to the ranch and sitting near the porch while Miss Mary told them stories of her life.

Camp Mary White inspired generations of young leaders. Among those to work at the camp as a counselor in her youth was Janet Napolitano, who later served as the secretary of homeland security in the Barack Obama administration—the first woman to hold that post. "Looking back," Napolitano wrote in recollection of her time at the camp for the dedication of this Historic Marker in 2009, "it is fair to say that people like Miss Mary helped build the road that many woman have now traveled, myself included."

Although the camp closed in 2003, former counselors and campers formed the Friends of Camp Mary White three years later to help restore the camp buildings and preserve the history and traditions of the camp itself. These former campers meet at the camp every year in an annual reunion, drawn to the place that holds so many fond memories for them. While together, they still refer to one another by the nicknames they were given as campers.

More to explore: *Marjorie Bell Chambers, Philmont Scout Ranch*

269. Matilda Coxe Stevenson (1849–1915)

Location: Cibola County. East of Inscription Rock, in a pullout on the south side of NM 53, between mile markers 42 and 43. See map 1.

Marker text: Matilda Coxe Stevenson was the first female anthropologist to study the Native Americans of New Mexico. Her research focused on the religious practices of indigenous peoples, particularly of the Zuni, and on the lives of native women and children. In 1885, she founded the Woman's Anthropological Society of America, a national organization, in part to address the inequality of the sexes in the field of Anthropology.

On June 8, 1885, ten women in Washington, D.C., founded the Women's Anthropological Society of America. It was the first such organization in anthropology created by women, and it was dedicated to recognizing and encouraging the work of female anthropologists, who often found themselves excluded from scientific careers—largely because the prevailing belief at the time held that such fields were best pursued by men. "We are satisfied to work out our own problems," a historical sketch of the society noted in rebuttal of that belief, "in anticipation of the time when science shall regard only the work, not the worker."

To serve as the first president of the society, members chose a person to whom the anthropological world owes a great debt: Matilda ("Tilly") Coxe Stevenson.

Stevenson was born in San Augustine, Texas, on May 12, 1849. Her family later moved to Washington, D.C., where her father opened a law firm in which Stevenson worked. Through her interest in mineralogy, she met and, in 1872, married ethnologist and explorer Colonel James Stevenson. Matilda accompanied her husband as his assistant in his surveys into Arizona and Mexico, helping him prepare catalogs of his acquisitions but also writing her own ethnographic reports of the indigenous people she encountered. When the Bureau of Ethnology was formed at the Smithsonian Institution in 1879, its head, Major John Wesley Powell—famous as the leader of one of the Great Surveys of the Southwest—dispatched Colonel Stevenson as the head of an expedition to study the Zunis and Hopis of the Southwest. Matilda Stevenson traveled with her husband, and in so doing became the first woman anthropologist to study in this part of New Mexico.

At Zuni, Stevenson found that her gender affinity with the women of the pueblo made it easier for her to learn about them and their children than could her male counterparts. Her studies focused on the religious practices of the Zuni people as well as on the lives of the women and children at the pueblo. After six months with the Zuni, the Stevensons and others in the party traveled to the other pueblos in New Mexico, and then to Arizona. Stevenson compiled her first report, *Zuni and the Zunians*, in 1881, and another, *The Religious Life of the Zuni Child*, in 1884. The following year, she helped form the Women's Anthropological Society of America.

After the death of her husband in 1888, Stevenson continued her work in New Mexico as an employee of the Bureau of Ethnology. She visited Zia Pueblo and returned to Zuni several times as well, intent on capturing the practices she felt were fast vanishing from the cultures she studied. Her work *The Zuni Indians: Their Mythology, Esoteric Fraternities, and Ceremonies* remains a valued anthropological resource today.

Stevenson passed away on June 24, 1915, in Oxon Hill, Maryland.

More to explore: *Pueblo of Zuni*

270. McComas Incident

Location: Grant County. South of Tyrone, in a pullout on the west side of NM 90, between mile markers 19 and 20. See map 5.

Marker text: In March 1883, Judge and Mrs. H. C. McComas were killed in this vicinity by a group of Chiricahua Apaches led by Chatto. An extensive manhunt failed to rescue their six-year-old son, who had been taken captive. This incident was part of a violent outbreak toward the end of the Apache wars.

Note: Chatto's name is sometimes spelled Chato.

Sadly, the terrible story of the McComas incident has no satisfactory epilogue. After being carried away by Chiricahua Apaches, little Charley McComas was never seen nor heard from again. Charley McComas. Harlan Collection, Book 2, Image 349. Photo courtesy Silver City Museum.

On March 27, 1883, Silver City residents Judge Hamilton C. McComas, his wife, and their six-year-old boy Charley left their home in Silver City on a planned week-long trip to Shakespeare, a small mining town near Lordsburg. Judge McComas had been summoned by an older son, who lived near Shakespeare, to assist with legal matters for a mining client. Mrs. McComas and Charley, eager to see their family member, went along for the trip. After spending the first night at a hostelry along the way, the McComases resumed their trip the next day, March 28, traveling over what was then known as the Lordsburg Road. Around noon, they pulled up alongside a walnut tree just outside Thompson Canyon in the Burro Mountains, a spot some ten miles west of here, and prepared a picnic.

Although New Mexico was marching boldly toward the turn of the century, the territory at that time still had many of the hallmarks of a frontier. For the previous thirty years, the region had been immersed in broad cultural strife, as encroachment by Anglo and Hispanic settlers into parts of the territory that had previously been the homelands of Indians like Navajos and Apaches had put cultures and intentions in direct (and often hostile) contact. Attacks and fierce reprisals on both sides, racist sentiment, fear, misguided government policies, and misunderstandings had escalated to the point where the conflict could only be referred to with a broad-brushed name: the Apache Wars. Although the violence was dwindling by the time the McComas family set out from Silver City that spring morning in 1883, and would largely be over by 1886, there was still enough animosity to incite isolated attacks on settlers by Chiricahua Apaches, led by their chief, Chatto, between the Sierra Madres in Mexico and southeastern Arizona that year. Before the curtain drew to a close on the Apache Wars, the McComases were to become unwitting players in the final act.

With little warning, the genteel picnic was suddenly interrupted. Judge McComas and his wife and young son found themselves set upon by the

Apache chief Chatto and about two dozen of his warriors. The family climbed hurriedly aboard their buckboard and attempted to escape. They had ridden only a few yards before a bullet caught Judge McComas. Severely wounded, the judge nonetheless managed to jump from the wagon and return to the walnut tree, where he shot several times at the Indians. Another round of bullets found him, and he fell to his death. Juniata McComas charged the horses, but a bullet killed one of the animals after a short distance and stopped the wagon from its getaway. As she reached to retrieve Charley, an Apache warrior struck her in the back of the head with the butt of his rife three times, killing her.

The judge and his wife, who only minutes earlier had been enjoying their family meal together, now lay dead. Hastily, the Indians stripped their bodies of valuables and left them naked in the canyon. They then fled south to the Sierra Madres in Mexico—with six-year-old Charley, still alive, as their captive.

Lieutenant Colonel George Forsyth and the Fourth Cavalry from Fort Cummings, north of Deming, as well as a militia from Shakespeare, set out in separate expeditions through the Playas Valley toward Mexico in an attempt to rescue Charley, but both groups returned without success. Soon after, General George Crook from Fort Whipple, Arizona, set out on another attempt, leading his troops to an Apache camp in the Sierra Madres in northern Mexico. With most of the warriors away from the camp, the soldiers found mostly women and children, who fled into the mountains upon the approach of the cavalry. Among the items retrieved at the campsite was a family album that Mrs. McComas had carried with her.

As time progressed, and with no sightings of Charley to satisfy the public desire for resolution, rumors arose to fill the void. Several stories claimed that the boy had been killed during or soon after the canyon massacre itself. Others maintained that the boy had fled into the reaches of the Sierra Madres when Crook's men stormed the Apache camp and had then either been killed by one of the Apache women or died from exposure after getting lost. This account was corroborated by Captain John G. Bourke, who served under General Crook, when he wrote that he believed Charley had "escaped, terror-stricken, to the depths of the mountains; that the country was so rough, the timber and brush-wood so thick that his tracks could not be followed, even had there not been such a violent fall of rain during the succeeding nights." Still other, more romantic, stories later arose that Charley had grown to adulthood riding with the Apaches, even becoming a chief. But through the years, no trace of Charley was ever found, and no person ever came forward to claim his birthright.

More to explore: *Captive Women and Children of Taos County, Lordsburg, Point of Rocks, Shakespeare, Silver City*

271. McNees Crossing

Location: Union County. North of Clayton, in a pullout on the east side of NM 406 between mile markers 18 and 19. See map 3.

Marker text: Here the Santa Fe Trail crossed the North Canadian River. The site is named for two young men, McNees and Monroe, who were shot at this crossing in 1828. Here too, a group of travelers celebrated Independence Day in 1831, the first documented 4th of July observation on the plains. Original trail ruts can still be seen near the crossing.

Note: An American Legion monument and the river crossing are reachable through a gate on the right side of the highway a short distance north of this Historic Marker.

Young traders Daniel Monroe and Robert McNees were returning to their home in Franklin, Missouri, with a trade caravan from Santa Fe in the fall of 1828. Monroe and McNees rode ahead of their convoy along the Santa Fe Trail into the rolling hills of what is now far northeastern New Mexico. Near the small earthen embankment where the trail crossed Corrumpa Creek, both men lay down to rest while waiting for the remainder of the caravan to arrive. As they slept, hostile Indians crept to the site, secured the traders' rifles, and turned them on the men—killing McNees and severely wounding Monroe. The assailants then fled.

Members of the caravan carried the dying Monroe nearly forty miles to the Cimarron River, but he passed away soon after. During a funeral ceremony near the river, a small group of Indians rode up on the opposite bank. The visitors may not have been involved in the murder, but vengeful members of the caravan nonetheless vented their aggression through rifle fire. All but one of the Indians were killed.

The deaths of Monroe and McNees were among the first fatal incidents along the Santa Fe Trail. Corrumpa Creek is sometimes known as McNees Creek, in honor of the slain young trader. The site of the tragedy took the name McNees Crossing. Despite the unfortunate incident that occurred there, the crossing became a regular camping place for caravans along the Santa Fe Trail.

McNees Crossing might have remained a place known only for its sorrowful past had it not been for a visit by a shy, studious, former schoolteacher turned frontiersman. Josiah Gregg, suffering from consumption and chronic dyspepsia, was following his doctor's orders to trek west for a more healthful climate when the one-hundred-wagon merchant caravan he had joined reached McNees Crossing in early July 1831. Gregg recorded the travelers' jubilant celebration of what was the first documented Fourth of July observance on the Plains:

Scarce had gray twilight brushed his dusky brow, when our patriotic camp gave lively demonstrations of that joy which plays around the heart of every American on the anniversary of this triumphant day. The roar of our artillery and rifle platoons resounded from every hill, while the rumbling of the drum and the shrill whistle of the fife, imparted a degree of martial interest to the scene which was well calculated to stir the souls of men. There was no limit to the huzzas and enthusiastic ejaculations of our people; and at every new shout the dales around sent forth a gladsome response.

A stone pedestal placed at the site by the American Legion in 1939 marks the location of the holiday merriment.

More to explore: *Point of Rocks, Rabbit Ear Mountain, Santa Fe Trail (series)*

272. Mela Leger
Bilingual Education Pioneer (1928–2006)

Location: Guadalupe County. At the south end of Dilia, about sixteen miles north of Interstate 40, near the intersection of US 84 and NM 119, in a pullout on the east side of US 84 between mile markers 77 and 78. See map 3.

Marker text: At four, Manuelita de Atocha (Mela) Lucero Leger read Spanish language newspapers to her blind grandfather in Colonias. Although New Mexico's constitution protects Spanish-speaking students, school children were often punished for speaking Spanish. As a pioneer in bilingual education, Mela changed that by founding one of the nation's first bilingual multi-cultural schools, developing curriculum, training teachers and helping write the historic 1973 Bilingual Education Act.

In 1973, the state legislature of New Mexico passed the Bilingual Multicultural Education Act, recognizing the value of multicultural education and permitting schools in the state to offer bilingual multicultural education to students. One of its strong supporters and advocates—without whom the bill would not have included some of the far-reaching provisions it did—was educator Manuela de Atocha Lucero Leger. Known as "Mela" to her family and friends, Leger knew from personal experience the need for such a bill in New Mexico.

Mela was born on July 3, 1928, in Villanueva, New Mexico, south of Las Vegas. As a girl, she spent time with her grandparents in the small village of Colonias east of here. Although she had not yet entered school, she read Spanish-language newspapers to her grandfather, who was blind. Mela was, literally, his eyes to the world. But when Mela did enter school, she found herself punished for speaking the language which, to that point in her life, had been her key to understanding the world and to communicating with her own family.

This dichotomy of culture and educational practice has a history. When New Mexico became a state in 1912, the state constitution provided for the training of teachers in both English and Spanish and also offered some protection for children of Spanish descent in the classroom. Article 12, Section 10 of the constitution stated that such children "shall never be denied the right and privilege of admission and attendance in the public schools, or other public educational institutions of the state, and they shall never be classed in separate schools, but shall forever enjoy perfect equality with other children in all public schools and educational institutions of the state." And yet, students often were discouraged from speaking their native language in the classroom—be that Spanish or a Native American language. And the culture and values inherent in that language were not seen as assets in a student's education.

Later in her life, Leger would help change this, and help bring the momentum of multicultural education in the state to fruition. After graduating from Loretto Heights College in Denver, Colorado (at the time a four-year college for women), she met and married Ray Leger, then later earned a master's degree in teaching from New Mexico Highlands University. As a teacher, Leger was in a position to affect the experience of Spanish-speaking children in New Mexico schools. Recognizing the value of bilingual education in leveraging the culture, values, and native language of students to advance their own learning, she founded a multicultural elementary school in Las Vegas, and her husband became superintendent. It was one of the first such schools in the country. There, she developed materials appropriate to the instruction of Spanish-speaking students, allowing those young people to use their first language to learn while also employing specific methods to develop skills in English. Her classroom experience, expertise, and growing nationwide recognition made her a successful advocate and proponent for bilingual education. And she did all this while also raising seven children.

Mela's work and thinking on the importance of multicultural education took legislative shape in the early 1970s. Working with New Mexico state legislators, Leger helped develop some of the language that would become part of the Bilingual Multicultural Education Act of 1973. It was the first bilingual law in the country.

Mela continued to shape the cause of multicultural education, bilingual teacher certification, and educational standards through her membership on the Bilingual Advisory Committee of the State Board of Education. She also advanced professionally in the field, working at New Mexico Highlands University as the director of the Bilingual Education Material Center, and later in Albuquerque as a teacher trainer in the Southwest Bilingual Education Training Resource Center at the University of New Mexico.

From her experience growing up in Colonias to enhancing the education of students statewide, Leger changed the course of the history of education in New Mexico.

Mela Leger passed away on December 31, 2006.

More to explore: *María Dolores Gonzáles—La Doctora, Susie Rayos Marmon (see under Pueblo of Laguna)*

273. Mesa and Pecos Valley

Location: Chaves County. Forty miles north of Roswell, in the Mesa Park Rest Area on the east side of US 285, between mile markers 148 and 149. See map 6.

Marker text: Pecos Valley section of Great Plains province stretches westward to foothills of Capitan, Jicarilla and Gallinas Mountains. Southern High Plains, 50 miles to east, are capped by water-bearing Ogallala Formation; Poquita Mesa to east is Ogallala remnant. Nearby depressions are sinkholes in porous Permian limestones. Elevation 4,500 feet.

The eastern third of New Mexico is part of the sprawling eternity of rolling plains, tablelands, and low bluffs that together shape the Great Plains. The immense sweep of the Great Plains is composed of several smaller, distinctive sections. Three sections appear in New Mexico and include the Pecos Valley and the High Plains in the southeastern part of the state. A third, the Raton, makes up the northeastern corner of New Mexico.

Starting about ten million years ago, drainage from the Sangre de Cristo Mountains and other uplifting ranges west of here carried gravel and other deposits into these plains. Over many years, those sediments collected into a vast, thick layer of rock debris known as the Ogallala Formation, named by geologist Nelson Horatio Darton for the town of Ogallala, Nebraska.

Persistent streams and watercourses later cut their way into these depositional plains, eroding long valleys like the Pecos Valley. The headwaters of the Pecos River begin on the southern slopes of the Sangre de Cristo Mountains and roll through southeastern New Mexico into Texas. Nineteenth-century ranchers drove cattle along the course of the mighty river, and the region soon thereafter opened to settlement. A pamphlet written in 1894 to lure homesteaders boasted that "there are people living here who have drunk Pecos River water for five to fifteen years and . . . they are as healthy people as can be found in the world."

Because of their rock composition, some higher areas of the plains were resistant to the effects of erosion. One of them to the east is Poquita Mesa, a remnant of the Ogallala Formation. The largest region left unexcavated is the High Plains section, which begins about fifty miles east of here. This flat plateau forms the central interior of the

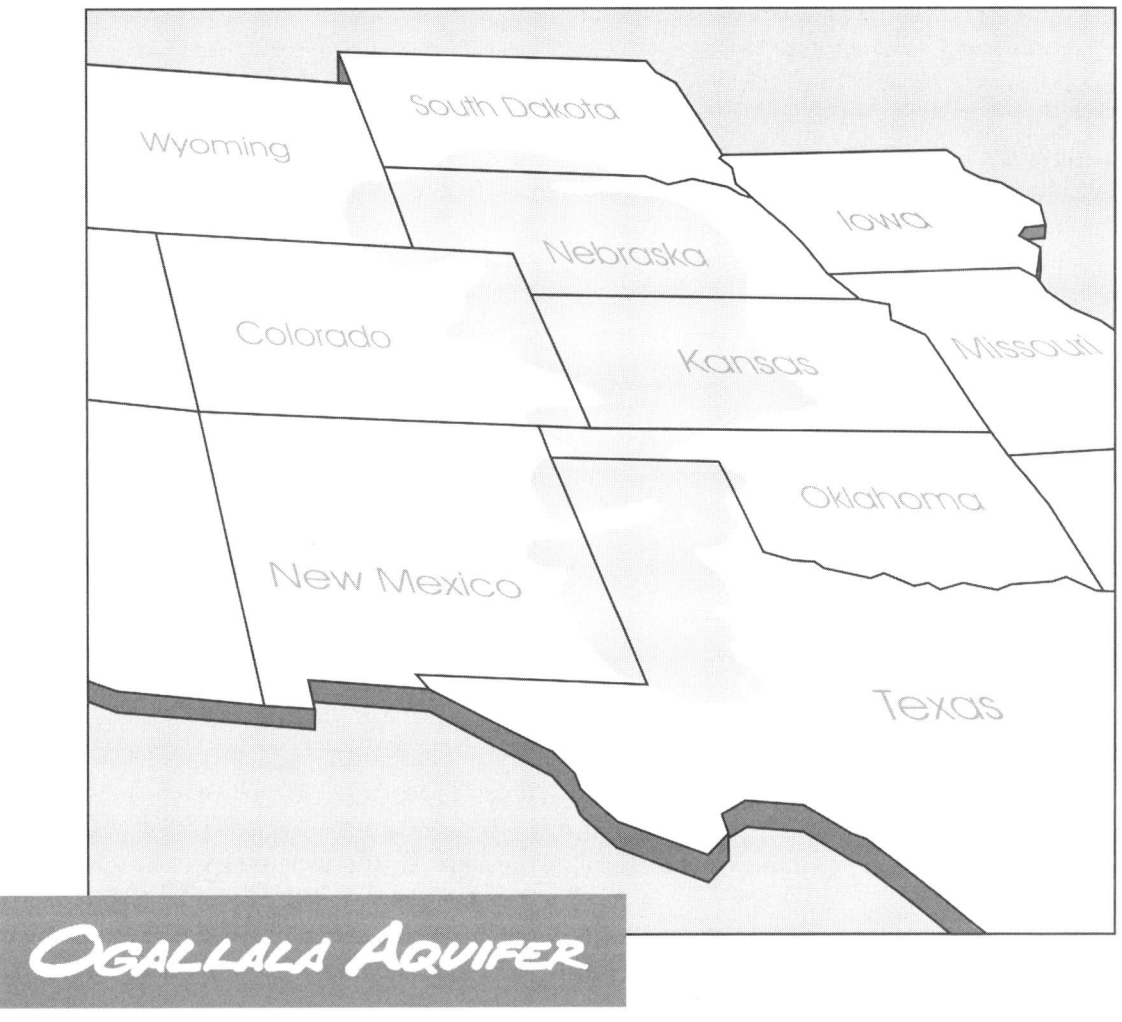

Ogallala Aquifer

Water from the Ogallala aquifer helps irrigate crops in a wide stretch of the southwestern United States. Illustration by David Carter.

Great Plains and reaches from the northern border of Nebraska through the Texas Panhandle into eastern New Mexico. Antelope, deer, coyote, and prairie dogs are all common on the lush grasslands of the High Plains. Beneath the High Plains rests a large body of water saturated into the Ogallala Formation. Stretching more than 170,000 square miles and claiming residency in the states of South Dakota, Nebraska, Wyoming, Colorado, Kansas, Oklahoma, Texas, and New Mexico, the Ogallala Aquifer is one of the largest underground bodies of water in the world. Farmers today extract this precious liquid both to irrigate their fields and to water their livestock. Sinkholes have formed in the porous Permian limestone of the Ogallala Formation throughout the southern High Plains, perhaps, as some geologists believe, in alignment with joints in the underlying formation.

The Capitan, Jicarilla, and Gallinas Mountains in Lincoln County border the Pecos Valley on the west.

More to explore: *Goodnight-Loving Trail (series), Pecos Valley, Sangre de Cristo*

274. Mesa del Contadero

Location: Socorro County. About twenty-five miles south of San Antonio on a small rise on the east side of NM 1, at mile marker 37. See map 5.

Marker text: The Chihuahua Trail passed by the large volcanic mesa on the east bank of the Rio Grande, marking the northern end of the Jornada del Muerto (Journey of the Dead Man). "Contadero" means "the counting place," or a narrow place where people and animals must pass through one-by-one.

The imposing 6,108-foot-high darkish mesa in the distance to the southeast of this Marker is the Mesa del Contadero. In Spanish, *contadero* means "counting place," a description that hints at the role this mesa played in the history of the state. The steep western wall of the landmark stood close to the bank of the Rio Grande and thus created a natural stockade where herdsmen traveling the Camino Real, the most significant trade and colonization route between Santa Fe and Mexico during the early years of New Mexico history, could inventory their cattle and sheep before the caravan continued. The Camino Real was also sometimes known as the Chihuahua Trail. A *paraje*, or camping site along the route, developed south of the mesa after 1598. It became known as El Contadero.

The isolated mesa marked the northern end of the Jornada del Muerto, or "Journey of the Dead Man." The Jornada, an arid ninety-mile stretch of desert along the Camino Real, challenged those who crossed it with barren terrain, infrequent watering holes, and the unremitting possibility of Apache attack. Heavily armed caravans moving south from the paraje of El Contadero into the Jornada joined up and traveled together for their own protection.

In September 1851, the US Army established Fort Conrad in the southern shadow of the mesa to provide military escorts to travelers along this segment of the Camino Real. When the flimsy cottonwood and adobe buildings at the fort began to deteriorate only a few years later, the army abandoned Fort Conrad and erected a new fort to the south, Fort Craig. The Bureau of Land Management today preserves the ruins of Fort Craig.

With the protection offered by the military presence in the area, small Spanish hamlets developed—and several would become victims of watery deluges. One was the village of San Marcial, founded along the western bank of the Rio Grande just north of the mesa around 1866. San Marcial grew in size with the arrival of the railroad around the turn of the century and soon included several stores, a Harvey House, restaurants, a school, and other mainstays of an incipient town. Then, in the late summer of 1929, contumacious waters from the Rio Grande flooded the town; floodwaters reportedly spread three miles across. According to one newspaper account, some residents were taken by boat from a second-floor window of the Harvey House! Although San Marcial survives in much more modest form today, other small communities in the area did not recover from the flood.

Another unfortunate village south of the mesa also became the victim of flooding. Known as Contadero, it was drowned by the waters of the newly formed Elephant Butte Reservoir in 1924.

More to explore: *El Camino Real—The King's Highway, Fort Craig, Jornada del Muerto, Rio Grande, Sally Rooke—Heroine of the Dry Cimarron Flood*

Melvin Mills's namesake town survives today, although it has seen hard times. The original caption for this photo, taken in 1935, reads: "The town of Mills, New Mexico. The grain elevator in background at right has been long ago abandoned. The bank is closed." Photo by Dorothea Lange, May 1935. Library of Congress, Prints and Photographs Division, FSA-OW Collection, LC-USF34-001627-E DLC.

275. Mills Canyon

Location: Harding County. Just south of Roy in a turnout on the east side of NM 39 at mile marker 67. See map 3.

Marker text: The site of one of New Mexico's most spectacular horticultural enterprises, the Orchard Ranch, established by Melvin W. Mills of Springer and notable for its skillfully engineered irrigation system. The ranch cultivated 12 miles of land along the Canadian River. Vegetable gardens and several thousand fruit trees flourished in the 1880s and later. A destructive flood wiped out orchards, irrigation system, buildings, and other improvements in 1904. They were never replaced.

This is the orchard that Melvin built: along a twelve-mile stretch of bottomland at the floor of the Canadian River Canyon in 1881, District Attorney Melvin Whitson Mills planted trees—some fourteen thousand total. His orchard included peach trees, pear trees, apple trees, mulberry, apricot, chestnut, pecan, and plum, in addition to landscaped vineyards and vegetable gardens. Of particular note was the extensive irrigation system, which carried waters from the river through tunnels that partially ran underground. To his credit, Mills had created one of the most bountiful horticultural endeavors in the state. "His orchard," an account later testified, "was pointed out as one of New Mexico's show places."

It might still be today, had the fall of 1904 remained dry, had an incessant rain not fallen from September 28 to 30 and bulged the Canadian River more than four feet, sending its waters into a fervent rush over the property. The torrent spared little in its assault, drowning the orchard and gardens, pulling down fences and corrals, demolishing the outbuildings. The opulent orchard ranch had become the victim of the largest deluge of the Canadian River yet recorded by the US Geological Survey.

Until then, Melvin Whitson Mills had been a powerful force in the development of north-central New Mexico. Born on October 11, 1845, to Quaker parents living in Ontario, he moved with his family to Michigan as a child and later graduated from law school in Ann Arbor. In 1869, Mills came to New Mexico and opened a law firm in the nascent mining town of Elizabethtown. As often praised as he was vilified, especially after defending a notorious murderer in a sensational Elizabethtown trial, the young lawyer invested in ranching and mining operations and helped found the communities of Cimarron and Springer. He later platted the town formerly known as Tailholt near the Canadian River Canyon and his orchard and gave it the name Mills. After marrying Michigan native Ella House in January 1877, with whom he adopted four children, Mills moved to Springer and built there an opulent three-story, thirty-two-room mansion. He became district attorney for Rio Arriba, Taos, Colfax, and Mora Counties. Still not content, Mills retired from public service and set out to build something grand. He arranged a profitable contract to supply fresh fruits and vegetables to the finest Harvey Houses, a chain of famous hotels and restaurants serving travelers along the Santa Fe Railway, and then he planted the first seeds of his Orchard Ranch.

The loss of the orchard devastated Mills, emotionally and financially. The last harvest eked from the surviving fruit trees came in 1912, but it was too little to sustain the operation. Financially unsteady, Mills lost his home in Springer—although it would not be the last time he would see it. By 1925, Mills, then age eighty, had become bedridden with stomach pains. In his decline, he made one last request: that he be allowed to die in his former Springer mansion. The owner obliged. Mills died in his home on August 19, 1925.

Today, only stone ruins of the buildings that made up his Orchard Ranch remain at the bottom of the canyon. His namesake town, Mills, survived the Depression, barely, and stands today as one of the few reminders of the man himself.

More to explore: *Canadian River Canyon, Dulcelina Salce Curtis, Elizabethtown, Sally Rooke—Heroine of the Dry Cimarron Flood, Springer*

---

276. Mogollon

Location: Catron County. About ten miles west of the town of Mogollon, at the intersection of US 180 and NM 159, on the east side of the road. See map 5.

Marker text: The mountains and the town were named for Juan Ignacio Flores Mogollón, governor of New Mexico from 1712 to 1715. The name also is applied to the Pueblo Indians who abandoned the area in the early 1400s. These mountains were inhabited by Apaches until the late 19th century.

There are four "Mogollons" intersecting here: a prehistoric Indian culture, a Spanish governor, a range of mountains, and a town.

The mountains came first, created by volcanic activity twenty-five to forty million years ago. They stretch roughly thirty miles from Silver City, south of here, to Reserve, north of here. The mountains were probably named for Juan Ignacio Flores Mogollón, who served as governor in New Mexico from 1712 to 1715 while New Mexico was still under the authority of the Spanish Crown. In a series of historical spillovers, the governor's name, applied to the mountains, also became the name of the prehistoric Indian culture that had lived here centuries before the governor took office: the Mogollon, who had made a home in these mountains from 300 BC until at least AD 1400. Evidence of their occupation can be found throughout southwestern New Mexico and at sites like the Gila Cliff Dwellings north of Silver City. And finally, the name is also reflected in the settlement of Mogollon, a town that developed around mines prospected along the western slopes of the Mogollon Mountains in the mid-nineteenth century.

Running expeditions through these mountains in the mid-1870s, army quartermaster sergeant James C. Cooney of the Eighth Cavalry at Fort Bayard was one of the first to uncover outcrops of silver-bearing ore in a canyon along Mineral Creek. Despite the threat of Apache strikes in the mountains, Cooney declined an army commission in 1876 and rejoined civilian life to establish the small, eponymous town of Cooney around his strike. He would prospect for only a few more years before being killed by Apaches in a raid that struck the village of Cooney and the nearby village of Alma in April 1880. He was forty years old. His friends blasted a cavity inside a huge, eighteen-foot-long shroud-like boulder along Mineral Creek near where he was killed, and then they interred the Irishman's casket inside it. They used copper and silver ore from the Cooney mine to seal the entry hole and fashioned a cross of stones in memoriam across it. The unusual grave remains intact today and can be visited along Mineral Creek Road.

Cooney's death did not prevent other miners from descending on the Mogollon Mountains, especially after Indian hostilities quieted in the 1880s. The first registered success belonged to John Eberle and his Last Chance Mine, sunk near Silver Creek in 1889. Other mines soon developed in the district, both placer and underground workings, with names reflecting the thoughts foremost on the mind of their owners: Eureka, Confidence, and Deep Down. Eberle's Last Chance Mine continued to be the big producer, although the Little Fannie, sunk on what is now Fannie Hill by Frank Vingo in 1887, was no slouch. The original Cooney mine itself generated more than a million dollars, with its operations overseen by James Cooney's brother, Michael.

Within the confines of Silver Creek Canyon arose what was to become Cooney's sister camp, Mogollon. Stores, hotels, churches, a theater, an ice plant, and homes—John Eberle's being the first—went up along Main Street, which ran along the narrow floor of the canyon. The mountain overlooking the town now bears Eberle's name in recognition. Despite the havoc wreaked on the town by floods, tailing slides down the mountain slopes, and a devastating fire that leveled the community in 1894, the residents of Mogollon persisted, and their camp soon grew in size as it accepted residents leaving the settlement of Cooney.

Activity in the Mogollon district continued for more than forty years. Fluctuations in silver prices during World War I, coupled with the depletion of mineral resources in the mountains and difficulties accessing both transportation and water, eventually cut short Mogollon's glory days. Today, the town retains its rugged ambiance and offers a scenic glimpse into the mining history of southwestern New Mexico.

More to explore: *The Catwalk, Fort Bayard, Gila Cliff Dwellings National Monument*

277. Monica Fuentes Gallegos (1851–1909) and Carlota Fuentes Gallegos (1857–1936)

Location: Harding County. Twenty-four miles north of Logan, in a pullout on the south side of NM 39, between mile markers 24 and 25. See map 3.

Marker text: Monica and Carlota Gallegos, widowed sisters, ranched 375,000 acres. Monica operated a general store and saloon and issued scrip in her name. When Black Jack Ketchum raided the ranch in 1890, Monica shot him in the arm. The sisters built a school and, in 1876, the Church of the Immaculate Conception, furnished with large Italian statues. Their vision ensured economic and social stability in Gallegos.

The historical landscape of Harding County abounds with hardy individuals who braved the frontier, just as the physical landscape abounds with the legacies of their fortitude. The small ranching community of Gallegos, visible to the northwest of this Marker, is one such place. The matriarchs of the Gallegos family, Monica and Carlota Gallegos, were sisters who left their indelible marks on this part of northeastern New Mexico.

Monica and Carlota Fuentes were born seven years apart. Monica was the oldest, born in 1851; Carlota followed in 1857. They met two brothers and married them—Monica married Francisco Gallegos, and Carlota married Emeterio Gallegos—in a double wedding held on November 27, 1872, in Anton Chico, New Mexico, west of this Historic Marker. With their husbands, the Gallegos sisters came to this location, along Ute Creek north of present-day Tucumcari, a site earlier settled around 1840 by Francisco and Emeterio's father, Jesús María Gallegos. The location was originally known as Rincon Colorado, or "Red Corner," because of the red mesas in the area, but it soon took the family name and became Gallegos.

The Gallegos family and friends they invited from around Las Vegas, New Mexico, established a cattle ranch at Gallegos. Their large enterprise included a number of outbuildings. Chief among those was a small adobe church, known as the Church of the Immaculate Conception, which the Gallegos family built in 1876 for use by the ranch hands and settlers who had come to work the ranch. When a tornado demolished that structure around 1910 (accounts differ on the date), the Gallegos family had it rebuilt with reinforced sandstone (and holes in the adobe through which they could aim their rifles if they were under assault and needed to seek shelter inside). An area outside the church was designated the *campo santo*, or cemetery. The interior was furnished with life-size, lifelike statues, including one of Saint Joseph, imported to the ranch from Italy; a statue of the baby Jesus was adorned with a golden crown made from the melted jewelry of the Gallegos sisters.

Monica Gallegos had three children, Filiberto, Flaucia, and Sara. Her sister Carlota had twelve.

As their family grew, so did the ranch, eventually reaching 375,000 acres and employing about a hundred ranch hands. The ranch settlement even included a school for the children of the ranch workers. Those families often bought their food and other provisions from the Gallegos Mercantile Store and Saloon—and they paid for their purchases with a special coin that the Gallegos family issued in the name of the ranch! The coin, minted in the East, was used in place of actual currency on the ranch but had no value off it. This arrangement offered a degree of protection against theft of the large amounts of money that might otherwise have been required to operate the ranch.

It's not hard to imagine that such an enterprise might be attractive to outlaws. A Gallegos family history recounts a tale of an encounter with the dark side of New Mexico history at the ranch in the fall of 1890. The story goes that notorious train robber Thomas "Black Jack" Ketchum made an unwelcome appearance at the ranch house one winter morning, hoping to steal his way to better fortune. Black Jack is known to have frequented the Tucumcari area, being involved in a shootout near Tucumcari in June 1896, and he worked at the Bell Ranch nearby before that. (And, perhaps damningly, stole from the owner.) Monica Gallegos, who was pregnant with her third child at the time, along with her two other children, holed up inside and fired bullets out at the outlaw to keep him at bay. The standoff was said to have lasted some six hours, before Monica escaped during the night and fled secretively through the snow with her children to the safety of another part of the ranch.

Monica lost her husband in 1898, and she herself passed away on April 25, 1909. While Carlota's husband died around 1910, Carlota herself lived to be seventy-nine, passing away in 1936. The family, as well as their children, are all buried inside the Church of the Immaculate Conception.

More to explore: *Black Jack Ketchum (series), Yetta Kohn*

278. Mother Magdalen and the Sisters of Loretto

Location: Santa Fe County. In Santa Fe, on Alameda Street, in Santa Fe River Park. See map 2.

Marker text: Four Sisters of Loretto, Mother Magdalen Hayden and Sisters Roberta Brown, Rosana Dant and Catherine Mahoney, arrived in Santa Fe from Kentucky on September 26, 1852. In January 1853 they established Our Lady of Light Academy, later known as Loretto, the first school for young women in the Territory of New Mexico.

Between 1863 and 1879 the Sisters with the help of local people raised funds to build the Loretto Chapel. During the next 150 years, 263 women of Hispanic heritage joined the Sisters of Loretto. Mother Lucia Perea was the first to be named superior in Santa Fe in 1896.

The Catholic Church in New Mexico in the mid-nineteenth century, under the leadership of Bishop (and later Archbishop) Jean-Baptiste Lamy, implemented far-reaching social improvements—including building the first hospitals and some of the first educational establishments in the state. Much of the credit for the success of these efforts belongs to the women of the church, in particular the Sisters of Loretto and, later, the Sisters of Charity.

The Sisters of Loretto, originally known as the Friends of Mary at the Foot of the Cross, were founded by three women in Kentucky in 1812 to help bring education to poor children. While traveling in Kentucky in 1852, soon after he had been appointed to the New Mexico Territory, Bishop Lamy met with the order and requested their assistance in his efforts to establish proper schools in his area. New Mexico and the Southwest had just come under the control of the United States, and Lamy felt that the Church had a responsibility to attend to the educational, medical, and spiritual needs of the people there. He wanted, in particular, to establish a school for girls in Santa Fe.

That summer, six Sisters of Loretto left Kentucky to help him meet that goal. Lamy met them in Saint Louis and continued with them, first by steamer and then over the Santa Fe Trail west to New Mexico. Sadly, the superior, Mother Matilda, died of cholera en route, and another Sister fell ill and turned back. Nonetheless, four stalwart Sisters arrived in Santa Fe on September 28 ready to work: Sisters Roberta Brown, Rosana Dant, and Catherine Mahoney, along with Mother Magdalen Hayden, who had been appointed superior upon Mother Matilda's death. They were four women who would change the history and the very character of Santa Fe.

In less than a year, the Sisters had opened Our Lady of Light Academy, the first school for young women in New Mexico. The academy was both a boarding school and a day school. Later, the school was renamed the Loretto Academy for Girls. From there, the Sisters of Loretto went on to open several other schools throughout New Mexico, many of which remain open today.

Beginning in 1863, the Sisters elicited funds from the community to build a chapel on the school grounds. French-born Lamy hired French architect Projectus Mouly to design the chapel, an elegant, Gothic revival structure, modeled after the Sainte-Chapelle in Paris. When completed in 1873, it became known as Loretto Chapel.

Today, many people know Loretto Chapel by the legend of the "miracle staircase" inside it. The circular wooden staircase leading to the choir loft has no central pole or other visible means of support. One popular legend says that the chapel was built with only a ladder providing access to the choir loft. The nuns prayed for a safer way to climb to the loft, and soon after, a stranger appeared who offered to build a staircase in exchange for food and a place to sleep. He left shortly thereafter, leaving the nuns with a new staircase, one that supported its own weight. Some believe the mysterious carpenter to have been Saint Joseph.

Since the arrival of the Sisters of Loretto in New Mexico, a number of local women, many Hispanic, have joined the order. In 1896, Mother Lucia Perea became the first woman of Hispanic descent to be named superior.

Although it no longer functions as a Catholic church, Loretto Chapel remains open to the public. The mysterious staircase can be viewed but can no longer be climbed for safety reasons.

More to explore: *San Antonio de Padua Catholic Church, Santa Fe, Sisters of Charity*

Mount Taylor: *see Grants*

279. Mountainair

Location: 1. Torrance County. On the east end of Mountainair, in a pullout on the north side of US 60, at the intersection of US 60 and Wilson Avenue. See map 4.

2. Torrance County. On the west end of Mountainair, in a pullout on the south side of US 60, at the intersection of US 60 and Limit Avenue. See map 4.

Marker text: Founded in 1902, Mountainair developed as a major center for pinto bean farming in the early 20th century, until the drought of the 1940s. The region had been occupied earlier by Tompiro and eastern Tiwa pueblo Indians from prehistoric times through the mid-17th century, when it served as a major center for Spanish Franciscan missionaries.

John W. Corbett, a former newspaper publisher from Kansas, and his business partner, Colonel E. C. Manning, arrived at the eastern end of Abó Pass in 1901 and surveyed there a 120-acre townsite. Situated near the southeastern base of the Manzano Mountains, the community took the name Mountainair. The Atchison, Topeka, and Santa Fe Railway arrived in the town in 1903 in the form of the Belen Cutoff, a line that ran from Belen east through Clovis and into Texas. Mountainair incorporated that same year.

Farmers in the Estancia Basin surrounding Mountainair soon made pinto beans the basis of the valley's dry-farming economy. These farmers shipped an average of 14,751,400 pounds of "pintos" into the world each year, according to a 1937 story in the *Santa Fe New Mexican*—enough to lead the town to christen itself the "Pinto Bean

Capital of the World." The *Mountainair Independent* ran recipes for bean sandwiches, beans with white sauce, bean patties, and even cream of pinto bean and tomato soup. Farmers stacked their pickups full of vines every fall and took them to the Farr Elevator Company in Mountainair for threshing, where a hundred-pound sack of beans would net eighty-five cents. After the harvest, residents celebrated their bounty at the Bean Festival and Rodeo, where all events received the royal blessing of the radiant Bean Queen.

By the mid-1940s, however, the prosperity was fading. A prolonged drought withered the fields of the Estancia Valley and forced many farmers to seek government relief. Many in Mountainair vacated their homesteads and moved elsewhere.

It was not the first time that drought had affected the interests of people living in the valley. Scattered around Mountainair are the ruins of multistoried dwellings abandoned by Tompiro and eastern Tiwa Pueblo Indians in the 1600s. Only three of these villages—Abó, Quarai, and Gran Quivira—are accessible today. Early Spanish settlers knew the region as Las Salinas for the extensive saline lake deposits in the valley.

Using Indian labor, Franciscan priests oversaw the construction of grand-scale missions at Abó, Quarai, and Gran Quivira in the early 1600s. These missions served as places of worship and schools where priests indoctrinated the Indians into Christianity and taught them to speak Spanish. Discordant relations between the priests and the Indians, as well as between secular and civil authorities in Spanish colonial New Mexico, caused conflict in Las Salinas for decades. In the 1660s and 1670s, extended droughts added to the difficulties and created a tumult of famine and disease, and attacks by nomadic Indians weakened the pueblos. The Spanish and the Indians abandoned the area, and by 1677 the Salinas missions and pueblos lay deserted.

Mountainair today serves as a center from which to explore the pueblos of Salinas National Monument and hosts travelers along US 60. It has also become a budding center for artists.

More to explore: *Abó Pass Trail, Abó Ruins, Cedarvale, Gran Quivira Ruins, Laguna del Perro, Quarai Ruins, Tajique*

---

280. Nara Visa

Location: Quay County. In Nara Visa, at the intersection of US 54 and King Street, in front of the Community Center. See map 3.

Marker text: This area is rich in prehistoric evidence, and home of the buffalo and Plains Indians. Explored by the early Spanish, the area was settled when the Rock Island Railroad was built through in 1901.

> The brick building, built in 1921, was home for a fine school. The adobe gym was built in 1935 by WPA laborers. The buildings are listed on the National and State Historic Registers. Now a Community Center, it is the heart of community activity.

Long before the settlements of modern Quay County took shape, this region was home to great herds of buffalo, which roamed the grasslands of eastern New Mexico, Texas, and Oklahoma. Plains Indians like the Comanches hunted the beasts through the 1700s, buffalo meat serving as a staple of their diet. Archaeological evidence such as shallow pits and artifacts at various sites around Quay County and the surrounding plains speak to the earlier presence of prehistoric humans in this area. In the spring of 1541, searching for the fabled cities of gold, Spanish explorer Francisco Vásquez de Coronado passed nearby on a hunt that would lead him into Kansas; he returned through this location as well, empty handed.

The arrival of the railroad in the late eighteenth and early nineteenth century ushered in the modern history of the region. Anticipating the arrival of the railroad, early settlers set up camp close to the proposed site of tracks. When the Chicago, Rock Island, and Pacific Railroad came through as planned in 1901 on its way south to Tucumcari, a small settlement developed along the line to serve as a livestock shipping point for area ranches. It took the name Nara Visa. Most likely the name was a corruption of the surname of a local ranching family, Narvaez.

As the community of Nara Visa took shape, more permanent buildings appeared, including a saloon, churches, stores, a billiard parlor, a feed store, and a bank. The townsite was platted in 1907.

In February 1921, having outgrown the original small building that had been serving as a schoolhouse, the Board of Education contracted with the Bone Construction Company of Amarillo, Texas, to erect a new school building. That building was completed at the eastern end of town in time for fall classes that year. Listed today on the National Register of Historic Places as "an outstanding example of a rural school in New Mexico during the time the eastern part of New Mexico was being settled," the grand brick building featured a two-story, pitched-roof middle section and two flat-roofed wings on either side—the eastern wing housing an auditorium. Later, in 1936, local residents working with the Works Progress Administration (WPA) began fashioning adobe bricks to be used in the construction of a new gymnasium for the school. Erected as a separate building on the east side of the school building itself and completed the following year, the gym contained both a basketball court and two additional classrooms. Students attending classes at the Nara Visa school were doing so in one of the grandest early school buildings in the state.

Today, although the school and gymnasium still stand, they no longer serve in their original capacities. After shifting population trends forced the school to close in 1968, the residents of Nara Visa repurposed the facility for use as a community center, where locals could hold meetings, weddings, and other events. It continues in that role today.

Speaking of which, if you plan to attend a meeting in Nara Visa, be sure to set your watch ahead one hour so you don't arrive late. Given its close proximity to Texas, Nara Visa observes Central Time, while the rest of New Mexico observes Mountain Time.

More to explore: *Cedarvale, Comanche Country, La Cienega School, Old Armijo School*

281. Navajo Indian Reservation

Location: McKinley County. Near the Tohatchi Middle School in Tohatchi, on the north side of US 491 between mile markers 23 and 24. See map 1.

Marker text: Occupants of northwest New Mexico since the 16th century, the Navajos today comprise the most populous Indian group in the United States. The 17th, 18th, and 19th centuries witnessed alternate periods of conflict and trading with their neighbors. The Navajo's economy traditionally has been based on stockraising, weaving, silversmithing, and more recently on mineral development.

Many geographic features in northwestern New Mexico bear Navajo place names, testifying to the long-standing presence of Navajos in the Four Corners region of southern Utah, Arizona, Colorado, and New Mexico. Navajos, who call themselves Dineh, or "the People," are the most populous Native American tribe in the United States. Their reservation, with tribal headquarters in Window Rock, Arizona, is the largest in the country.

Oral tradition among Navajos holds that the Dineh were required to pass through three underworlds before emerging into the fourth, which became their home. Navajos know the region of their earliest occupation, a sacred land near present-day Blanco in the Four Corners area, as Dinetah. By the sixteenth century, Navajos were hunting animals and growing corn within a homeland bounded by four revered mountains: Sierra Blanca Peak to the east near Alamosa, Colorado; Mount Taylor to the south near Grants; the San Francisco Peaks to the west near Flagstaff, Arizona; and Mount Hesperus to the north in the La Plata Mountains.

Through the nineteenth century, Navajos' relations with other Indian tribes alternated between conflict and partnership. Navajos often stole the livestock of the more sedentary Pueblo Indian villages along the Rio Grande, yet they also tapped into the trading networks between the Pueblos and tribes of the Plains, like the Comanches. The arrival of the Spanish in New Mexico in the sixteenth century and subsequent generations of Spanish, Mexican, and later Anglo migration into northwestern New Mexico introduced new cultural exchanges—and new tensions. As settlers encroached upon traditional Navajo homelands and hunting grounds, Navajo warriors raided their villages and camps in an effort to hold back Anglo settlement.

A bleak episode in Navajo history unfolded after the Southwest came under the control of the United States. In 1862, military commander General James H. Carleton established the Bosque Redondo Reservation in southeastern New Mexico with the misguided intent of creating a new home for Navajos, resettling them into an agricultural lifestyle there (and simultaneously removing them from a part of the state desired by the government for settlement and mineral development). Through a series of harsh raids and a scorched-earth campaign, soldiers led by Colonel Christopher "Kit" Carson forced more than 2,500 Navajo men, women, and children to walk three hundred miles or farther to the new reservation. Navajos know this compulsory exile as the Long Walk. Many died in the agonizing journey, and many more perished at the reservation from disease exacerbated by drought and famine. Finally, in 1868, the army negotiated the closing of the Bosque Redondo with Navajo leaders. The result was the Navajo Treaty, which established a permanent reservation in the Navajo homeland of the Four Corners.

Ranching and the sale of arts and crafts have been the traditional basis of the Navajo economy. Navajos are known for their beautiful handwoven rugs and sand paintings as well as for their silver and turquoise jewelry. Since the 1920s, proceeds from the mining of coal and natural gas reserves of the San Juan Basin and elsewhere within the Navajo Nation have added to the economic pedestal of the Dineh.

More to explore: *Farmington, Fort Sumner and Fort Sumner State Monument (series), Manuelito Area*

New Goodnight Trail: *see Goodnight-Loving Trail*

New Mexico Bureau of Mines and Mineral Resources Museum: *see New Mexico Tech*

New Mexico Historic Women Marker Initiative

Location: Throughout the state.

Marker text: The New Mexico Historic Women Marker Initiative was founded in 2005 by members of the New Mexico Women's Forum in a statewide effort to recognize women's contributions to New Mexico history on the state's Official Scenic Historic Markers. The Initiative ensures that women's diverse histories will be remembered and told, and will inspire and provide a guide for future generations. The 2006 Legislature funded the project.

Note: This Marker text appears on the backs of most of the Historic Markers erected as part of the Historic Women Marker Initiative.

Before 2005, only one woman was recognized with her own official New Mexico Scenic Historic Marker—and she didn't even exist. That woman, commonly known as the Kneeling Nun, is a rock formation near Silver City resembling a penitent Sister in prayer.

A handful of other women were mentioned in Historic Markers about other topics: Susan McSween in the Three Rivers Marker in Otero County, Maria Martinez in the Marker for the Pueblo of San Ildefonso, Mabel Dodge Luhan in the Marker for Kit Carson Park Memorial Cemetery in Taos, Elizabeth Garrett in the Marker for the New Mexico School for the Blind and Visually Impaired in Alamogordo, Frieda Lawrence in the D. H. Lawrence Ranch Marker near Taos, and Bethel Vernon Fuller in the Lordsburg-Hidalgo Library Marker in Lordsburg. And of course, the presence of women could be inferred through plural nouns like colonists and pioneers, farmers and ranchers, wives and sisters and mothers, legislators, teachers, soldiers, and scientists. But the explicit presence of women in the official Markers was not in proportion to their presence in the history of the state, nor to their importance in creating that history.

In 2005, three friends who were members of the International Women's Forum (New Mexico), an organization of women leaders, brought a proposal to the governor's office and the New Mexico state legislature in Santa Fe to erect a series of Historic Markers dedicated specifically to recognizing the contributions of women in the history of the state. In addition to making sure that those stories were known, the project also hoped that the contributions of these women would inspire future generations to their own successes. A selection committee was formed, including members of the International Women's Forum (New Mexico), the Historic Preservation Division, the Department of Transportation, the Commission on the Status of Women, and representatives of the Native American community, joined by community historians, genealogists, and photographers. Since that time, the selection committee has worked with the commissioners of every county and many of the pueblos and Indian tribes to research, write text for, and erect more than sixty Markers throughout the state specifically dedicated to women. And more are planned.

Now, joining Francisco Vásquez de Coronado, Juan de Oñate, Billy the Kid, Pat Garrett, Albert Fountain, and other historical figures on the stage set by the Historic Markers along New Mexico roadways are women like Santa Clara Pueblo artist Pablita Velarde, who brought Pueblo scenes to life in her paintings; Nina Otero-Warren, the first woman to run for Congress in New Mexico; Dr. Meta Christy, the first black osteopath in the state; Peggy Pond Church, who captured the essence of the Pajarito Plateau in her sensitive poems; Sally Rooke, whose heroism saved a number of lives while costing her own; Louise Massey Mabie, who brought talent and grace to the radio airwaves through the Depression; Dr. Dolores Gonzáles, a pioneer of bilingual education; and Evelyn M. Vigil and Juanita T. Toledo, who rescued a style of pottery that many feared lost to history. These women are joined by many others who have had important roles in the long and vibrant history of the state.

It turns out they were there all along. It took the New Mexico Historic Women Marker Initiative and the hard work of the selection committee and New Mexico county commissioners to bring them center stage. Or, in this case, to the faceplates of those big brown signs on the side of the road.

282. New Mexico School for the Blind and Visually Impaired

Location: Otero County. In Alamogordo, in front of the New Mexico School for the Blind and Visually Impaired, 1900 North White Sands Boulevard. See map 6.

Marker text: The New Mexico School for the Blind and Visually Impaired was founded on granted land in 1903 by the new territorial governor. The teacher and later regent was the blind daughter of lawman Pat Garrett, Elizabeth Garrett, who solicited the support of Helen Keller for the school's expansion. Ms. Garrett also wrote the state song, O, Fair New Mexico.

As New Mexico entered the twentieth century, blind and deaf students in the state were coeducated at a school in Santa Fe. But the educational needs of blind students were found to be very different from those of deaf students. So, in 1903, the territorial legislature approved the creation of a new school to serve blind and visually impaired students exclusively. Alamogordo resident William Ashton Hawkins, a member of the territorial legislature, successfully lobbied to have the school built in Alamogordo. The town of Alamogordo and the larger county of Otero in which it sits donated twenty acres of land for the purpose, and New Mexico governor Miguel Otero himself appointed the first board of regents. Opening in 1906 as the New Mexico Institute for the Blind, the school underwent a number of name changes over time and is today known as the New Mexico School for the Blind and Visually Impaired, often abbreviated NMSBVI. Enrollment in the first year of the school included eleven boys and ten girls.

That number soon grew, and by 1925 the school was in need of expanded facilities. Through Elizabeth Garret, the daughter of lawman Pat Garrett (most famous for having killed outlaw Billy the Kid), who was blind herself and served as a regent, the school solicited help from Helen Keller. Keller was a well-known advocate for the blind and the subject of the dramatic series *The Miracle Worker*. At Garrett's request, Keller spoke before the New Mexico state legislature in Santa Fe on March 9, 1925, in support of an appropriation to the school for new construction. The bill passed.

Today, the Alamogordo campus offers elementary school classes from kindergarten to sixth grade, as well as a secondary school for grades seven through twelve. Students at the school may be blind, or they may have low or impaired vision. Instruction in braille is given, and adaptive technologies such as screen readers are used in classrooms. In addition to core studies such as math, English, and history, the NMSBVI teaches students independent living skills that will help them succeed on their own after graduation. Students are encouraged to participate in community events and often attend classes in the Alamogordo public school system.

A number of NMSBVI students live on campus throughout their time at the school; others attend only during the day. Buildings and facilities at the school include classrooms, a gym and auditorium, an administration building, a central garden and gazebo, and residence halls. One of those residence halls, Garrett Hall, the dormitory for girls, remembers in its name former NMSBVI teacher and regent Elizabeth Garrett.

In addition to her teaching skills, Garrett was also an accomplished poet and songwriter—she was once called the "Songbird of the Southwest." She wrote the NMSBVI school song, with a first stanza that allowed students to sing their school spirit: "There's a school in Alamo / That we think is great / 'Tis in fair New Mexico / Called our Sunshine State / All our hearts beat loyally / Everyone is true / To our dear old Alma Mater / Love it? Course we do!"

Garrett wrote another song of note, "O Fair New Mexico." Upon request by New Mexico governor Washington E. Lindsey, Garrett performed the song personally before the state legislature in 1917; the following day, legislators voted unanimously to make it the official state song of New Mexico. Its lyrics speak to the beauty of the state: "Under a sky of azure / Where balmy breezes blow / Kissed by the golden sunshine / Is Nuevo Mejico."

Speaking of golden things, the New Mexico School for the Blind and Visually Impaired's mascot is a golden bear.

More to explore: *Alamogordo (see under La Luz), Pat Garrett Murder Site, State History of Education Museum*

283. New Mexico Tech

Location: Socorro County. In Socorro, on the campus of New Mexico Tech, at the intersection of College and Leroy Avenues. See map 5.

Marker text: Founded in 1889 as New Mexico's School of Mines, New Mexico Institute of Mining and Technology offers degrees through the doctorate in a number of science and engineering disciplines. In addition to its academic functions, the institute also conducts extensive research and development activities.

284. New Mexico Bureau of Mines and Mineral Resources Museum

Location: Socorro County. In Socorro, on the campus of New Mexico Tech, at the entrance to the museum. See map 5.

Marker text: Based on personal collection willed to the New Mexico School of Mines by C. T. Brown in 1928, this museum displays thousands of mineral specimens from around the world with special emphasis on minerals found in New Mexico. Highlights include smithsonite from Kelly (Magdalena District), linarite from Bingham, Grants District uranium, Carlsbad potash, Silver City copper, Harding pegmatite minerals, and numerous fossils.

Note: Cony T. Brown did not will his collection to the school, as noted in the Marker text. His son sold the collection to the museum for a minimal cost.

New Mexico was not yet a state when the territorial legislature voted in February 1889 to establish three institutions of higher learning, among them the University of New Mexico in Albuquerque and the New Mexico College of Agriculture and Mechanical Arts (now New Mexico State University) in Las Cruces. The third was the School of Mines, intended, as the act stated,

to furnish facilities for the education of such persons as may desire to receive instruction in chemistry, metallurgy, mineralogy, geology, mining, milling, engineering, mathematics, mechanics, drawing, the fundamental laws of the United States and the rights and duties of citizenship, and such other courses.

Local merchant Juan José Baca, who served in the legislature and owned mines in this part of central New Mexico, proposed in the early 1890s that the School of Mines be built in Socorro. The town seemed an expedient choice. Midway between Albuquerque and Las Cruces and surrounded by the mining camps of Magdalena, Kelly, and Carthage, Socorro was also home at the time to the Billing Smelter, the largest enterprise in the state for processing mineral ores.

Members of the legislature agreed, and soon construction crews had finished work on a new building in Socorro to serve as the sole structure of the new college. Called "Old Main" even in its youth, the edifice held the original lecture rooms, library, and laboratories of the institution. The School of Mines opened its doors in September 1893 to a class of seven students. Enrollment increased every year thereafter, and the school added additional buildings to house the new capacity. Since 1927, the school has also been the headquarters for the New Mexico Bureau of Mines and Mineral Resources, today known as the Bureau of Geology and Mineral Resources.

In its early years, the college housed a geology museum in one room of Old Main. According to a history written by Paige Christiansen, the collection included more than four thousand minerals, ores, and rocks properly organized and classified. Regrettably, disaster took an irreplaceable toll in July 1928 when a fire gutted Old Main and destroyed the extensive collection.

So the school tried again. In 1938, in anticipation of the fiftieth anniversary of the institution, the geology department purchased at greatly reduced cost from benefactor Tom Brown a collection of some 1,500 specimens gathered by his father, Maine-born Cony T. Brown. The elder Brown, a successful local mining engineer, former president of the Socorro State Bank, state legislator, and regent of the School of Mines itself, had remained devoted in his lifetime to the development of the institution. New Mexico historian Ralph Twitchell considered him "one of the most capable mining men in the Southwest." Brown's contributions to the town of Socorro and to the school are remembered in the name of the building that replaced Old Main: Brown Hall.

Cony T. Brown was a determining influence in the development of New Mexico Tech. His mineral collection formed the basis of the current Bureau of Geology Museum. According to Bureau of Geology officials, Brown likely posed against this backdrop of cornstalks in 1922 to accentuate his exceptional six-foot, three-inch height. Courtesy Frank and Peggy Paxton Dailey, New Mexico Bureau of Geology and Mineral Resources, Historic Photograph Archives, Socorro.

To recognize its expanded educational facilities, the school in 1915 was renamed the New Mexico Institute of Mining and Technology. It is often known today simply as New Mexico Tech.

More to explore: *Kelly, Magdalena, Socorro*

285. Nina Otero-Warren (1881–1965)

Location: Valencia County. In Los Lunas, at the Rail Runner Station on Juan Perea Road. See map 4.

Marker text: Maria Adelina Isabel Emilia (Nina) Otero-Warren was born into two of New Mexico's prominent Spanish colonial families near Los Lunas. A leader in New Mexico's suffrage movement, in 1922 she was the first woman in state history to run for Congress. A political and social reformer, she worked as Santa Fe Public Schools Superintendent and for the WPA. In 1936, she wrote Old Spain in Our Southwest.

Nina Otero-Warren's greatest contribution to the history of women's rights might have been in a life spent leading by example. She was the first woman in New Mexico to run for Congress. Portrait of Nina Otero-Warren. Bergere Family Photograph Collection 1975-024, Image 217012, courtesy New Mexico State Records Center and Archives.

After María Adelina Isabel Emilia Otero-Warren, known to most as "Nina," announced her candidacy for the US House of Representatives on the Republican ticket for New Mexico in the election of 1922, coverage in the press was generally supportive—despite one article that focused more on her hairstyle than her policy positions. She lost the election to Democrat John Morrow of Raton, but she won a place in New Mexico history as the first woman in the state to run for Congress.

Otero-Warren was born in 1881 near Los Lunas, New Mexico. Her mother, Eloise Luna, and her father, Manuel Basilio Otero, were descended from two prominent families with roots reaching back to the Spanish colonial era. (Indeed, Los Lunas is named after the Luna family.) Nina's father was killed when she was young, but her mother remarried into the Bergere family and moved the family to Santa Fe. Nina attended school at Maryville College of the Sacred Heart in Saint Louis, Missouri, but returned to New Mexico after graduation. Her family had political connections: her uncle was a justice on the New Mexico Supreme Court, and one of her cousins was governor. In Santa Fe, Nina met and married First Lieutenant Rawson Warren of the Fifth US Cavalry in 1908. Their marriage lasted only two years, and Otero-Warren never remarried.

With burgeoning national interest in the suffrage movement after 1910, Otero-Warren began to campaign actively for women's right to vote, even leading the New Mexico chapter of the National Women's Party, then known as the Congressional Union. In 1917, Otero-Warren became the first female superintendent of the Santa Fe County Public Schools. While still holding that position, she was appointed to serve as a member of the State Board of Health upon its formation in 1919. She was so well regarded in that position that when she tried to resign from the post two years later, the governor rejected her resignation.

In 1920, Otero-Warren became the Republican Party's nominee for the US Congress—the first woman in the state to run for that seat. Her campaign focused on helping veterans after World War I, maintaining the budget, and emphasizing social welfare issues. "I will . . . work for all possible federal aid," she wrote in a candidacy notice in August 1922, "which will help the state to progress in matters of education and in matters of health and child welfare."

When the election went to her opponent, Otero-Warren returned to education, serving as the inspector of Indian schools in Santa Fe. With the onset of the Great Depression, she worked to address the problem of illiteracy by serving as the supervisor of literacy programs for the Works Progress Administration in New Mexico. In addition to writing a manual for teachers on teaching English as a second language, she also created language guides, written in both Spanish and English, that explained common tasks such as writing and mailing letters. The guides introduced new vocabulary words and were useful to adult learners as well as young people.

Otero-Warren's abiding pride in her own cultural traditions and history as well as the folklore of the region found their public expression in her writing. In 1936, she wrote the book *Old Spain in Our Southwest*, offering recollections of her own life as well as short essays and vignettes on the ways of life of Spanish-speaking people in rural New Mexico. Sections of the book included descriptions of baptismal and marriage rituals, saint's days, and a history of education in New Mexico.

Otero-Warren died at her home in Santa Fe on January 3, 1965.

More to explore: *Inez Bushner Gill, Maralyn Budke (see under Inez Bushner Gill), María "Concha" Concepción Ortiz y Pino de Kleven, Marjorie Bell Chambers, Santa Fe*

286. Oil and Gas

Location: Lea County. East of Hobbs, in Ken Towle Park, on the north side of US 62/180, between mile markers 108 and 109. See map 6.

Marker text: Completion of the discovery well of the Hobbs Pool six miles south, April 12, 1929, focuses attention upon the potential of New Mexico as a major source of oil and natural gas. Steady development under the State Conservation Program gradually moved New Mexico into sixth nationwide in oil production and fourth in gas production.

While Lea County attained first place in the value of oil and gas production, these positions achieved during the 1950s and 60s were maintained as the decade of the 1970s opened.

It's hard to imagine southeastern New Mexico today without the presence of the oil and gas industry, so prevalent has that industry become in defining the economic foundation of this corner of the state, and indeed part of the very character of the region. The pump jacks that pull oil from the ground around Hobbs are as much a part of the landscape here as yucca plants in southwestern New Mexico or stunning red mesas around Abiquiú. Yet the region was settled originally on farming and ranching, and its early years are filled with stories of cattle drives, and giant cattle empires and the barons who ran them. It took the discovery of oil under Artesia in 1924 to add oil and gas into the economic mix that sustains the region today.

A few years later, the discovery of the Hobbs Pool would further solidify the presence of the oil and gas industry here. On June 13, 1928, in a location just to the southwest of Hobbs, workers with the Midwest Refining Company struck the liquid gold they had hoped to find here. Their discovery well, known as State no. 1, found oil at a depth of more than four thousand feet. (Several exploratory wells might be drilled in the search for oil in a given location; the "discovery well" is the first one of those to produce.) The well had tapped into reserves underlying the Permian Basin, a 68,000-square-mile geographic designation that includes parts of eastern New Mexico and western Texas. In New Mexico, the basin encompasses Lea County, also including parts of Roosevelt County to the north and Chaves and Eddy Counties to the west.

Oil had been discovered in other parts of the Permian Basin in Texas prior to 1929. With the discovery of the Hobbs Pool, Hobbs and Lea County became major contributors as well. A report written for the New Mexico School of Mines (now the New Mexico Institute of Mining and Technology) in 1931 had this to say about the potential of the Hobbs Pool:

It is conservatively estimated that the present productive zone in the lower Permian will ultimately yield at least 150,000,000 barrels of oil. With proper handling of wells and the exploitation of other known productive horizons this amount of oil may easily be doubled. Enormous quantities of gas are also present in the field and will probably some day be utilized both for supplying commercial markets and for assisting in forcing more oil from the ground. All productive wells flow naturally.

The discovery was the impetus for the development of this part of the state as a major source of oil and natural gas. Further, it brought new economics, which brought new ways of life and new development to nearby communities like Hobbs.

Since that time, New Mexico has become one of the top oil- and gas-producing states in the country. At one time, New Mexico ranked sixth in the country in oil production and fourth in gas production. Those numbers fluctuate annually. According to statistics from the US Energy Information Administration, New Mexico in 2013 ranked still ranked sixth in the country in terms of crude oil production, behind states like Texas, Alaska, and California. And, in 2011, the state ranked seventh in natural gas production. Much of that is credited to the wells right here in Lea County.

The site of Midwest State no. 1 can be seen near the intersection of South Grimes Street and East Stanolind Road in southeast Hobbs.

More to explore: *Artesia, Hobbs, Llano Estacado and Oil (see under Llano Estacado [series]), Lovington*

287. Oil Country

Location: Lea County. East of Eunice, in a rest area at the northeast end of the intersection of NM 18 and NM 176/234 (Andrews Highway). See map 6.

Marker text: Southern part of Llano Estacado, Staked Plains, overlies prolific oil and gas geological formations of Pennsylvanian and Permian age; Monument Jal field to west, Drinkard field to south and Elliot Littman to north. At surface, Ogalalla Formation yield gravel and caliche; at depth, it supplies precious water. Elevation: 3,395 feet.

"Where cattle grazed," as a 1940s guide to New Mexico by the Works Progress Administration observed about the area around Eunice, "truckloads of workers and machinery rush by." Those workers and machinery are part of the extensive (and lucrative) oil industry, which dominates the economy of southeastern New Mexico. Pump jacks scattered across the plains here, known as the Llano Estacado, or "Staked Plains," silently and rhythmically genuflect as they pull black "liquid gold" from deep within the earth day and night. This is oil country.

It's also natural gas country. Soon after oil was discovered in the area in 1924, natural gas was discovered here, too. Both lie deep within underground geological formations dating to the Pennsylvanian epoch of the Carboniferous period, occurring more than 350 million years ago, and the Permian period, the last before the rise of the dinosaurs. The latter period also gave name to the Permian Basin, the large sedimentary basin encompassing far southeastern New Mexico and western Texas, so named for the large number of rocks from the Permian period to be found here. It is also the name by which the oil- and gas-producing region of southeastern New Mexico is known—the place all those workers are rushing through. According to the New Mexico Bureau of Geology and Mineral Resources, the Permian Bain accounts for 95 percent of the oil production in New Mexico and 33 percent of the state's natural gas production.

Oil- and gas-producing fields exist where oil and gas in source rocks underneath the surface have risen upward through more porous rock layers until becoming "trapped" by harder rock layers, creating what can be extensive reservoirs. Oil may flow upward in wells naturally if enough pressure exists to move it, but it can also extracted by pump jacks, the ubiquitous rocking machines that account for much of the scenery here. Because they are strong and obliging machines, pump jacks are sometimes known as "nodding donkeys."

The field west of this Historic Marker is known as the Monument Jal Field, for the towns of Monument and Jal. To the south is the Drinkard Field, and to the northeast is the Elliott Littman Field.

The earth here also yields stores of underground water, collected in an aquifer that is part of the extensive Ogalalla Formation stretching from western Texas to the southern part of South Dakota. On the surface, the Ogalalla Formation is topped with gravel and caliche (a sedimentary rock formed when calcium carbonate binds gravel, sand, and other minerals together), much of which as been washed down over the Great Plains from the slopes of the Rocky Mountains.

More to explore: *Hobbs, Jal, Oil and Gas*

288. Old Armijo School

Location: Bernalillo County. In south Albuquerque, in front of the school at 1021 Isleta Boulevard, SW. See map 4.

Marker text: Constructed in 1914, this building was designed by Atanacio Montoya, a progressive educator who introduced many reforms into early 20th century rural schools. It served as the school for the Village of Armijo until 1948. This school incorporated architectural features that were considered quite innovative and advanced for its time and is the only surviving structure of its kind.

When Atanacio Montoya became superintendent of schools for Bernalillo County in 1912, he faced the challenge of improving access to education in a New Mexico that only that year had achieved statehood. Having grown up in the small agricultural village of Casa Colorada south of Belen, Montoya was especially interested in the education of the underprivileged and those children living in rural communities. As an editorial in the *Santa Fe New Mexican* later recounted:

It is a truism, often expressed, that the country affords no instance of government neglect more notable than the failure to look after the education of the Spanish-speaking rural people of New Mexico. These people have been in every sense of the word underprivileged in education opportunities. Mr. Montoya, familiar for years with these conditions, who has himself done more than any other one educator here to remedy them, is apparently leaving no stone unturned to see that they have their belated opportunity.

One of those stones was the Old Armijo School in the town of Armijo south of Albuquerque. Known at the time as the Ranchos de Atrisco District Four School, the building when completed in 1914 illustrated a thoughtful and progressive-minded approach to facilities design. Large windows and a modern lighting system in the four classrooms ensured that no student sat in darkness or in an area that was too bright. Square classrooms allowed the teacher's voice to infiltrate the entire room. Students no longer had to run to an outhouse when the need arose, as the building introduced the luxury of indoor restrooms. Even the chalkboards were improved: Montoya freed teachers from scratching on antiquated black screens and gave them instead smoother green boards.

Montoya knew that the greatest asset of the school was not the building but the personnel within it. This was knowledge gained by experience. Montoya, who was thirty-six when appointed superintendent, had received his degree from the University of New Mexico and then taught at his alma mater as a professor of Spanish. He thus emphasized the hiring of quality teachers throughout the Bernalillo School District. Teachers were required to possess at least a second-grade teaching certificate and to prove their mental acuity by passing an examination before they were hired. Current teachers got a raise that almost doubled their yearly salary.

"The mission of the teacher," Montoya once said, "is more important than that of the priest, the minister, or the parent in these county schools."

Montoya continued to effect change in New Mexico schools in a greater capacity when he was later elected state school superintendent. The Armijo school served students and faculty until 1948, when population shifts in the Albuquerque area led to its closing. Today the building is used as a community meeting place.

More to explore: *Cedarvale, La Cienega School, Lincoln-Jackson School, Los Padillas, Nara Visa, State History of Education Museum*

Old Colfax County Courthouse: *see Springer*

Old Dowlin Mill: *see Ruidoso*

Old Fort Sumner and "Billy the Kid's" Grave: *see Fort Sumner and Fort Sumner State Monument (series)*

Old Silver City "Memory Lane": *see Silver City*

289. Old Spanish Trail

Location: Rio Arriba County. In Chama, at the Visitors Information Center, at the intersection of US 64 and NM 17. See map 2.

Marker text: In 1829–30, Antonio Armijo traveled from Abiquiú to California to trade for mules, thus extending the Old Spanish Trail and opening it to trade between Santa Fe and Los Angeles. His route turned west, near present-day Abiquiú Dam, to Largo Canyon, which led him to the San Juan River.

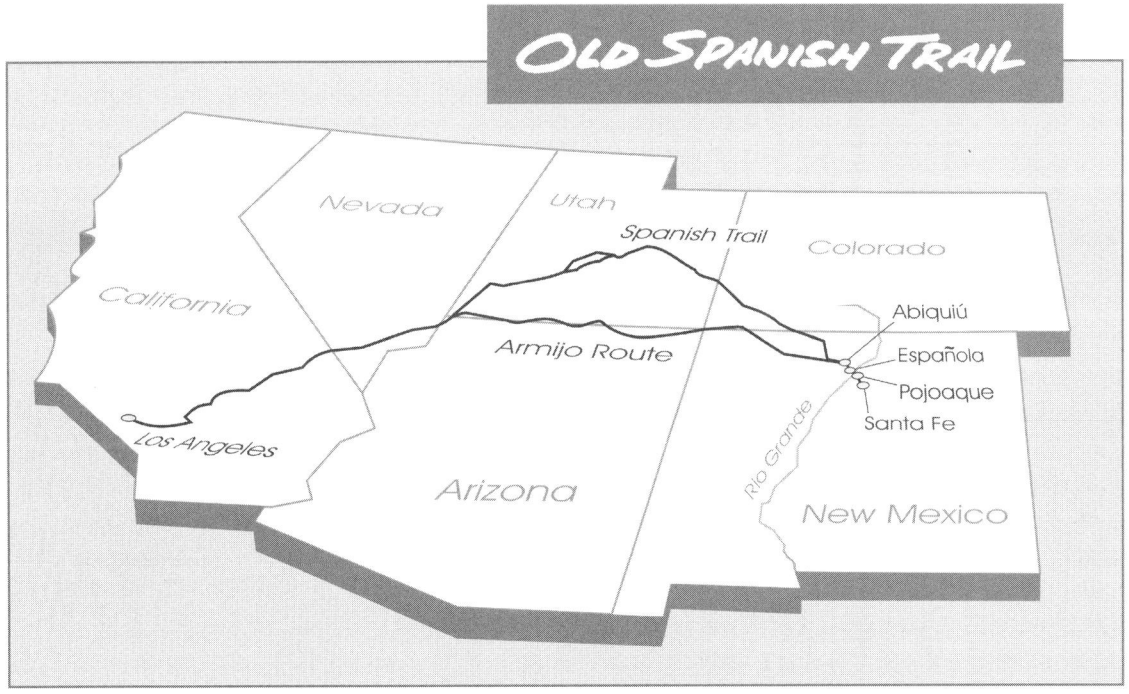

Antonio Armijo's legacy was being the first to travel the full length of what would become known as the Spanish Trail. The trail ran through north-central New Mexico, Arizona, Utah, Nevada, and then into California. Illustration by David Carter.

History credits northern New Mexico trader Antonio Armijo as the first to traverse the full length of what would become known as the Old Spanish Trail, an overland route between New Mexico and California. Armijo and his crew traveled the trail in 1829 with the blessing of New Mexico governor José Antonio Cháves, who summed up both the purpose and outcome of their mission in a letter dated May 14, 1830, to the minister of interior affairs in Mexico City:

On the eighth of November of last year, a company of about sixty men left this territory for California with the purpose of trading for mules with the products of this country. They have been traveling through unknown deserts until now, and have succeeded in discovering a new way of communication.... From the itinerary which I am sending Your Excellency it can be assumed that the distance which separates California from this territory is not great.

Portions of the Spanish Trail had existed prior to Armijo's journey. Much of the route, in fact, traced a network of trails already laid by Comanches, Navajos, and other Indians of the Southwest. In addition, some sections had been earlier trod by other Spanish travelers, including Franciscan priests Fray Francisco Atanasio Domínguez and Fray Silvestre Vélez de Escalante, who followed the trail in 1776 in their aborted attempt to open a route between Spanish missions in New Mexico and Monterey, California.

Armijo kept a diary of his eighty-six-day journey, which started near what is now Abiquiú Dam on November 7, 1829. With a sixty-man convoy in tow, Armijo passed through present-day Santa Fe National Forest, then continued northwest through what is now the Jicarilla Apache Indian Reservation. From there, the men followed Largo Canyon for four days until refreshing themselves at the San Juan River just east of present-day Bloomfield on November 15. They continued along the present boundary between Arizona and Utah, passed south of Las Vegas, Nevada, and finally arrived at San Gabriel Mission near Los Angeles on January 31. There, according to an official report of the journey, "they were hospitably received by the inhabitants, who were very surprised to see them arrive from the direction which until then was unknown."

For two decades thereafter, trade caravans laden with goods left Santa Fe in the fall to bump their way overland to the Pacific coast. John C. Frémont, a member of the Army Corps of Topographical Engineers assigned to survey portions of the West in the mid-nineteenth century, traveled sections of the route in California and followed it to Utah. Frémont was the first to use the term "Spanish Trail" in describing the path, a name by which it is still recognized today.

Although variant routes arose on the trail over time, travel diminished with the forging of other trails to California after 1848 and the arrival of the railroad four decades later.

More to explore: *Domínguez-Escalante Trail*

Oñate's Route: *see El Camino Real—The King's Highway*

Palisades Sill: *see Cimarron Canyon State Park*

290. Pajarito

Location: Bernalillo County. In Pajarito, at the intersection of NM 314 (Isleta Boulevard) and Pajarito Road, on the east side of NM 314. See map 4.

Marker text: In the 17th century, the Spanish established a series of farming and ranching communities, called estancias, along the western bank of the Rio Grande. The Camino Real normally followed the east bank of the river, but a western branch of the road was developed along what is now Isleta Boulevard to incorporate these estancias and later communities such as Pajarito (little bird) and nearby Los Padillas.

The predominantly Hispanic neighborhood of Pajarito is one of many small, unincorporated villages that today make up the South Valley of Albuquerque. While each of these neighborhoods retains it own distinct identity, they share a common culture, demographic makeup, and history.

That history began with the Pueblo Indians, who had farmed along the Rio Grande long before the Spanish arrived in New Mexico in the late sixteenth century. Spanish priests established missions at some of the Indian pueblos, including the one at nearby Isleta around 1613. At the same time, Spanish colonists began to establish ranches in the river valley north and south of present-day Albuquerque. These ranches, known as estancias, lay mostly along the western bank of the Rio Grande. A loose collection of some twenty such farming and ranching properties existed in the southern valley by 1670. But change came ten years later in the form of the Pueblo Revolt, an uprising among the Pueblo Indians during which the Spanish throughout New Mexico were expelled from the state and forced to flee south for safety.

After the return of the Spanish twelve years later, a new string of settlements began to emerge here, their owners subsisting by farming and raising sheep. The villa of Alburquerque was established in 1706 (the first *r* would later be dropped), and a number of other farming settlements began to form around it. One took a name, Parajito, that translated into English as "Little Bird." Pajarito, established in 1711, grew over time, and by 1770 was home to almost forty families.

The community, along with others that adjoined it like Atrisco to the north and Los Padillas to the south, lay along the west bank of the river. The villages were on the opposite bank from the major commercial trade route known as the Camino Real, or Royal Road. The Camino Real stretched from Santa Fe to Mexico and allowed for the transfer of goods, along with the arrival of new settlers and colonists. After crossing the Rio Grande from the west bank to the east near present-day El Paso, the Camino Real continued north through the state on the east bank. But, over time, variations in the course of the Royal Road developed. One such variation near here crossed the river just north of Isleta Pueblo to allow access to the communities on the west bank, like Los Padillas and Pajarito, and continued north. That route followed closely the course of Isleta Boulevard today.

Friedrich Adolph Wislizenus, a German-born explorer who traveled to New Mexico with a military expedition in 1846, left a description of the farming activities around Albuquerque as he saw them, giving us a glimpse of what life in Pajarito may have been like at the time:

*The country around Albuquerque appears to be well cultivated. Though the soil is sandy, and apparently not fertile, by irrigation they produce abundant crops, often twice a year. They cultivate mostly maize, wheat, beans, and red pepper (*chile colorado*). The fields are without fences. A canal, by which water from the river is led into the plain, provides by its ramifications the whole cultivated ground with the means of irrigation. How quick this* *sandy, apparently sterile soil in the valley of the [Rio Grande] is by affluence of water changed into the most fertile, is astonishing.*

Travel over the Camino Real ebbed after the arrival of the railroad in New Mexico in 1880.

The origin of the name of the community, Pajarito—Little Bird—is unknown. Place-names historian Robert Julyan suggests that it might have come from "birds in the cottonwood groves along the Rio Grande."

More to explore: *Albuquerque, El Camino Real—The King's Highway, Los Padillas*

291. Palo Flechado Pass
Elevation: 9,101 feet

Location: Taos County. At Palo Flechado Pass in Carson National Forest, in a pullout on the west side of US 64, between mile markers 272 and 273. See map 2.

Marker text: Palo Flechado (tree pierced with arrows) Pass was used by natives and newcomers traveling from the eastern plains to Taos by way of the Cimarron river. The name may be attributed to the Flecha de Palo Apache band (first mentioned by Juan de Ulibarri in 1706) inhabiting the plains east of the mountains in the early 1700s or to a Taos Indian custom of shooting one's remaining arrows into a tree near the pass following a successful buffalo hunt.

For many years before the arrival of the Spanish in New Mexico, Plains Indians like the Apaches, Comanches, and Kiowas traveled along the Cimarron River and through a pass in the Taos Range, a route equivalent to that of US 64 today. The name of the pass they crossed, Palo Flechado, translates as "Tree Pierced with Arrows." As there is no shortage of timbers in the pass, there is also no shortage of explanations for the name. One account credits its origin to arrows shot into trees by the Plains Indians to mark the course of their journey over the summit. Another favors the idea that the arrows were found in a tree after a fight between Indian tribes. Still another claims that the arrows were part of a traditional ritual among Indians to shoot spare arrows into a tree after a successful buffalo hunt.

One of the first Spanish accounts of this region can be found in the diary of Sergeant Major Juan de Ulibarri. In 1706, the Spanish governor, don Francisco Cuervo y Valdés, sent Ulibarri to the land northeast of Taos Pueblo to recover several Picurís Indians who had fled from their pueblo a decade earlier and were being held captive by Apaches. According to his diary, Ulibarri led a crew of twenty-eight soldiers, thirteen militiamen, and about a hundred Pueblo Indian guides from Santa Fe on July 13. They crossed the summit of the Sangre de Cristo Mountains and continued northeast through the Moreno Valley. Near the Canadian River, Ulibarri encountered bands of Jicarilla Apaches who cast aspersions on other, more hostile Indians "on the road in the distance"—including an Apache band called Flecha de Palo. After Ulibarri's ensemble had traveled sixteen leagues farther toward present-day Raton Pass, several members of the Flecha de Palo Indians, along with Indians of other bands and a chief, Ysdalnisdael, came peacefully to meet them. The Indians, Ulibarri's report noted, assured him that they were

very good people; that they had not stolen anything from anyone, but occupied themselves with their maize and corn fields which they harvest, because they are busy with the sowing of corn, frijoles, and pumpkins.

Another variation of the name was in use in 1719, as recorded in the journal of Governor Antonio de Valverde y Cosío on his expedition that year against the Ute and Comanche Indians in northeastern New Mexico. Following a path similar to that of Ulibarri more than a decade earlier, Valverde reached a river known to the Apaches as La Flecha. In his expedition years before, Ulibarri had named that river Río de Santa Magdalena. Valverde renamed it Nuestra Señora del Rosario. It is known today as the Cimarron River.

The elevation at Palo Flechado Pass is 9,107 feet.

More to explore: *Comanche Country, Taos, Taos Canyon*

Pancho Villa State Park: *see Columbus*

Pancho Villa's Raid: *see Columbus*

292. Paraje de Fra Cristobal

Location: 1. Socorro County. South of San Antonio, in the Fort Craig Rest Area on the east side of Interstate 25, between mile markers 113 and 114. See map 5.

2. Socorro County. South of San Antonio, in the Fort Craig Rest Area on the west side of Interstate 25, between mile markers 113 and 114. See map 5.

Marker text: The mountain range seen along the east bank of the Rio Grande is named after Father Cristobal de Salazar of the 1598 Juan de Oñate expedition. The northern edge of the twenty-one mile range is said to resemble the profile of the good friar. This paraje, or encampment, was a place of rest for caravans on the Camino Real as they entered or exited the Jornada del Muerto.

Visible in the far distance to the southeast of this rest area is the Fra Cristobal Range, named for sixteenth-century Franciscan priest Cristobal de Salazar. Salazar came to New Mexico with the colonizing expedition of his uncle, don Juan de Oñate, in 1598. A romantic etymology claims that the contours along the northern edge of the twenty-one-mile range are reminiscent of the friar's face and hand—and when the range is viewed at a certain angle, an imaginative person can indeed see such an outline. The more likely story for the name, though, is just as interesting.

Oñate's expedition north along the Rio Grande through New Mexico followed a course that became known as El Camino Real, or the Royal Road. Oñate (and others who traveled the route later) established small camping places, called *parajes* in Spanish, at intervals along the roadway. These parajes gave travelers and their livestock a place to rest from the journey. One was located along the east bank of the river nearby, where a break in the rugged lava terrain allowed access to the water. The spot lay at the northern end of the Jornada del Muerto, or "Journey of the Dead Man," a stark stretch of the Chihuahuan Desert to the south.

In 1599, Fray Cristobal set off with a return caravan to Mexico to bring additional troops and supplies for the new colony. Fray Cristobal is believed to have reached the paraje here, a campsite that still lacked a name, where, perhaps made ill by the strain of the journey, he passed away. Eventually, the paraje acquired Fray Cristobal's name, albeit with an alternate form of "Fray."

At the Paraje de Fra Cristobal, as the

encampment became known, southbound travelers rested, sometimes for several days, before entering the dreaded Jornada. Caravans left the campsite in the evening and traveled through the night to avoid the blistering desert heat of day. In 1847, Susan Shelby Magoffin, traveling with her trader husband to Mexico along the Camino, passed through the paraje. Expecting, as did many others, to see some form of habitation, her feelings upon not being so rewarded are clear:

There is not even the dusky walls of an adobe house to cheer its lonely solitude . . . it is only a regular camping place with a name. At present I can say nothing of its beauties—the bleak hill sides look lovely enough and feel cold enough.

Eventually, adobe houses did arise when the paraje expanded into a small settlement, called Paraje, around 1855. Paraje had 195 residents within five years. According to a history compiled by the state's Historic Preservation Division, the village had a store, a post office, a hotel, a church, and a school, most built from adobe and stone. Residents eked out a living by selling produce to soldiers at nearby Fort Craig. But when the military deactivated Fort Craig in 1885, Paraje, too, approached its final days. The waters of Elephant Butte Reservoir covered the abandoned village in 1927.

More to explore: *El Camino Real—The King's Highway, Elephant Butte Dam, Fort Craig, Jornada del Muerto*

293. Paraje de los Brazitos

Location: Doña Ana County. About ten miles south of Las Cruces and just north of Vado, at the intersection of NM 227 and NM 478. See map 5.

Marker text: Here the Camino Real between Santa Fe and El Paso passed along the eastern bank of the Rio Grande near a *brazito* or small branch of the river that created a small island. At this *paraje*, or stopping place, American troops defeated a Mexican Army force on Christmas Day, 1846, in what was the only battle of the Mexican War fought in present-day New Mexico.

294. Brazito Battlefield

Location: Doña Ana County. At the New Mexico Visitors Center, just north of the New Mexico–Texas border on Interstate 10. See map 5.

Marker text: One of the few battles of the Mexican War to be fought in New Mexico occurred near here on Christmas Day, 1846. U.S. troops under Colonel Alexander W. Doniphan defeated a Mexican army commanded by General Antonio Ponce de León. Two days later, Doniphan entered El Paso without opposition.

Christmas Day 1846 was an otherwise pleasant day. The waters of the Rio Grande flowed quietly past the Paraje de los Brazitos, a resting place near the small village of Brazito. The settlement had taken its name from the *brazitos*, or branches of the river, which had created a small island in this vicinity. The location had served as a spot where weary travelers along the Camino Real, the major trade and colonization route from Mexico to New Mexico, could rest from the fatigue of the journey.

Soldiers of the Missouri Mounted Volunteers who had camped along the river that day were resting from their own fatigue. The United States was at war with Mexico over possession of the Southwest, and on this Christmas Day the soldiers sang "Yankee Doodle" as they took a break on their march to Chihuahua. Although he had heard rumors of a Mexican force gathering, their commander, young, red-haired, Kentucky-born Colonel Alexander William Doniphan, ignored the suspicious cloud of dust to the south and joined his men in a round of the popular card game three-trick loo.

Doniphan was soon trumped. An advance guard returned with word that about a thousand Mexican troops led by General Antonio Ponce de León were headed toward the American camp. In short order, the Mexican soldiers were in sight.

From a fashion standpoint, Doniphan had already lost the battle. The Mexican Army, dressed, as soldier Isaac George later observed, "in a uniform of blue pantaloons, green coats trimmed with scarlet, and tall caps plated in front with brass," cut an impressive sight. Their force, later estimated in an official report at 490 mounted equestrians, 100 infantry soldiers, 500 militiamen, and a howitzer cannon, was superior in power—and pageantry—to the tattered, unwashed, buckskin-clad Missouri Volunteers. Additionally, Doniphan had split his army in two sections, and the second section, with artillery, still lagged behind.

The first gunfire came from Mexican soldiers, who had advanced within four hundred yards of the Americans. Lacking sufficient troops for a frontal assault, Doniphan directed his men to lie in the grass at intervals in an attempt to lure the Mexican Army within closer range. The ruse worked. When the Mexican soldiers were within ten yards, the Americans sprang from the ground and, as George put it, "let fly such a galling volley of yager balls into their ranks, that they wheeled about and fled in the utmost confusion." Sometime in the battle, General Ponce de León himself was injured. Seeing him leave the field, some of the Mexican soldiers also withdrew, perhaps, as some historians believe, thinking that their army was in retreat. American Captain John Reid and a small group of mounted soldiers took advantage of the situation and charged the Mexicans' howitzer, dragging it back to the American side. Befuddled and sensing defeat, the Mexican soldiers scattered.

As many as sixty-three Mexican soldiers were killed in the hour-long scuffle, the only battle of the Mexican-American War to occur in New Mexico. More than 150 were wounded. Seven American soldiers were injured. All recovered. The Americans took eight wounded Mexican soldiers prisoner, only two of whom survived. According to an account by soldier Frank S. Edwards, one of the prisoners was a boy about fifteen years old, who that evening "crawled a little away from the tent he had been laid in, and expired."

Two days later, Doniphan and his men moved on to El Paso and received a much warmer welcome: citizens there heralded the arrival of the Americans with white flags and baskets of fruit.

More to explore: *Bartlett Garcia Continental Survey Point, El Camino Real—The King's Highway, Jornada del Muerto*

295. Paraje de Robledo

Location: Doña Ana County. At the entrance to Fort Selden in Radium Springs on US 85. See map 5.

Marker text: This *paraje* or resting place was named for Pedro Robledo, a member of the Juan de Oñate expedition, who was buried nearby on May 21, 1598. This camping place was a welcome sight for caravans entering or exiting the dreaded *Jornada del Muerto*, a part of the trail which had limited water. Its strategic location along the Camino Real made it an ideal site for the establishment of Fort Selden in 1865.

Sixty-year-old Pedro Robledo and his wife, four sons, and daughter were part of the caravan of four hundred soldiers, priests, settlers, and servants pushing northward on the official colonization effort of Spain into New Mexico in 1598. Leading the effort was don Juan de Oñate, who had won the approval of the viceroy to establish the first European colony in New Mexico. Oñate's route between Mexico City and northern New Mexico became known as El Camino Real, the Royal Road. Spain was at its height of global power, and Oñate's new colony was to be the underpinning of Spanish settlement in the north.

Robledo would never see the marvelous colony they had set out to establish. Camped near here, members of the expedition awoke on the morning of May 21 to find that he had passed away during the night. In a journal of the expedition, Robledo was described as being "of good stature, entirely gray, 60 years of age." Robledo was buried that same day near the site of his death, and his bereaved wife and children continued north with the expedition the following day. His was the first death encountered on the journey by the colonists.

Robledo's gravesite along the Rio Grande became a camping place, or *paraje*, for others who later traveled Oñate's route. Known as the Paraje de Robledo, and sometimes as La Cruz de Robledo, or "the Cross of Robledo," it lay near the southern entrance to the dreaded Jornada del Muerto, "the Journey of the Dead Man." The Jornada was a deathly ninety-mile stretch of desert between present-day Doña Ana and Socorro, where the Camino Real strayed from the invigorating waters of the Rio Grande, and travelers often became the victims of exhaustion, thirst, or attacks by Apache Indians.

Hostilities in the Jornada continued after the Southwest came under the control of the United States in the mid-nineteenth century. In 1865, the army selected a site near the Paraje de Robledo as the location for a new military outpost, Fort Selden. Soldiers at the fort escorted travelers on the Camino Real and guarded settlers eking out their existence in the Mesilla Valley in villages like Mesilla and Doña Ana.

Soldiers also used a nearby hill as a heliograph relay point to bounce the rays of the sun into visual communiqués between military installations in southwestern New Mexico and even to Fort Bliss in El Paso. That hill took its name from the intrepid settler more famous in death than in life: Robledo Mountain.

Operations at Fort Selden continued until Indian disturbances quieted in the 1880s. The army decommissioned the fort in 1891.

More to explore: *Doña Ana, El Camino Real—The King's Highway, Fort Selden, Jornada del Muerto*

296. Paraje San Diego

Location: Doña Ana County. Ten miles north of Las Cruces, in the rest area on the west side (southbound) of Interstate 25, at mile marker 23. See map 5.

Marker text: This *paraje*, or stopping place, provided travelers along the Camino Real with a final opportunity to water their stock and prepare their caravans before leaving the Rio Grande Valley and entering the desolate Jornada del Muerto. Caravans on their way to Santa Fe started in the evening and traveled non-stop until they reached the Paraje de Fra Cristobal 100 miles to the north.

Like interstate rest areas today, *parajes* were resting places along the historic Camino Real, or Royal Road, the main passageway between Mexico and Taos until well into the nineteenth century. A paraje in this location, near a shallow crossing of the Rio Grande, took the name San Diego, honoring Saint Didacus. Here, travelers bearing north on the Camino Real left the Rio Grande and traversed a stretch of land so parched and desolate it became known as the Jornada del Muerto, or "Journey of the Dead Man." They traveled for just under a hundred miles until reaching the safety of the Paraje de Fra Cristobal near present-day Socorro.

In 1766, Nicolás de Lafora, a Spanish soldier and explorer who compiled maps of the Spanish frontier for the viceroy, left this account of the Paraje San Diego:

Here a halt is usually made because at this point begins the Jornada del Muerto where there is seldom any water. Thus water is generally taken on here. After the mules have drunk, travelers set out on the road, starting in the evening to take advantage of the night's coolness. They travel two nights, one day and part of another without stopping in order to reach Fray Cristobal.

With the arrival of stagecoaches, railroads, and later automobiles, travel along the historic Camino Real ended.

More to explore: *El Camino Real—The King's Highway, Paraje de Fra Cristobal*

297. Parteras of New Mexico

Location: McKinley County. At the east end of Gallup, in Babe Ruth Park, near the intersection of Joseph M. Montoya Boulevard and Ford Drive. See map 1.

Marker text: Historically, the practice of midwifery was essential to the birthing process in New Mexico. In this large, mostly rural state with few doctors, midwives, called parteras in Spanish, have helped women give birth to thousands of babies. When the University of New Mexico's medical school opened in 1961, the State began to train and certify midwives. Today, licensed midwives frequently work with doctors and hospitals.

298. Emma Estrada (1933–1997)

Marker text: Emma Estrada was a partera, or midwife, for over thirty years. She delivered more than seven hundred babies during an era when mothers in rural, sparsely populated areas had no choice but to deliver at home. She became the first licensed partera in New Mexico, and worked with doctors to assure the best medical care. She is remembered for her quiet confidence and devotion.

Note: Marker faceplates are on opposite sides of the same sign. See map 1.

The practice of midwifery was common in the early years of New Mexico—mostly because doctors were not. The large distances between villages ensured that even where women had access to a doctor, those women were not always able to make the journey to get the care they needed. It was easier, and in many ways safer, to trust the delivery of a newborn to a local midwife, called a *partera* in Spanish. Especially in the traditionally Hispanic villages of northern New Mexico, parteras were often highly regarded and well-known members of the community, and an expectant mother might prefer to be assisted by someone she knew over a doctor she didn't. Even after the dawn of the twentieth century brought greater access to health care, the large and rural nature of the state, costs involved with doctor-assisted deliveries, traditional cultural practices, and even language barriers ensured that parteras remained commonplace. One of the best-known parteras working in the last century was Gallup native Emma Estrada. Estrada was one of the longest-serving parteras in New Mexico history and one of the first in the state to be fully licensed in the work.

As is traditional, Estrada learned the art of midwifery from other local parteras (often, the apprentice learned the practice from her mother or grandmother). Estrada began her own work in and around the Gallup region. She used her own cloths and instruments, carrying them in a suitcase to her deliveries, which might occur five times a month or more. Estrada often merged her work with that of local medical professionals. As she explained in an interview in the *Gallup Independent*, doctors in Gallup might certify that a woman was healthy enough for home birth, then call Estrada to be present and to administer birth care, freeing the doctor to see other patients. Although the work naturally had a special joy associated with it, it was often also a business arrangement—Estrada could earn up to a hundred dollars per delivery. "When we were short of money," Estrada related in the interview, "my children would tell me, 'Mama, go sell a baby.'"

In New Mexico, the relationship between parteras and health care providers has generally been a good one. The difficulty of providing adequate health care in a rural state all but necessitates the assistance of local caregivers such as midwives, and the state has respected the presence of a tradition that reaches back even to colonial days. The challenge, however, has been to ensure that midwives follow certain standards of care and cleanliness and know how to respond if something goes wrong during the birth.

To that end, in 1980, the New Mexico Department of Health implemented stricter regulations for practicing midwives. Estrada was one of only two parteras in the state to pass the first licensing exam. The New Mexico Public Health Division formally recognized Estrada in 1989 for her "outstanding contribution to the cause of public health for the State of New Mexico" in being the first partera in the state to become a fully licensed midwife.

In 1997, after bringing more than an estimated seven hundred new lives into the world, Emma Estrada herself quietly departed from it.

More to explore: *Curanderas—Women Who Heal, Dr. Annie Dodge Wauneka, Dr. Meta L. Christy*

299. Pat Garrett Murder Site

Location: Doña Ana County. Just west of Organ, in a pullout on the south side of US 70. See map 5.

Marker text: Pat Garrett, the Lincoln County Sheriff who shot and killed William "Billy the Kid" Bonney at Fort Sumner in 1881, was himself murdered at a remote site nearby on February 29, 1908. Wayne Brazel, a local cowboy, confessed to shooting Garrett but was acquitted of all charges. The motive and circumstances surrounding Garrett's death are still being debated.

Sheriff Pat Garrett has entered history as the peace officer who felled Billy the Kid in 1881. His own death adds a strange epilogue to the story and remains one of the most perplexing unsolved mysteries of the West.

Patrick Floyd Jarvis Garrett was born on June 5, 1850. He left the Louisiana plantation owned by his family at age eighteen to hunt buffalo on the Texas Panhandle. At the conclusion of the violent Lincoln County War in 1879, a two-year battle between political and economic divisions in Lincoln County, Garrett was appointed as Lincoln County sheriff. Foremost among his tasks was to bring to justice young Billy the Kid, who had killed the previous sheriff during the fracas. After the Kid escaped from jail, Garrett tracked him to Fort Sumner and, on July 14, 1881, shot him to death. Garrett subsequently moved to Organ and served as Doña Ana County sheriff from 1896 to 1902. After a stint as collector of customs in El Paso, he returned with his family in 1906 to live and work on his Organ ranch.

Garrett had leased a portion of his property to cowboy Wayne Brazel, who used the land to raise goats. Although varying accounts exist, it appears that another man, Carl Adamson, later offered to buy the land from Garrett on the condition that Brazel's goats, which had destroyed the land for cattle grazing, be removed. Brazel refused. Tensions high, the three men agreed to meet in Las Cruces to hammer out a compromise.

On February 29, 1908, Garrett and Adamson set out together from Garrett's Organ ranch toward Las Cruces. They met up with Brazel on the road along the way, and the three uneasily agreed to travel the remaining distance together.

Lawman Pat Garrett's daughter, Elizabeth, wrote "O Fair New Mexico," which was adopted as the English-language Official State Song in 1917. Pat Garrett. New Mexico State University Library, Archives and Special Collections.

Later that day, Wayne Brazel turned himself in to Doña Ana County sheriff Felipe Lucero, confessing that he had just killed Pat Garrett.

The eminent lawman was dead. Garrett had been shot twice, once in the head and once in the stomach. Brazel alleged that, when the party stopped briefly near Alameda Arroyo some five miles distant from Las Cruces, Garrett had threatened him with a shotgun; in self-defense, Brazel had fired first. Evidence seemed contrary: the bullet entering Garret's skull had come from behind. Additional sets of hoof prints and horse droppings uncovered near the arroyo provided support for the theory, believed by many then and now, that Garrett had been ambushed. One conjecture even suggests that Adamson and Brazel were in league together in the crime.

Brazel was indicted on a charge of first-degree murder. Albert Fall, a renowned lawyer in southern New Mexico and afterward one of the first US senators for New Mexico, provided Brazel's defense when the case opened on April 19, 1909. Fall argued his case effectively, and the jury quickly returned a verdict. Not guilty.

Pat Garrett was buried on March 5, 1908, in the Odd Fellows Cemetery in Las Cruces and later reinterred in the Masonic Cemetery. Speculation about the true cause of his death excites emotions and debate to this day.

More to explore: *Fort Sumner and Fort Sumner State Monument (series), Lincoln, New Mexico School for the Blind and Visually Impaired, Organ Mountains (see under San Augustin Pass)*

300. Pecos

Location: San Miguel County. In Pecos, at the intersection of NM 50 and NM 63. See map 3.

Marker text: The upper Pecos River Valley was on the frontier of Pueblo Indian civilization from at least the 13th to the 19th centuries, when the nearby Pueblo of Pecos was abandoned. Despite raids by various Plains Indians groups, Spanish-speaking settlers around 1825 founded what is today the village of Pecos.

301. Ghost Marker: Pecos National Historical Park

Marker text: Humans have inhabited the Pecos Valley for at least 12,000 years. The fifteenth century Towa-speaking trading pueblo, Cicuyé, had over 2,000 inhabitants. During the sixteenth and seventeenth centuries, Franciscan churches were built and rebuilt here under the direction of the Spanish. By the 1780's disease, raids and drought had decimated the population, and in 1838 the last 17 inhabitants moved to Jemez to live with their Towa-speaking relatives.

Within the boundaries of Pecos National Historic Park are ruts from the Santa Fe Trail, the site of the 1862 Civil War Battle at Glorieta Pass, and the 20th century cattle ranching operation of the Forked Lightning Ranch, where movie actress Greer Garson once lived. Today the valley is home to long-time residents and attracts many visitors.

Note: This text was written to replace the text on a previous Marker, which has since gone missing. See map 3.

302. Evelyn M. Vigil, Phan-un-pha-kee (Young Doe) (1921–1995) and Juanita T. Toledo, Pha-wa-luh-luh (Ring-Cloud Around the Moon) (1914–1999)

Location: Sandoval County. At the pueblo of Jemez, in a picnic area on the north side of NM 4, at mile marker 7. See map 4.

Marker text: Evelyn M. Vigil, a descendant of the last remaining Pecos residents that moved to Jemez Pueblo in 1838, led the revival of Pecos Pueblo style pottery. She spent time at Pecos National Historic Park studying materials and techniques used by the Pecos people. With the aid of Juanita T. Toledo, another Pecos descendant, Evelyn helped to recreate the glazeware that was made there from 1250 to 1700.

Pecos National Historical Park today preserves and protects the ruins of the spectacular pueblo of Pecos and the Spanish mission church of Nuestra Señora de los Angeles. Once among the largest pueblo villages in North America, Pecos Pueblo arose in the fifteenth century on a ridge offering unassailable protection from attacks by other Indians. Because their village lay near the river, the Towa-speaking Indians who lived here named the region Pa-kyoo-laor Peko, a name that references the abundance of water they found in these southern foothills of the Sangre de Cristo Mountains. Later, the Spanish pronunciation became Pecos.

Spanish explorer Francisco Vásquez de Coronado visited Pecos in 1540. His chronicler described the pueblo as

a village of nearly five hundred warriors, who are feared throughout that country. It is square, situated on a rock, with a large court or yard in the middle. . . . The houses are all alike, four stories high. . . . There are corridors going all around it at the first two stories, by which one can go around the whole village. These are like outside balconies, and they are able to protect themselves under these. The houses do not have doors below, but they use ladders, which can be lifted up like a drawbridge, and so go up to the corridors which are on the inside of the village.

In 1625, Spanish Franciscans constructed at the pueblo an imposing mission church, Nuestra Señora de los Angeles, in their endeavor to proselytize the native residents of the village. Raids by Plains Indians, the spread of disease, and the encroachment of Spanish land grants into the area all helped reduce the population of Pecos Pueblo. In 1838, fewer than twenty residents remained. They left their pueblo that year and moved west across the Rio Grande to join Jemez Pueblo, the last remaining Towa-speaking village in New Mexico.

Before leaving their pueblo for Jemez, the Pecos Indians turned over the painting that had hung in their mission church to the care of Pecos residents. It hangs today in the local Catholic church of San Antonio de Padua.

Spanish settlement had progressed by that time around the pueblo and into the adjacent river valley. The San Miguel del Vado grant, awarded by the Spanish government in 1794 and including land twenty miles southeast of Pecos Pueblo, along with the Pecos grant surrounding Pecos Pueblo, opened the region southeast of Santa Fe to Spanish settlement. By 1825, early pioneers had formed a small village just a few miles from the pueblo in an area then known as the Cañon de Pecos. Their village took the name Pecos.

As the Indians had before them, Spanish settlers in Pecos suffered from attacks by various Plains Indians, including Comanches. These attacks continued until 1874, after which time most of the free-roaming Comanches had resettled onto reservations. Residents of Pecos settled into an agricultural lifestyle along the bracing waters of the Pecos River—a watercourse itself named for the pueblo.

Other histories played out here as well, and their legacies are included within the boundaries of the park itself. The stage stop and ranch belonging to Martin Kozlowski, and ruts of the Santa Fe Trail that crossed nearby, are preserved here. The ranch was an important stopping point for wagoneers, merchants, and settlers traveling to and from Santa Fe over the historic trail. About six miles to the northwest, in Glorieta Pass, Union and Confederate troops met in the Civil War Battle of Glorieta Pass. That battle is sometimes called the "Gettysburg of the West." Union soldiers used Kozlowski's ranch as a hospital.

In addition, the Forked Lightning Ranch, which is down the road from the Pecos Visitors Center, became the home of MGM movie star Greer Garson in the twentieth century. Garson, who first appeared on screen in the 1939 movie *Goodbye, Mr. Chips*, remained a popular star throughout the 1940s and into the 1950s. After marrying her third husband, E. E. "Buddy" Fogelson, a Texas oilman, she and her husband retired to the Forked Lightning Ranch. The ranch was bestowed to Pecos National Historical Park upon the passing of Garson and her husband, and the park's Visitors Center is named for Fogelson.

In the 1970s, a remarkable bit of forensic archaeology resurrected an important Pecos Pueblo tradition. When the Pecos Indians left their Pueblo for Jemez in the early nineteenth century, knowledge of the specific method and materials potters at the pueblo had used in creating their glazeware pottery was lost. It might have remained so forever were it not for two twentieth-century potters, Evelyn M. Vigil and Juanita T. Toledo, both descendants of the last residents of Pecos and both accomplished potters in their own right. Vigil and Toledo joined rangers and volunteers at Pecos National Historical Park in a project to re-create historic Pecos Pueblo–style pottery. They worked methodically with a variety of different types of local clays, tempers, and natural pigments—even varying the intensity of the heat for the firing as well as the type of wood used for the fire—experimenting through trial and error for five years until they finally found the combination that matched the thin-walled pottery and glazes made at the pueblo from 1250 to 1700. In the process, they rescued an ancient tradition from the reaches of time.

More to explore: *Comanche Country, Pueblo of Jemez, San Antonio de Padua Catholic Church, Settlements of the San Miguel del Vado Land Grant (see under San Miguel del Vado National Historic District), Vásquez de Coronado's Route*

303. Pecos Valley

Location: Roosevelt County. East of Kenna on US 70, between mile markers 389 and 390. See map 6.

Marker text: Plain bordering east side of Pecos Valley. Caprock escarpment, or west edge of Llano Estacado (Stockaded Plain) 15 miles to southwest on horizon. Capitan Mountains and Sierra Blanca on western skyline are east edge of Basin and Range province. Railroad Mountain, low east-west ridge 5 miles to south, is igneous dike. Elevation 4,110 feet.

This Historic Marker lies within part of the transition zone between two sections of the Great Plains: the Pecos Valley to the west and the High Plains to the east.

Among the valleys in southeastern New Mexico, none is more famous than the Pecos Valley, named for the Pecos River flowing through it. Mountains may be more photogenic, but it is valleys like the Pecos that offer unencumbered travel, abundant watercourses, and plentiful grasslands for grazing and farming. In 1891, a pamphlet by the New Mexico Bureau of Immigration described the Pecos Valley in this way:

For miles and miles, as far as the eye can reach, this marvelous valley stretches away, from north to south and from west to east; its surface smooth and even as a floor and covered with a rich gramma grass, which, for years past, has furnished sustenance to hundreds of thousands of cattle and sheep.

Beautiful Sierra Blanca Peak rises on the far western skyline a hundred miles distant. Even from this point, Sierra Blanca can be seen to live up to its English translation, "White Mountain," with a dome of snow cresting its highest peak (11,973 feet) almost year-round. The mountain, part of the Sacramento Range, is located in the Mescalero Apache Indian Reservation and is a popular skiing and recreational area.

The Capitan Mountains can be seen northeast of Sierra Blanca. This range tends east-west for some twenty-three miles. The highest peak, Capitan Peak, reaches 10,083 feet. It was in these mountains in the summer of 1950 that firefighters rescued a bear cub from a forest fire. The little cub was later flown to Washington to become the living symbol of forest fire prevention, Smokey Bear.

The Capitan Mountains and Sierra Blanca lie along the eastern edge of the Basin and Range Province. This physiographic region, characterized by mountains isolated between valleys, defines the topography of most of southwestern New Mexico.

The Caprock escarpment to the southwest delimits the eastern edge of the Pecos Valley. This north-south tending line of bluffs, stretching roughly from US 380 near the town of Caprock south to US 180, levels to a smooth top as the Pecos Valley gives way to the flat expanse of the Llano Estacado. One translation of Llano Estacado is "Stockaded Plain," possibly for the Caprock itself, which at a distance appears like a defensible fortress wall. The Llano Estacado is one of the flattest stretches of land in the world.

Visible about five miles to the south is Railroad Mountain, an elevated igneous dike that runs eastward for about thirty-five miles. A dike is an earthen ridge formed when magma seeps through a vertical crack and hardens. Railroad Mountain was named either for its resemblance to the kind of raised earthen bed often used for railroad tracks or for the fact that it looks somewhat like a train en route to a faraway grassy destination.

More to explore: *Basin and Range Country, Capitan, Mesa and Pecos Valley, Sierra Blanca, Smokey Bear Historical Park*

Peggy Pond Church: *see Marjorie Bell Chambers*

304. Peralta

Location: Valencia County. At the south end of Peralta, in a triangular area formed by the intersection of NM 47 and Peralta Boulevard. See map 4.

Marker text: One of the last skirmishes of the Civil War in New Mexico took place here on April 15, 1862. The Sibley Brigade, retreating to Texas, camped at the hacienda of Governor Henry Connelly, a few miles from Peralta. Here the Confederates were routed by Union forces under Col. Edward R. S. Canby.

Peralta was one of a cluster of small farming villages founded along the banks of the Rio Grande south of present-day Albuquerque during the Spanish colonial era. Named for its early founders, Andres and Manuel de Peralta, the village was home to a population that rarely exceeded one thousand people throughout the seventeenth century. It also holds the distinction as the site of one of the last engagements of the Civil War in New Mexico.

Under the command of Brigadier General Henry Hopkins Sibley, Texas Confederates had begun marching north along the Rio Grande in late February 1862 with plans to secure what military installations they could and reach the gold fields in southern Colorado. In the Battle of Valverde near Socorro, they narrowly defeated Union troops from Fort Craig under the command of Colonel Edward R. S. Canby. They bypassed the fort and continued north. By mid-March, Sibley and his men had taken Albuquerque and reached the state capital in Santa Fe. Fearing for his safety, Governor Henry Connelly fled to Las Vegas, New Mexico—but the Confederate Army never made it that far. After federal soldiers burned their supply wagons later that month at the Battle of Glorieta Pass between Santa Fe and Las Vegas, Sibley and his troops were forced to flee south from the state. Colonel Canby and some 2,400 soldiers followed in pursuit.

In their retreat, the Confederate Army's Fifth Texas Regiment, under the command of Colonel Thomas Green, traveled along the east bank of the Rio Grande as Sibley and the main body of troops moved along the west. On April 15, Green's men reached the large ranch owned by Connelly just north of Peralta, where they camped for the night. Enlisted men bivouacked in the large fields outside the home while the officers reveled inside the house. Unknown to the soldiers, Colonel Canby's Union troops had amassed just to the north and were deploying themselves for a morning attack.

As daylight broke, Confederates became aware of the Union camp when Canby's troops blew reveille. A light artillery skirmish ensued. Soon after, Union troops charged an approaching seven-wagon supply and ammunitions train led by Lieutenant James Darby and thirty-four men of Company I, Fifth Regiment, who had lagged behind the main Confederate force. Union soldiers advanced to within fifty feet of the wagons, then rushed them intently, capturing the supplies and mules as well as a howitzer. Darby and his men offered little resistance.

In the meantime, the Texans had marched closer to the town of Peralta and the woods near the river, where they stationed themselves in defensive positions in trenches and behind adobe walls. One of Canby's men devised a plan to attack the town, but Canby did not allow it. Canby felt that such an attack would kill innocent Peralta citizens and that, further, as noted by Colorado Volunteer member Ovando Hollister, "the horses, weak and weary, would have stuck in the mud, while the riders were picked off by an unseen foe." Instead, both sides fired on each other at intervals throughout the day. General Sibley attempted to cross the cold river waters to reinforce Green's regiment, but Union cavalry officers kept him at bay.

Although they held a strong position in Peralta, Green and his Confederate soldiers, their supply wagons now commandeered and their bodies and temperaments exhausted, had little energy or motivation to wage an effective defense. Weather finally intervened on their behalf. A strong wind whipped up a blinding desert sandstorm around two that afternoon, effectively benumbing both armies. After Union soldiers withdrew from the field that evening, Green and his men crossed the river to rejoin Sibley and the remainder of the Confederate brigade. Their retreat continued the next morning.

Hollister considered the skirmish at Peralta to be the "most harmless battle on record," but it was not without casualties. Estimates of the number of Union soldiers killed range from one to four, with three wounded; for the Confederates, four were killed and eight wounded.

More to explore: *Albuquerque, Cañoncito at Apache Canyon, Fort Craig, Glorieta Pass Battlefield*

305. Percha Creek

Location: Sierra County. About three miles west of Kingston on NM 152, in a parking area by the bridge on the south side of the road. See map 5.

Marker text: Built in 1927, this historic Warren deck truss bridge spans Percha Creek, cutting through an impassable but beautiful gorge below. The bridge was constructed during a difficult project to build the Black Range Highway, now NM 152. This structure has been preserved by the New Mexico Department of Transportation and is listed on the National Register of Historic Places.

Percha Creek Canyon, just west of Hillsboro, is a splendid gorge marked by brilliant sunlight and dark shadows, cool breezes, and the pleasant sound of waters from Percha Creek as they trickle past on their way to rendezvous with the Rio Grande. Although beautiful, this chasm in the Black Range Mountains proved to be an impasse to early travelers. The New Mexico State Highway Department tackled the problem in the 1920s as it surveyed a route through the mountains to connect the mining camps of Hillsboro, Kingston, and Silver City. In what the *New Mexico Highway Journal* in February 1929 cited as "evidence of the progressive spirit of the citizens of Grant and Sierra counties," residents of those counties agreed to two mill levies to help finance this "Black Range Highway."

Engineers with the Ware Company of El Paso conquered the canyon with a bridge with a Warren deck truss design—marking the first time such a design had been used in the state's fledgling road program. Patented in 1848 by two Englishmen, Captain James Warren and Theobald Willoughby Monsani, the Warren design features a system of tension-bearing isosceles triangles known as trusses to support the bridge deck. Those trusses at Percha Creek run forty feet long and are held aloft by two concrete foundations, themselves gripped by rocky holds in the canyon walls. The 120-foot depth of the gorge offered sufficient clearance for the trussing to be located underneath the roadway—a requirement of the form. Placing the supports beneath the blacktop also left more clearance for traffic on the roadway itself. Completed in 1927, the bridge at Percha Creek runs 210 feet long and stretches 19 feet wide.

An efficient and relatively inexpensive design, the Warren deck truss is today one of the most popular of bridge types. Five other examples exist in the state. One crosses the San Francisco River on US 180 near Luna in Catron County. Another crosses the Canadian River on US 54 at Logan in Quay County. A pair cross Nogal Canyon on Interstate 25 near the Elephant Butte Reservoir in Socorro County. The last crosses Seboyeta Creek on NM 297 at Seboyeta in Cibola County.

The Percha Creek Bridge, oldest of them all, continued as part of the road network through the Black Range until the Highway Department bypassed it with the present structure in 1995. To recognize the importance of the original bridge in meeting the transportation needs of early Black Range residents, the Highway Department preserved it intact.

The bridge was added to the National Register of Historic Places in 1997. The nomination form for the listing notes how the location of the bridge at Percha Creek "imbues the bridge with a strong feeling of its historic appearance and the role it played in providing a highway link to one of the state's most remote mining districts."

More to explore: *Hillsboro Historic District, Rio Felix Bridge, Rio Grande Bridge at Radium Springs, Rio Grande Gorge Bridge, Silver City*

306. Philmont Scout Ranch

Location: Colfax County. Just south of Cimarron, in a pullout on the west side of NM 21 at mile marker 1. See map 3.

Marker text: Oklahoma oilman Waite Phillips gave this 127,000 acre property to the Boy Scouts of America in 1938 and 1941. The first National Boy Scout Camp ever established, Philmont now hosts young men from all over the world. Kit Carson, Lucien B. Maxwell, and Dick Wootton were important in the history of the area.

Ask a Boy Scout how he spent his summer vacation and his answer may well include stories of Philmont Scout Ranch. At nearly 140,000 acres, Philmont is the largest private youth camp in the world—host to some eighteen thousand trustworthy, brave, and reverent young scouts every summer.

Philmont is the philanthropic legacy of oilman and rancher Waite Phillips. Born in Iowa in January 1883, Phillips later moved to Oklahoma and grew rich in oil and banking enterprises. In the 1920s, he began purchasing land in the western foothills of the Sangre de Cristo Mountains near the village of Cimarron and later moved with his family to live on what he called his Villa Philmonte Ranch. The name was a hybrid of Phillips and the Spanish word for mountain, *monte*.

An outdoorsman himself, Phillips in November 1938 deeded 35,857 acres of his mountainous New Mexico ranch to the Boy Scouts of America for use as a wilderness campsite in furthering the character-building mission of that organization. It was the first such Boy Scout camp in the country. Phillips again used wordplay when he named this site Philturn—an amalgam of his name and one of the Boy Scout mottoes, "Do a good turn daily."

When it opened for the summer of 1939, the Philturn Rockymountain Scoutcamp, as it was called at the time, welcomed 189 scouts to its program. Two years later, Phillips did another good turn: he deeded to the Boy Scouts an additional stretch of land adjacent to the first, along with other properties he owned. His donation increased the size of the camp by more than 91,000 acres.

Phillips once said: "Put a boy in touch with nature and the job of inspiring him with high ideals is an easier one than in any other environment." It was beliefs such as this that motivated Phillips to create what is today known as the Philmont Scout Ranch.

Other noteworthy figures earlier inspired by Cimarron country, which surrounds Philmont, include Kit Carson, Lucien B. Maxwell, and

Dick Wootton. Mountain man Carson spent time along the Cimarron River and lived at Rayado before serving as colonel of the First New Mexico Volunteers during the Civil War. His friend, Lucien B. Maxwell, owned the two-million-acre Maxwell Land Grant upon which Philmont was later built—believed to be the largest tract of land ever owned by a private individual. For his part, Richens Lacy "Uncle Dick" Wootton also made a living off the land. In 1864, he blazed a passable road over rocky Raton Pass between New Mexico and Colorado, along the Mountain Branch of the Santa Fe Trail, and charged travelers a fee to traverse it.

More to explore: *Cimarron, Hyde Memorial State Park, Kit Carson Park (see under Taos), Mary White, Raton, Santa Fe Trail (series), Seton Village*

307. Pilar

Location: Taos County. At the Rio Grande Gorge Visitors Center in Pilar, on the west side of NM 68, between mile markers 28 and 29. See map 2.

Marker text: In 1795, twenty-five families were granted land along the Río Grande at Pilar, then known as Cieneguilla. The Battle of Cieneguilla was fought at Embudo Mountain near here in March 1854. A large force of Utes and Apaches inflicted heavy losses on sixty dragoons from Cantonment Burgwin near Taos.

308. Ghost Marker: Cantonment Burgwin (1852–1860)

Marker text: Never officially designated a fort, this post was built to protect the Taos Valley from Utes and Jicarilla Apaches. It is named for Capt. John H. K. Burgwin, who was killed in the Taos uprising of 1847. It was abandoned in 1860 and is now the site of the Fort Burgwin Research Center.

Note: This Marker appears in an inventory of Historic Markers compiled by the State Historic Preservation Office but is not in the field. See map 2.

309. Ghost Marker: Embudo Stream Gaging Station

Marker text: Established in 1888. Site of the first United States Geological Survey training center for hydrographers. Those trained here made some of the earliest hydrological studies in the nation, leading to stream-gaging of many streams throughout the country, and thus providing important evaluation of the nations surface water resources.

Note: This Marker appears in an inventory of Historic Markers compiled by the State Historic Preservation Office but is not in the field. See map 2.

In 1795, the Spanish colonial government of New Mexico conveyed a tract of land alongside the Rio Grande here as a community land grant, with the intent that the area be settled and a village formed. First to put down roots that year were members of twenty-five families, a total of 185 people. Their community was called Cieneguilla. The word translates in English to "little marsh" and was no doubt a reference to the marshy land formed by streams and runoff from the Rio Grande from which the community drew water for its crops. The Denver and Rio Grande Western Railroad came through in the 1880s, establishing Embudo Station nearby. A post office opened

1903 with the name Cieneguilla, but only a short while later, in 1918, the name changed to Pilar, which is the name the town uses today.

That same water source that had drawn Spanish settlers here in the eighteenth century had earlier made the land attractive to the Jicarilla Apaches. The Jicarillas had lived in the Sangre de Cristo Mountains and southern Colorado long before the Spanish arrived, and had once settled their own small farming village near the site of Cieneguilla.

In August 1852, the US Army erected Cantonment Burgwin about eighteen miles to the northeast, in the foothills of the Sangre de Cristo Mountains, to protect the region from Apache attacks. The post took its name for Captain John Henry K. Burgwin, who had been killed in a January 1847 rebellion in Taos by residents unhappy with the US takeover of New Mexico, which until then had been part of Mexico. The designation of "cantonment" rather than fort was to indicate that the post was to be temporary, although it remained in operation for a full eight years. It had an officers' quarters, enlisted men's barracks, hospital, guardhouse, and mess hall, most constructed of wood and adobe, with two interior courtyards and parade grounds. Two years after the post opened, soldiers stationed there were part of an important historical engagement known today as the Battle of Cieneguilla.

Sixty men of companies F and I, First Dragoons, marched out from Cantonment Burgwin on March 29, 1854, on an expedition under the command of Lieutenant John Wynn Davidson. The men were under orders to observe a camp of Jicarilla Indians nearby. In a canyon in the Embudo Mountains near present-day Pilar the next morning, in what was possibly an ambush, the soldiers came under attack by some two hundred Apache and Ute Indians, who rained arrows down on them from the top of the canyon. Davidson's account of the incident to Major George Alexander Hamilton Blake, commander at Cantonment Burgwin, on April 1, offers a few scant details. According to Davidson, the Apaches "at once sounded the war whoop." Feeling that "there was but one thing to do" in response to such an act, Davidson charged his men up the canyon in an attempt to drive them away. The Indians "rallied at once," Davidson wrote, "and charged the command at close quarters seven times." After a fight that lasted two or three hours, the troops withdrew with their wounded. Twenty-two men had been killed, almost half the command, and thirty-six wounded.

Among the wounded was Private James A. Bennett, shot in the legs by a single rifle ball, who retreated from the battle in part by grabbing the stirrups of two horses and allowing himself to be dragged away. After reaching Cantonment Burgwin, Bennett recuperated at the fort, fearing an Indian attack in reprisal. "What a pleasant situation," he wrote in his journal, "to lie in bed, helpless, and expect to be massacred at any moment." Bennett recovered from his injuries.

Soon after, Lieutenant Davidson's tactics in the field were called into question by a contemporary, Lieutenant David Bell of the First Cavalry, who wrote that Davidson was boasting of the number of Indians killed in the engagement, was driven by his own prejudices against the Indians, and had, in fact, engaged the Apaches without just cause and at significant loss of life. "If he had been under the command of any officer other than Major Blake," Bell wrote of Davidson and his commanding officer, "he would have been tried for disobedience of orders." On March 26, 1856, the Court of Inquiry that had been convened to investigate Lieutenant Bell's allegations issued its report. The court found that Captain Davidson "could not under the circumstances, with honor, have avoided the battle near the Cieneguilla on the 30th of March 1854." In fact, the report went on to say that Davidson had exhibited skill, prudence, coolness, and courage in the engagement, and that the statements of Lieutenant Bell were "malicious criticism."

A study of the battlefield conducted in 2009 by David M. Johnson and others with the US Forest Service sheds new light on the episode. After an archaeological survey of the area, from which more than a thousand artifacts were recovered and studied, Johnson and his team were able to reconcile the reports of the battle with the reality they found in the field itself. They concluded that, although much of the written report of the battle was accurate, it was probably true that the number of Apaches claimed to have been in the engagement likely was higher than were actually present. As for the suggestion that Davidson attacked without provocation, Johnson points out that the Court of Inquiry was likely loathe to question Davidson's decision to fight rather than retreat, seeing it as a question of honor, despite the decision having cost the lives of many men. "Perhaps it is true that in 1854 a soldier could not retreat from an enemy's camp without engaging in a fight once the 'war whoop' had commenced," the report notes, "or his honor and reputation would be impugned. In this setting, at this time, Davidson may have done the only thing he could to protect his honor."

Cantonment Burgwin was vacated in May 1860. The ruins of the fort were later rebuilt, expanded, and repurposed as the Fort Burgwin Research Center, today part of Southern Methodist University's satellite campus in Taos.

Another occasion of historic import, one that was certainly less violent, took place near Cieneguilla in December 1888. In that month, scientists with the Irrigation Survey, a newly formed department of the US Geological Survey, arrived at Embudo, about eleven miles south of Pilar, to establish the first stream gaging station in the country and train in the field of hydrology. Stream gaging is a method for measuring the flow of a river. The effort was in response to a suggestion offered by Major John Wesley Powell, leader of one of the four Great Surveys of the West and later head of the US Geological Survey, in his *Report on the Lands of the Arid Region of the United States*, that an inventory of streams in the western states be conducted and that the flow of those streams be measured and recorded so that their potential to irrigate the land could be evaluated. Although the Irrigation Survey was closed in 1890, the Embudo stream gage remains today, a few hundred feet downstream from its original location. Today, the US Geological Survey maintains the station, along with more than seven thousand stream gages around the country, as part of the National Streamflow Information Program.

More to explore: *Dulcelina Salce Curtis, Jicarilla Apache (Tribe), Taos*

310. Pinos Altos

Location: Grant County. South of the town of Pinos Altos on the east side of NM 15, between mile markers 6 and 7. See map 5.

Marker text: Once the seat of Grant County, Pinos Altos survived conflicts with the Apache. A gold discovery in 1860 by three 49ers from California stimulated a boom that led to the establishment of this mining camp which produced over $8,000,000 of gold, silver, copper, lead and zinc before the mines played out in the 20th century.

It was May 1860, and ex–California Gold Rush prospector Henry Birch and his friends, Colonel Jacob Sniveley and James Hicks, were panning for gold among the cool pines along nearby Bear Creek. When Birch stopped to drink from the stream, he noticed small flecks of gold glittering in the sparkling waters. Those small shimmering flecks were enough. Hundreds of prospectors soon arrived to work both placer and lode mines in the foothills of the Black Range Mountains. Among them were brothers Thomas and Virgil Marston, who opened the successful Pacific Mine that same year. Merchants came too, including former Doña Ana brothers Sam and Roy "Law West of the

Pecos" Bean, who worked as the proprietors of a small store. The camp took the name Birchville on behalf of its founder.

Henry Birch was not the first to seek wealth in this region, nor would he be the last. The Santa Rita del Cobre copper mine near present-day Bayard had been worked since 1804, and other prospectors claimed to have discovered gold in the gulches long before Birchville took shape. None of this activity escaped the attention of the Apaches, who begrudged the miners and settlers now canvassing their mountainous hunting grounds. The Apaches harassed settlers in the nascent settlement and other villages in the mountains in an attempt to dispel the new pioneers. In one daring assault on Birchville on September 22, 1861, Apache warriors surged four hundred strong into the town. When the bloody incursion was over, fifteen Indians and three miners lay dead—one of them, Thomas Marston.

To help protect settlers from further attacks, the army in 1867 established Fort Bayard a few miles south of Birchville. With soldiers now on patrols through the region, Birchville citizens felt confident enough in the stability of their rustic village to plat a townsite that same year. They also opened a post office, but chose as the formal name of their village not Birchville but Pinos Altos, or "Tall Pines." When the territorial legislature created Grant County in 1869, Pinos Altos became county seat.

It would hold that honor only a few years. Silver City, a town developed by former Pinos Altos resident John Bullard, rapidly became the preeminent settlement in Grant County and eclipsed Pinos Altos as county seat in 1871. Mining continued in Pinos Altos on a small scale through the turn of the century. Before the mines played out, Pinos Altos had produced, by some estimates, more than $8 million in combined gold, silver, copper, lead, and zinc—enough to lead the National Park Service to call the village the "Eldorado of New Mexico."

More to explore: *Fort Bayard, Santa Rita Copper Mines, Silver City*

311. Plains of San Agustín

Location: Socorro County. Between Magdalena and Datil, on the south side of US 60 at mile marker 90. See map 5.

Marker text: Northeast part of Plains of San Agustín, occupied some thousands of years ago by large intermontane lake, is downdropped graben bordered by uplifted volcanic masses. San Mateo and Luera Mountains and Pelona Mountain are southeast and Horse Mountain and Datil Mountains are northwest. Elevation 7,030 feet.

This expansive, forty-five-mile-long, smooth grassy valley is a *graben*, a German word meaning "grave." The gloomy allusion is a descriptive term for land that has dropped between parallel faults, in much the same way that pallbearers lower a coffin into a grave. Rainwater and runoff from the uplifted volcanic masses that formed the circumscribing mountains filled the graben, creating an ancient intermontane ("between mountains") lake. The San Mateo and Luera Mountains, as well as Pelona Mountain, rise in the southeast. Horse Mountain and the Datil Mountains can be seen to the northwest.

The basin today is known as the Plains of San Agustín, named for Saint Augustine of Hippo (AD 354–430), one of the most important early theologians of what became the Roman Catholic Church.

The namesake of this large basin, Saint Augustine of Hippo (AD 354–430), was an important theologian in the development of the early Christian church. Today, radio astronomers use the grassy plain as a backdrop from which to eavesdrop on the heavens. Photo by John Mulhouse. Used with permission.

Spread across this plain are the twenty-seven radio antennas that form the National Radio Antenna Observatory. Scientists at the NRAO use these antennas to eavesdrop on the universe. Each antenna stands 94 feet tall, stretches 82 feet in diameter, and weighs 235 tons. The antennas are mounted on railroad tracks so scientists can more easily maneuver them into different formations, or arrays, depending on research needs. The largest of these arrays spans a range with a width of twenty-two miles and is known as the "Very Large Array," or VLA. It was the need for a large stretch of flat, open land to accommodate such large arrangements that made the Plains of San Agustín ideal for the placement of the VLA.

More to explore: *Basin and Range Country, Edge of the Plains, Magdalena*

312. Playas Siding

Location: Hidalgo County. West of Playas, on the south side of NM 9, between mile markers 25 and 26. See map 5.

Marker text: In 1902, Phelps, Dodge and Company built the El Paso and Southwestern Railroad to link El Paso, Texas with the copper mines of Bisbee, Arizona, and eventually, with several other mining towns throughout the region. Highway 9, New Mexico's "Border Route" between Columbus and Rodeo, parallels the old rail line, and actually utilizes a portion of the abandoned EP & SW railroad bed between Columbus and Anapra.

Along this lonely stretch of highway lie the scattered hulls of railbeds, broken wooden bridges, and empty cattle pens—a potter's field of scraps marking the erstwhile course of the El Paso and Southwestern Railroad. Constructed in 1902 by the Phelps Dodge Corporation and abandoned in the mid-1960s, the line ran across the level, arid terrain of southwestern New Mexico to link the company-owned Copper Queen copper mine near Bisbee, Arizona, with the smelter in El Paso, Texas.

At intervals along the 250-mile chain of track that ran through New Mexico, construction crews established several small railroad sidings where trains could take on water or cargo. Some blossomed into communities that survive today, like Columbus and Rodeo. Others exist only in memory, their names evoking the characteristics endemic to this far southwestern corner of the state: Vista, Malpais, Victorio, Antelope.

In the sun-swept valley here, lodged between the Animas Mountains to the west and the Little Hatchet Mountains to the east, the railroad established Playas Siding. The name came from Playas Lake, a nearby basin fed by cloudbursts that often as not go unseen by human eyes in this sparsely populated setting. Playas Siding served as a shipping point for area ranchers grazing their livestock over wide reaches of the Playas and Animas Valleys. Cowboys loaded cattle destined for El Paso onto railroad cars via the wooden cattle pens that time has left nearly intact along the roadside here.

A small but productive flurry of mining activity hit the Little Hatchet Mountains to the southeast before the turn of the century, with mines like the King, the American, and the Hornet producing silver, lead, and copper. A small camp appeared on the scene and took the name Hachita, the Spanish word for "Little Hatchet." Originally, Hachita lay a few miles closer to the mountains than it does today. With the arrival of the line, miners at Hachita reopened their post office in a new community beside the tracks. The railroad offered a cost-effective means of transporting ores from Hachita mines. Eventually, Old Hachita became a ghost town, but its reincarnated self, Hachita, remains today.

Driving along New Mexico Highway 9 between Columbus and Anapra today is like driving in the ghostly wake of the original train route, which was abandoned in 1961. Parts of the highway between Hachita and El Paso also closely parallel the US-Mexico border; the stretch was sometimes known as the Border Route. Where once rolled railroad cars now roll the green-and-white vehicles of the US Border Patrol.

More to explore: *Columbus, Cumbres and Toltec Scenic Railroad (see under Chama), Hachita, Yucca Plains*

313. Point of Rocks

Location: Colfax County. East of Springer, in a pullout on the north side of US 56/412, between mile markers 23 and 24. See map 3.

Marker text: Point of Rocks was a major landmark on the Santa Fe Trail. Located in Jicarilla Apache country, it was near here that the party of Santa Fe merchant J. M. White was attacked in 1849. Kit Carson was a member of the military party organized to rescue White's wife and daughter.

The escarpments and small plateau that form the historic Point of Rocks district guided travelers along the Cimarron Cutoff of the Santa Fe Trail. Wagon masters driving their caravans along the grasslands past Point of Rocks often used a spring at the site as a camping place and to water their livestock. Trader and trail historian Josiah Gregg called that spring "a charming little fount of water." Charming though it might have been, travelers often camped away from the rock formation to avoid being ensnared by hostile bands of Indians. Even this was no guarantee of safety, as one tragic story recounts.

It was October 1849, and physician and trader James M. White and his family were returning home to Santa Fe with a merchant caravan along the Cimarron Cutoff. As travelers sometimes did, White, his wife Ann, their daughter, a servant woman, and two other men rode ahead of the wagon train. Several miles east of Point of Rocks, Jicarilla Apache Indians ambushed the lone party in an aggressive attack, killing Mr. White and the other men. The Indians spared Ann White, her daughter, and the servant, but took them captive.

Word of the incident quickly reached Taos, where Captain William Grier of the US Army ordered his First Dragoons into their saddles on a charge to recapture the hostages. Mountain man and army guide Kit Carson soon joined the chase. For almost two weeks, the rescue party followed an elusive trail, finding motivation where they could. "In nearly every camp," Carson later wrote in his autobiography, "we found some of Mrs. White's clothing, and these discoveries spurred us to continue the pursuit with renewed energy."

At last, near present-day Tucumcari, the troops came unnoticed upon the Apache camp. Carson wrote later that he had wanted to press the advantage of their stealth and attack, but another guide convinced Captain Grier to parley with the Indians instead, in hopes of winning the return of the captives through diplomacy. The moment of indecision proved a fatal misstep. Upon spying the soldiers, the Indians fled. According to Carson, Ann White did not realize that the soldiers were present and used the confusion to make a desperate attempt at escape. She did not travel far—no more than two hundred yards—before an Indian arrow pierced her heart. Carson found her body on the ground, still warm.

Among the items soldiers recovered in the camp was a paperback book romanticizing Kit Carson's exploits on the frontier. The irony was not lost on Carson, who later conceded:

I have often thought that Mrs. White must have read it, and knowing that I lived nearby, must have prayed for my appearance in order that she might be saved. I did come, but I lacked the power to persuade those that were in command over me to follow my plan for her rescue.

In 1850, Congress offered a $1,500 reward "for the redemption of the daughter of Mr. and Mrs. James M. White, who was captured by the Indians on the borders of New Mexico," but the money went unclaimed. Despite efforts by her uncle to discover her whereabouts, the little girl was never seen again.

More to explore: *Captive Women and Children of Taos County, Kit Carson Park (see under Taos), McComas Incident, Santa Fe Trail (series)*

314. Portales

Location: Roosevelt County. In Portales, across from Eastern New Mexico University on US 70. See map 6.

Marker text: Portales derives its name from the porch-like appearance of a cave entrance at nearby Portales Springs. It developed as a major peanut producing region in the early twentieth century, after the Pecos Valley Railroad opened the area for commercial agricultural development. Eastern New Mexico University was founded here in 1934.

315. Los Portales

Location: Roosevelt County. North of Portales on the west side of US 70, near the intersection of US 70 and NM 467. See map 6.

Marker text: Nearby is Los Portales, the site of a fresh water spring located among overhanging natural formations, which according to Hispanic folklore reminded Spanish explorers of porches. During the late 19th century, this spring became an important stopping place along the trail between Fort Sumner and west Texas. William "Billy the Kid" Bonney and other outlaws frequently used the spring as a hideout.

Across the spacious sweep of southeastern New Mexico, reliable water sources were vital stops for early travelers. A freshwater spring here became known as Los Portales, a name supposedly derived because the caliche-rock ledges and overhangs surrounding the spring were said to resemble the patio porches, or *portales*, of Spanish ranch homes. In the early 1880s, Los Portales became a stop along the cattle trail blazed by cowboy Jim Stinson. The Stinson Trail ran from west-central Texas into eastern New Mexico, then continued past Fort Sumner and Vaughn until it reached the New Mexico Land and Cattle Company ranch in Estancia, where Stinson was manager.

The rock formations at Los Portales also offered an opportune place for outlaw William "Billy the Kid" Bonney to sequester cattle stolen from ranches of the eastern plains and Texas Panhandle. W. S. Koogler, in the *Las Vegas Gazette* in December 1880, wrote of the Kid and his associates Charlie Bowdre and Tom O'Folliard:

They spend time in enjoying themselves at Portales, keeping guards out and scouting the country for miles around before turning in for the night. Whenever there is good opportunity to make a haul they split up in gangs and scour the country, always leaving behind a detachment to guard their roost and whatever plunder they may have stored there.

Homesteader Doak Good established a small ranch near the spring around 1881, said to be the first such operation in the area. According to early pioneer histories, Good later tangled with fellow homesteader Jim Newman over water rights for their cattle and left after killing a gunman he believed Newman had sent to murder him. "Uncle Josh" Morrison, by later opening a small store, created the first commercial enterprise at Los Portales. Settlement would not linger here for long, however. In 1899, work crews reached the valley to lay track for the Pecos Valley and Northeastern Railroad six miles west of the springs. Built under the direction of southeastern New Mexico land promoter James J. Hagerman, the railroad was an extension of an existing line running from Pecos, Texas, to Roswell. Given the inevitable construal of its abbreviation, PV&NE, workers nicknamed the line the "Pea Vine." Morrison moved his store to the new railroad camp and opened a post office. Among the items he took with him was the name, and the settlement of Portales was fathered.

Shortly thereafter, in 1903, the state legislature approved the creation of Roosevelt County and established the budding town of Portales as county seat.

The Pea Vine allowed for the convenient shipment of cattle and opened the grasslands for commercial ranching and agricultural development. After 1910, Portales farmers began to harvest the first Valencia peanuts in the region. Today, New Mexico is the leading producer of Valencia peanuts in the country, a distinction celebrated annually at the Portales Peanut Valley Festival.

In 1934, Eastern New Mexico Junior College in Portales opened its doors as a two-year institution to train teachers for rural schools. Later, regents added a third and fourth year and the college became Eastern New Mexico University. It is today the third-largest university in the state.

More to explore: Eastern New Mexico University, Lincoln

316. Pueblo of Ácoma

Location: Cibola County. In the rest area off exit 102 from Interstate 40. See map 1.

Marker text: Built atop a great mesa for defensive purposes, Ácoma has been continuously occupied since the 13th century. A dramatic battle between the Ácomas and Oñate's forces occurred here in 1599. The mission church of San Esteban was built between 1629 and 1641, and today looks much as described by Fray Francisco Atanasio Domínguez in 1776.

317. Old Ácoma "Sky City"

Location: 1. Cibola County. At the scenic overlook near the entrance to Acoma Pueblo on BIA 38. See map 1.

2. Cibola County. In Acoma, in the parking lot of the Acoma Sky City Marketing Department Building, near the intersection of Silver Dollar and Pueblo Lane. See map 1.

Marker text: Legend describes Ácoma as a "place that always was." Archaeological evidence shows it has been occupied since at least the 13th century. Established on this mesa for defensive purposes, Ácoma was settled by inhabitants of nearby pueblos which had been abandoned. Nearly destroyed by the Spanish in 1599, Ácoma was quickly reestablished by ancestors of its present occupants.

Note: This Marker makes a geographic reference to "this mesa." The mesa referenced is south of here, at the site of the original pueblo.

Built atop a towering, 357-foot-high red mesa, the "Sky City" of Acoma Pueblo is the home of the Keresan-speaking Acoma tribe. Archaeologists believe that ancestors of the Acoma people living in older villages in the outlying areas may have moved onto this mesa around 1100, possibly so they could more easily defend themselves against attacks. In the late thirteenth century, Mesa Verdeans and others migrating from drought conditions elsewhere may have joined them. Many Acomas believe, however, that their people have always lived on the mesa, and the name Acoma has been translated to mean "a place that always was."

Spanish contact with Acoma came in 1540, when the conquistador Francisco Vásquez de Coronado sent Captain Hernando de Alvarado to investigate the pueblo. Alvarado described Acoma this way:

The village was very strong, because it was up on a rock out of reach, having steep sides in every direction. . . . There was a wall of large and small stones at the top, which they could roll down without showing themselves, so that no army could possibly be strong enough to capture the village.

One tried, though—the soldiers of don Juan de Oñate. Oñate came to New Mexico in 1598 to colonize the land for Spain. In early December, his nephew, Juan de Zaldívar, led a regiment of sixteen soldiers to Acoma to trade tools for food. A battle erupted at the pueblo, the genesis of which remains unclear—either the soldiers molested Acoma women, or Zaldívar felt that a conspiracy was in the works to do him in. In the scuffle, Acoma Indians killed Zaldívar and eleven of his soldiers. Oñate sent a second nephew, Vicente de Zaldívar, to exact punishment. Zaldívar and his men ascended the south mesa under camouflage of darkness and besieged the village, killing eight hundred people. At a trial presided over by Oñate, the Indians were found guilty of treason to Spain. So that others might be intimidated against similar uprisings, all Acoma males over twenty-five years old had one foot amputated.

Between 1629 and 1641, Fray Juan Ramírez oversaw the completion of the pueblo mission of San Estevan del Rey. Fray Francisco Atanasio Domínguez visited the church in 1776 while making an inventory of missions in New Mexico. He noted the dimensions and details of the sanctuary, the choir loft "in the usual place" and "supported by . . . wrought beams which rest on a strong cross timber," the "beautiful windows with wooden gratings," the baptismal font, the high altar, the sacristy, and even the vestments and missals.

Although most Acomas today live elsewhere, the pueblo atop the lofty mesa remains home to a handful of families year-round. The tribe assembles here during the annual feast day of Saint Stephen, on September 2.

More to explore: *El Morro National Monument Inscription Rock, Espejo's Expedition, Oñate's Route (see under El Camino Real—The King's Highway), Pueblo of Laguna, Pueblo of Santa Ana, Pueblo of Zia, Vásquez de Coronado's Route (series)*

318. Pueblo of Isleta

Location: Bernalillo County. At the west end of Isleta Pueblo, in a small triangular pullout created by the merging of NM 314 (Isleta Boulevard) and NM 45. See map 4.

Marker text: Isleta, or "little island" in Spanish, is the largest of the Rio Grande pueblos. Many Isletans moved to El Paso with the Spanish during the 1680 Revolt; others resettled the pueblo around 1710. Parts of the mission, San Agustín de la Isleta, date from about 1613.

319. Pueblo of Isleta Tuei

Location: Bernalillo County. In Isleta Pueblo, in the parking lot of Joseph L. Jojola/Celso Montoya Park, on NM 147. See map 4.

Marker text: This Southern Tiwa Pueblo is said to have derived its name from the frequent flooding of the Rio Grande, which surrounded the village, giving it the appearance of a little island. Isleta was noted for the excellence of its crops and orchards. The western branch of the Camino Real crossed the river north of here.

The pueblo of Isleta is a southern Tiwa pueblo, meaning that its residents traditionally spoke the Tiwa language. Isleta and Tuf Shurn Tui (formerly Sandia Pueblo), both located near Albuquerque, make up the southern Tiwa pueblos, while Taos Pueblo and Picurís Pueblo, near Taos, make up the northern Tiwa pueblos. Today, Tiwa, along with Spanish and English, is spoken at the pueblo.

When Bishop Pedro Tamarón y Romeral, the sixteenth bishop of the archdiocese of Durango, Mexico, visited the region in 1760, he wrote an account of the origin of the Spanish name of the pueblo—Isleta, or "Little Island." Tamarón wrote: "It is called Isleta because it is very close to the Río Grande del Norte, and when the river is in flood, one branch surrounds it. It is not inundated because it stands on a little mound."

Around 1613, a Franciscan priest, Juan de Salas, oversaw construction of a mission church on the north end of the pueblo plaza. It is one of the oldest mission churches in New Mexico. The adobe walls are almost three feet thick, with windows to light the interior. The chapel bears the original dedication San Antonio de Padua.

In 1680, many of the pueblos in New Mexico rose to expel the Spanish, who were, among other things, hampering their religious practices. Although some Isleta residents fled at the outbreak of the revolt to Arizona to seek shelter at Hopi settlements there, many others remained at the pueblo. They were soon joined about 1,500 Spanish settlers, gathered together by the alcalde (similar to a mayor) of the lower colonial district of New Mexico, Lieutenant General Alonso García. Fearing that Governor Antonio de Otermín in Santa Fe had been annihilated in the insurrection, García led the colonists and many of the Isletans south. In fact, Otermín had not been killed. He arrived soon after at Isleta with a number of additional colonists, priests, and Indian allies in retreat from Santa Fe. The company rested at Isleta before continuing south themselves. The two groups reconnected near present-day Socorro. From there, they continued together to the mission church of Nuestra Señora de Guadalupe, near present-day El Paso.

The approach of winter and lack of sufficient arms kept Otermín from attempting a reconquest of New Mexico until the following spring, by which time the Isletans with him at El Paso had formed a new pueblo there. They called their new pueblo Ysleta del Sur—"Isleta of the South." The community remains today.

After the return of the Spanish to New Mexico, Isleta Pueblo was resettled around 1710, mostly by Isletans who had remained in New Mexico or fled to live with the Hopis at the outbreak of the Pueblo Revolt. Although the mission church had been set afire during the revolt, the walls of the nave were intact. The Isletans rebuilt their church. Because the mission at Ysleta del Sur had been dedicated to Saint Anthony, they chose to change the dedication of the church at Isleta as well, to San Agustín de Isleta—Saint Anthony of Isleta.

Isleta lay along the course of the Camino Real, which linked the communities of the northern New Mexico frontier with Mexico and allowed for trade and settlement of the region. While the Camino Real generally followed the east bank of the river north through the state, one branch crossed the river just north of Isleta to reach the small farming communities, like Los Luceros and Pajarito, that developed on the west bank in the early 1700s.

In 1776, the Franciscan priest Fray Francisco Atanasio Domínguez visited Isleta on a tour of mission churches in New Mexico. Although he was not taken with the overall physical shape of the mission, writing, "if I describe it, I shall only cause confusion," he was nonetheless enamored of the pueblo's crops and orchard:

This convent has a beautiful kitchen garden among the Indians' lands, from which a large amount of green vegetables is gathered. There are vinestocks in it, but wine is not made because they are few. Cotton is also sown in it, and a small amount is gathered for candles. It has small peach trees. There are seven [small fields]. If wheat is sown, they take 3 fanegas [a unit of measurement approximately equal to one and a half bushels] each, which usually yield, when wheat is planted in two of them, some 80 fanegas. Three almudes [a unit of measurement approximately equal to four and a half gallons] of maize can be planted in each [field], and if maize is planted in three of them, 80 fanegas of maize are usually harvested from these three that remain. Obviously they are good. They are irrigated by very deep wide ditches taken from the Rio del Norte [the Rio Grande], and the pueblo takes care of everything, including depositing the harvest in the convent storerooms.

More than three thousand people today live at Isleta, making it the largest of the Rio Grande pueblos. The traditional name of the pueblo is Tue-I.

More to explore: La Salineta, Pueblo of Tuf Shurn Tui

320. Pueblo of Jemez

Location: Sandoval County. At the pueblo of Jemez, in a picnic area on the north side of NM 4, at mile marker 7. See map 4.

Marker text: Jemez is the sole surviving pueblo of the seven in the "provincia de los Hemes" noted by Spaniards in 1541, and the last at which the Towa language is still spoken. In 1838, the remaining inhabitants of Pecos Pueblo moved here. The mission of San Diego de Jemez was last rebuilt in the 1880s.

When Spanish conquistador Francisco Vásquez de Coronado led an expedition to New Mexico in 1540, his chronicler noted the following year that

Captain Francisco de Barrionuevo was sent up the river toward the north with several men. He saw two provinces, one of which was called Hemes and had seven villages. . . . [T]he inhabitants of Hemes came out peaceably and furnished provisions.

Today, the pueblo of Jemez is the last of those seven villages and the last in New Mexico in which some residents still speak the Towa language, along with English and Spanish.

Ancestors of the Jemez Indians settled along the Jemez River and its tributaries centuries before the Spanish arrived. Among their villages was one known to the Indians as Giusewa. Missionary work by Spanish friars at Giusewa in the early seventeenth century led to the founding of the church of San José de los Jémez. Ruins of this mission, along with those of the Giusewa Pueblo itself, can be seen today at the Jemez Historic Site (formerly Jemez State Monument). Later, the Spanish colonial government consolidated the Jemez pueblos to ameliorate the work of the priests. By 1622, the Jemez Indians were living in two main villages, Astialakwa and Giusewa. Further Navajo depredations eventually forced the villages to join into one, Walatowa—modern Jemez Pueblo.

When Major John G. Bourke of the US Army visited the pueblo in 1881, he recounted the sad ruins of the mission church, San Diego de los Jémez, which was burdened with the wear of more than a hundred years' service:

There is no church; the church fell down about ten days ago—the great amount of rain this summer falling upon [the] earth roof proved too much for the resisting power of the old beams which gave way, falling in a heap of ruins upon the altar.

The Jemez people rebuilt the mission of San Diego in 1888 atop the ruins of the old. They have remodeled the structure several times since.

For many centuries, Jemez Pueblo had a linguistic counterpart in the pueblo of Pecos, in the foothills of the Sangre de Cristo Mountains southeast of Santa Fe, whose residents also spoke the Towa language. As disease, Comanche raids, and encroachments by Spanish settlers onto pueblo land weakened Pecos Pueblo, the Indians at Jemez invited those remaining at Pecos to join their pueblo. In 1838, the last seventeen residents of Pecos accepted, leaving their village at Pecos and moving permanently to the pueblo of Jemez.

Jemez celebrates two feast days, the Jemez feast day on November 12 and the Pecos feast day on August 2.

More to explore: *Evelyn M. Vigil and Juanita T. Toledo (see under Pecos), Jemez State Monument, Pecos*

321. Pueblo of Laguna

Location: Cibola County. In the scenic view pullout overlooking Laguna Pueblo, on the north and south sides of Interstate 40, between mile markers 113 and 114. See map 1.

Marker text: Keresan-speaking refugees from Santo Domingo, Ácoma, Cochiti and other pueblos founded Laguna after the Pueblo Revolt of 1680 and the Spanish reconquest of 1692. Named by the Spaniards for a marshy lake to the west, the pueblo still occupies its original hilltop site today.

322. San José de la Laguna Mission

Location: Cibola County. In the scenic view pullout overlooking Laguna Pueblo, on the north and south sides of Interstate 40, between mile markers 113 and 114. See map 1.

Marker text: The picturesque mission church of San José de la Laguna was built around 1706 by Fray Antonio Miranda and shows the single-aisle floor plan commonly used in pueblo churches. It has been repaired many times and acquired its distinctive white stucco exterior in 1977.

The church contains a beautiful and well-preserved altar screen made between 1800 and 1808 by a folk artist known only as the "Laguna santero." The interior walls are mud-plastered and white-washed, and the floor is made of packed earth. The handsome wooden ceiling is laid in a herringbone pattern.

323. Susie Rayos Marmon
"Ga-wa goo maa" (Early Riser), 1877–1988

Location: Cibola County. On Interstate 40, in the pullout on the south side of the interstate overlooking Laguna Pueblo, between mile markers 113 and 114. See map 1.

Marker text: Educated at the Carlisle Indian School in Pennsylvania under the U.S. policy of acculturating Indian children through schooling and removal from their homelands, Susie was instrumental in bringing education back to Laguna. A lifelong teacher, oral historian, and storyteller, Susie was honored with a school in her name in Albuquerque in 1989 and received many national and state citations for her commitment to educating students.

The origins of Laguna Pueblo are rooted in an uprising among the Pueblo Indians against the Spanish in 1680. Known as the Pueblo Revolt, the rebellion drove the Spanish from New Mexico for more than a decade. Fearful of reprisals from the Spanish after their return in 1692, refugees from the pueblos of Santo Domingo, Cochiti, Jemez, and others fled the Spanish advance to the safety of nearby Acoma Pueblo. They remained at Acoma until 1697, when many came together to found a new village in this location. Modern Laguna Pueblo arose on a sandstone slope near the San José River, where waters had pooled into a small marshy lake, or *laguna* in Spanish. That lake has since gone dry.

On July 4, 1699, New Mexico governor Pedro Rodríguez Cubero officially dedicated the pueblo and conferred its patron saint, San José.

Shortly thereafter, Father Antonio Miranda began work on the picturesque mission, San José de la Laguna, or "Saint Joseph of the Lake." Built between 1699 and 1701, the church exhibited in its wooden hand-carved pulpit, adobe altar, packed-earth floor, and single-aisle floor plan features typical of southwestern pueblo missions of the time. One of the most aesthetic of objects adorning the church is the well-preserved wooden altar screen with twisted pillars. The artist has not been identified; he has been referred to simply as the Laguna Santero. (A *santero* is a person who carves religious figures, often from wood.) According to the National Park Service, the talented santero also carved the altar screens in the San Miguel Chapel in Santa Fe and at the mission churches of Zia, Santa Ana, and Acoma Pueblos. Laguna residents added the austere white stucco exterior to the church in 1977.

For many years, the US government had a policy of removing Native American children from their homes and educating them in boarding schools run by the Bureau of Indian Affairs, like the Santa Fe Indian School in Santa Fe, where they were acculturated to the language and lifestyles of the predominant Anglo culture. Although initially well intentioned, the policy separated children from their homelands and their own powerful cultures and educational influences, and forced them to suppress their own native heritage in favor of being "Americanized." One Laguna woman, Susie Rayos Marmon, helped change this.

Born at Laguna in 1877, Marmon herself was schooled away from home, removed from the pueblo as a girl and enrolled first in the Presbyterian Mission School in Albuquerque, and later the Carlisle Indian Industrial School in Carlisle, Pennsylvania. After graduating in the early 1900s, she remained in Pennsylvania, enrolling in the Bloomsburg Teachers College (now Bloomsburg University) in Bloomsburg, Pennsylvania, where she graduated in 1906. She then entered the career that would serve as her lifelong vocation: teaching.

Marmon first accepted a position teaching at Isleta Pueblo, south of Albuquerque, but later returned to Laguna to teach at the place where she had been born. With a change in government policy in the 1930s toward self-governance in Indian tribes, Marmon helped bring education to the pueblo. Marmon taught every subject, from English to science. Because the school at Laguna was the only one at the pueblo, she taught most everyone who lived in the reservation—including her own children. In a 1989 interview with the *Albuquerque Journal*, Marmon's nephew remembered learning from his aunt in the one-room schoolhouse. "She was my first teacher, and she was strict," he recalled.

Marmon remained a teacher at Laguna through four generations, retiring from the profession when she was in her sixties. Her dedication and long service were recognized and rewarded by her students and her peers. Governor Garrey Carruthers declared April 15, 1987, as Susie Rayos Marmon Day. At the time, Marmon was an incredible 110 years old.

Marmon passed away the next year, on April 4, 1988.

Laguna Pueblo is today the largest Keresan-speaking pueblo in the state and one of the largest in population of all the New Mexico pueblos. The pueblo's feast day is September 19.

More to explore: *Gallup, Grants, Pueblo of Acoma, Pueblo of Santa Ana, Pueblo of Zia*

324. Pueblo of Nambé

Location: Santa Fe County. In pullout on the south side of the intersection of NM 503 and US 85. See map 2.

Marker text: In Tewa, the name Nambay-Onghwee or Nambé, means people of the round earth. Occupied around 1300, this Tewa pueblo was first described by Castaño de Sosa in 1591 as a square structure, two stories high, with a central plaza, whose people irrigated their crops. It served as a primary cultural and religious center for this community. It was nearly destroyed when the Spanish conquerors arrived in New Mexico and learned of its importance.

325. The St. Francis Women's Club

Location: Santa Fe County. At Nambé Pueblo, on the west side of NM 503, between mile markers 3 and 4. See map 2.

Marker text: The St. Francis Women's Club was instrumental in raising funds to rebuild San Francisco de Asís Church, which had been condemned and demolished in about 1960. Their main fundraiser was the annual Fourth of July ceremonial, featuring dances of Nambe and participating Pueblos. By 1974, the group raised enough money to rebuild the church, and, in the process, helped to renew cultural traditions at Nambe.

When Spanish explorer Gaspar Castaño de Sosa approached the Tewa-speaking Nambé Pueblo on January 9, 1591, he found a multistoried pueblo in house blocks arranged around a central plaza. Castaño and his men, about twenty in all, spent the night at the pueblo, where the Indians gave them a variety of flavorsome produce grown in well-irrigated fields. As noted by the expedition's chronicler: "We slept here inside the pueblo, and they gave us maize, flour, beans, squash, tortillas, and turkeys, all in great abundance for the people that were there."

Ancestors of the residents of Nambé have occupied this pueblo in the sloping foothills of the Sangre de Cristo Mountains south of Santa Fe since around 1300. The word *nambé* comes from the original Tewa name for the pueblo, Nambay-ongwee, which may be a reference to the ruins of an earlier pueblo village still present on the reservation. Another translation ascribes the meaning as "people of the round earth."

Spanish Franciscan priests had established a small mission church in Nambé by 1617, but relations between the Indians of New Mexico and the Spanish grew darker over subsequent decades. In a show of solidarity known today as the Pueblo Revolt, the Nambé people joined with other pueblos in August 1680 to push the Spanish from the region. Nambé Indians martyred their resident priest, Fray Tomás de Torres, and destroyed their mission church. The Indians remained defiant after Governor Diego de Vargas returned the state to Spanish control in 1692. With other Pueblo Indians, they formed a stronghold on a mesa near the pueblo of San Ildefonso. After Governor Vargas denied their access to the planted fields below, the Indians eventually left the mesa and resettled their home.

Encroachment onto pueblo lands by the Spanish, along with a devastating spread of epidemics among the Nambé people, brought about a marked population decline in the pueblo in subsequent centuries. When Major John G. Bourke of the US Army visited in 1881, he recorded "an inconsiderable pueblo of six or seven families." Although Nambé remained sparsely populated through the turn of the century, its numbers have since increased.

Fray Francisco Atanasio Domínguez, on an inspection of New Mexico missions in 1776, complained of the mission church at Nambé, San Francisco de Nambé, that the "furnishings are complete emptiness." In fairness, he also noted the brass candlesticks, large wooden pulpit, and "big table with a good drawer." That church collapsed in the early 1900s through weathering and neglect. A second one built in 1910 fared little better, being condemned around 1960 and demolished soon thereafter.

After the demise of that church, women at the pueblo took on the task of raising money to erect a solid, sustainable sanctuary. Members of the group known as the Saint Francis Women's Club organized an annual fundraiser, open to the public, which was held on July 4 every year. The fundraiser took the form of a ceremonial, at which dancers from Nambé and other participating pueblos performed traditional dances, and hungry attendees bought food and drinks. The festival, which also helped revitalize cultural traditions at Nambé, had raised enough money by 1974 that the residents of Nambé were able to hire architect Allen L. McNown to help rebuild their church.

That new church, known as San Francisco de Asís Church, was dedicated the following year. It remains standing today, a structural testament both to faith as well as to the hard work of community members. In that church, Nambé residents today celebrate the annual feast day of Saint Francis of Assisi on October 4.

More to explore: *Castaño de Sosa's Route, Pueblo of San Ildefonso, Pueblo of Santa Clara, Pueblo of Tesuque*

326. Pueblo of Picurís

Location: Taos County. At the eastern entrance to the pueblo, in a pullout on the north side of NM 75, at the intersection of NM 75 and Indian Road 201. See map 2.

Marker text: The pueblo of Picurís, first visited by Spaniards in 1591, was described as being 7 to 8 stories high. In the 18th century, Picurís cooperated with the Spaniards against the raids of the Plains Indians. The church, the third at this pueblo, dates from the 1770s.

327. Maria Ramita Simbola Martinez "Summer Harvest" (1884–1969), Cora Durand (1904–1981), Virginia Duran (1904–1998)
Picurís Pueblo

Location: Taos County. At the western entrance to the pueblo, in a pullout on the north side of NM 75, at the intersection of NM 75 and Indian Road 205. See map 2.

Marker text: Maria Ramita Simbola Martinez, Cora Durand, and Virginia Duran helped to preserve the distinctive micaceous pottery tradition that is important in Picurís and other nearby pueblos. Made with locally mined mica-rich clay, these unusual pots have a glittery sheen. They are fired at a low temperature which makes them ideal for cooking. While valued for their utility, these pots are also now considered works of art.

The first Spanish view of the Tiwa-speaking pueblo of Picurís comes from Gaspar Castaño de Sosa, a Spanish explorer who led an illegal colonization expedition into New Mexico in 1590. Castaño visited Picurís on January 13 and 14 of the following year. Trapped by the snow and suspicious of the actions of the Indians, who were carrying stones and standing on the roof, Castaño stayed only one night. His chronicler left this laconic recollection: "The pueblo had a very large force of people and in great number, and the houses were seven and eight stories high."

Today, the pueblo of Picurís consists of mostly one-story structures built around two central plazas.

Ancestors of the Picurís Indians had settled in

the mountains of northern New Mexico by the thirteenth century. When don Juan de Oñate brought the land under Spanish control in 1598, he called the pueblo the "Great Pueblo of the Picuries." Oñate had probably borrowed the name by which Keresan-speaking Indians referred to the pueblo, Pee-Koo-ree-a.

As part of Spanish missionary endeavors among the pueblos, Franciscan priest Fray Martin de Arvide arrived in Picurís in 1621 and directed the construction of the original mission church. During the Pueblo Revolt of 1680, Picurís Pueblo united with other New Mexico pueblos to expel the Spanish from the region. In the process, they sacked their church. After the Spanish reasserted control twelve years later, priests erected a second small mission at the pueblo to replace the first.

In the early 1700s, Picurís Indians allied with Spanish soldiers in punitive expeditions and scouting campaigns against the raiding Apache, Ute, and Comanche Indians, in part to recover Picurís Indians whom these tribes had taken captive. Despite these efforts, Picurís Pueblo continued to suffer attacks by Comanche Indians, including one in 1769 in which the Comanches pillaged the pueblo and set the church afire. The damaged structure was later demolished, and a new one, the present San Lorenzo Mission Church, built near the plaza.

For several centuries, potters at the pueblo have produced pottery distinguished by its earthen tones and glittery sheen. These vessels contain mica, a silicate mineral, present in the clay dug from nearby mountains; it is the mica that gives the pots their shimmering quality. Mica also retains heat, making these vessels excellent for use in cooking. Traditionally, the micaceous pottery created at the pueblo was used for that purpose—some pots even becoming known as "bean pots" for their suitability in cooking large amounts of pinto beans. Waterproof, the pots were also commonly used for storing food and water, as well as serving food. Over the past century, with increased tourism to the Southwest as well as subsequent interest by collectors, the beautiful pots have also now become regarded for their artistic beauty as well.

While many potters at the pueblo produce these finely crafted wares, three women in particular became known for their prominence and ability in this area: Maria Ramita Simbola Martinez, Cora Durand, and Virginia Duran.

Born on April 1, 1884, Maria Ramita Simbola learned the art of pottery from her mother, Soledad. Ramita, who was given the name "Summer Harvest" at the pueblo, later married Juan José Martinez and raised six children with him. To supplement their income and support their family, Martinez sold her wares at local markets. Often, her husband decorated the pots himself.

Potter Cora Lopez was born on August 23, 1904. She later married Roland Durand; together, they had four children. Like many pueblo potters, Durand learned the art of pottery making from others in her family, particularly her grandmother. She, in turn, taught her grandson, Anthony Durand, who carried forward the family name in pottery making until his death in 2009.

Born in the same year as Durand, 1904, Virginia Duran emphasized the sheen in her pottery by rubbing a "slip" of mica onto the pot before firing. A slip is liquefied clay that potters can use to coat a pot and create a thin veneer, often to protect the pot or to change the color or characteristics of the clay.

By carrying the tradition of pottery making through the turn of the century and into the twentieth century, these women helped preserve one of the important cultural traditions of Picurís Pueblo.

The pueblo of Picurís celebrates its feast day on August 10.

More to explore: *Castaño de Sosa's Route, Comanche Country, Pueblo of Isleta Tuei, Pueblo of Tuf Shurn Tui, Virginia T. Romero*

328. Pueblo of San Felipe

Location: Sandoval County. On the San Felipe Reservation, near the intersection of Indian Reservation Road 84 and Hagan Road, in a pullout on the north side of Indian Reservation Road 84. See map 4.

Marker text: San Felipe, named St. Phillip the Apostle by Spanish explorer Francisco Sanchez Chamuscado in 1581, was abandoned during the Pueblo Revolt of 1680. Reestablished on the mesa top, this too was abandoned before 1706, when the pueblo was constructed on its present site. The mission church appears today much as it did in the 18th century.

Note: The Marker misspells the name of the apostle Saint Philip.

Sixteenth-century Spanish explorer Francisco Sánchez Chamuscado, traveling with the Spanish priest Fray Agustín Rodríguez and a small entourage to visit and proselytize the Native American populations in the state, reached a Keresan-speaking pueblo here in 1581. In its early history, the pueblo is believed to have consisted of two separate villages on either side of the river. A chronicle of the expedition left a description of the pueblo as it existed at the time:

And so they continued up the same river for twenty days, through eighty leagues of uninhabited country, until they came to a settlement to which they gave the name of the province of San Felipe. There they found a permanent pueblo with houses two stories high and of good appearance, built of mud walls and white inside, the people being dressed in cotton mantas *with shirts of the same.*

Chamuscado had conferred on the pueblo the Spanish name by which it is known today, San Felipe. The name is Spanish for Saint Philip, one of the twelve apostles.

Anger and resentment over the subjugation of their way of life led the Pueblo Indians of New Mexico to rise up against the Spanish in the year 1680. During this, the Pueblo Revolt, the pueblos united in rebellion to drive Spanish colonists from the region. Fearing reprisals, the Indians at the pueblo of San Felipe fled their pueblo when Governor Antonio de Otermín returned briefly the year following the revolt, rebuilding atop Horn Mesa to the north with refugees from other nearby pueblos. Otermín burned their former pueblo. After Spanish resettlement around 1692, the Indians moved to a new site atop nearby Santa Ana Mesa, but sometime before 1706, they abandoned that pueblo and constructed a new village on the west bank of the Rio Grande. The pueblo remains at this site today, although the San Felipe Reservation itself extends to both sides of the river.

The mission church at the pueblo of San Felipe retains much of the same character of its original construction. On an inspection tour of missions in the Southwest in 1776, Fray Francisco Atanasio Domínguez visited the pueblo and left a description of the church at the time. Domínguez noted the "adobe with thick walls" and single nave design, and the buttresses, which stretched from "the front corners of the church to near its door," with a balcony "between the tower buttresses and over the door." He also described the roof of the nave, saying that it "consists of forty wrought and corbelled beams, and the clerestory rises on the one that faces the sanctuary." Given the somewhat isolated geographical location of San Felipe, Domínguez described the pueblo itself as being "like something tucked in a corner."

The pueblo of San Felipe feast day is held on May 1.

More to explore: *Pueblo of Acoma, Pueblo of Laguna*

329. Pueblo of San Ildefonso

Location: Santa Fe County. At the entrance to the pueblo, at the intersection of NM 502 and Indian Road 401. See map 2.

Marker text: In the 1500s, migrants from the Pajarito Plateau joined their Tewa-speaking relatives at San Ildefonso. The pueblo is famous as the home of the late María Martínez and other makers of polished black pottery. The modern church, a replica of that of 1711, was finished in 1968.

330. María Montoya Martínez
Poveka, Pond Lilly (ca. 1886–1980)

Location: Santa Fe County. At the entrance to the pueblo, at the intersection of NM 502 and Indian Road 401. See map 2.

Marker text: María Martínez was a self-taught potter who helped elevate Pueblo pottery to a respected art form. She and her husband Julian were successful polychrome potters and together revived black pottery. Their work improved the economic conditions of the community. Recognized internationally, María was an innovator with strong spiritual and cultural awareness. Her skills and techniques have been carried on successfully by subsequent generations.

The Tewa-speaking pueblo of San Ildefonso may be best known today for its tradition of crafting distinctive black-on-black polished ware pottery. The art was heavily influenced by the eminent Pueblo Indian potter María Martínez. With her family and husband, Julian—who later served as governor of San Ildefonso—Martínez was one of the most respected artists working in the medium in the twentieth century, both domestically and internationally. Her innovative pottery and distinctive style helped make Pueblo Indian pottery a respected art form. Although Martínez passed away in 1980, other potters at San Ildefonso have continued to produce the fine, jet-black ceramics that have brought the pueblo worldwide recognition and helped improve the pueblo's economy. The María Martínez Family Pottery Collection is today housed at the Millicent Rogers Museum in Taos.

María Martínez and her jet-black pottery style influenced generations of San Ildefonso potters. Here she polishes a pot with a polishing stone prior to firing and decorating. María Martínez, potter, San Ildefonso Pueblo, undated. Courtesy Palace of the Governors Photo Archives (NMHM/DCA), neg. no. 44192.

In her pottery designs, Martínez was inspired by prehistoric pot shards that her husband had helped excavate at ancestral Tewa sites on the Pajarito Plateau, a mesa west of the Rio Grande on which the city of Los Alamos today stands. Around 1300, drought forced the migration of the early Native Americans on the plateau into the Rio

Grande Valley. Ancestors of the Indians at San Ildefonso settled near here in a village they called Pohwoge. When don Juan de Oñate, the first Spanish governor of New Mexico, visited the pueblo in 1598, he renamed it to honor Saint Ildephonse, the archbishop of Toledo in the seventh century.

By 1617, Spanish Franciscans had completed work on a mission church at the pueblo. It would see service for more than seventy years, until the pueblos united in a coordinated dissension to oust the Spanish colonists from New Mexico. San Ildefonso participated in this, the Pueblo Revolt of 1680, by martyring their two missionaries, Fray Antonio Sánchez de Pío and Fray Luis de Morales, and setting fire to the mission church. When the Spanish returned under the command of don Diego de Vargas in 1692, San Ildefonso residents fled to nearby Black Mesa along with other Tewa and Tano Indians to avoid the Spanish forces. With a small army of men, Vargas seized the fields below the mesa and forcibly prevented the Indians from reaching their food supply. Eventually, the San Ildefonso people, along with others living on the mesa, surrendered their stronghold and returned to their villages.

Priests erected a new mission church in the pueblo around 1711. According to an inventory of pueblo missions conducted in 1776, the mission had among its possessions a "small wooden tabernacle with a key" and "six small brass candlesticks which the King gave." The report also noted that "the whole wall around the sanctuary is painted blue and yellow from top to bottom like a tapestry, and not too badly." That church collapsed after years of service. In 1968, San Ildefonso residents rebuilt it in replica west of the plaza.

The San Ildefonso feast day is held on January 23.

More to explore: *Oñate's Route (see under El Camino Real—The King's Highway), Pueblo of Nambé, Pueblo of Picurís, Pueblo of Santa Clara, Pueblo of Tesuque, Virginia T. Romero*

331. Pueblo of Santa Ana

Location: Sandoval County. Ten miles west of Bernalillo, at the entrance to the pueblo, near mile marker 11 on the north side of US 550. See map 4.

Marker text: The Keres-speaking pueblo of Santa Ana was established on its present site in 1693, as part of Diego de Vargas' reconquest of New Mexico. The spot, exposed to flooding, was poorly suited for farming, and today the residents live on their farms along the Rio Grande instead of the pueblo, which is used as a ceremonial site.

Historians believe that ancestors of the Keresan-speaking Santa Ana people migrated to the Jemez Valley from pueblos in the Galisteo Basin southeast of Santa Fe sometime between 1200 and 1300. Pueblo oral history recounts an origin underground and to the north, with a subsequent emergence by the ancestors into the present world. By the late 1500s, the Indians were living at the approximate site of Santa Ana today. They called their home along the north bank of the Jemez River Tamaya. When the Spanish colonized New Mexico in 1598, they conferred on the pueblo the patron saint Santa Ana.

New Mexico history changed dramatically in 1680, when most of the northern Indian pueblos allied against the oppression brought by the Spanish government. Santa Ana Pueblo joined the uprising, known as the Pueblo Revolt, and helped expel Spanish colonists, priests, and government officials from the region. Governor Diego de Vargas returned the state to Spanish rule in 1692. He found that the Santa Ana people had fled in the meantime to a mesa in the Jemez Mountains. Within a year, the Santa Ana people returned to the area and established modern Santa Ana Pueblo at its present site.

The location, though, was prone to flooding from the Jemez River and therefore poorly suited for farming. In the eighteenth century, residents of Santa Ana began to purchase land that was more arable along the Rio Grande at the nearby village of Ranchitos. Today, many Santa Anans live year-round outside the pueblo at Ranchitos and other farming villages along the banks of the Jemez River and the Rio Grande near Bernalillo. They use the pueblo itself mainly as a ceremonial site. It is open to the public on the Santa Ana feast day, July 26.

More to explore: *Galisteo Basin, Pueblo of Acoma, Pueblo of Laguna, Pueblo of Zia*

332. Pueblo of Santa Clara

Location: Rio Arriba County. Just south of the pueblo entrance, on the west side of NM 30, at mile marker 7. See map 2.

Marker text: Founded around the fourteenth century, Santa Clara traces its ancestry to Puyé, an abandoned site of cave dwellings on the Pajarito Plateau. Increasing tensions with the Spanish led to its participation in the Pueblo Revolt of 1680. The mission church, once thought to be the narrowest of its kind, has been reconstructed several times since the 17th century.

333. Pablita Velarde
Tse Tsan, Golden Dawn (1918–2006)

Location: Rio Arriba County. Just south of the pueblo entrance, on the west side of NM 30, at mile marker 7. See map 2.

Marker text: Pablita Velarde was an internationally acclaimed artist whose paintings largely depicted Pueblo life. She was commissioned by the WPA arts program to paint murals at Bandelier National Monument. Selected as one of New Mexico's "Living Treasures," she received many awards, including the French Palmes Académique, the New Mexico Governor's Award for achievement in the arts, and the Lifetime Achievement Award from the Eight Northern Pueblos.

Santa Clara Pueblo, situated along the western bank of the Rio Grande just south of Española, is one of six Tewa-speaking pueblos in New Mexico. Residents of Santa Clara trace an ancestral link to the former inhabitants of Puyé, a village of abandoned caves and cliff house ruins on the elevated Pajarito Plateau to the southwest. When environmental factors caused the Indians at Puyé to abandon their pueblo around 1550, they migrated eastward to settle closer to the river.

The first Spanish governor of New Mexico, don Juan de Oñate, visited the village in its present location on his colonizing mission in 1598. Oñate dedicated the pueblo to Santa Clara, thus giving it the Spanish name by which it is commonly known. Santa Clarans know their village as Kha-'Po.

By the time Franciscan missionary Fray Alonso de Benavides arrived at the pueblo around 1622 to minister to the parish, political and religious dissonance between the Spanish and Pueblo Indians in New Mexico was rising. That festering discontent discharged in a fury on August 10, 1680, as the pueblos united to emancipate themselves from Spanish control. Santa Clara resident Domingo Naranjo served as one of the leaders of this rebellion, known today as the Pueblo Revolt. When General Diego de Vargas returned New Mexico to Spanish governance twelve years later, residents of Santa Clara initially pledged a peaceful submission, but later sought sanctuary with other Tewa- and Towa-speaking Indians on a nearby mesa. There they rebuffed repeated attacks by Vargas and his soldiers until the governor turned from the mesa to the planted fields at its base and prevented the Indians from reaching their primary food supply. Faced with the threat of starvation, the Santa Clarans eventually resettled their village.

In 1706, the residents of Santa Clara completed a small church to replace the one erected under the supervision of Fray Benavides. That original church had been damaged in the revolt. Unfortunately, the second church fared little better: it had fallen to ruin by 1758. A new building was begun that year under the direction of resident priest Fray Mariano Rodríguez de la Torre. The Father's new church took an unusual shape. Lacking sturdy and long timber for vigas, or rooftop supports, Fray Rodríguez instead placed several thinner vigas close together. The constriction created what was then considered the narrowest church in New Mexico: a building measuring 14 feet in width and 110 feet in length. Fray Francisco Atanasio Domínguez, in his inventory of New Mexico missions in 1776, could not decide whether the best comparison was to a long, thin cannon, or to a wine cellar—so he used both. This church, too, collapsed when its newly installed pitched roof failed to withstand a torrential rain in 1909. The present structure was erected in 1918.

On September 19 of that same year, a woman was born at the pueblo who would go on to become one of the most recognized of Native American women painters. Her Tewa name was Tse Tsan, or "Golden Dawn," but the art world knows her by the name Pablita Velarde. As a girl in the early 1930s, Velarde attended the Santa Fe Indian School. It was there that she met her first art instructor, Dorothy Dunn, who encouraged the interest in art that Velarde had shown even as a child, and who would become a lifelong mentor. Velarde and her sister were the only girls in Dunn's painting class. Dunn described her as having "a merry disposition revealed through a provocative sense of humor" and noted that she had "a daring loyalty to the people and principles in which she believed." After graduating, Veldarde took a handful of short career detours, serving as a maid, a nurse's aide, and later the nursemaid to the family of naturalist Ernest Seton, before being offered a position with the Depression-era Works Progress Administration. There, she was commissioned to paint scenes of pueblo life for the museum at Bandelier National Monument—the park protecting the ruins of structures built by the ancestors of some of today's Pueblo Indians, including Santa Clarans.

Between the years 1937 and 1943, working when the government had funds to pay her, Velarde painted more than seventy pieces depicting traditional dances, processions, and people working, set in the eight northern New Mexico pueblos, including Santa Clara, Zia, San Ildefonso, and others. Together, these beautifully colorful works could be considered a visual encyclopedia of pueblo life in New Mexico at the time. Scenes like that depicted in *Basket Dance at San Ildefonso Pueblo* showed Indian dances, while *Silversmith* showed a pueblo man crafting a piece of silver. For her work, Velarde was paid five dollars a day.

Despite working at a time when Native American women were not encouraged toward painting, Velarde continued producing beauty on the canvas throughout her life. Her work at Bandelier brought her national attention, as did her showings in exhibitions. She used a number of media during that time, including watercolor, oil, tempera, casein, and other natural pigments. She was commissioned to paint murals in banks and stores throughout the Southwest, including at Los Alamos and Houston, Texas, and was sought out as a lecturer and art instructor.

Her work, as described by her former teacher Dunn, possessed "the glowing color, the naturalness and noise, and the deep, rich symbolism of Pueblo life itself."

Velarde's talent was recognized through a number of prestigious awards, including one from the French government in 1954, the Ordre des Palmes Académiques, or "Order of Academic Palms," which honors achievements in education and culture. Other awards closer to home included the New Mexico Governor's Award for Excellence in the Arts in 1977, a Lifetime Achievement Award from the Eight Northern Pueblos, and selection as a "Santa Fe Living Treasure" in 1988.

"I want the earth to remember me through my work," Velarde once said.

Velarde passed away on January 12, 2006. Her work remains on display in a number of galleries worldwide, including the Indian Pueblo Cultural Center in Albuquerque.

Craftspeople at Santa Clara Pueblo are also regarded for their skill in fashioning highly polished black pottery. The pueblo celebrates its feast day on August 12.

More to explore: *Oñate's Route (see under El Camino Real—The King's Highway), Pueblo of Nambé, Pueblo of San Ildefonso, Pueblo of Tesuque, Puyé Ruins, Seton Village*

334. Pueblo of Santo Domingo
Kiua

Location: Sandoval County. At the entrance to the pueblo, in a pullout where the exit ramp from NM 22 intersects with Indian Service Route 88, near the railroad tracks. See map 4.

Marker text: The Keresan people of Santo Domingo have occupied this area of the Rio Grande Valley since prehistoric times despite several floods that have forced relocation and reconstruction of the original pueblo. Strategically located along the roads that have led to La Bajada, this pueblo and its people have played an important role in the history of the Camino Real.

335. Kewa Women's Co-Op

Location: Sandoval County. In Santo Domingo, in a pullout on the south side of NM 22, near the intersection of NM 22 and Interstate 25. See map 4.

Marker text: According to oral and recorded history, the Santo Domingo people have always made and traded jewelry. From prehistoric times heishi, drilled and ground shell beads, have been strung into necklaces. Generations of Santo Domingo women have passed down this art. Recent descendents have formed the Kewa Women's Co-Op to retain heishi and other traditions including pottery, embroidery, weaving, and Pueblo foods.

As oral tradition in Santo Domingo Pueblo holds, the earliest ancestors of the Keresan-speaking residents of the pueblo emerged from the earth to the north at a place called Sipapu, then migrated in later generations to the Rio Grande from Mesa Verde and Chaco Canyon. The Indians' presence in this part of north-central New Mexico predates Spanish occupation by many centuries. The name of the pueblo today comes from the patron saint later conferred on it by the Spanish: Saint Dominic, founder of the Dominican Order.

Given its location in the valley of the Rio Grande, the pueblo has long been subject to the demands of a vagarious river. A flood washed away the sixteenth-century pueblo, called Gipuy, along the east bank of the river. In response, the Santo Domingo people resettled on the west bank and erected a new pueblo, which they called Huashpa tzena. Santo Domingoans again suffered flooding when, in the late 1600s, the waters of the Rio Grande overflowed their banks and ravaged Huashpa tzena. The Indians constructed a new pueblo, which they called Kiva, at the current site of the village. As described by Fray Francisco Atanasio Domínguez in 1776:

The pueblo consists of six blocks, or buildings, of dwellings. . . . They are all separate from one another, with a street in the form of a cross dividing the four. The houses have upper and lower stories . . . with a beautiful plaza overlooked by the [facades of the four house blocks] and those of the church and convent. The whole pueblo is surrounded by a high adobe wall with two gates.

Santo Domingo lay along the course of El Camino Real, or the Royal Road, New Mexico's major overland connection with Mexico until the late nineteenth century. At Santo Domingo Pueblo, the Camino Real left the Rio Grande and turned sharply northeastward on its approach to La Bajada Hill. La Bajada, meaning "the descent," is a prominent escarpment just south of Santa Fe over which northbound caravans struggled in their ascent from the Rio Grande Valley into Santa Fe.

The residents of Santo Domingo today enjoy recognition for a long tradition of jewelry making, dating back to prehistoric times. Among their best-known types of jewelry, often crafted by women at the pueblo, are the beads known as *heishi*. These small beads are formed from ground shells and are usually strung, often with polished stones, into beautiful necklaces. Pottery, jewelry making, and weaving traditions have been passed down over many generations and remain a source of revenue for the pueblo today. The current restoration of the historic Santo Domingo Trading Post, lost to fire in 2001, will help Santo Domingo residents continue to market these fine handcrafted products.

Today, Santo Domingo Pueblo is also often known as Kewa Pueblo. Pueblo members celebrate their feast day on August 4.

More to explore: *El Camino Real—The King's Highway, La Bajada, Pueblo of Acoma, Pueblo of Laguna, Pueblo of Santa Ana, Pueblo of Zia, Rio Grande*

336. Pueblo of Tesuque

Location: Santa Fe County. Near the pueblo of Tesuque, in the parking area for Camel Rock, on the US 284/285 frontage road, near mile marker 175. See map 2.

Marker text: The name Tesuque is a Spanish variation of the Tewa name Tetsugeh, meaning "narrow place of cottonwood trees." The small Tewa-speaking pueblo of Tesuque was established before 1200, and was first visited by Europeans in 1591. It is one of the most traditional of the Tewa speaking pueblos and played an important role in the 1680 Pueblo Revolt, which drove the Spanish from New Mexico.

337. Tesuque Rain Gods

Location: Santa Fe County. Near the pueblo of Tesuque, in the parking area for Camel Rock, on the US 284/285 frontage road, near mile marker 175. See map 2.

Marker text: Seated clay figurines known as rain gods or "rain catchers" spring from Tesuque Pueblo's deep-rooted figurative pottery tradition. Popularized in the 1880s, Tesuque women made and sold the figurines in a variety of colors and designs, and earned income by selling them to curio dealers and tourists. Rain gods typically hold pots while other gods hold children, animals and other objects. The tradition is practiced to this day.

Historians believe that the pueblo of Tesuque, the southernmost Tewa-speaking pueblo in New Mexico, has been in existence since before 1200. One of the first Europeans to visit was Spanish explorer Gaspar Castaño de Sosa, who arrived at Tesuque about an hour before sunset on a cold January 7, 1591. Upon entering the pueblo, which then was located about three miles to the south, Castaño's chronicler noted: "All the people came out to receive us. . . . They brought us many tortillas, maize for the horses, and some turkeys, showing themselves very friendly to us and without fear."

That pueblo came to be known by the name Tesuque. That was the Spanish pronunciation of the original Tewa name for the pueblo, Tet-sugeh, meaning "narrow place of cottonwood trees."

By 1680, resistance had grown among the Pueblo Indians to Spanish rule in New Mexico. Tesuque Indians were among the chief instigators of the subsequent uprising, known today as the Pueblo Revolt. Two of the fastest Tesuque Indian runners, Nicolás Catua and Pedro Omtua, sprinted among the pueblos with instructions to begin the coordinated uprising on August 13. Both men were intercepted and taken to Santa Fe by officers of the Spanish governor. Fearing that the plot might be exposed, Tesuque chiefs began the rebellion immediately; local Spaniard Cristóbal de Herrera, killed by the Tesuques that day, thus earned the distinction of being the first casualty of this change in tactic. Full-scale revolt broke out among the pueblos the following morning. Tesuque Indians martyred their resident priest, Fray Juan Bautista Río, and set fire to their mission church of San Lorenzo de Tesuque.

In 1692, Spanish general Diego de Vargas entered a more passive New Mexico and again asserted Spanish control over the region. Fearful of being punished for their actions, the Indians at Tesuque abandoned their pueblo two years later and combined forces with residents of eight other northern pueblos to create a defensive stronghold on a mesa near the pueblo of San Ildefonso. Governor Vargas broke their resolve through the threat of starvation: with his officers, he took possession of the planted fields in the river valley. In September of that year, the Tesuque Indians left the mesa and established a new village near the western foothills of the Sangre de Cristo Mountains eight miles north of Santa Fe—still the location of the pueblo.

In his inventory of New Mexico missions in 1776, Fray Francisco Atanasio Domínguez described the Tesuque mission church as having "thin walls, single nave construction," and a ceiling that "consists of thirty beams with a little carving which rest on the small corbels (three of them are ready to fall)." By 1881, they had indeed fallen—along with most of the rest of the edifice. The Tesuque people built a new church, which still stands, and incorporated into its structure the sacristy of the old church.

The arrival of the railroad to New Mexico around that same time brought tourists and curio seekers to nearby Santa Fe. The small, seated, clay figures known as "rain gods," traditionally crafted by women at Tesuque Pueblo, became popular with these visitors as well as with collectors of American Indian art. In response to the increased demand, Tesuque women produced large numbers of the clay figurines, varying their shapes, sizes, and colors. A typical rain god would be made seated and holding a bucket in his lap, in which rainwater would be captured—leading to the alternate name of the figures, "rain catchers"—but other gods might be holding babies or animals. Despite the large number produced, each showed the craftsmanship of the pottery tradition long in evidence at the pueblo. Rain gods remain popular today, and continue to be made and sold by pueblo artists.

Three Tesuque Pueblo ceremonies are open to the public: the annual feast day of the patron saint of the pueblo, San Diego, on November 12; the Christmas Day celebration on December 25; and the Corn Dance on the first weekend in June.

More to explore: *Castaño de Sosa's Route, Pueblo of Nambé, Pueblo of San Ildefonso*

338. Pueblo of Tuf Shurn Tui

Location: Sandoval County. In Tuf Shurn Tui Pueblo, on the east side of NM 313 between mile markers 3 and 4, near the intersection of NM 313 and the Sandia Loop. See map 4.

Marker text: The Southern TIWA Pueblo was established before 1300 A.D. In the year 1614 The Pueblo Spanish Mission and church complex were important along the Camino Real. Tuf Shurn Tui (Sandia) was destroyed several times during the Pueblo Revolt in 1680 and 1681. The Pueblo inhabitants sought refuge among the Hopi in Puyuki. The ancient Pueblo was re-occupied by descendants of these refuges in 1748.

Original: This Southern Tiwa Pueblo was established about 1300 A.D. The Pueblo and its Spanish Mission Church complex were important sites along the Camino Real by 1614. Sandia was destroyed during the Pueblo Revolt of 1680, and its Indian inhabitants sought refuge among the Hopi villages in Arizona. The ancient pueblo site was reoccupied by descendants of these refugees in 1748.

Note: The text on this marker has typographical errors that make it difficult to understand. For clarity, text from a previous Historic Marker here (which had the title "Pueblo of Sandia") has also been included.

Tuf Shurn Tui (formerly known as Sandia Pueblo) is one of four surviving pueblos in New Mexico whose residents have historically spoken a dialect of the Tiwa language. Tuf Shurn Tui, with Isleta Pueblo, lies south of the northern Tiwa pueblos of Taos and Picurís, and the two are therefore considered southern Tiwa pueblos. Although English and Spanish have over time become the predominant spoken languages of New Mexico pueblos, renewed interest in the traditional cultures of their people have encouraged many at Tuf Shurn Tui and other pueblos to study the indigenous language of their ancestors.

The native name of the pueblo makes reference to the bountiful river valley that has sustained life for the pueblo's inhabitants since before AD 1300. Here, the Indians irrigated their farmlands with water from the Rio Grande and hunted deer and rabbits in the foothills of the Sandia Mountains. When first seen by the Spanish conquistador Francisco Vásquez de Coronado in 1540, this part of the middle Rio Grande Valley was home to as many as twenty pueblos, which in totality the Spanish called the Province of Tiguex. Members of Coronado's expedition visited the pueblo, although it was not in the same location as it is today. They gave the pueblo the name Sandia, a Spanish word meaning "watermelon." The name may have come from squash gourds grown by the Indians in the pueblo, which were, some historians believe, mistaken by the Spanish for watermelons.

Years of strife between the colonizing Spanish and the native Indian populations led to the Pueblo Revolt of August 1680. In the bloody confrontation, the Tuf Shurn Tui people sacked and burned their Spanish mission church, Nuestra Señora de los Dolores de Sandia, "Our Lady of the Sorrows of Sandia." New Mexico governor Antonio de Otermín himself set fire to the pueblo as he and other colonists escaped south from Santa Fe to safety in El Paso. During an unsuccessful attempt at reconquest the following year, Otermín again torched the pueblo. The residents of Tuf Shurn Tui eventually fled their pueblo. Some historians believe that they may have sought refuge with Hopi Indian villages farther west in Arizona and helped establish there the pueblo of Payupki. Descendants of the original refugees, and possibly other Pueblo Indians as well, resettled the pueblo around 1748—more than fifty years after the Spanish had reclaimed New Mexico. The Province of Tiguex had been reduced to Isleta and Tuf Shurn Tui Pueblos.

The pueblo of Tuf Shurn Tui celebrates the Feast of Saint Anthony on June 13.

More to explore: *Pueblo of Isleta Tuei, Vásquez de Coronado's Route (series)*

339. Pueblo of Zía

Location: 1. Sandoval County. At entrance to Zia Pueblo, in a pullout on the east side of the road, just off US 550. See map 4.

2. Sandoval County. Just east of the entrance to Zía Pueblo, in a pullout on the south side of NM 550, between mile markers 17 and 18. See map 4.

Marker text: In 1583, Antonio de Espejo recorded this pueblo as one of five in the Province of Punamé. Following the sacking of Zía by Spanish troops in 1689, the pueblo was reestablished, but never attained its former size. The Zía ancient sun symbol is incorporated in the design of the state flag of New Mexico.

340. Trinidad Gachupin Medina (ca. 1883–1964)

Location: Sandoval County. Just east of the entrance to Zia Pueblo, in a pullout on the south side of NM 550, between mile markers 17 and 18. See map 4.

Marker text: Trinidad Gachupin Medina was the most widely known Zia potter of her time. She was recognized for her large polychrome storage jars. Sponsored by trader Wick Miller, she toured the United States from 1930 to 1946, demonstrating pottery making at department stores and national exhibitions, including the World's Fair held in Chicago. Generations of Zia potters continue this tradition, which she helped to preserve.

In 1923, the New Mexico chapter of the Daughters of the American Revolution hosted a design competition for a new state flag. Dr. Harry Mera, a Santa Fe physician and anthropologist with the New Mexico Museum of Anthropology, along with his wife, Reba, submitted the winning entry: a modification of the ancient sun symbol the Meras had seen on a pot from Zia Pueblo. The Meras' design set the symbol in burgundy against a backdrop of gold, making use of the Spanish royal colors. A simple yet powerful motif, the Zia symbol may today be one of the most recognized emblems in the state.

Archaeologists believe that the Keresan-speaking residents of Zia are descendants of the Ancestral Puebloan people of the Four Corners region, who migrated to the Jemez Valley sometime in the thirteenth century. When Spanish explorer Antonio de Espejo arrived here from Mexico in 1583, he noted five pueblos in a region he named the Province of Punamé. The word *punamé*, Espejo recorded, meant "people of the West." Largest among these pueblos was one the natives knew as Tsiya, which Spanish-speaking settlers later came to spell and pronounce Zia.

In writing of the main village of Punamé, which was probably Zia Pueblo, Espejo's chronicler estimated the population at more than four thousand men—although many historians believe that this figure may be too large. Espejo also noted the dress of the men, who wore blankets, cloaks, shawls, and "leather shoes in the shape of boots." The women wore "a blanket over their shoulders tied with a sash at the waist." The Zians gave Espejo and his men gifts of turkeys, corn, and tortillas.

Smoldering resentment of Spanish authority among the native people in New Mexico broke out in revolt in 1680 when the Pueblo Indians successfully expelled the ruling Spanish from the state. Residents of Zia joined the uprising. Several failed attempts by the Spanish to reassert control over New Mexico followed in the subsequent decade. During one undertaken in 1689, Spanish soldiers led by Governor Domingo Jironza Pétriz de Cruzate lay siege to Zia Pueblo. The men sacked the pueblo and took seventy Zia Indians as captives.

In 1692, General Diego de Vargas reestablished Spanish control and began the work of resettling the state. Vargas convinced the Zia people, who had since fled to the Jemez Mountains and erected a small village near Jemez Pueblo, to reestablish their village. Even after resettlement, the population in the pueblo declined markedly, with estimates showing that only one hundred people lived there in 1890. An upswing began in the twentieth century, and Zia today is again a thriving village.

One of the most renowned of Zia potters after the turn of the century was Trinidad Gachupin Medina. Born Trinidad Gachupin at the pueblo in 1883, she married José D. Medina in 1904 and raised one son. After learning the skill of pottery making, she began to specialize in large storage jars of multiple colors, often decorated with animals, flowers, geometric designs, and other patterns.

In 1930, Medina accepted an interesting invitation from merchant Wick Miller, who ran a trading post in nearby San Ysidro. Miller wanted to bring knowledge of pottery making and other Indian crafts to a larger audience. He offered to sponsor Medina to be part of a traveling exhibition, in which she would demonstrate the art of pottery making at Zia Pueblo in various venues across the country.

With Miller, Medina traveled throughout the United States off and on for a period of sixteen years, from 1930 to 1946. Her position took her to exhibitions, fairs—even department stores. She was even one of the attractions at the giant Chicago World's Fair in 1933. On these occasions, Medina was usually seated on a blanket in the center of an exhibit space, often with another Native American artist demonstrating another craft alongside her, both of them surrounded by a large railing to separate them from the crowd—an arrangement Medina once remarked made her feel "like a cow in a corral." Nonetheless, the exposure helped her become one of the best-known potters working in the United States at the time, and it helped increase awareness of Zia culture and craftsmanship.

Today, potters at Zia Pueblo continue the centuries-old tradition, creating beautiful, thin-walled wares that often feature designs of birds and other animals. These pots are widely regarded for their excellent craftsmanship and aesthetic beauty.

Nearby Zia Lake on the Zia Reservation is a recreational attraction open to the public. The Zia Pueblo feast day is observed annually on August 15.

More to explore: *Espejo's Expedition, Espejo's Trail, Pueblo of Acoma, Pueblo of Jemez, Pueblo of Laguna, Pueblo of Santa Ana, Virginia T. Romero*

341. Pueblo of Zuni

Location: McKinley County. On the Zuni Reservation, on NM 53, between mile markers 13 and 14. See map 1.

Marker text: The six original Zuni pueblos were the legendary "Seven Cities of Cibola" sought by Vásquez de Coronado in 1540. They were abandoned during the Pueblo Revolt, and the present pueblo was settled in 1699 after the Spanish reconquest. In 1970, Zuni became the first Indian community to administer its own reservation affairs.

342. Zuni Olla Maidens

Location: McKinley County. On the Zuni Reservation, in a pullout on the south side of NM 53, at mile marker 17. See map 1.

Marker text: The Zuni Olla Maidens are an all-women's group renowned for their skill and ability to balance fragile water jars or ollas on their heads. Historically, Zuni women collected water in ollas from nearby springs for everyday use. Today, they perform in parades and community events, walking with water jars placed on their heads while singing their own compositions and those traditionally sung by Zuni men.

Spurred by tales of mythical golden cities in the interior lands, the Spanish government sent Franciscan priest Fray Marcos de Niza and his guide, a slave named Estevan, north from Mexico in 1539 to investigate. Estevan, traveling ahead, spied the Zuni village of Hawikuh. The Zuni Indians killed him—possibly, as some historians believe, because he made threats toward them. Fray Marcos returned to Mexico having only glimpsed the village, if he had seen it at all. Perhaps he believed that the pueblo really was made of gold, or perhaps he was just fibbing, but Fray Marcos was full of stories of golden cities. The following year, Spain sent Francisco Vásquez de Coronado on a quest to examine further these "Seven Cities of Cibola." (Although the Spanish reported seven cities here, archaeologists have identified only six Zuni villages.)

Some historians believe that Coronado's July 1540 entrance into Hawikuh interrupted a sacred ceremony, a theory that offers one explanation for the melee that broke out between his men and the Zuni Indians. Coronado wrote to Spanish officials in August 1540 of his own fate in the ensuing battle:

Thus, for myself, they knocked me down to the ground twice with countless great stones which they threw down from above, and if I had not been protected by the very good headpiece which I wore, I think that the outcome would have been bad for me.

Coronado's men took possession of Hawikuh by force. Although disappointed that the Zuni pueblos were not made of gold, Coronado did not give up hope that such cities existed elsewhere and used the village as his headquarters for further explorations.

Zuni at the time of Coronado's arrival numbered about three thousand occupants. For at least three centuries and possibly longer, the Zuni had subsisted here by hunting and by farming corn, beans, and squash. Zuni oral history recounts an origin in the underworld and a later search by the Zuni people for the center of the universe. In that search, the early people settled along the north bank of what is now the Zuni River, the site of present-day Halona, the name by which the Zuni know their pueblo.

Spanish Franciscan priests in 1629 established a mission church at Hawikuh and another, Nuestra Señora de Guadalupe, at Halona. Both came under attack in 1680, when the Pueblo Indians in New Mexico banded together to expel the Spanish in an upheaval now known as the Pueblo Revolt. Zuni Indians destroyed the churches in the insurrection and abandoned most of their villages. When the Spanish reasserted control twelve years later, the Indians consolidated into one village, Halona.

In 1970, the Bureau of Indian Affairs granted Zuni officials the authority to govern judicial and legal pueblo affairs inside the pueblo, except any infractions that violated federal law. Zuni Pueblo was the first in New Mexico given such control.

Historically, Zuni women gathered water from nearby springs and carried it to the village in ceramic jars, known as ollas, perched atop their heads—leaving their hands free for other objects or for holding their children. Today, a group of women from the pueblo, known as the Zuni Olla Maidens, honor that ancestral tradition by performing what is called the Pottery Dance. At parades, public exhibits, and other venues, these women dance with water jars balanced delicately on their heads, attired in traditional leggings, moccasins, and dresses. The beautiful, choreographed performances may feature songs that are either composed by the members themselves or traditionally sung at the pueblo. The Olla Maidens have performed across the United States.

More to explore: *Matilda Coxe Stevenson, Vásquez de Coronado's Route (series)*

343. Puerto de Luna

Location: Guadalupe County. In the village of Puerto de Luna, in a pullout on the west side of NM 91, between mile markers 9 and 10. See map 3.

Marker text: Established by the early 1860s, Puerto de Luna is one of southeast New Mexico's oldest permanent settlements. An important farming and ranching center, the town was the Guadalupe County seat from 1891 until 1903. A strong oral tradition maintains that William "Billy the Kid" Bonney had many friends here and frequently visited the village and patronized Alexander Grzelochowski's general store.

Note: The store owner's surname is misspelled on this Marker. It should be Grzelachowski.

Although Puerto de Luna may seem almost hidden here along NM 91, its strategic location in the Pecos Valley has given it a role in several chapters of New Mexico history. This was the county seat of Guadalupe County for just over a decade around the turn of the century, and it was also here that famous New Mexico outlaw Billy the Kid ate his last Christmas dinner.

One story attached to the origin of the name is worthy of note for its romantic use of historical anecdote, even if it probably isn't true. The story goes that Francisco Vásquez de Coronado, one of the first Spanish explorers of New Mexico, paused here one evening in 1540 on his way to survey the eastern plains and was so taken by the glow of the moon he saw between two nearby mountains that he was moved to declare the spot the Puerto de Luna, or "Gateway to the Moon." More likely, the name recognizes the Luna family, prominent sheepherders in the area in its early years.

Puerto de Luna formed around 1863. That date makes Puerto de Luna one of the oldest settlements in southeastern New Mexico. Situated along the course of a cattle-driving trail running along the Pecos River, Puerto de Luna soon became a significant village, supporting a population estimated at more than a thousand people. Agriculture and ranching were the mainstays of the village, with the surrounding area supporting beautiful apple and peach orchards. A post office opened in 1873.

Around that time, Puerto de Luna became the home of Polish-born merchant Alexander Grzelachowski. Prior to settling in Puerto de Luna, Grzelachowski had served a calling as a Catholic priest, first in Ohio and later among villages and pueblos in northern New Mexico, coming to the Southwest with Archbishop Jean-Baptiste Lamy at age twenty-seven. Although Grzelachowski left the priesthood after some twenty years of service, including work as a military chaplain in the Civil War Battle of Glorieta Pass near Santa Fe, he retained the nickname he had been given during that time: Padre Polaco, the Polish Father. Grzelachowski moved with his family to Puerto de Luna in 1874, age fifty, and opened a store, which soon became the supply center for area ranches. One of the largest structures in the village, the store building took the shape of a long rectangle and featured a territorial-style porch. The building held both the Grzelachowski store as well as living quarters for the former priest's large family.

One of those who frequented the Grzelachowski store was William Bonney—better known as Billy the Kid. As a member of the "Regulators" posse, Billy the Kid and his companions attended dances in Puerto de Luna, and the Kid came to know Grzelachowski cordially. Their relationship, however, didn't stop the Kid from once stealing the shop owner's horses.

On December 25, 1880, Lincoln Country sheriff Pat Garrett and his deputies, who had apprehended Billy the Kid for the murder of the former Lincoln County sheriff, William Brady, passed through Puerto de Luna with their prize captive, along with some other prisoners. Garrett was escorting the outlaw to Las Vegas, New Mexico, where he was to stand trial for the murder. It was

Christmas Day, about two in the afternoon. As both Garrett and the Kid knew Padre Polaco, they stopped at his home. (Garrett was also married to a woman from Puerto de Luna.) "My friend Grzelachowski gave us all a splendid dinner," Garrett later wrote of the Christmas meal the former priest prepared for the men before they continued their journey north that afternoon.

The dinner with his friend Grzelachowski would be the Kid's last Christmas dinner. In July of the following year, after the Kid escaped from the Lincoln County jail, Sheriff Garrett tracked him to a house in Fort Sumner and shot him dead.

When Guadalupe County was formed in 1891, Puerto de Luna was named county seat. Alexander Grzelachowski donated land for a courthouse, which was completed at a cost of $19,650. The courthouse served country residents faithfully for more than a decade, but the fortunes of Puerto de Luna were soon to change. When the Rock Island Railroad connected with the El Paso and Northeastern in Santa Rosa, about ten miles north, economic and political clout in the county shifted, and in 1903 the county seat was moved to Santa Rosa. After losing its original purpose, the courthouse in Puerto de Luna was put into service as a school, a role it served for many years before being shut down.

Although Puerto de Luna has diminished in importance since its early days, it retains an authentic historic character, offering visitors today a true gateway to another era.

More to explore: *Glorieta Pass Battlefield, Lincoln, San Antonio de Padua Catholic Church, Santa Rosa, Vásquez de Coronado's Route (series)*

344. Puyé Ruins

Location: Rio Arriba County. At the entrance to Puyé Ruins, at the intersection of NM 30 and BIA 601. See map 2.

Marker text: This spectacular site on the Pajarito Plateau is located in the reservation of Santa Clara Pueblo. It includes a pueblo on the mesa top and rooms cut from the volcanic rock. Puyé, occupied from about 1250 to 1550, is considered the ancestral home of Santa Clara and other Tewa-speaking pueblos.

High atop a mesa on the southern rim of Santa Clara Canyon stand the spectacular ruins of the pueblo of Puyé, a name derived from the Tewa Indian word that designates a place where rabbits gather. The site rests on the reservation of Santa Clara Pueblo, and indeed, residents of the pueblo consider the former inhabitants of Puyé to be their ancestors.

By analyzing pottery fragments, grinding stones, and other artifacts, archaeologists have estimated that human occupation of the mesa began sometime in the late 1100s. The early Native American population that arose here was living on what is now known as the Pajarito Plateau, a prominent cliff of volcanic tuff formed from eruptions of the Valles Caldera more than a million years ago. Using the materials at hand, they pieced together a large pueblo from tuff deposits quarried from the mesa's edge. By the mid- to late thirteenth century, these early architects had erected the village that is today called Puyé.

At one time, the Community House of Puyé, perhaps the most impressive feature of the site, may have reached two or even three stories high and offered shelter to a full community of some 1,500 people, according to archaeological estimates. A large courtyard plaza at the interior of the pueblo served as a common meeting and social area. Holes cut into the cliff formed natural stairways that the Indians traversed as they scurried up and down the mesa between the Community House and the sheer base of the cliff.

Into the bedrock of soft volcanic tuff along that base, the Indians dug several *cavate*, or caves, which served as small dwellings and perhaps as storage areas. Legend among the Santa Clara people states that the Indians burned the walls and ceilings to rid them of insects. Many of these rooms formed the back sections of larger masonry structures projecting from the side of the cliff. Although these talus rooms, as they were known, have since collapsed, an example of one has been reconstructed for visitors to examine.

Landscaped features around Puyé, including the remains of garden plots and a reservoir the Indians carved in the tuff to catch rainwater, show the extent of agricultural industry engaging the time of the Indians at Puyé. The Indians also fashioned beautiful pottery. Petroglyphs of animals and concentric circles on the cliff walls demonstrate other forms of artistry.

Crop failures and drought conspired against a sustainable existence on the plateau. By 1600, Puyé lay empty. Anthropologists believe that the Indians migrated east down the mountain to establish villages closer to the waters of the Rio Grande.

More to explore: *Gila Cliff Dwellings National Monument, Pueblo of Santa Clara*

---

345. Quarai Ruins
Salinas National Monument, 1 Mile West

Location: Torrance County. On NM 55, at entrance to Quarai Ruins. See map 4.

Marker text: On the edge of the Plains stands the abandoned Tiwa Pueblo Indian village of Quarai (ca. 1200–1670s), the southernmost of the Tiwa villages, located along the eastern flanks of the Manzano Mountains. The Spanish Franciscan mission church of La Purísima Concepción (1630) is the most complete remaining examples of the large Salinas churches.

Quarai, magnificent even in ruins, stands where the eastern foothills of the Manzano Mountains give way to the rolling Great Plains. Here, around AD 1300, Tiwa-speaking Indians built a room-block housing unit, known today as Mound A or the South Mound. Historians believe that the Indians may have later abandoned this structure for many years, returning to erect a much larger masonry pueblo sometime in the sixteenth century. This was the southernmost pueblo in the state where Indians spoke the Tiwa language, although two others, Tajique and Chililí, were nearby. For food, the Indians at Quarai cultivated corn and beans, ate piñon nuts, and hunted rabbits, turkeys, and deer. What they could not acquire from the land they received in trade, as Quarai and other pueblos in the valley were part of a far-reaching trade network involving the Rio Grande pueblos and the Plains Indians.

As part of the missionary endeavors of the Catholic Church in the late sixteenth and early seventeenth centuries, Franciscan priests came to minister to the Indians of the Estancia Valley. They called the region Las Salinas for the saline deposits in nearby playas. Quarai, which the Spanish knew as Cuarac (historians believe that Quarai may be a later spelling of Cuarac), received its first priest in 1626 with the arrival of Fray Alonso de Benavides. Benavides left an account of the appearance of the Indians in the valley, stating that they "all clothe themselves with cotton blankets and skins and . . . try to adorn themselves as best they can, especially with necklaces and earrings made from turquoise."

Sometime in the 1630s, the resident priest at Quarai directed Indian laborers in the construction of a Spanish mission church in the pueblo, La Purísima Concepción. The church reflected in its grand scale the ardent devotion of the Franciscans to their charge. The red sandstone walls towered forty feet high and stretched six feet wide at their broad foundations. The cruciform, or cross-shaped, structure of the building featured a twenty-seven-foot-wide nave, which led to a transept fifty feet wide and an apse where the altar stood. A choir loft hung immediately over the inside doorway. A convento alongside the church held the priest's private quarters and reception rooms.

Inside the fortress-like stone walls, frictions between priests and laypersons in the New Mexico of the seventeenth century grew into feuds. Local landowners and civil authorities known as encomenderos clashed with mission priests over the role of the Church in the Indian villages. In one spectacle of the gulf created by the system, Nicolás de Aguilar, encomendero of the Salinas Valley, interrupted a sermon by Fray Nicolas de Freitas in La Purísima, with castigations to the priest that the loyalty of the Indians belonged to the king, not the Church.

Such political pressures, together with disease, lack of supplies, attacks by nomadic Indians, and widespread famine, further hobbled Quarai. In 1677, Fray Diego de Parraga, then the resident priest, loaded the mission bell into a wagon and led his people to the nearby pueblo at Tajique. Later, the Indians joined pueblos along the Rio Grande, and the shadows cast by the towering red walls of La Purísima fell over an empty village.

More to explore: *Abó Ruins, Gran Quivira Ruins, Laguna del Perro, Tajique*

346. Quemado

Location: Catron County. On the west end of Quemado, on the south side of US 60. See map 5.

Marker text: Spanish word for "burned," Quemado is located in an extinct volcanic area. This community was first settled in 1800 by Jose Antonio Padilla, who brought sheep and started the stock raising industry in this part of the state. Quemado was once famous for its colony of rodeo celebrities in Largo Canyon south of town.

Rancher José Antonio Padilla was one of the first to settle in this part of west-central New Mexico. Padilla moved here with his family from Belen, south of Albuquerque, around 1880. Over time, a small settlement grew around his cattle and sheep ranch. When a post office opened in 1886, the village took the name Quemado. The word is Spanish for "burned" and may have originated either from the legacies of prehistoric volcanic activity in the region or from nearby Rito Quemado, "Burned Stream." Reportedly, the stream received its name because early settlers burned the vegetation along its banks to destroy natural cover behind which hostile Apaches might hide to ambush unsuspecting visitors.

In the late 1800s and early 1900s, ranchers drove livestock through Quemado on their way from western New Mexico and eastern Arizona to the railhead farther east at Magdalena. The route they took was known as the Magdalena Stock Driveway. As the livestock industry grew in south-central New Mexico, sheep raisers and cattle ranchers in Quemado added their own cattle and sheep to the drives.

During the Great Depression, Quemado earned recognition for its colony of rodeo celebrities who practiced their art in Largo Canyon south of town. A writer for the Works Progress Administration in 1933 described the town as the "Rodeo Center of New Mexico." These stars included names

"They travel everywhere," a Depression-era writer waxed about the rodeo celebrities from Quemado, "winning fame for themselves and for their homeland, New Mexico." Quemado, New Mexico. Bronc busting at the rodeo. Photo by Russell Lee, June 1940. Library of Congress, Prints and Photographs Division, FSA-OWI Collection, LC-USF347-036948-D-B.

famous in rodeo circuits at the time. Among them was Donald Nesbitt, the former world champion "All-Round Cowboy"; Walter Heacock and his brothers Steve and Chuck; and Dick Griffith, a "top-notch fancy trick rider and Brama bull rider." Also included in the ranks was Eleanor Heacock, who spent a year "headlining with the Ringling Brothers Circus as a trick rider."

Today, Quemado survives as a small outpost along US 60. Many visitors during the summer come for Quemado Lake, a popular outdoor recreational area twenty miles to the south.

More to explore: Lea County Cowgirls, Magdalena

347. Rabbit Ear Mountain

Location: 1. Union County. Northwest of Clayton, in a pullout on the south side of US 64/87, between mile markers 427 and 428. See map 3.

2. Union County. Southwest of Clayton, in a pullout on the north side of US 56/412, at mile marker 81. See map 3.

Marker text: These two striking mounds were the first features to become visible to Santa Fe Trail traffic crossing into New Mexico from Oklahoma, and so became important landmarks for caravans. From here, traffic on this major 19th century commercial route still had about 200 miles to travel before reaching Santa Fe.

Among the distinctive land forms of northeastern New Mexico are the two lopsided protrusions of Rabbit Ear Mountain. Note the singular "ear." As tempting as the plural may be, the mountain was not named for a tenuous resemblance to the ears of a hare but rather for the legend of an Indian by this name who somehow became associated with the mountain. One account claims that the mythical Indian chief, possibly Cheyenne or Comanche, died nearby and was buried on the mountain—but the true story is lost to time.

Geologically the eroded remains of a Tertiary period volcano, the unusual double prominence was a milestone for travelers along the Cimarron Cutoff of the Santa Fe Trail, who took their landmarks where they could get them. For four days and more than thirty miles, these twin peaks guided westbound wagon trains as they moved from Oklahoma into northeastern New Mexico. Travelers rested and grazed their animals near the mountain in a short break from the journey, before resuming the two hundred miles yet to go before reaching Santa Fe.

More to explore: *McNees Crossing, Point of Rocks, Santa Fe Trail (series)*

348. Raton

Location: Colfax County. In Raton, on the east end of town, in a pullout at mile marker 350 on the north side of US 64. See map 3.

Marker text: Once the Willow Springs freight stop on the Santa Fe Trail, the town of Raton developed from A.T. & S.F. repair shops established when the railroad crossed Raton Pass in 1879. Valuable coal deposits attracted early settlers. Nearby Clifton House was a stagecoach stop until the Trail was abandoned after 1879.

349. Ghost Marker: Raton Pass

Marker text: This important pass on the Mountain Branch of the Santa Fe Trail was used by Brigadier General Stephen Watts Kearny for his 1846 invasion of New Mexico, and by Colorado Volunteers who defeated the Confederates in 1862. Richens L. "Uncle Dick" Wooten operated a toll road from 1866 to 1879, when the Santa Fe Railroad crossed the pass.

Note: This Marker, once probably located at the top of Raton Pass, has gone missing. See map 3.

350. Ghost Marker: Willow Springs

Marker text: In 1861, the U.S. Army established a government forage station here by a small spring. A well was dug, and the station became a water stop for Barlow and Sanderson stagecoaches. With the arrival of the railroad in 1879 and the founding of Raton, the station was incorporated in to the new town and eventually was razed.

Note: This Marker appears in an inventory of Historic Markers compiled by the State Historic Preservation Office but is not in the field. See map 3.

351. First Automobile in New Mexico

Location: Colfax County. In Raton, at the Tourist Information Center, at the intersection of US 64 and South Second Street. See map 3.

Marker text: Robert L. Dodson bought a steam-powered Locomobile in Denver with plans to drive it to Albuquerque. Accompanied by a Locomobile representative, on November 30, 1900, the pair became the first motorists to traverse treacherous Raton Pass into New Mexico. The trip to Raton, largely on wagon roads, took five days. A few days later the Locomobile arrived in Albuquerque to fanfare and some consternation.

After wagons on the Mountain Branch of the Santa Fe Trail descended the heights of Raton Pass from southern Colorado into New Mexico, their drivers could freshen up at the three-room log cabin and tavern known as the Willow Springs Ranch. Located at the southern base of the Raton Mountains, the property borrowed its name from nearby Willow Creek. Local cowboys ranching their stock in this part of northeastern New Mexico likewise frequented the tavern, as did passengers on the Barlow and Sanderson Company stage line when it crossed the pass in the 1870s. Before them, Union troops, including the Colorado Volunteers, marched over the pass and went on to defeat Confederate soldiers at the Civil War Battle of Glorieta Pass near present-day Pecos. Earlier still, General Stephen Watts Kearny and his Army of the West had traversed the pass when the United States took control of the Southwest from Mexico in 1846. Already, the benefits of the location that would become the site of Raton were clear.

The railroad certainly noticed. In December 1878, the first engine of the Atchison, Topeka, and Santa Fe Railway labored into New Mexico, and it, too, largely followed the route of the Mountain Branch across Raton Pass. Officials chose the site of the old tavern and stage station as their division headquarters and repair shop for locomotives. In 1880, the post office, originally opened as Willow Springs, became Raton. The new name, reflecting both the pass and mountain range, is often translated from the Spanish as "mouse," although it can also mean ground squirrel or rat.

Development in early Raton was scaffolded by the large deposit of bituminous coking coal known as the Raton Coal Field beneath the town. The combination of railroad enterprise and coal mining in early Raton brought an industrious character to the town, as reflected in its nickname of the time, "Pittsburgh of the West." Settlers arrived by rail to work the mines, and by 1881 the population had ballooned to three thousand. Stores, banks, hotels, saloons, and homes arose, many fronting what was then the main road through town, First Street. In 1897, the town supplanted Springer as the county seat of Colfax County.

The need for coal waned as railroads switched to diesel after World War I, but Raton survived the downturn by catering to travelers over Raton Pass, as it had since its inception.

The first of those travelers to arrive by automobile came on November 30, 1900. On that day, Robert L. Dodson and B. L. Cainwell crossed the pass on their five-day trip from Denver to

Raton was the first documented city in New Mexico to be visited by an automobile, as the steam-powered "Locomobile" crossed Raton Pass into town on November 30, 1900. Locomobile. Cobb Memorial Collection, Box 10, Folder 5, Item 000-119-0747, Center for Southwest Research, University Libraries, University of New Mexico.

Albuquerque in their Locomobile—a steam-powered car that was, as the name implied, a cross between a locomotive and an automobile. Cainwell was a representative of the company that made the vehicle. After traveling five days from Denver to Raton Pass over existing dirt wagon roads, the duo bumped their way over the pass, then continued another two days to Albuquerque. According to Dodson's grandson, Doug Sylvester, the Locomobile scared the horses in Albuquerque so much when it arrived in town that there were threats to lynch the men. The mighty machine was a great attraction in Albuquerque, and Dodson sometimes drove it in community parades.

Among the sites of historical note nearby is Clifton House, about seven miles to the south. Although only ruins remain today, Clifton House was once a lavish hostelry and resting area for travelers on the Santa Fe Trail and for those riding the Barlow and Sanderson stagecoaches through this part of northeastern New Mexico. The railroad, which gave life to Raton, robbed it from the Clifton House.

More to explore: *Clifton House Site, La Bajada, Santa Fe Trail (series)*

352. Red River Valley

Location: Taos County. Just east of the town of Red River, on the south side of NM 38 between mile markers 10 and 11. See map 2.

Marker text: The Red River Valley nestled in the Sangre de Cristo Mountains is one of the most spectacular areas of the state. Abundant game attracted trappers to the valley in the early 1800s and prospectors followed in 1860s with gold, silver and copper mines operating until 1925. Labor and environmental history of the 20th century have been largely defined by the discovery and mining of molybdenum in the Red River Canyon. Designated as a "mountain playground" in the 1920s, the Red River has endured as a vibrant destination for tourism.

The New Mexico State Highway and Transportation Department has designated the eighty-five-mile loop drive over NM 38, NM 522, and US 64, connecting the communities of Taos, Eagle Nest, and Angel Fire, as the Enchanted Circle Scenic Byway. This idyllic drive through the whispering ponderosa pines and Douglas firs of the 1.5-million-acre Carson National Forest—named for mountain man and army scout Christopher "Kit" Carson, who frequented the Sangre de Cristo Mountains in the 1820s as a beaver trapper and guide—offers some of the most breathtaking views in New Mexico. Wheeler Peak is here, all 13,161 feet of it, meriting recognition as the highest peak in New Mexico.

Among the first to venture their hand at mining in what is now called the Red River Valley in the late 1800s were three trapper brothers, Orrin, Jerome, and Sylvester Mallette of Fort Garland, Colorado. Another former Coloradan, land promoter Edward I. Jones, purchased the Mallette brothers' claim in 1894 and, with two other developers, platted the townsite of Red River City alongside the similarly named Red River. Heady with gold fever, rugged prospectors and settlers tramped into the mountain highlands village, and, by 1905, the community had evolved from a sloppy collection of tents and cabins into an orderly town of some three thousand residents, complete with a schoolhouse, hospital, stores, and saloons.

Miners worked their way to gold, silver, lead, and copper veins such as the Bunker Hill Claim, the Jay Hawk Mine, and the Inferno Prospect. According to the National Park Service, the Questa Moly mine produced some of the largest quantities of molybdenum in the world in the early twentieth century. Molybdenum is an ore used to strengthen metal. Despite such victories, however, transportation problems and inefficient smelters tempered the miners' success. Earnest mining in the valley had stopped by the early 1930s.

The picturesque location of Red River ensured that there was no bust in its cycle. The bracing mountain breezes and cool crystal waters of the valley lured visitors after the turn of the century and transformed Red River into a resort and vacation playground, complete with guest ranches and "tourist courts." Today, Red River continues its role as active resort community and is a haven for hikers, cyclists, skiers, and tourists who come to appreciate Carson National Forest. Among the recreational opportunities available at Red River and other communities along the Enchanted Circle Scenic Byway are skiing, horseback riding, camping, golfing, and fishing at Eagle Nest Lake.

More to explore: *Eagle Nest Lake State Park, Kit Carson Park Memorial Cemetery (see under Taos), Wheeler Peak*

353. Red Rocks

Location: Rio Arriba County. North of Abiquiú, on the east side of US 84, between mile markers 215 and 216. See map 2.

Marker text: The colorful formations exposed here are the slope forming Chinle Shale of Triassic age deposited in streams, lakes, and floodplains some 250 million years ago and the cliff forming Entrada Sandstone of Jurassic age deposited as windblown sand some 160 million years ago. These are typical landforms of the Colorado Plateau province.

The striking vermilion-colored rocks here, flanking the northern rim of the Rio Chama Valley, are characteristic of those found in the physiographic province known as the Colorado Plateau: a 130,000-square-mile desert terrain of mesas, cliffs, and canyonlands stretching through northern Arizona, southern Utah, southwestern Colorado, and northwestern New Mexico. Generations of southwestern artists, including Georgia O'Keeffe, have found inspiration in the stark and transcendent beauty of the plateau.

Two significant geological layers are exposed along this roadway: the Chinle Shale and Entrada Sandstone Formations. Geologists categorize such rock strata as formations—simply, layers of closely related rock with a recognizable top and bottom. Formation names typically specify both the location most often associated with that type of rock as well as the principal rock found within the layer, and therefore tell much about the origin and composition of the rock within.

The Chinle Shale takes its name from the village of Chinle near Canyon de Chelly National Monument in Arizona. It contains a predominance of shale formed during the Triassic period, some 205 to 250 million years ago. Such Triassic rocks often contain dinosaur fossils, and, indeed, scientists have found specimens of *Coelophysis*, the official state fossil, in this layer of shale. The Chinle Shale is also largely responsible for the Painted Desert of Arizona.

Younger still is the Entrada Sandstone, formed during the Jurassic period some 160 million years ago when windblown sand collected and deposited into sandstone beds. The Entrada Sandstone takes its name from Entrada Point in Utah. As confirmed by the terrain fronting the roadway here, this brilliant sandstone can form dramatic, sheer vertical cliffs.

More to explore: *Colorado Plateau, Georgia O'Keeffe*

354. Reserve

Location: 1. Catron County. On the east side of Reserve, in a pullout on the north side of NM 12. See map 5.

2. Catron County. East of Reserve, in a pullout at the intersection of US 180 and NM 12. See map 5.

Marker text: Located in the San Francisco Valley, Reserve was named Upper San Francisco Plaza by its original Hispanic settlers in 1874. The name was later changed to Reserve in recognition of the U.S. Forest Service headquarters located here. Apaches made frequent attacks on the community, which lay within Apache hunting lands.

355. Ghost Marker: Fort Tularosa

Marker text: Fort Tularosa was established in 1872 south of present-day Aragon. Two companies of infantry were stationed here to guard the Apaches placed at the Tularosa Southern Apache Reservation. The post was deactivated in 1874 when the Apaches were transferred to another reservation. The fort's garrison was then transferred to Fort Craig, south of Socorro.

Note: This marker appears in an inventory of Historic Markers compiled by the Historic Preservation Division but is not in the field. See map 5.

Holed up in a cabin in Reserve amid an onslaught of gunfire from rowdy cowboys, Elfego Baca reportedly used a small statue of Santa Ana as a decoy in one window while he returned fire from another. He emerged a celebrity. Elfego Baca. William A. Keleher Pictorial Collection, Box 1, Folder 3, Item 000-742-0006, Center for Southwest Research, University Libraries, University of New Mexico.

Spanish-speaking settlers developed three kindred villages in the San Francisco Valley in the early 1870s: Upper San Francisco Plaza, Middle San Francisco Plaza about a mile south, and Lower San Francisco Plaza two miles beyond that. Together, the settlements were collectively called Frisco. Apache Indians, who had long considered the valley and surrounding mountains their traditional hunting grounds, frequently assailed villagers in all three plazas. These attacks continued until the 1880s, when Geronimo and other Apache leaders either were killed or slowly assented to US government control.

In April 1872, the US Army had begun construction of a small log fort, Fort Tularosa, about twenty miles to the northeast. The fort was intended to protect what would become the new reservation and Indian Agency of the Chiricahua Apache Indians, but dissatisfaction with the location among the Indians, along with other economic factors, led to its abandonment two years later. The two companies at the fort were transferred to Fort Craig, south of Socorro.

Upper San Francisco Plaza was the site of one of the more legendary instances of perseverance in New Mexico history. It happened in October 1884, when nineteen-year-old store worker Elfego Baca arrived with Socorro County deputy sheriff Pedro Sarracino to protect local residents from a band of unruly cowboys employed by rancher John Bunyan Slaughter. (The village at the time was within the boundaries and jurisdiction of a then much-larger Socorro County.) Baca disarmed one of the men and took him to jail, an action that chafed the ruffian's friends. When an angry mob of cowboys marshaled to seek revenge, Baca hastily retreated to a small adobe shack outside the village. There he withstood round after round of gunfire as he watched the cowboys through cracks in the adobe. When Baca emerged a day and a half later, alive and unharmed, having killed four cowboys and wounded another eight, a new legend of the Southwest was born. Baca returned to Socorro, where residents there later elected him sheriff. His exploits are portrayed in the Walt Disney Studios television miniseries *The Nine Lives of Elfego Baca*.

In 1899, largely at the urging of naturalist Aldo Leopold, the Forest Service established the Gila Forest Reserve, later the Gila National Forest, in this part of southwestern New Mexico. This set-aside of 574,000 acres of pristine, rugged mountain wilderness surrounding the Frisco villages was the first such stretch of land in the country specifically reserved as a protected wilderness area. When residents of Frisco opened a post office in 1901, they recognized this precedent in the name they selected for their community: Reserve.

Reserve today thrives as a gateway to the Gila, a resort community, and the county seat of Catron County.

More to explore: *Gila Cliff Dwellings National Monument*

356. Riley

Location: Socorro County. In Magdalena, on Main Street, in front of the library and village office. (Riley itself is twenty miles north of this Marker on Forest Road 354.) See map 5.

Marker text: Twenty miles north of Magdalena, Riley was a small agricultural village originally named Santa Rita by its Hispanic founders in the mid-nineteenth century. By the late 1880s, mining drove the town's economy and in 1890 it was granted a post office under the name "Riley." The mines gave out, and the town was slowly abandoned. Former residents still gather every May to observe Santa Rita days.

Forest Road 354 north from Magdalena leads through an open desert that sees few visitors. Passing along the eastern rim of Cibola National Forest, the road eventually meets and crosses the Rio Salado. Just after doing so, it reaches the tiny settlement of Riley. Now a ghost town, Riley's sunbaked adobe houses, stone schoolhouse, and church (still maintained) tell a story of the history of an area of the state not often recounted.

The small village began around 1882, when Pedro Aragon and other farmers, many from the village of Polvadera nearby, chose a site for a new settlement along the east bank of the Rio Salado, where they could pull water from the river to irrigate their fields of corn and beans. In its early years, the community was known as Santa Rita. Residents built adobe homes and constructed a sturdy, one-room stone schoolhouse for their children. Two stores were in operation, and a church served the spiritual needs of the villagers. Like the name of the town, the church, too, bore the dedication of Santa Rita when it was established in 1883.

The early families who lived here had chosen to name their settlement for a woman who had known great suffering in her life. Born near Spoleto in Italy in 1381, Rita of Cascia survived an unloving husband and an abusive marriage to become a nun. As a Sister, she prayed before a crucifix to suffer as Christ had, and was struck in the forehead by a thorn that fell from the cross. Saint Rita is the patron saint of impossible cases.

A post office opened in Santa Rita in 1890. Because the name Santa Rita was already in use elsewhere in the state, the community officially took the name Riley, probably for the surname of a local sheep rancher.

By the time the settlement of Riley had been established, mining operations had been underway in the mining districts to the south. Magdalena Mines (now Magdalena) and Kelly (now a ghost town) were in full swing by 1885. In Riley, too, mining took hold. Four separate mines operated around the community, pulling gold, silver, and lead from the earth. A small vein of coal had been mined south of the village since its founding, but new claims arose after the turn of the century. Gregorio Romero filed claim on one coal mine in 1917; F. L. Dugger filed on another, named the Hot Spot Mine, in 1927. For a time, the settlement subsisted on agriculture, mining, and sheepherding.

Eventually, the mines around Riley were depleted of the reserves that could be easily accessed, and the cost of maintaining them and shipping the materials out became prohibitive. Dependent on the Rio Salado for irrigation, farming also could be a difficult enterprise, especially in years of Dust Bowl drought. The post office closed in 1931. Although Riley hung on until the early 1950s, residents eventually left, and the small town became a ghost town.

Today, given its remote location, many of the structures of the town still stand. The schoolhouse remains largely intact, although time has taken its toll, and ruins of some adobe homes serve as relics of bygone times. The most impressive structure is the church, which locals from nearby communities have maintained now for many decades. The church observes Mass every May 22, the day Saint Rita died, designated as her feast day.

More to explore: *Carthage-Tokay-Farley, Elizabethtown, Kelly, Magdalena, Shakespeare, Socorro*

357. Rincón

Location: Doña Ana County. In Rincon, on the north side of NM 140 (Rincon Road), next to a playground and across from the railroad tracks, between Corea Street and Baker Street. See map 5.

Marker text: Rincón was originally named El Rincón de Fray Diego in honor of a 17th century Franciscan who died here. Established as a settlement called Thorne in 1881, it became Rincón in 1883. With the establishment of the Santa Fe Railroad, Rincón became the area's main business and trading center. The line forked here, one track going west to Deming, the other south to El Paso.

Note: Despite the spelling used in this Historic Marker, the name of the town of Rincon is most often seen without an acute accent over the *o*.

Rincón is a Spanish word that translates in English to "corner" or "nook." The original name of the village, El Rincón de Fray Diego, is said to reference a Franciscan priest with the surname Diego who passed away near here in the seventeenth century. Although there is no specific mention of such an event in the historical record, it would certainly have been possible. Present-day Rincon is only a short distance from the historic Camino Real, until the late nineteenth century the major trade and settlement route between New Mexico and Mexico. Starting in the late seventeenth century and for two hundred years thereafter, merchants, settlers, and missionaries came to New Mexico over the course of the Camino Real. Rincon is close to a section of the trail known as the Jornada del Muerto, or "Journey of the Dead Man," a dreaded stretch in which the Camino

Real leaves the Rio Grande and crosses ninety miles of barren desert. As the name implies, the Jornada did claim its share of travelers' lives. Further, another geographic feature nearby bears the name of a man who perished along the Camino Real. The Robledo Mountains twenty miles south of here remember colonist Pedro Robledo, who died on the trail on the first Spanish colonizing expedition in 1598.

Trade and travel over the Camino Real ended with the arrival of the railroad in New Mexico. When engineers with the Santa Fe Railway established a depot here in 1881, they went with another name entirely for the site: Thorne. Their name was likely a misspelled reference to Fort Thorn, a military installation established in 1853 near present-day Hatch, about five miles north. Decommissioned in 1859, only the ruins of the adobe buildings of Fort Thorn would have remained by the time the rails came through twenty years later. And even those have now vanished.

The name Thorne didn't last long either. When a post office opened here in 1883, the settlement at last took the official name Rincon.

Rincon was a dividing point on the Santa Fe Railway. From a point just south of the Rincon depot, tracks split to move trains to two separate destinations. One line continued south another eighty miles to El Paso. The other went west, toward Deming, some fifty miles distant, where they connected with the Southern Pacific on March 8, 1881, to complete the country's second transcontinental railroad. A few years later, the railroad built a Harvey House in Rincon, one of a string of elegant restaurants and hotels managed by Fred Harvey along the course of the railroad.

With the arrival of the railroad, Rincon developed into a small business and trading center serving this part of the upper Mesilla Valley, with many residents working for the railroad. At one point, the community had a population of several hundred people. A glimpse of life in the town at the time, albeit an unflattering one, comes from the wife of Dr. Charles A. Brown, who had been hired by the railroad to administer to the health of its employees locally. In a letter to her father written in September 1884, Mrs. Brown expressed her displeasure with the town:

Rincon is a hard place! A man don't dare go through the streets with . . . ten dollars in his pocket after night. "The Roll"ers just knock them down and "roll" him over and take the money. . . . There [are] 3 grocery stores, 1 dry good store, and 5 saloons.

With few such enterprises left today, Rincon is no longer the "hard place" Mrs. Brown described. The original depot, a grand, two-story wooden structure, has been replaced by a more modest building, while the Harvey House and other original structures have been torn down. The town remains easily accessible from the interstate, a quiet agricultural community with a past tied closely to the railroad.

More to explore: *Deming, Doña Ana, El Camino Real— The King's Highway, Harvey Girls, Hatch, Paraje de Robledo*

358. Rio Felix Bridge

Location: Chaves County. One mile north of Hagerman at the bridge site on the Rio Felix, in a pullout on the east side of NM 2, at mile marker 18. See map 6.

Marker text: Completed in 1926, the Rio Felix Bridge was one of the most important structures in New Mexico's highway system. The bridge was placed across the river at nearly a 45-degree angle to increase stability during floods. Constructed with three 144-foot Pratt Truss spans, it is the longest bridge of its type in New Mexico. Bypassed in 1984, the bridge is listed in the National Register of Historic Places for its design, enhancing local farming and tourism at Carlsbad Caverns.

The historic Rio Felix Bridge is no longer in use, but its grand stature conveys even to the contemporary traveler a sense of its historic significance. Its successor, the modern highway bridge crossing NM 2, sits just twenty yards away, and a wistful traveler could be forgiven for imagining that the older bridge is mentoring the younger.

In fact, by comparing the two, changes in the approach to bridge construction here in the years between the original bridge's construction in 1926 and the newer bridge's in the 1980s become apparent. Immediately evident is the forty-five-degree angle at which the older bridge crosses the river, an angle not duplicated in the newer. This angle was required to match the original course of the highway. But engineers knew that a bridge at such an angle, if not engineered properly, would be subject to a broadside of water during flooding. So the architect placed the piers of the bridge at an angle to the bridge deck itself and, not incidentally, in line with the flow of the river. This arrangement ensured that water moved smoothly around the foundations of the bridge and not straight into them, lessening potential damage from any sustained watery deluge.

Also apparent are the three beautiful overhead trusses of the original bridge. (A truss is simply a framework that supports a structure and, in the case of a bridge, distributes the load across it.) Those trusses, built by the Boardman Company of Oklahoma City, stretch 144 feet each. They run above the roadway, not underneath—preventing damage by flooding. They are a Pratt truss design, a particular type of truss often used for longer bridge spans. Indeed, the old Rio Felix Bridge is the longest Pratt truss bridge in New Mexico.

Construction on the bridge was completed in 1926 as part of an effort by the state to provide highway access to farming communities in this part of New Mexico, and also to Carlsbad Caverns for tourists traveling south.

The National Park Service added the original Rio Felix Bridge to the National Register of Historic Places in 1997, noting its "long association with highway transportation in New Mexico dating to the first decades of statehood."

More to explore: *Percha Creek, Rio Grande Bridge at Radium Springs, Rio Grande Gorge Bridge (see under Rio Grande Rift)*

359. Rio Grande

Location: Doña Ana County. At the west end of Las Cruces, on the south side of US 70 as it crosses the Rio Grande at La Llorona Park, west of Motel Boulevard, between mile markers 145 and 146. See map 5.

Marker text: The Rio Grande (Spanish for Big River) has been an integral part of the history of New Mexico for thousands of years. Running through the entire state, it is both its backbone and lifeblood. It originates in the southern Rocky Mountains of Colorado and then forms the boundary between Texas and Mexico before spilling into the Gulf of Mexico. Over 1,800 miles long, it is one of the great rivers of the world.

The Rio Grande has provided water for irrigated crops and sustenance to countless peoples who lived and traveled along its banks. The river flow through the Mesilla Valley is now highly channeled and controlled by several dams, the largest of which is Elephant Butte Dam, seventy miles north. Consequently, the river no longer changes course or floods as it frequently did in the past.

The Rio Grande, a Spanish name meaning "Big River," flowing through the center of New Mexico, has greatly influenced the course of human events that have transpired around it. The river had its inception some four million years ago as rainwater and snowmelt from the uplifting Rocky Mountains and other ranges in New Mexico collected in basins and combined into what is known as the ancestral Rio Grande. Very different from the river of today, the ancestral Rio Grande ended in a small lake in El Paso. A second river, the lower Rio Grande, continued to the Gulf of Mexico. Over time, the upper and lower rivers combined to form the 1,800-mile-long Rio Grande, which flows today from the San Juan Mountains in southern Colorado through New Mexico, forms the boundary between Texas and Mexico, and then continues to the Gulf of Mexico. It is one of the longest rivers in the world.

The Rio Grande has lived a hundred lives since its birth. At first, it was a pathfinder. Some of the first roads in the state followed its course and were laid by Pueblo Indians, who farmed in villages alongside the river. These trails ran across the river valley to other Indian pueblos and allowed trade between Indian groups to flourish. When the conquistador don Juan de Oñate led his colonizing expedition north from Mexico City into what is now New Mexico in 1598, he, too, largely followed the course of the waters. Oñate called the river Rio del Norte, or "River of the North."

The river succored Spanish and, later, Mexican farming settlements, as settlers grew chile and cotton along the rich bottomlands of the river valley. A 1726 description by Spanish cartographer Álvarez Barreiro, as translated by Thomas H. Naylor and Charles W. Polzer, remains apt today:

The [Rio Grande] is the most generous of all [rivers in New Mexico]. . . . All its banks are level land, so all the water needed can be drawn from it for the Spanish settlements as well as for the Indian pueblos along its banks. This relationship of river and land is equally useful through the whole stretch of country from the royal presidio of El Paso to the pueblo of Isleta on the west side of the river.

Sometimes the river revoked what it bestowed. In 1769, floodwaters ravaged farmlands in Tomé. Repeated flooding along the middle and lower Rio Grande wiped out communities like Corrales and San Marcial and forced settlers to abandon their homes or rebuild. At times, settlers left flood-worn valleys and founded entirely new villages. Farmers escaping the devastation wrought by flooding in El Paso in 1839 moved north to form the village of Doña Ana. In 1862, other settlers left the fields of the lower Mesilla Valley for the drier territory of what would later become Tularosa.

To calm the intemperance of the river, the US Congress in 1907 approved the construction of a dam somewhere south of Socorro. After crews poured and formed 655,000 barrels of cement, officials dedicated the Elephant Butte Dam east of Truth or Consequences on October 16, 1916. The dam works in conjunction with other irrigation channels and dams, like the Leasburg Diversion Dam in Leasburg and the Mesilla Dam near Mesilla, to channel the flow of the river for irrigation on the farms along the lower Rio Grande.

More to explore: *Doña Ana, Elephant Butte Dam, Leasburg Dam State Park, Oñate's Route (see under El Camino Real—The King's Highway), Rio Grande Rift, Rocky Mountains, Tularosa*

360. Rio Grande Bridge at Radium Springs

Location: Doña Ana County. South of Radium Springs, in a pullout on the west side of NM 185, at the Radium Springs bridge. See map 5.

Marker text: This structure—one of the best surviving examples of timber and beam bridge construction in the state—was erected in 1933. The superstructure consists of 19 spans, each 25 feet in length. The roadway is 475 feet long. During the 1920s and 30s, timber beam bridges were an economical and easily maintained solution for crossing arroyos and waterways. Although the bridge no longer carries motorized traffic, it continues to serve pedestrians, bicyclists and equestrians.

For good reason, the New Mexico Highway Department has preserved intact several of the original bridges built as part of the state's fledgling road system. These bridges, like the Rio Felix Bridge near Hagerman and the Percha Creek Bridge near Kingston—which might otherwise have been demolished when new highway alignments or road improvements were implemented—have instead been left in place for admiration and study. They are like ghost towns in a way, allowing modern travelers to see firsthand how our road-tripping ancestors lived—and, more specifically, how they crossed the chasms and rivers of New Mexico's varied and often challenging topography.

One such bridge on the historical itinerary is here, the Rio Grande Bridge, just south of Radium Springs on NM 185.

The Rio Grande Bridge at Radium Springs is a beam bridge (as opposed to a truss, arch, or other structural bridge type). A beam bridge, the simplest and most common bridge type, uses flat beams to cross a chasm—much like laying a plank of wood across a stream. To hold the weight of the bridge, the beams often rest on supports known as piers. For longer distances, a beam bridge might consist of several shorter sections of beams, all connected, resting on several piers. These different sections are known as spans.

The Rio Grande Bridge at Radium Springs consists of nineteen spans, each stretching 25 feet in length. This makes the bridge 475 feet long. (It is 29 feet wide.) The spans are supported underneath by a total of eighteen piers. The piers themselves each comprise seven piles, which are, in effect, upright timbers that resemble telephone poles. Diagonal boards connecting these piles to one another help reinforce the structure of the overall pier, and in turn, the bridge itself. When first constructed in 1933, the bridge had only six piles on every pier; it was later widened, necessitating an extension of the piers—a task accomplished by simply adding one additional pile to each pier.

Because of their simple construction, beam bridges are relatively inexpensive to build and maintain. The New Mexico Highway Department, in establishing a modern road system for the state after statehood in 1912, used the type often.

Although the historic Rio Grande Bridge at Radium Springs no longer carries motorized traffic, it is open for pedestrians, cyclists, and bridge aficionados. The timber spans and piers, not easily visible from atop the bridge, can be seen from the side or from underneath the bridge. Because the bridge sits very close to the modern bridge that replaced it, comparisons between the two are possible.

More to explore: *Percha Creek, Rio Felix Bridge, Rio Grande*

Rio Grande Gorge Bridge: *see Rio Grande Rift*

Rio Grande Gorge State Park: *see Rio Grande Rift*

361. Rio Grande Rift

Location: Taos County. At the south end of Tres Piedras, near the intersection of US 64 and US 285, in a pullout on the east side of US 64/84. See map 2.

Marker text: A tremendous split in the earth's crust has resulted in the Rio Grande rift basin filled with thousands of feet of alluvium from bordering mountains and lava flows from deep within the earth. About 650 feet of this basin-fill is exposed in the Rio Grande Gorge at the bridge crossing.

362. Rio Grande Gorge State Park

Location: Taos County. In the rest area at the west end of the Rio Grande Gorge Bridge, between mile markers 243 and 244 on US 64, overlooking the gorge. See map 2.

Marker text: With spectacular views and some of the finest public fishing in New Mexico, this park runs along the banks of the Rio Grande from the Colorado border through the park. The "great river" offers exciting whitewater boating through a deep canyon. There are four major camping/picnicking areas along the river.

Note: This Historic Marker incorrectly identifies a stretch of land along the river as the Rio Grande Gorge State Park. While some seventy miles along the Rio Grande once did make up a state park, the region is no longer designated as such, and the park no longer exists.

363. Rio Grande Gorge Bridge

Location: 1. Taos County. In Tres Piedras, at intersection of US 285 and US 64. See map 2.

2. Taos County. North of Taos, in a pullout on the west side of NM 522, between mile markers 1 and 2. See map 2.

Marker text: Second highest bridge on the National Highway System, rises 650 feet above the stream of the Rio Grande. Dedicated Sept. 10, 1965, it is a lasting monument to the untiring efforts of Governor Jack M. Campbell and the citizens of northern New Mexico to open this scenic area to the public.

364. Jack M. Campbell Highway
Taos to Tierra Amarilla

Location: Taos County. Near the former site of Rio Grande Gorge State Park, in a small pullout along US 64, on the east end of the Rio Grande Gorge Bridge, between mile markers 243 and 244. See map 2.

Marker text: This road passes through some of the most spectacular scenery in the American Southwest. It is a key section of the east-west highway which brings visitors to this region from throughout the United States. Since this route became a reality through the leadership and perseverance of Governor Jack M. Campbell (1963–1966), the members of the New Mexico State Highway Commission voted unanimously on September 23, 1965 to name this portion of U.S. 64 in his honor.

The Rio Grande has chiseled a deep passage through layers of volcanic basalt and gravel in this part of north-central New Mexico to create the breathtaking, vertigo-inducing Rio Grande Gorge. The basalt comes courtesy of the volcanoes from the now-extinct Taos Plateau to the north. The gorge is part of a much larger rut known as the Rio Grande Rift, which cuts roughly through the center of the state and takes its name from the Rio Grande running over it.

Such a spectacular feat of nature could only be spanned by an equally spectacular feat of man. Begun in July 1963 and completed in 1965 at a cost of $2,153,000, the 1,272-foot-long, 36-foot-wide Rio Grande Gorge Bridge plays an integral role in connecting east-west travel above the Española Valley. Typical of continuous steel deck truss designs, the supporting triangular patterns of the bridge are located underneath the bridge floor, an arrangement possible only where canyons are deep enough to allow adequate clearance without the threat of damage by flooding. The gorge here, which runs 1,200 feet wide and approximately 600 feet deep, more than sufficiently meets those requirements. At the time it was built, the bridge was the second-highest suspension bridge in the nation, topped only by the Royal Gorge Bridge in Colorado. It has since lost that distinction—but it retains the title as the longest bridge in New Mexico.

The bridge and the completion of US 64 across it had been the dream—and part of the political platform—of former New Mexico governor Jack M. Campbell. A former marine and FBI agent, Campbell later explained to a reporter in a March 1, 1996, story in the *Santa Fe New Mexican*:

I didn't have very many friends up in this part of the state. It helped me considerably to promise the bridge. It helped me in Taos, Raton, Farmington and all along that northern border because people had to go all the way down to Española and come back up to get to the other side. . . . It was a major architectural and engineering undertaking. I saw it as an opportunity both for the state and my campaign—and it worked.

State transportation officials dedicated the bridge on September 10, 1965, toward the end of Campbell's second two-year term in office. Shortly thereafter, on September 23, the New Mexico State Highway Commission unanimously approved a resolution to dedicate the section of US 64 between Taos and Tierra Amarilla as the Jack M. Campbell Highway. Oddly, that twenty-five-mile stretch of highway was not officially renamed for thirty years, being dedicated at a ceremony at the bridge on July 23, 1996.

Governor Campbell lived to see the dedication. He passed away in Santa Fe three years later, on June 14, 1999, after a protracted illness.

More to explore: *Percha Creek, Rio Felix Bridge, Rio Grande, Rio Grande Bridge at Radium Springs*

365. Rio Salado Sand Dunes

Location: Socorro County. North of Socorro, in the Walking Sands Rest Area, on the east side of Interstate 25, at mile marker 167. See map 5.

Marker text: Dunes along this part of the Rio Grande Valley are formed by sand blown northeastward from the normally dry bed of the Rio Salado (salty river). The Rio Grande is in a deep trench between the uplifted Los Pinos Mountains to the east and the Ladrones Mountains to the northwest. Rocks from the crest of the Ladrones are found four miles deep below the dunes.

366. Rio Salado Sand Dunes
Elevation: 4,850 feet

Location: Socorro County. North of Socorro, in the Walking Sands Rest Area, on the west side of Interstate 25, at mile marker 167. See map 5.

Marker text: Winds blowing across the usually dry, sandy riverbed of Rio Salado formed dunes along this part of the Rio Grande Valley. The Rio Grande, just southwest of here, follows a massive geological trench shaped millions of years ago when huge blocks of land sank as the earth in central New Mexico slowly began pulling apart. The resulting Rio Grande Rift uplifted Los Pinos Mountains to the east. Northwest are the Sierra Ladrones. Rocks on their 9,000-foot crests are similar to those buried four miles beneath these dunes.

Note: The Rio Grande is to the east of this Historic Marker, not the southwest.

Sometimes the striking geography of New Mexico is as much the result of what does not happen as what does. The Rio Salado, which rises in northeast Catron County and flows south, then southeast, into the Rio Grande Valley, depends on runoff from mountains to the west for its survival. Except in heavy rains, the river rarely makes it this far, its waters dried up by evaporation or absorbed into surface gravels as they flow through this generally arid region of south-central New Mexico. Winds blowing across the dry riverbed stir sand and dust, particles of which have collected here over many years to form the vegetated sand dunes that surround this rest area.

When flowing, the Rio Salado, a name that translates as "Salty River," eventually joins the Rio Grande a short distance to the south. The Rio Grande is the longest river in New Mexico and one of the longest in the world. The course of the Rio Grande follows a huge geological trench in the crust of the earth known as the Rio Grande Rift. The incipient rift took shape millions of years ago as the earth in central New Mexico slowly began pulling apart and huge blocks of land sank downward between the cracks. Mountain runoff collecting in basins along the course of the rift eventually joined to form the Rio Grande.

The same down-dropping that created the rift also forced large blocks of land on its margins to uplift into mountains. The long, low, north-south-trending Los Pinos Mountains ("Pines Mountains") visible to the northeast on the opposite bank of the Rio Grande were formed this way. The highest peak is Whiteface Mountain at 7,530 feet.

To the northwest stand the Ladrones Mountains, known also by their Spanish name, Sierra Ladrones. Rocks on the nine-thousand-foot crests of this range are offset from the rocks found below these dunes by about four miles. According to legend, the steep defiles of the massive Sierra Ladrones served as hiding places for bandits and horse thieves through the nineteenth century. These unscrupulous activities earned the mountains their disreputable name, Thieves Mountains. The highest peak here is Ladrones Peak, which reaches an arresting 9,176 feet.

More to explore: *Camino del Llano, Fort Craig Rest Area, Rio Grande, Waldrop Park*

367. Rockhound State Park

Location: Luna County. At the entrance to Rockhound State Park, in a pullout on the south side of NM 143 (inside the gate). See map 5.

Marker text: Located on the rugged slopes of the Florida Mountains, this is one of the most unusual parks in the nation. Here "rockhounds" are encouraged to take home samples (up to 15 pounds) of rocks and minerals. The park also offers camping and picnicking facilities, hiking trails and a playground.

Note: This Marker incorrectly states that Rockhound State Park is on the slopes of the Florida Mountains. The park is actually on the slopes of the Little Florida Mountains. The names are similar, but they are separate ranges.

At Rockhound State Park, the adage to "leave only footprints, take only photographs" does not apply—this is one of the few parks in the United States where visitors are allowed to remove part of the park itself.

The park, established in 1966, is geared to "rockhounds," a name given to amateur rock and mineral collectors. Each visitor may remove up to fifteen pounds of rocks and minerals—provided he or she does so for individual study and admiration, and not for commercial gain. The slopes of the Little Florida Mountains are happy to oblige this interest and offer a varied inventory from which to stock a growing collection. Here collectors can find obsidian, agate, and onyx, among others. Lucky collectors may even happen on geodes, hollow rocks with dramatic and beautiful crystalline formations inside.

After growing tired from rockhounding, visitors can camp overnight in the developed campsites within the park and enjoy a breakfast the next morning at several picnic tables. Three miles of interpretive hiking trails wind through the park.

More to explore: *Bisti Wilderness, City of Rocks State Park*

368. Rocky Mountains

Location: Colfax County. East of Raton, in a pullout on the north side of US 65 between mile markers 364 and 365. See map 3.

Marker text: The Sangre de Cristo ranges of the southern Rocky Mountains visible here include the Spanish Peaks in Colorado, and the Culebra and Cimarron Ranges in New Mexico. Reaching altitudes of more than 13,000 feet, the well watered and forested mountains offer numerous recreational activities including skiing, hiking, fishing, hunting and climbing.

The beautiful snowcapped peaks on the far western horizon are too spectacular to be anything but the Rocky Mountains. This range, a southern extension of the Rockies, has the name Sangre de Cristo, or "Blood of Christ." The view includes the Spanish Peaks in south-central Colorado. East Spanish Peak, forested with aspen, ponderosa, and bristlecone pine, reaches an altitude of 13,625 feet.

The highest peak in New Mexico, Wheeler Peak, also rises in the Sangre de Cristo Range. Although not as high as East Spanish Peak, the 13,161-foot reach of Wheeler Peak requires no apology.

South of the Spanish Peaks lay the prominent subranges of Culebra and Cimarron. The Culebra Range, mainly a Colorado landform, extends briefly into northern Taos County in New Mexico.

The north-south-tending Cimarron Range is showcased by Baldy Mountain, which spires to 12,441 feet. Lush forests, meadows, soaring cliffs, and sublime snowcapped peaks compose the Cimarron country.

A Denver and Rio Grande Western Railroad pamphlet published in 1917 offered this enticement for travelers, a description of the Rockies that remains fitting today:

To the camper is proffered tent-life at perfection; to the wayfarer awheel, the best of roads, magnificently planned; to the wilderness seeker, a myriad of trails rarely trodden, but hospitably waiting . . . to the natural scientist, animal and plant life of all zones from the temperate to the frigid, and rock formations as varied . . . to the artist, marvelous vistas of valley, range and plain, most beautiful effects of sunshine, cloud and shadow, entrancing sunrises and sunsets; to the weary and ill, peace and health; to the well of mind and body, added vigor and feats for testing their endurance.

More to explore: Organ Mountains (see under San Augustin Pass), Sandia Mountains (see under Albuquerque), Wheeler Peak

369. Rodeo Station

Location: Hidalgo County. In Rodeo, on the west side of NM 80. See map 5.

Marker text: The El Paso and Southwestern railroad was completed in 1902 by Phelps, Dodge and Company to link El Paso, Texas with the copper mines at Bisbee, Arizona. New Mexico Highway 9, the "Border Route" between Columbus and Rodeo parallels the rail line, and actually follows a portion of the abandoned railroad bed. The Southern Pacific's "Golden State Limited" and "Californian" passenger trains passed through Rodeo until 1962.

370. Rodeo Intermediate Field
Civil Aeronautics Authority #57A

Location: Hidalgo County. Just north of Rodeo, in a pullout on the west side of NM 80, at the intersection of NM 80 and NM 9. See map 5.

Marker text: The intermediate field system, developed by the U.S. Department of Commerce, greatly increased safety in early commercial aviation. Rodeo Intermediate Field 57A was established in 1930 to enhance navigation for Standard Airlines—later TWA—from California to El Paso, and served as an army auxiliary field during WWII. Its building foundations, earthen air strips and red directional arrow pointing the way to El Paso still are visible today.

Note: To view the remnants of Rodeo Intermediate Field, drive east on NM 9 from this sign for about two and a half miles. Park in the small dirt pullout on the south side of the highway, between mile markers 2 and 3, just before the road curves to the north. The field can be viewed beyond the fence to the north.

Squatting two miles shy of the Arizona border, the community of Rodeo lies in the far southwestern corner of New Mexico affectionately known as the "Bootheel" for its resemblance on maps to the heel of a cowboy boot. Along with timetables and lost luggage, Rodeo was one of the things left behind by the El Paso and Southwestern Railroad in the early twentieth century. The line reached this valley in 1902, when the Phelps Dodge Corporation extended rails from the company-owned Copper Queen copper mine near Bisbee, Arizona, eastward to El Paso. Constructed initially to haul ores from the mines to the company smelter for processing, the railroad changed the face and character of the Bootheel.

William "Pop" Bond was one of the first to

homestead along the planned route of the line in 1901. As railroad crews laid ties through the San Simeon Valley, they established a stop near where Pop had come to live. It was one of several along the route that would allow trains to take on water or cargo. According to place-names historian Robert Julyan, the stockyard and corrals that formed here, used by local cowboys as a shipping point for their cattle, may have been the genesis of the name of the community that grew around Pop's homestead. A "rodeo" can also be an enclosed pen for cattle. When platted in 1907 by Texas cattleman James Harrison Parramore, whose twelve-thousand-head San Simeon Ranch lent its name to the valley, the community of Rodeo was the westernmost stop for the line in New Mexico.

The El Paso and Southwestern ran passenger service trains over the line. These trains were "modern" in every early twentieth-century sense of the term. An early brochure described them as "Solid Vestibuled Trains with Combination Café and Parlor Observation Cars" and boasted that they were "the swellest thing out." Among the named trains that later ran the route were the Golden State Limited and the Californian, featuring refined sleeping cars and dining service in resplendent coaches. In late October 1924, the line came under the ownership of the Southern Pacific Railroad. Trains ran through the San Simeon Valley through World War II and into the early 1960s, until finally rolling to a declining economic stop in mid-December 1961. By late 1965, the Southern Pacific had torn up the rails and ties between Douglas and El Paso, and the line was gone. Today, New Mexico Highway 9 north of Rodeo closely follows the original train route for some distance.

Rodeo served a role in the history of another form of transportation as well—aviation. In the 1930s, the Civil Aeronautics Authority, a division of the US Department of Commerce responsible for air traffic safety, established an "intermediate field" just north of the town. Intermediate fields, a necessary component of early civilian aviation, primarily served as emergency landing strips in case a pilot needed to make an unscheduled landing, but they were also used for navigational purposes. Comprising a landing strip, a radio building, and another service building, Rodeo Intermediate Field 57A was one of three in this part of southwestern New Mexico to aid pilots flying for Standard Airlines (later Trans World Airlines, or TWA) between San Diego and El Paso by way of Rodeo. A giant red concrete arrow on the ground at Rodeo Intermediate Site pointed the way to El Paso—an especially helpful directional aid for pilots flying visually and without the assistance of navigational instruments, as was often the case in early aviation. Later, during World War II, the site was used as an auxiliary field for the military, providing a location for emergency landings and also a base from which to conduct test flights. As navigational instruments in civilian aircraft become more sophisticated after the war, intermediate fields were no longer needed and were abandoned.

Portions of the foundations of some of the buildings at Rodeo Field, as well as the red arrow, are still visible. The radio building was moved into Rodeo itself and is now part of Rodeo Cottages, viewable at the northeast corner of Chestnut and Second Streets—the word "Rodeo" can still be seen painted on its pitched roof.

More to explore: *Cumbres and Toltec Scenic Railroad (see under Chama), Playas Siding*

371. Rodey

Location: Doña Ana County. Just north of Rodey, in a pullout on the west side of NM 185, near the intersection of NM 185 and County Road E019 (Fourth Street in Rodey). See map 5.

Marker text: Said to be the oldest village in the area, settled around 1865 and once walled for defense against Apaches. This village, still inhabited, originally was called Colorado, for the reddish hills just to the West; old timers still recognize and use this name. The name Rodey recalls Bernard Shandon Rodey, an Irishman who came to Albuquerque as stenographer for the A&P Railroad and later became a lawyer and political figure.

Located just southeast of the community of Hatch, Rodey is situated in the midst of some of the most fertile agricultural land of the Mesilla Valley. No surprise, then, that much of the economy of the community is tied to farming, as it has been since the village was founded around 1865. Although Hatch, originally settled in 1851, is older, Rodey is still one of the oldest settlements in the Hatch Valley.

When first founded, the community took the name Colorado, a Spanish word that translates to "red." Likely the name was a reference to the colorful red earth on the hills to the west. To protect settlers in the area from raids by Apaches, the army had earlier erected Fort Thorn a short distance to the north in 1853, but the fort had been abandoned by the time the small settlement was established. Instead, the early residents of the community provided their own defense by way of architectural adaptation: their houses had thick walls, few windows, and doors that opened into a common area bordered by other houses. In this way, the structures of their village formed a defensible barricade against outside attacks.

When a post office opened here in 1904, the name Colorado was already in use and not available as the settlement's official name. Instead, residents chose to name their community Rodey. The name honored territorial representative Bernard Shandon Rodey, a prominent figure in nineteenth- and early twentieth-century New Mexico.

Bernard Rodey was born in Ireland on March 1, 1856. At age six, he emigrated to Canada with his family, who were escaping the economic effects of the potato famine in Ireland. Rodey came to

Although territorial legislator and statehood champion Bernard Shandon Rodey was probably aware of the small southwestern New Mexico village named in his honor, it's not known if he ever visited. Bernard Shandon Rodey. Cobb Memorial Collection, Box 3, Folder 9, Item 000-1190220, Center for Southwest Research, University Libraries, University of New Mexico.

the United States in 1877, age twenty-one, and a few years later accepted a position as the private secretary to the general manager for the Atlantic and Pacific Railroad, a job that brought him to Albuquerque. After only a short time in that role, he put his stenography skills to work as a court reporter. Exposure to the courts allowed Rodey to train himself in the law, and the up-and-coming lawyer went on to open his own law practice in Albuquerque—the prestigious Rodey Firm, still in operation today.

In 1889, Bernard Rodey won election to the New Mexico territorial legislature, where he co-authored House Bill 186, an act that would "establish and provide for the maintenance of the University of New Mexico," as well as a school in Socorro (now the New Mexico Institute of Mining and Technology) and another in Las Cruces (now New Mexico State University). Called the Enabling Act, the legislation passed in February of that year. For his efforts, Rodey was dubbed the "Father of the University of New Mexico."

The desk where Rodey sat when he wrote the act is on display in Hodgin Hall, the alumni relations building at the University of New Mexico in Albuquerque.

Soon after arriving in New Mexico, Rodey began a campaign to seek statehood for the New Mexico Territory. Running on a platform of statehood, he won election to the US House of Representatives and represented the territory in Congress from 1901 to 1905, advocating passionately on behalf of his cause. According to an article in the *St. Louis Globe Democrat* on June 8, 1902, Rodey even had a rubber stamp made that read "Work for statehood for New Mexico," which he used to stamp all his outgoing mail. Statehood did arrive. Although it came in 1912, after Rodey had left Congress, he was around to see the fruits of his tireless efforts. Fifteen years later, Rodey passed away, in Albuquerque, just a few days after his seventy-first birthday.

More to explore: *Albuquerque, Hatch, Rincón*

372. Rose Powers White (1894–1969)
Guardian of History

Location: Roosevelt County. Northeast of Portales, at the entrance to the Blackwater Draw Rest Area and Blackwater Draw Museum, on the south side of US 70, between mile markers 429 and 430. See map 6.

Marker text: Rose Powers White worked tirelessly to compile histories of early pioneers of southeastern New Mexico. She published numerous articles and was frequently asked to lecture to organizations and school groups. She served as president of the New Mexico Folklore Society in 1953, and with her husband, R. E. "Eddie" White, donated land to Eastern New Mexico University and to the School for Exceptional Children.

Much of what we know today about the pioneer history of southeastern New Mexico, and particularly that of the early settlers of Portales and other ranching communities on the Llano Estacado, might have been lost had it not been for the work of Rose Powers White.

Born in Las Vegas, New Mexico, and trained as a teacher at the Las Vegas Normal School, White put her degree to work as a math and English teacher in Vaughn and, later, Santa Rosa schools. She came to the Portales area in 1923 after marrying local rancher and, later, bank president Robert Edward "Eddie" White. Then, as now, Portales had all the hallmarks of the epic Old West: sprawling ranches, a history of cattle drives, a railroad, and even visits by outlaw Billy the Kid. Such elements were not only characteristic of the region, they were also part of its history—a rich diorama that White was inspired to capture on paper.

Working frequently as an oral historian, White visited with the people of southeastern New Mexico, listening and capturing their stories. Starting with her own in-laws, who operated the H-Bar Ranch where Rose and her husband lived, she interviewed the pioneers who had helped settle this region when the area was, as she later wrote, "open prairie, with no fences nor law officers to hamper the freedom-loving pioneers who were the first permanent settlers." The stories, along with many others from local ranches and settlers, captured life and culture in southeastern New Mexico from those who both created and lived it. Among her interview subjects was Colonel Jack M. Potter, a ranch owner, author, historian, and former New Mexico state representative; Dr. John Sidney Pearce, the first physician in Portales; and many other local ranchers. Her stories captured the changing character of the Llano Estacado, the flatlands of southeastern New Mexico, with the arrival of the railroad, homesteaders, and schools and churches.

The Whites left their mark on Roosevelt County in a physical way as well. Rose and Eddie were strong supporters of education. After Eddie helped successfully lobby the state legislature in 1927 to locate the Eastern New Mexico normal school (now Eastern New Mexico University) in Portales, the Whites donated a portion of land upon which the campus was erected. They also donated land for what was known as the Training Center for Exceptional Children, a school for the education of children with disabilities.

White shared the stories she gathered by writing columns for local newspapers and by giving talks at civic and school groups. Through her work and interests, she became affiliated with the New Mexico Folklore Society, headquartered in Albuquerque, which had been formed with the express purpose of preserving the stories and culture of the state. In 1952, she served as vice president of the society, and a year later as the president.

At the same time, White also helped found the Portales-based Roosevelt County Pioneers in September 1952. The group, many of whose members had families that had homesteaded southeastern New Mexico, recognized families who had lived in southeastern New Mexico and Roosevelt County for three decades or longer. Powers served as the organization's president and later still as secretary and (in her words) "chief work-horse" until leaving the position in 1968. She passed away a year later, in May 1969.

Many of White's pioneer histories were compiled into book form by her daughter, Ruth White Burns, and published under the title *A Man Was a Real Man in Them Days: Pioneers of the Llano Estacado, 1860 to 1900*.

More to explore: *Eastern New Mexico University, Eve Ball, Llano Estacado, Portales*

373. Roswell

Location: 1. Chaves County. On the north side of Roswell, in a pullout on the north side of US 285. See map 6.

   2. Chaves County. On the east side of Roswell, on the north side of US 380, between mile markers 157 and 158. See map 6.

   3. Chaves County. On the south side of Roswell, on the east side of US 285, between mile markers 106 and 107. See map 6.

Marker text: Roswell was a watering place for the Pecos Valley cattle drives of the 1870s and 1880s. It was incorporated in 1891 and is the seat of Chaves County, named for Col. J. Francisco Chaves, Civil War soldier and delegate to the U.S. Congress from the Territory of New Mexico. In the 1930s, Dr. Robert Goddard conducted experiments in liquid fuel rocket flights here.

374. Roswell Pioneer Plaza

Location: Chaves County. In downtown Roswell, in Pioneer Plaza, across from the courthouse. See map 6.

Marker text: This plaza incorporates two of downtown Roswell's most historic buildings. East of this location is the Chaves County Courthouse, built in 1911. It is one of the best surviving examples of courthouses built in the Beaux Arts Revival "monumental civic style" architecture. The nearby Conoco service station was built in the 1920s. It is one of the few remaining architecturally intact gasoline stations from this early period of New Mexico's transportation history.

Nebraska-born Van C. Smith and his business partner, Aaron O. Wilburn, established a small townsite here in 1865 to supply cowboys driving cattle through southeastern New Mexico. Smith named the settlement for his father, Roswell Smith. Near where the Hondo, Spring, and Pecos Rivers converged in the vast twelve-thousand-square-mile Pecos Valley, Roswell offered not only a respite from ennui but a place for ranchers and their cattle to relax, eat, and sleep. Smith and Wilburn built a corral, a store, and a post office at their settlement. In early Roswell, form followed function: Main Street was left wide so drovers on cattle drives could more easily maneuver their herds straight through the center of town.

In 1877, Tennessee-born Captain Joseph Calloway Lea arrived in Roswell with his wife, Sally, and son, Harry, to try his hand at ranching. Lea purchased Smith's share of the land and eventually acquired the remaining property from Aaron Wilburn. Lea convinced the territorial legislature in 1889 to create a new county around the settlement: Chaves County, named at Lea's request for his friend, speaker of the house José Francisco Chaves. Roswell became the county seat and soon claimed more than two thousand residents. Three years later, Roswell incorporated as a city with Lea, a seminal force in the development of the town, as mayor.

Regrettably, soon after he assumed his new duties, the "Father of Roswell" contracted pneumonia and passed away. Captain Lea was sixty-three at the time of his death.

In the 1930s, a plateau outside Roswell helped launch the country into the space age—literally. There, Massachusetts-born physicist Robert Goddard set up a laboratory to continue experiments he had proposed in his 1919 report, "A Method for Gaining Extreme Altitudes." Goddard's experiments at his Roswell lab eventually culminated in rockets that reached heights of up to a mile and a half and traveled 550 miles per hour. When the US government took notice after World War II, the work of the Roswell physicist helped make possible Neil Armstrong's "giant leap for mankind."

Something came back down out of those skies near Roswell in 1947, but just what that thing was is a question that has spawned an entire cottage industry of speculation and bumper stickers. Military officers at the Roswell Army Air Field in July of that year recovered the remains of a crashed object north of town and brought the pieces back to the base. The air force issued a press release that a "flying disk" had been retrieved, but very quickly retracted the statement and claimed instead that the debris was that of a weather balloon. In a definitive report issued in 1994, the air force states that the object was indeed the remains of a weather balloon, part of an effort known as Project Mogul, and not, as has been claimed, an unidentified flying object, or UFO. Despite these statements, a community of believers persists, many of them drawn to Roswell in a search of answers and commemorative mugs, and alien visages are today a common site around the town.

On March 24, 2001, Roswell residents celebrated the community's first annual Pioneer Day with a parade and an unveiling of a statue of local cattleman John Chisum on Pioneer Plaza downtown. From atop his bronze horse, Chisum can see two of the most historic buildings in Roswell: the Chaves County Courthouse and the old Conoco service station. The courthouse (across Main Street) was erected in 1911 to replace an earlier wooden building that had fallen into disrepair. Designed by Colorado architect Isaac Hamilton Rapp on land deeded for the purpose by Captain Lea, the monumental structure partially follows the Beaux-Arts architectural style and features an impressive green dome. Rapp is also known as the architect behind the design of the governor's mansion in Santa Fe. The Conoco station, at the corner of Main and Fifth Street, went up in the 1920s to cater to a mobile decade. The beautiful cottage-like building embodies the spirit of early twentieth-century auto touring in its Tudor revival architecture, gabled roof, and large service bay doors. In more recent years, the building has been called to service as the location of various local organizations, including the Roswell Hispano Chamber of Commerce and the Chaves County Crime Stoppers.

More to explore: *Chisum Trail (see under Ruidoso), Chisum's South Spring Ranch (see under Artesia), Mesa and Pecos Valley, Pecos Valley*

Roswell Pioneer Plaza: *see Roswell*

375. Ruidoso

Location: Lincoln County. On the west side of Ruidoso, at the intersection of US 70 and Glade Drive. See map 6.

Marker text: Originally known as Dowlin's Mill, the town was located on the Chisum Trail which ran from the Pecos River to Arizona. By 1885 it had attracted a store, a blacksmith shop, and a post office which was named Ruidoso after the local stream. Several incidents of the Lincoln County War occurred here, including the murder of Paul Dowlin in May 1877.

376. Old Dowlin Mill

Location: Lincoln County. In Ruidoso, on the north side of US 70, also called Sudderth Street. See map 6.

Marker text: Famous New Mexico landmark for nearly 100 years. Original building still stands and water turns massive water wheel during the summer. Billy the Kid, Pat Garrett, and Colonel Pershing visited here.

377. Ghost Marker: Chisum Trail

Marker text: Sometimes confused with the Chisholm Trail from Texas to Kansas, the Chisum Trail was used by New Mexico rancher John S. Chisum to supply cattle to the Indian agencies in Arizona. In 1875, Chisum sent 11,000 head over this route, which winds from Roswell to Las Cruces, then roughly follows modern I-10 west to Arizona.

Note: This Marker appears in an inventory of Historic Markers compiled by the State Historic Preservation Office but is not in the field. See map 6.

Captain Paul Dowlin, the post trader at nearby Fort Stanton, along with this brother Will, began construction on a gristmill in Lincoln County around 1868. To gather sufficient waterpower to propel the double-wide, overshot wheel, the brothers pieced together a three-mile-long open chute to flume water from both the Carrizo River and the Rio Ruidoso. As the wheel turned, it powered flint stones that ground grain into flour, and at the same time it churned a sawmill. A bachelor, Paul Dowlin lived on the upper story of the mill and used the first floor for equipment and millwork.

In May 1877, Paul Dowlin sold half the interest in the mill to merchant Frank Lesnett, whom he knew from Fort Stanton. Lesnett, recently married, sent for his Chicago bride, Annie, to join him in Lincoln County. Annie's arrival at the mill was less than auspicious. Greeting her on the grass near the front lawn of the mill on the day of her arrival were splattered stains of human blood. Only a day before, disaffected employee Jerry Dillon, who had worked for Dowlin for about five years, shot his boss in the head and took flight to Texas. The May 8, 1877, edition of the *Santa Fe Weekly New Mexican* offered this sullen recounting of the incident:

The murder was cold-blooded; and further advices state that after firing two shots with a carbine, Dillon drew a revolver and continued firing until Dowlin fell. During the firing Dowlin kept advancing on Dillon—although unarmed—begging Dillon to stop firing for God's sake and listen to reason.

The Lesnetts continued operations at the mill despite Dowlin's death. In 1882, Frank Lesnett bought out the remaining interest held by Will Dowlin to become the sole owner. Still called the Dowlin Mill, the landmark served duty as general store and post office for the fledgling community that was growing around it: Ruidoso.

Ruidoso was a stop along the cattle trail of John Chisum (not to be confused with Jesse Chisholm, trader and guide on the Chisholm Trail between Kansas and Texas). In 1875, rancher Chisum pioneered a route running more than 150 miles from Roswell westward through Ruidoso and farther still to military forts near Las Cruces, where he supplied beef contracts to the army. Chisum's enterprise had made him one of the most successful ranchers in the country at the time.

According to Annie Lesnett, Lincoln County outlaw Billy the Kid played with the Lesnett children at the mill and gave them rides on his pony. Other visitors to the mill included Pat Garrett, who served as Lincoln County sheriff in the early 1880s. Even Colonel John J. "Black Jack" Pershing came by while stationed at nearby Fort Stanton. Pershing would go on to exploits of a more daring nature while leading troops in World War I.

By 1885, Ruidoso had a new blacksmith shop and post office, and the Dowlin Mill faded as a center of activity. Today the mill is a popular historical attraction and store.

More to explore: *Chisum's South Spring Ranch (see under Artesia), Fort Stanton, Lincoln, Pat Garrett Murder Site*

378. Sabino y Lemitar

Location: Socorro County. At the western end of the village of Lemitar, on the south side of NM 408, across from the cemetery. See map 5.

Marker text: The Camino Real passed near here below the bluffs on the east bank of the Rio Grande. Apache raids prevented permanent Spanish settlement of this area until the early 1800s, when the village of Sabino was established on the east bank of the river and Lemitar on the west side. A ford across the river linked the villages, and a west bank branch of the Camino Real soon developed.

Today, the village of Sabino can be found only on historical maps. Named for the Spanish word for a scrub-cedar juniper that vegetates this region, Sabino was settled as early as 1833 along the east bank of the Rio Grande just north of Socorro. It was one of several outposts established along the lower Rio Grande to expand the southern Spanish frontier in the state. Sabino remained a small community throughout its short existence. Just over a hundred people lived there in 1860, down from a peak population of twice that ten years earlier. Among the residents was Juan Armijo, brother of Manuel Armijo—the last Mexican governor of New Mexico before the United States claimed the territory in 1846.

Manuel Armijo, in fact, had a home for a short time across the river in the village of Lemitar. Lemitar may have also been named for local vegetation: *lemitas* are the green berries of the squaw-bush plant. Founded about 1831, Lemitar was built as a series of small buildings facing a central plaza, with the outside walls of the homes left windowless for better defensibility against Indian attack. Lemitar was a *paraje*, or stopping place, along El Camino Real, the key trade and colonization route between Mexico City and Taos. Although the Camino Real ran along the east bank of the river, a second branch here followed the west bank between San Felipe Pueblo and Socorro.

A small ferry across the Rio Grande linked the two villages. W. W. H. Davis, governor of the New Mexico Territory from 1856 to 1857, wrote of crossing in that ferry:

The river was quite high and rapid, and the only means of crossing was in an old canoe made out of cottonwood log, the horses being obliged to swim. . . . We had some difficulty in getting them to take the water; but, once fairly in and striking out for the opposite shore, we converted them into a convenient motive power, and made them drag canoe and passengers to the other side, where we arrived in safety.

Although settlers had abandoned Sabino before 1870, Lemitar lived on, even serving as county seat of Socorro County from 1854 to 1867. The community church, Sagrada Familia de Lemitar, is listed on the National Register of Historic Places as "one of the oldest extant Spanish village churches in the Rio Abajo." The Rio Abajo, or lower river, was a geographic designation of the land south of Santa Fe through the Mexican era. The small adobe church, near the center of the village, dates from 1836.

More to explore: *Cañoncito at Apache Canyon, El Camino Real—The King's Highway*

379. Sally Rooke, Heroine of the Dry Cimarron Flood (1843–1908)

Location: Union County. In Folsom, in front of the Folsom Museum, at the intersection of NM 325 and NM 456. See map 3.

Marker text: On the night of August 27, 1908, while working as a telephone operator, Sally received a call that a wall of water was rushing down the Dry Cimarron River towards Folsom. She perished that stormy night at her switchboard warning of the danger, saving countless lives. Telephone operators across the country contributed 4,334 dimes to honor their colleague with a memorial.

The headline of the *Santa Fe New Mexican* on Friday, August 28, 1908, recounted in chilling detail the events of the night before: "Death Dealing Flood Practically Wiped Out Union County Town Last Night; Disaster Came Without Warning at Midnight while People Were Asleep."

The target of the watery wrath was Folsom, New Mexico, a ranching community of about eight hundred people. Named in honor of the wife of President Grover Cleveland, Francis Folsom, the town of Folsom after the turn of the century had a hotel, commercial buildings, a school, a saloon, and a train depot, among other enterprises, and was the center of ranching operations for the large number of local ranches.

It also had a local telephone exchange and a dedicated operator to work it, Sarah J. Rooke. Going by the name "Sally," Rooke had come to Folsom from Iowa in 1905—age sixty-five—after visiting a friend who lived in the area and falling in love with northeastern New Mexico. Rooke's work required the use of a switchboard, through which she manually patched phone calls by inserting cords into jacks to connect the lines. In the early years of telecommunications, the switchboard operator was often the heart and soul of a community.

Sally Rooke was at her home, which was also where the switchboard office was located, on the night of Thursday, August 27, 1908, a heavy rain falling outside, when she received a call around 11:00 p.m. from the Owens Ranch near Johnson Mesa, about ten miles upstream. The evening cloudburst had swelled the Dry Cimarron River to overflowing, Mrs. Owens warned Rooke anxiously, and the waters were sweeping through the valley toward the town. Indeed, "every river and arroyo was transformed into a roaring torrent," the paper explained the next morning. The watery deluge on its way to Folsom was destined to be the worst flood yet recorded of the Dry Cimarron.

Despite being directly in the path of the onslaught, Sally Rooke did not abandon her station to seek her own safety. Instead, she recognized the unique opportunity her switchboard offered her and set to work. Quickly, she began calling residents of Folsom, the town she had adopted as her own only a few years earlier—the town, it turned out, where her quick thinking would, for many residents, mean the difference between life and death. Rooke rang as many numbers as she could reach, rousing her sleeping neighbors and warning them to seek safety, her switchboard effectively serving as an emergency alert system. According to Alcutt McNaghten, the local telegraph operator, when Rooke reached him at the telegraph station to solicit his assistance in warning the townspeople of the danger, she told him in plaintively direct words that there was "an awful flood coming down the river."

Debris clogging the railroad bridge west of town held the waters back for a short time, but eventually the blockade gave way. By midnight, a wall of water reportedly higher than four feet and stretching the length of five city blocks was pushing through the dirt streets of the town, tearing apart buildings and crushing them to debris. Some residents hid in their attics to escape; one woman climbed atop her piano as the waters swirled below her. Several gathered at the train depot for safety. "Together we could only watch and hope," McNaghten later recalled. "As we watched, we saw a building near the end of the Folsom Hotel disintegrate like an egg crate."

McNaghten recounted another chilling sight that night:

The Wenger house and its four occupants was seen with the lights still burning floating down Grand Avenue, and the screams of the occupants for help could be heard above the roar of the waters. About two miles below town the flood waters created a whirlpool which caught the Wenger house and spun it around and around until it hit the river bank. After the flood, the largest piece of the house that could be found was half of a door.

The terrible floodwaters only began to recede around three in the morning.

With both telephone and telegraph lines down, word of the disaster reached the outside world slowly. When it did, the scale of the terrible tragedy became clear. The flood had carried away almost every building in town that wasn't built of stone. Worse, it had claimed seventeen lives—including that of telephone operator Sally Rooke.

Rooke had stayed at her post until the very end, until the waters rushed through her house on Grand Avenue and took her with them.

Sally Rooke's body was lost to dirt and debris for seven months, until it was recovered downstream the following spring by a local rancher and identified by a ring Rooke had worn. She was buried in the cemetery overlooking the town. Initially, her grave was unadorned. But in July 1925, a story ran in the *Mountain States Monitor*, the internal magazine of the Mountain States Telephone and Telegraph Company, recounting Rooke's lifesaving act of courage. The editorial board requested that employees of the company contribute toward the dedication of a memorial in Rooke's honor. "Let's erect a monument at the grave of Sally Rooke," they suggested. "Let's mark the spot where she rests with imperishable granite and engrave upon the stone the story of her heroic deed. In this way we can manifest our appreciation of her sacrifice."

Sally Rooke's heroic act the night of August 27, 1908, received attention around the nation, with even the *New York Times* stating: "In the face of certain death she stayed in a doomed building sending alarms to every resident who had a telephone." Photo of Sally Rooke. Courtesy Telephone Museum of New Mexico, and the Folsom Museum. Used with permission.

The editorial board of the *Monitor* calculated that if each employee contributed a dime, enough money would be raised for a memorial. Operators and employees of the company responded, contributing a total of 4,334 dimes—$433.40. With the proceeds, a plaque was inset into a giant boulder and placed at Rooke's gravesite in a dedication ceremony held on May 15, 1926. The inscription on the plaque reads in part: "With heroic devotion she glorified her calling by sacrificing her own life that others might live." The memorial still stands today.

More information on Sally Rooke can be found in the Folsom Museum, and a full exhibit on her life and her final heroic act is on display at the Telephone Museum of New Mexico in Albuquerque.

More to explore: *Dulcelina Salce Curtis, Mills Canyon*

380. Salmon Ruin

Location: San Juan County. At the entrance to Salmon Ruin on US 550 (formerly NM 44), just west of Bloomfield. See map 1.

Marker text: In the late 11th century, influence from Chaco Canyon, 45 miles south of here, began to be felt at this site and at nearby Aztec Ruins National Monument. The Chacoans abandoned this large and well-built masonry pueblo by 1150, and shortly thereafter, Mesa Verde people reoccupied it for approximately fifty years.

Peter and Mary Salmon came to the Bloomfield area from Indiana in 1877 to make a home along the banks of the San Juan River. Around 1893, their son George homesteaded an adjacent plot of ground. George, his wife, and generations of Salmon children protected artifacts on the property that would later bear their name in recognition: stone ruins, pottery shards, tools, and bones, relics of an advanced prehistoric civilization whose members had homesteaded the land long before the Salmons arrived.

Historians believe that the Ancestral Puebloan people began to build a village here in the latter part of the eleventh century. At the site of present-day Salmon Ruin, these early Native Americans erected a large masonry pueblo, with at least 110 rooms on the ground floor alone and a second level of 67 rooms, possibly more. An underground kiva in the plaza was the center of social gatherings and religious observations. A second kiva, now called the Tower Kiva, commanded the center of the pueblo.

This remarkable village was one of several related communities that archaeologists believe were somehow associated with the Ancestral Puebloan site of Chaco Canyon, home to one of the most advanced civilizations in prehistoric America. Salmon, which archaeologists believe may have supported a community of four hundred people, ranked as one of the largest Chacoan "outliers." A dirt road reaching twenty feet wide in places crossed the San Juan Basin between the two villages. This Great North Road was one of many spokes in a network known as the Chaco Road System, which had as its nucleus the pueblos at Chaco Canyon and as its end points most often the principal outlier communities like Salmon. As the theory known as the Chaco Phenomenon suggests, the road network may have been part of an infrastructure connecting geographically disparate supply centers. That is, outlier communities such as Salmon may have provided food and raw materials to the hub at Chaco in exchange for laborers both to gather those items and to maintain other work endeavors.

Around 1130, the Chacoans at Salmon left their pueblo. Historians are not sure what caused the departure, but many believe that crops, water, and other resources the Indians depended on for stability may have failed them. The pueblo sat empty for another forty-five years, occupied only sporadically during a phase archaeologists dub the Intermediate Occupation.

The Secondary Occupation of Salmon began around 1185, when a new people arrived from southwestern Colorado, possibly from the Ancestral Puebloan cliff dwellings known today as Mesa Verde. Archaeological excavations conducted by Cynthia Irwin-Williams and students from Eastern New Mexico University in the 1970s show that the new residents, some several hundred people, made modifications to the pueblo at Salmon. In a room the Chacoans had used for making tools, for example, they built subdivisions to store corn. In another room that the Chacoans had used as a living area, they dumped refuse. They even remodeled square rooms to accommodate their own circular kivas.

Then, prehistory repeated itself. No later than 1285, the Mesa Verde people, too, abandoned the site, and Salmon was again empty.

More to explore: *Aztec Ruins National Monument, City of Bloomfield*

381. San Augustin Pass

Location: Doña Ana County. East of Las Cruces, in a pullout at the crest of the Organ Mountains on San Augustin Pass on the south side of US 70. See map 5.

Marker text: This pass has always provided the best access through three mountain ranges, the Organ to the south and the San Andres and San Augustin to the north. It was chosen as the route for U.S. 70, one of the nation's first coast-to-coast highways. Road cuts revealed Tertiary monzonite near the summit. Nearby, Organ Mountain mines yielded copper, lead, silver, gold and zinc. Gypsum sands glisten to the northeast, and to the west is Rio Grande Valley.

382. Ghost Marker: Organ Mountains

Marker text: Spectacular Organ Mountains to east tower over water-rich Rio Grande Valley. High sharp peaks and massive cliffs of igneous rocks are part of ancient volcanoes. Copper, silver, gold, lead and zinc were mined from Organ Mining district at north end of mountains. Basin and Range country is to west.

Note: This Marker was once at this location but has been replaced with the Marker for San Augustin Pass. See map 5.

Antonio de Otermín, governor of New Mexico from 1677 to 1683, had an easy task when it came time to name the range just south of this Historic Marker. He wisely chose Los Organos, or "the Organs," undoubtedly for the likeness of the north-south running string of peaks to a pipe organ. The immense rock cliffs that form those peaks are composed mostly of Tertiary period quartz monzonite. Their highest peak is Organ Needle at 9,012 feet.

The northern end of the Organs gives way to the San Augustin Mountains, extending northward from US 70. Running only about eight miles north to south, the San Augustin Mountains are a smaller subrange of the much larger San Andres Mountains, which extend from just north of here for about seventy-five miles, terminating at Mockingbird Gap near US 380 south of Socorro.

The mountains here are part of a large geographic region of interspersed mountain ranges and low-lying valleys known collectively as the Basin and Range Province, which extends from southeastern Oregon through Nevada, western Utah, parts of California, and southwestern sections of Arizona, New Mexico, and Texas. True to type, the eastern flank of these mountains slopes into the Tularosa Basin, a flat breadth of land stretching eastward to the Sacramento Mountains. The western side enters the water-rich Rio Grande Valley, for many years the setting of cotton, pecan, and chile farms. Part of that valley includes the ninety-mile waterless stretch known as the Jornada del Muerto, or "Journey of the Dead Man," which vexed early caravan travel.

In the 1880s, a small mining camp known as Organ developed in the northern foothills of the Organ Mountains. Miners extracted lead, copper, silver, gold, and zinc from the mountains in mines like the Doña Dora and the Mormon, and the town of Organ grew to 1,800 residents. Pat Garrett, the sheriff most noted for having killed Billy the Kid, had a ranch nearby. Full-scale mining operations ended after the turn of the century. The town survives today, although most of the original buildings have since been torn down.

The San Augustin Wayside Interpretive Pavilion in San Augustin Pass, the location of this Historic Marker, offers motorists atop the mountain a dramatic view of the Organ peaks and the gypsum white sands of the Tularosa Basin in the western distance. The pass allows traffic through the range over US 70, one of the first transcontinental highways, originally running from North Carolina's Atlantic coast to Los Angeles. Today, much of that route has been given over to interstates, but US 70 remains an impressive 2,385 miles long, stretching today from the community of Atlantic, North Carolina, to Globe, Arizona.

For many years, a cave in the western foothills of the Organ Mountains served as a home for El Ermitaño, the Hermit. The Hermit had migrated to the area from another cave in a mountain near Las Vegas, New Mexico, in the mid-nineteenth century. Living a life of solitude, the Hermit spent his time in religious meditations within the secluded earthen comfort of his small, one-man cavern. Because he administered natural cures to the poor and suffering, he became a beloved, albeit distant, neighbor of the residents of Mesilla. They were shocked, then, to discover his murdered body outside his cave one April morning in 1869. Death had come to the holy man by an unknown assailant. The Hermit's cave, known today as La Cueva, is open to the public as part of the Organ Mountains Recreation Area.

More to explore: *Hermits Peak, Pat Garrett Murder Site, Sandia Mountains (see under Albuquerque)*

383. San Antonio
On the Camino Real

Location: Socorro County. On US 380 just west of San Antonio, near exit 139 from Interstate 25. See map 5.

Marker text: Established in the mid 1600s, the mission of San Antonio de Senecú was the last outpost on the Camino Real before the Mesilla Valley to the south. Around 1820 Hispano settlers from the north re-occupied the area after the Pueblo Revolt. Conrad Hilton got his start here, carrying luggage from the train station to his father's hotel located in his family's adobe house.

The name San Antonio is a holdover from the seventeenth century, when Spanish priests around 1629 established the mission of San Antonio de Senecú to introduce Christianity to the Piro-speaking pueblo of Senecú near here. Historians are not certain of the exact location of the pueblo but believe that it was somewhere near present-day San Marcial. When the Pueblo Revolt of 1680 drove the Spanish temporarily from New Mexico, many of the Indians at Senecú likewise deserted their pueblo and fled with the retreating Spanish colonists to El Paso. The majority did not return to New Mexico when the Spanish reasserted control twelve years later. Their mission church, however, was remembered in the name of the new farming community that formed north of the abandoned pueblo around 1820—San Antonio.

Through the nineteenth century, San Antonio stood as one of the last outposts on El Camino Real before the Mesilla Valley to the south. The Camino Real was the major travel route connecting New Mexico with the controlling authorities in Mexico. South of San Antonio, travelers on the Camino Real passed through a large and relatively uninhabited region, a hostile stretch where nomadic Apache Indians threatened and where water and food were scarce.

Today, San Antonio may be best known as the birthplace of famous hotelier Conrad Hilton. After the Atchison, Topeka, and Santa Fe Railway cut through San Antonio in the 1880s, Conrad's parents, Augustus H. and Mary Hilton, modified the family home to serve as a hotel and store for travelers and railroad workers. Young Conrad, the Hiltons' first son and one of eight children in the family, served as a bellhop in the hotel and a stock boy in the store. As Conrad later recalled in his autobiography, *Be My Guest*:

Carl [Conrad's brother] and I met every train, at

midnight, at three in the morning, at high noon. We hustled. We took morning calls to awaken sleepy travelers. We carried luggage and trunks and showcases. I opened the store at eight and closed it at six, for there was always a chance of selling a can of tomatoes and business had to go on.

Conrad also confessed that he only once considered entering the hotel business as a young man in San Antonio and, even then, "strictly as a bellboy." In 1919, when he was twenty-two years old, he purchased the Mobley Hotel in Cisco, Texas, with money he had originally intended to use to buy a bank. The Mobley was his first hotel—but certainly not his last. By 1960, Conrad Hilton was chairman of one of the largest hotel chains in the world. His first hotel in New Mexico was the Hilton, now the Hotel Andaluz, in Albuquerque. Hilton died in 1979, age ninety-one.

More to explore: *Albuquerque, Carthage-Tokay-Farley, El Camino Real—The King's Highway, San Pedro*

384. San Antonio de Padua Catholic Church

Location: San Miguel County. In Pecos, on NM 63, between mile markers 6 and 7, across from the school. See map 3.

Marker text: This is one of the finest surviving examples of Bishop Lamy's French-inspired gothic architecture in New Mexico. Completed in 1906, it is constructed of locally quarried stone instead of traditional adobe. Among its adornment is a painting of Nuestra Señora de Los Angeles (Our Lady of the Angels), given to the nearby Pueblo of Pecos by the King of Spain in the early eighteenth century.

Dedicated to Saint Anthony, the patron saint of Padua in northeastern Italy, the French-inspired Gothic church of San Antonio de Padua in Pecos is listed on the National Register of Historic Places as the embodiment of "French and Spanish elements which came together in the mid-19th century to form the continuing tradition of New Mexico Catholicism." Origins of the French influence can be traced to the first archbishop in the state, French-born Jean-Baptiste Lamy, who came to the New Mexico Territory by papal decree in 1851. As Vicar Apostolic, Lamy left a legacy of ecclesiastical

Archbishop Jean-Baptiste Lamy oversaw the construction of more than forty chapels in New Mexico. Although erected after Lamy's death, the San Antonio de Padua Catholic Church in Pecos shows his stylistic influence. Archbishop Jean-Baptiste Lamy. Courtesy Palace of the Governors Photo Archives (NMHM/DCA), neg. no. 65116.

and architectural reform in New Mexico and became, in the process, a subject worthy of the main role in Willa Cather's classic novel *Death Comes for the Archbishop*.

Lamy passed away in 1878, but his influence continued to be felt within the Church for generations. Among those following in his tradition was French priest Father Maxime Mayeux, who arrived to minister to the spiritual needs of the Pecos parish in 1894. Pecos at the time was a small farming village alongside the similarly named Pecos River and the ruins of Pecos Pueblo. Under the watch of Father Mayeux and his successor in 1904, Father Edward Paulhan, Pecos parishioners began construction of the San Antonio de Padua Catholic Church at the site where an earlier village church had burned to the ground.

Like Lamy, Mayeux and Paulhan likewise found inspiration in Gothic French architecture. Accordingly, they imbued the design of San Antonio with touches that must have reminded them of the cathedrals of Paris. The granite and sandstone walls and steeped pitched roof of the cruciform building stood in contrast to the adobe and flat-roof constructions often found in Spanish mission churches in New Mexico. Sandstone arches crowned the stained-glass windows, while inside, two crystal candle-burning chandeliers brought flickering elegance to the resplendent interior. Burials were made on the outside northern and eastern sides of the building.

Bishop John Baptist Pitaval performed a dedication ceremony for the church on August 1 and 2, 1906, the year of its completion. Pecos residents still celebrate the feast day of Nuestra Señora de Los Angeles every August 2.

Among the treasures adorning the interior of the church is the beautiful painting entitled *Nuestra Señora de Los Angeles de Porciuncula* (*Our Lady of the Angels of Porciuncula*), hung aloft by chains over the altar. The work depicts a heralded Virgin Mary with a partially outstretched right arm. Mexican artist Juan Correa, whose works portrayed religious subjects, painted the oil sometime around 1700. It is one of only nine Correa paintings known to exist outside Mexico. The king of Spain had earlier presented the work to the Indians of nearby Pecos Pueblo to hang in the mission church of their pueblo, once one of the largest mission churches in New Mexico. When the last few residents of Pecos left their pueblo in 1838 to live with their Towa-speaking relatives at Jemez Pueblo, they asked the residents of Pecos to look after the painting. It has remained in Pecos, protected and adored, since that time.

More to explore: *Pecos, Santa Cruz, St. Anthony's Catholic Church*

385. San Francisco de Asís Church
Ranchos de Taos, New Mexico

Location: Taos County. In Ranchos de Taos, in a parking lot at the back of the church, on the east side of US 68. See map 2.

Marker text: This Mission Church is one of the oldest churches in America dedicated to San Francisco de Asís. It was constructed between 1813 and 1815 under the direction of the Franciscan Fray José Benito Pereyro. It is an outstanding example of adobe mission architecture. This Church continues to this day to be a place of worship and an integral part of the community.

The picturesque San Francisco de Asís Church anchoring the historic Ranchos de Taos Plaza is one of the most recognized mission churches in the Southwest. Its cruciform design, thick adobe walls, curved buttresses, and twin bell towers are excellent examples of the features typically associated with Spanish colonial mission architecture. Here, those features form a composite that is, as the National Survey of Historic Sites and Buildings poetically stated, "almost like a piece of abstract sculpture." Indeed, the San Francisco de Asís Church has charmed the creative instincts of generations of photographers and painters, finding one of its most eminent representations on the canvas of artist Georgia O'Keeffe.

The church is an integral part of the village of Ranchos de Taos. That village developed in the late 1770s as a string of small adobe buildings framing a central plaza—a square now bisected by Highway 68. In 1810, the resident priest of nearby Taos Pueblo, Fray José Benito Pereyro, added to his assignments by agreeing to minister to the settlers of Ranchos de Taos as well. It was under Pereyro's direction that settlers completed the mission church of San Francisco de Asís sometime around 1815. A patch of ground in the churchyard, enclosed by a four-foot-high adobe wall, served as the *campo santo*, or cemetery.

In its dedication, the mission honors Saint Francis of Assisi, the patron saint of the Taos Valley. Born at Assisi in Umbria, Italy, in 1181 or 1182, Saint Francis was the son of a wealthy merchant. After meeting impoverished lepers when he was in his early twenties, Francis dedicated his life to serving the less fortunate. Although his father objected to these ministrations and threatened disinheritance, the beneficent Francis continued his devotions by giving clothes and alms when he could, while living the life of a poor man, begging for money and food to survive. His piety attracted followers, so Francis founded the Friars Minor, a diminutive name said to have been chosen intentionally in the hopes of keeping its members humble. Saint Francis died on October 3, 1226.

The church in Ranchos de Taos is one of the oldest in the country to bear his patronage.

More to explore: *El Santuario de Chimayó (see under Chimayó), Georgia O'Keeffe, Santa Cruz, Taos*

386. San Gabriel on the Camino Real

Location: Rio Arriba County. North of Española, on the east side of US 68 between mile markers 4 and 5, near the intersection of US 68 and NM 74. See map 2.

Marker text: Governor Juan de Oñate set up his headquarters in San Juan Pueblo in 1598, but by 1601 he had moved the Spanish capital across the Rio Grande to Yuque-Yunque Pueblo. Named San Gabriel, it served as the seat of government until 1610, when Oñate's successor founded a new capital at Santa Fe.

After years of fits and starts, the viceroy in Mexico chose don Juan de Oñate, son of a wealthy silver mine owner, to expand the holdings of sixteenth-century Spain in the New World by establishing the first European colony in what is now New Mexico. Oñate set out from Santa Barbara, Mexico, in January 1598 with an entourage that would rival Queen Sheba's: some four hundred soldiers, priests, settlers, and servants; eighty-three oxcarts and wagons filled with trunks of personal possessions, equipment, and food; and more than seven thousand head of cattle, goats, sheep, and horses.

Oñate and a small group of soldiers often rode ahead to prepare the way for the main caravan. In early August, they reached a region in north-central New Mexico that Francisco Vásquez de Coronado, a Spanish explorer who led an earlier expedition here in 1540, had called the province of Yuque-Yunque. Extending from the confluence of the Chama River and the Rio Grande south to present-day Santa Fe, the province contained six Tewa-speaking Pueblo Indian villages. One of these was Yunque-Ouinge, from which Coronado had derived the name. On August 10, Oñate and his men entered the pueblo known as Ohke. Having given other pueblos along the route Spanish names, Oñate renamed Ohke as San Juan Pueblo—a name it retained until the pueblo returned to its original name of Ohkay Owingeh in 2005, the name by which it is known today.

Historians question how the sequence of events unfolded after the remaining colonists arrived less than two weeks later. The colonists may have moved into San Juan Pueblo temporarily, and then migrated across the river into the pueblo of Yunque-Ouinge. Or they may have moved to Yunque-Ouinge immediately. Alternatively, as archaeologist Florence Hawley Ellis has proposed, it is possible that Yunque-Ouinge was not a separate pueblo but rather still part of San Juan. Regardless of the chronology, by 1601 the Spanish colonists had crossed to the opposite bank of the river and established there the seat of government in the pueblo they renamed to honor the Catholic saint tasked to sound the trumpet on Judgment Day: San Gabriel.

Judgment, in fact, came for Oñate only a few years later. In 1606, the king of Spain recalled the governor from New Mexico under charges that he had mismanaged the incipient colony. Despite Spanish hopes to the contrary, the new seat of government had seen little resplendence in its founding years. The majority of early colonists returned to Mexico, unwilling to endure the overcrowding, scarcities of food, and, as one wrote, "great deprivations they were suffering."

In 1610, don Pedro de Peralta arrived to establish a new capital in a more promising location to the south: Santa Fe.

More to explore: *Oñate's Route (see under El Camino Real—The King's Highway), Santa Fe, Vásquez de Coronado's Route (series)*

San Isidro Catholic Church: *see Agua Fria*

San José de la Laguna Mission: *see Pueblo of Laguna*

387. San Miguel del Vado National Historic District

Location: San Miguel County. In San Miguel, in the parking lot of the San Miguel del Vado Catholic Church, on the west side of NM 3 between mile markers 68 and 69. See map 3.

Marker text: This community was established in 1794 on a Spanish land grant of the same name. Located at the Santa Fe Trail's principal crossing of the Pecos River, it was a port of entry where caravans entering New Mexico stopped to pay customs taxes to the Mexican government. It was also the San Miguel County seat until 1864. Construction of the church began in 1806.

388. Settlements of the San Miguel del Vado Land Grant

Location: San Miguel County. In San Miguel, in the parking lot of the San Miguel del Vado Catholic Church, on the west side of NM 3 between mile markers 68 and 69. See map 3.

Marker text: Soon after the Spanish government approved the San Miguel del Vado Land Grant in 1794, settlements such as San Miguel, Puertecito, San José, Las Mulas, Entranosa, Guzano, Bernal, La Cuesta and El Pueblo were established along the banks of the Pecos River. Others such as San Juan, Rivera, El Barranco, Sena, Lovato, La Fragua and El Cerrito were founded later in the 19th century.

Note: Marker faceplates are on opposite sides of the same sign.

On November 26, 1794, at an unsettled tract of land near where the waters of the upper Pecos River became shallow enough to cross by wagon, Lorenzo Márquez and other residents of Santa Fe and Peña Blanca walked over the terrain, pulled up the grass, and shouted: "Long live the king!" With them was Captain Antonio José Ortiz, the alcalde (similar to a mayor) of Santa Fe, who officially conveyed ownership to this, the land grant of San Miguel del Vado—Saint Michael of the Ford.

Several close-knit farming villages arose within the boundaries of the grant, including Puertecito, San José, Las Mulas, Entranosa, Guzano, Bernal, La Cuesta (now Villanueva), and El Pueblo. These were among the first Spanish-speaking settlements in the region. The chief village in the cluster, San Miguel, soon grew to be the largest settlement southeast of the Santa Fe capital. By 1811, villagers had completed work on their church, which still stands. The sturdy, three-foot-thick adobe walls of the structure reached twenty feet high, and two towers on either end of the facade served as lookout points from which residents could survey the surrounding countryside for hostile Indians.

Greater prominence came to the village with the opening of the Santa Fe Trail after Mexico declared its independence from Spain in 1821. It was to San Miguel, in fact, that Mexican soldiers first escorted William Becknell, the Missouri trader credited with opening the trail that year, when they encountered his caravan approaching Santa Fe. The Mexican government established a customs operation in San Miguel in 1830 and required that wagon masters crossing the Pecos River on their way to the capital at Santa Fe pay a tariff on their goods. Most often, however, these transactions took place in Santa Fe, and later, the port of entry moved there.

In 1844, the Mexican government created San Miguel County and made San Miguel, from which the county had taken its name, the county seat. Villagers built a courthouse behind the church on the plaza, and other settlements began to form, including Lovato and El Cerrito. Puertecito, founded earlier, changed its name to Sena.

The railroad changed everything. When crews with the Atchison, Topeka, and Santa Fe Railway arrived in Las Vegas, New Mexico, in 1879, political clout in San Miguel County shifted to that budding city. Ironically, Las Vegas had been founded in 1835 by residents from San Miguel who were seeking new pasturelands. San Miguel lost the county seat to Las Vegas in 1864.

Its historic character, however, has never been lost. In recognition of the important role the settlement played in New Mexico history, the National Park Service added the historic district of San Miguel del Vado to the National Register of Historic Places in July 1972.

More to explore: Las Vegas, Santa Fe Trail (series)

389. San Patricio

Location: Lincoln County. Above San Patricio, on the south side of US 70, at mile marker 281. See map 6.

Marker text: This farming and ranching community was the scene of many events associated with the Lincoln County War. In July 1878, a posse ransacked the village while searching for William "Billy the Kid" Bonney and others of the faction known as "Regulators" who frequently visited the town or had hiding places in the vicinity. More recently, renowned artist Peter Hurd made his home here.

The location of San Patricio along the Rio Ruidoso made it a frequent stopping place for William "Billy the Kid" Bonney in the 1870s. Situated between the town of Lincoln, the economic hub of Lincoln County in the late nineteenth century, and the Tunstall Ranch on the Rio Felix to the south, where the Kid had previously worked, San Patricio was at that time little more than fifteen adobe buildings and a plaza. According to Billy's friend George Coe, the Spanish-speaking people in villages like San Patricio in this part of southeastern New Mexico liked the Kid and "were his friends and strong allies."

Two battles in San Patricio were tributaries to a much larger fray known today as the Lincoln County War. The first engagement occurred on June 27, 1878, as Deputy Jack Long and his posse, dispatched by Lincoln County sheriff George Peppin, came to the hamlet to engage the Kid and his gang, known as the Regulators. The Kid was on the run after having shot and killed the previous sheriff of Lincoln County, William Brady, to avenge the death of his former boss, John Tunstall. A gun battle between Long's posse and the Regulators echoed through the dirt streets of the village for the better part of four hours until the Kid and his men finally fled into the foothills of the Capitan Mountains.

Less than a week later, on July 3, Lincoln County deputy José Chavez y Baca led a second posse into San Patricio. Before the sun had even risen, the men found themselves amid a salvo of gunfire as the Regulators fired on them from San Patricio rooftops. In short order, Chavez y Baca and his men had retreated from the town. James Dolan, a merchant in Lincoln County and one of the chief players in the Lincoln County War, returned later that day and pursued the Regulators along the Rio Hondo. However, Dolan and his company, too, fell back after a second gunfight with the Kid a short distance from San Patricio.

More recently, and certainly more quietly, San Patricio was the home of artist Peter Hurd, famous for his watercolor paintings of southwestern scenes. Born in Roswell, New Mexico, in 1904, Hurd attended the New Mexico Military Institute from 1917 to 1920. He studied in his youth with artist N. C. Wyeth in Pennsylvania, which occasioned his meeting Wyeth's daughter, Henriette—an artist herself and sister of painter Andrew Wyeth, who created the iconic *Christina's World* among many other works. Henriette and Peter were married in 1929. The two soon returned to live in New Mexico and settled in San Patricio. Hurd died in 1984.

More to explore: *Couse-Sharp Historic Site, Fort Sumner and Fort Sumner State Monument (series), John H. Tunstall Murder Site, Lincoln*

390. San Pedro

Location: Socorro County. East of San Antonio, in a pullout on the south side of US 380, between mile markers 2 and 3. See map 5.

Marker text: Established in the 1840s on the east bank of the Rio Grande, San Pedro became an important trading center along the Camino Real. The sister village of San Antonio, it was once known for its extensive vineyards and other agricultural produce. The village waxed and waned over the years, declining significantly in the 1940s, and is now almost abandoned.

In the early 1840s, settlers established the small village of San Pedro near the southwestern perimeter of the Los Pinos Mountains. It took a layout typical of villages of the time: an arrangement of homes, a church, and farmlands surrounding two earthen plazas. Census records show a population of 223 people making a home here in 1860. In its initial years, San Pedro was joined with the village of San Antonio, only a few miles to the west on the opposite bank of the Rio Grande, via a small ferry across the river.

San Pedro lay along the course of El Camino Real, the chief nineteenth-century route between Mexico and Taos, as the trail passed along the eastern bank of the Rio Grande. Although use of the trail would decline with the coming of the railroad at the end of the nineteenth century, the community served in the meantime as an important and active trading point for Camino Real travelers headed north or south.

Waters from the Rio Grande made the valley surrounding San Pedro fit for cultivation. Grapes grew well, and San Pedro residents planted extensive vineyards. At the peak of the village grape harvests, San Pedro residents were shipping, according to historian Ralph Twitchell, 250 barrels of wine a year from the railroad at San Antonio. Legend says that the favorite wine of Jean-Baptiste Lamy, the French-born archbishop of the New Mexico diocese in the mid-nineteenth century, came from grapes harvested at San Pedro vineyards.

In 1883, the coal mining community of Carthage developed a few miles east of the village. Many residents of San Pedro worked in the coal mines of Carthage and later Tokay, an adjunct coal mining community established near Carthage around 1918. By 1926, the coalfields at Carthage had been exhausted.

Today, the windswept cemetery and the abandoned San Pedro schoolhouse, constructed by the Works Progress Administration in 1936, are the most prominent reminders of the historic past of the small village.

More to explore: *Carthage-Tokay-Farley, El Camino Real—The King's Highway, San Antonio*

391. San Rafael

Location: Cibola County. Just east of the village, in a pullout on the east side of NM 53, between mile markers 83 and 84. See map 1.

Marker text: San Rafael, formerly known as El Gallo, is located at a spring near the Malpais, the great lava flow to the east. The area was visited by members of Vásquez de Coronado's expedition in 1540. In 1862, it was selected as the original site of Fort Wingate, focus of the campaign against the Navajos.

The terrain of wrinkled black rock to the east, landscaped by lava expelled from nearby Mount Taylor and other area volcanoes, was known to Spanish colonists as the malpais, or badlands. In August 1540, an advance guard with the expedition of Spanish conquistador Francisco Vásquez de Coronado traversed this stretch of west-central New Mexico on their way eastward from Hawikuh, present-day Zuni Pueblo, to Acoma Pueblo and farther still to the Rio Grande. At the head of the twenty-man ensemble was Hernando de Alvarado, Coronado's captain of artillery, along with an Indian guide from Pecos Pueblo whom the Spanish had nicknamed Bigotes, or Whiskers, because he wore a large moustache. These men would have passed the lava flows on their trip, although many historians believe that they likely skirted the basalt furrows in the south to avoid crossing the scabrous terrain.

A spring near the malpais later became known to Spanish colonists as Ojo del Gallo, or "Spring of the Rooster," likely for the abundant wildfowl in the region. Over time, the name was shortened to El Gallo.

After the American occupation of the Southwest in 1846, the army selected El Gallo as the original site of the military post known as Fort Wingate. Soldiers at the fort, which was established on October 22, 1862, were to assist in the orchestrated government campaign to force Navajos of the Four Corners region to the Bosque Redondo Reservation in southeastern New Mexico. Leading a contingent of soldiers from the fort in early summer of 1863, army officer Colonel "Kit" Carson drove more than eight thousand Navajos on a forced journey by foot to the reservation. Indians stopped briefly at Fort Wingate on their exile, a journey that became known as the Long Walk.

When abject conditions at Bosque Redondo finally led to its closure in 1868, Navajos negotiated with the government to return to their homeland in northwestern New Mexico. The army dismantled Fort Wingate and moved it from El Gallo to a site closer to the new Navajo reservation, where it would serve as a base from which soldiers could help resettle the Indians.

With the reservation of the old fort now opened to the public domain, Spanish-speaking farmers and sheepherders, along with military veterans, moved in. These early settlers established a new farming village near the former site of Fort Wingate, west of the malpais and south of the up-and-coming railroad community of Grants. When a post office opened in 1881, their community took the name San Rafael.

More to explore: *Fort Sumner and Fort Sumner State Monument (series), Fort Wingate, Grants, Navajo Indian Reservation, Pueblo of Acoma, Pueblo of Zuni, Vásquez de Coronado's Route (series)*

392. Sangre de Cristo

Location: Taos County. South of Ranchos de Taos, in a rest area on the south side of US 68, between mile markers 33 and 34. See map 2.

Marker text: From left to right along the eastern horizon, two of New Mexico's highest mountain ranges are visible, the Truchas Range and the Santa Fe Range. Both are part of the Sangre de Cristo Mountains of the Southern Rockies where glacier carved alpine peaks rise to elevations exceeding 13,000 feet.

The stunning view to the east of the Marker comes courtesy of the Rocky Mountains. Here, from the left to right, rise the beautiful Truchas Peaks and the Santa Fe Mountains. These mountains form the southernmost reach of the Rocky Mountains, which extend into north-central New Mexico and contain the tallest peaks in the state.

The Truchas Peaks take their name from the Rio Truchas, or "River of Trout," which flows out of these mountains. A number of peaks make up the Truchas region, with the four most prominent being North Truchas, Middle Truchas, West Truchas, and South Truchas. South Truchas is the highest, reaching 13,012 feet—just shy of the highest mountain in the state. The Truchas Peaks are a subregion of the Santa Fe Mountains.

The Truchas Peaks and the Santa Fe Mountains lie within the larger subrange known as the Sangre de Cristo Mountains, which extend from south-central Colorado to just east of Santa Fe. The name is Spanish and translates to "Blood of Christ." The spiritual reference is an allusion to the red hue of the mountains at sunset and sunrise, which, as the tale goes, reminded early missionary priests in New Mexico of the blood of their savior. Indeed, the mountains do produce a delightfully crimson glow in the mornings and evenings, especially in winter.

More to explore: *Rocky Mountains, Truchas, Truchas Peaks*

393. Santa Cruz

Location: Rio Arriba County. In the courtyard of the Santa Cruz Catholic Church in Ojo Caliente. See map 2.

Marker text: La Santa Cruz Catholic Church was built after 1793 and was licensed on January 13, 1811 and blessed on January 3, 1812. The restoration of the historic Santa Cruz Catholic Church of Ojo Caliente, New Mexico began in April 1991, by the community of Ojo Caliente and other volunteers, assisted by the New Mexico Community Foundation, it was completed on September 16, 1994. The blessing and rededication by Archbishop Michael Sheehan occurred on September 24, 1994.

394. Ghost Marker: Ojo Caliente

Marker text: Ojo Caliente ("hot spring" in Spanish) was a strategic point for the defense of the Chama and upper Rio Grande Valleys. Colonization began in the early 18th century, but pressure from the Utes and Comanches delayed permanent settlement until 1793. Lt. Zebulon Pike reported a population of 500 in 1807. See map 2.

Note: This marker appears in an inventory of Historic Markers compiled by the Historic Preservation Division but is not in the field.

For centuries, health seekers have patronized the hot mineral springs that give the village of Ojo Caliente, or "Hot Springs," its name. Archaeological digs in the surrounding valley and cliffs have unearthed the remains of at least three prehistoric Tewa Indian pueblos, including those known today as Ponsipa'akeri and Posi, and historians believe that the Indians who lived in these villages from the fourteenth to the mid-sixteenth centuries may have visited the hot water springs. When Spanish settlement progressed here with the founding of the village of Ojo Caliente in 1793, the Spanish, too, frequented the springs. Much later, the bubbling springs were developed as a commercial resort.

It wasn't until about 1793 that raids by Utes and Comanches on villages had slowed enough to allow permanent settlement to take hold. Lieutenant Zebulon Pike, exploring the Southwest for the US Army and captured by Spanish troops, passed through the region while being escorted to Chihuahua as a prisoner. He noted: "This village may contain 500 souls. The greatest natural curiosity is the warm springs, which are two in number, about 10 yards apart."

Among the first structures built in Ojo Caliente was the Santa Cruz Catholic Church, erected at the south side of the central village plaza. The church took shape with strong adobe walls and vigas, or wooden supports, which held aloft the ceiling. Villagers licensed the chapel on January 3, 1811, and dedicated it a year later, on January 13, 1812.

Ernest Ingersoll, who traveled the Rocky Mountain region in the 1880s, left a description of the church as it appeared in 1885:

The church itself of course was built of adobe, the facade being supported on the right of the door by a great sloping buttress, which was not only a brace, but had served in place of a ladder to those who built the roof and parapets. . . . Recent rains had evidently damaged the walls very much, for great hollows had been washed in them. . . . Centuries have rolled over its adobe walls, and its roof of closely set logs and adze-carved brackets has echoed to the clank of men in armor, as well as to the chant of . . . farmers and shepherds.

In the 1950s, residents built a second church behind the chapel, dedicated it as Saint Mary's, and began to worship there. The original chapel of Santa Cruz fell to disrepair over time, victimized by weather and pigeons, and once even saw duty as a barn. According to newspaper reports, thieves over time carried off the santos and other religious artifacts that had adorned the interior.

Fearing that the aging structure had become unsafe, the archdiocese in Santa Fe made plans to tear it down—but interest among residents in preserving the historic chapel prevented its demolition. The spring of 1991 brought a major renovation, supervised and supported in part financially by the philanthropic New Mexico Community Foundation. Using materials donated by local businesses, workers and community volunteers rejuvenated the aging church by applying new stucco to its walls and even repairing a broken corner of the building.

At an outdoor mass held on September 24, 1994, Archbishop Michael Sheehan blessed and rededicated the restored Santa Cruz church.

More to explore: *El Santuario de Chimayó (see under Chimayó), San Antonio de Padua Catholic Church, San Isidro Catholic Church (see under Agua Fria), Truth or Consequences*

395. Santa Cruz de la Cañada

Location: Santa Fe County. In Santa Cruz de la Cañada, on NM 53, before the Iglesia de Santa Cruz de la Cañada Catholic Church. See map 2.

Marker text: In 1695, Governor Diego de Vargas founded his first town, Santa Cruz de la Cañada, designed to protect the Spanish frontier north of Santa Fe. The church, which still stands, was constructed in the 1730s. In 1837, residents revolted against Mexican authorities, resulting in the death of Governor Albino Pérez.

396. Santa Cruz Plaza

Marker text: In 1695, Governor Diego de Vargas founded Santa Cruz de la Cañada south of the Santa Cruz river. The town was later moved to this site north of the river. The church facing the plaza dates from the 1730s. Santa Cruz was an important stop on the Camino Real between Santa Fe and Taos.

Note: Marker faceplates are on opposite sides of the same sign. See map 2.

When New Mexico returned to Spanish control in 1692 after the Pueblo Revolt twelve years earlier, Governor Diego de Vargas began the process of resettling Indian and Spanish villages in the state and establishing new ones. Vargas wanted to found a new town north of Santa Fe, in part to buffer the capital from the incursions of nomadic Indian tribes like the Apaches and Comanches. In early 1695, Governor Vargas directed sixty Spanish families to assemble on Santa Fe Plaza "with pack mules, horses, a ration of corn and beef, corn for planting, implements picks, hoes, shovels, axes." On April 21, those families followed Vargas and a small posse of soldiers north, arriving the next day at a spot south of the Santa Cruz River. After the new residents swore their allegiance to the Crown and the Church, soldiers fired three volleys in celebration of this, the first town founded by Vargas: La Villa Nueva de Santa Cruz de Españoles Mexicanos del Rey Nuestro Señor Carlos Secondo, or "the New Town of Santa Cruz of the Mexican Spaniards for the King, Our Lord, Charles II."

By 1730, residents of Santa Cruz de la Cañada had moved their village to its present location on higher ground north of the river. Given the constant threat of raids by marauding bands of Indians, the settlement was laid out as a fortified plaza, with adobe houses surrounding a central square. Sometime around 1733, work began on the village church, known as La Iglesia de Santa Cruz. Several years of toil eventually produced a beautiful cruciform chapel with fronting twin bell towers. The cross of the church was decorated with silver.

Designated by Vargas as a villa, the highest classification of a Spanish town, Santa Cruz was an important village. Population estimates show one hundred families living there in 1744. The town lay along the Camino Real, the royal highway between New Mexico and Mexico. The northernmost section of the Camino Real ran between Santa Fe and Taos and passed through Santa Cruz. Until the decline of the route in the nineteenth century, the village was a stop for trade caravans and those bringing supplies to the colony.

In 1837, Santa Cruz residents took part in a turbid affair that became known as the Chimayó Rebellion. In August of that year, angry Hispanic farmers and supportive Pueblo Indians marshaled in Santa Cruz to protest the taxes levied on them by the Mexican governor, Colonel Albino Pérez. Governor Pérez sent a militia to stop the insurrection, but the mob quickly routed these forces and reached the capital at Santa Fe. As recorded by young trader and author Josiah Gregg in his book *Commerce of the Prairies*:

Knowing that they would not be safe in Santa Fe, the [governor and his officers] pursued their flight southward, but were soon overtaken by the exasperated Pueblos; when the Governor was chased back to the suburbs of the city, and savagely put to death. His body was then stripped and shockingly mangled: his head was carried as a trophy to the camp of the insurgents, who made a foot-ball of it among themselves.

More to explore: Albuquerque, El Camino Real—The King's Highway, Taos

397. Santa Fe

Location: Santa Fe County. In Santa Fe, on the south side of Cerrillos, near its intersection with Camino Carlos Rey. See map 2.

Marker text: Santa Fe, the oldest capital city in the United States, was established in 1613 as the seat of Spanish colonial government for the Province of New Mexico. The Palace of the Governors, used by Spanish, Mexican, and Territorial governors, has flanked the historic plaza since its construction in 1610, and now comprises part of the Museum of New Mexico.

398. Ghost Marker: Kearny's Route

Marker text: In 1846, U.S. forces under Brigadier General Stephen Watts Kearny invaded New Mexico and, on August 18, raised the U.S. flag in Santa Fe. Afterwards, he marched unopposed into Bernalillo and Albuquerque. As a result of his occupation, New Mexico passed from the jurisdiction of Mexico to that of the United States.

Note: This Marker once existed near Santa Fe but was removed and has not been replaced. It mentions the route that Brigadier General Stephen Watts Kearny followed through New Mexico and his arrival in Santa Fe, and so is reproduced here as a Ghost Marker. See map 2.

In 1613, don Pedro de Peralta, third governor of the province of Nuevo Mejico, established a new seat of government for Spanish settlement north of Mexico—La Villa Real de Santa Fe, "the Royal Village of Holy Faith." Peralta's capital replaced the one established in 1598 by don Juan de Oñate north of here, and over time Spanish-speaking colonists living at the old site migrated to Santa Fe. The early village took shape as a square of private homes and government offices surrounding a packed-earth plaza, twice the size then as today's Santa Fe Plaza. Chief among the buildings was El Palacio Real, the Palace of the Governors, which held the offices and living quarters of the governor, a corral, and the first town jail. In its original design, the building featured a large, round tower on the west end, where munitions were stored; another on the east housed a small chapel. The distinctive portal was added in the early 1700s.

The province continued under Spanish rule until 1821, the year Mexico declared its independence from Spain. Soldiers raised the Mexican flag over the Palace of the Governors in September of that year to signify the new administration. The change in governance also meant a change in economic policy—New Mexicans would now be allowed to trade with eastern settlements, an act previously forbidden. Almost immediately, Santa Fe became the western terminus for commerce and settlement over the Santa Fe Trail. The growing alliance between Mexican citizens of New Mexico and United States citizens abetted by the trail was manifested on August 18, 1846, when Brigadier General Stephen Watts Kearny and his Army of the West marched into Santa Fe and peacefully raised the Stars and Stripes over the Palace of the Governors. New Mexico was now part of the United States.

The flag that flew over the capital city would change one last time. During the Civil War, Confederates advanced from Texas north along the Rio Grande corridor through New Mexico. Before the Rebels arrived in Santa Fe in March 1862, Governor Henry Connelly fled the capital for safety to Las Vegas, New Mexico, in the southeastern foothills of the Sangre de Cristo Mountains to the east. The Confederate flag flew over the Palace of the Governors for two weeks, until Union and Confederate troops tangled at the Battle of Glorieta Pass between Las Vegas and Santa Fe. During the battle, Union soldiers burned the Confederate supply wagons. The loss forced the Rebels to withdraw from the state.

In 1885, the state legislature erected a larger capitol office building off the plaza, followed by a new mansion for the governor in 1907. New Mexico became a state five years later, with Santa Fe continuing as its capital city—the oldest capital city in the country.

A Federal Writers' Project guidebook to the state written in the 1940s effectively summed up the unique combination of history, geography, and culture that is the allure of Santa Fe today:

The charm of the Royal City is quickly felt. The ancient narrow streets and the brown adobe houses are thick with deeds and memories. In the evening the fragrance of piñon smoke fills the air, for Santa Fe is a city of fireplaces. It is a town of patios where hollyhocks nod, where towering cottonwoods splatter with shade, here a crumbling gateway, there an ancient wall whose adobe bricks show through the broken earthen plaster . . . for here are blended, as nowhere else in the United States, the full rich patterns of three distinct cultures—Indian, Spanish, and American.

More to explore: *Glorieta Pass Battlefield, Las Vegas, San Gabriel on the Camino Real, Santa Fe Opera, Santa Fe Trail (series)*

399. Santa Fe Opera

Location: Santa Fe County. Just north of Santa Fe, near the entrance to the opera, in an island created by the intersection of Opera Drive and Avenida Monte Sereno. See map 2.

Marker text: Located on a former guest ranch of 199 acres, the Santa Fe Opera was founded in 1956 as the Opera Association of New Mexico by John Crosby, a New York–based conductor. The first season began in July of 1957. The Santa Fe Opera is internationally known for introducing new and innovative operas as well as for its productions of works from the standard operatic repertoire.

Some of humanity's greatest moments of love and tragedy have taken place on a piñon-covered hillside just north of Santa Fe. Here, Italian *innamorati* have gaily toasted wine and love, yearning counts have won the hearts of beautiful maidens with help from baritone barbers, and sisters tricked into infidelity by their charlatan suitors have recounted their romantic woes in parallel thirds. Bravo!

The man who would found the Santa Fe Opera Company first came to New Mexico from New York in his youth, not to sing but to breathe. Hopeful that the cool desert air might help their son's asthma, the parents of young John Crosby sent him to spend a year at the Los Alamos Ranch School in the early 1940s. After later serving in the army, graduating from both Yale and Columbia, and studying musical composition with mentors who would follow him through life, Crosby returned to New Mexico in 1957. He was driven by the idea that the state, known even then as an artistic center, could successfully host a professional opera company—one that would keep productions accessible by performing in English.

Opening night for that new company in 1957 saw a love-torn Japanese geisha ending her life before an audience moved to tears in Puccini's masterpiece, *Madame Butterfly*. Ten curtain calls that evening were as much in appreciation for Crosby's vision as for the performance. In its first season, the Santa Fe Opera enjoyed a full house at almost every performance.

The acclaim of the upstart company soon spread. Opera aficionados from around the globe came to enjoy performances, including the premieres of American operas like *The Tower* by Marvin David Levy. Some of the performers they heard on stage were budding stars gaining professional experience by singing in the chorus or by serving in understudy roles. These novices were part of the Santa Fe Opera Apprentice Artists Program, the first of its kind in the country, another innovative idea from Crosby.

On July 27, 1967, before the master jeweler Cardillac could murder the unfortunates who purchased his art in what would have been the American premiere of Paul Hindemith's *Cardillac*, a devastating fire ravaged much of the opera house. Fortunately, the destruction proved only an entr'acte. Within a year, the design firm of McHugh and Kidder had completed a sophisticated new building to serve the company. The innovative house featured an exquisitely sweeping roof, a curvature that has since become the architectural signature of the world-renowned Santa Fe Opera.

John Crosby remained director of the Santa Fe Opera until his retirement in 2000.

More to explore: *Garcia Opera House, Louise Massey Mabie, Santa Fe*

SANTA FE TRAIL: Series of Historic Markers (Various Locations around Northeastern and North-Central New Mexico)

General Introduction

Dubbed the Great Prairie Highway by the National Park Service, the Santa Fe Trail is one of the best-known, and perhaps the most romanticized, of the pathways of westward expansion. It is one of the defining historical features of northeastern and north-central New Mexico.

Because of the importance of the trail to the history of the state, several Historic Markers have been placed around northeastern and north-central New Mexico to denote areas of trail interest. They are grouped here in a series, including information on the formation of the trail; the two main variations in its route, the Mountain Branch and the Cimarron Cutoff; and some of the women who traveled on the trail. The Markers are listed here in three groups: those dealing with the opening of the trail, those dealing with the Cimarron Cutoff, and those dealing with the Mountain Branch.

On May 8, 1987, President Ronald Reagan signed legislation designating the Santa Fe Trail as a National Historic Trail.

More to explore (Santa Fe Trail Series): *El Camino Real—The King's Highway, Las Vegas, Santa Fe, Trail of the Forty-Niners, Women of the Camino Real (see under El Camino Real—The King's Highway)*

Schooners traveling twenty miles in a day crossed the prairies over the Santa Fe Trail, a celebrated overland route named for its western terminus in Santa Fe. The trail split at Dodge City, Kansas, into the Mountain Branch and the Cimarron Cutoff. Illustration by David Carter.

400. Santa Fe Trail

Location: Mora County. In the Interstate 25 rest area just north of Watrous, on the east side of the interstate, at mile marker 375. See map 3.

Marker text: Opened by William Becknell in 1821, the Santa Fe Trail became the major trade route to Santa Fe from Missouri River towns. The two main branches, the Cimarron Cutoff and the Mountain Branch, joined at Watrous. Travel over the Trail ceased with the coming of the railroad in 1879.

Note: See the general introduction to this series of Markers, as well as the other Markers making up the series, for further background on the Santa Fe Trail.

401. Santa Fe Trail

Location: Colfax County. In Cimarron, in the dirt area on the north side of the intersection of Tenth and Euclid Streets, in front of the Cimarron Inn. See map 3.

Marker text: Opened by William Becknell in 1821, the Santa Fe Trail became the major trade route to Santa Fe from Missouri River towns. The two main branches, the Cimarron Cutoff and the Mountain Branch, joined at Watrous. Travel over the Trail ceased with the coming of the railroad in 1879.

Note: See the general introduction to this series of Markers, as well as the other Markers making up the series, for further background on the Santa Fe Trail.

William Becknell and a small caravan of traders left Franklin, Missouri, in September 1821, pulling wagons piled high with cargo, heading west. When Becknell set out on his journey, New Mexico was under the control of Spain, and its citizens were allowed to purchase only merchandise offered by designated Chihuahua merchants. Exactly how far Becknell had planned to go isn't clear, but perhaps he hoped that anticipated changes in the political structure of the Spanish government in New Mexico would work in his favor, and the closed borders of the Mexican Southwest would be opened to outside trade.

He was right. In the meantime, Mexico declared itself free from Spain and, as one of the foundations of its new independence, opened its doors to outside trade. After encountering the Mexican army south of Las Vegas, New Mexico, in November 1821, Becknell and his men were allowed to proceed to Santa Fe, the capital city. Finding Santa Fe consumers eager to buy, Becknell reaped incredible profits. Other merchants, hoping to do likewise, followed in his footsteps—literally. The route Becknell followed became a well-traveled interstate of commerce and settlement and fostered the exchange of information between the Mexican Southwest and the American Midwest. This was the Santa Fe Trail.

The Santa Fe Trail over time divided into shortcuts, detours, and cross trails along its course as travelers searched for fresher pastures for their stock or gentler terrains for their wagon wheels. Just west of Dodge City, Kansas, the trail made its largest divide, splitting into two separate and distinct branches. The Mountain Branch journeyed northwestward to Colorado and then south over Raton Pass into New Mexico. Its counterpart, the more direct Cimarron Cutoff, which Becknell pioneered on his second trip, ran southward from Dodge City through the westernmost corner of Oklahoma and into northeastern New Mexico. The two branches rejoined near present-day Watrous, New Mexico.

402. Puertocito de la Piedra Lumbre

Location: San Miguel County. Southeast of Las Vegas, in a pullout on the north side of NM 283, between mile markers 0 and 1. See map 3.

Marker text: Near this spot on November 13, 1821, a band of six Missouri traders led by William Becknell, encountered a force of more than 400 Mexican soldiers, militia, and Pueblo Indians under the command of Captain Pedro Ignacio Gallego. The peaceful meeting and the subsequent arrival of Becknell in Santa Fe, marked the beginning of the Santa Fe Trail as a commercial link between the United States and Mexico.

Cerca de este sitio el 13 de Noviembre, 1821, seis commerciantes de Missouri, dirijidos por William Becknell, encontraron una fuerza de mas de 400 soldados Mejicanos, milicia, y indios de pueblo mandados por el Capital Pedro Ignacio Gallego. Este encuentro pacifico y a llegada de Beckness a Santa Fe, inició el Camino de Santa Fe como una ruta commercial entre Los Estados Unidos de N.A. y Mejico.

Note: See the general introduction to this series of Markers, as well as the other Markers making up the series, for further background on the Santa Fe Trail.

A pivotal moment in the opening of the Santa Fe Trail occurred on November 13, 1821, near this spot just southeast of present-day Las Vegas, New Mexico. Here, there is a gap in the mountains that had taken the name Puertocito de la Piedra Lumbre, or "the Little Gap of the Fire Rock" (flint). (The location is today known as Kearny Gap.) On that day, during his first journey on what would become the Santa Fe Trail, William Becknell and his small band of Missouri traders encountered a military force of some four hundred Mexican soldiers led by Captain Pedro Ignacio Gallego. The troops were on a scouting mission against raiding Comanches and were surprised to find the Americans. Both Becknell and Gallego kept a written account of the meeting—Becknell in his journal, and Gallego in his military reconnaissance notes. Because of this, the historic encounter can be viewed from two different points of view.

Captain Gallego's version first:

About 3:30 p.m. encountered six Americans at the Puertocito de la Piedra Lumbre. They parlayed with me and at about 4 p.m. we halted at the stream at Piedra Lumbre. Not understanding their words nor any of the signs they made, I decided to return to El Vado [with Becknell and his men], in the service of your excellency [New Mexico governor Facundo Melgares].

Becknell's version tells a somewhat different story:

On Tuesday morning the 13th, we had the satisfaction of meeting with a party of Spanish troops. Although the difference of our language would not admit of conversation, yet the circumstances attending their reception of us, fully convinced us of their hospitable disposition and friendly feelings. Being likewise in a strange country, and subject to their disposition, our wishes lent their aid to increase our confidence in their manifestations of kindness. . . . We encamped with them that night, and the next day about 1 o'clock, arrived at the Village of St. Michael [San Miguel del Vado], the conduct of whose inhabitants gave us grateful evidence of civility and welcome.

Captain Gallego had escorted the party to the nearby village of San Miguel del Vado, the principal settlement in the region at the time. Becknell was allowed to proceed to Santa Fe, with an interpreter he hired at San Miguel. There he met with the governor, who "asked many questions concerning my country, its people, their manner of living, etc." and who was willing to open trade. Becknell—and generations of traders after him—found in Santa Fe an eager market for their goods.

The historic encounter here that November day in 1821 was the beginning of the development of the Santa Fe Trail as an important trade and settlement link between the United States and Mexico. For his role, Becknell is sometimes referred to as the "Father of the Santa Fe Trail."

More to explore: *San Miguel del Vado National Historic District, Santa Fe, Santa Fe Trail (series)*

403. Santa Fe Trail

Location: Union County. Just east of Clayton, in a pullout on the north side of US 64, between mile markers 83 and 84. See map 3.

Marker text: The Santa Fe Trail was the major trade route between New Mexico and Missouri from 1821 until arrival of the railroad in 1880. The Cimarron Cutoff, a major branch of the Trail, passed through this portion of northeast New Mexico. Some of the best preserved segments of the Trail route are located at nearby Kiowa National Grasslands, along the Santa Fe National Historic Trail.

Note: This Marker contains a location-specific reference, the Kiowa National Grasslands, which are about fifty miles west of this Historic Marker.

Note: See the general introduction to this series of Markers, as well as the other Markers making up the series, for further background on the Santa Fe Trail.

The Cimarron Cutoff, a major branch of the Santa Fe Trail running southward from Dodge City through the westernmost corner of Oklahoma and into northeastern New Mexico, shaved more than fifty miles from the journey. The cutoff had disadvantages: in addition to lacking water, it crossed an open prairie, which left prairie schooners vulnerable to attacks by hostile bands of Comanches and other Plains Indians. Still, because of its shorter length, the cutoff remained the choice of most early trailers.

So many, in fact, that the record of their passing furrowed itself physically into the earth. Heavy traffic on the trail during its busy years wore deep ruts into the earth still visible today. These historic furrows are especially in evidence at the nearby Kiowa National Grasslands, a 263,954-acre region of grasslands in northeastern New Mexico that reaches into bordering Oklahoma and Texas.

404. Santa Fe Trail

Location: Union County. Just east of Clayton, in a pullout on the north side of US 64, between mile markers 83 and 84. See map 3.

Marker text: William Becknell, the first Santa Fe Trail trader, entered Santa Fe in 1821 after Mexico became independent from Spain and opened its frontier to foreign traders. The Mountain Branch over Raton Pass divided here. One fork turned west to Cimarron, then south and joined a more direct route at Rayado.

Note: This Marker contains a location-specific reference that is inaccurate for this location and probably was intended for a sign closer to Raton (about eighty miles west of here). The reference is to the division of the Mountain Branch into two separate (short) branches. Just south of Raton, the Mountain Branch split into two distinct paths. One arced a short bit to the west and passed through the village of Cimarron, then continued south. The other continued due south without the short detour. The two branches joined at Rayado, about fifty miles south of Raton.

Note: See the general introduction to this series of Markers, as well as the other Markers making up the series, for further background on the Santa Fe Trail.

405. Santa Fe Trail

Location: Mora County. In the Interstate 25 rest area just north of Watrous, on the west side of the interstate, between mile markers 375 and 376. See map 3.

Marker text: The difficulty of bringing caravans over rocky and mountainous Raton Pass kept most wagon traffic on the Cimarron Cutoff of the Santa Fe Trail until the 1840s. Afterwards, the Mountain Branch, which here approaches Raton Pass, became more popular with traders, immigrants, gold seekers, and government supply trains.

Note: See the general introduction to this series of Markers, as well as the other Markers making up the series, for further background on the Santa Fe Trail.

406. Santa Fe Trail

Location: Union County. Just east of Clayton, in a pullout on the north side of US 64, between mile markers 83 and 84. See map 3.

Marker text: The difficulty of bringing caravans over rocky and mountainous Raton Pass kept most wagon traffic on the Cimarron Cutoff of the Santa Fe Trail until the 1840s. Afterwards, the Mountain Branch, which here approaches Raton Pass, became more popular with traders, immigrants, gold-seekers, and government supply trains.

Note: This Marker contains a location-specific reference, the approach of the Mountain Branch to Raton Pass.

Note: See the general introduction to this series of Markers, as well as the other Markers making up the series, for further background on the Santa Fe Trail.

407. Santa Fe Trail Cimarron Cutoff

Location: Colfax County. In Cimarron, in the dirt area on the north side of the intersection of Tenth and Euclid Streets, in front of the Cimarron Inn. See map 3.

Marker text: The difficulty of bringing caravans over rocky and mountainous Raton Pass kept most wagon traffic on the Cimarron Cutoff of the Santa Fe Trail until the 1840s. Afterwards, the Mountain Branch, which here approaches Raton Pass, became more popular with traders, immigrants, gold-seekers, and government supply trains.

Note: This Marker contains a location-specific reference, the approach of the Mountain Branch to Raton Pass.

Note: See the general introduction to this series of Markers, as well as the other Markers making up the series, for further background on the Santa Fe Trail.

Craggy, rock-ribbed Raton Pass, a rugged corridor over the Raton Mountains between Colorado and New Mexico, proved a formidable challenge to wagon caravans of Santa Fe hopefuls traveling the Mountain Branch of the Santa Fe Trail. This pass alone was sufficient reason to stick with the Cimarron Cutoff, a shortcut that sacrificed the safety and water found along the Mountain Branch for the advantage of a shorter trip over the level prairies. Getting a wagon to the top of the pass might take an entire day, and the defile was so narrow in places that often only one wagon could move through at a time.

Lieutenant James W. Abert of the US Army left a firsthand account of the difficulties he faced crossing Raton Pass in 1846:

We commenced the passage of one of the most rocky roads I ever saw; no one who has crossed the Raton can ever forget it. A dense growth of pitch pine interferes with the guidance of the teams; in many places the axletrees were frayed against the huge fragments of rock that jutted up between the wheels as we passed; pieces of broken wagons lined the road, and at the foot of the hill we saw many axletrees, wagon tongues, sand-boards, and ox yokes, that had been broken and cast aside.

Shortly after American soldiers claimed the Southwest for the United States, Raton Pass saw a new wave of settlers and immigrants. Among those traveling west in the mid-nineteenth century were fortune seekers caught in the mad scamper to California in the Gold Rush of 1849. During the Civil War, government supply trains headed to army forts in New Mexico also traversed the pass, fearing that the open prairies of the Cimarron Cutoff might leave them vulnerable to Confederate attack. After the war, many travelers who pushed their prairie schooners over the Mountain Branch were immigrants coming to homestead a patch of land. Unforgiving Raton Pass may have been a metaphor for their rough and rocky experiences.

Travel on the Santa Fe Trail receded in the 1880s when the arrival of the railroad in New Mexico brought a more efficient method of transporting goods over long distances.

408. Women of the Santa Fe Trail

Location: Colfax County. South of Raton, in a highway rest area on the west side of Interstate 25, between mile markers 434 and 435. See map 3.

Marker text: The Women of the Santa Fe Trail endured untold hardships traveling across the Great Plains. In 1829, six Hispanic women were the first known female travelers going east on the trail. In 1832, Mary Donoho was the first woman whose name was recorded to travel west along the trail. Susan Shelby Magoffin and Marion Sloan followed and both wrote about their experiences.

Note: See the general introduction to this series of Markers, as well as the other Markers making up the series, for further background on the Santa Fe Trail.

Ironically, the very act that allowed commerce over the Santa Fe Trail to flow into New Mexico—the declaration of independence of Mexico from Spain—also led to the trail's use for the expulsion of citizens out of New Mexico. One such group of sixteen people in 1829 included six Hispanic women—the first recorded instance of women traveling on the Santa Fe Trail. The names of the six women in the group are not known, but their crimes are: they (and the others in their families) remained loyal to Spain after Mexican independence, and for this civic sin they were banished from the New Mexican territory.

Under somewhat happier circumstances, the

first woman recorded by history to come west over the trail from Missouri to Santa Fe was Mary Watt Donoho. With her husband, William, and their infant daughter, Donoho traveled the trail in 1833. After settling in Santa Fe, the Donohos opened a hotel on the plaza; it is believed that the two children they had while running the hotel are the first two Anglo babies born in Santa Fe. The Donohos' hotel sustained them for some time, but political unrest in New Mexico in 1837 caused them to return to Missouri. They took with them two formerly captive women they had ransomed from Comanches.

When Kentucky trader Samuel Magoffin, whose trade business had made him familiar with travel on the Santa Fe Trail, set out for Santa Fe again in June 1846, he asked his young wife, Susan Shelby Magoffin, to accompany him. Only eighteen years old at the onset of their journey from Independence, Missouri, Susan Magoffin kept a diary of her trip, which offers rich insights into the rigors of travel over such a distance into lands that were unfamiliar, particularly to a young woman of society. Following behind the Army of the West, which had been tasked to raise the American flag in the Southwest and bring the land under American control from Mexico, the Magoffins reached Santa Fe on August 31, 1846. Susan Shelby Magoffin appreciated the beauty of the land they crossed, writing of "mountains far more lofty than any I've seen, deep [valleys] below that looked blue as great was the distance to them; the clouds seemed resting on the mountains around us. Oh, for the genius of an artist that I might pencil such scenes otherwise than in my memory." Sadly, Magoffin suffered on the trip, miscarrying in July at Bent's Fort in Colorado and later contracting yellow fever. After some time in Santa Fe, she continued with her husband down to Mexico.

Another account of travel over the Santa Fe Trail from a woman's point of view came from Marion Sloan Russell, who made a total of five journeys on the trail in her lifetime and left a poetic narrative of her travels. After Sloan's mother and stepfather separated when she was a child, her mother set out with young Mary and her brother on the trail—their first trip—in 1852. Although they intended to reach California, a robbery outside Albuquerque delayed them, and they decided instead to stay in New Mexico. In her narrative of the trip, written later, Sloan describes playing in the enclosure formed by the circled wagons in the evening, marveling at the many buffalo they saw, and huddling inside the wagon during the fierceness of storms on the prairie. "I remember so clearly the beauty of the earth," she recalls, "and how, as we bore westward, the deer and the antelope bounded away from us. There were miles and miles of buffalo grass, blue lagoons and blood-red sunsets and, once in a while, a little sod house on the lonely prairie—home of some hunter or trapper." In Santa Fe, Sloan's mother established a boarding house on the plaza. They went back to Kansas in 1856 but returned four years later, settling again in Santa Fe. Sloan later married an army officer, Lieutenant Richard D. Russell, and after some time at Fort Union and other places in northern New Mexico eventually settled with her husband on a cattle ranch near Trinidad, Colorado. She died there at age ninety-one.

409. Santa Rita Copper Mines

Location: Grant County. Just east of Hanover, at the junction of US 180 and NM 152. See map 5.

Marker text: Copper has been mined here since 1804. For five years, development by Francisco Manuel Elguea resulted in some 6,000,000 pounds of copper being transported annually to Mexico City by mule train. Brief periods of activity were halted by Apache opposition until the coming of the railroad in the 1880s, when the area became a major copper producer.

Among the earliest worked and most vibrantly producing mines in New Mexico is the Santa Rita copper mine east of Silver City. Apaches hunting in the Mimbres and Black Range Mountains knew of copper outcroppings here since at least 1800, the year they relayed word of the deposits to Lieutenant José Manuel Carrasco of the Spanish military. After securing financial backing from Chihuahua entrepreneur Francisco Manuel Elguea, Carrasco petitioned the Spanish government for the Santa Rita del Cobre ("Saint Rita of the Copper") land grant, with dimensions encompassing the deposits. Carrasco then left the enterprise, selling out to Elguea in 1804.

Elguea used convicts, most of them transported from Mexico, to do the grunt work in the mine. One unsubstantiated estimate of the return reports that six million pounds of copper went south to Mexico City by mule train each year, although some historians believe that that number may be too large—and the mules too small! The copper was a commodity in the Royal Mint, Elguea having successfully lobbied officials in Mexico City to purchase his ores for coinage.

A unique fort around the mine provided some measure of defense and protection from Apache attacks while the men labored. As later described by the mapping expedition of John Russell Bartlett in 1851, the structure was

of triangular form, each side presenting a front of about 200 feet, with circular towers on the corners. It is built of adobe, with walls from three to four feet in thickness, and a single opening on the eastern side.

A replica of the Santa Rita fort stands now as a tourist attraction in nearby Pinos Altos.

Elguea died in 1809. Thereafter, Apache raids reduced efforts at Santa Rita to infrequent intervals. Mining continued in the late nineteenth century with the pacification of the region and the arrival of the Santa Fe Railway into southwestern New Mexico. Around that time, the outbuildings of the mine formed the beginnings of a small village, which took the name Santa Rita.

The modern history of the Santa Rita district began when the Kennecott Copper Corporation purchased the mines in 1909. Kennecott expanded the workings into a large, open pit, which produces to this day. As previously cloistered tunnels were breached in the expansion, workers at times uncovered the gruesome skeletal remains of Elguea's convict laborers within.

Over time, the excavations eventually engulfed the adjacent village of Santa Rita.

Today, the Santa Rita mining operations are owned and operated by Freeport-McMoRan Copper and Gold. Although the town of Santa Rita is gone, the exclusive Babies Born in Space Club is open to those who came into the world in the cradle of the old Santa Rita Hospital—now open "space." The club roster includes Harrison "Jack" Schmitt, former astronaut and US senator for New Mexico, and Ralph Kiner, inductee in the Baseball Hall of Fame.

More to explore: Bayard, Kneeling Nun, Pinos Altos, Silver City

410. Santa Rosa

Location: 1. Guadalupe County. At the west end of Santa Rosa, in a pullout on the south side of the Interstate 40 business loop (US 84 / Historic Route 66), near the intersection of River Road and the Interstate 40 business loop. See map 3.

2. Guadalupe County. At the west end of Santa Rosa, in a pullout on the south side of the Interstate 40 business loop (US 84 / Historic Route 66), just before the Interstate 40 interchange. See map 3.

Marker text: The Spanish explorer Antonio de Espejo passed through this area in 1583, as did Gaspar Castaño de Sosa in 1590. Santa Rosa, the Guadalupe County seat, was laid out on the ranch of Celso Baca y Baca, a politician and rancher in the late 1800s. It was named for his wife, Doña Rosa.

If travelers occasionally find themselves lost in Santa Rosa, they can take comfort in knowing they are not the first. In December 1590, Gaspar Castaño de Sosa led a colonizing expedition north into what is now New Mexico from Mexico. After passing near present-day Santa Rosa and camping to the north, members of the hopeful new colony, as noted by the expedition's chronicler, "expressed the opinion that we had lost our way." Castaño comforted them, at which "some were content and others were incredulous." Although the colonists eventually continued on their way, Spanish officials arrested a contrite Castaño the following year for leading an unlicensed expedition and returned him to Mexico. Seven years before Castaño's visit, Spanish explorer Antonio de Espejo had also passed near Santa Rosa—although in the opposite direction. Espejo was returning southward to Mexico along the Pecos River from an expedition to rescue two Franciscan priests who had stayed behind from an earlier excursion.

Settlement here began around 1865 with the arrival of don Celso Baca y Baca, who may have been drawn to the area for its natural artesian springs—legend says he chose to settle in this part of east-central New Mexico in hopes that his sickly daughter would find curative benefit in those waters. Baca established a ranch on nearby El Rito Creek and named the small community that developed around it Santa Rosa. That was the name of his wife, doña Rosa Viviana Baca y Baca, as well as the name of the chapel he built in the community, the Capilla de Santa Rosa, or "Chapel of Saint Rose."

The town of Santa Rosa developed quickly with the arrival of the Chicago, Rock Island, and Pacific Railroad in 1902. A pamphlet written that year by the New Mexico state government described the settlement thus:

Santa Rosa is a prosperous and growing railroad, trade and stock center with a population of 1,000. It has two weekly newspapers, a bank, several churches, the Roman Catholic, Baptist and Methodist denominations being represented, railroad shops and round houses.

By 1907, Santa Rosa had acquired enough influence to replace Puerto de Luna as the county seat of Guadalupe County. Arable soil made the county a "Mecca for land hungry farmers," according to a 1908 article in the *Santa Fe New Mexican*. Depression-era projects revitalized the natural artesian springs bubbling here, notably the eighty-one-foot-deep Blue Hole. Santa Rosa continues to promote its springs by dubbing itself "the City of Lakes."

More to explore: *Castaño de Sosa's Route, Espejo's Expedition, Espejo's Trail, Puerto de Luna, Santa Rosa Lake State Park*

411. Santa Rosa Lake State Park

Location: Guadalupe County. At the north side of Santa Rosa toward the lake, in a pullout on the east side of NM 91 between mile markers 0 and 1. See map 3.

Marker text: Pronghorn antelope may be seen grazing near this reservoir on the Pecos River at the edge of the Llano Estacado—the famed "Stockaded Plains." The park offers water sports; fishing for catfish, bass, and walleyes; camping; picnicking sites; a visitor center and a boat ramp.

412. Louis S. Page and Joe O. Page Highway

Location: Guadalupe County. In Santa Rosa, in a parking lot area just north of the intersection of South Second Street and the Interstate 40 business loop (US 84, also called Parker Avenue). See map 3.

Note: This Marker contains no faceplate text other than the title of the sign.

New Mexico Highway 91 begins from just past the Interstate 40 underpass at the north end of Santa Rosa (connecting from North Eighth Street). Leading northward out of the boundaries of Santa Rosa itself, the highway curves to the east and then travels northwestward for about nine miles, ending at Santa Rosa Lake State Park. Along the way, the road travels through a sparse but beautifully scenic landscape of relatively flat, unbroken desert grassland so common in Guadalupe County and this part of eastern New Mexico.

Along its course, the highway parallels the Pecos River, always about a mile and a half to the west, until the highway and river cross at the edge of Santa Rosa Lake. This land was home to Comanches and other Indians until the late nineteenth century. Visitors are likely to see antelope grazing on the grasslands leading to Santa Rosa Lake State Park.

This stretch of highway has been named the Louis S. Page and Joe O. Page Memorial Highway. The designation commemorates New Mexico state senators Louis S. Page and his son, Joe O. Page, both from Santa Rosa. The senior Page represented Guadalupe County in the New Mexico legislature in the 1950s and 1960s. His son, a former elementary school principal, was elected to the New Mexico Senate in 1988 and also represented Guadalupe County, as well as De Baca and San Miguel Counties. Both were Democrats. Sadly, Joe Page died in office less than a year after his swearing in. A heart attack claimed his life on September 25, 1989. He was fifty-four years old.

More to explore: *Comanche Country, Ken Towle Park*

413. Seton Village

Location: Santa Fe County. Southeast of Santa Fe, in a pullout on the west side of NM 300 (Old Las Vegas Highway), near the intersection of NM 300 and County Road 58 (Seton Village Road). See map 2.

Marker text: Ernest Thompson Seton (1860–1946), naturalist, artist, writer, authority on Indian lore, and first Chief Scout of the Boy Scouts of America, lived here during the last part of his life. The village includes his home, art collection, library, and Indian museum.

Ernest Thompson Seton became one of the leading naturalists in the country and was a founder of the Boy Scouts of America. The expansive home he built near Santa Fe was the manifestation of his love for the outdoors. Ernest Thompson Seton, on bench. Photo by Bain News Service, Library of Congress, Prints and Photographs Division, George Grantham Bain Collection, LC-B2-455-10.

At age fourteen, young Ernest Thompson Seton founded what he called the Robin Hood Club with friends. It was the first of many efforts at formalizing and sharing his love for the outdoors, a passion that would later culminate in making Seton one of the most prominent naturalist leaders in the United States.

Born in England on August 14, 1860, Ernest Seton moved to Canada with his family at age ten. After studying art on scholarship at the Royal Academy in London, Seton traveled to the United States on exploratory trips, experiencing firsthand the variety of the natural world he had loved from an early age. In 1902, Seton founded the League of Woodcraft Indians in Connecticut. The club was intended, as Seton later explained, to "teach the outdoor life for its worth in the building up of the body and the helping and strengthening of the soul." When Seton met with other like-minded individuals, including Lord Robert Baden-Powell, who had formed an outdoor youth corps in England, his ideas merged with those of the budding scouting movement, leading to the establishment of the Boy Scouts of America. Seton served as the first Chief Scout in the United States and helped write the first Boy Scout manual.

At the same time, Seton continued to spread his naturalist message through lectures, paintings, and published works, including a total of forty-two books. Characteristic of his writing is the 1898 *Wild Animals I Have Known*, offering first-person narratives of his encounters with various animals, like the wolf Lobo, the "King of Currumpaw" (a ranch in New Mexico), and Raggylug, a cottontail rabbit. Many of the stories gave the animals anthropomorphic traits, including human-like emotions and intent. "The real personality of the individual, and his view of life are my theme," Seton wrote, "rather than the ways of the race in general, as viewed by a casual and hostile human eye." Other similar books included *The Biography of a Grizzly* and *Animal Heroes*. He also produced guide books—often influenced by Native American practices and traditions—such as *The Book of Woodcraft and Indian Lore* and *Sign Talk of the Cheyenne Indians*. Seton illustrated the books himself.

In 1930, Seton purchased land south of Santa Fe and constructed a "village" of his own making, where he lived with his wife. Centered around a forty-five-room stone edifice known as the "castle," which served as Seton's home as well as a library and instructional center, the property also included guesthouses, a craft shop, lodges, a museum, and other structures. Two of Seton's homes on the property were built around old railway cars. At Seton Village, Seton continued his promotion of outdoor life by hosting meetings of the American Woodcraft League and lecturing.

Ernest Thompson Seton died in his castle home at Seton Village in 1946, at age eighty-six.

Seton Village today is owned by the Academy for the Love of Learning, which acquired the property from Seton's daughter. Unfortunately, a devastating fire in 2005 destroyed Seton's castle, but the ruins have been preserved as a garden.

More to explore: Hyde Memorial State Park, Mary White, Pablita Velarde (see under Pueblo of Santa Clara), Philmont Scout Ranch

Settlements of the San Miguel del Vado Land Grant: *see San Miguel del Vado National Historic District*

414. Seven Rivers Cemetery

Location: Eddy County. South of Artesia, in the Earl Boulden Park Rest Area on the west side of US 285 at mile marker 61. See map 6.

Marker text: Seven Rivers was located south of Artesia near the confluence of seven branches of a stream that flowed into the Pecos River. Settled in the mid-1860s, the town flourished as a trading post and refuge for participants in the Lincoln County War. The community declined until only the cemetery was left. When Brantley Dam was constructed in 1988 the cemetery was relocated behind Twin Oaks Memorial Park north of Artesia.

Now completely vanished under the waters of Brantley Lake, the community of Seven Rivers is a ghost town of a ghost town. Yet for many years, the small settlement was a key player in some of the epic sagas of southeastern New Mexico, including the historic cattle drives of the western frontier, as well as the infamous Lincoln County War.

Although a small community had existed here as early as the late 1860s, attacks by hostile Indian bands hampered the growth of the settlement until the early 1870s. By that time, a small trading post and a collection of ranches here were taking advantage of their location along the famous Goodnight-Loving Trail to cater to cowboys moving cattle along the Pecos River to markets at Fort Sumner and other points north of here. More homesteaders arrived, and the small community they formed took the pleasant name Seven Rivers, for a series of streams and stream branches that converged nearby.

In 1875, cattleman John Chisum established his sprawling South Spring Ranch near Roswell, grazing his herds throughout the Pecos Valley. Chisum was partners with Charles Goodnight and Oliver Loving as well as merchants and ranchers Alexander McSween and John Tunstall of Lincoln, New Mexico, about a hundred miles northwest of here. (Seven Rivers was, at the time, part of the then much larger Lincoln County, which encompassed the entire lower southeastern corner of New Mexico.) Those associations put Chisum at odds with the economic faction headed by Lawrence G. Murphy and James J. Dolan, merchants in Lincoln and suppliers of cattle to fulfill the government contract for Fort Sumner—and the chief rivals to McSween and Tunstall.

Meanwhile, Seven Rivers rancher Henry "Hugh" Beckwith, one of the earliest to settle in Seven Rivers, organized what became known as the Seven Rivers Warriors. The Warriors were a group of local ranchers and residents based mostly in Seven Rivers, all hostile to Chisum for his prominent cattle holdings and his usurpation of the open range, which left little grazing land available for their own livestock. The Warriors, whose members included Lincoln County deputy sheriff Bob Beckwith, who was Hugh's brother, as well as US Deputy Marshal Robert Olinger, aligned with Murphy and Dolan in Lincoln. Chisum suspected, probably correctly, that rustlers aligned with or aided by the Warriors were stealing his cattle and selling them to Murphy and Dolan.

This could only end badly.

Following the murder of John Tunstall on February 18, 1878, a series of reprisals and Old West–style revenge killings broke out throughout Lincoln County between the Murphy-Dolan faction and their supporters, including members of the Seven Rivers Warriors, against the Tunstall-McSween-Chisum faction, which included Billy the Kid, a ranch hand to John Tunstall. The fracas has become known to history as the Lincoln County War. The fighting culminated in a weeklong gunfight in the streets of Lincoln in July 1878. Members of the Seven Rivers Warriors were present and took part in the hostilities. When it was over, Alexander McSween, Deputy Bob Beckwith, and several others were dead.

The lawlessness did not stop in Lincoln—in fact, it seemed to follow the Warriors back to Seven Rivers, with several members later turning their anger (and their shotguns) against one another. But the shootout on the streets of Lincoln did mark a turning point in the hostilities. New Mexico governor Lew Wallace pardoned all the participants except Billy the Kid. It was during a jailbreak from the Lincoln County jail in Lincoln in April 1881 that the Kid gunned down another Warriors member, Deputy Marshal Robert Olinger.

As peace returned to Lincoln County, the village of Seven Rivers developed commercially. Stores, a restaurant and hotel, and a saloon soon opened, and a townsite was platted in 1886. The community at that time was home to some three hundred people. Three years later, when Eddy County was created, Seven Rivers was named the county seat. But before a courthouse could even be built, a vote the following year moved the county seat to the upstart settlement of Eddy, south of Seven Rivers. Eddy, today known as Carlsbad, still retains the county seat. The rise of Carlsbad came at the expense of Seven Rivers, and the settlement was soon abandoned.

The story of Seven Rivers has an interesting epilogue. Although the town itself was gone by 1900, the cemetery remained. Knowing that the reservoir created by the construction of Brantley Dam would immerse the graves, the US Bureau of Reclamation in 1988 undertook a project to relocate the entire cemetery. A report on the effort by the Bureau of Reclamation at the conclusion of the project details the process undertaken. The bureau first surveyed the site to locate and identify as many graves as possible, then notified the next of kin of the need to relocate the bodies. Beginning in January 1988, bodies were carefully exhumed, forty-five in total, and with great care and respect moved to a patch of land at the back of the Twin Oaks Memorial Park in nearby Artesia. That small patch could be considered a replica of the Seven Rivers cemetery, as care was taken to reinter the bodies in the same relative places and orientations to one another as they were when originally buried. Headstones were repaired where possible and placed with the deceased, with markers reading "Unknown" for those whose identities could not be determined.

As part of the relocation effort, archaeologists conducted forensic analysis to learn what the dead had to reveal about life in Seven Rivers. Sadly, many of the graves are those of infants or young children, victims of diphtheria or other diseases. In addition, the report noted, "a striking number of deaths were caused by violence"—most of that brought about by knife or gun wounds. The bodies included one known member of the Seven Rivers Warriors, William H. Johnson. They also included Wilson S. Keith, killed by Indians near Seven Rivers while on a cattle drive in 1873.

A stone memorial marks the site of the Seven Rivers Cemetery within the Twin Oaks Cemetery. The names of the dead and their birth and death dates, where known, are listed. Of these pioneers, the memorial reads, in part: "All played a part in settling a last frontier."

In remembrance of the pleasantly named town with a rough-and-tumble past, the stretch of US 285 between Artesia and Carlsbad has been named the Seven Rivers Highway.

More to explore: *Artesia, Carlsbad, Fort Sumner and Fort Sumner State Monument (series), Lincoln, Roswell*

415. Shakespeare

Location: Hidalgo County. Just west of Lordsburg, in the New Mexico Tourist Information Center, exit 20A off Interstate 10 (reachable from Lordsburg by driving along West Motel Boulevard over the interstate). See map 5.

Marker text: Located at the north end of the Pyramid Mountains, near the old stage stop at Mexican Springs, Shakespeare was first known as Pyramid Station. Later named Ralston, a diamond swindle caused its collapse in 1874. The town was revived as Shakespeare in 1879, named for the Shakespeare silver mining company, but the economic depression of 1893 closed the mines and made it a ghost town.

416. Women of Shakespeare
Emma Marble Muir (1873–1959), Rita Wells Hill (1901–1985), Janaloo Hill Hough (1939–2005)

Location: Hidalgo County. Just west of Lordsburg, in the New Mexico Tourist Information Center, exit 20A off Interstate 10 (reachable from Lordsburg by driving along West Motel Boulevard over the interstate). See map 5.

Marker text: Emma Marble Muir arrived at the mining town of Shakespeare in 1882. She and her daughter, Rita Wells Muir, learned to appreciate and preserve the town's history. Rita and her husband bought Shakespeare as part of their ranch in 1935. Rita passed the ranch to her daughter, Janaloo Hill Hough.

Janaloo and her husband continued fighting for the history and preservation of Shakespeare. Investing their own resources, they rebuilt some of the buildings destroyed by a fire in 1997. Without the dedication of this mother, daughter and granddaughter, the ghost town of Shakespeare would not exist today.

When prospectors discovered silver in the Burro Mountains in 1869, a small camp of adobe buildings developed near the local watering hole known as Mexican Springs. The location had only a year before been visited by John Evensen and Jack Frost, workers for the National Mail and Transportation Company, who established a stage stop at the springs. The silver strike soon attracted the attentions of William C. Ralston, founder of the Bank of California. Ralston made elaborate claims about the richness of the mines here and backed them financially by attracting outside investors. Ralston renamed the settlement at Mexican Springs after himself: Ralston.

By 1871, improperly filed claims and sparse returns had undermined Ralston's investment and emaciated the population of his town. Salvation arrived, so it seemed, in the fall of 1872, when prospectors Philip Arnold and John Slack visited William Ralston in California holding a bag of diamonds and rubies and claiming to have stumbled on a mountain full of such gems at a southwestern location they would not disclose. Ralston convinced the men to lead a party of mining experts, all blindfolded, to verify the discovery. When the men returned with tales of diamonds scattered on the ground, eager miners flooded the community of Ralston, knowing of its association with William Ralston and thus believing it to be the site of the jackpot. But surveyor Clarence King, who had earlier explored the region as the head of one of the four Great Surveys undertaken by the government in the 1860s, suspected cunning. King discovered the magic mountain to be east of Salt Lake City, nowhere close to Ralston, and, even worse, he learned that some of the supposedly raw diamonds had already been cut! Newspapers later reported that Arnold and Slack had purchased inferior gemstones in Amsterdam, then spread them over the ground in deceit—even going so far as to push diamonds into anthills. The most innocent victim of the swindle, the town of Ralston, suffered a sharp drop in population as miners left to stake their hopes (and claims) elsewhere. The town was nearly deserted by 1875, the same year William Ralston's Bank of California collapsed and Ralston himself drowned in San Francisco Bay. It's not clear whether his drowning was an accident or suicide.

Although off to a rocky start, the community of Ralston nonetheless did sit within an area rich in silver, and in April 1879 English mining engineer Colonel William G. Boyle and his brother, General John Boyle, reorganized the community. The brothers formed the Shakespeare Gold and Silver Mining Company and changed the name of the town to Shakespeare. Main Street became Avon Avenue, and the hotel was named the Stratford, after the birthplace of their literary patron, Stratford-upon-Avon. The Bard's namesake town grew to include three saloons, an assay office, and a store, and by 1880 was home to one hundred residents. Among the notable people to visit during the boom years was Lew Wallace, governor of New Mexico from 1878 to 1881 and author of the novel *Ben-Hur*, who came at least once to check on his mining interests.

From this point, the history of Shakespeare is taken up by three remarkable women, without whom its history—and perhaps its very existence—might have been lost forever.

It begins with the arrival of young Emma Marble, who came to Shakespeare with her family in 1882 after her parents bought the old National Mail and Transportation Company stage stop from John Evensen. As a child, she learned of the history of the town from Evensen, who had witnessed most of that history firsthand. Marble later married local rancher, state representative, and president of the First National Bank of Lordsburg, John T. Muir. While teaching in local schools, Emma Marble Muir also researched and wrote about the history of the town of Shakespeare. During this time, the mines around Shakespeare played out, and the devaluation of silver in 1893 caused by the country adopting the gold standard ended mining activity in the town. The budding railroad community of Lordsburg, two miles south, drained the remaining residents, and Shakespeare was on its way to becoming a ghost town.

When the town was sold again in 1935, Muir

befriended the new owners, Rita Wells Hill and Frank Hill. The Hill family, including daughter Janaloo, lovingly restored much of the town and also came to appreciate its history. Much of that history was shared with them by Muir before she passed away in February 1959.

Rita Wells Hill, who had appeared in silent films earlier in her life, once again found herself in the spotlight when the State Highway Department selected a portion of the land owned by the Hills near Shakespeare for a highway interchange in the early 1970s. After exhausting other legal measures to prevent the seizure of her land, Hill, then in her seventies, built a small shack near the site of the interchange and stayed inside it, refusing orders to leave and causing a local headline to declare: "Lady's Intransigence Baffles N.M. Officials." Hill ultimately lost the battle, and the interchange was put into place. She passed away in 1985.

Janaloo Hill, her daughter, carried forward the mantle of Shakespeare and the strong will of the women associated with it. With her husband, Manny Hough, Hill maintained the town, captured and recorded its history, and led tours for visitors. After a devastating fire gutted some of the buildings in the town in 1997, she and her husband restored the structures. Janaloo Hill Hough passed away in 2005.

The town these women preserved and loved so much remains open to the public today.

More to explore: *Carthage-Tokay-Farley, Dawson, Elizabethtown, Lordsburg, Riley*

417. Shalam Colony (1884–1907)

Location: Doña Ana County. North of Las Cruces, at the intersection of US 185 and County Road D052 (Shalam Colony Trail), between mile markers 5 and 6 on US 185. See map 5.

Marker text: In 1884, Shalam Colony was established on the banks of the Rio Grande near the village of Doña Ana by John Ballou Newbrough and a group of Utopian followers called Faithists. Newbrough's "Book of Shalam" set forth a plan for gathering the outcast and orphaned children of the world and raising them to be the spiritual leaders of a new age. Shalam Colony was closed in 1901.

One morning in 1881, New York dentist John Ballou Newbrough was startled to see what he believed was an otherworldly glow of light on the back of his hands. The light, which Newbrough felt was inspired by angels, directed his hands to a typewriter, and he began typing, "very vigorously," for about a half hour. The same thing happened the next morning, according to Newbrough, and the next, and the next, for almost a year. The result was a nine-hundred-page illustrated tract that would enter the annals of revelation-based religious literature and inspire a colony of religious-minded followers to found a spiritual community off the banks of the Rio Grande just north of Doña Ana: Shalam Colony.

Born in Ohio on June 5, 1828, Newbrough worked his way through medical school to become a dentist before taking a quick sojourn west as a gold rush prospector. Returning to New York, he opened his own dental practice, where he often treated poor patients for free. Newbrough dabbled in spiritualism, before the guiding light moved his hands over the typewriter keys and his life changed forever.

Newbrough's marathon automatic writing sessions resulted in a holy book he called *Oahspe*. The name was said to be a combination of short words from a forgotten language, with *O* representing the earth, *ah* representing air, and *spe* representing spirit. Soon after the publication of the book

Founded by adherents known as Faithists, Shalam Colony was intended to serve as a refuge for the raising and care of orphaned children and to function as a utopian colony. It was in operation for more than fifteen years. New Mexico State University Library, Archives and Special Collections.

in 1882, adherents to the new text arose, calling themselves Faithists. They vowed to forgo liquor, live passively, and devote their industry to the service of others. At the first convention of Faithists in 1883, adherents in particular elected to follow a directive given in the *Oahspe Book of Shalam*. That scripture instructed the Faithists to create a utopian refuge for children orphaned or abandoned by Uzans (non-Faithists), and raise them as a new generation of sinless leaders:

8. *Now, I pray Thee, O Father, what shall thy servant do?*
9. *Jehovih answered Tae, saying: Go, seek, and bring out of Uz orphan babes and castaway infants and foundlings.*
10. *And these shall be thy colony, which shall be My new kingdom on earth.*

John Newbrough himself was among those who arrived in New Mexico in 1884 to establish that new colony on land that Newbrough had bought along the banks of the Rio Grande near Doña Ana. With help from Doña Ana residents, who worked with them to raise adobe buildings and irrigate their fields, and aided by wealthy patrons, including Massachusetts wool merchant Andrew H. Howland, Newbrough's small parish soon took shape. Known as Shalam Colony, the communal village included a church known as the Temple of Tae, a large forty-room dormitory for the Faithists known as the Fraternum, a separate dormitory for the children called the Children's House, and several other buildings. The colony also contained fields of vegetables and a fruit orchard, sales from which supplied income to the community.

In 1887, John Newbrough married another

Faithist adherent, Frances van de Water Sweet. Together, the couple traveled to major cities, including Kansas City, Chicago, and New Orleans, where they collected abandoned and unwanted babies and brought them back to New Mexico. The children, boys and girls alike, were of all races. At its height, Shalam Colony had about fifty children, all of whom received instruction in Faithist practices, along with art, history, and other disciplines. They were given new names, taken from the texts of *Oahspe*.

Newbrough succumbed to a bout of pneumonia in April 1891, leaving his colony in the hands of Andrew Howland, the principal financier. Howland married Newbrough's widow two years later. The two maintained the colony for a period of time thereafter, even adding a second small "suburb" known as Levitica to house additional residents. That enterprise did not last, however, as residents there quarreled and caused other problems, forcing Howland to send them away.

Eventually, the cost of keeping operations going at Shalam Colony grew burdensome. Apparently, too, the children proved challenging, especially as they reached their teenage years. After placing the remaining children into families or other orphanages, Howland and his family sold the grounds and moved to El Paso.

Shalam Colony, the utopia on the Rio Grande, ended in 1901.

More to explore: *Doña Ana, Las Cruces*

418. Ship Rock

Location: San Juan County. On the west side of US 491 near the junction with Indian Road 13. See map 1.

Marker text: This huge volcanic neck was formed in Pliocene time, over 3,000,000 years ago. It rises 1700 feet above the surrounding plain and is famed in the legends of the Navajo as "Sa bit tai e" (the rock with the wings). They hold that it was the great bird that brought them from the north.

419. Ghost Marker: Shiprock

Marker text: This area has been part of the Navajo homeland for centuries. The town of Shiprock is named for the great peak nearby, which figures importantly in Navajo legend. Early in the 20th century, Shiprock was made headquarters of the Northern Navajo Agency.

Note: The Historic Marker for the town of Shiprock is missing. The name of the town is spelled as one word, while the volcanic neck is two. See map 1.

Ship Rock may be the most recognized geologic feature in northwestern New Mexico; it is certainly one of the most enchanting. This striking, 1,700-foot spire is a textbook case of a volcanic neck. That neck began to form some three million years ago. When the fervid anger of the earth could no longer be contained, the volcano that would produce Ship Rock erupted, sometimes trembling so violently in its fury that its dome cracked and lava roared out the sides. In the fiery discharge, lava oozed upward through the conduit, or neck, of the volcano and out its vent. As lava still inside the neck cooled, it solidified into towering magma pillars imprisoning the shape of their upward thrust. Over millions of years, weathering denuded the outer form of the volcano, leaving only the interior—solidified, Pliocene-epoch rage.

Perceptions of Ship Rock have varied throughout New Mexico history. In the cosmology of the

Navajo Indians, Ship Rock is the vestige of a giant bird. Many years ago, that bird carried Navajos in flight from the north, where they once lived, to the Four Corners region. Because of its place in their beliefs, Navajos know Ship Rock by a name that means "winged rock." Those wings are the elongated volcanic ridges extending outward from the core. Called dikes, these ridges formed when lava flowed through cracks in the volcano and later solidified.

Still other perceptions were laid over the great rock when Spanish and Anglo settlers first saw its towering hulk. Many likened the spires to a Gothic cathedral or to a large pipe organ. To most, though, the landform resembled a landlocked desert windjammer. In its tortured face, many saw rigging, masts, and sails unfurled in the warm breeze. That perception has been preserved in the name, Ship Rock.

The nearby community of Shiprock takes its name from the rock, but blending the words. It began in 1903 as the site of the Northern Navajo Indian Agency, established here by the US government to serve the Indians of the Navajo Nation. Now under the auspices of the Bureau of Indian Affairs, the Shiprock Agency continues today.

More to explore: *Capulin Volcano National Monument, Colorado Plateau, Navajo Indian Reservation, Wagon Mound*

420. Sierra Blanca

Location: Otero County. Between Ruidoso Downs and Mescalero, in a pullout on the east side of US 70, between mile markers 253 and 254. See map 6.

Marker text: Sierra Blanca, a complex ancient volcano, rises more than 7,300 feet above Tularosa Basin to peak at 12,003 feet. Vertical geologic movement between ranges and basin is about 2 miles. San Andres Mountains on west side of Tularosa Basin are uplifted on east side and tilted westward. Elevation 4,670 feet.

Note: The highest point of Sierra Blanca has been remeasured to 11,973 feet.

Reaching an imposing 11,973 feet, Sierra Blanca is the highest summit in the Sacramento Mountains and the highest mountain in southern New Mexico. Sierra Blanca lives up to its translated epithet, "White Mountain," by remaining capped with snow until late summer.

Sierra Blanca rises more than seven thousand feet from the floor of the Tularosa Basin. The basin is a large, flat expanse of sunken land cradled on the west by the San Andres Mountains and on the east by the Sacramentos. The mountains and basin are related by membership in the Basin and Range Province, a vast region of north-south-tending mountain ranges interspersed with broad, flat valleys. The Tularosa Valley lies within the even larger Rio Grande Rift, an elongated stretch of sunken earth that formed millions of years ago as land through the center of the state pulled apart along fault lines. The San Andres Mountains to the west are likewise members of the rift. They are uplifted on the east side to tilt westward.

Sierra Blanca is a complex volcano, but understanding it need not be. A complex volcano is simply a series of multiple flows, ash layers, and domes, with two or more vents. Sierra Blanca last erupted about thirty-five million years ago.

Mescalero Apaches consider the mountain, a portion of which lies on their reservation, to be sacred.

More to explore: *Basin and Range Country, Rio Grande Rift, Tularosa*

421. Sierra Grande

Location: Union County. In highway rest area on north side of US 64, at mile marker 392. See map 3.

Marker text: Largest extinct volcano in northeastern New Mexico. Sierra Grande rises to an elevation of 8,720 feet, one of many volcanoes, cinder cones, and flows that cover more than 1,000 square miles of area in northeastern New Mexico and southeastern Colorado eastward to the Oklahoma state line.

Sierra Grande rises to a respectable 8,270 feet, making it the largest extinct volcano in northeastern New Mexico and one of the largest in the state.

The gently sloping leviathan is a shield volcano, formed when lava escaped from its central vent and hardened into the shape of a dome. Sierra Grande never has reason to feel lonely: Union County alone is home to more than eighty volcanoes. They are part of an extensive region of lava flows and cinder cones (mountains formed when ash and pebble-size cinders coalesce around a volcanic vent to form a circular or oval dome) known as the Raton-Clayton Volcanic Field. Covering more than a thousand square miles, the volcanic field stretches into southeastern Colorado and eastward to the Oklahoma state line. It includes nearby Capulin Volcano National Monument, itself an extinct cinder cone.

More to explore: *Capulin Volcano National Monument, Malpais, Ship Rock*

422. Silver City

Location: Grant County. At the west end of Silver City, on the east side of US 180, between mile markers 111 and 112. See map 5.

Marker text: Silver City is located in the midst of rich mineral deposits. The Santa Rita Copper Mines, opened in 1805, were the second such mine operating in what is now the U.S. A silver strike in 1870 began the commercial mining for which the area is still known. The Apache chiefs Victorio, Geronimo and Mangas Coloradas figure in its history.

423. Ghost Marker: Mangas Coloradas

Marker text: Mangas Coloradas (Spanish for Red Sleeves) was a chief of the Mimbreño Apaches, who derived their name from the nearby Mimbres Mountains. Mangas Coloradas, a contemporary of legendary Apache chiefs Victorio and Cochise, led his people during the 1850s until he was captured near Pinos Altos in 1863. He was killed the night of January 18, 1863, while being held prisoner at Fort McLane, near present-day Hurley.

Note: This Marker may have once been located somewhere in Grant County but has since gone missing. See map 5.

424. Ghost Marker: Old Silver City "Memory Lane" (Established ca. 1882)

Marker text: In this pioneer cemetery, still in use today, lie the remains of early settlers, merchants, miners, politicians and railroad men who contributed to the development of southwestern New Mexico. Among those buried here are Kathrine Antrim (1829–1874), mother of Billy the Kid; Ben V. Lilly (1853–1936), renowned hunter and guide for Theodore Roosevelt; John Bullard (1841–1871), town founder; and Leonidas S. Lytle (1846–1924), Medal of Honor recipient in 1875.

Note: Although appearing in a state inventory, this Historic Marker was apparently never built. See map 5.

The history of mining near present-day Silver City dates to the early 1800s, when Chihuahua entrepreneur Francisco Manuel Elguea opened the nearby Santa Rita copper mines to provide copper for the Royal Mint in Mexico City. Elguea's mines produced millions of pounds of copper a year. According to a report from the US Geological Survey in 1910, Santa Rita ranked "next to the Lake Superior district of Michigan as the earliest known important copper district within the territory now included in the United States."

This migration of miners and settlers into the region incensed the native Apaches. In retaliation for the loss of their camping grounds, Apache leaders like Geronimo, Victorio, and Mangas Coloradas led raids to harass miners and their enterprises. Mangas Coloradas, whose name translates from Spanish to "Red Sleeves," was a chief of the Mimbreño Apache tribe. The name comes from the Mimbres River to the east of Silver City. On the night of January 18, 1863, Mangas Coloradas was shot by soldiers while meeting to arrange a truce with American troops at the now vanished Fort McLane fifteen miles south of Silver City.

About six years later, in early 1869, Missouri-born brothers John and James Bullard began to farm a small plot of land in Cienega Marsh while residing in nearby Pinos Altos. John Bullard identified outcroppings of silver near his farm. Bullard formed a new community around his strike and named it for his discovery: Silver City. Bullard did not live to see his new town grow; on July 11, 1871, in a rancorous frame of mind, he stormed an Apache camp along the Gila River to avenge an attack on his town. Indians shot him through the heart with an arrow and killed him.

The community Bullard left behind, however, flourished. In 1874, its growing prosperity as the commercial center for mining efforts in the Black Range Mountains made it a natural choice for the county seat of Grant County. A report that year by Rossiter Raymond, commissioner of mining statistics, described the community and its architectural progress this way:

It has a population of about one thousand, consisting chiefly of miners and their families, although most of the trades and professions are well represented. Some of the buildings of Silver City will compare favorably with those of larger towns in the East. Brick is being extensively manufactured, and that material will be used almost exclusively for building purposes in the future.

One by one, the great Apache leaders succumbed to the nineteenth century. Mexican citizens trapped Victorio in a canyon in Chihuahua on October 15, 1880, and killed him. Geronimo surrendered to the US Army in 1886 and was moved to a reservation. With their passing, attacks on settlers in Silver City declined.

When heavy rains sent a twelve-foot-high wave crashing through town in 1895, and a second flood just eight years later wiped out much of what the first had left behind, Main Street in Silver City became a twenty-five-foot-deep gulch. Residents moved Main Street to Bullard Street, one block north, and had the Civilian Conservation Corps reinforce the sides of the gulch with masonry walls in 1935. They even gave it a name, San Vicente Arroyo. It is today known affectionately as the Big Ditch and is one of the prominent attractions in town.

Silver City is home to Western New Mexico University, founded in 1893.

Many of the players in the history of Silver City and surrounding region now rest at Memory Lane Cemetery at the east end of town. John Bullard, the town founder, is here, as is Ben Lilly, who developed a reputation as a mountain lion hunter in the Gila Wilderness and who once led President Theodore Roosevelt on a hunt. Catherine Antrim, the mother of Billy the Kid, also lies here, quite a distance from her son's grave in Fort Sumner, New Mexico. The cemetery also holds the grave of the US Army's First Sergeant Leonidas S. Lytle, recipient of the Medal of Honor in 1875 for "services against hostile Indians."

More to explore: Bayard, Ladies Auxiliary of Local 890, Pinos Altos, Santa Rita Copper Mines

425. Sisters of Charity

Location: Santa Fe County. Fifteen miles south of Santa Fe, in the Bicentennial Rest Area and Visitors Center, on the east side of Interstate 25. (The rest area is also known as the La Bajada Rest Area.) See map 2.

Marker text: The first Sisters of Charity arrived in New Mexico Territory in 1865 from Cincinnati at the request of Bishop Lamy with the mission of serving all people regardless of race, religion or ability to pay. Hundreds of sisters followed. They established some of the most significant institutions of the state including St. Vincent Hospital & Orphanage and St. Elizabeth Shelter for the Homeless in Santa Fe.

Sisters Pauline Leo and Vincent O'Keefe, Civil War nurses, with Sisters Theodosia Farn and Catherine Mallon arrived in Santa Fe in 1865.

Sister Mary de Sales Deleney, an Irish immigrant with an eighth-grade education, became the first woman doctor licensed in the Territory.

Sister Blandina Segale, an Italian immigrant, authored *At the End of the Santa Fe Trail.*

Hermana Dolores Chavez de Gutierrez, a New Mexico Territory native, became a benefactor of St. Vincent Hospital and Orphanage.

Note: The name of Sister Mary de Sales Leheney is misspelled on this Marker as "Deleney."

First by rail, then boat, then crowded into a stagecoach bumping its way over the western countryside, four members of the Sisters of Charity religious order traveled in the late summer of 1865 from Ohio to their new lives in Santa Fe. The Sisters of Charity, based in Cincinnati, had become well known across the country for the charitable care they gave to soldiers on the battlefields of the Civil War. As part of their mission, Sisters would travel to new locations around the country and establish orphanages, hospitals, and girls' schools. So, at the end of the Civil War, Santa Fe's bishop, Jean-Baptiste Lamy—who had earlier served in Cincinnati and was familiar with the Sisters—requested their presence in New Mexico as well, where he wanted their assistance opening hospitals and engaging in other charitable works.

Arriving in Santa Fe on September 13, 1865, were Sister Superior Vincent O'Keefe and Sister Pauline Leo, both of whom had previously served as Civil War nurses, along with Sister Theodosia Farn and Sister Catherine Mallon, the latter having only taken her vows the very morning the Sisters set out for New Mexico! The Sisters quickly realized that the Southwest was not like the land they had left. Sister Catherine had this to say about their new domicile, a modest adobe behind a small church that had formerly served as the home of the bishop himself:

Imagine the surprise of persons coming from places where houses are built with every convenience and sanitary device, suddenly to find themselves introduced into several oblong walls of adobes, looking like piled brick ready to burn, to enter which, instead of stepping up, you step down onto a mud floor; rafters supporting roof made of trunks of trees, the roof itself of earth which they were told had to be carefully attended, else the rain would pour in; door openings covered with blankets; the whole giving you a prison feeling. . . . Strangers to the country, the customs, and the language, do you wonder that a lonesome feeling as of lingering death came over them?

Notwithstanding such feelings, the Sisters quickly made New Mexico their home. Not yet a state, the territory of New Mexico had no official hospitals, and Bishop Lamy saw it as his charge to begin to establish them. In the very building that had once been Lamy's home, the Sisters in 1866 established Saint Vincent's Hospital and Orphanage—the first hospital in New Mexico. The facility was dedicated to serving the needy of all races and religions, without regard for the patient's ability to pay. In a sign of the times, the first orphan to be brought to the orphanage at the hospital was a small Navajo child rescued from a battlefield by Brigadier General James H. Carleton, commander of the military department of New Mexico. Later, the facility was expanded to include a second floor and an annex, and the small adobe church that stood behind it was replaced by the elegant Saint Francis Cathedral (today known as the Basilica Cathedral of Saint Francis of Assisi).

In a plot of land just next to that church, the Sisters also erected the large, French second empire–style building that housed Saint Vincent's Sanatorium, serving patients suffering from tuberculosis who came to New Mexico for the dry, mild climate of the Southwest. Unfortunately, the building burned on June 16, 1896. A new structure was built on the same spot after the turn of the century and reopened for the same purpose. Later, with tuberculosis on the decline, the building became a convent and was renamed Marian Hall.

The Sisters of Charity formed a strong bond with the Sisters of Loretto, who had also come to New Mexico at Bishop Lamy's request, to help establish new schools in the state.

Over time, the original four Sisters of Charity were joined by others. Sister Mary de Sales Leheney was an Irish immigrant from Cincinnati who joined the sisterhood in 1882. Despite having only an eighth-grade education and little work experience beyond her previous job in a shoe factory, Sister de Sales's work alongside surgeons at Saint Vincent's Hospital would lead to her being the first woman to receive (in 1901) a license to practice medicine in the territory of New Mexico. Sister Blandina Segale, who was born in Italy, moved with her family to the United States in 1854 and joined the Sisters of Charity at age sixteen. The letters she wrote of her experiences were later published as the semi-autobiographical *At the End of the Santa Fe Trail*, offering a firsthand account of the work of the Sisters of Charity in New Mexico. A number of local women also joined the order, including Hermana Dolores Chavez de Gutierrez, a native of Albuquerque, who joined at the age of sixty.

Although they received community support for their endeavors, including a stipend from General Carleton for care of his soldiers, the Sisters struggled with inadequate funds. To help finance their operations, all of which were nonprofit, the Sisters traveled (often on foot) among the booming mining camps around Santa Fe, where good times often meant some degree of fortune for the miners. In the camps, the Sisters solicited money for their cause.

Today, the legacy of Saint Vincent's Hospital continues as Christus Saint Vincent Regional Medical Center, although no longer under the auspices of the Sisters of Charity and in a different location. In the mid-1980s, the Sisters of Charity helped establish the current Saint Elizabeth Shelter in Santa Fe to serve homeless people. The park that fronted the old Saint Vincent's Sanatorium is today known as Cathedral Park.

More to explore: *Dr. Meta L. Christy, Mother Magdalen and the Sisters of Loretto, Santa Fe*

426. Site of San Augustin Springs

Location: Doña Ana County. Just east of Organ, in a pullout on the north side of US 70 at the base of the Organ Mountains. See map 5.

Marker text: Here on July 27, 1861, less than 300 Confederate troops intercepted 500 Union soldiers retreating from Fort Fillmore to Fort Stanton. Exhausted from the heat and famished for water, the Union troops straggled across the desert in a five-mile evacuation train. Unable to fight, Major Isaac Lynde surrendered his command without firing a single shot.

Before the outbreak of the Civil War, soldiers at Fort Fillmore, which stood a few miles south of Mesilla, occupied their time patrolling the Mesilla Valley for hostile Indians. In 1861, however, they faced a new enemy: a Confederate army.

In early summer, Confederate lieutenant colonel John Robert Baylor formed the Second Texas Mounted Rifles and marched his three-hundred-man regiment north from San Antonio, Texas, into New Mexico. His was an advance unit of the much larger Confederate force, led by Brigadier General Henry H. Sibley, that would follow about a half a year later to advance the Rebel plan to capture the Southwest. On the afternoon of July 25, Baylor reached Fort Fillmore. Rather than attack the fort outright, Baylor chose instead to enter and hold the nearby village of Mesilla, where sympathies ran decidedly Southern. In fact, residents there greeted the soldiers with a celebratory welcome.

Around five o'clock that afternoon, Union major Isaac Lynde, the post commander at Fort Fillmore, led eighty infantrymen and mounted riflemen, as well as cannons, to engage the Confederate army in the streets of Mesilla. Lynde sent a flag to the Texas forces with demands to surrender. Baylor responded: "We [will] fight first, and surrender afterward." Union troops met the challenge by firing a few rounds from their howitzers. These had little effect, and the battle was given over to companies of artillery. In a brief but noisy scuffle that ended in a startling upset—one that likely even surprised the Mesilla residents who had gathered on a nearby hill to watch—Confederates killed two federal soldiers and wounded six others. Lynde retreated. Fearing further harassment, Lynde ordered Fort Fillmore abandoned. On July 27, with some seven hundred of his men, including eight companies of infantry and four of cavalry, Lynde headed eastward away from the Texas forces, hoping to survive a march of more than one hundred miles to Fort Stanton near Lincoln.

That morning, Baylor and his soldiers climbed atop a Mesilla building and spied the retreating Union column as it dragged toward the foothills of the Organ Mountains. Riding in pursuit, Confederate scouts encountered a disheveled evacuation train struggling through the desert. "The road for 5 miles was lined with the fainting, famished soldiers," Baylor later wrote, "who threw down their arms as we passed and begged for water." Soldiers in the rear guard were suffering from dehydration or were drunk, some having filled their canteens with liquor from the sutler's store before they abandoned the fort. Confederate troops took the sickly soldiers prisoner and returned them to Mesilla.

Baylor reached Lynde's temporary camp near San Augustin Springs that afternoon. Major Lynde surrendered unconditionally.

On August 1, Baylor issued a proclamation declaring Mesilla the capital of the Confederate "Territory of Arizona." It would be almost a year before Union victories would force the Confederates to retreat from the state.

More to explore: *Fort Craig, Glorieta Pass Battlefield, La Mesilla, Peralta*

427. Smokey Bear Historical Park

Location: Lincoln County. In Capitan, on the north side of US 380, in front of the old Smokey Bear Museum. See map 6.

Marker text: This park commemorates Smokey Bear and describes the history and development of this national symbol of forest fire prevention. The original Smokey is buried here within sight of the mountain where he was found orphaned by a fire raging in the Lincoln National Forest. The park offers extensive historical exhibits as well as a trail that identifies native plants.

Lack of rainfall in the summer of 1950 had left Lincoln National Forest so dry that a fire ignited on Capitan Peak on May 4 kept firefighters scrambling for three straight days. No sooner had work crews quarantined the flames in Las Tablas Canyon than a second inferno, as eager as the first, accelerated through Capitan Gap. Army soldiers from Fort Bliss in El Paso, along with the "Red Hats"—Mescalero Indian firefighters from the nearby Mescalero Indian Reservation—helped battle the blaze for two days and two nights until it, too, was under control.

Resting at the base camp, firefighters chatted about a small bear they had seen howling and running loose in Capitan Gap. A fire crew soon came upon the creature clinging to a tree: an orphaned black bear cub barely two and a half months old. The men affectionately nicknamed the cub Hot Foot Teddy, but soon changed his name to Smokey, after the cartoon character advocating forest fire prevention, Smokey Bear. Created by the Ad Council in 1944, the Smokey Bear cartoon by that summer had been successfully warning campers about the dangers of careless camping for six years.

Later that May, Ray Bell, chief law enforcement officer in the New Mexico Department of Game and Fish, and Elliott Barker, the New Mexico state game warden, approached the Forest Service to discuss making the little bear the living counterpart of the cartoon Smokey. Forest Service officials liked the idea, and the Capitan cub was flown to Washington, D.C., to become the majordomo of America's forests.

In commercials, posters, and even songs, the cartoon Smokey grew to become one of the most recognized symbols in America. The real Smokey, meanwhile, continued as a popular attraction at his home at the National Zoo in Washington. According to some officials, Smokey was a bit of a grouch, growling at his keepers and refusing the attentions of visitors. He was beloved nonetheless. Smokey received so many cards and letters, in fact, that the US Postal Service assigned him his own zip code: 20252.

In 1962, zoo officials gave Smokey a partner, Goldie, another black bear from the mountains near Magdalena, New Mexico. Later, they introduced the couple's adopted son, Little Smokey, a cub found near Cloudcroft, New Mexico. When Smokey Bear retired on May 2, 1975, after twenty-five years of service as the national symbol of fire prevention, Little Smokey succeeded him.

As Smokey grew older, Capitan residents lobbied their representatives in the US Congress to prepare for his eventual return home. In 1974, Congress passed a concurrent resolution directing that "upon his death, the body of Smokey Bear . . . be returned to Capitan, New Mexico, for proper disposition and a permanent memorial in or near Capitan."

Smokey Bear passed away on November 8, 1976. A TWA flight that afternoon carried his remains back to his state of birth. The cherished New Mexico icon was laid to rest under a boulder in Smokey Bear Historical Park in Capitan, within sight of the mountains where his career had begun.

More to explore: *Capitan, Lincoln, Three Rivers*

428. Smuggler's Trail

Location: Hidalgo County. On the north end of Animas, near the high school, on NM 338. See map 5.

Marker text: Smugglers once crossed this area with mule trains of contraband from Mexico, to be traded for merchandise in Arizona. In the summer of 1881, a group of Mexican smugglers were killed in Skeleton Canyon by members of the Clanton gang, including Old Man Clanton, Ike and Billy Clanton, and Curly Bill.

429. The Clanton Hideout

Location: Hidalgo County. On the north end of Animas, near the high school, on NM 338. See map 5.

Marker text: The infamous Clanton gang had two crude dugouts here in the 1880s that served as hideouts and a base for wide-ranging outlaw activities, particularly in connection with the Curly Bill Gang's depredations along the Smuggler's Trail that passed by here. Old Man Clanton was ambushed below the border in revenge for a Skeleton Canyon massacre.

Note: Marker faceplates are on opposite sides of the same sign.

The Clanton Gang, who would later become renowned for their role in the gunfight at the O.K. Corral in Tombstone, Arizona, also played a bit part in the history of southwestern New Mexico. Newton Hayes "Old Man" Clanton, the patriarch of this notorious group of cattle-rustling outlaws, operated a ranch in the Animas Valley in the late 1800s. With him were his sons, Ike and Billy, and William "Curly Bill" Brocius, leader of his own band of ne'er-do-wells in the Tombstone area.

The Clantons sometimes used two mountain dugouts near present-day Cloverdale as a rendezvous point and hideaway. These hollows were near what was commonly called the Smuggler's Trail. Over this covert route from Mexico, across the Playas Valley, through the rugged Peloncillo Mountains to Tucson, Arizona, and back, illegal traders drove mules laden with sacks of contraband and Mexican bullion. The Smuggler's Trail was a lucrative corridor, both for those who traversed it and for those who preyed on those who traversed it.

In one incident on August 1, 1881, cowboys ambushed a pack train of about twelve Mexican smugglers in a canyon in the Peloncillo Mountains, robbed them of some $4,000 in Mexican coins, and massacred four men. Locals reportedly collected bones from the skeletons of the smugglers as souvenirs, a gruesome act said to have earned the canyon its name: Skeleton Canyon. Many believed that Curly Bill's gang was behind the attack, but history has never chosen sides. Regardless, the incident was an appropriate prelude for the violence that would end the life of Old Man Clanton.

On the morning of August 12, less than two weeks after the Skeleton Canyon massacre, Clanton and Arizona rancher Billy Lang left Clanton's Animas Valley ranch on a cattle drive to Tombstone. With them were four other cowboys: Charlie Snow, Billy Byers, Harry Ernshaw, and Jim Crane. By nightfall, the men had driven their stock to Guadalupe Canyon, just below the Mexican border, where they camped for the evening.

The cowboys would never know, nor would history reveal, whether the attackers who ambushed their camp at dawn the next morning were smugglers retaliating for the Skeleton Canyon massacre or outlaws simply out for plunder. The shadowy assailants climbed the hills and shot down into the canyon on the men. The sleeping forms of Jim Crane and Dixie Gray, another cowboy who had joined the men after they were on the trail, made easy targets. Attackers took down Charlie Snow as he tried to make his escape by horseback over a nearby mountain, where he had earlier that morning ridden to check for bears. Billy Byers, who survived the incident, described the canyon chaos from that point in an interview with the *Arizona Weekly Star* on September 1, 1881:

As soon as I saw what was up I looked for my rifle, and not seeing it I grabbed my revolver, and seeing them shooting at us from all sides, started to run, but had not gone forty feet when I was shot across my body, but I didn't fall, and in a few more steps was hit in my arm, knocked the pistol out of my hand and I fell down. When I was down Harry and Will passed me, both running for the canyon. Soon Will fell, shot through the legs, and he then turned his revolver loose, and I think killed one Mexican and wounded another, as one man was killed and another badly wounded, and [Will] was the only one that did much fighting. Soon I saw some Mexicans coming from the direction Will and Harry had run, wearing [the cowboys'] hats.

Only Harry Ernshaw and Billy Byers survived the ordeal, the latter by stripping naked and playing dead. Old Man Clanton himself witnessed very little of the attack that morning. He was shot, according to Byers, "at the first fire, and almost instantly killed."

More to explore: *Black Jack Ketchum (series), Lincoln*

430. Socorro

Location: Socorro County. At the west end of Socorro, in a pullout on the east side of US 60 between mile markers 137 and 138. See map 5.

Marker text: The Piro Indian pueblo Teypana was visited by Juan de Oñate in 1598. The people of the village reportedly supplied corn to Oñate who bestowed the name Socorro ("aid" in Spanish) on the pueblo. In 1626, the mission of Nuestra Señora de Socorro was built at the nearby pueblo of Pilabó. Abandoned during the Pueblo Revolt of 1680, the present town was founded in 1815.

431. Ghost Marker: Socorro Plaza (Kittrell Park)

Marker text: Established in 1816 at the time of the original Spanish land grant, this plaza developed into the traditional social, political and economic hub of the community. Excellent examples of Mexican and Territorial period architecture surround the plaza, which is named after Dr. L. E. Kittrell, a local dentist who landscaped the plaza in the 1880s.

Note: This Marker, which once stood on the plaza, is now missing. See map 5.

After struggling through the uninviting desert south of here at the head of the first official colonization mission by Spain into New Mexico in 1598, don Juan de Oñate and his advance guard reached an assemblage of Piro-speaking Indian villages along the Rio Grande in this vicinity. These villages had been noted by the earlier Spanish expedition of Francisco Vásquez de Coronado in 1541. The Indians living at a pueblo called Teypama (also written as Teypana) offered Oñate and his famished soldiers water to drink and corn to eat. In gratitude, Oñate christened the pueblo El Pueblo de Nuestra Señora del Socorro, or "the Village of Our Lady of Aid." Over time, the name "Socorro" somehow transferred to another nearby pueblo, Pilabó, which stood at the site of modern Socorro.

By August 1626, priests had finished work on the mission church of Nuestra Señora de Socorro in Pilabó, from which they ministered to the spiritual needs of the Indians at the pueblo and other settlers living along the middle Rio Grande Valley. The residents at Pilabó abandoned both the pueblo and mission in 1680 when Pueblo Indians in New Mexico led an insurgency against the ruling Spanish. Colonists living along the lower Rio Grande fled south, joined by many Indians from Pilabó and other pueblos. Near El Paso, the Indians formed a new community, Socorro del Sur, or "Socorro of the South," where their descendents still live today.

Raids by hostile Apaches kept the region sparsely populated until around 1815, when seventy families arrived to establish a new community atop the old—literally. They erected the adobe houses of their small farming village over the vestiges of the burned-out pueblo and incorporated parts of the walls of the earlier mission into their picturesque new church, San Miguel. They also incorporated the name: Socorro.

Socorro sat on the west bank of the Rio Grande, opposite the Camino Real, or Royal Road, the main route between Mexico and Taos until the late nineteenth century. A small road on the western bank connected the village to the Camino Real on the eastern bank. Fort Craig, established nearby in 1853, protected travelers on the route and settlers along the Rio Grande Valley.

Socorro shifted from small farming village to active commercial center in the mid-nineteenth century as mining ventures took hold in camps like Kelly and Magdalena in the mountains to the west. The downtown plaza grew in prominence as houses and business facilities opened around the streets lining and leading to it, including the homes of Juan Nepomuceno Garcia, one of the oldest adobe homes along the plaza, and Juan José Baca, built before 1880. The plaza became known as Kittrell Park, in honor of a local dentist, Dr. L. E. Kittrell, who, in the 1880s, helped to landscape the plaza commons.

In 1889, the territorial legislature chose Socorro as the site of the New Mexico School of Mines to help further the study of mining and earth science in the state. The institution is today known as the New Mexico Institute of Mining and Technology.

More to explore: *Fort Craig, Garcia Opera House, Kelly, Magdalena, New Mexico Tech, Oñate's Route (see under El Camino Real—The King's Highway)*

432. Soda Dam

Location: Sandoval County. At Soda Dam, in a pullout on the east side of NM 4. See map 4.

Marker text: This spectacular formation has built up over the centuries by deposits of calcium carbonate from a spring that bubbles to the surface at this point. The river flows under a dome that is still building. The dam is 300 feet long, 50 feet high, and 50 feet wide at the bottom.

The Jemez Mountains are a hotbed of geothermal activity. At this point along NM 4, water rich with calcium carbonate seeps upward from deep within the earth. The cooler surface air causes the minerals in the water to precipitate, or pull apart in solid form, and then materialize into a crystalline limestone. Limestone created this way, often found at hot springs like this one, is known as travertine. Over many centuries, the resulting buildup took the shape of a massive rock mantle—Soda Dam.

Despite the name, this "dam" has not truly blocked the movement of the Jemez River. Water spurts through a hole near the bottom of the rock levee, cascading in a small but capricious waterfall. That spout has become a refreshing recreational attraction for visitors to the Jemez Mountains, who come to be doused under its cool waters.

Although Soda Dam today is an imposing fifty feet high and three hundred feet long, it is only a shadow of its former self. Road crews penetrating the mountains in the 1950s sliced through the original formation, which at the time stretched to the other side of NM 4. Nor is the shroud a finished work; deposits of calcium carbonate continue to amass today.

More to explore: *Jemez Mountains, Valle Grande*

433. Southern Rockies

Location: Santa Fe County. South of Santa Fe, on US 285, near the turnoff to Lamy. The text for Galisteo Basin appears on the opposite side of the sign. See map 2.

Marker text: These foothills and the higher glaciated peaks to the north are the southern tip of the Rocky Mountains. This particular segment is known as the Sangre de Cristo ("Blood of Christ"), a formidable barrier that rises above 13,000 feet in a chain of peaks that tend from Santa Fe on the south to Salida, Colorado on the north.

Note: There are no longer glaciated peaks in this part of the Rocky Mountains.

The breathtaking Sangre de Cristo Mountains north of here are the southernmost grasp of the Rocky Mountains. The tallest peak in New Mexico is within this range: Wheeler Peak, near Angel Fire, with an imposing 13,161-foot reach. In the early years of western exploration, travelers respected these lofty mountain spires as much for their snow-capped beauty as for their rugged formidability. A map of the region plotted by the War Department in October 1827 warned that there was "no passage north of this place" and added further intrigue by labeling the range simply, "Impassable Mountains."

The Sangre de Cristos reach their northern limits some two hundred miles north of here, near Salida, Colorado. The eastern slopes of the mountains ease into the level eastern third of the state and the Great Plains. The western slopes drop into the upper Rio Grande Valley.

A popular legend ascribes the name Sangre de Cristo, which translates as "Blood of Christ," to a priest martyred on the mountains during the Pueblo Revolt of 1680. Just before his final breath, the priest is said to have prayed to God for a sign of his own redemption, which arrived in the blood-like glow of sunset on the towering peaks. A less romantic but likely more accurate account associates the name with the Penitente religious brotherhood of northern New Mexico, whose members practiced their ascetic religious devotions (which sometimes involved self-flagellation) in the remote folds of these mountains.

More to explore: *Rocky Mountains, View of the Rockies, Wheeler Peak*

434. Spanish Entrada Site

Location: Sandoval County. Just north of Rio Rancho, on the west side of NM 528, between mile markers 13 and 14. See map 4.

Marker text: Among the many prehistoric and historic sites located nearby is a camp where Francisco Vasquez de Coronado's troops may have spent the winter of 1540–41. Coronado also visited the ancient pueblo of Kuaua located to the north. Kuaua's ruins are preserved and interpreted at the Coronado State Monument near Bernalillo.

Note: Coronado State Monument is now known as the Coronado Historic Site.

Shallow dugouts west of Bernalillo indicate the presence of a campsite nearby, probably used around 1540. Archaeologists believe that the camp may have been that of Francisco Vásquez de Coronado, leader of one of the first Spanish explorations of New Mexico. Coronado had come to New Mexico to search for the Seven Cities of Cibola, mythical cities of gold rumored to exist somewhere in this unexplored interior land or possibly on the Great Plains. While exploring what is now New Mexico, one of Coronado's men, Hernando de Alvarado, encountered the pueblos along the upper Rio Grande near here and suggested to Coronado that the location would make a good place for the expedition to shiver out the approaching winter of 1540–1541.

Archaeologists believe that the site excavated near Bernalillo probably served as the provisional camp where Coronado and his three hundred soldiers first settled that winter. It is, according to the National Park Service, the only site in the southwestern United States known to be associated with an entrada, or Spanish exploratory expedition. The soldiers used the campsite only temporarily. The cold winter air later forced Coronado and his men to abandon the site and appropriate a nearby Indian pueblo, referred to as Alcanfor in a chronicle of the expedition. It is not known which pueblo that was.

During his time in the area, Coronado very likely visited the pueblo known as Kuaua. The ruins of Kuaua are preserved in what is now the Coronado Historic Site (formerly Coronado State Monument). Visitors to the Coronado Historic Site today can see reconstructions of some of the foundation walls of the pueblo and also visit the interior of a kiva, a ceremonial chamber in the pueblo. Archaeologists working on the ruins in the 1930s recovered beautiful murals that had been painted on several layers of the kiva walls. Because these murals do not depict any animals introduced by the Spanish, like sheep or horses, they are believed to be among the best precontact murals extant. Some of the originals of those murals can be seen at the Visitors Center, and reproductions have been painted onto the replastered walls of the kiva itself.

More to explore: *Bernalillo, Tiguex Province, Vásquez de Coronado's Route (series)*

435. Springer

Location: Colfax County. At the north end of Springer, in a pullout on the west side of Railroad Avenue (the Interstate 25 business loop), near the intersection of Railroad Avenue and NM 468. See map 3.

Marker text: Located in the old Maxwell Land Grant and near the Cimarron Cutoff of the Santa Fe Trail, Springer served as Colfax County seat from 1882 to 1897. Several men were killed here in one of the late flareups of the Colfax County War, a dispute between land grant owners and settlers.

436. Old Colfax County Courthouse

Location: Colfax County. In Springer, in front of the museum on the Interstate 25 business loop through town. See map 3.

Marker text: Built in 1879 at a cost of $9,800, this building served as the Colfax County Courthouse from 1882 through 1897, when the country seat was moved to Raton. This building housed the New Mexico reform school for boys from 1910 to 1917 and has been a public library, town hall and city jail.

While his brother Charles was overseeing construction of Eagle Nest Dam in the Moreno Valley, Iowa-born Frank Springer, who had moved to New Mexico with his brother in February 1873, worked as an attorney for Lucien Maxwell and his two-million-acre land grant in northeastern New Mexico. In payment for Springer's services, Maxwell deeded him a 320-acre plot along the Cimarron River, near the Cimarron Cutoff of the Santa Fe Trail. The settlement that developed took the brothers' name, Springer.

The arrival of the Santa Fe Railway in the 1880s

transformed Springer into a commercial shipping and supply post for area ranches. Anticipating a shift in the economic center of Colfax County, District Attorney Melvin W. Mills led an effort in the legislature to transfer the county seat from Cimarron to Springer, then rallied Springer citizens to build a courthouse in anticipation of success. Following a simplified second empire style and looking every bit the territorial courthouse, the symmetrical, two-story brick building featured a pitched roof, arched windows, and a projecting three-story tower—the top floor of which held a gallows. Court was to be held on the second story, with the judge's chambers to the rear. Later, a brick jail cell was added at the back of the building. Mills was victorious; Springer became county seat in 1881.

In March 1885, Springer was the site of one of the last flare-ups of the Colfax County War, a feud between settlers and Maxwell Land Grant and Railway Company officials over who properly owned the grant land. The Springer squabble began when George Curry, a young merchant in Raton, led a group of citizens in disarming a militia sent to that town by the land company. Soon after, Springer deputy Jesse Lee arrested one of Curry's men on a disorderly conduct charge not related to the incident. According to his autobiography, Curry believed that the jailing was appropriate and rode to the Springer Courthouse with his men to cooperate with Deputy Lee. A crowd had gathered in anticipation of their arrival. Unaware of Curry's peaceful intention and fearful that the mob was out to kill them, Lee and another deputy shot and killed one of Curry's men, Dick Rogers. Curry described the scene and the assaults on his men from that point:

Hearing the shooting, the crowd rushed toward the courthouse. Tom Whealington, on horseback, carried his rifle in his hand. My brother, John, who was armed with a revolver, was shot and mortally wounded when still about fifteen yards from the courthouse. I had him removed to the Springer hospital where he died about two o'clock the following morning. Whealington, who had dismounted in an attempt to pick up the body of Dick Rogers, was killed instantly [by the deputies]. Bob Lee and Ed King, both armed, escaped injury. I was unarmed and might have been killed, but had taken refuge behind a small brick building, near where my brother lay wounded.

Although Curry was charged with sixteen crimes and misdemeanors from the incident, he "pleaded guilty to a charge of unlawful carrying of firearms, and was fined five dollars." This black mark on his record did not prevent Curry from being elected governor of New Mexico in 1907, or from representing New Mexico in the US House of Representatives from 1912 to 1913. His contributions to the state are remembered in the name of Curry County in eastern New Mexico.

In 1897, Springer lost the county seat to Raton, a budding railroad and coal-mining community about forty miles to the north. Angered, Springer county clerk Manuel M. Salazar refused to release county records until officials removed them under force.

Absent its erstwhile judicial responsibilities, the courthouse found other ways to be of service. From 1910 to 1917, the building was the first home for the New Mexico Reform School, later renamed the New Mexico Industrial School for Boys, an institution created, as a report by the board of trustees in 1936 stated, "for the training and directing of juvenile delinquents." Later, that institution was moved to another site outside of town. At various times thereafter, the old courthouse housed the Springer Public Library and municipal offices. In 1965, with growing interest in the Santa Fe Trail, residents voted to make the building a museum dedicated to trail history. Today it holds artifacts from Springer history, a miniature wagon used in a re-creation of the journey over the Santa Fe Trail, a shoe from the "gentle giant" and shoe salesman Robert Wadlow, and its most curious piece: the first and only electric chair in New Mexico, previously used at the state penitentiary in Santa Fe.

More to explore: *Colfax County War, Eagle Nest Lake State Park, Mills Canyon, Santa Fe Trail (series)*

437. St. Anthony's Catholic Church

Location: Taos County. In Questa, in the parking lot of the church, at 10 Church Plaza, just off NM 522. See map 2.

Marker text: St. Anthony's Church was built in the 1840s. Once recognized by Archbishop Lamy as being grand and beautiful, the church boasts four foot adobe walls and substantial vigas harvested from the surrounding mountains. The church was dedicated to San Antonio, the patron saint associated with the return of lost articles and missing persons. For decades it has stood at the center of the solemnity, witnessing hundreds of baptisms, weddings and funerals.

The village of Questa in north-central New Mexico was settled around 1830 on a cuesta, the Spanish word for ridge. Early residents, wanting a church in their new village, agreed to work on the structure every Saturday until it was completed. The cruciform church, considered the oldest building still standing in Questa, was built with enormous double adobe walls running four feet wide in places. Hand-carved vigas, timbers used to support the roof, were cut from trees harvested from the surrounding mountains; they spanned twenty-five feet across the roof. The church took Saint Anthony as its patron. Saint Anthony had also been recognized in the original name of the village, San Antonio del Rio Colorado ("Saint Anthony of the Red River"). Saint Anthony is the patron saint of lost articles and missing persons.

A Works Progress Administration–sponsored pioneer history by Frank V. Garcia of Questa described the dedication ceremony of the church:

The thirteenth day of June [circa 1840] was to be the great day of the fiesta. On that day all the men mounted their horses and wheeled them into two lines. . . . Four women carried the image of San Antonio which had been donated by Doña Maria, Don Benito's wife; all the other women and the children followed. The women chanted the hymn Historios de San Antonio *and all the men joined in the chorus. The procession went to the four corners of the valley so that San Antonio might see the conditions of the crops.*

As hardy as it was beautiful, the church earned the approval of Bishop Jean-Baptiste Lamy, head of the Catholic Church in New Mexico. In a baptismal book for the Questa area, Lamy in 1860 noted: "This plaza of Rio Colorado now has a large and beautiful chapel."

Since its founding, the church has been a mainstay of life in the community. Generations of couples have been married within its solemn walls. Local residents have baptized their children there, attended services with their families, and held funerals for their loved ones.

By 2008, however, snow, weathering, and time had taken their toll on the building, and the massive structure was showing signs of age. When the western wall collapsed in the fall of that year, the archdiocese in Santa Fe made a decision to demolish the historic building. But enterprising Questa residents wanted to save their church. They organized a committee to restore the structure and successfully convinced the archdiocese to turn over the church to the community for six years for reconstruction. Community volunteers since that time have been working diligently on the restoration.

Today, the wall has been repaired, and services are still held at the historic church. The parish also serves nearby Red River, Costilla, and Amalia.

More to explore: *La Cienega School, Red River Valley, San Antonio de Padua Catholic Church*

438. State History of Education Museum

Location: Chaves County. In Lake Arthur, in the courtyard of the Lake Arthur school at the far east end of Broadway Street. See map 6.

Marker text: Constructed in 1906, the Lake Arthur Elementary School has been memorialized as the oldest continuously used school building in New Mexico. In 1989, the New Mexico legislature designated the structure as the official New Mexico State History of Education Museum. The museum was dedicated on October 12, 1989 and features displays and artifacts from New Mexico's school districts.

In late 1906, local contractor Ed Ewins constructed the first school building in Lake Arthur: this beautiful brick edifice, holding four rooms, a wide staircase between floors, and windows overlooking the front schoolyard. Elementary school classes were taught on the lower floor; high school on the upper—an arrangement that led teachers to joke that the building made literal the term "higher education." Students came to school every morning in the Lake Arthur "school bus," a renovated Model T with benches where the back seat had been.

By the 1960s, after the town had erected a new elementary and junior high school, the old building was used only for storage. Timothy Raftery, superintendent for the Lake Arthur schools in 1988, briefly considered having the building torn down, but he later conceived the idea of using the old school as a museum to chronicle the legacy of education in New Mexico. Raftery and supporters in the community devised an appropriate name for their project: the State History of Education Museum. Even the acronym would be effective—SHOEM—because, as Raftery later recounted: "We *show 'em* in Lake Arthur."

Citizens of Lake Arthur spent nearly $3,000 bringing their old schoolhouse up to code. Volunteers created displays that included composition books, photos of schoolchildren from surrounding communities in the early 1900s, school desks, and yearbooks donated by former students. They even repaired the school bell, a rusted relic reportedly salvaged from an old ship. In years past, the sound of that bell was a call to Lake Arthur residents to come to the school for a news announcement, or to provide assistance because of a fire in the vicinity. According to Raftery, as the bell rang again for the first time in more than forty years, long-time residents who remembered the signal gathered in the schoolyard, wondering what emergency was calling them to service now.

Volunteers also worked to ready the pièce de résistance: the SHOEM Hamilton piano. At the time, New Mexico had eighty-eight school districts. Using a label maker, helpers stamped each of the eighty-eight piano keys with the name of one of those districts. From Alamogordo (lowest A) to Hondo (middle C) to Zuni (highest C), they were, as a sign above the piano proudly declared, "88 School Districts in Harmony."

Meanwhile, State Representatives Robert B. Corn, Barbara A. Casey, and Richard T. Knowles introduced a resolution in the first session of the Thirty-Seventh Legislature memorializing the school building as the oldest still in use in the state and officially declaring it the State History of Education Museum.

On October 12, 1989, members of the State Board of Education rang the schoolhouse bell at the opening ceremonies for this, the only museum in New Mexico dedicated to education. Some four hundred visitors spent the evening eating barbecue and admiring the displays, but the night did not end until the president of the school board, a former music teacher herself, sat at the SHOEM piano and began to play.

More to explore: *Cedarvale, La Cienega School, Lincoln-Jackson School, Los Padillas, Nara Visa, Old Armijo School*

St. Francis Women's Club: *see Pueblo of Nambé*

439. Storrie Lake State Park

Location: San Miguel County. Inside Storrie Lake State Park, opposite the parking lot at the pay station. See map 3.

Marker text: Long a popular spot for rainbow trout fishing, Storrie Lake also features boating, swimming, and camping/picnicing sites, a boat ramp, a playground and a visitor information center.

As NM 518 continues its journey north of Las Vegas, it curves along the easternmost edge of beautiful Storrie Lake, one of the most popular recreational spots in this part of New Mexico. The lake is a popular site for boating, swimming, and fishing—stocked with three-inch fingerlings, rainbow trout, and channel catfish, among others. Although water sports are the primary attraction of Storrie Lake State Park, visitors can also enjoy camping (both developed and primitive) and picnicking sites.

The lake is named for local engineer Robert Storrie. In 1916, Storrie began construction of an earthen dam here in order to create a reservoir on the Gallinas River and harness the water for irrigation. He completed the project five years later. The 1,100-acre reservoir that was created borrowed Storrie's name. The state created Storrie Lake State Park in 1959, and the site was dedicated the following year.

A Visitors Center today welcomes travelers to the park.

More to explore: *Elephant Butte Lake State Park, Las Vegas, Sumner Lake State Park*

440. Strike Valleys

Location: San Miguel County. North of Sapello, on the east side of NM 518, between mile markers 15 and 16. See map 3.

Marker text: Between Sapello and Mora, State Road 3 follows a narrow strike valley eroded into soft shale between ridges of resistant sandstone called hogbacks, both the result of uplift of the Rocky Mountains. To the east stretch the Great Plains and to the west, the Sangre de Cristo Mountains rise to elevations exceeding 13,000 feet. Elevation here 7,000 feet.

Note: State Road 3 is now NM 518.

Geologists use the words "dip" and "strike" to help describe certain geologic features. Dr. Pat Brady of Sandia National Laboratories explains their meaning:

To a geologist, the strike is the single horizontal line that can be imagined on an inclined planar geological feature—such as a bed or a fault. The dip of the bed or fault is the angle it makes with the horizontal.

The word "strike" can also be used to define any geologic feature that follows the same direction as the defining horizontal line. For example, a strike fault is a crack in the earth that runs parallel to the course that the strike in the layers of rock runs. A strike valley, then, is a valley that follows the same direction as a strike. NM 518 follows such a strike valley between the small northern New Mexico communities of Sapello and Mora.

On either side of this valley lie small ridges, called hogbacks because the steep tilt of their rock layers resembles the hairs on a hog. Hogbacks form when erosion-resistant rocks overlie layers that are more prone to erosion.

This strike valley helps separate two distinct physiographic provinces. To the west rise the foothills of the Sangre de Cristo Mountains, part of the southern Rocky Mountains Province. The highest peak in New Mexico, Wheeler Peak at 13,161 feet, is among the crests found here. Prospectors have mined this range for zinc, lead, and even gold, and the remains of several defeated mining camps, including Elizabethtown—the first incorporated city in New Mexico—still lie scattered among the crests and valleys.

To the east stretches a second distinct physiographic province: the Great Plains. Here, the land flattens to form the broad plains and grasslands that sweep across the eastern third of New Mexico and the better part of the interior of the country.

Driving along NM 518 is like driving through a transition zone, between the highest peaks in New Mexico to some of its lowest-lying plains.

More to explore: *Elizabethtown, Hogback, Hogbacks, Magdalena Fault, Oil and Gas, Southern Rockies, Wheeler Peak*

441. Sugarite Canyon State Park

Location: Colfax County. Near the entrance to the park, at the intersection of NM 526 and NM 72. See map 3.

Marker text: This heavily wooded mountainous park, located on the Colorado–New Mexico border, was formerly the site of a thriving coal camp. There are two fishing lakes in the New Mexico portion of the canyon, and another lake lies just across the border in Colorado. Wild turkey and deer are plentiful in the park vicinity, and facilities include hiking trails and camping/picnicking sites. The colorful history of the canyon and region is described in the visitor's center.

The history of Sugarite Canyon State Park begins with the discovery of coal in a canyon here in 1909. The original name of the canyon, Chicorica, may have been derived from a Comanche term for turkey, or perhaps for the chicory plants growing in the canyon. Later settlers pronounced the name somewhat differently, coming closer to *Sugar-reet*, which is the pronunciation of the name that eventually eclipsed the original canyon name: Sugarite.

A mining camp developed to house workers with the St. Louis, Rocky Mountain, and Pacific Company, who mined the coal from the canyon. The camp, which borrowed the name of the canyon and was also called Sugarite, was large, with several stone homes built on a lower terrace of the canyon wall, a large, two-story school, a store, mine buildings, and about a thousand residents. Miners shipped their coal harvests to nearby Raton to fuel the railroad that had arrived over Raton Pass at the turn of the century. "The mine produces a good grade of bituminous coal," the New Mexico mine inspector wrote of the mines here in 1903, "thickness of vein, 5 feet, nearly horizontal."

Sugarite was a short-lived settlement. When the mines closed in 1941, the community itself was soon abandoned.

Almost fifty years later, the ruins of the mining camp, as well as 3,600 acres of land around them, were set aside as a state park. That makes Sugarite Canyon State Park one of the youngest state parks in New Mexico, established in July 1985.

Today, visitors can learn about the history of the mining town of Sugarite at the Visitors Center, which is housed in the original town post office. They can then follow a trail up the steep canyon and hike through many of the ruins of the old town itself. In addition to spectacular scenic views throughout the park, wild turkey, deer, and other wildlife often make an appearance. Camping and picnicking sites are available at Lake Alice and Lake Maloya, as well as the opportunity to catch rainbow and cutthroat trout. Non-gasoline-powered boating is available at Lake Maloya. Lake Dorothey, while still part of the park, lies just across the border in Colorado.

More to explore: *Elizabethtown, Kelly, Riley, Shakespeare*

442. Sumner Lake State Park

Location: De Baca County. At the intersection of US 84 and NM 203, the turnoff to Sumner Lake State Park. See map 6.

Marker text: Sumner Lake was originally named Alamogordo Lake after Alamogordo Creek. The lake and surrounding land became a state park in 1960. In 1974, the lake and state park were renamed Sumner in honor of Colonel Edmond Vose Sumner who in the mid 19th Century established forts Craig, Fillmore, Thorn, and Union.

Situated on the southeastern plains of New Mexico, Sumner Lake State Park is a welcoming, if secluded, recreational area. Camping is available in a number of developed and primitive campgrounds across the six thousand acres of the park, and the lake itself is a popular spot with boaters and swimmers. Fishers will find walleye, channel catfish, and largemouth bass, among others. An impressive feature of the lake is the large concrete dam and spillway. Interpretive signs near a scenic overlook by the lake tell the story of the construction of the dam.

The history of the park begins in 1937, when the US Bureau of Reclamation constructed a 164-foot-high dam near the junction of the Pecos River and Alamogordo Creek, creating in the process a 4,500-acre reservoir then known as Alamogordo Lake. The lake and surrounding land became a state park in 1960 under the name Alamogordo Lake State Park. But in 1974, the state chose to rename the park Sumner Lake State Park, hoping to avoid confusion with the town of Alamogordo in southwestern New Mexico.

The new name honored Colonel Edmond Vose Sumner, the leader of the US Army's Ninth Military District, which included New Mexico, from 1851 to 1853. Under Sumner's command, the army established the military installations of Fort Fillmore near Las Cruces in 1851, Fort Union near Watrous in 1851, Fort Craig near Socorro in 1853, and Fort Thorn near Hatch in 1853. Of these, only the ruins of Fort Craig and Fort Union remain today. Both are open to the public.

Colonel Sumner's name is also remembered in the military encampment of Fort Sumner, about sixteen miles south of here. The fort was dedicated to him shortly after his death in 1863 by Brigadier General James H. Carleton, who established the fort and the Bosque Redondo Navajo Reservation it helped protect. The settlement that grew around the fort also took the name Fort Sumner.

More to explore: *Fort Sumner and Fort Sumner State Monument (series), Storrie Lake State Park*

443. Sunnyside Springs

Location: De Baca County. Just north of Fort Sumner, in a pullout on the west side of US 84, between mile markers 1 and 2. See map 6.

Marker text: Nearby is a "sweet water" spring which has been used through the centuries by Plains Indians, Spanish Explorers, and most recently, ranchers and settlers. A stagecoach station was located at the spring, which was a popular stopping place for travelers. The spring was named after Sunnyside, the nearby settlement whose name was changed to Fort Sumner in 1910.

The area of present-day Fort Sumner served as an Indian campground for years before Europeans arrived. The Indians likely drank from a small spring in this stretch of plains, about a mile north of what is now Fort Sumner. Spanish explorers probably also visited the spring in the sixteenth century as they made their way along the Pecos River. It took another three hundred years before the waters would acquire a name: settler Milnor Rudolph dubbed them Sunnyside Springs when he made a home here in the late 1870s. A small village of adobe buildings, tents, and saloons soon developed. When a post office opened in 1878, Rudolph named the town after the springs, Sunnyside.

Meanwhile, wealthy landowner Lucien Maxwell had purchased the abandoned buildings of Fort Sumner, a former army installation that oversaw the Indian reservation of Bosque Redondo just a few miles south. A second settlement, known as Fort Sumner, grew around the Maxwell estate. For several years thereafter, Sunnyside and Fort Sumner were sister communities.

When the Atchison, Topeka, and Santa Fe Railway reached the area in 1905, residents of Fort Sumner moved their homes and businesses north to be closer to the railroad. Sunnyside residents, who then lived in a village that consisted of, according to the National Park Service, "several saloons, three restaurants, and a number of tents," did likewise. Even so, it took an act of Mother Nature to end the community of Sunnyside entirely. The *Santa Fe New Mexican* reported that on July 2, 1908, a cyclone wiped out much of the village, killing at least five people, wounding another forty, and destroying homes and businesses. (Although fortunately rare in New Mexico, tornadoes do strike on occasion.) Stalwart Sunnyside residents rebuilt parts of their settlement, but soon after voted to incorporate their community into Fort Sumner.

Milnor Rudolph bears one other relevant historical footnote: after Sheriff Pat Garrett shot Billy the Kid to death in a bedroom of the Maxwell house at Fort Sumner on July 14, 1881, Rudolph was asked to head the coroner's jury. The jury declared "that the act of said Garrett was justifiable homicide and we are of the opinion that the gratitude of the whole community is owed to said Garrett for his deed, and that he deserves to be rewarded."

More to explore: *Fort Sumner and Fort Sumner State Monument (series), Pat Garrett Murder Site*

444. Tajique

Location: Torrance County. In the town of Tajique, on the west side of NM 55. See map 4.

Marker text: The pueblo mission of San Miguel de Tajique was established in the 1620s. In the 1670s, famine, disease and Apache raids caused the abandonment of the Jurisdiccion de las Salinas (1598–1678) which included Tajique. Modern occupation of Tajique began in the 1830s with a land grant made to Manuel Sanchez.

Southwestern Torrance County was once the site of several pueblos of Tompiro- and Tiwa-speaking Indians, which together formed a transition zone between the Rio Grande pueblos to the west and the Comanche and Apache Indians of the eastern plains. These villages included the pueblos of Abó, Quarai, Gran Quivira, and another at the base of the Manzano Mountains along the south bank of what is now Tajique Creek. This broken stone pueblo, home to three hundred Tiwa-speaking Indians in 1630, was Tajique, a name likely derived from a Spanish pronunciation of the original Indian name.

The Spanish knew the Estancia Basin as the Jurisdicción de las Salinas because of the nearby salt-filled playas. Franciscan priests arrived to administer Las Salinas in the early seventeenth century. Fray Geronimo de la Llana, although he lived at Quarai, oversaw the construction of an adobe mission church at Tajique in the early 1600s. The chapel bore the dedication San Miguel de Tajique. As described by an inventory conducted at the time: "The pueblo of Tajique has a very good church and convento [living quarters and offices for the priest], choir and organ, and there are 484 souls under its administration."

In the 1670s, famine, pestilence, drought, and attacks by Apaches crippled the missions and pueblos of the Estancia Valley. Indians at Quarai, along with their resident priest, Fray Diego de Parraga, abandoned their pueblo in 1677 and migrated to Tajique. Soon thereafter, bowing to the same pressures, Indians at Tajique, too, deserted their village and moved elsewhere.

Modern Tajique arose in March 1834 when the Mexican government awarded an unsettled tract of land here to local settler Manuel Sánchez. Nineteen others from the nearby village of Valencia joined him. The new settlement took the name of the pueblo of old, Tajique.

More to explore: *Abó Ruins, Gran Quivira Ruins, Laguna del Perro, Quarai Ruins*

445. Taos

Location: 1. Taos County. On the south end of Taos, on the east side of Paseo del Pueblo, near the intersection of Frontier Road and Paseo del Pueblo. See map 2.

2. Taos County. In El Prado (north of Taos), in a pullout on the east side of US 64, between mile markers 252 and 253. See map 2.

Marker text: The Spanish community of Taos developed two miles southwest of Taos Pueblo. It later served as a supply base for the "Mountain Men," and was the home of Kit Carson, who is buried here. Governor Charles Bent was killed here in the anti-U.S. insurrection of 1847. In the early 1900s, Taos developed as a colony for artists and writers.

446. Kit Carson Park

Location: Taos County. In Taos, at the entrance to Kit Carson Memorial State Park off Paseo del Pueblo Norte. See map 2.

Marker text: This municipal park was acquired by the Town of Taos in 1988 from the State of New Mexico. It is dedicated to the citizens of Taos and to the historic figures of our community who have made this a great place to live and visit. Please help us keep it clean and safe!

447. Kit Carson Park Memorial Cemetery

Location: Taos County. In Taos, at the Kit Carson Memorial State Park Cemetery. See map 2.

Marker text: This historic cemetery is the final resting place for many prominent Taoseños. Notables buried here are: Christopher "Kit" Carson, a legendary scout, Padre Antonio Martinez, a famous educator and church leader, and Mabel Dodge Lujan. Others buried here are the soldiers and other local citizens killed during the January 1847 rebellion here in Taos. The rebellion was sparked by a fear by some that the annexation of New Mexico as a Territory by the United States would result in a loss of their land rights. Governor Charles Bent was killed during the rebellion.

Note: The name "Mabel Dodge Lujan" is a misspelling on this Marker; the correct spelling is Mabel Dodge Luhan.

By the time Mexico declared its independence from Spain in 1821, the small Spanish village officially known as Don Fernando de Taos had become a rendezvous headquarters and supply base for Spanish, American, and French fur trappers and mountain men. These rugged mountain capitalists trapped beaver in the streams of the Sangre de Cristo Mountains and elsewhere throughout the Rocky Mountains. Taos also served as the location of the Taos Fair, an annual event during which Spanish settlers, mountain men, and otherwise hostile Comanches, Utes, and other Indians met peaceably to trade hides, pelts, food, and, regrettably, enslaved Indian captives.

Most legendary among the trappers who frequented the New Mexico highlands may well be Christopher "Kit" Carson. Carson first arrived in the New Mexico territory from Missouri in 1826. He later married Josefa Jaramillo, the daughter of a prominent Taos family, and purchased a house near Taos Plaza. The building is open to the public today as the Kit Carson Museum. In addition to trapping, Carson became an army expedition scout, a guide, and an agent to the Ute Indians, although his later harsh campaigns against Apaches and Navajos elicit resentment among many Native Americans today. Carson National Forest in the Sangre de Cristo Mountains carries his name.

Another name famous in the annals of nineteenth-century Taos is that of Charles Bent, a former surveyor and member of the Supreme Court of the territory of Missouri. Bent arrived in New Mexico over the Santa Fe Trail in 1831. When American troops marched into New Mexico to claim the Southwest for the United States fifteen years later, their leader, Brigadier General Stephen Watts Kearny, established a civil government in the territory. He appointed Bent, an educated leader and successful businessman, as the first American governor of New Mexico.

Although the American occupation was initially peaceful, it would not remain so. Among those most vocally opposed to the loss of Hispanic land rights by the new American system of land ownership was a prominent Taos priest, Antonio José Martínez. Padre Martínez had come to Taos from Abiquiú in 1826. To him is credited the first printed book in New Mexico—a textbook to be used in the girls' and boys' school he established in Taos, the territory's first coeducational school.

The American takeover rankled some Mexican and Indian residents of New Mexico, who feared—often correctly—that the change in government would mean the loss of their land rights. Mexican citizens joined with Indian allies from Taos Pueblo to plot a revolt known today as the Taos Rebellion. On the morning of January 19, 1847, after a night of insurgence that left the Taos sheriff dead, the rebels stormed Governor Bent's small adobe home one block north of the plaza. While Bent attempted to negotiate a peaceful solution, his wife, her sister, and her daughter from a previous marriage struggled desperately to claw their way through an adobe wall to freedom. Before they could escape, the rebels, in a gruesome display of recalcitrance, scalped Bent with the taut string of a hunting bow, then killed two of the older male children. Several hundred insurgents continued their assault by burning Turley's Mill, a gristmill and mountain man rendezvous point a few miles north of Taos, and killing seven men there, including the owner, Simeon Turley. Several other American citizens were slain in the insurrection before the Missouri Volunteers from Santa Fe, under the command of Colonel Sterling Price, along with a militia made up chiefly of mountain men, charged into town. The new American justice system was swift: the leaders of the revolt were found guilty of treason and hanged.

A later invasion was more peaceful. In 1914, artists Ernest Blumenschein and Bert Phillips led a small cadre of artists to found the Taos Society of Artists in the town. Their paintings of southwestern landscapes and Indians found a successful market in the East, and Taos soon became, as noted by the National Park Service, "the most important art center west of the Mississippi River." Taos socialite and wealthy art patron Mabel Dodge Luhan influenced the society and other Taos artists and writers, including D. H. Lawrence and his wife, to whom Luhan gave her Kiowa Ranch north of Taos as a home. Lawrence's ashes are held in a shrine on the ranch property. Taos remains an artistic haven for painters, musicians, and writers today.

Several former Taoseños including Kit Carson, Governor Bent, his wife María, Padre Martínez, and Mabel Dodge Luhan now rest quietly in the Kit Carson Memorial State Park Cemetery. The men killed at Turley Mill, including Simeon Turley, are buried in a common grave. The cemetery is part of the larger Kit Carson Memorial State Park, acquired by the community of Taos from the state in 1988. After concern arose about the name of this park, which honors a man not well regarded by Native Americans, the community of Taos voted to rename the park. As of spring 2015, a new name had not yet been chosen.

Buried in the Taos cemetery named in his honor, mountain man and government scout Christopher "Kit" Carson was a key figure in early Taos. His house is now a museum. Colonel Kit Carson. William A. Keleher Pictorial Collection, Box 1, Folder 15, Item 000-742-0032, Center for Southwest Research, University Libraries, University of New Mexico.

More to explore: *Couse-Sharp Historic Site, Cumbres Pass, Taos Canyon, The Three Fates*

448. Taos Canyon

Location: Taos County. At Las Petacas Campground in Carson National Forest, east of Taos, on the south side of US 64 between mile markers 258 and 259. See map 2.

Marker text: In 1692, after having been driven from New Mexico by the Pueblo Revolt of 1680, the Spanish began to reestablish their rule. In one of the last battles of the reconquest, in September 1696, Governor Diego de Vargas defeated the Indians of Taos Pueblo at nearby Taos Canyon.

The Pueblo Revolt of 1680 marked a turning point in relations between the Spanish and the native people in New Mexico. The revolt, an uprising among the Pueblo Indians of the upper Rio Grande against Spanish authority, expelled Spanish colonists from New Mexico for twelve years. In 1692, after a handful of abortive attempts by his compatriots, Spanish officer Diego de Vargas successfully entered Santa Fe and reestablished the capital city for Spain. Intent on restoring the civil infrastructure in New Mexico, Vargas, now the governor, made it one of his primary tasks to rebuild Spanish and Indian settlements that had been abandoned. He found that the strong emotions that had led to the rebellion in the pueblos had diffused in the intervening decade. Still, the new governor faced pockets of resistance—one of them at Taos Pueblo.

Vargas left Santa Fe on September 21, 1692, with a detachment of soldiers and Indian allies to visit Taos Pueblo personally. By the time he arrived, the Indians had fled to Taos Canyon, fearful that Vargas had come to punish them for their insurgent role in the revolt. According to his diary, Vargas attempted to negotiate with the Indians, promising pardons should they return quietly to their pueblo. The Indians refused, firing a volley of arrows to underscore their point.

On the second day, Vargas sent companies of his men to flank the sides of the timbered canyon, which lay within what is now Carson National Forest. Another detachment remained at the canyon mouth. Vargas and his soldiers charged into the defile, only to find that the Indians had retreated farther into the mountains.

The next day brought no change in tactic. Vargas again sent detachments to flank the ridges as he rode on horseback into the canyon. The Indians remained on the mountain, and Vargas was left without an enemy to fight, although he did manage to burn and loot the campsite and take more than a few Indians captive. As he had done successfully with other holdouts in the pueblos along the Rio Grande, he also seized the fields where the Indians had planted their crops and vowed to hold them until a peaceful surrender had taken place.

The tactic worked. Knowing that they could not long sustain themselves without access to their fields, the Indians slowly emerged from the canyon and returned home. More came forward over subsequent weeks as the air became crisp with the approach of winter. In mid-October, Vargas wrote in his journal that he felt the time had come for him to "withdraw and leave [the Taos Indians] to the freedom of their pueblo."

More to explore: *Taos*

Tesuque Rain Gods: *see Pueblo of Tesuque*

449. The Three Fates
Mabel Dodge Luhan (1879–1962), Frieda Lawrence (1879–1956), Dorothy Eugénie Brett (1883–1977)

Location: Taos County. North of El Prado (just north of Taos), in a pullout on the west side of NM 522, between mile markers 1 and 2. See map 2.

Marker text: Three extraordinary women contributed to the unique artistic culture of Taos in the 20th Century. Sometimes called "The Three Fates," they had a long, passionate and often contentious relationship with each other. Mabel Dodge Luhan created a haven for artists, writers and musicians at her Taos home, including D. H. Lawrence and his wife Frieda. They arrived in Taos in 1924 with their friend, Dorothy Brett.

Frieda von Richthofen was born into Prussian aristocracy and married Lawrence in 1914. She was his most ardent supporter and served as inspiration for many of his characters. Dorothy Brett, known simply as Brett, was born into English aristocracy. She provided moving depictions based on Taos Pueblo spiritualism in her paintings known collectively as "The Ceremonies." Together, these women created a vibrant world of artistic experimentation and creation.

450. D. H. Lawrence Ranch
University of New Mexico

Location: Taos County. At entrance to the Lawrence Ranch, at the intersection of NM 522 and County B 009, between mile markers 10 and 11 on NM 522. See map 2.

Marker text: The Kiowa Ranch, home of novelist D. H. Lawrence and his wife Frieda in 1924–25, was given to them by Mabel Dodge Luhan. Frieda continued to live at the ranch after his death, and later married Angelo Ravagli. In 1934 they built a shrine for Lawrence's ashes. Aldous Huxley was among the many visitors to the ranch.

Three prominent figures in the drama that was the development of the Taos art culture in the twentieth century could have been pulled from any epic novel of English literature. New York–born Mabel Dodge Luhan, a wealthy art patron, had first come to Taos in 1917 at age thirty-eight and established a haven and intellectual community for artists, writers, and musicians. Frieda von Richthofen, born into Prussian aristocracy, was the wife of famous English novelist D. H. Lawrence—a figure whom Luhan greatly admired. Lady Dorothy Eugénie Brett, a painter, was friends with Frieda and D. H. and accompanied them to Taos. Across many years and through a tumultuous history together, this trio of remarkable women became known as "the Three Fates," a reference to the figures of Greek mythology to whom was entrusted the outcome of each individual's life.

An invitation in 1922 by Luhan to Lawrence asking him to visit Taos initiated this coalescence of talents. Luhan (then Sterne), daughter of a wealthy family and by then a prominent Taos art benefactor, hoped that Lawrence and his wife might be stirred artistically by the people, landscape, and lore of the state. (She had done the same, successfully, with artist Georgia O'Keeffe.) A budding artist colony had taken root in Taos and would soon emerge in Santa Fe, and northern New Mexico was becoming favored by writers, poets, and painters alike.

Lawrence was intrigued by the idea, in part because he saw in Taos an opportunity to start a commune he had long envisioned, which he called Rananim. Lawrence himself would soon become one of the best-known icons of English literature. Simultaneously extolled as a genius of the sensual and derided as an artistic pornographer, his best-known classics today include *Lady Chatterley's*

Lover, *Women in Love*, and *Sons and Lovers*. He had met his wife, Frieda, in England in 1912. Lawrence had once been a former pupil of Frieda's first husband, Ernest Weekley, a French professor at University College in Nottingham. Frieda divorced her husband and married Lawrence. (It is believed that Lawrence based the relationship in *Lady Chatterley's Lover* on his relationship with Frieda, given her aristocratic background.) Frieda suffered from depression; Lawrence from tuberculosis, coupled with a sometimes violent temper.

Frieda and Lawrence arrived in Taos on September 11, 1922—the day of Lawrence's thirty-seventh birthday. Lawrence's struggle with tuberculosis required that he and Frieda stay only a short time in Taos before leaving for Mexico, but Luhan convinced them to return in 1924. Accompanying them on their second arrival was their friend, painter and literary patron Lady Dorothy Eugénie Brett. Lady Brett was most often known simply as "Brett."

The lives of Luhan, Frieda, and Brett entwined through relationships that were passionate and sometimes strained, but they helped imbue the community of Taos with a character of artistic creativity that still permeates the town today. At times, the three women competed for Lawrence's attention.

Luhan's domineering personality certainly added to the strife. But she was also quite generous. She offered Lawrence her 160-acre Flying Heart Ranch on Lobo Mountain twenty miles north of Taos as a gift. Although Lawrence refused it, Frieda accepted, renaming the ranch Kiowa. (In return, Frieda gave Luhan the manuscript for Lawrence's *Sons and Lovers*.) D. H. and Frieda lived on the ranch, as did Brett in a small cabin of her own. It was a generous endowment, rewarded in part by the creativity it inspired. Lawrence penned much of his short novel *St. Mawr* sitting at a table under a pine tree at the ranch, whose spiring branches were later made famous by Georgia O'Keeffe in her painting *The Lawrence Tree*. Among the other artists drawn to Kiowa was English writer Aldous Huxley, author of *Brave New World*, a classic novel partly set in New Mexico.

Brett herself found inspiration nearby as well—she attended a number of ceremonies conducted at Taos Pueblo and painted a series of highly colorful renditions of the dances and the people of the pueblo. The paintings are known collectively as *The Ceremonies*. When not painting, Brett often typed Lawrence's manuscripts.

When D. H. Lawrence eventually succumbed to his illness in France in 1930, Frieda returned to Taos and the Kiowa Ranch, later marrying her Italian lover, Angelo Ravagli. After having Lawrence's body exhumed and cremated in 1935, she had the ashes brought to Kiowa, where she interred them in a concrete altar inscribed across the front with the initials "D. H. L." This she had placed inside a petite, pitched-roof building on the ranch to serve as a permanent memorial to her late husband.

Frieda Lawrence herself passed away on August 11, 1956, in Taos, the day of her seventy-seventh birthday, and was laid in a grave near the shrine. Mabel Dodge Luhan died in 1962 and is buried in Kit Carson Memorial Cemetery in Taos. Dorothy Brett passed away on August 27, 1977; her ashes were spread along the base of Lobo Mountain on the ranch.

More to explore: *Georgia O'Keeffe, Taos*

451. Three Rivers

Location: Otero County. In Three Rivers, in front of the Three Rivers Trading Post, on US 54, at the turnoff to the Three Rivers petroglyphs. See map 6.

Marker text: Located in the Tularosa Basin east of the great lava flows known as the malpais, Three Rivers was once prominent in the cattle empires of Albert Bacon Fall, John S. Chisum, and Susie McSween Barber, "the cattle queen of New Mexico." Charles B. Eddy's El Paso & Northeastern Railroad reached here in 1899.

452. Three Rivers Petroglyphs

Location: Otero County. In Three Rivers, in front of the Three Rivers Trading Post, on US 54, at the turnoff to the Three Rivers petroglyphs. See map 6.

Marker text: Three miles to the east is a mile-long array of pictures pecked into the solid rock walls of a volcanic ridge. They include both geometric and animal forms. They were likely made by prehistoric Mogollón Indians between ca. A.D. 1000 and 1400.

Three Rivers is located just east of a forty-mile-long volcanic lava flow known as the malpais, a Spanish word meaning "badlands." The wrinkled black skin of the malpais formed about five thousand years ago when lava discharged by Little Black Peak, a small but industrious volcano to the north, spread through the upper reaches of the Tularosa Valley. From AD 900 until around 1200, this valley was home to the Jornada Mogollon, prehistoric Indians who inscribed more than twenty thousand petroglyphs of animals, human beings, and abstract designs on rocks in hills near the lava flows. One petroglyph of a human face shows evidence of the Indians' appreciation for the seasons: during the winter solstice, the sun shines on only half the face.

A small ranching village developed near Three Rivers Creek in the early 1870s. When a post office opened in 1883, the community took the name Three Rivers for a nearby convergence of three creeks. One of the early settlers was Susan McSween, who moved to the Three Rivers area from Lincoln with her second husband, attorney George Barber. McSween's former husband, Alexander, had been killed in July 1878 in what became known as the Lincoln County War. In her new home, McSween and her husband established the Three Rivers Land and Cattle Company with

Although born in Kentucky, lawyer, soldier, rancher, and US senator Albert Bacon Fall made New Mexico the backdrop for his epic life. His Tres Ritos Ranch at Three Rivers was his last gasp of greatness in the state. Albert Bacon Fall. William A. Keleher Pictorial Collection, Box 1, Folder 25, Item 000-742-0049, Center for Southwest Research, University Libraries, University of New Mexico.

cattle given to them by John Chisum, former partner of Alexander McSween in Lincoln and one of the richest cattle ranchers in southeastern New Mexico at the time. Susan McSween met such success in the cattle business that history awarded her the title "Cattle Queen of New Mexico."

In 1899, railroad developer Charles Eddy extended his El Paso and Northeastern Railroad from El Paso north through the Tularosa Basin to Santa Rosa, passing near Three Rivers. The population of the village reached 163 by 1900.

Eventually, much of the land around Three Rivers fell into the hands of Albert Bacon Fall, an influential lawyer who later would become one of the first two men to represent New Mexico in the United States Senate. By assuming control of water rights on Three Rivers properties, Fall essentially evicted most residents of the village. In 1902, he acquired the McSween ranch; Susan McSween had earlier divorced her husband and retired to the nearby town of White Oaks, where she resided until her death in 1931. Fall continued amassing land, often through foreclosure, until his Three Rivers ranch became an empire of more than a million acres.

Trouble lay ahead for Fall. Convicted of accepting a bribe in the Teapot Dome Scandal while serving as secretary of the interior under President Warren G. Harding in 1921, Fall, then in reduced health, parceled and sold his ranch to pay his debts.

With the loss of its principal organizers, Three Rivers was by that time a settlement of diminished prospects. Eventually, the train discontinued stops at the village, and the school closed. The village survived in modest form, however, and today exists as a peaceful collection of ranch properties, a church, and a handful of small buildings.

More to explore: *Albuquerque Petroglyphs (see under Albuquerque), Beclabito Dome, Lincoln, Malpais, Tularosa, White Oaks*

453. Three Wise Women
Eva Scott Fenyes (1849–1930)
Leonora Scott Muse Curtin (1879–1972)

Location: Santa Fe County. Fifteen miles south of Santa Fe, in the Bicentennial Rest Area and Visitors Center, on the east side of Interstate 25. (The rest area is also known as the La Bajada Rest Area.) See map 2.

Marker text: Three generations of one family worked more than 100 years to preserve the cultural heritage of New Mexico. Eva Fenyes created an artistic and photographic record of missions and adobe buildings, and preserved Spanish Colonial and Native American crafts. Leonora S. M. Curtin wrote Healing Herbs of the Upper Rio Grande, which documented the ethnobotany of the region and the plants used by traditional healers.

Leonora Curtin Paloheimo (1903–1999)

Location: Santa Fe County. Fifteen miles south of Santa Fe, in the Bicentennial Rest Area and Visitors Center, on the east side of Interstate 25. (The rest area is also known as the La Bajada Rest Area.)

Marker text: Leonora Curtin Paloheimo worked to preserve New Mexico's varied cultures. She researched Native American languages for the Smithsonian. During the Depression, she founded The Native Market as an outlet for Spanish American artisans who handcrafted traditional furniture and household items. She and her Finnish husband, George Paloheimo, established New Mexico's first living history museum, El Rancho de las Golondrinas, in 1972.

Note: Marker faceplates are on opposite sides of the same sign.

Between them, Eva Scott Fenyes; her daughter, Leonora Scott Muse Curtin; and Leonora's daughter, Leonora Curtin Paloheimo, brought more than one hundred years of dedicated adherence to the idea of preserving the cultural heritage of the Southwest. Each of them did so in her own way, helping to preserve the traditions, architecture, and healing wisdom of this part of the country from the mid-nineteenth century to the present day.

Born on November 9, 1849, into a wealthy New York family, Eva Scott Fenyes married Lieutenant William S. Muse in 1878 and gave birth to a daughter, Leonora, the next year. When she came to New Mexico in the 1880s, Fenyes had already traveled through Europe and Africa, become an accomplished artist, divorced her first husband, and married physician Adalbert Fenyes. She became an expert in Spanish colonial arts and an advocate for the preservation of southwestern culture. Her magnum opus, which she began after moving to Pasadena, California, in 1898, was a series of more than three hundred watercolor paintings of missions and older adobe buildings in California—all created in an attempt to document the architecture of a time and place before it vanished. She stopped only on her death in 1930.

Arriving in New Mexico with Fenyes in the 1880s was her daughter, Leonora, whose father was Fenyes's first husband. Like her mother, Leonora had a fascination with learning and with travel. She met and married her husband, lawyer Thomas Edouard Curtin, in Santa Fe. The couple had one child, a girl, also named Leonora. When the elder Leonora's husband died in 1911, mother and daughter divided their time between California and their house in Santa Fe. The senior Leonora's particular interest was ethnobiology, the study of plant use by various cultures.

Traveling among the traditionally Spanish-speaking villages of northern New Mexico, she studied the use of native herbs by community healers. Her work culminated in the 1947 book, *Healing Herbs of the Upper Rio Grande*. Written in the first person and including many personal anecdotes from Leonora's visits, the book documents the herbs of northern New Mexico and their use for medicinal purposes. It is considered a classic in the field of ethnobotany.

Born on December 7, 1903, Leonora Frances Curtin carried the tradition of her grandmother and mother into a third generation. She worked for a time at the Smithsonian Institution studying the languages of the Pueblo Indians, and during the Great Depression she sponsored a market in Santa Fe to provide artists with a forum for selling their work. With her mother, she purchased a small ranch, La Cienega, just south of Santa Fe in the 1930s. For many years, she traveled to remote villages with her husband, a Finnish diplomat she had met in New York in 1946, purchasing buildings and historic farm equipment. These she had transported to La Cienega, creating in that place a living history museum of a Spanish colonial village. The village, first opened to the public in 1972 and still open today, is known as El Rancho de las Golondrinas, or "Ranch of the Swallows."

Fenyes, her daughter, and her granddaughter called their home in Santa Fe the Acqeuia Madre House because of its address on Acequia Madre Street. But their friend Charles Lummis, journalist and author of the New Mexico classic *Land of Poco Tiempo*, referred to it as "the house of the three wise women."

More to explore: *Curanderas—Women Who Heal, El Rancho de las Golondrinas/Old Cienega Village Museum, Historic Los Luceros, Santa Fe*

454. Tierra Amarilla

Location: 1. Rio Arriba County. Just north of Tierra Amarilla, in a pullout at the intersection of US 64/84 and NM 162, between mile markers 174 and 175 on US 64. See map 2.

2. Rio Arriba County. Just south of Tierra Amarilla, in a pullout at the intersection of US 84 and NM 162, between mile markers 253 and 254 on US 84. See map 2.

Marker text: In 1832 the Mexican government made a large community land grant to Manuel Martínez and other settlers, but settlement was delayed by raids by Utes, Jicarilla Apaches and Navajos. Tierra Amarilla, first called Nutritas, became the Rio Arriba County seat in 1880. In 1967 it was the focus of conflicts between National Guardsmen and land rights activist Reies López Tijerina.

In 1832, the Mexican government awarded the Tierra Amarilla grant in north-central New Mexico to Manuel Martínez and other residents of nearby Abiquiú so they might have new lands upon which to cultivate farms and to pasture sheep. *Tierra amarilla* is a Spanish term that means "yellow earth" and refers to the abundant yellow clay found in the Chama River Valley. Raids by Utes, Jicarilla Apaches, and Navajos kept Spanish colonists from establishing a permanent settlement on the land grant until the early 1860s, when the US Army established Camp Plummer (later renamed Fort Lowell) nearby to protect settlers. Thereafter, a cluster of small Hispanic villages evolved in the valley, including Los Ojos, La Puente, and Encinada, with the largest being Las Nutritas, or "Little Beavers."

In 1877, a visiting army officer, Lieutenant C. A. H. McCauley, left this description of the region:

The Tierra Amarilla is the center of the Mexican population of northwestern New Mexico, the industry of the inhabitants being limited to agriculture and pastoral pursuits. . . . Las Nutritas is the largest of the group, to which sometimes the name of the section itself is applied. . . . The post office of the section was located here, mails being weekly only and from no direction save from Santa Fe to the south; population, 250.

When the territorial legislature created Rio Arriba County in 1880, Las Nutritas residents erected a new courthouse to serve as the county seat. The village did so under a new name: Tierra Amarilla.

In that courthouse, the village of Tierra Amarilla made modern history as the focal point of conflicts between northern New Mexico land rights activists and the US government. On June 5, 1967, forty-year-old Reies López Tijerina led about twenty members of his Alianza Federal de Mercedes, or Federal Alliance of Land Grants, on a raid of the Rio Arriba County courthouse in Tierra Amarilla to make a citizen's arrest of the district attorney. In doing so, Tijerina, a former evangelist, hoped to bring attention to the unscrupulous means by which the government and Anglo settlers had usurped Hispanic land grant properties.

After about ninety minutes of shooting within the courthouse walls, during which a state policeman and a jail worker were wounded, Tijerina and his followers fled to nearby Canjilon with a sheriff's deputy and a reporter as hostages. The National Guard, the New Mexico State Police, and the FBI pursued the band, eventually capturing Tijerina in Bernalillo five days later. He was given two years and eight months in jail as a combined sentence for both the raid and for a previous takeover of Echo Amphitheater near Abiquiú.

More to explore: *Abiquiú, Colfax County War*

455. Tiguex Province

Location: Bernalillo County. In Rio Rancho, in a pullout on the south side of NM 528, between Rio Vista Drive NE and Rio Pinos Road NE. See map 4.

Marker text: More than one hundred prehistoric and historic pueblos and other archaeological sites and over 15,000 petroglyphs or rock art sites give ample evidence of the occupation of this valley for at least 12,000 years. Spanish explorers who came into the area in the sixteenth century gave the name "Tiguex Province" to the dozen or more Tiwa-speaking Indian pueblos (towns) they found in the middle Rio Grande Valley.

Francisco Vásquez de Coronado, on a search for gold for Spain, arrived in New Mexico in 1540. While remaining near the pueblo of Zuni in western New Mexico, he sent an advance guard led by Hernando de Alvarado to explore the region along the Rio Grande. Following the river north, the men reached this part of the middle Rio Grande Valley in the fall of that year. They found the area populated with a number of Indian pueblos. The residents of these small villages spoke dialects of a common language known as Tiwa. The Indians called the region Shia-way. The Spanish heard the name differently, as Tiguex (originally pronounced TEE-wesh; the pronunciation TEEG-way is also becoming common). They then extended that name to the collection of Tiwa-speaking pueblos, calling this Tiguex Province.

At the time, Tiguex Province stretched from present-day Bernalillo (about ten miles north of this Historic Marker) to Isleta Pueblo south of Albuquerque (about twenty miles south of this Historic Marker). It included at least twelve pueblos, possibly many more.

Hernando de Alvarado left this description of Tiguex Province as it first appeared to European eyes:

This river of Our Lady flows through a very wide open plain sowed with corn plants; there are several groves, and there are twelve villages. The houses are of earth, two stories high; the people have a good appearance, more like laborers than warlike race; they have a large food supply of corn, beans, melons, and fowl in great plenty; they clothe themselves with cotton and the skins of cows and dresses of the feathers of the fowls; they wear their hair short. Those who have the most authority among them are the old men.

Of the Tiwa-speaking pueblos in the original Tiguex Province, only two survive today. Isleta Pueblo lies just south of Albuquerque, and the pueblo of Tuf Shurn Tui (formerly known as Sandia Pueblo) lies to the north.

This part of New Mexico has seen human occupation in different locations and for different periods of time for more than twelve thousand years. Symbols and figurines inscribed into rock left by some of these early inhabitants, drawings known as petroglyphs, can be found at Petroglyph National Monument in the canyons of west Albuquerque. Archaeologists have identified the ruins of more than a hundred Puebloan structures and other sites associated with human activity in this region, both historical and prehistoric. Many of those sites are now protected archaeological resources whose location is not made publicly available. The ruins of one, however, Kuaua, is open to visitors as the Coronado Historic Site in Bernalillo.

More to explore: *Albuquerque, Bernalillo, Spanish Entrada Site, Vásquez de Coronado's Route (series)*

456. Tijeras Canyon

Location: Bernalillo County. East of Albuquerque in Tijeras Canyon, along old Route 66 between mile markers 7 and 8, just past the road to City Hall. See map 4.

Marker text: This pass between the Sandia and Manzano Mountains has been a natural route for travel between eastern New Mexico and the Rio Grande Valley since prehistoric times. Known as Cañon de Carnué in the Spanish colonial period, it takes its present name from the village of Tijeras, Spanish for "scissors."

As far back as nine thousand years ago, nomadic Paleo-Indians traveled this concourse between the Sandia and Manzano Mountains. Tijeras Canyon was later home to Tiwa-speaking Indians, who erected several small villages in the mountainous confines around 1100. These Indians eventually concatenated their population into two larger pueblo villages—the ruins of one of them now taking the name Tijeras Pueblo—before migrating from the area sometime after 1400.

After the founding of Albuquerque in 1706, Spanish settlement progressed into these piñon- and juniper-covered mountains, now within the boundaries of Cibola National Forest. In February 1763, a small group of Spanish-speaking pioneers established a settlement near the canyon. Their village took the name San Miguel de Carnué. The word *carnué* was probably a phonetic corruption of the original Tiwa name for the site. That corruption continued for years in the name of the canyon itself: Cañon de Carnué. Despite the defensive layout of their settlement, the early residents of San Miguel de Carnué could not withstand the onslaught of Apache Indian attacks. They deserted their village a scant eight years after having founded it.

The region waited until 1819 for new settlers. In that year, intrepid local settler Juan Ignacio Tafoya and twenty-six others arrived to have a go at it. Their land grant, awarded by the Spanish government as the Cañon de Carnuel grant, encompassed the canyon and the former village of San Miguel. As the community took hold, it gradually evolved into the present-day villages of Carnuel and Tijeras. Spanish for "scissors," the word *tijeras* may be a reference to two canyons that meet at this point, juxtaposed in such a way that they create a shape suggestive of crossed scissor blades.

More to explore: *Albuquerque*

457. Tomé

Location: Valencia County. In Tomé, off NM 47 to the Church Loop, in the courtyard and park before the Immaculate Conception Church and Museum. See map 4.

Marker text: For centuries, the prominent *cerro*, or steep hill, of Tomé was a significant landmark for travelers along the Camino Real. Settled as early as 1650, this area was abandoned following the Pueblo Revolt of 1680 and remained uninhabited until the Tomé Land Grant was established in 1739. During the late 18th and early 19th centuries, Tomé was the center of government for the Rio Abajo district.

Geologically an eroded volcanic plug, Tomé Hill for years served as a beacon along the historic trail between Mexico and New Mexico known as El Camino Real. Throughout the eighteenth and nineteenth centuries, wagon caravans bearing supplies and communications passed near the prominent *cerro*, or steep knoll, as their drivers followed the Rio Grande through the middle of the state. Travelers resting at the hill no doubt noticed the scratched petroglyphs of animals and geometric shapes carved into boulders on its sides, symbolic art drawn by early Native Americans many centuries before the arrival of the Spanish.

Around 1659, Spanish military officer Tomé Domínguez de Mendoza II petitioned for and received a parcel of land on a plain west of the then-unnamed hill. Mendoza and his family erected a large ranch alongside the banks of the river, and for a short time in 1664 Mendoza served as interim governor of the New Mexico province. His was one of the first Spanish households in the area—but it did not survive to enjoy the merit. In 1680, the Pueblo Indians in New Mexico revolted against the Spanish colonists and forced them from the state. Domínguez de Mendoza and other local settlers and Indians he assisted escaped the rebellion alive, but thirty-eight of his relatives did not.

The region remained uninhabited until July 1739, when a group of Spanish colonists and *genízaros*, or detribalized Indians, received the Tomé land grant in this region from Governor Domingo de Mendoza. These settlers established a village on their grant about a mile south of the abandoned Domínguez ranch. Their hamlet borrowed the previous patriarch's name to become Nuestra Señora de la Concepción de Tomé Domínguez.

Tomé, as it was commonly called, lay deep in the territory frequently assailed by Apaches and Comanches. In response, settlers constructed their village as a string of defensible homes and a church confining and thus securing a central plaza. Tomé residents raised livestock and farmed the river valley, persisting despite Indian raids and several demoralizing floods. An alcalde, a position similar to a mayor, directed the course of civic affairs in the village and outlying areas, and Tomé soon became prominent in the Rio Abajo district, the designation of land and settlements along the lower Rio Grande. These civic affiliations continued after the Southwest came under the control of the United States. In 1850, when the territorial legislature created Valencia County, Tomé served as the first county seat.

Eventually, however, political and economic weight in Valencia County transferred to Los Lunas. Tomé lost the county seat in 1876.

Every Good Friday, Tomé residents join with family, friends, and neighbors from surrounding communities to embark on a religious pilgrimage centered at Tomé Hill. Members of the congregation stride in procession up the Way of the Cross path to the summit of the hill in this most devout expression of the villagers' abiding communion with the land.

More to explore: *Comanche Country, El Camino Real— The King's Highway, El Rancho de las Golondrinas/ Old Cienega Village Museum*

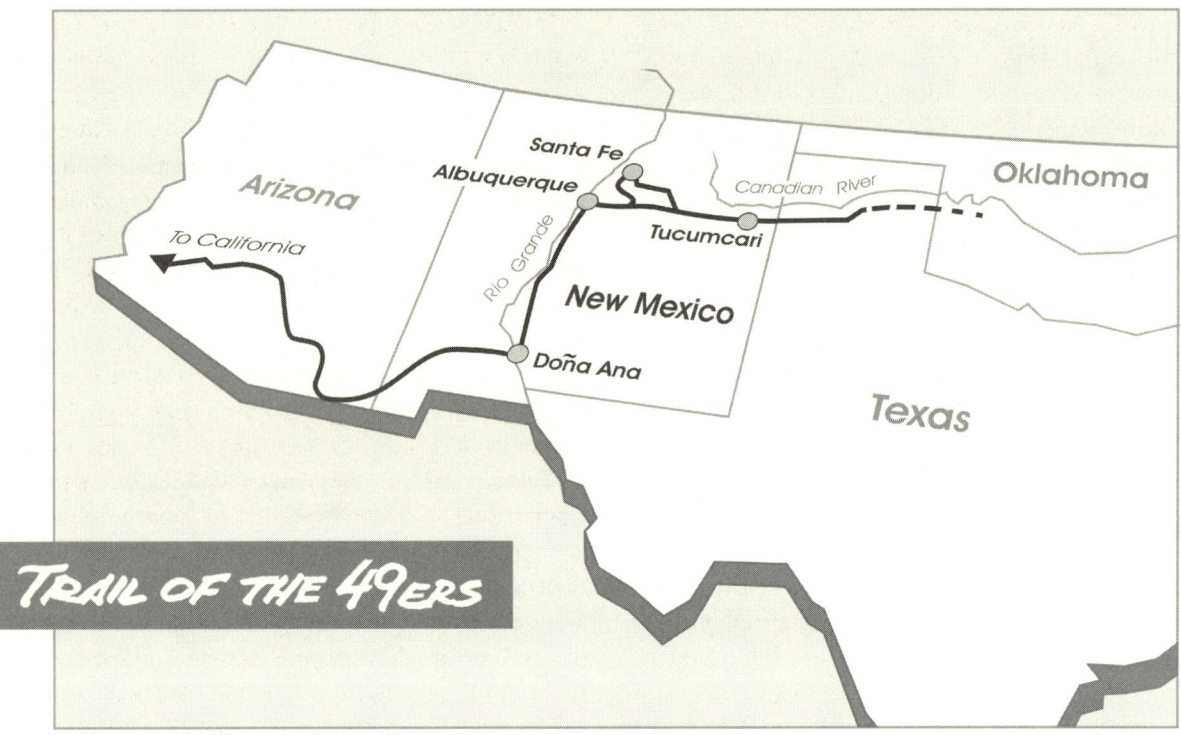

"The accounts of the abundance of gold in that territory," President James K. Polk told the nation in December 1848, "are of such extraordinary character as would scarcely command belief were they not corroborated by authentic reports of officers in the public service." Many of the '49ers who went west on Polk's nod of approval followed this route. Illustration by David Carter.

458. Trail of the Forty-Niners

Location: Guadalupe County. In the rest area on the north side of Interstate 40 between Clines Corners and Santa Rosa, at mile marker 150. See map 3.

Marker text: To give gold-seekers another route to California, Capt. Randolph B. Marcy and Lt. James H. Simpson opened a wagon road from Arkansas to New Mexico in 1849. Marcy's Road, although very popular with the Forty-Niners, still was never as well-traveled as the Santa Fe Trail. Here the route parallels I-40 to Albuquerque.

Workers building a sawmill for John Augustus Sutter along the American River near Sacramento, California, in 1848 eyed flakes of gold shimmering on the riverbank—and suddenly the country had an infrastructure problem. Gold-seeking "forty-niners," so dubbed because most started on their epic journey west in the spring of 1849, followed popular and crowded routes like the Oregon Trail and the Santa Fe Trail on their way to the Pacific coast. Large volumes of traffic on these trails had left the prairies littered with broken wagons and hand-dug latrines. New roads were needed.

That year, the government tapped Captain Randolph Barnes Marcy of the US Army, a Massachusetts-born graduate of West Point, along with Lieutenant James Hervey Simpson, a member of the Army Corps of Topographical Engineers, to escort an emigrant train west from Fort Smith, Arkansas, and open a new route for gold seekers. With a detachment of soldiers from the First and Second Dragoons along with companies of the Fifth Infantry, a doctor, eighteen wagons, and a six-pound iron gun, Marcy and Simpson set out on their prairie quest on April 5, 1849. The party followed the Canadian River through the grasslands of Oklahoma, north Texas, and into eastern New Mexico. From Tucumcari, where they parlayed briefly with local Comanche Indians to arrange safe passage, their route paralleled present-day Interstate 40 to Albuquerque. They arrived in Santa Fe around 4:00 p.m. on June 28.

"I have never passed over a country," Marcy wrote, "where wagons could move along with as much ease and facility, without the expenditure of any labor in making a road, as upon this route."

Although Marcy's road ended in Santa Fe, most of the emigrants continued on their own from Albuquerque to California. They followed the Rio Grande south, then turned west near Doña Ana and kept to a wagon road pioneered three years earlier by Lieutenant Colonel Philip St. George Cooke and the Mormon Battalion. They entered Arizona, and then they continued with high hopes to the gold fields of California.

In 1859, Marcy penned *The Prairie Traveler*, a handbook for those making the overland journey west. His book included chapters on "Fording Rivers," "Best Methods of Marching," "Cures for the Bite," "Repairing Broken Wagons," and "Quicksand." Also listed were the most popular trails between Mississippi and California, including his own. Marcy took the opportunity his book presented to lament his belief that he had never received due credit for having blazed his trail. "This route," he wrote, "is set down upon most of the maps of the present day as having been discovered and explored by various persons, but my own name seems to have been carefully excluded from the list."

Lieutenant Simpson also felt passed over in recognition of having opened the road. In a letter later submitted to the army's chief of engineers, Simpson wrote: "I confess that I have felt hurt by these omissions, and think it due to myself and history that I should thus officially refer to them."

The men did not have long to express regret. With most of the surface gold depleted by 1864, the mad rush to California had ended.

More to explore: *Comanche Country, Cooke's Wagon Road, El Camino Real—The King's Highway, Gold and Turquoise, Jornada del Muerto, Santa Fe Trail, Tucumcari Mountain*

Trinidad Gachupin Medina: *see Pueblo of Zia*

459. Trinity Site

Location: Socorro County. East of San Antonio, at the intersection of NM 525 and US 380 (the road to Stallion Gate, White Sands Missile Range) between mile markers 12 and 13 on US 380. See map 5.

Marker text: The nuclear age began with the detonation of the world's first atomic bomb at the Trinity Site on July 16, 1945. The site may have been named Trinity by J. Robert Oppenheimer, director of the Los Alamos Nuclear Physics Laboratory, who said at the blast, "Now, I am become Death, the destroyer of worlds," quoting from the Bhagavad Gita. The detonation of the bomb marked the culmination of the Manhattan Project.

460. Jumbo

Location: Socorro County. Just off the downtown plaza in the town of Socorro, near the intersection of Court Street and Plaza Street, by Veterans Memorial Park. See map 5.

Marker text: This is a fragment from Jumbo, a huge steel vessel designed to contain the explosion of the first nuclear device at the Trinity Site some 35 miles southeast of here on July 16, 1945. Jumbo was 25 feet long, 12 feet in diameter, and weighed 214 tons. Its steel walls were 14 inches thick. Although Jumbo was not used in the tests, it was 800 feet from ground zero at the time and escaped without damage except for a steel superstructure around it which was crumpled by the blast. Jumbo was used in later experiments which resulted in the ends being blown out. This piece of Jumbo is a souvenir of the worlds first nuclear explosion. Dr. Marvin Wilkening, an observer in 1945.

Note: The text of this Historic Marker was written by physicist Marvin Wilkening (1918–2006), who was present at the detonation of the atomic bomb at the Trinity Site and later served as professor emeritus at the New Mexico Institute of Mining and Technology in Socorro.

Early travelers over the barren desert between Las Cruces and Socorro known as the Jornada del Muerto, or "Journey of the Dead Man," could scarcely imagine that the land they were crossing would one day help usher in the nuclear age. They had more immediate concerns. The Jornada lacked water and firewood and was a hotbed of Apache attacks. Yet the same isolation that made the land so unaccommodating for early travelers made it attractive to twentieth-century scientists as a place to test an entirely new weapon of war.

Work on that weapon began when the US government formed the top secret Manhattan Project in June 1942. Its mission: to build an atomic bomb that would help end World War II in advance of any similar weapon the Germans might develop. Major General Leslie R. Groves was placed in charge of the operation, with Dr. J. Robert Oppenheimer, a physicist from the University of California, chosen to lead the scientists designing the bomb. Included in the ranks were noted physicists Enrico Fermi and Marvin Wilkening (the latter would later write the text for the "Jumbo" Historic Marker on Socorro Plaza). The men worked at a hidden lab on Pajarito Plateau north of Santa Fe, a research center that survives today as Los Alamos National Laboratory.

In 1944, construction began on a base camp at the northern end of the desolate Jornada del Muerto, then part of the Alamogordo Bombing Range, which would serve as the site of the trial run for the device the scientists had developed. Soldiers built protective bunkers for the scientists, technicians, and camera operators who would conduct the operations. Called South 10,000, West 10,000, and North 10,000, the names of these bunkers referenced both their direction and the number of yards they stood distant from ground zero, where the bomb was to be detonated. Work crews also converted the abandoned George McDonald ranch house into a laboratory where scientists could assemble the plutonium core. Oppenheimer chose a name for the site inspired by the opening line of a poem by John Donne: Trinity.

Originally, the bomb was to have been placed in a giant steel encasement measuring twenty-five feet long and twelve feet in diameter. This massive outer shell was called Jumbo, a reference to its size as well as its weight: 214 tons! If the bomb failed to explode as expected, Jumbo would mitigate the damage from the blast and keep deadly plutonium contained. Although Jumbo was brought to the Trinity Site, it was not used, as scientists felt confident that the bomb would explode as expected.

On July 14, 1945, technicians placed the bomb, dubbed "Fat Man," atop a one-hundred-foot-high steel tower. Light rain at dawn on July 16, the target date for the test, stalled the detonation for about ninety minutes. At last, the rain let up, and the countdown began (Wilkening later recalled that it was the first time he had ever heard someone count backward). Oppenheimer himself pushed the button to trigger the world's first nuclear bomb explosion, and, in the words of eyewitness Brigadier General Thomas F. Farrell:

The whole country was lighted by a searing light with the intensity many times that of the midday sun.... Thirty seconds after, the explosion came ... to be followed almost immediately by the strong, sustained, awesome roar which warned of doomsday and made us feel that we puny things were blasphemous to dare tamper with the forces heretofore reserved to the Almighty.

The nuclear age began at 5:29:45 a.m. mountain time on Monday, July 16, 1945.

In a television interview given years later in 1965, Oppenheimer described his feelings at the time by quoting from the Bhagavad Gita, a classic of sacred Indian scripture, which recounts in verse the conversation between Prince Arjuna and his spirit guide, Krishna, before a great war. Oppenheimer said:

We knew the world would not be the same. A few people laughed. A few people cried. Most people were silent. I remembered the line from the Hindu scripture, the Bhagavad-Gita. Vishnu is trying to persuade the prince that he should do his duty, and to impress him takes on his multi-armed form and says, "Now I am become Death, the destroyer of worlds." I suppose we all thought that, one way or another.

Jumbo, having been hoisted onto a steel support tower eight hundred yards away from the blast site, escaped unharmed. (The same could not be said for the support tower, which was destroyed in the blast.) Most of the structure of Jumbo remains intact and is on display at the Trinity Site, although the ends were blown out when the army used the structure for a bomb detonation in 1946. A fragment has been placed near the plaza in Socorro, giving visitors the opportunity to inspect firsthand its fourteen-inch-thick wall.

The Trinity Site today lies within the White Sands Missile Range. Although restricted to the public most of the year, the site is open for visitors on the first Saturday in April and October.

More to explore: *El Camino Real—The King's Highway, Jornada del Muerto, La Luz, Peggy Pond Church (see under Marjorie Bell Chambers)*

461. Truchas

Location: Rio Arriba County. In Truchas, in a turnout on the south side of NM 76, between mile markers 15 and 16. See map 2.

Marker text: In 1754, Governor Tomás Vélez Cachupín granted land on the Río Truchas to families from Santa Cruz and Chimayó. The village was originally called Nuestra Señora del Rosario de Truchas (Our Lady of the Rosary of Trout). Located on the far northern frontier and subject to attack by Plains Indians, Governor Vélez Cachupín stipulated the houses should form a square with only one entrance.

In 1754, Governor Tomás Vélez Cachupín granted land about twenty-five miles north of Santa Fe to a handful of Spanish families from Santa Cruz and Chimayó, two small villages in the Santa Cruz Valley to the east. Because of its location along the banks of the Rio Truchas, the hamlet that developed was named Nuestra Señora del Rosario de Truchas, or "Our Lady of the Rosary of the Trout." Most often, it was simply called Truchas.

Safety was a tenuous prospect in the northern hinterlands of New Mexico in the mid-eighteenth century. With fortified villages such as Truchas to serve as high-country outposts, safeguarding against depredations by Apaches, Comanches, and other Plains Indians, the Spanish could create a buffer zone to shield the capital in Santa Fe. Cachupín thus ordered that the settlement be built in a pattern typical of such Spanish villages. Specifically, houses were to sit side by side, joined together and facing an open public square, or plaza. The outer walls of the buildings were to have no windows, and there was to be only one entrance, wide enough to allow passage for only a single cart, "in a manner that the inhabitants and families may be able to defend themselves from invasions and assaults."

Truchas subsisted as a farming village for generations. In 1800, it was home to 150 people, most of whom spent their time tending fields of wheat and alfalfa and grazing sheep.

When a new highway opened Truchas to the outside world in the 1960s, one unlikely visitor eventually came knocking: Hollywood. Robert Redford chose the picturesque, somnolent village as the setting for his 1988 film *The Milgaro Beanfield War*, based on a novel by New Mexico author John Nichols. One hundred and twenty crew members descended on the community through the fall and spring of 1986 and 1987, according to estimates from the New Mexico Film Office. In appreciation to the town after the movie was completed, Redford donated thousands of dollars to help build the Truchas Community Center.

More to explore: *Chimayó, Comanche Country, Córdova, El Rancho de las Golondrinas/Old Cienega Village Museum, Truchas Peaks*

462. Truchas Peaks

Location: Rio Arriba County. North of Truchas, in a pullout on the east side of NM 76, at mile marker 17. See map 2.

Marker text: Ice age glaciers carved these beautiful alpine peaks, among the highest in the New Mexico Rockies, rising to 13,101 feet. Precambrian quartzite, some of the oldest rock in New Mexico, forms the core of the Truchas ("trout") Peaks, part of the Pecos Wilderness which encompasses some of the most pristine mountain terrain in the state.

It's hard not to be impressed with the view to the east here: those are the spectacular Truchas Peaks. *Truchas* is a Spanish word meaning "trout." The name comes from the Rio Truchas, or River of Trout, which begins on the western slopes of these mountains and flows westward to the small village of Truchas just north of here.

The Truchas Peaks are a sub-region of the Santa Fe Mountains. Among their highest peaks are North Truchas at 13,024 feet, Middle Truchas at 13,066 feet, and Truchas Peak (also called South Truchas Peak), the highest, at 13,102 feet. Until 1948, Truchas Peak was believed to be the highest peak in New Mexico. But that year, a mountain lover and photographer from Santa Fe, Harold Walter, determined that, in fact, Wheeler Peak, which lies in the Taos Mountains farther north, was higher, at 13,161 feet. The height of these craggy peaks puts them in the high-altitude alpine tundra, a region where trees do not grow.

The Truchas Peaks and Santa Fe Mountains are within the Sangre de Cristo Mountains, which form the southernmost extension of the Rocky Mountains in New Mexico. Precambrian quartzite, a metamorphic rock, makes up the core of these mountains, as it does much of the Sangre de Cristo range.

The Truchas Peaks are a prominent part of the

Pecos Wilderness, a region of more than 223,000 acres of pristine mountain terrain. The Pecos is within Santa Fe National Forest and home to Rocky Mountain bighorn sheep, deer, bears, turkeys, and other forest denizens.

More to explore: *Rocky Mountains, Sangre de Cristo, Truchas*

463. Truth or Consequences

Location: Sierra County. At the north end of Truth or Consequences on the north side of Broadway Street. See map 5.

Marker text: In 1581, Captain Francisco Sanchez Chamuscado took possession of this region for the King of Spain, naming it Ojo de Zoquete (mud spring) in the Province of San Felipe. Native Americans first used these springs for healing; in the early 20th century, European-Americans settled here and named it Hot Springs. Truth or Consequences ("T or C") took its present name in 1951 in response to a contest from Ralph Edwards' popular radio program.

464. Truth or Consequences

Location: Sierra County. At the west end of Truth or Consequences (technically in Williamsburg), at the intersection of Broadway and Hyde, near the fairgrounds, on the south side of the road. See map 5.

Marker text: In 1581, Captain Francisco Sanchez Chamuscado took possession of this region for the King of Spain, naming it the Province of San Felipe. Significant European settlement of the area, however, did not occur until the mid-1800s. Once called Hot Springs because of its curative natural hot springs, "T or C" in 1950 took its present name from Ralph Edwards' radio program.

It was March 31, 1950, and 1,589 people turned out for the vote. They went to the VFW Hall, the Community Center, the Fireman's Hall on Date Street, and the Catholic Church on Fifth. The little town of Hot Springs was about to make what the local paper would call "the most unprecedented action taken by a city anywhere." When the election was over and all votes had been tallied, the result was 1,294 in favor and 295 opposed. Citizens of the southwestern New Mexico town of Hot Springs had agreed to change the name of their settlement to Truth or Consequences.

Captain Francisco Sánchez Chamuscado of the Spanish military probably could not have imagined such an event when he passed through the region in 1581 on an expedition up the Rio Grande from present-day El Paso. On August 21, Chamuscado took possession of the land and named it the Kingdom of San Felipe in honor of the king of Spain, Philip II. Modern settlement of the area began after soldiers of the US Army erected Fort McRae near present-day Elephant Butte in 1863 to protect travelers and early residents in the river valley from Indian attacks. The construction of Elephant Butte Dam south of the fort in 1910, although creating a reservoir that engulfed the ruins of Fort McRae, encouraged the development of a town. In 1914, a post office opened, taking the name Hot Springs.

That name spoke to the geothermal hot springs bubbling from abundant underground reservoirs around the town. For generations, Indians had used those springs to comfort their fatigued bodies. Early settlers and soldiers at Fort McRae had likewise savored their restorative warmth; the area was sometimes known as Ojo de Zoquete, or "mud springs." Since its inception, the town had capitalized on its geothermal gifts by enticing motorists with the promise of the redemptive powers of the waters. The town of Hot Springs was a recreational destination and health resort.

Burton Roach, manager of the Hot Springs Chamber of Commerce, saw further opportunity to attract tourists when he learned in 1949 that Ralph Edwards had offered to broadcast the tenth-anniversary show of his popular television program *Truth or Consequences* from any town that would change its name to match that of the show. Roach arranged a special town election to decide the issue and got the paper to run editorials in support of the idea. The propaganda worked: residents voted overwhelmingly to adopt the new name.

On April 1, 1950, Ralph Edwards broadcast *Truth or Consequences* live from the renamed town.

More to explore: Caballo Mountains, Elephant Butte Dam, Magnolia Ellis

465. Tucumcari

Location: Quay County. In Tucumcari, at the east end of town, in a pullout on the north side of East Tucumcari Boulevard (the Interstate 40 business loop), between South Mountain Road (US 54) and Quay Road. See map 3.

Marker text: This area was troubled by both Comanches and *Comancheros*, New Mexicans who traded illegally with the Indians, until the military campaigns of 1874. With the coming of the railroad in 1898, the small community of Liberty, eight miles to the north, moved here to form the nucleus of Tucumcari, which was incorporated in 1908.

Tucumcari owes its existence in part to the construction of Fort Bascom a few miles to the north in 1863. Because the army forbade the sale of alcohol within the boundaries of the fort, a new settlement formed west of the military reservation to serve the recreational needs of the soldiers and the cattle ranchers of the eastern plains. It was named Liberty.

Residents of Liberty needed the protection of the fort as much as the soldiers needed the break from duty that Liberty offered. Comanche Indians had roamed this area since the early 1700s, alternately fighting and negotiating with the Anglo settlers and cattle ranchers who slowly came to claim the territory as their own. *Comancheros*, Americans and Mexicans who bartered illegally with Comanches, Kiowas, and other tribes for blankets, livestock, and even captive slaves, likewise upset the tranquility of the Plains. Embattled by an onslaught of campaigns by the US Army in 1874, the last of the Comanches had left their homes on the Plains and moved to reservations within a year. Comanchero trade slowly abated and finally ceased altogether.

The army abandoned Fort Bascom in 1870, but Liberty survived as a ranching and supply community. In 1898, workers with the Chicago, Rock Island, and Pacific Railroad began to lay tracks through the area from the northeast to connect with another railroad at Santa Rosa. Soon, a tent city of homesteaders and railroad workers sprouted close to the railroad, eight miles south of Liberty. The population shot up to four hundred in only two months, and the bustling and lawless camp became known for a time as Six-Shooter Siding. When the community opened a post office in 1901, it first took the less scandalous tag of Douglas, but within a year, the name changed to Tucumcari for nearby Tucumcari Mountain.

An early account of Tucumcari written by a New Mexico government employee in 1902 described the settlement this way:

It has one weekly newspaper, a church, a public

school, one bank, and 750 inhabitants. . . . A round house, coal chutes, yardage, etc., necessary to the new town as a divisional and junctional railway point have been constructed.

When the territorial legislature created Quay County in 1903, they designated Tucumcari as county seat. Residents voted to incorporate their town five years later.

More to explore: *Fort Bascom, Llano Estacado, Tucumcari Mountain*

466. Tucumcari Mountain

Location: Quay County. In Tucumcari, at the east end of town, in a pullout on the north side of East Tucumcari Boulevard (the Interstate 40 business loop), between South Mountain Road (US 54) and Quay Road. See map 3.

Marker text: Tucumcari Mountain has long been a landmark for travelers along the Canadian River. Pedro Vial mentioned it in 1793, while opening a trail between Santa Fe and St. Louis. In order to find the best route from Arkansas to California, Capt. Randolph B. Marcy led an expedition past here in 1849.

Captain Randolph Marcy's historical account of Tucumcari Mountain compared it to the dome of the US Capitol Building as it appeared in 1849. Notice any resemblance? US Capitol, ca. 1846. Capitol photo by John Plumbe, Library of Congress, Prints and Photographs Division, LC-USZC4-3595; Tucumcari Mountain photo by the author.

Although Tucumcari Mountain reaches an altitude of only 4,956 feet, it nonetheless overshadows the otherwise level landscape here. The mountain, visible two miles to the south of the Marker, was a natural landmark for travelers along the Canadian River, who could easily spot its slopes across the plains. An early mention of the mountain appears in the journal of Pedro Vial, a French explorer hired by the Spanish government in the late eighteenth century to open a trail between Santa Fe and Saint Louis. In his trip log for November 5, 1793, Vial notes the mountain: "Course to the south, leaving the river on the right. I recognized Tunconcaro, and stopped at a distance of 5 leagues, having traveled 7."

During the California Gold Rush of 1849,

Tucumcari Mountain again witnessed a historic expedition. That year, Captain Randolph B. Marcy trekked past, along with a detachment of soldiers, wagons, and gold-seeking prospectors. The US Army had sent Marcy to open a new overland route from Arkansas to the Pacific coast in hopes that it would supplement the overburdened Oregon Trail, Santa Fe Trail, and Mormon Trail in meeting the rising influx of westward-ho '49ers. Marcy and his emigrant train followed the length of the Canadian River through eastern New Mexico on a route largely paralleling that of present-day Interstate 40. They reached this area on June 17. Marcy also wrote of the mountain:

About three miles from our camp of last night we came in sight of the "Cerro Tucumcari." It appeared to be about thirty miles distant, a little to the right of our course, apparently perfectly symmetrical, and is a most conspicuous landmark. It presents, when seen at a long distance, very much the appearance of the dome of the Capitol at Washington.

Marcy's comparison made more sense in 1849, when the Capitol dome in Washington, D.C., was shaped more like the smooth top of a helmet than the elegant, wedding-cake design it later acquired. Still, the right and left flanks of the mountain do resemble the Senate and House chambers, respectively, and the general shape of the mountain compares favorably to the Capitol Building.

According to place-names expert Robert Julyan, the word *Tucumcari* is likely a corruption of a Comanche word meaning "lookout," for which purpose the tribe sometimes used the mountain.

More to explore: La Luz, Rabbit Ear Mountain, Ship Rock, Trail of the Forty-Niners, Tucumcari, Wagon Mound

467. Tularosa

Location: Otero County. At the south end of the town of Tularosa, on the east side of US 70, between mile markers 77 and 78. See map 6.

Marker text: The Tularosa Basin has been occupied by Indian groups for thousands of years. The first Hispanic settlers moved here from the Rio Grande Valley in 1862. Anglo settlers and cattlemen began moving into the region in the 1870s. The original 1862 townsite has been designated a State and National Historic District. Tularosa appears as "Oasis" in the novels of Eugene Manlove Rhodes.

468. Ghost Marker: Round Mountain

Marker text: This cone-shaped landmark about 10 Miles from Tularosa was once known as Dead Man's Hill, and has been the backdrop for several military encounters. In April 1868 a small group of soldiers and Tularosa settlers engaged in battle with about 200 Mescalero Apaches. See map 6.

Ruins of early dwellings and ancient petroglyphs on rocks nearby are the work of the prehistoric Jornada Mogollon people, who made a home in the Tularosa Basin as long ago as AD 900. Historians believe that these early Native Americans survived here in part by hunting buffalo and other animals that are now extinct. Later, the Tularosa Basin and much of southwestern New Mexico was among the lands roamed by nomadic Apache Indians.

The valley first saw Hispanic settlement in November 1862, when Mesilla Valley farmer

Cesario Duran and about a hundred of his neighbors left their flood-ravaged fields in Mesilla and Doña Ana and migrated over the San Andres Mountains to the Tularosa Basin. Only men came that fall. To prepare for the arrival of their families, these early settlers dug irrigation ditches and built defensive adobe homes to protect against Indian attacks. Springtime brought the women and children to the new village, which the men had located along a river with banks overgrown by bulrushes—*tules* in Spanish. Tularosa.

By the late nineteenth century, the land that had delivered prosperity to the Hispanic settlers began to attract the attention of Anglos, many from the open ranges of Texas. One by one, cattle ranchers bought land from the original Spanish settlers or their heirs and turned the Tularosa Basin into a commercial ranching empire. Pat Coughlan arrived in Tularosa in 1874, opened a store, and soon got his hands on enough property to claim the title "King of Tularosa." Oliver Milton Lee arrived in the valley from Texas in 1892 and, despite facing charges of having rustled cattle and, later, of having murdered prominent Mesilla attorney Albert Fountain, found his destiny as one of the most powerful cattlemen in southeastern New Mexico. Defending Lee at his murder trial was attorney and politician Albert Fall, another baron of southern New Mexico, who owned a ranch north of Tularosa at Three Rivers and, indeed, much of Three Rivers itself.

Observing it all, and sometimes participating, was novelist Eugene Manlove Rhodes, who had moved with his family to New Mexico in 1881. After stints as a miner and schoolteacher, Rhodes built a ranch in the Tularosa Basin. The novels and stories he would later write featured a western town known as Oasis, a settlement Rhodes had based on Tularosa. In one story, "Consider the Lizard," Rhodes wrote:

Oasis has all the drawbacks you mention and some you would never guess; civically speaking, it is "link'd with one virtue and a thousand crimes."

Yet—for all that deep and cool and generous shade, and the brave tinkling of her hundred acequias— *men in the world's showplaces think with a pang of that dim and far old town, and name her puny river with a kindling eye.*

The cone-shaped mountain about ten miles north of Tularosa looks like it should have a story associated with it—and it does. On April 2, 1868, a small cadre of soldiers returning east to Fort Stanton after escorting a wagon train south past the mountain encountered a band of some two hundred Apache Indians. A fight broke out, and after a military messenger got word back to Tularosa of the incident, the ranks of the soldiers (who had since holed up in a small adobe fort) were augmented by about twenty-five Tularosa militiamen. According to one story, the citizens of Tularosa appealed to God that if they were victorious in the battle, they would build a church and dedicate it to Saint Francis. The battle ended with one Apache casualty and a few wounded on both sides. Every year, parishioners of the Saint Francis de Paula Church in Tularosa celebrate the founding of their church through the promise made more than a century ago.

To recognize the historic character of the architecture in Tularosa, the National Park Service added the original forty-nine-block townsite to the National Register of Historic Places in February 1979. That district is today defined as the section bounded by First and Eighth Streets to the north and south, and A through H Streets to the east and west. "Tularosa," the report reads, "remains a rural farming town, where people still keep animals and small farms in their yards, and water runs through the ditches."

More to explore: *Carrizozo, Malpais, Three Rivers, White Oaks*

469. Ute Dam and Reservoir

Location: Quay County. In Logan, just east of the entrance to Ute Lake State Park, on the south side of NM 540, near Amigo Street. See map 3.

Marker text: Constructed and operated by the Interstate Stream Commission. Construction funds appropriated by the State Legislature. Original construction completed in 1963. Enlargement completed in 1984.

470. Ute Lake State Park

Location: 1. Quay County. In Logan, in a pullout on the east side of US 54, between Yucca Street and NM 39, between mile markers 326 and 327 on US 54. See map 3.

2. Quay County. In Logan, just east of the state park, in a pullout on the south side of NM 540, near Amigo Street. See map 3.

Marker text: Offering the best walleye fishing in New Mexico, this reservoir on the Canadian River also provides good fishing for both white and largemouth bass, channel catfish and crappie. Park facilities include camping/picnicking sites, a playground, boat ramps and a marina.

From the air, Ute Lake looks like a giant Gila monster crawling across the plains of southeastern New Mexico. The Gila monster is actually a reservoir formed by Ute Dam, which restrains water from the Canadian River and Ute Creek into a lake with a water surface of 8,200 acres. The name "Ute" comes from the Ute Indians, who once frequented these plains.

The man-made Ute Lake was formed in 1963, after the New Mexico state legislature authorized $5 million for the construction of an earthen dam in this location. The Interstate Streams Commission erected the dam from a design by the Bechtel Corporation. Ute Lake State Park was established around the lake the following year. Later, in 1984, the dam was enlarged, raising the level of the lake by twenty-seven feet.

The park sees more than 200,000 visitors a year, many of whom come to boat, picnic, hike, windsail, or even scuba dive. RV and tent camping is available at several separate campsites, including Zia Campground, Windy Point, and Yucca Campground. Primitive camping is available at Mine Canyon Campground, accessible at a separate entrance south of the village of Logan.

Fishing is a popular activity here, with the lake offering white and largemouth bass, channel catfish, and crappie. The names of roads along NM 540 leading to the park will catch the eye of any fisherman: Carp, Perch, Trout, Pike, and Walleye Drive.

More to explore: *Eagle Nest Lake State Park, Elephant Butte Lake State Park, Fenton Lake State Park*

471. Valencia

Location: Valencia County. In Valencia, in the courtyard of the Sangre de Cristo Catholic Church, at the corner of Main Street and Roberts Circle. See map 4.

Marker text: This community traces its beginnings to the hacienda established by Captain Francisco Valencia along this section of the Camino Real by the mid-17th century. Abandoned during the Pueblo Revolt of 1680, the area was resettled in 1740 by Christian Indians called genízaros. These settlers played an important role in the defense of the Spanish frontier.

In this part of the middle Rio Grande Valley south of Albuquerque in the mid-1600s, Captain Francisco Valencia, and later his son Juan de Valencia, lived in a hacienda, or large ranch home. The Valencia household lay on the eastern bank of the Rio Grande along the Camino Real, the main road connecting New Mexico with Mexico. Valencia, who had served as an officer with the army of Governor Antonio de Otermín, abandoned his ranch in 1680 when the Pueblo Indians in New Mexico revolted against the Spanish and forced early settlers from the state.

Twelve years later, Spanish governor Diego de Vargas followed the Rio Grande north to Santa Fe to reestablish Spanish control. Along the way, he camped with his men at the vestiges of the Valencia ranch. Writing in his journal for Saturday, September 6, 1692, Vargas was the first to call the area Valencia:

Arrived at this place, an abandoned farm of Juan de Valencia. . . . I remain at this place called Valencia so that the Holy Sacrament of penance may be administered to the members of the expedition, tomorrow, which is the feast of Our Lady.

In 1740, the governor, don Gervasio Cruzat y Góngora, granted a tract of land here to a group of about forty *genízaro* families. Genízaros were an important part of the ethnic makeup of colonial New Mexico. They were the sons and daughters of Indian captives, usually women, who had been taken from Plains Indians tribes like the Apaches, Comanches, and Kiowas, and raised as Christians in Spanish homes. During the mid-1700s, the Spanish government granted land to impoverished and landless genízaros in hopes of encouraging new settlements. In return, the genízaros were to provide defense against attacks by Apaches or Comanches. That they were doing a good job of this in Valencia is evidenced in a record written in 1744 by Fray Miguel de Menchero: "The people . . . are under obligation to go out and explore the country in pursuit of the [Apache], which they are doing with great bravery and zeal in their obedience."

A hundred years after that report, the territorial legislature in New Mexico created Valencia County here, which took its name from the town. The village of Valencia served as the first county seat until being superseded by Tomé and later Los Lunas.

More to explore: *Historic Los Luceros, Tomé*

472. Valle Grande

Location: Sandoval County. Overlooking the Valle Grande, in a pullout and parking area on the north side of NM 4. See map 4.

Marker text: About one million years ago, the magnificent valley before you was formed by collapse, after a series of tremendous volcanic eruptions ejected a volume of material more than 500 times greater than the May 1980 eruptions of Mt. St. Helens. This event climaxed more than 13 million years of volcanism in the Jemez Mountains. Minor volumes of magma, leaking to the surface as recently as 50,000 years ago, formed the dome-like hills between you and the skyline to the north, which is the opposite wall of the enormous Valles Caldera. The heat from young volcanism makes this area attractive for geothermal energy.

The Valle Grande, or Big Valley, is one of the most awe-inspiring features of the Jemez Mountains, with a history as dramatic as its panoramic, 176-square-mile vista.

The Valle Grande began with the creation of the Jemez Mountains themselves. More than ten million years ago, a field of volcanoes stretched across this part of north-central New Mexico. The Jemez volcano erupted about 1.6 million years ago in two colossal explosions. With the interior magma chamber spent, the mountains and rocks above it collapsed to form a large basin known as a caldera. Magma forced upward by the subsiding land hardened into an 11,254-foot-high resurgent dome, today known as Redondo Peak, near the southern center of the caldera. *Redondo* is a Spanish word meaning "round."

The human history of the region is exciting, too.

The Valle Grande is part of a large land grant known as the Baca Location no. 1, which had its genesis in an error arising from another land grant awarded in 1835. In that year, Juan Maese received from the New Mexico government a 500,000-acre tract of land near present-day Las Vegas. Trouble came in 1841, when don Luis María Cabeza de Baca received a grant of land that overlapped the one earlier awarded to Maese. Congress corrected the oversight in 1860 by allowing the Baca heirs to select five other 100,000-acre tracts of vacant land anywhere in the state. The Bacas' first choice, and hence the name Baca Location no. 1, encompassed the land now known as Valle Grande.

This pristine valley is home to an assortment of natural wonders. The rare limber pine grows here, a tree named for its ability to bend in a strong wind. The valley is also home to seventeen animals on the endangered species list, including the Mexican spotted owl and the Jemez Mountains salamander.

In 2000, Congress approved the acquisition of Baca Ranch from private citizens and brought the Valle Grande and other valleys in the caldera into public ownership.

More to explore: *Jemez Mountains, Organ Mountains (see under San Augustin Pass), Puyé Ruins, Soda Dam*

Valverde Battlefield: *see Fort Craig*

VÁSQUEZ DE CORONADO'S ROUTE: Series of Four Historic Markers (Various Locations)

General Introduction

In 1540, Spanish explorer Francisco Vásquez de Coronado set out from Compostela, Mexico, with a small expedition of soldiers, fevered with the hope of finding Quivira, a metropolis of seven cities built entirely of gold, which earlier explorers had hinted existed somewhere in the north. The story of their journey through New Mexico plays out over several Historic Markers strategically placed around the state. It begins shortly after the Spaniards enter New Mexico near the Zuni pueblo of Hawikuh in early July, disappointed to find that the pueblos of Zuni were not the golden wonderland they had expected.

The Markers that document Coronado's exploits have been grouped here into a series in this book so the story can be followed more easily. They are listed roughly in chronological order.

More to explore (Vásquez de Coronado's Route series): *Bernalillo, Pueblo of Zuni, Rio Grande, Spanish Entrada Site, Tiguex Province*

473. Vásquez de Coronado's Route

Location: Bernalillo County. South of Isleta Pueblo, on the east side of NM 314. See map 4.

Marker text: In the fall of 1540, Francisco Vásquez de Coronado's army traveled from Zuni to his chosen winter headquarters in the Tiguex province on the Rio Grande. Here the advance guard of the army followed the river from the Isleta area to Alcanfor, a pueblo near Bernalillo, where it camped for two winters.

Note: See the general introduction to this series of Markers, as well as the other Markers making up the series, for further background on Coronado's expedition through New Mexico.

After establishing a provisional base at present-day Zuni Pueblo in July 1540, Coronado sent advance guards on exploratory missions throughout the region. An emissary from Pecos Pueblo, whom the Spanish nicknamed Bigotes, led one of these men, Hernando de Alvarado, eastward to the Rio Grande. Near this point, Alvarado and his men turned north and followed the river until they reached twelve Indian villages in the vicinity of present-day Bernalillo. Alvarado named these villages the Province of Tiguex, likely from his interpretation of the Indian name. He then sent word back to Coronado that this would make a good place to huddle through the approaching winter. In agreement, Coronado and his army traveled that fall from Zuni to a Tiguex pueblo he called Alcanfor. Some historians believe Alcanfor is the now-abandoned pueblo of Kuaua, preserved at the Coronado Historic Site.

Although initially accommodating, the Indians at Alcanfor grew to resent the burden of providing food and supplies to the Spaniards. In a show of insurrection, Indians one day drove away many of Coronado's horses and shot arrows at the animals as they galloped off. In retaliation, Coronado ordered one of his men, don García López de Cardeñas, to attack the pueblo the Spaniards called Arenal. Cardeñas and his soldiers surrounded Arenal, climbed onto the roofs, and smoked out the Indians until they emerged making the sign of the cross—upon which the soldiers then fired at them. Soldiers tied several Indian prisoners to stakes and set them on fire.

The bloody confrontation worsened as fighting spread to other Tiguex villages. The Indians fled to Moho, their strongest pueblo, where they barricaded themselves against the Spanish onslaught for more than two months. Then, in a desperate attempt at escape, the beleaguered Indians emerged from their pueblo in the cold, dark air of a winter evening. Said Coronado's chronicler of the tragic result:

But they were driven back with great slaughter until they came to the [Rio Grande] river, where the water flowed swiftly and very cold. They threw themselves into this, and as the men had come quickly from the whole camp to assist the cavalry, there were few [Indians] who escaped being killed or wounded.

When spring arrived, Coronado and his men continued their search for gold deep into the plains of what is now Kansas.

474. Vásquez de Coronado's Route

Location: Socorro County. South of Socorro, in the Fort Craig Rest Area on the east side of Interstate 25, between mile markers 113 and 114. See map 5.

Marker text: In 1541 an expedition from the army of Francisco Vásquez de Coronado, New Mexico's first explorer, marched south 80 leagues to investigate the pueblos along the lower Rio Grande. The group reached that part of the infamous Jornada del Muerto, now covered by Elephant Butte Lake, where the river disappeared underground.

Note: See the general introduction to this series of Markers, as well as the other Markers making up the series, for further background on Coronado's expedition through New Mexico.

After spending his first winter in the land that is now New Mexico, Francisco Vásquez de Coronado sent one of his officers to explore the pueblo country along the lower Rio Grande. The captain of the expedition is unnamed in the chronicle of the journey. Traveling south, the officer and his small company of men passed the pueblo of Isleta, where Indians greeted them peacefully. They visited four Piro-speaking villages between Isleta and San Marcial; all four have now vanished.

The expedition continued along the Rio Grande to an area north of present-day Truth or Consequences. There, wrote Coronado's chronicler, they "found that the river disappeared underground like the Guadiana in Extremadura."

What the men had seen reminded them of one of the longest rivers of their Iberian Peninsula homeland. The point at which the river performed its disappearing act has now disappeared entirely, inundated by the waters of Elephant Butte Reservoir.

Although their Indian guides assured the captain that the river reemerged as a larger stream farther south, the expedition had covered the eighty leagues required. They turned back.

475. Vásquez de Coronado's Route

Location: Guadalupe County. In Santa Rosa, on the west end of town, in the parking lot of the Budget 10 Motel, at the intersection of US 54 and the Interstate 40 business loop. See map 3.

Marker text: In 1540 Francisco Vásquez de Coronado and a small army set out from Mexico to search for the fabled Quivira and its cities of gold. In the spring of 1541, the expedition halted near here for four days while they built a log bridge across the Pecos River. From there they continued their exploration deep into present day Kansas.

Note: See the general introduction to this series of Markers, as well as the other Markers making up the series, for further background on Coronado's expedition through New Mexico.

After wintering in the Indian villages near present-day Bernalillo in 1540, Francisco Vásquez de Coronado and his men continued their search for gold eastward the following spring. Upon reaching the Pecos River near here, as recorded by the expedition's chronicler, Pedro de Castañeda:

They stopped ... in order to build a bridge for crossing it. This was completed in four days with all diligence and quickness. Once finished, the entire army and livestock crossed over the bridge.

Historians do not believe that this bridge lasted long, perhaps no longer than a couple of weeks, before the waters of the Pecos washed it away. With few clues to follow, experts are unsure exactly where it existed. Some believe that the most likely spot is along the river near Anton Chico, northwest of Santa Rosa. Others feel that a more likely site is closer to Puerto de Luna. Historians Richard Flint and Shirley Cushing Flint have documented no fewer than ten hypothetical locations, finally stating their own opinion that it was built along the "Pecos River just below its junction with the Gallinas River." The exact route the army followed after crossing the bridge is also murky, and historians have likewise proposed several routes through the Texas Panhandle as possible paths.

Regardless, the chimera-chasing expedition eventually reached present-day Kansas. They found no gold cities, no gold bells hanging from trees, no gold silverware—only prairie grasses and the villages of the Plains Indians. Dejected, Coronado and his men returned to Tiguex for a second winter.

476. Vásquez de Coronado's Route

Location: Sandoval County. Near San Ysidro, on the north side of US 550 (formerly NM 44) at mile marker 19. See map 4.

Marker text: Francisco Vásquez de Coronado, preparing to spend his second winter in New Mexico, sent out expeditions from Tiguex, near Bernalillo, in the fall of 1541 to gather supplies. Captain Francisco de Barrionuevo went as far west as Jemez Pueblo, then visited others as far north as the Rio Chama.

Note: See the general introduction to this series of Markers, as well as the other Markers making up the series, for further background on Coronado's expedition through New Mexico.

Francisco Vásquez de Coronado had come to New Mexico in 1540 to check on reports of legendary golden cities that the Spanish believed lay somewhere in this northern land. After a year of searching turned up little evidence, Coronado prepared to spend a second winter in the state. With his officers, he made a headquarters in a region they called the Province of Tiguex, a string of Tiwa-speaking Indian villages along the Rio Grande near present-day Bernalillo. One of Coronado's aides-de-camp, Captain Francisco de Barrionuevo, journeyed north from Tiguex along the Rio Grande to gather provisions in preparation for the colder months to come. As recorded in the chronicle of Coronado's journey:

[Barrionuevo] found two provinces, one of which was called Hemes, containing seven pueblos [these were the seven Jemez pueblos] and the other Yuque-Yunque [a Tewa-speaking pueblo near present-day Ohkay Owingeh Pueblo]. The pueblos of Hemes came out peacefully and furnished provisions. Those of Yuque-Yunque abandoned two very beautiful pueblos which were on opposite sides of the river, while the army was establishing camp, and went to the sierra where they had four very strong pueblos which could not be reached by the horses because of the craggy land. In these two pueblos were found abundant provisions and beautiful glazed pottery of many decorations and shapes.

Barrionuevo continued north to Taos Pueblo before turning back.

477. Vaughn

Location: Guadalupe County. On the west end of Vaughn, in a pullout on the south side of US 60. See map 3.

Marker text: Vaughn, a division point in the transcontinental railway system, is located along the route of the Stinson cattle trail. In 1882, Jim Stinson, manager of the New Mexico Land and Livestock Co., drove 20,000 cattle in eight separate herds along this important trail from Texas to the Estancia Valley.

Attracted by the promise of southeastern New Mexico, a vast, unbroken rangeland swept by blue gramma and buffalo grasses, ranchers in the nineteenth century drove herds of cattle across this level thoroughfare. One of the first was cowboy Jim Stinson. In the 1880s, Stinson was the manager of the New Mexico Land and Cattle Company in Estancia, New Mexico, a ranch owned by wealthy San Franciscan Joel P. Whitney. In 1882, Stinson drove eight separate herds—a total of twenty thousand cattle—from west-central Texas into New Mexico. His path through New Mexico entered the state near present-day Portales, continued west to the Pecos River at Fort Sumner, and then moved farther still over some eighty miles of prairie before veering northwesterly to the Estancia Valley. The route is similar to that run today by US 60 from Clovis to Willard.

Drovers along the Stinson Trail rested and watered their cattle at natural springs along the way. One of those was atop a small, gently sloping rise here. A Depression-era writer later described the view from that rise as having "only the native grass and shrubbery to break the monotony of the desert calm."

After the turn of the century, something else would break that monotony: new beasts were being driven across the southeastern plains. In 1901, the Golden States route of the Chicago, Rock Island, and Pacific Railroad reached the area from the northeast. A small settlement grew near the camp that railroad workers had established at the spring. Two hotels, a Harvey House, and "tourist camps," or motels along the roadside, opened to serve travelers. Only a few years later, the Santa Fe Railway arrived from the southwest, making this new settlement the only point in the state where two railroads crossed.

When a post office opened in the settlement in 1907, the town took the name of an engineer with the Santa Fe Railway—Major G. W. Vaughn.

More to explore: *Portales*

478. Velarde on the Camino Real

Location: Rio Arriba County. Just north of Velarde on the south side of US 68, between mile markers 15 and 16. See map 2.

Marker text: Founded in 1875, this small farming community was first named La Jolla. It was once famous for finely woven blankets. Here the Camino Real left the Rio Grande and followed a canyon northeast to Embudo Creek where it began a climb over the mountains to Taos.

Velarde sits along the banks of the garrulous Rio Grande, safe from the highway, amid lush orchards and fields of chile and corn made possible by the charity of the river. Close ties to the earth have long marked the history of the community. Those ties began in 1712, when the area was part of the Sebastian Martin land grant and known as La Jolla. According to place-names historian Robert Julyan, that was likely an alternate spelling of *joya*, a Spanish word meaning "basin." La Jolla resident David Velarde opened a post office in 1885, and the settlement thereafter took the name Velarde.

Velarde lay along the course of the Camino Real, or Royal Road, between New Mexico and Mexico. Much of the course of the Camino Real followed the Rio Grande through the state to Taos. Just north of Velarde, however, the Rio Grande twisted westward, squeezed through a narrow funnel between canyons, and emerged at the small community of Embudo. Northbound travelers along the Camino Real continued without making the turn, departing from the Rio Grande after resting at Velarde and then continuing northeast to rejoin the course of the river where it combined with Embudo Creek some five miles distant. From there, wagon trains continued northeast over the mountains to Taos.

A reporter for the *Santa Fe New Mexican* blithely described the farms and residents of the village of Velarde in March 1892:

This land is highly cultivated and full of orchards and vineyards, and its 600 inhabitants are all independent, healthy and happy. Well they may be happy with their homes in such a lovely spot, adjacent to the banks of the noble Rio Bravo del Norte, full at this place of splendid trout.

In the late 1920s, the residents of Velarde planted some of the first commercial apple tree orchards in the Española Valley. These orchards thrived on the rich bottomland along the Rio Grande and enjoyed protection from frost through the shawl of the surrounding mountains. Apple blossoms burst forth fragrant and beautiful: Jonathans, Roman Beauties, Delicious, and Winesaps among them. Velarde farmers also grew Bartlett pears, Green Gage plums, Champion and Freestone peaches, and cherries. Even today, spring harvests see many Velarde residents hauling their fruits to market.

More to explore: *El Camino Real—The King's Highway, Mills Canyon, Rio Grande*

479. Vietnam Veterans National Memorial

Location: Colfax County. In Angel Fire, at the entrance to the memorial. See map 3.

Marker text: This chapel was erected in 1968 by Dr. Victor Westphall in memory of his son David Westphall and all U.S. personnel killed in the fighting in Vietnam. It was first dedicated as the Vietnam Veterans Peace and Brotherhood Chapel, and on May 30, 1983, it was rededicated as the Disabled American Veterans (DAV) Vietnam Veterans National Memorial.

The Vietnam War claimed the lives of 399 New Mexicans. One of them was twenty-eight-year-old Lieutenant Victor David Westphall III, rifle platoon commander, Bravo Company, First Battalion, Fourth Marines. On May 22, 1968, Lieutenant Westphall and his company were crossing a rise in Con Thien, South Vietnam, when they came under sudden ambush by more than a hundred Vietnamese soldiers. Young David Westphall was among the twenty-seven soldiers who lost their lives. An official report lists his casualty as, "HOSTILE, KILLED."

Later that fall, David's father, Dr. Victor Westphall, hired Santa Fe architect Ted Luna to design a chapel and memorial on the Westphalls' Val Verde Ranch in Angel Fire. The chapel would honor the memory of his first-born son and all others who had suffered the tragedies of the war in Vietnam. This, the Vietnam Veterans Peace and Brotherhood Chapel, arose on a hillside overlooking the Moreno Valley—a tranquil spot where, according to his father, David had liked to sit and read. The refined plan of the chapel featured sloping white walls soaring nearly fifty feet into the brisk mountain air and a narrow window extending from floor to ceiling. Originally dedicated on May 22, 1971, the anniversary of David's death, it was the first memorial in the world to honor Vietnam veterans.

Ownership of the chapel passed from the Westphall family to the Disabled American Veterans organization (DAV) in 1982. On May 30, 1983, the chapel was rededicated as the Disabled American Veterans Vietnam Veterans National Memorial. The DAV helped finance the construction of a Visitors Center to display information on the war in Vietnam and to serve as a reference center for the seventy thousand visitors who visit the chapel each year.

In 1987, Congress passed a resolution designating the site as a national monument. President Ronald Reagan added his signature, and Public Law 100-164 officially recognized the chapel and praised it as "a memorial of national significance."

More to explore: *Eagle Nest Lake State Park, Khe Sanh Veterans, Women Veterans of New Mexico*

480. View of the Rockies

Location: Colfax County. East of Springer, in a pullout on the north side of US 56/412, between mile markers 23 and 24. See map 3.

Marker text: Reaching altitudes of more than 13,000 feet, well watered and forested, the Rocky Mountains are host to numerous recreational activities including skiing, fishing, hunting, and camping. To the north can be seen numerous volcanic peaks that lie east of the Rocky Mountains in both Colorado and New Mexico. Elevation here 6,300 feet.

Treeless grasslands of the High Plains cover the eastern one third of New Mexico and stretch eastward into the mid continent. Surface water from the mountains beyond the underground aquifers permit ranching as the principal economic activity. Carbon Dioxide gas, a geologic resource, has been discovered and developed in the subsurface.

The vantage point at this Marker gives visual access to three major landscapes of New Mexico.

To the west is the southernmost end of the Rocky Mountains, specifically the range known as Sangre de Cristo, or "Blood of Christ." The name comes from the aspen-colored glow of the mountains at sunset. Within this range towers Wheeler Peak, the highest mountain in New Mexico, reaching 13,161 feet high.

North of here are several small volcanic peaks. These volcanoes are part of the extensive Raton-Clayton Volcanic Field, which stretches from Raton to the eastern edge of the state and extends north into Colorado. The field includes Capulin Volcano in northeastern New Mexico, an extinct cinder cone volcano. Capulin is accessible via a road that winds around it to the crater rim. A museum at the Capulin Volcano National Monument interprets the site for visitors.

Mountains give way to prairies in the view to the east. This is the High Plains region, a western subsection of the much larger Great Plains, which cover the eastern third of New Mexico and largely define the interior of the United States. The plains are underlaid with rock and sediment washed down from the Rocky Mountains. Much of that permeable sediment traps water, creating a giant underground pool known as the Ogallala Aquifer. Named for the town of Ogallala, Nebraska, the aquifer stretches from southwestern Texas to the southern part of South Dakota. A portion of it underlies southeastern New Mexico, giving farmers a water source for crop irrigation. Farming and ranching in southeastern New Mexico accounts for much of the economic activity of that part of the state.

More recently, naturally occurring carbon dioxide has been discovered in the region known as the Bravo Dome in northeastern New Mexico. The gas is used in the recovery and production of underground oil reserves.

The elevation here is 6,300 feet.

More to explore: *Capulin Volcano National Monument, Rocky Mountains, Sangre de Cristo, Southern Rockies*

481. Villanueva State Park

Location: San Miguel County. At the entrance to Villanueva State Park, just east of the village of Villanueva. See map 3.

Marker text: Couched between high red sandstone bluffs in a beautiful valley of the Pecos River, this park is located near the picturesque Spanish colonial village of Villanueva. The park offers hiking trails with historical markers and camping/picnicking sites.

Villanueva State Park nestles amid the giant red sandstone bluffs that surround it, cradling the banks of the Pecos River as those waters continue their journey south through the state. The park is a good place for those who want to leave the world behind, at least for a weekend.

Activities at Villanueva will interest anyone who enjoys spending time in nature. Trout fishing is available in the Pecos River, and the park offers camping and picnicking sites along the floor of the canyon. Almost three miles of hiking trails allow visitors to explore the canyon literally from top to bottom. Those trails include the River Trail, which parallels the river, as well as the Viewpoint Trail on the opposite bank of the river, which offers the opportunity for a hike along the canyon rim.

Villanueva State Park was established by the state in 1967. The park takes its name from the nearby historic community of Villanueva, founded as one of many small settlements that arose as part of the San Miguel del Vado land grant of 1794, while New Mexico was still under the domain of Spain.

More to explore: *Pecos, San Miguel del Vado National Historic District*

482. Virginia T. Romero (1896–1998)

Location: Taos County. At Taos Pueblo, near the intersection of NM 150, NM 522, and US 64, in a pullout on the east side of NM 150, between mile markers 0 and 1. See map 2.

Marker text: Virginia T. Romero, world-famous potter and mother of ten children, began her lifelong career in 1919. She supported her family by selling a variety of pots to locals and tourists for use in cooking, storing water, and as decorative art. She helped keep the micaceous pottery tradition alive in Taos Pueblo. Traditionally fired outdoors, these pots are dotted with flecks of mica, a shiny silicate mineral.

One day in 1919, a father in Taos Pueblo gave his twenty-three-year-old daughter a bag of clay and encouraged her to try her hand at pottery making, telling her it would support her through her life. From such beginnings, the young woman would go on to become one of the most famous of Taos potters: Virginia T. Romero.

Born Virginia Trujillo in September, 1896, Romero came on her talent naturally. While potters often learn their craft from techniques passed down from one generation to the next, Romero instead called on what appeared to be an innate ability. Although she recalled watching her mother making pottery, she had never thought to try it herself, until her father encouraged her—and then she found herself naturally able to work the clay. She was, of course, surrounded and supported by a long tradition of pottery making at Taos Pueblo. For more than five hundred years, potters at Taos (mostly women) have been making a soft, earthen brown pottery for which the pueblo has become well known.

In 1920, Virginia Trujillo married Joe Romero. As their family grew, eventually reaching ten children, Romero began to fire and sell pottery to help support them. She soon found that her pottery was of interest to collectors as well as casual buyers. New Mexico had become a state less than ten years earlier, and visitors to the region were discovering the beautiful handcrafted pottery, jewelry, and art that the Indians of the Southwest had traditionally crafted.

Romero helped keep this tradition alive at Taos Pueblo. As had generations before her, Romero used clay rich in mica gathered from deposits in the mountains nearby. Mica is a shiny silicate mineral valued for its ability to retain heat; pottery created from it presents a noticeable and pleasant shimmer. The heat-retaining property of the mica makes the pots excellent for use as cookware as well as for serving—for which purposes they were traditionally used. Today, the micaceous pottery of Taos Pueblo and other northern New Mexico pueblos, including Pojoaque, Nambé, Santa Clara, Picurís, and others, is collected as art by those who appreciate fine handicrafts of the Southwest. In addition to their practical use, the pots were also beautiful, displaying the talent and time-honored skill of the potter herself.

Romero used an outdoor oven known as a *horno* to fire her vessels, which she shaped from clay that she had ground particularly fine. She would soak the clay overnight before firing. Her finished pots occasionally included some integral ornamentation, such as undulating "coils" laid across the circumference. She did not paint them but instead let the natural bronze coloring supply a soft, earthen beauty. Romero often signed her vessels on the bottom, using her full name, Virginia T. Romero, and including "Taos Pueblo NM," as well as the date.

Virginia T. Romero passed away in 1998, but later generations of her family have continued the pottery tradition at Taos Pueblo. She is survived as well by her own legacy of craftsmanship. Today, her works are on display in museums across the Southwest and in private collections around the world.

More to explore: *Trinidad Gachupin Medina (see under Pueblo of Zia), Virginia Duran (see under Pueblo of Picurís)*

483. Wagon Mound

Location: Mora County. On the west side of the settlement of Wagon Mound, at the intersection of NM 271 and NM 120. See map 3.

Marker text: This last great landmark on the Santa Fe Trail was named for its resemblance to the top of a covered wagon. At Wagon Mound, travelers could cross from the Cimarron Cutoff to Fort Union, which is located on the Mountain Branch of the Trail. The two branches joined south of here at Watrous.

Afoot, a shoe, the canopy of a covered wagon—regardless of the image the butte inspired, the distinctive shape of the eroded lava flow known today as Wagon Mound guided many travelers along the Cimarron Cutoff of the Santa Fe Trail, the major trade and settlement route between the Midwest and Santa Fe during the nineteenth century. In an age when geologic landmarks doubled as odometers, Wagon Mound meant that westbound traders beholding its form had six days left before they reached the capital city.

From Wagon Mound, travelers so inclined could follow a short stem off the main trail west along the northern edge of the Turkey Mountains to reach Fort Union, an army post established in 1851 about thirty miles to the south. Soldiers at

Fort Union provided escorts to travelers on the Mountain Branch of the Santa Fe Trail, which entered New Mexico over Raton Pass and crossed near the fort. The Cimarron Cutoff and Mountain Branch rejoined farther south, near the village of Watrous.

A settlement taking the name Santa Clara soon grew near the butte. When residents opened a post office in 1881, the name thereafter became Wagon Mound.

More to explore: Fort Union National Monument, Santa Fe Trail (series), Ship Rock, Tucumcari Mountain, Watrous

484. Waldrop Park

Location: Chaves County. In a roadside rest area just east of Caprock on the south side of US 380 at mile marker 196. See map 6.

Marker text: This site is named for Victor H. Waldrop and stewardship for it is shared by the New Mexico Department of Transportation and local bird enthusiasts. Wind-blown sand deposited at the base of Mescalero Ridge forms a 60 mile expanse of open dunes and stabilized hummocks. This park has become popular with bird watchers. The scissor-tailed flycatcher and other species can be found throughout the dunes.

For the shade in this roadside park, a unique asset on these spacious and treeless plains, thank homesteader Victor H. Waldrop and his family. Born in Milam County, Texas, on April 18, 1884, Waldrop was the son of Virgil A. and Lilly Scott Waldrop. On September 3, 1906, he married May Robinson in Sweetwater, Texas, with whom he began a family. Like many other pioneers, Waldrop wanted to stake a claim to his own piece of the frontier under the Homestead Act. So, in 1914, he traveled in a covered wagon with his wife and four children and their possessions to start a new life on the plains of southeastern New Mexico.

Waldrop settled originally near Caprock, a town several miles to the east, which had only a year before opened its first post office. The founder of the town, Charles E. Crossland, also served as postmaster. To bring shade where nature offered none, Crossland planted cottonwood trees in the small village—perhaps also sowing the seed that later inspired Waldrop to create his own shady roadside oasis.

In 1924, Waldrop and his family moved from Caprock to the vicinity of the present-day Waldrop Park. They had chosen to settle in a spot along the road between Roswell and Tatum, a course later followed by US 380. Here, according to a family history later written by daughter Virginia Scarbrough, Waldrop opened a grocery store and service station to cater to the needs of those traveling between the two communities. As part of his efforts, Waldrop and his family planted a variety of trees to provide shade to anyone visiting his store.

Victor Waldrop died at midnight on June 13, 1956, age seventy-two, in his Roswell home, where he had later retired. His obituary in the *Roswell Daily Record* described him as a "retired grocer" and "long time county resident." His wife, May, survived him by twenty-nine years, passing away on April 30, 1985. Mr. and Mrs. Victor Waldrop are buried side by side in Southpark Cemetery in Roswell.

The state of New Mexico eventually acquired the property where the Waldrop service station had stood. They erected a small roadside park along US 380, where visitors can enjoy the shade of the trees Waldrop planted many years before. The park has been named in Waldrop's honor.

Waldrop Park lies a short distance from

Mescalero Sands, a sixty-mile-long stretch of quartz sand blown here from the Mescalero Escarpment (also known as Mescalero Ridge). The escarpment is a low-lying cliff that forms the western edge of the plains known as the Llano Estacado. A popular recreation spot, Mescalero Sands features sand dunes and hummocks (small mounds of dirt), vegetated and stabilized by shin oak, yucca, and other plants. The dunes attract the scissor-tailed flycatcher, the lesser prairie chicken, burrowing owls, Cassin's sparrows, and others, as well as ornithologists hoping to catch a glimpse of them.

More to explore: Bicentennial Celebration, Fort Craig Rest Area, Roswell

485. Watrous

Location: Mora County. At the south end of Watrous, at the junction of Interstate 25 exit 364 and NM 161. See map 3.

Marker text: The Mountain Branch and the Cimarron Cutoff of the Santa Fe Trail meet at Watrous. This important spot on the Trail was first known as La Junta, "junction" in Spanish. In 1879, with the coming the railroad, it was named for Samuel B. Watrous, a prominent local rancher.

Vermont-born merchant Samuel B. Watrous settled in the small community of La Junta, New Mexico, in 1849. La Junta took its name, a Spanish word meaning "junction," from its location near the confluence of the Mora and Sapello Rivers. The community was also the point of junction for the two main branches of the Santa Fe Trail, the Cimarron Cutoff and the Mountain Branch, a union that made the village an ideal place to establish a business to serve the needs of fatigued travelers. Watrous did so, constructing a twenty-room combination house and store with adobe brick fireplaces, and glass and doorframes fetched from the East over the Santa Fe Trail. His mansion endures today as a private residence.

Watrous met success in his entrepreneurial ventures and quickly became a wealthy rancher and merchant in the village. With his son, Joseph, he managed a freighting business using the Santa Fe Trail as a supply line. After the army established Fort Union nearby in 1851 to protect settlers crossing northeastern New Mexico, Watrous sold beef from his cattle ranch to the soldiers stationed at the fort. The community of La Junta grew along with Watrous's endeavors. By 1875, the small settlement had a mill, three stores, a hotel, and an express office. When crews with the Atchison, Topeka, and Santa Fe Railway began laying tracks through La Junta in 1879, Watrous deeded ten acres of land just east of the settlement for the railroad depot. Officials with the railroad named that depot, and hence the town itself, Watrous.

The June 28, 1879, edition of the *Santa Fe Weekly New Mexican* had this to say about the "new town" of Watrous:

This new town is very prettily located on the rich alluvial lands between the verdure covered bluffs on the east and the Sapello river, presenting a most beautiful landscape, overlooking south, west and north, that grand valley of La Junta, the gem of New Mexico, with the snowy range of the Rocky Mountains as a background.

Sadly, the story of Samuel Watrous ends on a discordant note. In 1886, Watrous's son Joseph shot himself to death. Watrous, apparently despondent over the tragic loss, committed suicide himself one morning a few months later.

More to explore: Fort Union National Monument, Santa Fe Trail (series), Wagon Mound

486. Wheeler Peak

Location: Colfax County. South of Eagle Nest, in a pullout on the west side of US 64, between mile markers 281 and 282. See map 3.

Marker text: Across Moreno Valley stands Wheeler Peak, 13,161 feet, highest peak in New Mexico. Rocks of Wheeler Peak and the Taos Range are highly resistant granites and gneisses of Precambrian age. Moreno Valley is underlain by soft sandstones and shales which are covered by stream and glacial deposits. Placer gold was mined at Elizabethtown north of here during the 1860s.

At 13,161 feet, Wheeler Peak towers to a defining superlative: it is the tallest mountain in New Mexico. Composed of Precambrian granite and gneiss, Wheeler Peak stands within the Taos Range and delineates the western edge of the Moreno Valley. The Taos Range uplifted to the west, and the Cimarron Range to the east. Streams and glaciers carried sand and gravel from the mountains to cover the valley floor, itself underlaid with soft sandstones and shales. The human history of the valley includes several chapters of mining lore. When prospectors discovered gold on Baldy Mountain north of here in the 1860s, the mining camp of Elizabethtown became the first incorporated city in New Mexico. Today, it is a ghost town.

In its name, Wheeler Peak recognizes the efforts of Massachusetts-born army surveyor Lieutenant George Montague Wheeler in opening the West for settlement. In 1871, Lieutenant Wheeler undertook the last of the four Great Surveys, a series of expeditions authorized by Congress after the Civil War to map the uncharted lands west of the 100th meridian. According to a roster of the expedition, Wheeler's team included four engineers, two medical officers, three astronomical assistants, seven topographers, three meteorologists, three geologists, and an escort of sixty soldiers. While in New Mexico between the years 1873 and 1875, Wheeler's surveyors performed the first recorded ascent of the peak later named in his honor.

Wheeler's was the only Great Survey conducted by the US military, which needed topographical maps to navigate the movements of soldiers and supplies between forts in the Southwest. Leading the other surveys were private scientists, famous men like Ferdinand Hayden and John Wesley Powell. The dissimilarity in background and purpose between the surveying camps caused a noticeable rift. Hayden and Powell felt that the intrusion of the War Department into regional mapping activities constituted a turf war, literally, and they countered by challenging Wheeler's abilities outright. In a statement submitted to the Committee on Public Lands in May 1874, James T. Gardner, a geologist with the Hayden survey, went so far as to fume that Wheeler's maps contained "great regions, as large as Connecticut and Rhode Island together, that he simply marched around and looked into, but did not enter."

Wheeler would ultimately lose this frontier feud. In 1879, the government created the United States Geological Survey and tasked it with mapping responsibilities. Government scientists, not military officers, would now have primary control of surveying the West.

Wheeler died on May 3, 1905, in New York City.

More to explore: *Elizabethtown, Gila Cliff Dwellings National Monument, Red River Valley, Rocky Mountains, Strike Valleys*

487. White Oaks

Location: Lincoln County. On the east end of White Oaks, on the south side of NM 349, between mile markers 8 and 9. See map 6.

Marker text: White Oaks grew rapidly after the discovery of gold in 1879. From tent city to bustling mining town, it was the largest town in Lincoln County with cultural events and an occasional bandit. Gold depletion and failure to grant railroad right-of-way caused its demise. Cedarvale cemetery—resting place of many White Oaks residents.

Four men prospecting in the hills of south-central New Mexico in 1879 discovered an outcropping of gold ore along the eastern slope of Baxter Mountain. Three of the prospectors, George Wilson, George Baxter, and Jack Winters, developed the North Homestake mine around the discovery. A story persists that the fourth, believed to be a fugitive, left the area after selling his stake in the claim—reportedly for the frontier bargain price of forty dollars, a pony, and a bottle of whiskey!

Cupped in the Jicarilla Mountains, the townsite that developed around the claim grew quickly, vaulting from tent city to the largest town in Lincoln County within a few years. Residents built a beautiful brick school building on a hill overlooking town, then added a church, an opera house, a bank, and several saloons, and reported on their progress in the *Old Abe Eagle* newspaper. It was enough enterprise to give the town the title role in local writer Emerson Hough's semiautobiographical and warm-hearted novel, *Heart's Desire: The Story of a Contented Town, Certain Peculiar Citizens, and Two Fortunate Lovers*. Hough based his "contented town" on White Oaks, an amenable name borrowed from nearby White Oaks Spring.

White Oaks miners pulled their profit from the mountains in mines like the Lady Godiva, Rip van Winkle, and Boston Boy. According to mining historian Fayette Jones, the productive and profitable 1,375-foot-deep Old Abe gold mine was the deepest dry shaft in the world before the turn of the century. Supervising operations at the Old Abe was Watson Hoyle, who used his earnings to erect the Victorian-style home known as the Hoyle

White Oaks has aged gracefully, with many of the buildings appearing very much today as they did when they were built. The White Oaks schoolhouse building is one of the more prominent structures in the town. Photo by John Mulhouse. Used with permission.

House, which still stands. Billy the Kid, a chief player in a feud centered in the nearby town of Lincoln, rode into town on horseback on occasion. Among other notables who made a more permanent home in White Oaks were lawyer William C. McDonald, who owned the Bar W Ranch nearby and later served as the first governor of New Mexico after statehood, and rancher Susan McSween Barber, whose prominent ranch near Three Rivers had earned her the title "Cattle Queen of New Mexico." Notable in a different way was Madame Varnish, who ran the casino and, some say, brothel.

In 1897, promoter Charles B. Eddy began to extend his El Paso and Northeastern Railroad north from El Paso through the Tularosa Valley to connect with the Chicago, Rock Island, and Pacific at Santa Rosa. White Oaks residents purchased land athwart the planned route in anticipation of their community becoming the right-of-way, but Eddy bypassed the town in favor of Ancho Canyon at the northern end of the Jicarilla Mountains. Estranged from rail connections and faced with the depletion of gold, White Oaks declined.

Perhaps not coincidentally, the protagonists in Hough's *Heart's Desire* also face the issue of railroad access to their town. In the novel, however, it is the citizens who turn away from the railroad. The character Uncle Jim dryly states: "Seems to me like we always got along here pretty well the way things *was*."

Many of the older buildings in White Oaks have likewise gotten along pretty well, and the town today offers a restored vision of its urbane past. Cedarvale Cemetery west of town is the resting place of many former White Oaks residents, including Susan McSween Barber, who died in 1931, and William McDonald, who died in 1918. One of the most poignant graves, though, is the mass grave dated March 9, 1895, for eight men, with the inscription "Died by Suffocation in Old Abe Mine."

More to explore: *Carrizozo, La Luz, Three Rivers, Tularosa*

---

488. Women of Cochiti

Location: Sandoval County. At the entrance to Cochiti Pueblo, in a pullout on the east side of NM 22, between mile markers 12 and 13. See map 4.

Marker text: Women in Cochiti are known for reviving the historic figurative tradition now referred to as Storytellers, adult clay figurines surrounded by children. The efforts of these women have bloomed into a vibrant cottage industry, inspiring many potters and have greatly enhanced the economic welfare of Cochiti. Storytellers are now widely collected as art, appearing in major museums and private collections around the world.

The pueblo of Cochiti in north-central New Mexico is renowned for its crafting of clay figures known as Storytellers. These sculptures display seated figures, most often with their legs outstretched before them. The figures are usually women, but they can also be men, and sometimes even animals. Invariably the figure is surrounded by small children, who may be depicted as reverent or rambunctious. The children may be seated in the lap of the main figure, held in her arms, crawling on her shoulders or waist, or sitting in the reaches of her dress as it spreads out around her. The main figure is often depicted with her mouth open in an oval shape as if speaking or singing. She is the "storyteller," and the children who surround her are enthralled by her tales. Storytelling at Cochiti, as in many pueblos and other ancient cultures, was and still is a means of passing along the customs, values, and history of the pueblo through many generations.

Figurative pottery like the Storyteller sculptures has long been a tradition at Cochiti Pueblo. Early figurative pottery at the pueblo included depictions of mothers carrying their children and often singing to them, a motif that some art historians believe may have been the basis for the Storyteller-style figures that followed.

The women of Cochiti began creating Storyteller figures in their current form in the 1960s. Since that time, the making of these figures has blossomed into a vibrant cottage industry, bolstering the pueblo's economic welfare. The beautifully crafted Storytellers produced at Cochiti Pueblo have become admired around the world. They are of interest to collectors of fine Native American art as well as to anyone who appreciates objects of beauty.

More to explore: *Zuni Olla Maidens (see under Pueblo of Zuni)*

Women of Shakespeare: *see Shakespeare*

Women of the Camino Real: *see El Camino Real—The King's Highway*

489. Women of the Judiciary
The Honorable Mary Coon Walters (1922–2001)

Location: Bernalillo County. In Albuquerque, at the University of New Mexico School of Law, 1117 Stanford Drive NE. See map 4.

Marker text: Ms. Walters, who was a transport pilot during World War II, was the only woman in her UNM law school class when she graduated at age 40. She served on the state Court of Appeals and as a probate judge. In 1984, she became the first female New Mexico Supreme Court justice. She was a role model and mentor to women in New Mexico's legal community.

490. Women of the Judiciary
Chief Justice Pamela B. Minzner (1943–2007)

Marker text: Pioneers prove their value in those that follow. Pamela Minzner took Mary Walters' seat on the Court of Appeals. Later, following Justice Walters to the New Mexico Supreme Court, she became the first woman chief justice. Renowned for her intellect, kindness, professionalism and gentle spirit, she, in turn, mentored hundreds in the legal profession. Today, women regularly serve on New Mexico's court benches.

Note: Marker faceplates are on opposite sides of the same sign. See map 4.

Mary Coon Walters and Pamela B. Minzner both lived lives of firsts. And through their mentorship of others in the legal profession, they ensured that those firsts opened doors for others who would come after them.

Walters was born Mary Coon on January 29, 1922, in Baraga, Michigan. Just after the start of World War II, at the age of twenty, she enlisted in the Women Airforce Service Pilots, commonly known by the acronym WASPs. (WASPs were women pilots who flew noncombat missions during the war.) Assigned to Hondo Army Air Field in Hondo, Texas, Coon flew as a C-45 transport pilot for the US Army Air Force. After the war, Walters enrolled in the University of New Mexico School of Law on the G.I. Bill. When she graduated in 1962 at age forty, she was the only woman in her class. Admitted to the New Mexico Bar that same year, she was continuing a tradition begun by the first woman in New Mexico admitted to the bar, Henrietta Pettijohn, in 1892.

When Governor Bruce King appointed Walters to serve on the district court in Albuquerque in 1971, she became the first female district judge in

New Mexico. She later worked as a probate judge in that city. (A probate judge oversees the legal execution of assets of a deceased person.) In 1978, she began service as one of ten judges on the New Mexico Court of Appeals—hearing cases on civil and noncapital criminal legal issues. At home, she and her husband, Asa Lane Walters, raised two children.

There was one more rung for her to climb in the state judicial system, and in 1984, she climbed it—being appointed by Governor Toney Anaya as one of the five justices of the New Mexico Supreme Court. The woman who once sat in the cockpit of World War II transport planes was now sitting on the bench of the highest court in her state, and further, she was the first woman in the history of the state to do so. Through her achievements, earned with hard work, intelligence, and passion, she served as a role model for women in the legal community.

Justice Walters passed away on April 5, 2001. Since 2003, in her honor, the Women's Law Caucus at the University of New Mexico School of Law has annually awarded the Justice Mary Walters Award to an "outstanding woman in the New Mexico legal community."

When Justice Walters left the court of appeals in 1984, her vacancy was filled by another accomplished woman, Pamela B. Minzner.

Minzner was born Pamela Burgy in 1943. After graduating from Miami University of Ohio in 1965, she was accepted to Harvard Law School, where she met and married her husband, Richard Minzner. The couple moved to New Mexico, and, in 1973, Minzner accepted a faculty position with the University of New Mexico School of Law. She remained at UNM until her appointment by Governor Toney Anaya to the State Court of Appeals eleven years later. During this time, she and her husband raised two children.

In 1999, after having served on the New Mexico Supreme Court for five years, Minzner added another first to the roster of achievements for women in the state, being appointed by Governor Bruce King as the court's first woman chief justice.

Those who knew Minzner appreciated her intelligence, kindness, and willingness to mentor others who, like her, chose to make their mark in the legal profession. Chief Justice Edward L. Chávez, who served with Justice Minzner on the Supreme Court, later wrote of her demeanor on the court: "She was as quick to compliment a justice on what she considered to be a well-articulated position as she was to respectfully voice her disagreement with a position. She never made her disagreements personal. She had a way of making one gain confidence in his or her position when she was in agreement, and her calm approach to disagreement was likely to make one revisit his or her position."

On August 29, 2007, in what would be her last official act, Chief Justice Minzner signed an order from the Supreme Court honoring her predecessor, Justice Mary Coon Walters, by posthumously granting her the honorary title of Chief Justice of the New Mexico Supreme Court and ordering that her portrait be permanently displayed in the Supreme Court Building in Santa Fe. Minzner died two days later.

Justices Walters and Minzner achieved much in their lifetimes—and they left behind a legacy that demonstrates the lasting significance of those achievements. Today, it is not unusual to see women judges in any court in New Mexico.

More to explore: *Doña Dolores "Lola" Chávez de Armijo, Inez Bushner Gill, Maralyn Budke (see under Inez Bushner Gill), Maria "Concha" Concepción Ortiz y Pino de Kleven, Marjorie Bell Chambers, Nina Otero-Warren*

Women of the Santa Fe Trail: *see Santa Fe Trail (series)*

491. Women Veterans of New Mexico

Location: Sandoval County. West of Placitas, in a pullout on the south side of NM 165, between mile markers 0 and 1, just east of the Interstate 25 interchange. See map 4.

Marker text: New Mexico has a proud history of military service. We are a state of culturally diverse citizens who are willing to defend our freedom and rights. Over 15,000 women in New Mexico have volunteered to serve in our military. New Mexican women have taken up arms throughout our history and their considerable contributions are a tribute to the pride and honor of all New Mexicans.

These three women, who lost their lives in military service, are representative of the region:

1st Lt. Tamara Archuleta
United States Air Force
Los Lunas, NM
Died 23 March 2003

Specialist Lori Piestewa
United States Army
Tuba City, Arizona
Died 23 March 2003

Captain Christel Chávez
United States Air Force
Albuquerque, NM
Died 7 August 2002

More than fifteen thousand women from New Mexico have served the country in the armed forces. This Historic Marker notes the names of three of them—three women who gave their lives in service to their country. Their deaths are quite recent, and the pain of their loss is still very present for family, friends, admirers, and those with whom they served. Their deaths are a reminder that the history of our state includes individuals of all races and genders who have sacrificed valiantly for our country—sometimes offering the ultimate sacrifice.

First Lieutenant Tamara Archuleta, known as Tammy to her family, was a native of Los Lunas serving as a pilot for the Forty-First Expeditionary Rescue Squadron of the US Air Force and based at Moody Air Force Base near Valdosta, Georgia. On March 23, 2003, she was the copilot on a mission to assist two Afghani children as part of Operation Enduring Freedom when the HH-60G Pave Hawk helicopter she and five airmen were in crashed, killing all aboard. First Lieutenant Archuleta was only twenty-three at the time of her death.

Private First Class Lori Ann Piestewa was a member of the Hopi Tribe, deployed from Fort Bliss in El Paso, Texas, in February 2003. On March 23, she was driving a Humvee with other members of the 507th Maintenance Company as part of the invasion of Iraq when the unit was ambushed near Nasiriyah. Three members of the unit were killed when the Humvee crashed into another vehicle; Piestewa and six others—included soldier Jessica Lynch—were taken prisoner. Piestewa died later that day in an Iraqi hospital. (Subsequently, US Special Forces staged a raid on the hospital, rescuing Lynch and recovering the bodies of other American soldiers.) After Piestewa's death, the army posthumously promoted her to specialist and awarded her the Purple Heart.

Captain Christel Angélica Chávez, an Albuquerque native, graduated from the Air Force Academy in 1998 and was stationed at Hurlburt Field in Okaloosa County, Florida, as a member of the Sixteenth Special Operations Wing. During a training exercise on the night of August 7, 2002, the C-130 Combat Talon aircraft Captain Chávez was copiloting crashed into a mountainside near San Juan, Puerto Rico. Captain Chávez and all ten others aboard were killed. Chávez was buried in Santa Fe National Cemetery, memorialized by an epitaph that reads in part: "A Star That Shined Bright."

More to explore: *Khe Sanh Veterans, Vietnam Veterans National Memorial*

492. Yetta Kohn (1843–1917)
Matriarch, Cattle Rancher, and Business Woman

Location: Quay County. In Tucumcari, at the Tucumcari Convention Center, 1500 West Historic Route 66. See map 3.

Marker text: Born in Bavaria and widowed in Las Vegas (NM), Yetta ran the family store and raised four children alone. She later moved to La Cinta on the Canadian River where she opened another store, became the postmistress, started a bank and operated a ferry. She eventually bought land that became the 4V Ranch, which expanded into the T-4 Cattle Company, operated today by her descendants.

As pioneers go, Yetta Louise Goldsmith Kohn was one of the finest.

Her story begins with her birth in Bavaria in southeastern Germany on March 9, 1843. At the age of ten, Yetta emigrated with family members to the United States, possibly escaping anti-Semitic sentiments in her native country. She met and married Samuel Kohn in Leavenworth, Kansas, sometime around 1860. The couple decided to "go West," so they traveled along the Santa Fe Trail from Kansas. According to a family history, one of their wagon-pulling oxen died en route, and

Widowed and left to raise four children by herself in the New Mexico Territory in the mid-nineteenth century, Yetta Kohn used fortitude, business sense, and willpower to rise above her circumstances and become one of the most prominent ranchers and businesswomen in the history of New Mexico. Portrait of Yetta Kohn. New Mexico Jewish Historical Society Collection, 1988-052, Box 12148, Folder 11, courtesy New Mexico State Records Center and Archives.

they were forced to substitute a cow. After initially giving it a go in Denver, the Kohns later settled in Las Vegas, New Mexico, where they opened a store and sold, among other things, wool. The census lists Yetta's occupation at the time as "seamstress."

The Kohns were one of only a small number of Jewish pioneers in New Mexico in the mid-nineteenth century, many of that small group having come to America from Germany. Those who came to New Mexico settled throughout the state, but most stayed in Santa Fe, Albuquerque, or Las Vegas, and many opened businesses. The Kohns operated their store at a time between the Civil War and the arrival of the railroad in 1880, a period that historian Henry J. Tobias calls the "golden age of German-Jewish merchant settlers in New Mexico."

But Yetta's luck took a bad turn in 1878, when Samuel passed away. Yetta was widowed, left alone to raise their three boys and one girl. Although her prospects at the time may have appeared bleak, Kohn managed bit by bit to reverse her fortunes. Within twenty years, she would be at the helm of one of the largest cattle operations in east-central New Mexico.

Her success came gradually. After running the store in Las Vegas for four more years, Kohn moved with her family in 1882 to a small parcel of homesteaded land at a settlement known as La Cinta, a village along the Canadian River about sixty miles southeast of Las Vegas (near present-day Conchas Lake). There, with the experience she had gained in Las Vegas, Kohn opened a grocery store. She also served as the postmistress for the village and on at least one occasion steered a ferry across the Canadian River. She then joined with other partners and invested in the basic commodity of the plains: cattle. Her holdings were the start of her first ranch, known as the 4V Ranch, managed later by her sons and daughter. After the turn of the century, Kohn moved her family to the new railroad community of Montoya, about twenty miles south of La Cinta. With her sons, she opened the large Kohn Brothers General Merchandise store there, as well as a bank. Kohn augmented her land and cattle holdings over the years, and under her guidance, the ranching operation grew, eventually subsuming the town of Montoya itself.

Sadly, Kohn outlived two of her sons. Charley died of an infected tooth while on his honeymoon in 1916; George died a few days later, possibly in grief from the loss of his brother.

That grief no doubt also affected the matriarch of the family. Yetta Kohn passed away herself the next year, on April 24, 1917.

The Kohn's cattle company was renamed in 1946 as the T-4 Cattle Company. It remains in operation today, run by her descendants.

More to explore: *Harriet Belle Amsden Sammons, Monica Fuentes Gallegos and Carlota Fuentes Gallegos*

493. Yucca—New Mexico's State Flower

Location: Grant County. In rest area on the south side of Interstate 10, at mile marker 49. See map 5.

Marker text: The Yucca is a member of the lily family. Its spring blossoms are pearly white. Early Indians used its tender shoots for food. Soap was made from its roots, sandals and basketry from the leaf fiber. A single variety of moth produces pollination.

494. Yucca Plains

Location: Grant County. In rest area on the south side of Interstate 10, at mile marker 49. See map 5.

Marker text: Wide alluvial plains of Southwest New Mexico are feature of basin and range province with isolated fault block mountains scattered like islands from a sandy sea. Volcanic rocks form most of Cedar Mountains to south and Pyramid Mountains to west but Burro Mountains to northwest are mainly ancient granites. Elevation 4,560 feet.

As practical as it is beautiful, the yucca will grow to thirty feet tall. Photo by Sam Kolman. Used with permission.

Seeking a flower suitable in beauty and regional character to represent New Mexico as the official state flower, members of the state legislature in 1927 asked the New Mexico Federation of Women's Clubs for an appropriate recommendation. Club members, in turn, surveyed schoolchildren throughout the state, who voted overwhelmingly in favor of the flowering pearly-white blossoms of the soapweed or palmilla plant, *Yucca elata*. On March 14, 1927, the legislature passed H.B. 371 and formally approved yucca blossoms as the "distinctive official flower" of New Mexico.

But the yucca is more than just a pretty face. The Mogollon Indians of southwestern New Mexico wove the fibrous leaves of the plant into sandals. Later, Native Americans pulverized yucca amole, soaked the pulp in hot water, and cleaned their hair and bodies with the sudsy soap this mix produced. Yucca leaves, which can grow two feet in length, doubled as brooms and building material for pueblo roofs, or were woven strand by strand into a tough and fibrous rope. Spanish settlers burned the stalks as firewood and used the leaves as food for hungry cattle during droughts. The yucca plant also played a role in the American occupation of New Mexico in 1846, as noted in the journal of soldier Isaac George, marching through the Jornada del Muerto desert just north of Las Cruces:

The soldiers, fatigued with marching, faint with hunger, and benumbed by the piercing winds, straggled along the road at night (for there was not much halting for repose), setting fire to the dry bunches of grass and stalks of soap-plant, or palmilla, which would blaze up like flashes of powder, and as quickly extinguish, leaving the men shivering in the cold. For miles the road was most brilliantly illuminated by sudden flashes of light, which lasted but for a moment, then again all was dark.*

The yucca is a member of the lily family. Reproduction depends on a single variety of moth. Small white yucca moths, *Tegeticula yuccasella*, mate inside the protective canopy of the flower, which also holds the eggs laid later by the female moths. The moth larvae feast on yucca seeds as they mature. During the evenings, the female yucca moth carries the sticky pollen from the stamen of one yucca plant to the pistil of another. Entomologists call this give-and-take between moth and flower "mutualism." Without the assistance of the yucca moth, the yucca would have no ability to reproduce in variation.

Legend says that the first Spanish settlers to reach New Mexico in the late sixteenth century also appreciated these flowers. Reportedly, these settlers, upon first beholding the beautiful yuccas spread out on the desert before them, named them *candelarios de Dios*—candles of God!

Yuccas can be found across the plains of this part of southwestern New Mexico. The region is part of the Basin and Range Province, one of the physiographic regions that geographers use to characterize the diverse physical landscape of the country. As the name implies, the Basin and Range Province includes fault-block mountains (mountains formed along fault lines) separated by large stretches of sediment-covered plains—a combination described eloquently in the Yucca Plains Historic Marker as "isolated fault block mountains scattered like islands from a sandy sea." The Cedar Mountains to the south and the Pyramid Mountains to the west are composed of rocks formed in part by tuff from volcanic eruptions during the Tertiary period, 1.8 million to 6.5 million years ago. The highest peak in the Pyramid Mountains is 6,008-foot Pyramid Peak, shaped something like a pyramid, from which the range takes its name. The Burro Mountains to the northwest are mainly ancient granites formed millions of years ago. That's a long time to be scenic, but they've been doing it well from the start.

More to explore: *Basin and Range Country, Hachita, Mogollon*

Zuni Olla Maidens: *see Pueblo of Zuni*

Bibliography

Books and Articles

Abert, James William, Lieutenant. *Expedition to the Southwest: An 1845 Reconnaissance of Colorado, New Mexico, Texas, and Oklahoma.* Edited by H. Bailey Carroll. Lincoln: University of Nebraska Press, 1999.

Ackerly, Neal W. *An Overview of the Historic Characteristics of New Mexico's Mines.* Santa Fe, NM: Historic Preservation Division, 1997.

Ackerly, Neal W., et al. *Acequia Systems of the Velarde Region: North-Central New Mexico.* Center for Anthropological Research, New Mexico State University. Santa Fe, NM: Historic Preservation Division, 1994.

Adams, Karen R. *Pollen, Parched Seeds and Prehistory: A Pilot Investigation of Prehistoric Plant Remains from Salmon Ruin, A Chacoan Pueblo in Northwestern New Mexico.* Eastern New Mexico University Contributions in Anthropology, vol. 9. Portales, NM: Llano Estacado Center for Advanced Professional Studies and Research, 1980.

Aday, Bennie Joe, Jr., and A. L. Gennaro. *Mammals (Excluding Bats) of the New Mexican Llano Estacado and Its Adjacent River Valleys.* Portales, NM: Natural Science Research Institute, Eastern New Mexico University, 1973.

Ailman, Harry B. *Pioneering in Territorial Silver City.* Edited by Helen J. Ludwall. Albuquerque: University of New Mexico Press, 1983.

Arellanes, Kathy, ed. *New Mexico Scenic and Historic Byways.* New Mexico Highway and Transportation Department. Albuquerque: University of New Mexico Printing Services, n.d.

Arellano, Anselmo F., and Julián Josué Vigil. *Las Vegas Grandes on the Gallinas, 1835–1985.* Las Vegas, NM: Editorial Teleraña, 1985.

Armstrong, Ruth W. *Cycle of Seasons in Corrales.* Santa Fe, NM: Sunstone Press, 1988.

Arnon, Nancy S., and W. W. Hill. "Santa Clara Pueblo." In *Handbook of North American Indians.* Vol. 9, *Southwest,* edited by Alfonso Ortiz. Washington, D.C.: Smithsonian Institution, 1979.

Ashcroft, Bruce. *The Territorial History of Socorro, New Mexico.* El Paso: Texas Western Press, 1988.

Baars, Donald L. *Navajo Country: A Geology and Natural History of the Four Corners Region.* Albuquerque: University of New Mexico Press, 1995.

Bailey, Jessie Bromilow. *Diego de Vargas and the Reconquest of New Mexico.* Albuquerque: University of New Mexico Press, 1940.

Bailey, Lynn R. *Bosque Redondo: An American Concentration Camp.* Pasadena, CA: Socio-Technical Books, 1970.

———. *The Long Walk: A History of the Navajo Wars, 1846–1868.* Los Angeles, CA: Westernlore Press, 1964.

Baker, Ellen R. *On Strike and on Film: Mexican American Families and Blacklisted Filmmakers in Cold War America*. Chapel Hill: University of North Carolina Press, 2007.

Ball, Eve. *Indeh: An Apache Odyssey*. Norman: University of Oklahoma Press, 1988.

Ball, Larry D. *The United States Marshals of New Mexico and Arizona Territories, 1846–1912*. Albuquerque: University of New Mexico Press, 1978.

Bancroft, Hubert Howe, and Henry Lebbeus Oak. *History of Arizona and New Mexico, 1530–1888*. San Francisco, CA: The History Company, 1889.

Bandelier, Adolph F. A., and Fanny R. Bandelier, eds. *Historical Documents Relating to New Mexico, Nueva Vizcaya, and Approaches Thereto, to 1773*. Vol. 3. Washington, D.C.: Carnegie Institution of Washington, 1937.

Barela, Josephina. *Ojo del Gallo: A Nostalgic Narrative of Historic San Rafael*. Santa Fe, NM: Sleeping Fox Enterprises, 1975.

Barker, Elliott S. *Smokey Bear and the Great Wilderness*. Santa Fe, NM: Sunstone Press, 1982.

Barrett, Elinore M. *Conquest and Catastrophe: Changing Rio Grande Pueblo Settlement Patterns in the Sixteenth and Seventeenth Centuries*. Albuquerque: University of New Mexico Press, 2002.

Barry, John W. *American Indian Pottery: An Identification Guide*. Florence, AL: Books Americana, 1984.

Bartlett, John Russell. *Personal Narrative of Explorations and Incidents in Texas, New Mexico, California, Sonora, and Chihuahua, 1850–1853*. Vol. 1. Chicago, IL: Rio Grande Press, 1965.

Bauer, Paul W., Jane C. Love, John H. Schilling, and Joseph E. Taggart Jr. *The Enchanted Circle: Loop Tours from Taos*. Scenic Trips to the Geologic Past, no. 2. Socorro, NM: New Mexico Bureau of Mines and Mineral Resources, 1991.

Beck, Warren A., and Ynez D. Haase. *Historical Atlas of New Mexico*. Norman: University of Oklahoma Press, 1969.

Beckett, Patrick H. *Las Cruces, New Mexico 1881: As Seen by Her Newspapers*. Las Cruces, NM: Coas Publishing and Research, 2003.

Benedict, Audrey DeLella. *A Sierra Club Naturalist's Guide to the Southern Rockies*. San Francisco, CA: Sierra Club Books, 1991.

Bennett, James A. *Forts and Forays: A Dragoon in New Mexico, 1850–1856*. Edited by Clinton E. Brooks and Frank D. Reeve. Albuquerque: University of New Mexico Press, 1996.

Binnewies, Robert O. *Palisades: 100,000 Acres in 100 Years*. Bronx, NY: Fordham University Press, 2001.

Blyth, Lance R. *Chiricahua and Janos: Communities of Violence in the Southwestern Borderlands, 1680–1880*. Lincoln: University of Nebraska Press, 2012.

Bodine, Marc W., Jr. *Geology of the Capitan Coal Field*. Socorro, NM: New Mexico Institute of Mining and Technology, 1956.

Boldurian, Anthony T., and John L. Cotter. *Clovis Revisited: New Perspectives on Paleoindian Adaptations from Blackwater Draw, New Mexico*. Philadelphia: University Museum, University of Pennsylvania, 1999.

Bourke, John Gregory. *An Apache Campaign in the Sierra Madre*. New York: Charles Scribner's Sons, 1958.

———. *The Snake-Dance of the Moquis of Arizona*. Chicago, IL: Rio Grande Press, 1962.

Bradford, James E. *Archaeology Survey: Gila Cliff Dwellings National Monument*. Santa Fe, NM: National Park Service, Division of Anthropology, 1992.

Brandt, Elizabeth A. "Sandia Pueblo." In *Handbook of North American Indians*. Vol. 9, *Southwest*, edited by Alfonso Ortiz, 343–50. Washington, D.C.: Smithsonian Institution, 1979.

Brooks, Connie. *The Last Cowboys.* Albuquerque: University of New Mexico Press, 1993.

Brown, Donald N. "Picurís Pueblo." In *Handbook of North American Indians.* Vol. 9, *Southwest,* edited by Alfonso Ortiz, 268–77. Washington, D.C.: Smithsonian Institution, 1979.

Brown, Joseph E. *The Mormon Trek West.* Garden City, NY: Doubleday, 1980.

Brown, William E. *The Santa Fe Trail: National Park Service 1963 Historic Sites Survey.* Saint Louis, MO: Patrice Press, 1988.

Browne, Walter Anderson. *The Llano Estacado: A Geographic Interpretation.* Nashville, TN: George Peabody College for Teachers, 1935.

Bryan, Howard. *Albuquerque Remembered.* Albuquerque: University of New Mexico Press, 2006.

———. *Robbers, Rogues, and Ruffians: True Tales of the Wild West in New Mexico.* Santa Fe, NM: Clear Light Publishers, 1991.

Bullock, Alice. *Mountain Villages.* Santa Fe, NM: Sunstone Press, 1973.

Bunting, Bainbridge. *Of Earth and Timbers Made: New Mexico Architecture.* Albuquerque: University of New Mexico Press, 1974.

Bureau of Immigration of the Territory of New Mexico. *Compilation of Facts Concerning the Pecos Valley.* Santa Fe, NM: New Mexican Printing Company, 1891.

———. *Guadalupe County, New Mexico.* Bulletin no. 16. Santa Fe, NM: New Mexican Printing Company, 1902.

———. *Union County.* Bulletin no. 15. Santa Fe, NM: New Mexican Printing Company, 1902.

Burroughs, Jean M., ed. *Roosevelt County History and Heritage.* Portales, NM: Bishop Printing Company, 1975.

Burton, Jeff. *Dynamite and Six-Shooter: The Story of Thomas E. "Black Jack" Ketchum.* Santa Fe, NM: Palomino Press, 1970.

Bushman, Claudia Lauper, and Richard Lyman Bushman. *Mormons in America.* New York: Oxford University Press, 1999.

Caffey, David L. *Frank Springer and New Mexico: From the Colfax County War to the Emergence of Modern Santa Fe.* College Station: Texas A&M University Press, 2006.

Caperton, Thomas J. *Rogue! Being an Account of the Life and High Times of Stephen W. Dorsey, United States Senator and New Mexico Cattle Baron.* Santa Fe: Museum of New Mexico Press, 1978.

Carleton, James H., Major. *Diary of an Excursion to the Ruins of Abo, Quarra and Gran Quivara in New Mexico in 1853, Under the Command of Major James Henry Carleton.* Santa Fe, NM: Stagecoach Press, 1965.

Carlson, Paul H. *The Buffalo Soldier Tragedy of 1877.* College Station: Texas A&M University Press, 2003.

Carson, Kit. *Kit Carson's Autobiography.* Edited by Milo Milton Quaife. Lincoln: University of Nebraska Press, 1966.

Cash, Joseph H., and Gerald W. Wolff. *The Comanche People.* Phoenix, AZ: Indian Tribal Series, 1974.

Chambers, Marjorie Bell, and Linda K. Aldrich. *Los Alamos, New Mexico: A Survey to 1949.* Los Alamos, NM: Los Alamos Historical Society, 1999.

Chapin, Charles E., et. al. *Coal, Uranium, Oil, and Gas Potential of the Riley-Puertecito Area, Socorro County, New Mexico.* Socorro: New Mexico Institute of Mining and Technology, 1979.

Chapman, Manville. *Blazed Trails: A Series of Colfax County Historical Narratives Based on the Mural Paintings in the Shuler Auditorium of Raton, N.M.* N.p., 1935.

Chavez, Fray Angelico. *The Dominguez-Escalante Journal.* Edited by Ted J. Warner. Salt Lake City: University of Utah Press, 1995.

———. "Doña Tules, Her Fame and Her Funeral." *El Palacio* 57, no. 8 (August 1950).

———. "Genízaros." In *Handbook of North American Indians*. Vol. 9, *Southwest*, edited by Alfonso Ortiz, 198–200. Washington, D.C.: Smithsonian Institution, 1979.

Chilton, Lance, Katherine Chilton, Polly E. Arango, James Dudley, Nancy Neary, and Patricia Stelzner. *New Mexico: A New Guide to the Colorful State*. Albuquerque: University of New Mexico Press, 1984.

Christensen, Thomas, and Carol Christensen. *The US-Mexican War*. San Francisco, CA: Bay Books, 1998.

Christiansen, Paige W. *Of Earth and Sky*. Socorro: New Mexico Institute of Mining and Technology, 1964.

———. *The Story of Mining in New Mexico*. Socorro: New Mexico Bureau of Mines and Mineral Resources, 1975.

———. *The Story of Oil in New Mexico*. Socorro: New Mexico Bureau of Mines and Mineral Resources, 1989.

Chronic, Halka. *Roadside Geology of New Mexico*. Missoula, MT: Mountain Press, 1987.

Civilian Conservation Corps. *Fort Bliss 1935 CCC Annual*. El Paso, TX: Fort Bliss, 1935.

Clark, Mary Grooms. *A History of New Mexico: A Mark of Time*. Canyon, TX: Staked Plains Press, 1983.

Coan, Charles F. *A History of New Mexico*. New York: American Historical Society, 1926.

Cobos, Rubén. *A Dictionary of New Mexico and Southern Colorado Spanish*. Santa Fe: Museum of New Mexico Press, 1983.

Coe, George. *Frontier Fighter: The Autobiography of George W. Coe*. Albuquerque: University of New Mexico Press, 1951.

Conkling, Roscoe P., and Margaret B. Conkling. *The Butterfield Overland Mail, 1857–1869*. Vol. 2. Glendale, CA: Arthur H. Clark, 1947.

Conway, Jay T. *A Brief Community History of Raton, New Mexico, 1880–1930, Commemorating Her Fiftieth Birthday*. Raton, NM: Colfax County Pioneers Association, 1930.

Cook, John R. *The Border and the Buffalo*. Topeka, KS: Crame and Company, 1907.

Cooke, Philip St. George. *The Conquest of New Mexico and California*. Albuquerque, NM: Horn and Wallace, 1964.

Cordell, Linda S., ed. *Tijeras Canyon: Analyses of the Past*. Albuquerque: University of New Mexico Press; Maxwell Museum of Anthropology, 1980.

Cottrell, Steve. *Civil War in Texas and New Mexico Territory*. Gretna, LA: Pelican Publishing, 1998.

Coulter, Mary. *Manual for Drivers and Guides Descriptive of the Indian Watchtower at Desert View and Its Relation, Architecturally, to the Prehistoric Ruins of the Southwest*. Grand Canyon National Park, AZ: Fred Harvey, 1933.

Cozzens, Peter, ed. *Eyewitnesses to the Indian Wars, 1865–1890*. Mechanicsburg, PA: Stackpole Books, 2003.

Crichton, Kyle S. *Law and Order, Ltd.: The Rousing Life of Elfego Baca of New Mexico*. Santa Fe: New Mexican Publishing Corporation, 1928.

Crosby, Harry H. *The American Heritage Book of Great Adventures of the Old West*. New York: American Heritage Press, 1969.

Current, Richard N., ed. *Encyclopedia of the Confederacy*. New York: Simon and Schuster, 1993.

Curry, George. *George Curry: An Autobiography*. Albuquerque: University of New Mexico Press, 1958.

Cusic, Don. *The Cowboy in Country Music: An Historical Survey with Artist Profiles*. Jefferson, NC: McFarland and Company, 2011.

D'Arcy, Gail. *Block by Block, Piecing Together Central New Mexico's Past: The Homesteaders*. Chico, CA: Memoir Books, 2009.

Davis, W. W. H. *El Gringo; or, New Mexico and Her People*. Santa Fe, NM: Rydal Press, 1938.

Davis-Floyd, Robbie E., Lesley Barclay, Jan Tritten, and Betty-Anne Daviss, eds. *Birth Models That Work*. Berkeley: University of California Press, 2009.

Dawdy, Doris Ostrander. *George Montague Wheeler: The Man and the Myth*. Athens: Ohio University Press, 1993.

Dawson, Joseph G., III. *Doniphan's Epic March: The 1st Missouri Volunteers in the Mexican War*. Lawrence: University Press of Kansas, 1999.

Dean, Rob, ed. *Santa Fe: Its 400th Year*. Santa Fe, NM: Sunstone Press, 2010.

DeBuys, William. *Enchantment and Exploitation: The Life and Hard Times of a New Mexico Mountain Range*. Albuquerque: University of New Mexico Press, 1985.

Densmore, Frances. "Music of Acoma, Isleta, Cochiti, and Zuñi Pueblos." Smithsonian Institution, Bureau of American Ethnology, Bulletin 165. Washington, D.C.: Government Printing Office, 1957.

Denver and Rio Grande Railroad. *Outdoor Life in the Rockies*. Denver, CO: Carson-Harper, 1917.

Domínguez, Fray Francisco Atanasio. *The Missions of New Mexico, 1776*. Albuquerque: University of New Mexico Press, 1956.

Duffus, R. L. *The Santa Fe Trail*. Albuquerque: University of New Mexico Press, 1972.

Dunlay, Tom. *Kit Carson and the Indians*. Lincoln: University of Nebraska Press, 2000.

Eagle Walking Turtle. *Indian America: A Traveler's Companion*. Santa Fe, NM: John Muir Publications, 1995.

Edelman, Sandra A. "San Ildefonso Pueblo." In *Handbook of North American Indians*. Vol. 9, *Southwest*, edited by Alfonso Ortiz, 308–16. Washington, D.C.: Smithsonian Institution, 1979.

Edelman, Sandra A., and Alfonso Ortiz. "Tesuque Pueblo." In *Handbook of North American Indians*. Vol. 9, *Southwest*, edited by Alfonso Ortiz, 330–35. Washington, D.C.: Smithsonian Institution, 1979.

Edwards, Frank S. *A Campaign in New Mexico with Colonel Doniphan*. Albuquerque: University of New Mexico Press, 1996.

Eggan, Fred. "Pueblos: Introduction." In *Handbook of North American Indians*. Vol. 9, *Southwest*, edited by Alfonso Ortiz, 224–35. Washington, D.C.: Smithsonian Institution, 1979.

Eisenhower, John S. D. *So Far from God: The US War with Mexico, 1846–1848*. New York: Random House, 1989.

Ellis, Florence Hawley. "Isleta Pueblo." In *Handbook of North American Indians*. Vol. 9, *Southwest*, edited by Alfonso Ortiz, 351–65. Washington, D.C.: Smithsonian Institution, 1979.

———. "Laguna Pueblo." In *Handbook of North American Indians*. Vol. 9, *Southwest*, edited by Alfonso Ortiz, 438–49. Washington, D.C.: Smithsonian Institution, 1979.

———. *San Gabriel del Yungue: As Seen by an Archaeologist*. Santa Fe, NM: Sunstone Press, 1989.

Ellis, Richard N. *New Mexico Historic Documents*. Albuquerque: University of New Mexico Press, 1975.

Espinosa, J. Manuel. *Crusaders of the Rio Grande: The Story of Don Diego de Vargas and the Reconquest and Refounding of New Mexico*. Chicago, IL: Institute of Jesuit History, 1942.

———. *First Expedition of Vargas into New Mexico, 1692.* Albuquerque: University of New Mexico Press, 1940.

Etulain, Richard W., ed. *Western Lives: A Biographical History of the American West.* Albuquerque: University of New Mexico Press, 2004.

Ewen, David. *Encyclopedia of the Opera.* New York: Hill and Wang, 1963.

Fallon, Denise, and Karen Wening. *Howiri: Excavation at a Northern Rio Grande Biscuit Ware Site.* Santa Fe: Museum of New Mexico, Laboratory of Anthropology, 1987.

Faragher, John Mack, ed. *American Heritage Encyclopedia of American History.* New York: Henry Holt, 1998.

Faust, Patricia L., ed. *Historical Times Illustrated Encyclopedia of the Civil War.* New York: Harper and Row, 1986.

Favour, Alpheus. *Old Bill Williams, Mountain Man.* Norman: University of Oklahoma Press, 1962.

Ferguson, Bobbie, and Richard Holloway. "And They Laid Them to Rest in the Little Plot Beside the Pecos": Final Report on the Relocation of Old Seven Rivers Cemetery, Eddy County, New Mexico. Denver, CO: US Bureau of Reclamation, 1993.

Fitzpatrick, George, and Harvey Caplin. *Albuquerque: 100 Years in Pictures, 1875–1975.* Albuquerque: Calvin Horn, 1975.

Flint, Richard, and Shirley Cushing Flint. "The Coronado Expedition: Cicuye to the Rio de Cicuye Bridge." In *The Coronado Expedition to Tierra Nueva: The 1540–1542 Route Across the Southwest*, edited by Richard Flint and Shirley Cushing Flint, 262–77. Boulder: University Press of Colorado, 1997.

Florin, Lambert. *New Mexico, Texas Ghost Towns.* Seattle, WA: Superior Publishing Company, 1971.

Foreman, Grant. *Marcy and the Gold Seekers.* Norman: University of Oklahoma Press, 1939.

Franzwa, Gregory M. *The Santa Fe Trail Revisited.* Saint Louis, MO: Patrice Press, 1989.

Frazer, Robert W. *Forts of the West: Military Forts and Presidios and Posts Commonly Called Forts West of the Mississippi River to 1898.* Norman: University of Oklahoma Press, 1972.

Frazier, Arthur H., and Wilbur Heckler. *Embudo, New Mexico: Birthplace of Systematic Stream Gaging.* US Geological Survey Professional Paper no. 778. US Department of the Interior. Washington, D.C.: Government Printing Office, 1972.

French, David Heath. "Factionalism in Isleta Pueblo." PhD diss., University of Washington, 1966.

García-Mason, Velma. "Acoma Pueblo." In *Handbook of North American Indians.* Vol. 9, *Southwest*, edited by Alfonso Ortiz, 450–66. Washington, D.C.: Smithsonian Institution, 1979.

Gardner, Martin. *Are Universes Thicker than Blackberries?* New York: W. W. Norton, 2003.

Garraty, John A., and Mark C. Carnes, eds. *American National Biography.* New York: Oxford University Press, 1999.

Garrett, Pat. *The Authentic Life of Billy, the Kid.* Santa Fe: New Mexican Printing and Publishing Company, 1882.

George, Isaac. *Heroes and Incidents of the Mexican War.* San Bernardino, CA: Sun Dance Press, 1971.

Geronimo Springs Museum. *Elephant Butte Dam, 1911–1986: Construction and History.* Truth or Consequences, NM: Geronimo Springs Museum, 1986.

Gibson, Arrell Morgan. *The Santa Fe and Taos Colonies: Age of the Muses, 1900–1942.* Norman: University of Oklahoma Press, 1983.

Giese, Dale F. *Forts of New Mexico: Echoes of the Bugle.* Silver City, NM: Phelps Dodge Corporation, 1995.

Gilbert, Bil. *The Trailblazers*. The Old West Series. New York: Time-Life Books, 1973.

Gjevre, John A. *Chili Line: The Narrow Rail Trail to Santa Fe; The Story of the Narrow Gauge Denver and Rio Grande Western's Santa Fe Branch, 1880–1941*. Española, NM: Rio Grande Sun Press, 1969.

Graham, Frank, Jr. *Man's Dominion: The Story of Conservation in America*. New York: M. Evans and Company, 1971.

Gregg, Josiah A. *Commerce of the Prairies; or, The Journal of a Santa Fé Trader, During Eight Expeditions Across the Great Western Prairies, and a Residence of Nearly Nine Years in Northern Mexico*. 5th ed. Philadelphia, PA: J. W. Moore, 1851.

Grinstead, Marion C. *Life and Death of a Frontier Fort: Fort Craig, New Mexico, 1854–1885*. Socorro, NM: Socorro County Historical Society, 1973.

Gunnerson, Dolores A. *The Jicarilla Apaches: A Study in Survival*. DeKalb: Northern Illinois University Press, 1974.

Gunnerson, James H. "Southern Athapaskan Archaeology." In *Handbook of North American Indians*. Vol. 9, *Southwest*, edited by Alfonso Ortiz, 162–69. Washington, D.C.: Smithsonian Institution, 1979.

Hackett, Charles Wilson. *Revolt of the Pueblo Indians of New Mexico and Otermin's Reconquest, 1680–1682*. Albuquerque: University of New Mexico Press, 1942.

Hafen, Leroy R., and Ann W. Hafen. *Old Spanish Trail: Santa Fe to Los Angeles*. Lincoln: University of Nebraska Press, 1982.

Haines, Helen. *History of New Mexico from the Spanish Conquest to the Present Time, 1530–1890*. New York: New Mexico Historical Publishing Company, 1891.

Haley, J. Evetts. *Charles Goodnight: Cowman and Plainsman*. Norman: University of Oklahoma Press, 1949.

Hall, Martin Hardwick. *Sibley's New Mexico Campaign*. Austin: University of Texas Press, 1960.

Hall, Stephen A. *Field Guide to the Geoarchaeology of the Mescalero Sands, Southeastern New Mexico*. Prepared for the State of New Mexico Historic Preservation Division and New Mexico Bureau of Land Management. N.p., 2002.

Hämäläinen, Pekka. *The Comanche Empire*. New Haven, CT: Yale University Press, 2008.

Hammett, Kingsley. *Santa Fe: A Walk Through Time*. Layton, UT: Gibbs Smith, 2004.

Hammond, George Peter, and Agapito Rey. *Expedition into New Mexico Made by Antonio de Espejo, 1582–1583*. Los Angeles, CA: Quivira Society, 1929.

Harbert, Nancy. *New Mexico*. Oakland, CA: Compass American Guides, 1992.

Harland Bartholomew and Associates. *A General Development Plan for the Future Use of the Lands of Isleta Pueblo, New Mexico*. Prepared for the US Department of the Interior, Bureau of Indian Affairs, United Pueblos Agency. Albuquerque, NM: Harland Bartholomew and Associates, 1962.

Harlow, Francis H., and Dwight P. Lanmon. *The Pottery of Zia Pueblo*. Santa Fe, NM: School of American Research, 2003.

Harris, Linda G. *Las Cruces: An Illustrated History*. Las Cruces, NM: Arroyo Press, 1993.

Harris, Richard. *National Trust Guide: Santa Fe*. New York: John Wiley and Sons, 1997.

Hart, Herbert M. *Old Forts of the Far West*. Seattle, WA: Superior Publishing Company, 1965.

Hart, Stephen Harding, and Archer Butler Hulbert. *The Southwestern Journals of Zebulon Pike, 1806–1807*. Albuquerque: University of New Mexico Press, 2006.

Harvey, Fred. *The Alvarado: A New Hotel at Albuquerque, New Mexico*. N.p., 1904.

Hayes, Alden. *A Portal to Paradise*. Tucson: University of Arizona Press, 1999.

Hertzog, Peter. *Outlaws of New Mexico*. Santa Fe, NM: Sunstone Press, 1984.

Hester, James J. *Blackwater Locality no. 1: A Stratified Early Man Site in Eastern New Mexico*. Ranchos de Taos, NM: Fort Burgwin Research Center, 1972.

Hilton, Conrad. *Be My Guest*. Englewood Cliffs, NJ: Prentice Hall, 1957.

Hine, Robert V. *Bartlett's West: Drawing the Mexican Boundary*. New Haven, CT: Yale University Press, 1968.

Hinshaw, Gil. *Lea: New Mexico's Last Frontier*. Hobbs, NM: Hobbs Daily News-Sun, 1977.

Hodge, Frederick W., ed. *Spanish Explorers in the Southern United States*. New York: Charles Scribner's Sons, 1907.

Hoebel, E. Adamson. "Zia Pueblo." In *Handbook of North American Indians*. Vol. 9, *Southwest*, edited by Alfonso Ortiz, 407–17. Washington, D.C.: Smithsonian Institution, 1979.

Hofsommer, Don L. *The Southern Pacific, 1901–1985*. College Station: Texas A&M University Press, 1986.

Horgan, Paul. *Lamy of Santa Fe*. Middletown, CT: Wesleyan University Press, 2012.

Howarth, Sam, and Enrique R. Lamadrid. *Pilgrimage to Chimayó: A Contemporary Portrait of a Living Tradition*. Santa Fe: Museum of New Mexico Press, 1999.

Howe, Wesley M. *From Basin to Peak: An Explorer's Companion to the Colorado–New Mexico San Juan Basin*. Lubbock: Texas Tech University Press, 1998.

Hurst, James W. *Pancho Villa and Black Jack Pershing: The Punitive Expedition in Mexico*. Westport, CT: Praeger, 2008.

Ingersoll, Ernest. *Crest of the Continent*. Chicago, IL: R. R. Donnelley and Sons, 1885.

Irwin-Williams, Cynthia, and Phillip H. Shelley, eds. *Investigations at the Salmon Site: The Structure of Chacoan Society in the Northern Southwest*. Portales: Eastern New Mexico University Printing Services, 1980.

Iverson, Peter. *Diné: A History of the Navajos*. Albuquerque: University of New Mexico Press, 2002.

Ives, Berry Cottrell, and Clyde Eastman. *Impact of Mining Development on an Isolated Rural Community: The Case of Cuba, New Mexico*. Research Report no. 301. Las Cruces: New Mexico State University, Agricultural Experiment Station, 1975.

Ivey, James E. *In the Midst of a Loneliness: The Architectural History of the Salinas Missions*. Southwest Cultural Resources Center Professional Paper no. 15. Santa Fe, NM: National Park Service, 1988.

Jaehn, Tomas. *Jewish Pioneers of New Mexico*. Santa Fe: Museum of New Mexico Press, 2005.

Johansen, Bruce E., and Donald A. Grinde Jr. *The Encyclopedia of Native American Biography*. New York: Da Capo Press, 1998.

Johnson, Maureen. *Placer Gold Deposits of New Mexico*. US Geological Survey Bulletin 1348. Washington, D.C.: Government Printing Office, 1972.

Jones, Fayette Alexander. *Old Mining Camps of New Mexico, 1854–1904*. Santa Fe, NM: Stagecoach Press, 1964.

Jones, Paul M. *Memories of Santa Rita*. N.p., 1985.

Jordan, Teresa. *Cowgirls: Women of the American West*. Lincoln: University of Nebraska Press, 1992.

Julyan, Robert. *The Mountains of New Mexico*. Albuquerque: University of New Mexico Press, 2006.

———. *The Place Names of New Mexico*. Albuquerque: University of New Mexico Press, 1996.

Kavanagh, Thomas W. *The Comanches: A History, 1706–1875*. Lincoln: University of Nebraska Press, 1996.

Keleher, William A. *Maxwell Land Grant: A New Mexico Item*. Santa Fe, NM: William Gannon, 1964.

Kelley, Vincent C., and Caswell Silver. *Geology of the Caballo Mountains; with special reference to regional sratigraphy and structure and to mineral resources, including oil and gas*. Albuquerque: University of New Mexico Press, 1952.

Kendall, Geo Wilkins. *Narrative of the Texan Santa Fe Expedition*. New York: Harper and Brothers, 1844.

Kennedy, Frances H., ed. *The Civil War Battlefield Guide*. Boston, MA: Houghton Mifflin, 1990.

Kenner, Charles L. *A History of New Mexican–Plains Indian Relations*. Norman: University of Oklahoma Press, 1969.

Kessell, John L. *Kiva, Cross, and Crown: The Pecos Indians and New Mexico, 1540–1840*. Washington, D.C.: National Park Service, US Department of the Interior, 1979.

———. *Missions of New Mexico Since 1776*. Albuquerque: University of New Mexico Press, 1980.

———. *Remote Beyond Compare: Letters of don Diego de Vargas to His Family from New Spain and New Mexico, 1675–1706*. Albuquerque: University of New Mexico Press, 1989.

King, Scottie. *Listen to the Wind . . . Ghost Towns of New Mexico*. Santa Fe: New Mexico Magazine, 1978.

Kohn, George C. *Dictionary of Culprits and Criminals*. Metuchen, NJ: Scarecrow Press, 1986.

Kramer, David, and Chris Wilson. *Spanning the High Desert: The Historic Highway Bridges of New Mexico*. Santa Fe, NM: Environmental Section, New Mexico State Highway and Transportation Department, 1996.

Kubler, George. *The Religious Architecture of New Mexico*. Albuquerque: University of New Mexico Press, 1990.

Lafora, Nicolás de. *The Frontiers of New Spain: Nicolás de Lafora's Description, 1766–1768*. Edited by Lawrence Kinnaird. Berkeley, CA: Quivira Society, 1958.

Lamar, Howard, ed. *Reader's Encyclopedia of the American West*. New York: Harper and Rowe, 1977.

Lambert, David. *The Field Guide to Geology*. New York: Facts on File, 1988.

Lane, Lydia Spencer. *I Married a Soldier*. Albuquerque: University of New Mexico Press, 1987.

Lange, Charles H. "Santo Domingo Pueblo." In *Handbook of North American Indians*. Vol. 9, *Southwest*, edited by Alfonso Ortiz, 379–90. Washington, D.C.: Smithsonian Institution, 1979.

Lawter, William Clifford, Jr. *Smokey Bear, 20252: A Biography*. Alexandria, VA: Lindsay Smith, 1994.

Lea County Genealogical Society. *Then and Now: Lea County Families*. Lovington, NM: Lea County Genealogical Society, 1979.

Leonard, Olen E. *The Role of the Land Grant in the Social Organization and Social Processes of a Spanish-American Village in New Mexico*. Albuquerque, NM: Calvin Horn, 1970.

Levine, Susan. *Degrees of Equality: The American Association of University Women and the Challenge of Twentieth-Century Feminism*. Philadelphia, PA: Temple University Press, 1995.

Lindgram, Waldemar, Louis C. Graton, and Charles H. Gordan. *The Ore Deposits of New Mexico*. US Geological Survey Professional Paper no. 68. US Department of the Interior. Washington, D.C.: Government Printing Office, 1910.

Lister, Robert H., and Florence C. Lister. *Aztec Ruins on the Animas: Excavated, Preserved, and Interpreted*. Albuquerque: University of New Mexico Press, 1987.

Lomelí, Francisco A., Victor A. Sorell, and Genaro M. Padilla, eds. *Nuevomexicano Cultural Legacy: Forms, Agencies, and Discourse*. Albuquerque: University of New Mexico Press, 2002.

Loomis, Noel M., and Abraham P. Nasatir. *Pedro Vial and the Roads to Santa Fe*. Norman: University of Oklahoma Press, 1967.

Looney, Ralph. *Haunted Highways: The Ghost Towns of New Mexico*. Albuquerque: University of New Mexico Press, 1968.

LoPopolo, Carlos. *The New Mexico Chronicles*. 2nd ed. Socorro, NM: Cincar Publishing, 1996.

Lozinsky, Richard P., Richard W. Harrison, and Stephen H. Lekson. *Elephant Butte: Eastern Black Range Region*. Socorro: New Mexico Bureau of Mines and Mineral Resources, 1995.

Lucero, Helen R., and Suzanne Baizerman. *Chimayó Weaving: The Transformation of a Tradition*. Albuquerque: University of New Mexico Press, 1999.

Lummis, Charles F. *Pueblo Indian Folk-Stories*. Lincoln: University of Nebraska Press, 1992.

Luxán, Diego Pérez de. *Expedition into New Mexico Made by Antonio de Espejo*. Translated by George Peter Hammond and Agapito Rey. Los Angeles, CA: Quivira Society, 1929.

Lysinger, Scott. "The Geology of the Moreno Valley." In *Lure, Lore, and Legends of the Moreno Valley*, edited by the Moreno Valley Writers Guild, 18–20. Angel Fire, NM: Columbine Books, 1997.

MacArthur, Douglas. *Reminiscences*. New York: McGraw-Hill, 1964.

Mack, Greg H. *The Geology of Southern New Mexico*. Albuquerque: University of New Mexico Press, 1997.

Magdalena Old Timers' Association. *Celebrating 100 Years of Frontier Living*. N.p., 1984.

Magoffin, Susan Shelby. *Down the Santa Fe Trail and into Mexico: The Diary of Susan Shelby Magoffin, 1846-1847*. Edited by Stella M. Drumm. New Haven, CT: Yale University Press, 1926.

Mangum, Neil C. *In the Land of Frozen Fires: A History of Occupation in El Malpais Country*. Santa Fe, NM: National Park Service, 1990.

Mansfield, Colonel Joseph King Fenno. *Mansfield on the Condition of the Western Forts, 1853–54*. Edited by Robert W. Frazer. Norman: University of Oklahoma Press, 1963.

Marcy, Randolph Barnes. *The Prairie Traveler: A Hand-Book for Overland Expeditions; With Illustrations, and Itineraries of the Principal Routes Between the Mississippi and the Pacific, and a Map*. Edited by Richard F. Burton. London: Trübner and Company, 1863.

Marks, Paula Mitchell. *And Die in the West: The Story of the O.K. Corral Gunfight*. New York: Touchstone Books, 1989.

Marshall, Michael P., and Henry J. Walt. *Rio Abajo: Prehistory and History of a Rio Grande Province*. Santa Fe, NM: Historic Preservation Division, 1984.

Marshall, Terry. *Carlsbad*. Carlsbad, NM: Riverside Research, 1998.

Matson, Eva Jane. *It Tolled for New Mexico*. Las Cruces, NM: Yucca Tree Press, 1992.

McAlavy, Don, and Harold Kilmer. *High Plains History of East-Central New Mexico*. Clovis, NM: High Plains Historical Foundation, 1980.

McDonald, Barbara. *Weavers of a Tapestry of Time*. Alamogordo, NM: Bennett Printing, 2002.

McDonald, Claude, and Fran Pallesen. "Native Americans in the Moreno Valley." In *Lure, Lore, and Legends of the Moreno Valley*, edited by the Moreno Valley Writers Guild, 21–27. Angel Fire, NM: Columbine Books, 1997.

McDonald, Mike. "The DAV Vietnam Veteran's National Memorial." In *Lure, Lore, and Legends of the Moreno Valley*, edited by the Moreno Valley Writers Guild, 109–18. Angel Fire, NM: Columbine Books, 1997.

McHenry, Robert, ed. *Webster's American Military Biographies*. Springfield, MA: G. and C. Merriam Company, 1978.

Metz, Leon. *Border: The US-Mexico Line*. El Paso, TX: Mangan Books, 1989.

———. *Pat Garrett: The Story of a Western Lawman*. Norman: University of Oklahoma Press, 1973.

Michno, Gregory F. *Encyclopedia of Indian Wars: Western Battles and Skirmishes 1850–1890.* Missoula, MT: Mountain Press, 2003.

Miller, John P., Arthur Montgomery, and Patrick K. Sutherland. *Geology of Part of the Southern Sangre de Cristo Mountains, New Mexico.* Socorro: New Mexico Bureau of Mines and Mineral Resources, 1963.

Miller, Joseph. *New Mexico: A Guide to the Colorful State.* Federal Writers' Project, Work Projects Administration. New York: Hastings House, 1940.

Minge, Ward Alan. *Ácoma: Pueblo in the Sky.* Albuquerque: University of New Mexico Press, 1991.

Minogue, Anna C. *Loretto: Annals of the Century.* New York: America Press, 1912.

Moorhead, Max L. *New Mexico's Royal Road: Trade and Travel on the Chihuahua Trail.* Norman: University of Oklahoma Press, 1995.

Morris, John Miller. *El Llano Estacado: Exploration and Imagination on the High Plains of Texas and New Mexico, 1536–1860.* Austin: Texas State Historical Association, 1997.

Murphy, Dan. *Salinas Pueblo Missions.* Tucson, AZ: Southwest Parks and Monuments Association, 1993.

Murphy, Larry. *Out in God's Country: A History of Colfax County, New Mexico.* Springer, NM: Springer Publishing, 1969.

Murphy, Lawrence R. *Philmont: A History of New Mexico's Cimarron Country.* Albuquerque: University of New Mexico Press, 1972.

Myrick, David F. *New Mexico's Railroads: A Historical Survey.* Albuquerque: University of New Mexico Press, 1990.

Nabokov, Peter. *Tijerina and the Courthouse Raid.* Berkeley, CA: Ramparts Press, 1970.

Nanninga, S. P. *The New Mexico School System.* Albuquerque: University of New Mexico Press, 1942.

Nash, Jay Robert. *Bloodletters and Badmen: A Narrative Encyclopedia of American Criminals from the Pilgrims to the Present.* New York: M. Evans and Company, 1995.

National Park Service. "Special Report on Puyé Ruins, New Mexico." Santa Fe, NM: National Park Service, Southwest Regional Office, 1966.

Nelson, Nels. C. *Pueblo Ruins of the Galisteo Basin, New Mexico.* Anthropological Papers of the American Museum of Natural History, vol. 15, part 1. New York: American Museum of Natural History, 1914.

Newark, Peter. *The Illustrated Encyclopedia of the Old West.* New York: Gallery Books, 1980.

Newbrough, John Ballou. *The Origin of Oahspe.* London: Kosmon Press, n.d.

New Mexico State Highway and Transportation Department. *New Mexico Historic Bridge Survey.* Santa Fe, NM: Federal Highway Administration, Region 6, 1987.

New Mexico State Legislature. "An Act to Locate and Establish the Eastern New Mexico Normal School at Portales, Roosevelt County, New Mexico." Senate Bill no. 22, Chapter 9, 1927.

Niethammer, Carolyn. *I'll Go and Do More: Annie Dodge Wauneka, Navajo Leader and Activist.* Lincoln: University of Nebraska Press, 2004.

Noble, David Grant. *Ancient Ruins of the Southwest.* Flagstaff, AZ: Northland Publishing, 1991.

———. *Pueblos, Villages, Forts, and Trails: A Guide to New Mexico's Past.* Albuquerque: University of New Mexico Press, 1994.

Noe, Sally. *Gallup, New Mexico, U.S.A.: Our Story.* Virginia Beach, VA: Donning Company, 1997.

Nolan, Frederick. *The West of Billy the Kid.* Norman: University of Oklahoma Press, 1998.

Nostrand, Richard L. *The Hispano Homeland.* Norman: University of Oklahoma Press, 1992.

Nunn, Tey Marianna. *Sin Nombre: Hispana and Hispano Artists of the New Deal Era*. Albuquerque: University of New Mexico Press, 2001.

Olsen, Michael L., and Harry C. Myers. "The Diary of Pedro Ignacio Gallego Wherein 499 Soldiers Following the Trail of Comanches Met William Becknell on his First Trip to Santa Fe." *Wagon Tracks: Santa Fe Trail Association Quarterly* 7, no. 1 (November 1992).

O'Neal, Bill. *Encyclopedia of Western Gunfighters*. Norman: University of Oklahoma Press, 1979.

Opie, John. *Ogallala: Water for a Dry Land*. Lincoln: University of Nebraska Press, 1993.

Ortiz, Alfonso. "San Juan Pueblo." In *Handbook of North American Indians*. Vol. 9, *Southwest*, edited by Alfonso Ortiz, 278–95. Washington, D.C.: Smithsonian Institution, 1979.

Osborne, Charles. *How to Enjoy Opera*. Loughton, Essex, England: Piatkus Books, 1983.

Otero-Warren, Nina. *Old Spain in Our Southwest*. Santa Fe, NM: Sunstone Press, 2006.

Owen, Gordon. *Las Cruces New Mexico, 1849–1999: Multicultural Crossroads*. Las Cruces, NM: Red Sky Publishing, 1999.

———. *The Two Alberts: Fountain and Fall*. Las Cruces, NM: Yucca Tree Press, 1996.

Owsley, Douglas W. *Bioarchaeology on a Battlefield: The Abortive Confederate Campaign in New Mexico*. Santa Fe: Museum of New Mexico, Office of Archaeological Studies, 1994.

Palmer, Gabrielle G., June-el Piper, and LouAnn Jacobson, eds. *El Camino Real de Tierra Adentro*. Santa Fe, NM: Bureau of Land Management, 1993.

Pannell, H. C. *The Lovington Schools, 1908-1965: A Chronology*. Lovington, NM: n.p., 1965.

Parent, Laurence. *Gila Cliff Dwellings National Monument*. Tucson, AZ: Southwest Parks and Monuments Association, 1992.

Parish, William J., ed. "Sheep Husbandry in New Mexico, 1902–1903." *New Mexico Historical Review* 38, no. 1 (January 1963): 56–77.

Parsons, Elsie Clews. "Isleta, New Mexico." *Forty-Seventh Annual Report of the Bureau of American Ethnology, 1929–1930*. Washington, D.C.: Government Printing Office, 1932.

Pearce, T. M. *New Mexico Place Names: A Geographical Dictionary*. Albuquerque: University of New Mexico Press, 1965.

Pearson, Jim Berry. *The Maxwell Land Grant*. Norman: University of Oklahoma Press, 1961.

Peaster, Lillian, and Guy Berger. *Pueblo Pottery Families*. Atglen, PA: Schiffer Publishing, 1997.

Pershing, Major General John J. *Punitive Expedition*. N.p., 1916.

Peterson, Susan. *Pottery by American Indian Women: The Legacy of Generations*. New York: Abbeville Press, 1997.

Pettitt, Roland A. *Exploring the Jemez Country*. Los Alamos, NM: Los Alamos Historical Society, 1990.

Pike, Albert. *Prose Sketches and Poems Written in the Western Country*. College Station: Texas A&M University Press, 1987.

Pike, Zebulon. *Southwestern Expedition of Zebulon M. Pike*. Edited by Milo Milton Quaife. Chicago, IL: Lakeside Press, 1925.

Plog, Stephen. *Ancient Peoples of the American Southwest*. New York: Thames and Hudson, 1997.

Potter, Jack Myers. *Cattle Trails of the Old West*. Clayton, NM: Laura R. Krehbiel, [1939?].

Powell, Colonel William H. *List of Officers of the Army of the United States from 1779 to 1900*. New York: L. R. Hamersly and Company, 1900.

Powers, Robert P., William B. Gillespie, and Stephen H. Lekson. *The Outlier Survey: A Regional View of Settlement in the San Juan Basin*. Albuquerque: National Park Service, Division of Cultural Research, 1983.

Prince, Le Baron Bradford. *Spanish Mission Churches of New Mexico*. Cedar Rapids, IA: Torch Press, 1915.

Raymond, Rossiter W. *Mining Industry of the States and Territories of the Rocky Mountains*. New York: J. B. Ford and Company, 1874.

Rebolledo, Tey Diana, ed. *Nuestras Mujeres: Hispanas of New Mexico; Their Images and Lives, 1582–1992*. Albuquerque, NM: El Norte Publications, 1992.

Reeve, Agnesa Lufkin. *From Hacienda to Bungalow: Northern New Mexico Houses, 1850–1912*. Albuquerque: University of New Mexico Press, 1988.

Reséndez, Andrés. *Changing National Identities at the Frontier: Texas and New Mexico, 1800–1850*. New York: Cambridge University Press, 2005.

Rhodes, Eugene Manlove. *Best Novels and Stories of Eugene Manlove Rhodes*. Edited by Frank V. Dearing. Lincoln: University of Nebraska Press, 1987.

Rickards, Colin. *Sheriff Pat Garrett's Last Days*. Santa Fe, NM: Sunstone Press, 1986.

Riley, Robert B. *Tajique, Torreon, Manzano, Punta de Agua: A Planning Framework for Revitalization*. Albuquerque: Center for Environmental Research and Development, University of New Mexico, 1969.

Riskin, Marci L., ed. *New Mexico's Historic Places: The Guide to National and State Register Sites*. Santa Fe, NM: Ocean Tree Books, 2000.

———. *The Train Stops Here: New Mexico's Railway Legacy*. Albuquerque: University of New Mexico Press, 2005.

Ritchie, Laurajean. *This Is Vacationland: The Southwestern New Mexico Counties of Catron, Grant, Hidalgo, and Luna, and Chihuahua, Mexico*. N.p.: Four County Tourism Task Force, 1970.

Robbins, Michael. *High Country Trail: Along the Continental Divide*. Washington, D.C.: National Geographic Society, 1981.

Roberts, Robert B. *Encyclopedia of Historic Forts: The Military, Pioneer, and Trading Posts of the United States*. New York: Macmillan, 1988.

Robinson, G. P., A. A. Wanek, W. H. Hays, and M. E. McCallum. *Philmont Country: The Rocks and Landscape of a Famous New Mexico Ranch*. US Geological Survey Professional Paper no. 505. Washington, D.C.: Government Printing Office, 1964.

Robinson, Sherry. *Apache Voices: Their Stories of Survival as Told to Eve Ball*. Albuquerque: University of New Mexico Press, 2000.

Roessel, Ruth, ed. *Navajo Stories of the Long Walk Period*. Chinle, AZ: Navajo Community College Press, 1973.

Rosales, F. Arturo. *Testimonio: A Documentary History of the Mexican American Struggle for Civil Rights*. Houston, TX: Arte Público Press, 2000.

Ross, Terence W. *Cumbres and Toltec Scenic Railroad: The Toltec Gorge Route*. Santa Fe, NM: Colorado and New Mexico Society for Preservation of the Narrow Gauge, 1971.

Ruiz, Vicki L. *From Out of the Shadows: Mexican Women in Twentieth-Century America*. New York: Oxford University Press, 2008.

Ruiz, Vicki L., and Virginia Sánchez Korrol. *Latinas in the United States: A Historical Encyclopedia*. Bloomington: Indiana University Press, 2006.

Rundell, Walter, Jr. *Oil in West Texas and New Mexico: A Pictorial History of the Permian Basin*. Midland: Texas A&M University Press, 1982.

Russell, Peter. *Gila Cliff Dwellings National Monument: An Administrative History*. Santa Fe, NM: National Park Service, Southwest Region, Division of History, 1992.

Ruxton, George F. *Adventures in Mexico and the Rocky Mountains*. Glorieta, NM: Rio Grande Press, 1973.
Sagar, Keith, ed. *D. H. Lawrence and New Mexico*. Salt Lake City, UT: Gibbs M. Smith, 1982.
Sánchez, Joseph P. "Bernardo Gruber and the New Mexico Inquisition." In *The Rio Abajo Frontier, 1540–1692: A History of Early Colonial New Mexico*, 120–28. Albuquerque, NM: Albuquerque Mueseum, 1987.
———. *Explorers, Traders, and Slavers: Forging the Old Spanish Trail, 1678–1850*. Salt Lake City: University of Utah Press, 1997.
Sandberg-Jarzen, Elaine V. "Dr. Victor Westphall." In *Lure, Lore, and Legends of the Moreno Valley*, edited by the Moreno Valley Writers Guild, 119–25. Angel Fire, NM: Columbine Books, 1997.
Sandersier, Andy. *The Lakes of New Mexico: A Guide to Recreation*. Albuquerque: University of New Mexico Press, 1996.
Sando, Joe S. "Jemez Pueblo." In *Handbook of North American Indians*. Vol. 9, *Southwest*, edited by Alfonso Ortiz, 418–29. Washington, D.C.: Smithsonian Institution, 1979.
Sanger, S. L. *Working on the Bomb: An Oral History of WWII Hanford*. Portland, OR: Continuing Education Press, 1995.
Scarbrough, Virginia. "Waldrop." In *Then and Now: Lea County Families*. Lovington, NM: Lea County Genealogical Society, 1979.
Schaaf, Gregory. *Southern Pueblo Pottery: 2,000 Artist Biographies*. Santa Fe, NM: Center for Indigenous Arts and Cultures (CIAC) Press, 2002.
Schilling, John H. *Scenic Trips to the Geologic Past: Silver City, Santa Rita, Hurley*. Socorro, NM: New Mexico Bureau of Mines and Mineral Resources, 1959.
Schroeder, Albert. "Pueblos Abandoned in Historic Times." In *Handbook of North American Indians*. Vol. 9, *Southwest*, edited by Alfonso Ortiz, 236–54. Washington, D.C.: Smithsonian Institution, 1979.
Schroeder, Albert, and Dan S. Matson. *A Colony on the Move: Gaspar Castaño de Sosa's Journal, 1590–1591*. Santa Fe, NM: School of American Research, 1965.
Scott, Douglas, Lawrence Babits, and Charles Haecker, eds. *Fields of Conflict: Battlefield Archaeology from the Roman Empire to the Korean War*. Westport, CT: Praeger Security International, 2007.
Scott, Eleanor. *The First Twenty Years of the Santa Fe Opera*. Santa Fe, NM: Sunstone Press, 1976.
Seckler, Herb. *Ruidoso Countryside: The Early Days*. N.p., 1987.
Seton, Ernest Thompson. *The Birch Bark Roll of the Woodcraft Indians*. New York: Doubleday, Page and Company, 1907.
———. *Wild Animals I Have Known*. New York: Charles Scribner's Sons, 1909.
Sheridan, Thomas E., and Nancy J. Parezo. *Paths of Life: American Indians of the Southwest and Northern New Mexico*. Tucson: University of Arizona Press, 1996.
Simmons, Marc. "The Allure of Turquoise Through the Centuries." In *The Allure of Turquoise*, edited by Arnold Vigil, 22–29. Santa Fe, NM: New Mexico Magazine, 1995.
———. *The Last Conquistador: Juan de Oñate and the Settling of the Southwest*. Norman: University of Oklahoma Press, 1991.
———. *New Mexico: An Interpretive History*. Albuquerque: University of New Mexico Press, 1988.
———. "The Spaniards of San Gabriel." In *When Cultures Meet: Remembering San Gabriel del Yunge Oweenge. Papers from the October 20, 1984, conference held at San Juan Pueblo, New Mexico*, edited by Florence H. Ellis, Myra E. Jenkins, and Richard Ford, 39–62. Santa Fe, NM: Sunstone Press, 1987.

———. *Spanish Government in New Mexico*. Albuquerque: University of New Mexico Press, 1968.

———. *Turquoise and Six-Guns: The Story of Cerrillos, New Mexico*. Santa Fe, NM: Sunstone Press, 1974.

———. *Witchcraft in the Southwest: Spanish and Indian Supernaturalism on the Rio Grande*. Flagstaff, AZ: Northland Publishing, 1974.

Simmons, Marc, and Hal Jackson. *Following the Santa Fe Trail: A Guide for Modern Travelers*. Santa Fe, NM: Ancient City Press, 1986.

Simmons, Marc, and Joan Myers. *Along the Santa Fe Trail*. Albuquerque: University of New Mexico Press, 1986.

Siringo, Charles A. *A Texas Cowboy; or, Fifteen Years on the Hurricane Deck of a Spanish Pony*. Chicago, IL: M. Umbdenstock and Company, 1885.

Smith, Toby. *Coal Town: The Life and Times of Dawson, New Mexico*. Santa Fe, NM: Ancient City Press, 1993.

Snyder, Sharon. *At Home on the Slopes of Mountains: The Story of Peggy Pond Church*. Los Alamos, NM: Los Alamos Historical Socicty, 2011.

Sonnichsen, C. L. *Tularosa: Last of the Frontier West*. Albuquerque: University of New Mexico Press, 1980.

Speirs, Randall H. "Nambé Pueblo." In *Handbook of North American Indians*. Vol. 9, *Southwest*, edited by Alfonso Ortiz, 317–23. Washington, D.C.: Smithsonian Institution, 1979.

Staski, Edward. *Research on the American West: Archaeology at Forts Cummings and Fillmore*. Santa Fe, NM: Bureau of Land Management, 1995.

Stegner, Wallace. *Beyond the Hundredth Meridian: John Wesley Powell and the Second Opening of the West*. New York: Penguin Books, 1992.

Straw Cook, Mary Jean. *Doña Tules: Santa Fe's Courtesan and Gambler*. Albuquerque: University of New Mexico Press, 2007.

Strong, Pauline Turner. "San Felipe Pueblo." In *Handbook of North American Indians*. Vol. 9, *Southwest*, edited by Alfonso Ortiz, 390–97. Washington, D.C.: Smithsonian Institution, 1979.

———. "Santa Ana Pueblo." In *Handbook of North American Indians*. Vol. 9, *Southwest*, edited by Alfonso Ortiz, 398–406. Washington, D.C.: Smithsonian Institution, 1979.

Swadesh, Frances Leon. *Los Primeros Pobladores: Hispanic Americans of the Ute Frontier*. Notre Dame, IN: University of Notre Dame Press, 1974.

Tainter, Joseph A., and David "A" Gillio. *Cultural Resources Overview: Mt. Taylor Area, New Mexico*. Albuquerque, NM: US Department of Agriculture Forest Service, Southwestern Region, 1980.

Tainter, Joseph A., and Frances Levine. *Cultural Resources Overview: Central New Mexico*. Albuquerque, NM: US Department of Agriculture Forest Service, Southwestern Region, 1987.

Talbot, Dan. *A Historical Guide to the Mormon Battalion and Butterfield Trail*. Tucson, AZ: Westernlore Press, 1992.

Taylor, Morris F. *O. P. McMains and the Maxwell Land Grant Conflict*. Tucson: University of Arizona Press, 1979.

Thomas, Alfred Barnaby. *After Coronado: Spanish Exploration Northeast of New Mexico, 1696–1727*. Norman: University of Oklahoma Press, 1935.

———. *Forgotten Frontiers: A Study of the Spanish Indian Policy of Don Juan Bautista de Anza*. Norman: University of Oklahoma Press, 1932.

Thomas, Gerald W., Monroe L. Billington, and Roger D. Walker. *Victory in World War II: The New Mexico Story*. Las Cruces, NM: Rio Grande Historical Collections, New Mexico State University Library, 1994.

Thompson, Goldianne, and William H. Halley. *Clayton: The Friendly Town in Union County, New Mexico.* Denver, CO: Monitor Publishing Company, 1962.

Thomson, Gerald. *The Army and the Navajo: The Bosque Redondo Reservation Experiment, 1863–1868.* Tucson: University of Arizona Press, 1976.

Tiller, Veronica E. Velarde. *American Indian Reservations and Trust Areas.* Washington, D.C.: US Department of Commerce, 1996.

———. *The Jicarilla Apache Tribe: A History, 1846–1970.* Lincoln: University of Nebraska Press, 1983.

Torrance County Historical Society. *Torrance County History.* N.p., Torrance County Historical Society, [1979?].

Toulouse, Joseph H., Jr. *The Mission of San Gregorio de Abó: A Report on the Excavation and Repair of a Seventeenth-Century New Mexico Mission.* Albuquerque: University of New Mexico Press, 1949.

Trieb, Marc. *Sanctuaries of Spanish New Mexico.* Berkeley: University of California Press, 1993.

Trimble, Donald E. *The Geologic Story of the Great Plains.* US Geological Survey Bulletin 1493. Washington, D.C.: Government Printing Office, 1980.

Trimble, Stephen. *Talking with the Clay.* Santa Fe, NM: School of American Research, 1999.

Trott, Jim. *Condition Assessment of the Clovis Period Well at Blackwater Draw Locality no. 1.* Santa Fe, NM: National Park Service, n.d. On file, National Register of Historic Places, Washington, D.C.

Tucker, Phillip Thomas. *Cathy Williams: From Slave to Female Buffalo Soldier.* Mechanicsburg, PA: Stackpole Books, 2002.

Tuska, Jon. *Billy the Kid: His Life and Legend.* Westport, CT: Greenwood Press, 1994.

Twitchell, Ralph Emerson. *The Leading Facts of New Mexican History.* 5 vols. Cedar Rapids, IA: Torch Press, 1911–1917.

Udall, Stewart L. *Majestic Journey: Coronado's Inland Empire.* Santa Fe: Museum of New Mexico Press, 1987.

———. *The Quiet Crisis.* New York: Holt, Rinehart and Winston, 1963.

Underhill, Ruth. *Life in the Pueblos.* Santa Fe, NM: Ancient City Press, 1991.

Ungnade, Herbert E. *Guide to the New Mexico Mountains.* Albuquerque: University of New Mexico Press, 1965.

Urban, Jack C. "Elizabethtown: New Mexico's 'El Dorado.'" *Lure, Lore, and Legends of the Moreno Valley*, edited by the Moreno Valley Writers Guild, 28–62. Angel Fire, NM: Columbine Books, 1997.

Utley, Robert M. *Billy the Kid: A Short and Violent Life.* Lincoln: University of Nebraska Press, 1989.

Valencia y Valdez, Gloria M., José Antonio Esquibel, Robert D. Martinez, and Francisco Sisneros, eds. *Aquí se Comienza: A Genealogical History of the Founding Families of La Villa de San Felipe de Alburquerque.* Salt Lake City, UT: Family Heritage Publishers, 2007.

Varney, Philip. *New Mexico's Best Ghost Towns: A Practical Guide.* Albuquerque: University of New Mexico Press, 1981.

Vélez de Escalante, Sylvestre. *The Domínguez-Escalante Journal: Their Expedition Through Colorado, Utah, Arizona, and New Mexico in 1776.* Translated by Fray Angelico Chavez. Edited by Ted J. Warner. Salt Lake City: University of Utah Press, 1995.

Villagrá, Gaspar Pérez de. *Historia de la Nueva México, 1610.* Translated and edited by Miguel Encinias, Alfred Rodríguez, and Joseph P. Sánchez. Albuquerque: University of New Mexico Press, 1992.

Voynick, Stephen M. *New Mexico Rockhounding.* Missoula, MT: Mountain Press, 1997.

Wallace, William S. "Short-Line Staging in New Mexico." *New Mexico Historical Review* 26, no. 2 (April 1956): 89–100.

Walsh, Michael, ed. *Butler's Lives of Patron Saints.* San Francisco, CA: HarperCollins, 1987.

Walter, Paul A. F. *The Cities That Died of Fear.* School of American Research. Santa Fe, NM: El Palacio Press, 1931.

Ward, Geoffrey C. *The West: An Illustrated History.* Boston, MA: Little, Brown and Company, 1996.

Warren, Nancy Hunter. *New Mexico Style: A Sourcebook of Traditional Architectural Details.* Santa Fe: Museum of New Mexico Press, 1986.

Waugh, John C. *The Class of 1846: From West Point to Appomattox; Stonewall Jackson, George McClellan, and Their Brothers.* New York: Warner Books, 1994.

Weigle, Marta. *Hispanic Villages of Northern New Mexico.* Santa Fe, NM: Lightning Tree, 1975.

Weigle, Marta, and Peter White. *The Lore of New Mexico.* Albuquerque: University of New Mexico Press, 1988.

Welsh, Jack D. *Medical Histories of Confederate Generals.* Kent, OH: Kent State University Press, 1995.

Westphall, Victor. *Thomas Benton Catron and His Era.* Tucson: University of Arizona Press, 1973.

Wexler, Alan. *Atlas of Westward Expansion.* New York: Facts on File, 1995.

Whisenhunt, Donald W. *New Mexico Courthouses.* El Paso: Texas Western Press, 1979.

White, Marjorie. "The Cloud-Climbing Route." In *Railroads and Railroad Towns in New Mexico,* edited by Ree Sheck and William Clark, 30–32. Santa Fe, NM: New Mexico Magazine, 1989.

Whitmore, Jane. *The Traditional Village of Agua Fria.* Santa Fe, NM: Historic Preservation Division, 1983.

Wilson, Alan. *Navajo Place Names: An Observer's Guide.* Guilford, CT: Jeffrey Norton, 1995.

Wilson, John P. *Quarai: Living Mission to Monument.* Santa Fe: Museum of New Mexico Press, 1973.

———. "Quarai: A Turbulent History." *Exploration* (1982): 20–25.

Wilson, Spencer, and Vernon J. Glover. *The Cumbres and Toltec Scenic Railroad: The Historic Preservation Study.* Albuquerque: University of New Mexico Press, 1980.

Winchester, Dean E. *The Hobbs Field and Other Oil and Gas Areas, Lea County, New Mexico.* Socorro: New Mexico School of Mines, 1931.

Winship, George Parker. *The Coronado Expedition, 1540–1542.* Chicago, IL: Rio Grande Press, 1964.

Wirth, Conrad L. *Civilian Conservation Corps Program of the United States Department of the Interior: March 1933 to June 30, 1943. A Report to Harold L. Ickes, Secretary of the Interior.* Washington, D.C.: Department of the Interior, Civilian Conservation Corps, January 1944.

Wiseman, Regge N., Maisha Baton, and Yvonne Roye Oakes. *Glimpses of Late Frontier Life in New Mexico's Southern Pecos Valley: Archaeology and History at Blackdom and Seven Rivers.* Santa Fe: Museum of New Mexico, Office of Archaeological Studies, 2001.

Wislizenus, Friedrich Adolph. *Memoir of a Tour to Northern Mexico Connected with Colonel Doniphan's Expedition, in 1846 and 1847.* Washington, D.C.: Tippin and Streeper, 1848.

Wolf, James. *Guide to the Continental Divide Trail.* Bethesda, MD: Continental Divide Trail Society, 1991.

Women's Anthropological Society of America. *Organization and Historical Sketch of the Women's Anthropological Society of America.* Washington, D.C.: Women's Anthropological Society of America, 1889.

Woodbury, Richard B. "Zuni Prehistory and History to 1850." In *Handbook of North American Indians.*

Vol. 9, *Southwest*, edited by Alfonso Ortiz, 467–73. Washington, D.C.: Smithsonian Institution, 1979.

Young, John V. *The State Parks of New Mexico*. Albuquerque: University of New Mexico Press, 1984.

Young, Otis E. *The First Military Escort on the Santa Fe Trail, 1829*. Glendale, CA: Arthur H. Clark, 1952.

Zamora, Dorothy A, et al. *Excavations at the Coal Mining Community of Carthage, Socorro County, New Mexico*. Santa Fe: Museum of New Mexico, Office of Archaeological Studies, 1997.

Congressional Publications

Congressional Globe, Washington, D.C., 1850.

Congressional Record, Washington, D.C., 1984.

US Congress. *Biographical Directory of the American Congress, 1774–1971*. Washington, D.C.: Government Printing Office, 1971.

US Congress. House. *Report of Lieutenant J. W. Abert, of His Examination of New Mexico, in the Years 1846–47*. 30th Cong., 1st Sess. H. Ex. Doc. 41.

US Congress. House. *Report of the San Juan Reconnaissance of 1887*. By C. A. H. McCauley. 45th Cong., 3rd Sess. Vol. 5, Report of Chief of Engineers.

US Congress. House. *Report on the Lands of the Arid Region of the United States with a More Detailed Account of the Lands of Utah*. By J. W. Powell. Washington, D.C.: Government Printing Office, 1879.

US Congress. Joint Special Committee on Indian Affairs. *Condition of the Tribes*. Washington, D.C., 1867.

US Congress. Senate. *Report of the Secretary of War*, in *Index to the Executive Documents, Printed by Order of the Senate of the United States, First and Second Sessions, Thirty-Fourth Congress, 1855–56*. 34th Cong., 1st and 2nd Sess.

US Congress. Senate. *A Report from Mr. Bartlett on the Subject of the Boundary Line Between the United States and Mexico*. 32nd Cong., 2nd Sess. Ex. Doc. 41.

US Congress. Senate. *A Tabular Statement, Showing the Number and Names of the American Citizens Who Have Been Killed or Robbed While Engaged in the Fur Trade, or the Inland Trade to Mexico, Since the Late War with Great Britain, the Amount of Robberies Committed; and What Places, and by What Tribes*. 22nd Cong., 1st Sess. Ex. Doc. 90.

US Congress. Senate. *Notes of a Military Reconnaissance, from Fort Leavenworth, in Missouri, to San Diego, in California, Including Parts of the Arkansas, Del Norte, and Gila Rivers*. By W. H. Emory. 30th Cong., 1st Sess. Ex. Doc. 7.

US Congress. Senate. *Statistical Report on the Sickness and Mortality in the Army of the United States*. 36th Cong., 1st Sess. Ex. Doc. 52.

US Congress. Senate Committee on Aeronautical and Space Sciences. *Congressional Recognition of Goddard Rocket and Space Museum, Roswell, New Mexico: with Tributes to Dr. Robert H. Goddard, Space Pioneer, 1882–1945*. Washington, D.C.: Government Printing Office, 1970.

US Congress. Senate Committee on Public Lands, 43d Cong., 1st sess. H. Rept. 612.

US Congress. Senate Subcommittee on National Parks, Historic Preservation, and Recreation, of the Committee on Energy and Natural Resources. *Hearings on Civil War Battlefields; Lackawanna Valley; Galisteo Basin; Shiloh and Gettysburg National Military Parks; and Studies for Inclusion in the NPS*. 106th Cong., 1st sess.

US Congress. Special Senate Committee. *Report on the Irrigation and Reclamation of the Arid Lands: US* 51st Cong., 1st sess. Report 928, pt. 5. Serial 2708.

US Statues at Large, Washington, D.C., 45th Cong., 3rd Sess.

Executive Branch Documents

US Board of Indian Commissioners. *Third Annual Report*. Washington, D.C.: [Government Printing Office?], 1871.

US Department of the Interior. *Cultural Resource Management Plan for Fort Craig Historic Site*. Las Cruces, NM: Bureau of Land Management, April 1983.

US Department of the Interior. *Fifteenth Annual Report of the Reclamation Service, 1915–1916*. Washington, D.C.: Government Printing Office, 1916.

US Department of the Interior. *Geology and Ore Deposits of the Bayard Area, Central Mining District, NM*. US Geological Survey Bulletin 870. Washington, D.C.: Government Printing Office, 1936.

US Department of the Interior. *Old Spanish Trail: Draft National Historic Trail Feasibility Study and Environmental Assessment*. Washington, D.C.: National Park Service, July 2000.

US Department of the Interior. *Report of the Governor of New Mexico to the Secretary of the Interior*. Washington, D.C.: Government Printing Office, 1903.

US Geological Survey. *Destructive Floods in the United States in 1904*. Water-Supply and Irrigation Paper no. 147. Washington, D.C.: Government Printing Office, 1905.

Journals, Magazines, Newsletters, and Reports

American Archaeology, 1999

Assembly (Association of Graduates, United States Military Academy, West Point), 1977

Boys' Life, 1936

City of Rocks State Park Management and Development Plan

Enchantment Magazine 1993

IMPACT: Albuquerque Journal Magazine, 1983–1988

La Confluencia

La Cronica de Nuevo México, 1985

Lite Geology, New Mexico School of Mines, 1992

Michigan Law Review, 1986

Missouri Historical Review, January 1910, vol. 5

Mountain States Monitor, July 1925

New Mexico Highway Journal, 1929–1930

New Mexico Historical Review, 1926, 1945, 1990, 1997

New Mexico Magazine, 1940–1996

New Mexico State Park Management and Development Plans, 2004–2009

Smithsonian magazine, 1997

Wagon Tracks 7, no. 1 (November 1992)

Newspapers

Albuquerque Journal, 1973–2001
Albuquerque Journal North, 1988
Albuquerque Tribune, 1969–1995
Arizona Daily Star, 1881
Bullion, Socorro, NM, 1885
Clayton County Leader, Clayton, NM, 1999
Corrales Current, 1995
Daily New Mexican (later, *Santa Fe New Mexican*), Santa Fe, 1875
Deming Headlight, Deming, NM, 1989
Farmington Daily Times, Farmington, NM, 1953–1959
Herald, Truth or Consequences, NM, 1950
Las Vegas Optic, Las Vegas, NM, 1994
Little Rock Gazette, 1916
Los Angeles Times, 2000
Mountainair Progressive, Mountainair, NM, 1941
New Mexican (later, *Santa Fe New Mexican*), Santa Fe, 1965
New York Times, 1901
Roll Call, Washington, D.C., 1999
Roswell Daily Record, Roswell, NM, 1945, 1956
Sandoval County Review, Cuba, NM, 1978
Santa Fe New Mexican, Santa Fe, 1869, 1886, 1908, 1971–2000
Santa Fe Reporter, Santa Fe, 1988–2000

Maps

New Mexico Bureau of Geology and Mineral Resources. *Geologic Map of New Mexico*, scale 1:500,000. Socorro: New Mexico Bureau of Geology and Mineral Resources, 2003.
New Mexico Bureau of Mines and Mineral Resources. *Ghost Town Map of New Mexico*. Socorro: New Mexico Bureau of Mines and Mineral Resources, New Mexico Department of Development, n.d.
Reddinger, Ted. *The Power of Place: Bernalillo, New Mexico*. N.p.: Bernalillo Main Street Association, n.d.
US War Department, Office of Chief of Engineers. *An Original Plot of the Survey from Fort Osage, Mo., to Santa Fe, Oct. 27, 1827*. Washington, D.C., 1827.

Manuscripts and Archival Sources

American Life Histories: Manuscripts from the Federal Writers' Project, 1936–1940, Library of Congress, Washington, D.C.
Bergere Family Papers, New Mexico State Records Center and Archives, Santa Fe, NM.
Concha Ortiz y Pino de Kleven Papers, Center for Southwest Research, University Libraries, University of New Mexico, Albuquerque, NM.

Fabiola Cabeza de Baca Gilbert Papers, Center for Southwest Research, University Libraries, University of New Mexico, Albuquerque, NM.

Historic American Buildings Survey, Library of Congress, Washington, D.C.

Kohn Family Papers, New Mexico Jewish Historical Society Collection, New Mexico State Records Center and Archives, Santa Fe, NM.

National Register of Historic Places, Department of the Interior, National Park Service, Washington, D.C.

New Mexico Osteopathic Medical Association, Albuquerque, NM.

Returns from US Military Posts, 1880-1916, National Archives and Records Administration, Washington, D.C.

State Register of Historic Places, Santa Fe, NM.

Women in New Mexico Collection, Center for Southwest Research, University Libraries, University of New Mexico, Albuquerque, NM.

Oral History Collections

Recollections included in the essays for Nara Visa and Camp Lordsburg are courtesy of the Oral History Program, New Mexico Farm and Ranch Heritage Museum, Las Cruces, NM.

American Indian Oral History Collection, Center for Southwest Research, University Libraries, University of New Mexico, Albuquerque, NM.

Archives/Special Collections, Brookens Library, University of Illinois at Springfield, Springfield, IL.

United Indian Traders Association Oral History Project, Special Collections and Archives, Cline Library, Northern Arizona University, Flagstaff, AZ.